Professional Resumes for Accounting, Tax, Finance, and Law

A Special Gallery of Quality Resumes by Professional Resume Writers

by David F. Noble

D1384946

Publishing

Professional Resumes for Accounting, Tax, Finance, and Law
A Special Gallery of Quality Resumes by Professional Resume Writers

Copyright © 2000 by David F. Noble

Other books by David F. Noble

> *Gallery of Best Cover Letters*
> *Gallery of Best Resumes*
> *Gallery of Best Resumes for Two-Year Degree Graduates*
> *Professional Resumes for Executives, Managers, and Other Administrators*
> *Professional Resumes for Tax and Accounting Occupations*
> *Using WordPerfect in Your Job Search*

Published by JIST Works, Inc.
8902 Otis Avenue
Indianapolis, IN 46216
Phone: 800-648-5478
E-mail: jistworks@aol.com
Web site: http://www.jist.com

Development Editor: Virginia Noble
Interior Design: Debbie Berman
Layout: Carolyn J. Newland
Cover Design: Aleata Howard
Proofreader: Becca York

Printed in the United States of America

04 03 02 01 00   9 8 7 6 5 4 3 2 1

Library of Congress Cataloging-in-Publication Data

Noble, David F. (David Franklin), 1935–
      Professional resumes for accounting, tax, finance, and law, : a
special gallery of quality resumes by professional resume writers /
by David F. Noble.
            p.   cm.
      Includes index.
      ISBN 1-56370-605-9
      1. Résumés (Employment)   2. Cover letters.   3. Accounting-
-Vocational guidance.   I. Title.
      HF5383.N6227   2000
      808'.06665--dc21   99-43465
                                                                              CIP

We have been careful to provide accurate and authoritative information throughout this book, but it is possible that errors and omissions have been introduced. Please consider this in making any career plans or other important decisions. Trust your own judgment above all else and in all things.

ISBN 1-56370-605-9

To Chris and Charlie
for many good times

Acknowledgments

This collection of professionally written resumes is a shortened and rear-ranged version of *Professional Resumes for Tax and Accounting Occupations: A Special Gallery of Quality Resumes by Professional Resume Writers,* copublished in 1999 by CCH Incorporated and JIST for distribution by CCH Incorporated (4508 West Peterson Avenue, Chicago, IL 60646-6085, 800-248-3248, http://www.cch.com). Both that book and this new, shorter version could not have been written without the resume and cover letter submissions of the writers featured in both books.

When I compiled the first Gallery (*Gallery of Best Resumes,* Indianapolis: JIST Works, Inc., 1994), I knew some of these writers only as names on a mailing list from the Professional Association of Résumé Writers (PARW), which I had recently joined. Since the publication of that first Gallery and its sequel (*Gallery of Best Resumes for Two-Year Degree Graduates,* Indianapolis, JIST Works, Inc., 1996), I have met personally many of these writers at annual meetings of the PARW—first at Scottsdale, Arizona, in 1996, and then at Boston in 1997—and additional writers at the first annual meeting of the National Résumé Writers' Association (NRWA) at Chicago in 1998. All of these writers continually explore new ways to display their clients' strengths to prospective employers. I am happy to showcase again the recent work of these professional writers in this new collection.

I am grateful to Mike Farr, Tim Orbaugh, and Barb Ruess of JIST for supporting the publication of this shorter edition. I want to thank Michael Cunningham, JIST's managing editor, for his direction of the project to completion. Many thanks go to Debbie Berman for her appealing book design, Aleata Howard for her book cover expertise, Carolyn Newland for her skillful layout of the book and readi-ness to incorporate last-minute changes, and Becca York for her good catches .

Finally, I am especially indebted to my wife, Ginny. Because of her editing and organization skills, she managed to reduce a 640-page book to 416 pages, reorganize it, retain all of the contributors of the first book, and keep track of all the neces-sary changes to cross-references.

Contents

This useful "idea book" of best resumes for accounting, tax, finance, and law has three parts: Best Resume Tips; a Gallery of 201 resumes written by professional resume writers; and an Exhibit of 22 related cover letters, together with tips for polishing cover letters. With this book, you not only have a treasury of quality resumes and cover letters but also learn how to view them as superior models for your own resumes and cover letters.

This book is for *job searchers* who are applying for new positions, *career changers* who are looking for professional roles with other employers, *job changers* who are proactively climbing the corporate ladder, *M.B.A. graduates* who are applying for higher levels in management, and *new university graduates* who are seeking entry-level positions in accounting, tax, finance, or law. Because of the wealth and spread of quality resumes in this new Gallery—from those for Senior Executives of multimillion-dollar companies to those of Bookkeepers with varied responsibilities—this book is for *any job searcher with leadership ability* who wants examples of top-quality resumes to create an outstanding resume for himself or herself.

This collection of professionally written resumes shows you how to play up your skills and work experience in your own resume to be more competitive as a job applicant in a competitive job market.

In this section, you learn experience-tested, resume-writing strategies, such as how to showcase your skills, knowledge, and achievements.

Part 2: The Gallery of Professional Resumes

This Gallery has six sections of professional resumes for occupations related to accounting, tax, finance, and law. Regardless of your position, you should check out all the resumes throughout the Gallery for design tips, ways to express ideas, and impressive formats. At the bottom of each resume and cover letter page are comments that call your attention to noteworthy features or solutions to problems.

Part 3: Best Cover Letter Tips

Best Cover Letter Tips at a Glance

Best Cover Letter Tips

A quality resume can make a great impression, but it can be ruined quickly by a poorly written cover letter. This section shows you how to eliminate common errors in cover letters. It amounts to a *crash writing course* that you won't find in any other resume book. After you read the following sections, you will be better able to write and polish any letters you create for your job search.

In this section, you learn how to evaluate 22 sample cover letters that accompanied resumes submitted for use in the Gallery. After you study this exhibit, you will have a better feel for designing your own cover letters to make them distinctive and effective.

Appendix A: List of Contributors

Use this Appendix to locate or contact a professional resume writer whose resume styles you admire. Besides working with clients locally, a number of the writers work with clients by phone, fax, or e-mail, as well as on the World Wide Web.

Appendix B: Salaries Table

Use the table in this Appendix as a quick reference for comparing annual salaries of selected occupations. Treat this table as the beginning of inquiry inasmuch as salaries for occupations are always changing for reasons stated in the introduction to the table.

Occupation Index (Current or Last Job)

This Index enables you to find sample resumes for current or recent job positions listed alphabetically and cross-referenced. For example, if you want to see resumes for current or past financial managers, look up either *Financial Manager* or *Manager, Financial,* in the Index. The numbers given are *resume* numbers, not page numbers.

Features Index

This Index enables you to find quickly examples of particular resume sections in the resumes included in this book. Suppose that you want to create a Summary of Qualifications for your own resume and would like to see how professional resume writers have written this kind of section. Look up Summary of Qualifications, and you will see the numbers of the resumes that have this kind of section.

Introduction

Like the earlier Galleries of best resumes, *Professional Resumes for Accounting, Tax, Finance, and Law* is a collection of quality resumes from professional resume writers, each with individual views about resumes and resume writing. Unlike many resume books whose selections "look the same," this book contains resumes that look different because they are *real* resumes prepared by different professionals for actual job searchers throughout the country. (Certain information in the resumes has been fictionalized by the writers to protect, where necessary, each client's right to privacy.) Even when several resumes from the same writer appear in the book, most of these resumes are different because the writer has customized each resume according to the background information and career goals of the client for whom the resume was prepared.

Instead of assuming that "one resume style fits all," the writers featured here believe that a client's past experiences and next job target should determine the resume's type, design, and content. The writers interacted with clients to fashion resumes that seemed best for each client's situation at the time.

This book features resumes from writers who share several important qualities: good listening skills, a sense of what details are appropriate for a particular resume, and flexibility in selecting and arranging the resume's sections. By "hearing between" a client's statements, the perceptive resume writer can detect what kind of job the client really wants. The writer then chooses the information that will best represent the client for the job being sought. Finally, the writer decides on the best arrangement of the information, usually from the most important to the least important, for that job. With the help of this book, you can create this kind of resume yourself or learn how to contact a professional writer who can create a custom resume for you. See Appendix A, "List of Contributors," for contact information about the professional resume writers whose works are featured in this book.

Most of the writers of the resumes in this Gallery are members of either the Professional Association of Résumé Writers (PARW) or the National Résumé Writers' Association (NRWA). Some of the writers belong to both organizations. Those who have CPRW certification, for Certified Professional Résumé Writer (see Appendix A, "List of Contributors"), received this designation from PARW after they studied specified course materials and demonstrated proficiency in an examination. Those who have NCRW certification, for National Certified Résumé Writer, received this designation from NRWA after a different course of study and a different examination. A few contributors are not currently members of either organization but are either past PARW members or are professional writers in Indiana, Michigan, and Ohio who were invited by the author to submit works for possible selection for previous Galleries by the author.

Why a Gallery for Accounting, Tax, Finance, and Law Professionals?

This new Gallery of best resumes focuses on professionals in the fields of accounting, tax, finance, or law because they have special resume needs that "lower level" workers don't tend to have. Professionals in these fields possess finely tuned technical skills, and many have completed graduate courses and taken intensive examinations to be certified or licensed to perform certain tasks. Plus, such professional workers usually have accumulated leadership experiences over a relatively longer work life. This greater amount of managerial experience may be from work for different companies or from different positions within the same company as the worker climbed the company ladder and received more responsibility with each new job title. A challenge in writing a resume for an experienced professional is to select from an abundance of experience the right information to display in a resume for a person's career goals, particularly when the appearance of "being overqualified" can be a handicap in a competitive job market.

A trade-off of greater experience is older age. A legitimate concern in resume writing for professionals is finding ways to play down a person's age while calling attention to the individual's experience and achievements.

Professional workers not only have more career-related experience but also tend to have multiple skills that have been put to work in a greater range of experience. For example, a person who is currently a vice president or CFO might have been a controller who started out as an accountant. The resume-writing challenge here is to determine which experiences to emphasize and which to downplay. A related task is knowing what to exclude. Some clients of professional resume writers want to include "everything," but the writers prefer to present only the most important information on one, two, or sometimes three pages.

How This Book Is Organized

Professional Resumes for Accounting, Tax, Finance, and Law, like the preceding Galleries, consists of three parts. Part 1, "Best Resume Tips," presents resume-writing strategies, design and layout tips, and resume-writing style tips for making resumes visually impressive. A reference is given to one or more Gallery resumes that illustrate the strategy or tip. These references are not exhaustive. If you browse through this Gallery, you may see other resumes that exhibit the same strategy or tip.

Part 2 is the Gallery itself, containing 201 resumes from 91 resume writers. These resumes are grouped according to six categories: accounting-related resumes, tax-related resumes, finance-related resumes, law-related resumes, other related professional resumes, and information systems/information technology resumes related to accounting. These categories are nominal distinctions (that is, in name only) that were useful for sorting resumes and should not be used to make functional judgments about the duties or responsibilities of any particular job title. Many accountants have tax responsibilities, many financial managers have accounting responsibilities, and so on.

Because of this overlapping in responsibilities from one field to another, you should look at all of the resumes in this collection and not just at those of your particular position. All of the resumes form a hunting ground for ideas that may prove useful to you for developing your own resume.

Resume writers commonly distinguish between chronological resumes and functional (or skills) resumes. A *chronological resume* is a photo—a snapshot history of what you did and when you did it. A *functional resume* is a painting—an interpretive sketch of what you can do for a future employer. A third kind of resume, known as a *combination resume*, is a mix of recalled history and self-assessment. Besides recollecting "the facts," a combination resume contains self-interpretation and is therefore more like dramatic history than news coverage. A chronological resume and a functional resume are not always that different; often, all that is needed for a functional resume to qualify as a combination resume is the inclusion of dates for some of the positions held. All three kinds of resumes are illustrated in the Gallery. In this Gallery, a functional resume with a work history is labeled a functional resume.

When there are a number of resumes for a particular job title, the resumes are generally arranged from the simple to the complex, and from the most recent to the least recent. That is, a resume for a financial manager who has had that title for five years will appear before a resume for a financial manager who has been in that role for seven years. Generally, as the number of years of service increases, the resumes become more complex. Many of the resumes are one page, but a number of them are two pages. A few are more than two pages.

The Gallery offers a wide range of resumes whose features you can use in creating and improving your own resumes. Notice the plural. An important premise of an active job search is that you will not have just one "perfect" resume for all potential employers, but different versions of your resume for different interviews. The Gallery is therefore not a showroom where you say, "I'll take that one." It is a valuable resource of design ideas, expressions, and organizational patterns that can help make your own resume a "best resume" for your next interview.

Creating multiple versions of a resume may seem difficult, but it is easy to do if you have (or have access to) a personal computer and a laser printer or some other kind of printer that can produce quality output. You will also need word processing, desktop publishing, or resume software. Remember that most professional resume writers have the hardware and software, and they can make your resume look like those in the Gallery. A local fast-print shop can make your resume look good, but you will probably not get there the kind of advice and service the professional resume writer provides.

Part 3, "Best Cover Letter Tips," contains a discussion of some myths about cover letters, plus tips for polishing cover letters. Much of the advice offered here applies also to writing resumes. Included in this part is an Exhibit of 22 cover letters. All of these letters accompanied resumes that appear in this Gallery.

Appendix A is a "List of Contributors," which contains the names, addresses, phone numbers, and other information of the professional resume writers who contributed resumes and cover letters for this book. The list is arranged alphabetically by state and city. Although most of these resume writers work with local clients, many of the writers work with clients by phone, e-mail, and the World Wide Web from anywhere in the United States.

Appendix B, a "Salaries Table," contains illustrative salary information for a number of the occupations referred to in the resumes.

You can use the "Occupational Index" to look up resumes by current or most recent job title. This index, however, should not replace careful examination of all of the resumes. To that end, you can use the "Features Index" to find resumes that contain resume sections important to you and your resume needs. Too many resumes for some other occupation may have features adaptable to your own occupation. Limiting your search to the Occupational Index may cause you to miss some valuable examples.

Who This Book Is For

Anyone who wants ideas for creating or improving a resume can benefit from this book. It is especially useful for active job seekers—those who understand the difference between active and passive job searching. A *passive* job seeker waits until jobs are advertised and then mails copies of the same resume, along with a standard cover letter, to a number of ads. An *active* job seeker believes that a resume should be modified for a specific job target *after* having talked in person or by phone to a prospective interviewer *before* a job is announced. To schedule such an interview is to penetrate the "hidden job market." Active job seekers can find in the Gallery's focused resumes a wealth of strategies for targeting a resume for a particular interview. The section "How to Use the Gallery" at the beginning of Part 2 shows you how to do this.

What This Book Can Do for You

Besides providing you with a treasury of quality resumes whose features you can use in your own resumes, this book can help transform your thinking about resumes. If you think that there is one "best" way to create a resume, this book will help you learn how to design a resume that is best for you as you try to get an interview with a particular person for a specific job.

If you have been told that resumes should be only one page long, the examples of multiple-page resumes in the Gallery will help you see how to distribute information effectively across two or more pages. If you believe that the way to update a resume is to add your latest work experiences to your last resume, this book will show you how to rearrange your resume so that you can highlight the most important information about your experience and skills.

After you have studied "Best Resume Tips" in Part 1, examined the professionally written resumes in the Gallery in Part 2, and reviewed "Tips for Polishing Cover Letters" in Part 3, you should be able to create your own resumes worthy of inclusion in any gallery of best resumes.

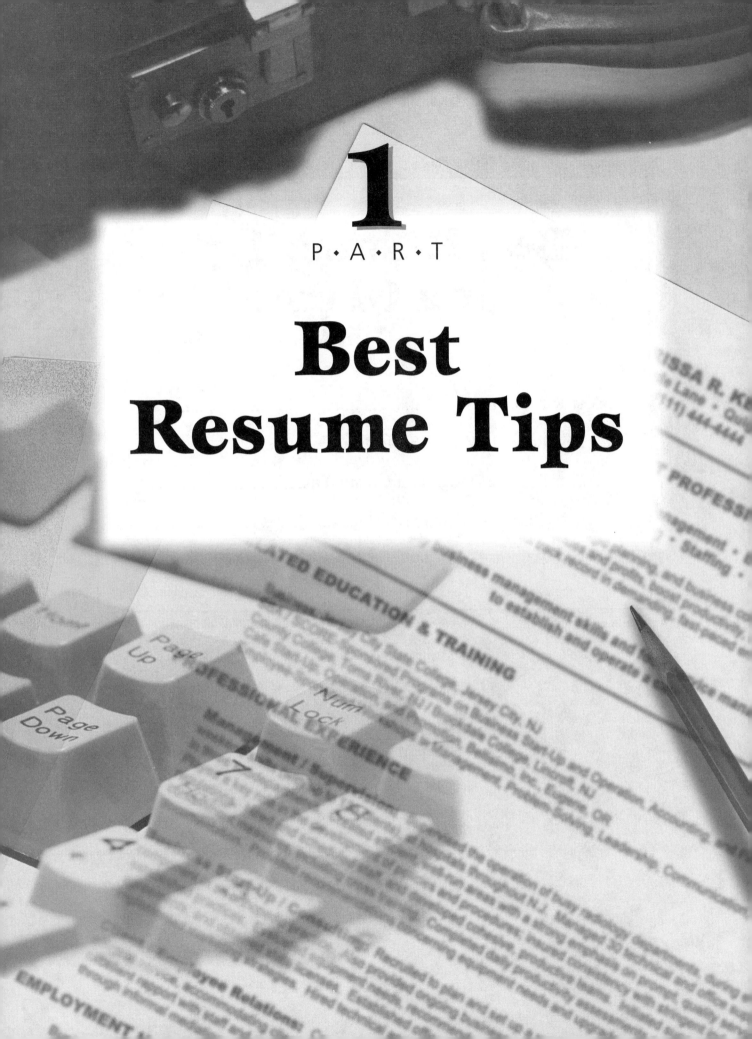

1

P·A·R·T

Best Resume Tips

Best Resume Tips
at a Glance

Best Resume Tips

In a passive job search, you rely on your resume to do most of the work for you. An eye-catching resume that stands out above all the others may be your best shot at getting noticed by a prospective employer. If your resume is only average and looks like most of the others in the pile, the chances are great that you won't be noticed and called for an interview. If you want to be singled out because of your resume, it should be somewhere between spectacular and award-winning.

In an active job search, however, your resume complements your efforts at being known to a prospective employer *before* that person receives it. For this reason, you can rely less on your resume for getting someone's attention. Nevertheless, your resume has an important role in an active job search that may include the following activities:

- Talking to relatives, friends, and other acquaintances to meet people who can hire you before a job is available

- Creating phone scripts to speak with the person who is most likely to hire someone with your background and skills

- Using a schedule to keep track of your appointments and callbacks

- Working at least 25 hours a week to search for a job

When you are this active in searching for a job, the quality of your resume confirms the quality of your efforts to get to know the person who might hire you, as well as your worth to the company whose workforce you want to join. An eye-catching resume makes it easier for you to sell yourself directly to a prospective employer. If your resume is mediocre or conspicuously flawed, it will work against you and may undo all of your good efforts in searching for a job.

The following list offers ideas for making resumes visually impressive. Many of the ideas are for making resumes pleasing to the eye; other ideas are for eliminating common writing mistakes and stylistic weaknesses.

Some of these ideas can be used with any equipment, from a manual typewriter to a sophisticated computer with desktop publishing software. Other ideas make sense only if you have a computer system with word processing or desktop publishing. Even if you don't have a computer, take some time to read all of the ideas. Then, if you decide to use the services of a professional resume writer, you will be better informed about what the writer can do for you in producing your resume.

Best Resume-Writing Strategies

1. **Although many resume books say that you should spell out the name of the state in your address at the top of the resume, consider using the postal abbreviation instead.** The reason is simple: it's an address. Anyone

wanting to contact you by mail will probably refer to your name and address on the resume. If they appear there as they should on an envelope, the writer or typist can simply copy the information you supply. If you spell out the name of your state in full, the writer will have to "translate" the name of the state to its postal abbreviation.

Not everyone knows all the postal abbreviations, and some abbreviations are easily confused. For example, those for Alabama (AL), Alaska (AK), American Samoa (AS), Arizona (AZ), and Arkansas (AR) are easy to mix up. You can prevent confusion and delay simply by using the correct postal abbreviation. As resumes become more "scannable," the use of postal abbreviations in addresses will become a requirement.

If you decide to use postal abbreviations in addresses, make certain that you do not add a period after the abbreviations, even before ZIP codes. This applies also to postal abbreviations in the addresses of references, if provided.

Consider, however, not using the state postal abbreviation when you are indicating only the city and state (not the mailing address) of a school you attended or a business where you worked. In these cases, it makes sense to write out the name of the state in full.

2. **Adopt a sensible form for phone numbers in the contact information and then use that form consistently.** Do this in your resume and in all of the documents you use in your job search. Some forms for phone numbers make more sense than others. Compare the following forms:

123-4567	This form is best for a resume circulated locally, within a region where all the phone numbers have the same area code.
(222) 123-4567	This form is best for a resume circulated in areas with different area codes.
222-123-4567	This form suggests that the area code should be dialed in all cases. But that won't be necessary for prospective employers whose area code is 222. This form should be avoided.
222/123-4567	This form is illogical and should be avoided also. The slash can mean an alternate option, as in ON/OFF. In a phone number, this meaning of a slash makes little sense.
1 (222) 123-4567	This form is long, and the digit 1 isn't necessary. Almost everyone will know that 1 should be used before the area code to dial a long-distance number.
222.123.4567	This form, which resembles a Web address, is becoming popular.

Note: For resumes directed to prospective employers *outside* the United States, be sure to include the correct international prefixes in all phone numbers so that you and your references can be reached easily by phone.

3. **If your resume has an Objective statement, make it focused, developed, or unique so that it grabs the reader's attention.** See Resume 62. If your Objective statement fails to do this, the reader might discard the resume without reading further. An Objective statement can be your first opportunity to sell yourself.

4. **If you can sell yourself better with some other kind of section, consider omitting an Objective statement and putting a Summary of Qualifications, a Profile, or an Areas of Expertise section just after the contact information.** See Resumes 76, 91, and 138.

5. **Consider replacing an Objective statement with a Profile in which you highlight the target field or intended position.** See Resumes 45, 52, and 200.

6. **Making a Qualifications summary long helps to position important information at the top of the first page.** See Resume 152.

7. **Casting Qualifications (or Areas of Knowledge, or Skills) in columns makes them easy to alter (by deleting some and adding others) if your target is a different job or industry.** See Resume 141.

8. **Spend considerable time determining how to present your skills.** You can present them as **Areas of Expertise** (Resumes 53, 65, 135, 157, and many others), **Areas of Knowledge and Expertise** (Resumes 107 and 114), **Competencies** (Resume 12), **Computer Proficiencies** (Resume 13), **Demonstrated Strengths** (Resume 60), **Key Management and Technology Abilities** (Resumes 187 and 196), **Notable Proficiencies** (Resume 178), **Professional Skills and Strengths** (Resume 118), **Qualifications Profile** (Resume 93), **Qualifications and Strengths** (Resume 24), **Skills Summary** (Resume 47), **Summary of Attributes** (Resume 123), **Technology Skills** (Resume 61), or **Technical Skills** (Resume 169).

    For a complete guide to all the features in the resumes, see the Features Index at the end of the book.

9. **In the Experience section or elsewhere, state achievements, not just duties or responsibilities.** Duties and responsibilities for a given position are often already known by the reader. Achievements, however, can be attention-getting. The reader probably considers life too short to be bored by lists of duties and responsibilities in a stack of resumes. See Resumes 97, 98, 135, 147, 148, and many others.

10. **In the Experience section and for each position held, consider explaining responsibilities in a brief paragraph and using bullets to point to achievements or contributions.** See Resumes 67, 91, 95, 111, and 112.

11. **When you indicate achievements, consider boldfacing them** (Resumes 100 and 107), **quantifying them** (Resumes 100, 111, and many others)**, or providing a separate heading for them** (Resume 110).

12. **When skills, abilities, and qualifications are varied, group them according to categories for easier comprehension.** See Resumes 8, 27, 36, 99, 146, 149, and many others as you browse through the Gallery.

13. **Include information that explains lesser-known companies.** See Resumes 69, 105, and 111.

14. **Group positions to avoid repetition in a description of duties.** See Resumes 26 and 192.

15. **As a general strategy, emphasize the important but withhold the irrelevant.** See Resume 66.

16. **Consider arranging positions topically rather than chronologically in order to see related strengths and experiences on one page.** See Resume 95.

17. **Consider arranging the information in the Qualifications section so that this information mirrors themes presented in the Summary section.** See Resume 14.

Best Resume Design and Layout Tips

18. **Use quality paper correctly.** If you use quality watermarked paper for your resume, be sure to use the right side of the paper. To know which side is the right side, hold a blank sheet of paper up to a light source. If you can see a watermark and "read" it, the right side of the paper is facing you. This is the surface for typing or printing. If the watermark is unreadable or if any characters look backward, you are looking at the "underside" of a sheet of paper—the side that should be left blank if you use only one side of the sheet.

19. **Use adequate "white space."** A sheet of white paper with no words on it is impossible to read. Likewise, a sheet of white paper with words all over it is impossible to read. The goal is to have a comfortable mix of white space and words. If your resume has too many words and not enough white space, the resume looks cluttered. If it has too much white space and too few words, the resume looks skimpy and unimportant. Make certain that adequate white space exists between the main sections. For resumes with a satisfying amount of white space, see Resumes 9, 24, 80, and 87. For resumes with adequate white space even with a small font size, see Resumes 21, 32, and 108. For white space provided through blank lines, see Resumes 74, 110, and many others. For white space accomplished through center-alignment, see Resumes 2 and 64.

20. **Margins in resumes for executives, managers, and other administrators tend to be narrower than margins in other resumes.** See Resumes 10 and 108. Narrower margins are often used in connection with smaller type to get more information on a one- or two-page resume.

21. **Be consistent in your use of line spacing.** How you handle line spacing can tell the reader how good you are at details and how consistent you are in your use of them. If, near the beginning of your resume, you insert two line spaces (two hard returns in a word processing program) between two main sections, be sure to put two line spaces between main sections throughout the resume.

22. **Be consistent in your use of horizontal spacing.** If you usually put two character spaces after a period at the end of a sentence, make certain that you

use two spaces consistently. The same is true for colons. If you put two spaces after colons, do so consistently.

Note that an em dash—a dash the width of the letter *m*—does not require spaces before or after it. No space should go between the *P* and *O* of P.O. Box. Only one space is needed between the postal abbreviation of a state and the ZIP code. You should insert a space between the first and second initials of a person's name, as in I. M. Jobseeker (not I.M. Jobseeker). These conventions have become widely adopted in English and business communications. If, however, you use other conventions, be sure to be consistent. In resumes, as in grammar, consistency is more important than conformity.

23. **Make certain that characters, lines, and images contrast well with the paper.** The quality of "ink" depends on the device used to type or print your resume. If you use a typewriter or a printer with a carbon tape, make certain that your paper has a texture that allows the characters to adhere permanently. (For a test, send yourself a copy of your resume and see how it makes the trip through the mail.) If you use an inkjet or laser printer, check that the characters are sharp and clean, without ink smudges or traces of extra toner. Mail yourself a laser-printed envelope to make sure that it looks good after a trip through the mail. A cover letter with a flaking impression for the address does not make a good impression.

24. **Use vertical alignment in stacked text.** Resumes usually contain tabbed or indented text. Make certain that this "stacked" material is aligned vertically. Misalignment can ruin the appearance of a well-written resume. Try to set tabs or indents that control this text throughout a resume instead of having a mix of tab stops in different sections. If you use a word processor, make certain that you understand the difference between tabbed text and indented text, as in the following examples:

Tabbed text:	This text was tabbed over one tab stop before the writer started to write the sentence.
Indented text:	This text was indented once before the writer started to write the sentence.

    Note: In a number of word processing programs, the Indent command is useful for ensuring the correct vertical alignment of proportionally spaced, stacked text. After you issue the Indent command, lines of wrapped text are vertically aligned automatically until you terminate the command by pressing Enter.

25. **For the vertical alignment of dates, try left- or right-aligning the dates.** This technique is especially useful in chronological resumes and combination resumes. For examples of left-aligned dates, see Resumes 70, 82, and others. For right-aligned dates, look at Resumes 91, 142, and many others. See Resume 83 in which dates of overall employment are put in the left column, while dates for each position are put after it to avoid the appearance of job hopping.

26. **Use as many pages as you need for portraying yourself adequately to a specific interviewer about a particular job.** Try to limit your resume to one page or two pages, but set the upper limit at four pages. No rule about the number of pages makes sense in all cases. The determining factors are a person's qualifications and experiences, the requirements of the job, and the

interests and pet peeves of the interviewer. If you know that an interviewer refuses to look at a resume longer than a page, that says it all. You need to deliver a one-page resume if you want to get past the first gate.

More important than the question of the number of pages is the issue of complete pages. A full page sends a better message than a partial page (which says "not enough to fill"). Therefore, one full page is better than 1.25 pages, and two full pages are better than 1.75 pages.

27. **When you have letters of recommendation, use quotations from them as testimonials.** Devoting some space (or even a full column) to the positive opinions of "external authorities" helps make a resume convincing as well as impressive. When placed effectively, such quotations can build respect, add credibility, and personalize a resume. See Resumes 4, 11, 40, 51, 85, and 137.

28. **Unless you enlist the services of a professional printer or skilled desktop publisher, resist the temptation to use full justification for text.** The price that you pay for a straight right margin is uneven word spacing. Words may appear too close together on some lines and too spread out on others. Although the resume might look like typeset text, you lose readability.

29. **If you can choose a typeface for your resume, use a serif font for greater readability.** Serif fonts have little lines extending from the top, bottom, and end of a character. These fonts tend to be easier to read than sans serif (without serif) fonts, especially in low-light conditions. Compare the following font examples:

Serif	Sans Serif
Century Old Style	Gill Sans
Courier	Futura
Times New Roman	Helvetica

Words like *minimum* and *abilities* are more readable in a serif font.

30. **If possible, avoid using monospaced type like this Courier type.** Courier was a standard of business communications during the 1960s and 1970s. Because of its widespread use, it is now considered "common." It also takes up a lot of space, so you can't pack as much information on a page with Courier type as you can with a proportionally spaced type like Times Roman.

31. **Think twice before using all uppercase letters in parts of your resume.** A common misconception is that uppercase letters are easier to read than lowercase letters. Actually, the ascenders and descenders of lowercase letters make them more distinguishable from each other and therefore more recognizable than uppercase letters. For a test, look at a string of uppercase letters and throw them gradually out of focus by squinting. The uppercase letters become a blur sooner than lowercase letters.

32. **Think twice about underlining some words in your resume.** Underlining defeats the purpose of serifs at the bottom of characters by blending with the serifs. In trying to emphasize words, you lose some visual clarity. This is especially true if you use underlining with uppercase letters in centered or side headings.

33. **If you have access to many fonts through word processing or desktop publishing, beware of becoming "font happy" and turning your resume into a font circus.** *Frequent* <u>font</u> changes *can distract* the reader **adversely,** AND SO CAN GAUDY DISPLAY TYPE.

34. **To make your resume stand out, consider using a nonstandard format or an unconventional display font in the contact information or in the headings.** See Resumes 9, 129, 176, and 188. What is usually fitting for resumes for some prospective jobs, however, is not always the most appropriate resume strategy for executive positions. Try to match the style of your resume to the target company's "corporate image" if it has one.

35. **Be aware of the value differences of black type.** Some typefaces are light; others are dark. Notice the following lines:

    A quick brown fox jumps over the lazy dog.

    A quick brown fox jumps over the lazy dog.

    Most typefaces fall somewhere in-between. With the variables of height, width, thickness, serifs, angles, curves, spacing, ink color, ink density, boldfacing, and typewriter double-striking, type offers an infinite range of values from light to dark. Try to make your resume more visually interesting by offering stronger contrasts between light type and dark type. Browse through the Gallery and notice the differences in light and dark type.

36. **Use italic characters carefully.** Whenever possible, use italic characters instead of underlining when you need to call attention to a word or phrase. You might consider using italic for duties or achievements. Think twice, however, about using italic throughout your resume. The reason is that italic (slanted) characters are less readable than normal (vertical) characters. You might have to hold the resume at an angle to make an all-italic resume more readable. Such a maneuver can irritate a reader.

37. **Use boldfacing to make different job titles more evident.** See Resumes 73, 86, 109, and many others.

38. **For getting attention, make a heading white on black if you use software that has this capability.** See Resume 158.

39. **If you use word processing or desktop publishing and have a suitable printer, use special characters to enhance the look of your resume.** For example, use enhanced quotations marks (" and ") instead of their typewriter equivalents (" "). Use an em dash (—) instead of two hyphens (--) for a dash. To separate dates, try using an en dash (a dash the width of the letter *n*) instead of a hyphen, as in 1998–1999.

40. **To call attention to an item in a list, use a bullet (•) or a filled square (■) instead of a hyphen (-).** Browse through the Gallery and notice how bullets are used effectively as attention getters.

41. **For variety, try using bullets of a different style, such as diamond (◆) bullets, rather than the usual round or square bullets.** Examples with diamonds are Resumes 35, 77, 135, 141, and many others. For other kinds of

"bullets," see Resume 91 (arrows and arrow tips); 113 (check marks); 34 (chevrons); 38, 139, and 188 (decorative); 152 (ellipses); 39, 97, and many others (filled squares); and 11 and 44 (shadowed squares). This list is not exhaustive. You will see more if you browse through the entire Gallery.

42. **Make a bullet a little smaller than the lowercase letters that appear after it.** Disregard any ascenders or descenders on the letters. Compare the following bullet sizes:

    • Too small ● Too large • Better • Just right

43. **When the amount of information justifies a longer resume, repeat a particular graphic, such as a filled square bullet (■) or a filled triangle (▲), to unify the entire resume.** See Resume 12.

44. **If possible, visually coordinate the resume and the cover letter with the same line enhancements or graphic to catch the attention of the reader.** See Resume 45 and Cover Letter 8.

45. **Use a horizontal line or a combination of lines to separate the contact information from the rest of the resume.** See Resumes 92, 123, 126, and many others.

46. **Use horizontal lines to separate the different sections of the resume and thus make them visible at a glance.** See Resumes 24, 44, 101, and many others.

47. **For variety in dividing sections of your resume, use partial horizontal lines that extend from the left margin to text, or from text to the right margin.** See Resume 46. Note that Resume 53 has partial lines that extend from centered headings to *both* the left and right margins.

48. **For better readability, use dot leaders to connect ranges of dates with positions held.** See Resume 5.

49. **To use space efficiently, consider presenting skills as phrases separated by bullets in a centered and doubly indented paragraph.** See Resume 65.

50. **If you have a word processing program, consider constructing the resume as a one-row, three-column table with lines hidden.** See Resumes 33 and 52.

51. **To avoid a cramped one-page resume that has small print, narrow margins, and reduced line spacing, consider using a two-page resume instead.** See Resume 30. (Those who insist on one-page resumes will not agree with this tip.)

52. **To call attention to a resume section or certain information, use horizontal lines to enclose it.** See Resumes 9, 111, 114, and many others.

53. **Change the thickness of part of a horizontal line to call attention to a section heading above or below the line.** See Resumes 98 and 165.

54. **Use a vertical line (or lines) to spice up your resume.** See Resumes 20, 33, 38, and 87.

55. **Use various kinds of boxes (single line, shadowed, or decorative) to make a page visually more interesting.** See Resumes 4, 76, 103, 112, 137, 147, and 179.

56. **Use a page border to make a page visually more interesting.** See Resumes 36, 82, 135, and 144.

57. **Consider using center-alignment to make short phrases and statements look better than if they were left-aligned.** See Resumes 86 and 140.

58. **Consider using double indentation to make a Profile or some other section stand out.** See Resumes 64 and 100.

59. **Consider using hanging indentation of section headings to make them stand out.** See Resume 56.

60. **Consider centering headings to make them easy to read down a page.** See Resumes 39 and 86.

61. **At the top of the first page but below the contact information, place a list of keywords that can easily be scanned for storage in an online resume database.** See Resumes 47 and 198.

Best Resume-Writing Style Tips

62. **Check that words or phrases in lists are parallel.** For example, notice the bulleted items in the Competencies section of Resume 12. All the entries contain nouns. Notice also the list in the Illustrative Experience section of Resume 148. All the verbs are in the past tense.

63. **Use capital letters correctly.** Resumes usually contain many of the following:

     - Names of people, companies, organizations, government agencies, awards, and prizes
     - Titles of job positions and publications
     - References to academic fields (such as chemistry, English, and mathematics)
     - Geographic regions (such as the Midwest, the East, the state of California, Oregon State, and northern Florida)

     Because of such words, resumes are mine fields for the misuse of uppercase letters. When you don't know whether a word should have an initial capital letter, don't guess. Consult a dictionary, a handbook on style, or some other authoritative source. Often a reference librarian can provide the information you need. If so, you are only a phone call away from an accurate answer.

64. **Check that capital letters and hyphens are used correctly in computer terms.** If you want to show in a Computer Experience section that you have used certain hardware and software, you may give the opposite impression if you don't use uppercase letters and hyphens correctly. Note the correct use of capitals and hyphens in the following names of hardware, software, and computer companies:

LaserJet III	Hewlett-Packard	dBASE
PageMaker	MS-DOS	Microsoft
WordPerfect	PC DOS	Microsoft Word
NetWare	PostScript	

The reason that many computer product names have an internal uppercase letter is for the sake of a trademark. A word with unusual spelling or capitalization is trademarkable. When you use the correct forms of these words, you are honoring trademarks and registered trademarks.

65. **Use all uppercase letters for most acronyms.** An *acronym* is a pronounceable word usually formed from the initial letters of the words in a compound term, or sometimes from multiple letters in those words. Note the following examples:

BASIC	Beginner's All-purpose Symbolic Instruction Code
COBOL	COmmon Business-Oriented Language
DOS	Disk Operating System
FORTRAN	FORmula TRANslator

An acronym like *radar* (*ra*dio *d*etecting *a*nd *r*anging) has become so common that it is no longer all uppercase.

66. **Be aware that you may need to use a period with some abbreviations.** An *abbreviation* is a word shortened by removing the latter part of the word or by deleting some letters within the word. Here are some examples:

adj. for *adjective*	*amt.* for *amount*
adv. for *adverb*	*dept.* for *department*

Usually, you can't pronounce an abbreviation as a word. Sometimes, however, an abbreviation is a set of uppercase letters (without periods) that you can pronounce as letters. AFL-CIO, CBS, NFL, and YMCA are examples.

67. **Be sure to spell every word correctly.** A resume with just one misspelling is not impressive and may undermine all the hours you spent putting it together. Worse than that, one misspelling may be what the reader is looking for to screen you out, particularly if you are applying for a position that requires accuracy with words. If you calculate the salary you don't get *times* the number of years you might have worked for that company, that's an expensive misspelling!

If you use word processing and have a spelling checker, you may be able to catch any misspellings. Be wary of spelling checkers, however. They can detect a misspelled word but cannot detect when you have inadvertently used a wrong word (*to* for *too*, for example). Be wary also of letting someone else check your resume. If the other person is not a good speller, you may not get any real help. The best authority is a good, *current* dictionary.

68. **For words that have a couple of correct spellings, use the preferred form.** This form is the one that appears first in a dictionary. For example, if you see the entry **trav · el · ing** *or* **trav · el · ling**, the first form (with one *l*) is the preferred spelling. If you make it a practice to use the preferred spelling, you will build consistency in your resumes and cover letters.

69. **Avoid British spellings.** These slip into American usage through books published in Great Britain. Note the following words:

British Spelling	American Spelling
acknowledgement	acknowledgment
centre	center
judgement	judgment
towards	toward

70. **Avoid hyphenating words with such prefixes as *co-*, *micro-*, *mid-*, *mini-*, *multi-*, *non-*, *pre-*, *re-*, and *sub-*.** Many people think that words with these prefixes should have a hyphen after the prefix, but most of these words should not. The following words are spelled correctly:

coauthor	microcomputer	minicomputer
coworker	midpoint	multicultural
cowriter	midway	multilevel
nondisclosure	prearrange	reenter
nonfunctional	prequalify	subdirectory

Note: If you look in a dictionary for a word with a prefix and can't find the word, look for the prefix itself in the dictionary. You might find there a small-print listing of a number of words that have the prefix.

71. **Be aware that compounds (combinations of words) present special problems for hyphenation.** Writers' handbooks and books on style do not always agree on how compounds should be hyphenated. Many compounds are evolving from *open* compounds to *hyphenated* compounds to *closed* compounds. In different dictionaries, you can therefore find the words *copy editor*, *copy-editor*, and *copyeditor*. No wonder the issue is confusing! Most style books do agree, however, that when some compounds appear as an adjective before a noun, the compound should be hyphenated. When the same compound appears after a noun, hyphenation is unnecessary. Compare the following two sentences:

> I scheduled well-attended conferences.
> The conferences I scheduled were well attended.

For detailed information about hyphenation, see a recent edition of *The Chicago Manual of Style*. You should be able to find a copy at a local library.

72. **Be sure to hyphenate so-called *permanent* hyphenated compounds.** Usually, you can find these by looking them up in a dictionary. You can spot them easily because they have a "long hyphen" (—) for visibility in the dictionary. Hyphenate these words (with a standard hyphen) wherever they appear, before or after a noun. Here are some examples:

all-important	self-employed
day-to-day	step-by-step
full-blown	time-consuming

73. **Use the correct form for certain verbs and nouns combined with prepositions.** You may need to consult a dictionary for correct spelling and hyphenation. Compare the following examples:

start up	(verb)
start-up	(noun)
start-up	(adj.)
startup	(noun, computer industry)
startup	(adj., computer industry)

74. **Avoid using shortcut words, such as abbreviations like *thru* or foreign words like *via*.** Spell out *through* and use *by* for *via*.

75. **Use the right words.** The issue here is correct *usage*, which often means the choice of the right word or phrase from a group of two or more possibilities. The following words and phrases are often used incorrectly:

alternate (adj.)	Refers to an option used every other time. OFF is the alternate option to ON in an ON/OFF switch.
alternative	Refers to an option that can be used at any time. If cake and pie are alternative desserts for dinner, you can have cake three days in a row if you like. The common mistake is to use *alternate* when the correct word is *alternative*.
center around	A common illogical expression. Draw a circle and then try to draw its center around it. You can't. Use *center in* or *center on* as logical alternatives to *center around*.

For information about the correct *usage* of words, consult a usage dictionary or the usage section of a writer's handbook.

76. **Use numbers consistently.** Numbers are often used inconsistently with text. Should you present a number as a numeral or spell out the number as a word? One approach is to spell out numbers *one* through *nine* but present numbers 10 and above as numerals. Different approaches are taught in different schools, colleges, and universities. Use the approach you have learned, but be consistent.

77. **Use (or don't use) the serial comma consistently.** How should you punctuate a series of three or more items? If, for example, you say in your resume that you increased sales by 100 percent, opened two new territories, and trained four new salespersons, the comma before *and* is called the *serial comma*. It is commonly omitted in newspapers, magazine articles, advertisements, and business documents; but it is often used for precision in technical documents or for stylistic reasons in academic text, particularly in the Humanities.

78. **Use semicolons correctly.** Semicolons are useful because they help to distinguish visually the items in a series when the items themselves contain commas. Suppose that you have the following entry in your resume:

Increased sales by 100 percent, opened two new territories, which were in the Midwest, trained four new salespersons, who were from Georgia, and increased sales by 250 percent.

The extra commas (before *which* and *who*) throw the main items of the series out of focus. By separating the main items with semicolons, you can bring them back into focus:

> Increased sales by 100 percent; opened two new territories, which were in the Midwest; trained four new salespersons, who were from Georgia; and increased sales by 250 percent.

Use this kind of high-rise punctuation even if just one item in the series has an internal comma.

79. **Avoid using colons after headings.** A colon indicates that something is to follow. A heading indicates that something is to follow. A colon after a heading is therefore redundant.

80. **Use dashes correctly.** One of the purposes of a dash (an em dash or two hyphens) is to introduce a comment or afterthought about preceding information. A colon *anticipates* something to follow, but a dash *looks back* to something already said. Two dashes are sometimes used before and after a related but nonessential remark—such as this—within a sentence. In this case, the dashes are like parentheses, but more formal.

81. **Avoid using the archaic word *upon* in the References section.** The common statement "References available upon request" needs to be simplified, updated, or even deleted in resume writing. The word *upon* is one of the finest words of the 13th century, but it's a stuffy word on the eve of the next century. Usually, *on* will do for *upon*. Other possibilities are "References available by request" and "References available." Because most readers of resumes know that applicants can usually provide several reference letters, this statement is probably unnecessary. A reader who is seriously interested in you will ask about reference letters.

2
P·A·R·T

The Gallery of Professional Resumes

The Gallery at a Glance

How to Use the Gallery

You can learn much from the Gallery just by browsing through it. To make the best use of this resource, however, read the following suggestions before you begin.

Look at the resumes in the category containing your field, related fields, or your target occupation. Use the Occupation Index to help you find resumes for certain fields. Notice what kinds of resumes other people have used to find similar jobs. Always remember, though, that your resume should not be "canned." It should not look just like someone else's resume but should reflect your own background, unique experiences, knowledge, and goals.

Use the Gallery primarily as an "idea book." Even if you don't find a resume for your specific occupation or job, be sure to look at all the resumes for ideas you can borrow or adapt. You may be able to modify some of the sections or statements with information that applies to your own situation or target field. Use the Features Index to find resumes containing certain kinds of resume sections.

Study the ways professional resume writers have formatted the names, addresses, and phone numbers of individuals. In most instances, this information appears at the top of the first page of the resume. Look at type styles, size of type, and use of boldface. See whether the personal information, known as contact information, is centered on lines, spread across a line, or located near the margin on one side of a page. Look for the use of horizontal lines to separate this information from the rest of the resume, or to separate the address and phone number from the person's name.

Look at each resume to see what section appears first after the contact information. Then compare those same sections (horizontally) across the Gallery. For example, look just at the resumes that have a Goal or an Objective statement as the first section. Use the Features Index to help you locate resumes with an Objective. Compare the length, clarity, and use of words. Do these statements contain complete sentences, or one or more partial lines of thought? Are some statements better than others from your point of view? Do you see one or more Objective statements that come close to matching your own objective?

Repeat such a "horizontal comparison" for any sections you like across the Gallery. Again, use the Features Index to locate sections of your choosing. As you make these comparisons, continue to note differences in length, the kinds of words and phrases used, and the effectiveness of the content. Jot down any ideas that might be true for you. Then put together sections for your own resume.

As you compare similar sections across the Gallery, pay special attention to the Profile, Summary of Qualifications, Areas of Expertise, and Experience sections. Notice how skills and accomplishments are worked into these sections. Skills and accomplishments are *variables* that you can select to put a certain "spin" on your resume as you pitch it toward a particular interviewer or job. Your observations here should be especially valuable for your own resume versions.

After you have examined the resumes "horizontally" (section by section), compare them "vertically" (design by design). To do this, you need to determine which resumes have the same sections in the same order, and then compare just those resumes. For example, look for resumes that have personal information at the top, a Summary of Qualifications, an Experience section, an Education section, and finally a line about references. (Notice that the section heads may differ slightly. Instead of the word *Experience*, you might find *Professional Experience* or *Employment*.) When you examine the resumes in this way, you are looking at their *structural design*, which means the order in which the various sections appear. The same order can appear in resumes of different fields, so it is important to explore the whole Gallery and not limit your investigation to resumes in your field or related fields.

Developing a sense of resume structure is extremely important because it enables you to emphasize the most important information about yourself. A resume is a little like a newspaper article read quickly and often discarded before the reader finishes. That is why the information in newspaper articles often dwindles in significance toward the end. For the same reason, the most important, attention-getting information about you should be at or near the top of your resume. What follows should appear in order of descending significance.

If you know that the reader will be more interested in your education than in your experience, put your Education section before your Experience section. If you know that the reader will be interested in your skills regardless of your education and work experience, put your Skills section at or near the beginning of your resume. In this way, you can help to ensure that anyone who reads only *part* of your resume will read the "best about you." Your hope is that this information will encourage the reader to read on to the end of the resume and, above all, take an interest in you.

Compare the resumes according to visual design features, such as the use of horizontal and vertical lines, borders, boxes, bullets, white space, and graphics. Notice which resumes have more visual impact at first glance and which ones make no initial impression. Do some of the resumes seem more inviting to read than others? Which ones are less appealing because they have too much information, or too little? Which ones seem to have the right balance of information and white space?

After comparing the visual design features, choose the design ideas that might improve your own resume. You will want to be selective here and not try to work every design possibility into your resume. As in writing, "less is more" in resume making, especially when you integrate design features with content.

An important note about style and consistency: The 201 resumes and 22 cover letters in this Gallery represent 91 unique styles of writing—the exact number of professional resume writers who contributed to this book. For this reason, you may notice a number of differences in capitalization. To showcase important details, many of the writers prefer to capitalize job titles and other key terms that usually appear in lowercase. Furthermore, the use of jargon may vary considerably—again, reflecting the choices of individual writers and thus making each resume truly "one of a kind."

Variations in the use (or *non*use) of hyphens may be noticeable. With the proliferation of industry jargon, hyphens seem like moving targets, and "rules" of hyphenation vary considerably from one handbook to another. In computer-related fields, some terms are evolving faster than the species. Thanks to America Online®, the term *on-line* is more often shown as *online,* but both forms are acceptable. And electronic mail comes in many varieties: *email, e-mail, Email,* and *E-Mail.* But the computer world is not the only one that has variety: both *healthcare* and *health care* appear in the resumes in this book.

Although an attempt has been made to reduce some of the more blatant inconsistencies in capitalization and hyphenation, differences are still evident. Keep in mind that the consistent use of capitalization and hyphenation *within* a resume is more important than adherence to any set of external conventions.

Note: In the comments below the resumes on the following pages, words in quotation marks are from written views of the resume writers themselves.

Accounting-Related
Resumes

SALLY GALLEN
5555 Beech Way
Prosperity, CA 55555
(555) 555-5555

OBJECTIVE

To obtain a position as an **Accounts Payable Supervisor** to contribute to the efficiency of the accounting department and profitability of the company overall.

SUMMARY OF QUALIFICATIONS

- Eighteen years' experience in accounting with increasing responsibility.
- Reputation for efficiency and accuracy.
- Organized and detail-oriented; special attention given to due dates to receive discounts, avoid late penalties and meet deadlines.
- Proficient in a wide variety of accounting and spreadsheet software packages.
- Exceptional customer service skills.
- Excellent interpersonal skills and enjoy working in a team environment.
- Self-motivated; fast learner with proven ability to learn on own initiative.

SKILLS

▸ Accounts Payable	▸ Accruals/Reversals	▸ Payroll Processing
▸ Accounts Receivable	▸ Stop Payments	▸ General Ledger
▸ Expense Report Processing	▸ Auditing	▸ Collections
▸ Account Reclassification	▸ Account Analysis	▸ Bank Deposits and Reconciliations

EMPLOYMENT HISTORY

Bookkeeper   3/XX to Present
Liquid Systems, International, Corporate, CA

Accounting Clerk   3/XX to 3/XX
GEM Stones, Inc., Riverdale, CA

Accounting Technician   7/XX to 2/XX
Statue Management Co., Palace, CA

Bookkeeper   4/XX to 6/XX
Cushman & Wakefield Co., Los Domingo, CA

Administrative Secretary   4/XX to 3/XX
National Furnishings Enterprises, Santa Maria, CA

Bookkeeper   7/XX to 3/XX
Golden State Construction Co., Commonton, CA

EDUCATION

Los Angeles Trade Technical College   XXXX to XXXX
Concentration in Secretarial Science

1

Functional. *Denise C. Ross, Anaheim, California*
This applicant for an Accounts Payable Supervisor position lacked previous formal supervisory experience. The writer therefore highlights skills especially relevant to this position.

Kay Castleton

10 Lion Drive
Troy, Illinois 62294
(618) 555-6552

Qualifications Summary

Experienced Bookkeeper with solid background handling payroll, expenses, invoicing, and specialized bookkeeping services for accounts ranging from small business partnerships to large corporations. A highly punctual, organized, and dependable employee who works well independently and completes projects with strong attention to detail and professional quality.

Key Strengths:

Expense Tracking
Trial Balance
Balance Sheet Statements
Bank Reconciliations

General Ledger
Profit and Loss Bookkeeping
Journal Entries
Financial Statements/Reports

Professional Experience

Bookkeeper, 19XX to present
COMPUTER-ASSISTED BOOKKEEPING, Collinsville, Illinois

- Sort and classify receipts into various purchase and expense categories. Code and enter purchase, expense, and wage expenditure information into computer.
- Total daily sales sheets.
- Calculate and prepare monthly state sales tax forms using daily sales reports.
- Calculate and prepare monthly, quarterly, and annual employer payroll tax reports (Illinois 501, 941, and UC-340; Federal 941, 940, W-3, and W-2).

Night Auditor, 19XX - 19XX
HOLIDAY INN, Collinsville, Illinois

- Balanced restaurant, lounge, and patio bar cash registers. Sent daily/nightly report of register readings and motel financial transactions to accounting.
- Ran trial balance on all charge and cash folios and balanced them with register readings.
- Figured room occupancy percentages and room occupancy/room revenue percentages.

Bookkeeper, 19XX - 19XX
MORLEN INSURANCE AGENCY, Highland, Illinois

- Sent monthly statements. Prepared payroll and aging schedule of accounts.
- Made daily bank deposits and typed invoices for new/renewal insurance policies.
- Maintained filing system.

Continuing Education

Accounting, Typewriting II (WordStar), Lotus 1-2-3
BELLEVILLE AREA COLLEGE, Belleville, Illinois

References Available on Request

2

Combination. *John A. Suarez, Troy, Illinois*
This Bookkeeper has had more job experience than higher education. The Qualifications Summary indicates the breadth of her experience and her relevant traits as a worker.

Liz Henry
55 550th Street
Bellerose, NY 55555
(555) 555-5555

PROFESSIONAL GOAL: ACCOUNTING POSITION

HIGHLIGHTS	‣ Highly motivated and competent accounting professional, with experience in management and employee supervision. ‣ Solid foundation in accounting principles and applications; Able to rapidly learn and master complex ideas. ‣ Highly analytical, mathematical, detail-oriented, and accurate. ‣ Excellent interpersonal skills—Readily develop positive relations with people from diverse economic and cultural backgrounds. ‣ Committed to achieving and exceeding corporate goals; Work effectively with team members to achieve desired results. ‣ Knowledge of Microsoft Excel, Access, Word, WordPerfect, and Lotus 1-2-3. ‣ Fluent in Polish, Ukranian, and Russian.

EDUCATION

NEW YORK UNIVERSITY - New York, NY
BA in Accounting, Minor in Economics - August, XXXX
Financed degree by working 2 part-time jobs

- Accounting GPA: 3.75
- Accounting Honor Society
- Dean's List - 5 semesters
- Overall GPA: 3.6
- Accounting Society
- Golden Key National Honor Society

RELEVANT COURSES

‣ Advanced Accounting	‣ Theory and Practice of Accounting
‣ Money and Banking	‣ Macro-Economic Analysis
‣ Cost Accounting	‣ Corporation Finance
‣ Auditing	‣ Statistics as Applied to Economics
‣ Business Law	‣ Federal and NYS Taxes on Income

EXPERIENCE

CLS - BROOKLYN - Brooklyn, NY - XXXX to present
Bookkeeper (XXXX to present)

‣ Record daily journal entries and reconcile accounts for company with up to $15,000 in daily sales.
‣ Manage and process accounts payable.
‣ Accurately prepare financial reports, such as P&L and transaction reports.

Assistant Manager / Salesperson (XXXX to XXXX)

‣ Directly supervised a team of 25 employees.
‣ Increased revenues by 15% by negotiating and landing corporate accounts and upselling to current customers.
‣ Resolved customer problems and ensured 100% customer satisfaction.
‣ Developed a loyal customer base by providing outstanding customer service.
‣ Promoted from **Cashier** (XXXX to XXXX).

NEW YORK UNIVERSITY - New York, NY - XXXX to present
Assistant, Accounting Department

‣ Complete administrative tasks to facilitate smooth office operations.
‣ Provide information and assistance to students and professors.

3

Combination. *Kim Isaacs, Jackson Heights, New York*
Highlights draw attention to this new graduate's main qualifications. The Relevant Courses section attempts to show their practical nature. The "distinctive border adds visual appeal."

SARAH GILL

3000 40 ½ Avenue South
Fargo, ND 58103

(701) 000-0000

- Ambitious, diversified **"take-charge" professional** with genuine desire and ability to enhance work environment
- Work well individually and as a **team player**; organized
- Noted for natural **"business sense"** to improve companies' profits
- Possess **creative and innovative ideas**
- Always **willing to take on additional responsibilities & challenges**
- Strong work ethic developed from farm background; **dependable**
- **Personable**; present warm first impression
- **Computer literate**: WordPerfect

● AREAS OF EXPERIENCE

- Customer service
- Sales
- Office management and procedures
- Supervising
- Scheduling and coordinating
- Ad promotions and marketing
- Telephone and mail responsibilities
- Expense monitoring

- Preparation and filing of insurance forms
- Account and ledger balancing
- Preparation of daily, monthly, and quarterly financial statements
- Accounts receivable, accounts payable, and payroll
- Collections
- Tax calculations
- Record keeping
- Cashiering

● PROFESSIONAL EXPERIENCE

Secretary/Receptionist/Bookkeeper   ANDERSON CHIROPRACTIC: Fargo, ND   9/95 - Present
Create a friendly, warm environment for patients; increase patient base through new/innovative marketing ideas.

Secretary/Receptionist   KENT FURNITURE STORE: Fargo, ND   10/94 - 5/95
Responsible for meeting time restraints and accurate preparation of documents.

Secretary/Receptionist/Bookkeeper   SMITH VISION CENTER: Bismarck, ND   11/92 - 7/94
Respected by customers and employer for natural ability to match vision products to customers' needs.

Sales Associate   ANDERSON'S: Bismarck, ND   9/89 - 12/92
Awarded three separate prizes for attracting most customers during store sales competitions.

Owner/Operator   SARAH'S DAYCARE: Bismarck, ND   4/87 - 9/89
Provided a safe, learning, and fun environment for seven children from infants to age nine.

Service Counter Manager/Cashier   H & K RED OWL: Valley City, ND   1/84 - 4/87
Quickly promoted from Cashier to Service Counter Manager.

● OTHER EXPERIENCE

North Dakota Air National Guard (82 - 85)
Administrative Secretarial Training

Avon Consultant (92 - Present)

● EDUCATION/CONTINUING EDUCATION

Lost Central High School: Lost, ND
Receptionist and Business Management Training - Smith Vision Center
Administrative Secretarial Training - ND Air National Guard

● TESTIMONIAL

*"Sarah has tremendous sales ability starting with a smile, answering questions and responding with an attitude 'I care.'
. . . I highly recommend Sarah as one of the top employees of our clinic and would hire her back without hesitation."*
– Dr. William A. Smith, Smith Vision Center

4

Combination. *Mary Laske, Fargo, North Dakota*
This resume is eye-catching because of its framed contact information, bulleted headings,
supportive information in italic under the positions, and quoted testimonial at the end.

SANDRA A. FOX

0000 Keystone Drive ● Titusville, Florida 00000 | (000) 000-0000

QUALIFICATIONS SUMMARY

Over 20 years' experience as **FULL-CHARGE BOOKKEEPER** with additional experience in office management and staff supervision. Establish accounting procedures to reduce expenses and protect revenue. Recognized as a results-oriented and solution-focused team leader. Proficient on *Data Modes* and *Real World* accounting software. Key areas of strength and experience include:

- General Ledger
- Payroll Preparation
- Payroll/State Taxes
- Quarterly Reports
- Accounts Payable/Receivable

- Sales Taxes
- Cash Disbursements
- Profit/Loss Breakdown
- CRT
- Personal Communicator

PROFESSIONAL EXPERIENCE

FULL-CHARGE BOOKKEEPER ....1991 - XXXX
Grambling Competition Center ● Hendersonville, Tennessee

Managed all bookkeeping and accounting operations for manufacturer of Sprint race cars with multiple companies. Reorganized entire office system in order to keep current on payroll taxes, filing, A/P, A/R, and inventory levels and to improve work flow procedures.

- Designed computer program to monitor $550,000 car parts and accessories inventory.
- Reconciled bank statements and maintained A/P and A/R accounts, collections, and cash deposits. Effectively dealt with bank officers in the transfer of international funds.
- Provided personalized customer service, handling all aspects of customer inquiries and complaints.
- Reestablished good credit relationships with vendors through the prompt payment of invoices.
- Processed medical insurance claims and explained policies and benefits to employees.

UNIT AUDITOR .... 1986 - 1991
Yummy Seafood Restaurant (1 of 90 restaurants) ● Nashville, Tennessee
Specialty Restaurant Corporation ● Anaheim, California

Oversaw all aspects of complete computerized bookkeeping system. Supervised and scheduled 3 employees.

- Audited all dining and bar room checks and reconciled to registers.
- Handled accounts receivable and payable, credit cards, inventory control, and cost control for food and beverage.
- Administered cash disbursements, payroll and related taxes, and prepared EDP sheets for end-of-the-month P & L statement.

FULL-CHARGE BOOKKEEPER .... 1978 - 1986
George O. Lawson Company ● Lebanon, Tennessee

Performed a full range of bookkeeping duties for corporation with $45+ million in annual revenue. Coordinated the workload of 6 clerical support staff (Accounts Payable, Accounts Receivable, Bid Preparation, Data Entry, Driver Reports, Receptionist).

- Developed specialized checks and balances system involving cash deposits, general ledger entries, payroll preparation, time cards, commissions, payroll taxes, 6-state sales taxes, quarterly reports, A/R and A/P, monthly book closings, profit/loss breakdown, expense sheets, sales entries, cash disbursements, and bank reconciliation.

5

Combination. *Carolyn S. Braden, Hendersonville, Tennessee*
The Qualifications Summary includes a two-column bulleted list of key accounting duties. Dot leaders make it easy to see the range of years during which each job was held.

KAYE MONTANA

10830 Olde Woods Way • Columbia, Maryland 21044 • (000) 000-0000

HIGHLIGHTS OF QUALIFICATIONS

- More than ten years of highly successful accounting and bookkeeping experience.
- Excellent supervision, management, and leadership skills.
- Effective communicator, both oral and written.

PROFESSIONAL EXPERIENCE

Church Bookkeeper/Accountant
- Manage and maintain records of all Church funds.
- Perform accounts payable, accounts receivables, and trial balance reports.
- Prepare monthly reports for Church Council's review.
- Maintain expense vouchers and vendor invoices.
- Maintain computerized employee payroll system and process adjustments.

Accounting Manager/Controller
- Maintained accounts payables, receivables, billing statements, forecasting, and budgeting.
- Balanced cash in vault room and disperse banks to cashiers. Made bank deposits, via Brinks Security.
- Compiled statistics and prepare several weekly reports to include sales, operating expenses, and commissions.
- Entered and processed weekly payroll for 75 employees. Resolved all pay discrepancies.
- Supervised an accounting assistant. Reviewed and evaluated employees' work performance.
- Facilitated employee-benefits orientations. Reviewed and processed paperwork. Met with union representatives.
- Served as liaison by assisting, coordinating, and solving discrepancies for vendors and department managers.

Accounting Assistant/Personnel
- Processed time cards and reviewed employees' checks for accuracy.
- Accounts payable (nonautomated) entered purchase on Summary Report.
- Balance vaults in cash room, issue daily banks to cashiers, make company deposits and transfer funds to corporate account.
- Perform human resource functions to include orientations, processing new hire paperwork, resolving payroll discrepancies and employee terminations.

Loan Officer/Member Service Representative
- Reviewed and analyzed credit bureau reports and debt ratios to process consumer loans.
- Disbursed proceeds and referred to Credit Committee.
- As Member Service Representative, provided services to members.
- Assisted with teller functions when needed.

Loan Processor/Collector
- Processed all consumer loans and mortgage payments.
- Reviewed applications for approval and notified applicants.
- Collected delinquent loans; student, personal, vacation, mortgage, and automobile loans.

EMPLOYMENT HISTORY

xxxx - Present	*Church Bookkeeper/Accountant*	Long Reach Church of God, Columbia, MD
xxxx - xxxx	*Accounting Manager/Controller*	Service America, Baltimore, MD
xxxx - xxxx	*Accounting Assistant/Personnel*	Service America, Baltimore, MD
xxxx - xxxx	*Loan Officer/Member Service Rep*	Montgomery County Teachers FCU, Kensington, MD
xxxx - xxxx	*Loan Processor/Collector*	Safeway Federal Credit Union, Landover, MD

EDUCATION

Bachelor of Science, Psychology, University of South Florida, Tampa, Florida, xxxx

COMPUTER SKILLS

MS Office, WordPerfect, Windows, Excel, Lotus, Smart Suite

6

Functional. *Audrey A. Boatwright, Columbia, Maryland*
This psychology major had "a diverse accounting and bookkeeping background." The underlined headings in the Experience section match the jobs in the Employment History.

ANGELA C. ARNOLD
18 French Court
City, State 00000
(555) 555-5555
E-mail: aaaaaa@aol.com

SUMMARY: *Accomplished Office Professional with extensive experience in construction and light manufacturing industries. Excellent accounting skills including Accounts Payable, Accounts Receivable, General Ledger, and Cost Accounting. Highly organized self-starter with strong interpersonal capabilities and superb attention to detail.*

PROFESSIONAL EXPERIENCE:

1989 - Present   **Office Manager, Acme Builders, Inc.; City, State.**
Residential developer and commercial construction contractor.
- Perform all accounting functions, including Payables, Receivables, Payroll, Journal Entries, and General Ledger; prepare Financial Statements.
- Post job costs to accounts in over 120 categories.
- Administer payments to subcontractors.
- Reconcile bank accounts; prepare tax filings.
- Schedule real estate closings; prepare closing summaries.
- Interact with buyers, attorneys, and banks.
- Prepare job specifications, changes, and correspondence; copy construction plans.
- Fulfill other customer service and general office functions.

1988 - 1989   **Bookkeeper / Office Manager**
Furniture Specialties, Inc.; City, State.
Furniture refinisher and upholsterer.
- Administered Payables and Receivables, made Journal Entries, maintained General Ledger, and prepared Financial Statements.
- Interacted with customers on the phone.
- Performed general administrative duties.

1986 - 1988   **Administrative Assistant / Bookkeeper**
Residential Construction / R.C. Systems, Inc.; City, State.
Building contractor and architectural firm.
- Prepared A.I.A. documents for use in job costing.
- Fulfilled bookkeeping and general secretarial duties.

1981 - 1985   **Bookkeeper / General Office, Royal Paving Co., Inc.; City, State.**
Commercial paving firm.
- Coordinated purchasing and administered Accounts Payable.
- Performed other accounting functions and general office duties.

1977 - 1981   **Bookkeeper / Credit Manager, Baby Buggies, Inc; City, State.**
Manufacturer of baby strollers. Promoted to Credit Manager after six months and assumed position as Bookkeeper after corporate merger in 1979.
- Prepared monthly statements; made cash flow projections.
- Administered Payables and Receivables.
- Reconciled bank accounts and prepared tax returns.
- Interfaced with Factor for financing of Receivables.
- Established lines of credit for customers.
- Collected on delinquent and past due accounts.

COMPUTER SKILLS:

Windows 95, MS Works (Word Processing, Spreadsheets, Database), MS Money, Lotus 1-2-3, Libra Accounting System, Paintshop, HTML, Internet.

LICENSE: New York State Licensed Notary Public.

Combination. *Arnold G. Boldt, Rochester, New York*
A resume for an experienced Bookkeeper who has become an experienced Office Manager who performs all accounting functions for a construction company. See Cover Letter 14.

AGNES WINSTON

98 Collingwood Drive ▲ Riverton, KY 00000
(555) 555-5555

_____ **PAYROLL & BENEFITS MANAGER** _____

Offering:
- ▲ Nineteen years of various bookkeeping/accounting experience with specialization in payroll and benefits
- ▲ Expertise in setting up and maintaining both in-house and online ADP/PC systems for payroll and related reports
- ▲ Adaptability to technological and organizational changes
- ▲ High tolerance for stress
- ▲ Independent action to anticipate and fulfill departmental needs
- ▲ Safeguard of matters requiring strictest confidentiality
- ▲ Computer knowledge of AS/400 and PC systems; ADP online payroll; MS Word and Excel software.

Areas of Expertise:

Payroll Processing
- ▲ Disbursed wages and salaries for small- to medium-sized companies.
- ▲ Calculated commissions, bonuses and pay deductions.
- ▲ Personally handled top-management payroll.
- ▲ Reconciled payroll with bank statements.
- ▲ Prepared, remitted and generated reports of federal and multistate taxes.
- ▲ Interfaced with accounts payable to routinize garnishee payments.

Personnel/Benefits Administration
- ▲ Controlled new hire paperwork, including confirmation of job offers, activation of payroll, explanation of benefit plans, and assistance with forms completion.
- ▲ Tracked employee attendance, vacations and other time away from job.
- ▲ Administered cafeteria plan benefits including health insurance, disability and 401K.
- ▲ Implemented merit pay increases.
- ▲ Deleted terminated employees and enrolled them in COBRA option.
- ▲ Acted as liaison with insurance broker regarding company vehicle accidents, workmen's compensation claims and business-related liabilities.

Other Bookkeeping/Accounting Functions
- ▲ Directly responsible for cash management and books of original entry, through general ledger.
- ▲ Involved with billing, accounts receivable entries, aging reports, account analysis and collections.
- ▲ Computed data for budget preparation.
- ▲ Prepared job costing schedules and related analyses.
- ▲ Managed petty cash fund.
- ▲ Handled foreign exchange transactions.

Administrative Experience
- ▲ Improved routine office procedures.
- ▲ Trained and supervised support staff.
- ▲ Purchased office, warehouse and miscellaneous supplies based on price and quality factors.
- ▲ Procured licenses, permits and renewals of same.

— Continued —

8

Combination. *Melanie A. Noonan, West Paterson, New Jersey*
Distinctive features are (1) the display font for the individual's name in the contact information, (2) the unusual heading Offering for the opening summary section, (3) the series of

AGNES WINSTON

Page 2

Current Employment:

Since 19XX   Mason & Devereau, Inc., Ashland, KY
Head Bookkeeper/Payroll Manager for $5 million liquor importer and distributor employing 122.

- ▲ Initiated payroll update through ADP, which expanded the utilization of functions.
- ▲ Recommended a qualified business broker, now in third year of service, who has been able to respond to specific company needs.
- ▲ Designed a personnel directory listing contact information for internal staff and sales people in different divisions and states, resulting in improved communications.
- ▲ Researched and developed an easy-to-update mail sorting system for more efficient access by sales staff.
- ▲ Established improved control of office supply inventory which restricted entry to the stockroom, thereby eliminating shortages and saving considerable replenishment expense.

Earlier Employment:

19XX to 19XX   COMMERCE DEVELOPMENT COUNCIL, Blue Grass, KY
Full Charge Bookkeeper/Personnel Administrator for consulting firm with staff of 25.

19XX to 19XX   GENEVA PACKING COMPANY, INC., Ashland, KY
Full Charge Bookkeeper for subsidiary of a cheese importing company (8-person branch office).

19XX to 19XX   DANIEL J. PARKER, CPA, Calhoun, KY
Bookkeeper in a small public accounting firm.

Education:

Blue Grass Community College, Bowling Green, KY
A.S. Business Administration, 19XX

Computer Learning Center, Hopkins, KY
Course in Microsoft Professional Office Applications

Regularly attend employment and disability seminars given by the state to keep up on new changes in legislation.

subheads for clustering duties and responsibilities in the Areas of Expertise section, and (4) the distinction between Current Employment and Earlier Employment. This distinction helps to call special attention to the person's current role as Head Bookkeeper/Payroll Manager by giving it a section of its own.

Phyllis Carson

P.O. Box 999
Granite Springs, NY 10527
(914) 248-1212

OFFICE MANAGEMENT / OFFICE ADMINISTRATION
Office Accounting / Bookkeeping / Credit & Collections

RESULTS-ORIENTED PROFESSIONAL with 14 years' increasingly responsible experience. Expertise in payables and receivables. Record of progressive advancement reflecting ability to augment fiscal efficiency, maximize operational productivity, and achieve substantive results. Decisive, proactive, and precise. Proficient with numerous customized accounting systems and state-of-the-art software packages, e.g., Lotus 1-2-3, Windows, and word processing programs.

Expert qualifications include:

- Office Administration
- Accounts Payable / Receivable
- Bank Reconciliations
- Computerized Accounting Systems

- Bookkeeping
- Billing / Collections
- Journal Entries
- Negotiation

PROFILE

- Organized, take-charge professional with exceptional follow-through abilities and detail orientation; able to oversee projects from concept to successful conclusion.
- Demonstrated ability to effectively prioritize a broad range of responsibilities in order to consistently meet deadlines.
- Strong track record in Retail, Real Estate, and Health Care/Medical environments.
- Possess in-depth knowledge of third-party reimbursement, no fault, workers' compensation, and Medicaid/Medicare.
- Highly adept in patient/customer collection procedures and processing medical claims.
- *Achieved reputation* for taking initiative to structure payment plans, resolving potentially problematic situations into win-win successes.

PROFESSIONAL EXPERIENCE

October xxxx through Present

ADVANCED ALLIANCE MANAGEMENT CORP., Jefferson Valley, NY
Collection Representative

- Successfully resolve and collect all outstanding patient accounts for radiological group operating from two locations.
- Obtain comprehensive billing information and documentation for self-pay accounts.
- Continually vigilant in reviewing aged trial balance for delinquent accounts.
- Rapidly respond to patient inquiries.
- Began part-time before transitioning to full-time April xxxx
- *Commended by supervisor* for *tactfully handling* financial hardship patients and developing successful payment plans.

9

Combination. *Mark D. Berkowitz, Yorktown Heights, New York*
This resume has distinctive features: (1) the three-dimensional name in the contact information; (2) staggered, dual horizontal lines; and (3) hollow diamond bullets with concave sides

October xxxx to April xxxx	**RICHARD'S HOME CENTER**, Mount Kisco, NY **Credit/Collection Manager**

- Successfully operated with firm's conviction that all cash due is collectable.
- Recognized for developing exceptional rapport with customers.
- Commended for *turning impending loss into profit* through *highly effective* on-the-spot *negotiations*.
- *Significantly increased cash flow* through implementation of shortened pay-out terms. Transformed previous 120-day collection terms down to 39-day average *effectively turning sales into cash* in less than 40 days.
- Oversaw all billing data entry, evaluating customer files and generating statements and invoices.

Office Manager/Bookkeeper
- Administered all payables and receivables.
- Prepared payroll for 25 staff utilizing ADP, an automated system.
- Handled all phases of banking.
- Assisted retained legal counsel on credit/collection matters in addition to other business issues.

January xxxx to October xxxx	**RASKIN, MATZA & COHEN**, New York, NY **Full Charge Bookkeeper** for real estate management firm specializing in rentals and cooperatives.

- Oversaw A/R, A/P and bank reconciliations for 20 entities.
- Prepared reports and accrued information for year-end audit for CPAs of each building.
- Prepared monthly cash management reports for various Boards of Directors.
- Developed and reviewed monthly and yearly budgets and financial reports for 20 entities.
- Was instrumental in converting company from manual bookkeeping system to highly efficient computerized system.

August xxxx to January xxxx	**HOWMET CORPORATION**, Greenwich, CT **Administrative Assistant**

- Served as right hand to Controller.
- Administered Travel Advance Account for two divisions.
- Performed monthly division balance.
- Analyzed General Ledger Accounts.
- Reconciled monthly budget report analysis for corporate departments.

EDUCATION   PACE BUSINESS SCHOOL, Yonkers, NY
Associate of Applied Science: Business Administration   xxxx
- GPA: 3.5

REFERENCES   Excellent references will be furnished on request.

for expert qualifications and special achievements. Pleasing white space is accomplished through a relatively large font size, greater leading (spacing) between lines and sections, and a wide left column for section headings and dates. This writer likes to use bold italic to call attention to significant phrases.

D. JACK WILLIAMS

(555) 555-5555 ● djack@atl.mindspring.com ● 3333-K Peachtree Drive ● Atlanta, Georgia 00000

EDUCATION

Masters in Business Administration - *Accounting Major*
Georgia State University, XXXX

Bachelor of Science - Management Major**,** Minors in *Accounting*, *Economics*, and *Spanish*
Georgia Institute of Technology, XXXX

RELEVANT COURSES

Auditing	Accounting Theory and Financial Statements
Corporate Income Tax	Principles of Accounting
Accounting Information Systems	Advanced Financial Accounting
Organizational Analysis	Industrial Relations
World Business	Strategic Management and Planning
Business Law and Ethics	Cost Accounting

ACCOUNTING INTERNSHIP EXPERIENCE

Accounting Assistant to the President   DIGITRAM, INC.- Atlanta, GA
- Experienced in all aspects of Accounts Receivable including:
      customer setup and terms approval ● order / data entry
      posting ● invoicing ● statements ● collections
- Prepare General Ledger, monthly Financial Statements, and monthly Bank Reconciliation.
- Authorized company check signer.
- Handle daily deposits.
- Maintain automated customer database.
- Customer contact including problem solving and trouble shooting, technical support, collections, and interfacing with international dealers.
- Maintain international customer communication through e-mail system.

EMPLOYMENT HISTORY

Customer Service Clerk*	The Kroger Company - Alpharetta, GA	XXXX-XXXX
Administrative Clerk*	Georgia Tech Foundation - Atlanta, GA	XXXX-XXXX
Customer Service Clerk*	Bruno's, Inc. - Norcross, GA	XXXX-XXXX

*Employment while full-time college student.

SKILLS

Lotus 1-2-3 ● Excel ● Peachtree Accounting ● MS Word ● MS Works ● Ami Pro

Foreign Language: Fluent in Spanish

HONORS/AFFILIATIONS

Dean's List, Georgia Institute of Technology

Alpha Kappa Psi - Professional Business Fraternity - Georgia Institute of Technology: Vice President, Membership Atlanta Alumni Chapter XXXX ● Audit Committee Member XXXX ● National Finance Committee Member XXXX ● Official Delegate to the National Convention XXXX.

10

Functional. *Karen D. Wrigley, Round Rock, Texas*
For this recent graduate with little work experience, the writer highlights subjects learned through courses, emphasizes internship experience, and de-emphasizes unrelated work.

REBECCA H. CALDERWOOD

Phone: (555) 555-5555
E-mail: rebeccacald@yahoo.com

500 55th Avenue
Forest Hills, NY 55555

ACCOUNTS PAYABLE / ACCOUNTING CLERK

Dedicated professional with 9 years of experience in general accounting and accounts payable. Detail-oriented and accurate—take pride in a job well done. Work well independently and in collaboration with team members. Adaptable and flexible—willing to pitch in and assist senior executives and colleagues with projects as necessary. Extensive experience with:

- ❑ Daily Cash Reports
- ❑ Material Projections
- ❑ Payroll Analysis
- ❑ General Ledger
- ❑ Order/Data Entry
- ❑ Bookkeeping
- ❑ Expense Accounts Analysis
- ❑ Accounts Payable/Receivable
- ❑ Inventory Management

Excellent written and verbal presentation skills; Bilingual English-Spanish. Computer literate with proficiency in Microsoft Excel, Windows 95, and QuickBooks Pro. Knowledge of Word and Lotus 1-2-3. Highly analytical and mathematical. Able to prioritize assignments and meet deadlines.

EXPERIENCE

ADVANCED GRAPHICS - Brooklyn, NY   XXXX to present
International leader in custom graphic design and desktop publishing
Accounting Clerk (XXXX to present)
- Analyze financial statements and prepare financial reports.
- Post all journal entries and prepare daily cash report for 2 companies.
- Analyze raw materials cost and prepare weekly perpetual inventory.
- Oversee 3-month-long analysis of $9 million in inventory.
- Reconciled double billing problem, saving company $90,000 over 4 years.
- Handled full-charge bookkeeping for joint venture (1997 to 1998).
- Managed $8-10 million annually in accounts payable and serve as backup for accounts receivable.

Accounts Payable Clerk (XXXX to XXXX)
- Processed accounts payable for $13 million annual disbursement.
- Handled financial transactions for 2 sets of books (XXXX to XXXX).
- Supervised an assistant; Promoted from **Order Entry Clerk** (XXXX).

TRANSPORTATION SYSTEMS COMPANY - New York, NY   XXXX to XXXX
Clerk (XXXX to XXXX)
- Completed order entry, helped with computerizing system, and tutored employees on Lotus 1-2-3.
- Covered for junior managers in their absence.
- Hired after an internship (XXXX) based on dedication and job performance.

EDUCATION

BROOKLYN COMMUNITY COLLEGE - Brooklyn, NY
A.A.S. degree - Computer Programming and Accounting, XXXX

ABILITY TECHNICAL SCHOOL - New York, NY
General Office Assistant Certificate, XXXX

Continuing Education / Certification:
- Bookkeeping Certificate, XXXX
- **SECURITIES, INC.** - Rego Park, NY - Income Tax Preparation Course, XXXX

"...Ms. Calderwood has been a valuable asset to our company since the day we hired her...She is thorough, accurate, and efficient in all aspects of accounts payable and computer applications...She is a fast learner and a top performer."— Daniel Pierce, Supervisor, Advanced Graphics

11

Combination. *Kim Isaacs, Jackson Heights, New York*
Two dual lines call attention to accounting skills, work ethic, verbal skills, computer literacy, and worker traits. The font looks mathematical, and the quotation adds credibility.

▼ ▼ ▼ **Donna Jacoby** ▼ ▼ ▼

277 Neal Street
Flagstaff, AZ 00000

(555) 555-5555

▼ **OBJECTIVE**

Staff accountant for an international company.

▼ **PROFILE**

Strong interest in accounting since high school, with work experience that reflects knowledge of a variety of accounting procedures. Proficient in administrating and maintaining accurate records, financial statements, analyses and reporting requirements for timely submission to management. Recognized as a productive, detail-oriented team contributor who works well under pressure and devotes whatever effort is necessary to meet scheduled deadlines.

▼ **COMPETENCIES**

General Accounting
- Accounts receivable, payable and general ledger transactions for incorporation into financial statements.
- Bank statement reconciliations and other banking functions.
- Audit and tax accounting support.
- Collection of past due accounts and arrangement of payment schedules.

Budgeting/Forecasting/Analysis
- Assistance with quarterly and annual budgets and forecasts, both internal and corporate.
- Review of various operating and balance sheet accounts for past activity, trends, costs, estimated/realized revenues, obligations incurred, etc., to project future income and expense.
- Interpretation of reasons for budget variances.
- Royalty reporting and forecasting related to licensed products.

Cost Accounting
- Reconciliation of inventory at multiple foreign and domestic warehouses and adjustment of journal entries to balance general ledger with perpetual inventory system.
- Review of standard costs for reasonableness, consistency of components within warehouses, determination of changes to be made and corrective actions.
- Recording of inventory receipts/transfers, assistance with cycle counts, and preparation of management reports showing monthly activity.
- Calculation of gross profits by business segment.

International Operations
- Letter of credit presentations with terms and conditions in accordance with corporate policy, legal and regulatory compliance, and international customs conformity.
- Direct collection on letters of credit, foreign and domestic.
- Accurate and complete evaluation of export documentation that includes forwarding cargo receipts, bills of lading, commercial invoices, shipping manifests, certificates of origin and certificates of inspection.

Computer Systems
- AS/400 to produce general ledger, recurring and adjusting journal entries and departmental chart of accounts.
- WordPerfect and Quattro Pro on PC for detail reports and special accounting projects.

12

Combination. *Melanie A. Noonan, West Paterson, New Jersey*
This writer uses a symbol—in this example, one or more downward-pointing filled triangles beside the applicant's name in the contact information and before each section heading—as

▼▼▼ **Donna Jacoby** ▼▼▼

– Page 2 –

▼ ACCOMPLISHMENTS

KUBBY LUV TOY CORPORATION, FLAGSTAFF, AZ   19XX—Date

Cost Accountant (since XXXX), promoted from **Junior Accountant** (XXXX–XX)

– Began as intern for this leading producer of stuffed toys, with manufacturing facilities in Hong Kong, Sri Lanka and Indonesia. Demonstrated knowledge and ability to perform beyond expectations and was hired permanently. Given sole responsibility for all international accounting procedures, directly reporting to corporate officers.

– Worked with IT department to consolidate cumbersome report of product sales and facilitate extraction of meaningful information and/or inconsistencies. Convinced management to assign high priority to the project, which required extensive purging of obsolete items. Resulting streamlined report now enables a more thorough and frequent review in 50% less time.

– Selected by Vice President to prepare statements of profitability on top 50 accounts (out of over 5,000 customers), making up 40% of company's sales. Coordinated with Director of International Operations and Inventory Manager to track allocated costs and variable expenses to determine accurate bottom-line figures required by CEO.

– Discovered and helped to resolve problem with distributor in the United Kingdom that had been charging duty for nondutiable goods because their public warehouse failed to include duty waiver forms with shipments. Implemented controls to prevent such recurrences.

▼ EDUCATION

Ben Franklin University, Prescott, AZ
B.S. Accounting, May 19XX
GPA: 3.7

Southwestern Community College, Flagstaff, AZ
A.A. Business Administration, December 19XX

CPA candidate under company sponsorship

▼ VOLUNTEER ACTIVITIES

– Assisted in organizing Walk-a-Thon for Juvenile Diabetes Foundation, 19XX.

– Math tutor for three junior high students.

a visual motif to unify a multipage resume. The bold page borders also help to tie together the two pages visually. Bold em-dash bullets are, like the triangles, a third unifying device. Why have such devices? For a practical reason: to help identify pages if they become separated. (Resume pages shouldn't be stapled.)

KAREN O'KEEFE
150 Serpentine Way
Bridgeton, DE 00000
(555) 555-5555

OBJECTIVE   Position with a public accounting firm that will provide further exposure to tax preparation, financial statements and auditing.

EDUCATION   Rutgers University, New Brunswick, NJ
Bachelor of Business Administration with specialization in Accounting, X/XX
- Dean's List all semesters; overall GPA: 3.57; Accounting GPA: 3.51
- Coursework included heavy emphasis on taxes. Senior project involved the application of tax rules without use of returns, worksheets or computer.

CPA candidate: 3 parts passed.

SUMMARY OF QUALIFICATIONS

- Experience in working with people and business data in situations which included multistate taxation, preparation of financial statements, streamlining of workflow systems, and training/support functions.
- Sound analytical, numerical reasoning, and interpersonal communication skills.
- Responsible attitude, with the organizational ability to prioritize and handle varied assignments simultaneously.
- Strong initiative to expand knowledge in any areas that would enable tax advantages and more profitable management of clients' cash resources.

COMPUTER PROFICIENCIES

- Computer Language Research: Automated Client Engagement (ACE)
- PeopleSoft: PS Financials
- Creative Solutions: Write-Up Solution and Ultra Tax 1065
- Intuit: QuickBooks
- Digitax 1040
- Lacerte 1120 and 1120S
- Microsoft Excel and Lotus 1-2-3 spreadsheet programs
- Microsoft Windows 95; Microsoft Word for Windows; PowerPoint
- Internet protocols

PROFESSIONALLY RELATED EXPERIENCE

X/XX–Present — Sansone Varner & Company, P.C., New Castle, DE
Staff Accountant at medium-sized public accounting/business consulting firm.
- Assignments included: client write-ups, bank reconciliations, and preparation of income tax basis financial statements in accordance with GAAP, as well as corporate, partnership, personal and payroll tax returns. Alerted management to issues that might affect clients' or firm's financial position.
- Developed increased technical knowledge while serving clients in varied industries such as real estate, managed health care, and sales organizations.
- Supported partners and managers and provided assistance to peers in meeting tight deadlines.
- Looked to as a knowledge source with computer applications; also instructed clients in the use of accounting software.
- Designed Excel worksheets with supporting schedules, which were used firmwide in the preparation of deferred construction costs for a major client having 30 contracting companies. This created increased efficiencies and allowed time to be spent more productively in analysis and consulting.
- Developed Lotus spreadsheet that facilitated tracking and analysis of managed care client's gains/losses from business securities.

… Continued

13

Combination. *Melanie A. Noonan, West Paterson, New Jersey*
The Objective and Education headings are short and are presented as side headings. The remaining headings are longer, and each is presented on one line without "wrapping."

KAREN O'KEEFE
- Page 2 -

X/XX–X/XX — ROTHMAN, NEDERLANDER AND LUCIANO, CPAS, P.C., New York, NY
Accounting Intern *for firm specializing in entertainment business clients.*
- Prepared weekly write-ups of gross sales revenues and expenses for producers of Broadway and traveling shows that included *Miss Saigon, Phantom of the Opera* and *Les Miserables*, aiding them in decision making concerning the shows.
- Assisted with bank reconciliations and payroll tax returns.

X/XX–X/XX — VOLUNTEER TAX ASSISTANT, Camden, NJ
- Assisted low income and senior citizens in the preparation of tax returns.

OTHER WORK EXPERIENCE

XX/XX–X/XX — WENCO FOOD SYSTEMS (WENDY'S) CORPORATION, West Brunswick, NJ
Assistant Manager*, responsible for shift of 15 people and the management of all restaurant and customer service functions.*
- Became accustomed to long hours and problem intervention in a high-volume environment.
- Increased efficiencies of daily store closing process by designing a flow chart of tasks, personnel assignments and time periods for completion. This saved two labor hours each evening as well as improved worker morale.

ORGANIZATION MEMBERSHIP

- Delaware Society of CPA Candidates

These longer headings extend beyond the indentation of the information below them. In the Experience section bold italic is used to highlight the positions, and small caps are used for company names. The role of Volunteer Tax Assistant also appears in small caps.

Julius E. Collins
999 Westgate Way
City, State 00000
555-555-5555

SUMMARY: *Seasoned professional with a 15+ year track record in Accounting, Financial Analysis, and Benefits Administration. Experience with Payroll, Receivables, General Ledger accounting, and overseeing pension plans - including annual filings.*

QUALIFICATIONS:

Accounting / Administrative Skills:
General Accounting:
- Administered Payable, Receivable, and General Ledger functions.
- Reconciled Accounts Receivable, Payroll, and Bank Statements.
- Coordinated transition of bookkeeping functions to computerized system.
- Prepared individual tax returns.

Accounting Supervision for Fortune 500 media company:
- Analyzed General Ledger accounts and conducted internal audits.
- Prepared Month-End Closings and Financial Reports.
- Participated in Budgeting and Profit Planning processes.
- Managed Accounts Receivable and Invoicing functions.
- Supervised four other accountants.

Administering pension plans for financial institutions providing services to retail, industrial and professional services firms:
- Prepared annual 5500 and PBGC filings for Pension Plans.
- Documented Plan Terminations and New Submissions.
- Calculated Payouts and Termination Balances.
- Researched state and federal regulations relating to Plan provisions.
- Communicated pertinent information to Plan participants.

PROFESSIONAL EXPERIENCE:

1988 - Present	**Staff Accountant,** Williams Properties, Inc.; City, State.
3/98 - 7/98	**Accountant,** Luxury Auto Accessories, Inc.; City, State. *(Temporary Assignment through Robert Half Accounting)*
1998	**Tax Preparer,** H & R Block; City, State.
1991 - 1993	**Senior Analyst,** Keystone Professional Services; City, State.
1990 - 1991	**Benefits Officer,** National Bank Employee Benefit Services, Inc.; City, State.
1987 - 1990	**Pension Administrator,** Actuarial Data of New York, Inc.; Fairport, New York.
1985 - 1987	**Sales Assistant,** Acme Insurance; City, State.
1985	**Accountant,** Wire-Well Electric; City, State.
1978 - 1983	City Publishing; City, State. **General Accounting - Section Supervisor (1981 - 1983). Accounts Receivable - Section Supervisor (1980 - 1981). Accountant (1978 - 1980).**

EDUCATION:

Bachelor of Science, Accounting; St. Matthew's College; City, State.

COMPUTER SKILLS:

Windows, ACC/PAC, Excel, Lotus, MS Word, Access.

14

Functional. *Arnold G. Boldt, Rochester, New York*
Three themes in the Summary—Accounting, Financial Analysis, and Benefits Administration—are treated in turn in the three groups of the Qualifications section.

ELEANOR T. LISBON
7456 Desktop Lane, Fields, IA 77777
(123) 456-7890

OBJECTIVE:

Seeking a challenging **General Accounting** position that would utilize my extensive skills and experiences.

QUALIFICATIONS:

Experienced, detail-oriented individual with strong knowledge of accounting procedures, including cash reconciliations, accounts payable and receivable, payroll and related taxes and preparation of financial reports; excellent organizational, administrative and problem-solving skills; knowledge of computer terminal usage.

WORK EXPERIENCE:

STAFF ACCOUNTANT, Electronics USA, Wilton, IA   September 1988 - May 1997
Reconciled cash ensuring monies were properly accounted for and in balance status; maintained accounts receivables; prepared payroll for 52 employees; tracked receipt and shipping of inventory via computer; assisted in troubleshooting problems encountered by fellow accounting staff. Other duties included handling petty cash and telephone reception.

STAFF ASSISTANT, Glibb, Glibb & Adlib, Oakton, IA   May 1987 - August 1988
Prepared monthly closing of books for small companies; compiled quarterly payroll taxes; reconciled bank statements. Other duties included performing general office work.

ACCOUNTING ASSISTANT, Realty Associates, Ridge, IA   October 1985 - May 1987
Managed timely and accurate completion of various accounting procedures and reports; related duties included overseeing accounts payable/receivable; made bank deposits and handled bank reconciliations; tracked payroll taxes.

FULL CHARGE BOOKKEEPER, Graphics, Inc., Dale, IA   April 1985 - October 1985
Performed all bookkeeping procedures including commission reports, bank reconciliations and customer billings.

ACCOUNTING DEPARTMENT SUPERVISOR, Federal Savings & Loan Association, Dale, IA
August 1978 - April 1985
Supervised ten bookkeepers; provided training and consultation; managed full accounting duties for one subsidiary corporation; prepared reports; analyzed accounts; reconciled bank statements; calculated interest payments on T-bills; coordinated CRT setup; handled accounting responsibilities for pension fund.

ASSISTANT SUPERVISOR, Major Corporation, Oakwood, IA   September 1974 - August 1978
Responsibilities included processing monthly sales, preparing accounts payable/receivable tax reports, analyzing profit and loss statements, overseeing bank reconciliations, logging journal entries on CRT, and auditing state and federal unemployment eligibility.

EDUCATION:

City College, Glenwood, IA
Completed various courses in accounting and business management disciplines.

References available upon request

15

Combination. *Cathleen M. Hunt, Chicago, Illinois*
A conservative look achieved through positions enhanced with bold, all-uppercase letters.
Ivory linen for the original added to this look. Experience in general accounting is evident.

COST ACCOUNTANT, CPA

1 Accounting Blvd.
New York, New York 99999
(000) 000-0000

QUALIFICATIONS

13 years' experience in all facets of accounting field
Analyze, compare, and interpret facts and figures quickly
Make sound judgments based on data obtained
Clearly communicate results of work, orally and in writing
Good working with people as well as with business systems and computers
Possess high standard of integrity

CERTIFICATION

Certified Public Accountant, State of New York, XXXX

RELATED PROFESSIONAL EXPERIENCE

ABC Manufacturing, New York, New York, XXXX - XXXX
Cost Accountant, XXXX - XXXX
- Studied and collected information to determine standard and actual costs of widget manufacturing including raw material purchases, inventory, and labor
- Analyzed data obtained and recorded results, using computer
- Examined changes in product design, raw materials, and manufacturing methods to determine effects on costs
- Evaluated actual manufacturing costs and prepared periodic reports comparing standard costs to actual production costs
- Provided management with reports comparing factors affecting prices and profitability of products explaining monthly budget variances to senior management
- Reported and interpreted discrepancies directly to upper management

Auditing Consultant, XXXX - XXXX
- Conducted special study and in-depth analysis of company's 401-K plan
- Audited internal controls of payroll deductions leading to proper accounting by 3rd-party investment company
- Results of audits assisted in maintaining good employee/management relations

New York Utilities Company, New York, New York, XXXX - XXXX
Cost of Service Analyst, XXXX - XXXX
- Performed and coordinated embedded and marginal cost of service studies
- Reviewed FERC and ICC rulings and orders for impact and incorporated appropriate changes into cost-of-service models
- Gathered necessary information and prepared various regulatory financial reports and rate filings
- Assisted in coordination and preparation of electric and gas rate filing schedules resulting in grant of rate increases
- Prepared cost studies and monthly billing calculations for contract customers

16

Combination. *Sally McIntosh, Jacksonville, Illinois*
This individual had been out of the workforce for five years to raise children. The writer's
strategy was to go back more than 10 years in the person's work history and indicate the

COST ACCOUNTANT, CPA - page 2

New York Utilities Company, continued
Internal Auditor, XXXX - XXXX
· Conducted audits for management to assess effectiveness of controls, accuracy of financial records, and efficiency of operations
· Provided proper checks and balances over company's various financial operations
· Uncovered internal control weaknesses in company's bidding practices
· Assessed and evaluated management's responses to audits
· Supervised employees during audits
· Audits performed included District/Area Offices and Storerooms, Power Plant Storerooms, Fuel Receiving and Accounting, Accounts Payable, Purchasing, Cash and Temporary Investments

Regulatory Accountant, XXXX - XXXX
· As sole regulatory accountant, prepared and coordinated annual regulatory reports to State Commerce Commission and Federal Energy Regulatory Commission, handling annual operating revenues of over $6,000,000
· Prepared financial statements for wholesale and retail rate cases
· Researched GAAP accounting and regulatory accounting questions that arose within the company
· Requested to teach Regulatory Accounting credit course to the Economics Engineering class
· Initiated computerization of financial statements
· Successfully filed for and was granted rate increases
General Accountant, XXXX - XXXX
· Reconciled NYUP's cash account to bank statements and general ledger balance for previous three years, allowing major accounting firm to issue unqualified opinion leading to positive effects on company's stock price
· Accurately handled 318 service-area bank statements and 15 disbursing banks' statements monthly
· Prepared monthly closing entries and annual inventory adjustments for storerooms

Other Positions Held: VITA, New York College, XXXX to Present

EDUCATION

Bachelor of Science degree in Accounting and Business Administration (Economics) New York City College, New, York, XXXX

Various continuing education courses, seminars, and workshops in accounting and related areas

REFERENCES

Available on request

wealth of experience she had gained in working for a public utility company. Statements about that experience take up the equivalent of a full page. That information is easy to read because it is spread across her four positions with that company.

ACCURATE K. ACCOUNTANT
2855 West Cactus Road
Phoenix, Arizona 85029
(602) 789-1200

CORPORATE FINANCE EXECUTIVE

Strategic Business & Financial Planning / Forecasting & Analysis / General Accounting & Reporting
Budgeting (Capital & Operating) / Cash Management & Optimization

---

SUMMARY OF EXPERIENCE

XYZ Communication Systems, Anyplace, Illinois   **9/95 to Present**
Position: Regional Financial Accountant
A manufacturing and service organization with over 15 branches nationwide, providing communication
solutions for a wide variety of businesses. Consolidated revenues of over $250 million.

- Provide direct financial support to branch management, coordinating financial needs of the Region with
  the corporate Finance Department in Anaheim.
- Responsibilities include supporting 7 branches in the Central & Southern Regions.
- Financial Statement analysis, budgeting & planning support, monthly booking/revenue forecasting.
- Schedule and conduct physical counts of the branch perpetual inventories as needed.
- Conduct regular reviews of branch adherence to company operating policies and procedures.
- Monitor and help control cash collection process by conducting monthly meetings with branch and
  collection personnel.
- Extensive spreadsheet analysis and preparation using Microsoft Office.

ABC Council of Realtors, Anytown, Illinois   **9/93 to 9/95**
Position: Director of Finance
A nonprofit association dedicated to the professional development of women in real estate. An affiliate of
the National Association of Realtors with revenues of over $2 million.

- Developed systems and procedures for the newly created Finance Department.
- Implemented program-based budget system.
- Prepared detailed financial reports including department and program/project analysis.
- Prepared written analysis of financial statements for review by Finance & Budget as well as executive
  committees.
- Reviewed account analysis and actual vs budget analysis using Lotus 1-2-3.
- Upgraded computer system based on current and future needs.
- Acted as liaison to outside consulting firm in the development of new membership system using Paradox
  for Windows.
- Evaluated and implemented computer software systems and arrange for staff training.

XXX International, Inc., Anytown Park, Illinois   **11/88 to 9/93**
Position: Supervising Senior Accountant
A manufacturer of hair care products with subsidiaries in over 17 countries. Consolidated revenues of
$220 million Internationally (one billion worldwide).

- Responsibilities included financial and accounting support to the International Group business units
  headquartered in Melrose Park.
- Supervised one professional and one clerk with the monthly closing and consolidation of the
  International Group financial records.
- Successfully designed and implemented programs for monthly reporting, budgeting, forecasting and
  strategic reviews using Lotus 1-2-3 and WordPerfect.

17

Chronological. *Bernie Stopfer, Phoenix, Arizona*
A substantial resume for an individual whose employment has been without gaps from April
of 1983 to the present even though the person has worked for five different employers during

ACCURATE K. ACCOUNTANT - Page Two

ZZZ, Inc., Anywhere, Illinois   **3/86 to 11/88**
Position: Senior Accountant
A manufacturer of micronutrients and injectable drugs consisting of four plants, two foreign and one
domestic subsidiaries, with consolidated revenues of $172 million.

- Responsibilities included monitoring two professionals and one clerk for monthly closing activities.
- Prepared monthly consolidated financial statements for four plants in addition to foreign and domestic
  subsidiaries, using IBM System 38 computer and Lotus 1-2-3 programs.
- Assisted manager of financial reporting in meeting all financial reporting requirements and SEC
  reporting.

QTE Technical Corporation, Somewhere, Illinois   **4/83 to 3/86**
Position: Assistant Controller
A wholly owned subsidiary of XYZ Corporation of Florida, a business comprising seven operating
subsidiaries involved in the machine tooling distribution industry, with consolidated revenues of
approximately $25 million.

- Responsibilities included preparing monthly consolidated financial statements for seven operating
  companies of XYZ Technical Corporation for corporate subsidiary General Ledger, intercompany
  accounting, working with IBM System 34 computer.
- Supervised small clerical staff consisting of accounts payable, billing and credit collections.

EDUCATION

B.S., Managerial Accounting, 1987 Loyola University, Chicago, Illinois

REFERENCES AVAILABLE BY REQUEST

that time. Some of the bulleted items indicate the individual's use of computing as that use shifted over the
years from IBM System 34 and 38 computers to microcomputers. Near the top of the first page, the two
lines enclose and thus call attention to the individual's many areas of accounting expertise.

JANE SMITH

1212 Easy Street, A-12   (714) 633-2783 (phone)
Some City, CA 90000   resumes100@aol.com (email)

Profile: Accounting professional with additional business and management education.

Key Skills: • Financial Record Analysis   • Statutory Compliance Review
                 • Periodic P&L Statements   • International Clientele Liaison

Employment History:

1997-Present   **Accountant – Worthwhile Agency**, Some City, CA
                • Formatted overdue A/R reconciliation schedules for major vendor customers.
                • Maintain daily journals and other accounting processes.

1995-1996   **Staff Auditor – Another Great Group**, Farther Away, CA
                • Analyzed financial records of recording and publishing companies.
                • Verified compliance with regulations by detailed audits.
                • Checked copyright ownership of several works.

1993-1994   **Staff Accountant – Asian Corporation**, Closer In, CA
                • Performed reviews and compilations for wholesale and distribution clients.
                • Computerized client data for time and labor savings.

1992   **Staff Accountant – Another Music Agency Corp.**, Nearer Yet, CA
                • Prepared profit reports for investors.
                • Prepared financial statements for each series and each investor.
                • Initiated an analytical review of profit reports for international participants.

1981-1991   **Accountant – Big Time Movie Group**, Near Hollywood, CA
                • Prepared corporate financial reports including journal entries & schedules.
                • Maintained and analyzed general ledger on a timely basis.

Education:

1998   Earned Certified Management Accountant Certificate
1985-1998   Accounting Courses: University of California, Irvine
1985   California Real Estate Broker's License

Other: Computer literate: Microsoft Office including Word, Excel, Access; Lotus.
                Bilingual: English/Spanish

                REFERENCES AVAILABLE UPON REQUEST

18

Combination. *Nita Busby, Orange, California*
A resume that is easily sized up and read because of its adequate white space and limited
amount of information. The contact information is arranged according to a balanced format.

James D. Schroeder
67 Yorktown Place
Parlin, New Jersey 08859
(732) 727-5926
E-mail: JDS0893@AOL.com

Objective

Growth-oriented position in accounting/business management with opportunity for professional development and continued education.

Education

BS in Accounting, May 1991
St. Peter's College, Jersey City, NJ

Summary

Increasing responsibilities in areas including:

- Accounts Payable
- Accounts Receivable
- Account Analysis
- Financial Statement Preparation

- Payroll
- Inventory Control
- Credit and Collections
- General Ledger Analysis

Experience

1994-Present

Accountant
SUMMIT HOLDINGS CORPORATION, Whippany, NJ

Initially hired to perform payroll functions, assumed accounts payable and accounting functions to decrease costs and increase efficiency.

- Created and managed payroll and accounts payable department for start-up company including real estate, warehousing, and shipping divisions totaling 60+ employees.
- Accounting responsibilities included general ledger analysis, monthly closings, and preparation and presentation of financial statements using MAS-90 accounting software.
- Responsible for managing cash accounts. Provided management with daily summary of change in investment and cash position.
- Assisted external auditors with annual audit.

1988-1994

Assistant to the Controller
TAYLOR WINE SALES OF NEW JERSEY, INC., Elizabeth, NJ

Hired as a College Intern, promoted to position of Assistant to the Controller in 1991.

- Performed numerous accounting functions including general ledger, accounts payable, and preparation of payroll for 100+ employees.
- Created backup functions and temporary personnel slots for key positions within the organization.
- Assisted the credit manager in supervisory functions relating to accounts receivable department.

Computers

Excellent computer skills, including the following software:

- Microsoft Excel
- Lotus 1-2-3
- Ami Pro 3.0
- ADP PC/Payroll

- EasyCalc
- Microsoft Word
- MAS-90

19

Combination. *Beverly Baskin, Marlboro, New Jersey*
A clear, easy-to-read resume. Diamond bullets ensure that the reader sees the "sweet spot": the location occupied here by the Summary. Italic enhances significant information.

Laura Miles

(513) 555-5555
4811 Bittertree Court, Cincinnati, Ohio 45242

PROFILE	**Accounting/Office Management professional** with diverse experience in wide range of industries.

- Highly organized, detail-oriented, and thorough; exceptional ability to follow through to completion.
- Creative problem solver skilled at finding root causes, analyzing problems and recommending solutions.
- Proficient in Lotus 1-2-3, WordPerfect, specialized construction industry and property management accounting programs. Self-trained on all software; highly adaptable to new learning experiences.
- Articulate and professional; excellent people skills; a positive attitude and strong work ethic.

**PROFESSIONAL
EXPERIENCE**
1994-Present

General Ledger Accountant • PROPERTY ACCOUNTING SERVICES, INC., Cincinnati, Ohio
Property Management Accounting and Payroll Service

- Serve as primary G/L accountant for the company's major client, a large property management firm. Reconcile bank accounts, compile and audit financial data, prepare monthly financial statements.
- Consistently meet stringent monthly deadlines for completion of large volume of accounting work.
- Complete extensive G/L work for other clients in various businesses. Clients' record-keeping styles are diverse and present challenging opportunities to restore order and bring reporting up to date.
- Analyzed and recommended improved accounting procedures and record-keeping policies for security deposits held for tenants of large property manager.
- Assumed position with all accounts behind schedule by 7 months. Implemented effective system that brought accounts up to date within 2 months and maintains current status on an ongoing basis.

1984-1994

Office Manager • SMITH & SONS, INC., Indianapolis, Indiana
General Contractor / Interior Finish Contractor

- Accounting responsibilities encompassed financial statements, payroll, quarterly tax reports, cash flow analysis, work in process, job cost, accounts receivable, accounts payable, collections.
- Responsible for smooth functioning of all office operations. Determined need for temporary help, coordinated requirements with agency, and supervised temporary accounting and office workers.
- Held independent decision-making authority for cash transfers, payment of vendors, and other business operational needs; owner absent 50 percent of the time.
- Handled weekly payroll that fluctuated from 45 to over 100 employees.
- Maintained detailed work-in-process records of job status and all job costs. Prepared regular reports that enabled quick review of expenses as compared to job progress and simplified gross profit calculations and interim and final billing.
- Served as contact person and liaison for customers, vendors and suppliers.
- Coordinated accounting information for CPA. Prepared detailed information for insurance audits.
- Following a 5-month hiatus, returned to the company to find accounts had been kept incorrectly and/or manually; restored order and fully computerized operations within 2 weeks.

1980-1984

Secretary / Accounts Payable • GREATER CINCINNATI BUSINESS ASSOCIATION, Cincinnati, Ohio
Chamber of Commerce

- Prepared minutes of board meetings, statistical reports, and general correspondence.
- Administered payroll, accounts payable, and insurance benefits.

1976-1980

Assistant Branch Manager / Administrative Assistant • ACME FINANCIAL, INC., Cincinnati, Ohio

- Gained thorough understanding of financial institution operations; handled all administrative duties.
- Progressed from entry-level position to Assistant Branch Manager.

EDUCATION

INDIANA UNIVERSITY Continuing Education, Indianapolis, Indiana: **Accounting**
CINCINNATI STATE UNIVERSITY, Cincinnati, Ohio: **Business Administration**

20

Combination. *Louise M. Kursmark, Cincinnati, Ohio*
Just one horizontal line with one vertical line can make a resume look more interesting.
"This resume led to an interview and subsequent acceptance of the first job applied for."

MATTHEW A. PORTER
8910 Stillwell Avenue, #1234
Lutz, Florida 33549
(813) 000-0000

PROFESSIONAL SUMMARY

Corporate Accountant offering over seven years of distinct experience and a demonstrated record of augmenting fiscal efficiency. Combine accounting expertise with proficiency in MIS technology to enhance software applications and maximize productivity; successful in launching goal-driven initiatives that generate substantive results. Well-versed in FAS 1000 and Unisys Mainframe Systems; software proficiency includes Windows, Lotus, dBASE, Quicken, and Excel. Conversant with corporate needs assessments, human resource functions, building client relations, and personnel supervision. Self-directed and conscientious; work well under pressure, with attention to details. Well-honed analytical, problem-solving, communication, interpersonal, and decision-making skills. **Areas of core competency include:**

➤ Corporate Accounting   ➤ Business Management
➤ Contract Negotiations   ➤ Operational Needs Assessments
➤ Automated Accounting Systems   ➤ Strategic Planning

ACCOUNTING SKILLS

Profit & Loss Statements/Projections … Financial Statements … Balance Sheets … Accounts Payable … Accounts Receivable
General Ledger … Payroll … Tangible/Intangible Property Taxes … Use Taxes … Excise Taxes … Sales Tax Reports
Budgeting … Fixed Asset Management … Month & Year-End Reconciliations/Adjustments/Closing Procedures

EMPLOYMENT HISTORY

TDF ASSOCIATION   **Tampa, FL**
Senior Accountant   **1995 - Present**
Spearhead accounting operations and supervise three accounting clerks. Integral role in developing software applications that enhance efficiency and maximize productivity. Directly manage $27MM in fixed assets; calculate/prepare various local, state and federal tax filings; formulate budgets for present/future fiscal year(s); maintain inventory controls; and handle licensing and registration for truck fleet.

• **Streamlined process for tracking inventory of fixed assets.**
• **Established systemized hauling rate calculations for use on spreadsheets.**
• **Created and implemented computerized spreadsheet forms.**

DAY CARE MANAGEMENT SERVICES   **Tampa, FL**
Regional Accountant/Business Manager   **1992 - 1995**
Pivotal role overseeing financial operations and business management of five-area, corporate-sponsored child care centers. Served as a liaison extensively interacting with high-profile clients, conducting contract negotiations and establishing a working rapport and "goodwill" among clients. Oversaw all accounting, report generation, computer troubleshooting, personnel management, and human resource functions.

• **Acted as interim Director of Tall Oaks (center for Salomon Brothers, Inc.) for approximately six months.**
• **Designed individual center-specific spreadsheets to track employee (client) benefits and cost allocations.**
• **Developed budgets, cost/break-even analysis and profit/loss projections for each location.**
• **Personally negotiated and adjusted budgets to gain approval of each client.**
• **Voted companywide to receive** *"Parent Partnership Award"* **for high-level performance in promoting "client goodwill."**

FLORIDA CORPORATION   **Vero Beach, FL**
Accountant   **1990 - 1991**
Handled general accounting duties.

EDUCATION

B.S. degree - Accounting, University of Florida, Gainesville, FL
Florida Academic Scholar - Richardson Foundation Scholarship

Professional 5th-Year Accounting, Florida Metropolitan University, Tampa, FL

Eligible for CPA Exam in 1998

21

Combination. *Diane McGoldrick, Tampa, Florida*
With compact information in wide lines and small print, this resume has the look of an executive resume for an individual wanting to become a Controller. See Cover Letter 17.

JANE S. SMITH
1965 Main Street
New York, New York 55555
(718) 555-5555

International Accounting/Financial Analyst Well versed in broad general accounting functions of medium to large corporations. Highly motivated, committed team player with strong organizational, analytical, and problem-solving skills.

HIGHLIGHTS of QUALIFICATIONS
* Expertise in current issues of international accounting, reinforced by eleven years' experience with multinational organizations
* Thrive on opportunities to assume responsibility
* Multilingual; fluent in French and Italian

<u>PROFESSIONAL EXPERIENCE</u>
General Foods, White Plains, NY
    SENIOR FINANCIAL ACCOUNTANT (1993-Present)
- Prepare Income Statement and Balance Sheet for two international energy companies
- Monitor monthly variance of actual vs. estimated earnings; compile and report to operations
- Compile foreign tax withholding data; recap revenue and expenses for filing US income taxes
- Summarize closing activities and variance analysis: month-month, quarter-quarter, year-year
- Assemble and provide data on foreign investments and revenue to Department of Commerce
- Calculate and record estimated Federal income tax accrual for three domestic subsidiaries
- Quality Coordinator; track customer/supplier activity, develop action plans for improvement

    FINANCIAL ACCOUNTANT (1991-1993)
- Developed internal controls for receivable collection of revenue and foreign tax
- Audited project contracts to ensure compliance to terms
- Supported project managers; provided assistance in budget development and budget analysis
- Developed RBase program to compile financial data for operations and tax departments
- Trained and supervised summer interns and part-time employees

    SENIOR ACCOUNTANT (1989-1991)
- Provided monthly and quarterly earnings analysis to management and Board of Directors
- Liaison to external auditors tracking annual audit fees of foreign subsidiaries
- Prepared monthly budget analysis report for Assistant Comptroller

Marymount College, New Rochelle, NY
    GRADUATE ASSISTANT TO DEPARTMENT CHAIR (19867-1989)
- Supervised accounting lab assistants; advised undergraduate accounting majors
- Organized departmental meetings; coordinated faculty schedules and appointments

PepsiCo Wines & Spirits International, Purchase, NY
    ACCOUNTING INTERN (1985-1986)
- Analyzed balance sheet accounts of division headquarters and Bermuda operations
- Translated and recorded currency conversion of foreign subsidiaries' financial statements

Drexel Burnham Lambert, New York, NY
    ACCOUNTING INTERN (1984)
- Assistant to manager of International Firm Trading/Accounting Department
- Maintained ledger of Hedge and Futures Accounts

<u>EDUCATION</u>
Postgraduate Certificate in Professional Studies, Accounting, Pace University, White Plains, NY (1994)
Master of Business Administration, Finance, Marymount College, Dobbs Ferry, NY (1988)
Bachelor of Arts, International Business/Accounting, Pace University, White Plains, NY (1984)

22

Combination. *Marian K. Kozlowski, Poughkeepsie, New York*
This individual has a record of increasing responsibility through promotion within the same company. Before that, her promotion from graduate assistant to department chair is stellar.

JANE B. DOE
555 Main Street • Anytown, USA 00000
(000) 000-0000

Objective:	**SENIOR ACCOUNTANT**

Profile:

- Reliable, efficient and hard-working individual, offering more than eight years of broad-based, senior-level experience in accounting.
- Strong problem-solving, analytical, and account-balancing skills.
- Consistently develop and implement more productive ways to complete tasks.
- Dedicated to excellence in job performance and professional development.

Computer Skills:

- Demonstrate working knowledge of Microsoft Word, Lotus 1-2-3, WordPerfect, DOS and spreadsheet development.

Education:

FOREST COLLEGE, Anytown, USA
Bachelor of Arts, Business Administration, 1983, Cum Laude

ANY STATE JUNIOR COLLEGE, Anytown, USA
Associate of Arts, Accounting, 1977

Experience:
1994 to Present

Senior Accountant, <u>Real Estate Development</u>, Anytown, USA
- Scope of responsibilities for eight business entities (corporations, partnerships and S Corps) consists of account review and balancing, journal entries, financial statements, comparative income statements, and year-end reporting.
- Prepare budgetary statements. Maintain job cost and fixed asset records.
- Compile and maintain working papers for the Financial Manager.
- Update revolving loan spreadsheets on a daily basis.
- Assisted in entering ADP payroll records onto new computer system.

Summers
1991 to 1994

Temporary Accountant, <u>Accountants On Call/Accountemps</u>, Anytown, USA
- Performed variety of long-term assignments involving payroll, accounts payable, Lotus worksheets and bank reconciliations.

1990 to 1992

Accountant (Part-Time), <u>Livingston Products</u>, Anytown, USA
- Prepared and analyzed financial statements.
- Maintained accounts receivable and accounts payable ledgers.
- Recorded and maintained direct materials expense and sales records.
- Set up manual systems for all accounting functions, including general ledger, cash accounts, accounts receivable, and accounts payable.

1985 to 1990

Finance Director, <u>Park District</u>, Anytown, USA
- Managed broad scope of financial operations, including general ledger, accounts receivable, accounts payable, fixed assets, payroll, purchasing and investments.
- Supervised accounting and clerical staff. Served as backup for payroll.
- Prepared the District's annual budget ($10 million).
- Compiled, analyzed and prepared financial reports.
- Oversaw all internal audit functions and prepared independent audit work papers.
- Managed information processing operations, including hardware and software maintenance of minicomputer network.

1983 to 1985

Account Analyst, <u>Insurance Company</u>, Anytown, USA
- Prepared bank reconciliations for 35 Allstate subsidiary bank accounts.
- Assisted in preparation of internal audits of a major insurance company.

References:

Provided Upon Request.

23

Combination. *Joellyn Wittenstein, Buffalo Grove, Illinois*
A master's degree in education and two years of teaching experience are not mentioned because they might confuse potential employers about this individual's career goal.

CHARLES I. CARTER

555 South Street
Phoenix, AZ 00000
(000) 000-000

EDUCATION

CPA	Successful Completion of the Certified Public Accounting Examination November 1996
Formal	*Bachelor of Science in Business Administration* • Cum Laude Miami University of Ohio • Oxford, OH • 1993 *Major: Accountancy* *Major: Finance* Completed Business Writing and Business Communications classes
	Minor: Computer Information Systems Northern Illinois University • DeKalb, IL • 1994 *Curriculum Emphasis:* *COBOL • Systems Analysis • Business Application Software*
Computer	*Proficient in the Use of:* Lotus 1-2-3 • dBASE IV • Ami Pro • WordPerfect • Windows • Microsoft Word • NOMAD • MONARCH • DBS [First of America Mainframe]

QUALIFICATIONS & STRENGTHS

Knowledgeable	Possesses solid accounting background acquired in working for a major bank, multiple-site business, and a CPA firm • Graduated cum laude from a nationally acclaimed undergraduate accounting program
Dedicated to Goal Achievement	Highly self-motivated, demonstrated tenacity, persistence, and ability to complete all tasks in a highly professional manner
Innovative	Creates change through developed analytic and problem solving skills directed at efficiencies in systems, processes, and procedures

PROFESSIONAL EXPERIENCE

Accountant II *Portfolio Analyst*	BANK CORPORATION Phoenix, AZ • December 1995 - 1998 Develop and prepare multidimensional and multilevel Arizona State Line of Business Consumer Installment, Consumer Revolving, and Home Equity portfolio analytics and models • Research portfolio data bases based upon unique parameters and stratifications • Produce reports relating to Portfolio Profit Plan, Plan versus Actual results, and 12-18 month Forecasts for a $1.1 billion portfolio • Support Chief Financial Officer and Consumer Portfolio Manager through monthly and ad hoc analyses • Provide data and assumptions for implementation and execution of profit plan into a balance sheet modeling software • Train new accounting staff
	Quality Service Representative • 1995 Selected by department to act as a representative • Communicate between departments on training and employee relation issues

24

Combination. *Betty Callahan, Vicksburg, Michigan*
A resume with much information but also much white space. This is accomplished through small type, dual lines enclosing centered headings with ample space, two inches of indentation

CHARLES I. CARTER_____

PROFESSIONAL EXPERIENCE
Continued

Accountant I
Burden Analyst

BANK CORPORATION
Phoenix, AZ • February 1995 - December 1995
Researched, compiled, and analyzed Arizona State Line of Business burden data in support of planning, forecasting, and profitability performance • Produced reports relating to Burden Profit Plan, Plan versus Actual results, and 12-18 month Forecasts • Maintained cost center structure to ensure use consistency of general ledger and cost centers • Trained new accounting staff

Staff Accountant
Accounting Intern

SENIOR SERVICES
Phoenix, AZ • 1991 - 1995
Performed write-up activities including bank reconciliations, standard and adjusting journal entries, working paper support for trial balance accounts, and data entry • Assisted in the implementation of a computerized billing system • [Worked as Accounting Intern, 5/91-11/93 and hired as Staff Accountant 11/93]

Accountant

PROFESSIONAL STRATEGIES
Phoenix, AZ • June 1993 - November 1993
Performed all day-to-day accounting functions required in liquidation of a multiple partner group of professionals

Bookkeeper
Training Supervisor

USA TODAY
Phoenix, AZ • 1990 - 1993
Reconciled daily sales to daily receipts and initiated computer system • Scheduled, trained, and supervised service staff • Also worked as expediter • [Promoted from Training Supervisor to Bookkeeper, 9/93]

Resident Assistant

NORTHERN ILLINOIS UNIVERSITY
DeKalb, IL • 1992 - 1993
Advised and assisted students in resolution of personal and academic problems, while ensuring University student conduct policies were maintained

ORGANIZATIONAL MEMBERSHIPS

Member

National Association of Investment Companies
1996 - Present

Beta Alpha Psi
Accounting Honorary Fraternity

References Available Upon Request

for the main information, and blank lines before and after clustered information throughout the rest of the resume. Underlining and italic are font enhancements that call attention to employers, other important information, and side headings. The Professional Experience section shows steady career growth.

Justin Gannett

619 Castle Street • Newtown, MA 00000 • (555) 555-5555

Qualifications

- Excellent interpersonal, communication and analytical/problem-solving skills.
- Consistently recognized by employers for outstanding performance.
- Ability to work well under pressure.
- Strong computer skills including extensive knowledge of FPRS and Microsoft Office.

Experience

ABC RETIREMENT SERVICES CO., Framingham, MA   xxxx–present
Payroll Specialist
- Ensure timely and accurate updating of client 401k contributions and loans for Fortune 500 corporations with assets averaging $1.4 billion.
- Provide customer service phone support during high-volume times.
- Audit and reconcile reports on a daily basis.
- Interact with internal/external parties in resolving participant/client inquiries.
- Train new associates.
- Modify and create monetary files using tape specs.
- Enhanced the established administrative procedures for several existing clients.
- Received "Spot Award" for dedication, customer responsiveness, teamwork, and problem-solving abilities.

ABC RETIREMENT SERVICES CO., Framingham, MA   xxxx–xxxx
Processor
- Processed participant loan repayment and rollover checks.
- Identified, researched, and resolved problems through analysis and corrective action.
- Chosen by management to serve as a "Knowledge Expert" for job function.

WALTHAM POLICE DEPARTMENT, Waltham, MA   Summer xxxx
Detective's Assistant
- Took reports over the telephone, conducted background checks, processed firearm applications, and fingerprinted people applying for citizenship and federal jobs.
- Recognized as "best intern ever."

Education

NORTH ADAMS STATE COLLEGE, North Adams, MA   xxxx
Bachelor of Science, concentration in Criminal Justice
Participated in one-semester internship with Berkshire County Attorney General's office.

25

Combination. *Wendy Gelberg, Needham, Massachusetts*
The purpose is "to demonstrate the candidate's suitability for promotion." The Qualifications section shows skills and work ethic. The rest documents an outstanding work record.

STEVEN J. DAVIDSON

555 Canaveral Place
Cocoa Beach, FL 55555
(555) 555-5555

Objective: Accounting or Payroll position utilizing detail, analytical and computer skills

SUMMARY OF QUALIFICATIONS
- 12+ years progressively responsible accounting and payroll experience
- Experience with government contracts, production/manufacturing and cost environments
- Administered multiple company ledgers and payrolls requiring multiple state tax reporting, financial statement preparation and corporate reporting
- Highly successful in establishing, streamlining and automating accounting systems
- Strength in recognizing, analyzing and solving problems
- Sharp in learning and comprehending new systems and methods

PROFESSIONAL EXPERIENCE
Accounting Manager, Marco Systems, Inc., Port Canaveral, FL, XXXX-XXXX
Accountant, Finance Dept., MICORP, Sebastian, FL, XXXX-XXXX
Payroll Clerk, Science South Engineers, Melbourne, FL, XXXX-XXXX
Sr. Payroll Specialist, Hartford Corporation, Cocoa Beach, FL, XXXX-XXXX

Accounting
- Processed Accounts Payable and Receivable and prepared Davis-Bacon Union fringe benefit reports
- Performed detail general ledger analysis and reconciliation as well as bank reconciliations
- Prepared adjusting journal entries for general ledger
- Supervised, audited, balanced, and performed all payroll functions through W-2 production for 500+ salaried, trade and hourly employees (multiple companies, states and projects)
- Solely responsible for general through year-end and corporate reporting
- Prepared client, interoffice and intercompany invoices

Accounting Systems Design & Problem Solving
- Assessed efficiency of accounting, implementing improvements to accuracy and cost-effectiveness
  - Gained control of delinquent, inaccurate fringe reports and brought them up-to-date at Marco Systems
  - As Payroll Clerk at Science South, developed tracking matrix for maximum hours worked
  - Revamped suspense file at MICORP, accurately journalizing and balancing it
  - Converted payroll and accounting software subsequent to corporate restructure at Marco Systems

Communications & Computers
- Developed cordial working relations, while explaining and clarifying others' clerical errors
- Acted as liaison at Marco Systems between Human Resources and Payroll to resolve conflicts
- Learned and mastered new software and accounting programs very quickly
- Assisted in implementation of computerized accounting/estimating systems
- Performed accounting using Vertical Marketing Software, Lotus 1-2-3 and WordPerfect
- Prepared and downloaded ORACLE Direct Deposit and Standard Register transfer files

EDUCATION
- Marco Systems, Inc., sponsored courses in MS Office, Lotus, Peachtree Accounting, WordPerfect
- Florida Continuing Education Center for Finance - 8 Financial institution related courses
- Valencia Community College courses in Business, Accounting I & II, Taxation

26

Functional. *Laura DeCarlo, Melbourne, Florida*
Redundancy in a resume is the appearance of similar information in the descriptions of similar jobs. Functional format here avoids redundancy in info about similar accounting jobs.

FRANK M. DILLARD

1111 SW 14th ♦ Anytown, ND 99999 ♦ (555) 555-5555

frankdill@internet.email

ACCOUNTING MANAGEMENT

Merging broad accounting experience and knowledge with excellent problem analysis, communication, and financial management skills

---

Highly motivated, disciplined professional with extensive experience in financial management, office administration, and project management. Strong individual contributor and leader who thrives in a team environment. Able to see shades of gray, anticipate potential difficulties, and creatively solve complex problems by checking all possibilities and asking "what if?" Tactful, diplomatic communicator and astute listener. Flexible, adaptable, quick learner who readily accepts challenges. Skilled at tracking data, preparing reports, generating business communications, and handling sensitive materials. Comfortable working with all ages, cultures, and levels. Possess secret clearance.

Financial Expertise Includes:

♦ Commercial Accounts
♦ Month- & Year-End Financial Statements
♦ GAAP
♦ Payables & Receivables
♦ Expense Planning & Control

♦ General Ledger
♦ Resource Utilization
♦ Payroll
♦ Financial Tracking
♦ Budgeting

Management Proficiencies Include:

♦ Supervision & Training
♦ Problem Analysis & Resolution
♦ Communications *(Written, Verbal & Listening)*
♦ Project Management
♦ Contract Administration

♦ Office Management
♦ Inventory Control & Management
♦ Interpersonal Relationships
♦ Client & Vendor Relations
♦ Strategic Planning

Computer & Software Knowledge Includes:

♦ PCs, Macintosh & Windows 95
♦ Excel 7.0

♦ Word 7.0
♦ Access 7.0

Managed budgets exceeding $25 million and supervised up to 245

EXPERIENCE

U.S. ARMY, NORTH DAKOTA STARC HEADQUARTERS, Bismarck, North Dakota   XXXX to XXXX
Assigned advisor/liaison duties between the U.S. Army and the North Dakota National Guard at State Training, Army Recruiting Control (STARC).

Accountant, United States Pay & Fiscal Office (XXXX to XXXX)
Travel Accounts Manager / Liaison, Department of Personnel Actions (XXXX to XXXX)
Travel Accounts Manager, Initial Active Duty Training (XXXX to XXXX)
Unit Administrator, Payroll (XXXX to XXXX)

♦ Managed the general ledger, a $5 million commercial account, payables and receivables, and travel and expense control for the Army in Nebraska.
♦ Balanced 3 journals weekly for a $25 million budget and tracked financial records daily.
♦ Processed and managed an $8 million payroll for 5,000 troops and coordinated paper flow for all promotions, reductions, transfers, GI Bill payments, and student loan repayments.
♦ Supervised 245 individuals handling administrative and operational activities throughout North Dakota.

Continued

27

Functional. *Carole S. Barns, Woodinville, Washington*
The individual "retired from the military just weeks before his resume was created with the goal of a new career." He earned his degree in accounting while he was on active duty and used

♦ Selected as one of 50 liaisons in the United States coordinating activities between Active and Reserve units.

♦ Assigned to Director of Personnel, Department of Personnel Actions, to manage and resolve a wide variety of human and environment problems.

♦ Provided technical guidance to lower-grade personnel.

♦ Found $550,000 in unbudgeted dollars to renovate office space during downsizing phase by tracking statewide, $11 million capital expense budget and collecting and consolidating material, supply, and labor credits.

♦ Approved expenditure of $1.25 million to assist the Nebraska National Guard in the construction of a dike to repair a 135-foot break caused by flooding of the Platte River.

♦ Authorized sending $3 million in equipment and initiated activation of 125 troops to assist North Dakota National Guard during disaster flooding.

♦ Briefed the Governor of North Dakota and the state's congressional delegation on National Guard disaster relief efforts during a national disaster declared by the President.

♦ Defined regulations and policies for company commanders.

♦ Assisted National Arbor Day Committee in its efforts with the National Guard to plant trees around all National Guard Armories.

♦ Established in 1988 the still-held record for drawing, use, and turnback of $8 million in ammunition.

EDUCATION & TRAINING

Bachelor of Arts, Business Administration/Accounting, *University of North Dakota*

"Accounts Payable Administration"
"Travel Administration & Entitlements"
United States Army Finance School

"Ethics, Hazcom, Weather & Prevention"
Nebraska National Guard

Excel 7.0, Access 7.0, Word 7.0, Windows 95
Nebraska Military Department

T.E.A.M. Quality Management Module 1, *for Military Reserve Component Leaders*
Focusing on change management, building trust, correcting and counseling, understanding motivation, leadership, attrition management, and personal development

"Diversity: Managing Cultural Differences"
"Sexual Harassment"
"Equal Opportunity"
U.S. Army

AWARDS & HONORS

Commendation Medal, North Dakota National Guard
For meritorious service

Individual Achievement Award, North Dakota National Guard
For demonstrating exceptional professional ability and customer service

"his financial expertise" in the Army. An impressive resume throughout. Notable features are the horizontal lines at the top of the first page and the diamond bullets pointing to financial expertise, management proficiencies, computer literacy, and career achievements. The Awards & Honors section is a strong ending.

CLARE FARRELL

6820 Cattrell Avenue ▪ Sunnyvale CA 94000
(408) 000-0000

OBJECTIVE: Growth-oriented position as an Accounting Manager or Assistant Controller.

KEY QUALIFICATIONS:

- Hands-on and management experience in a broad range of accounting functions, including general ledger, accounts receivable, accounts payable, cash management, fixed assets, job costs, corporate insurance, banking, taxes and financial statements.
- Proven ability to build and manage a cooperative, highly productive team.
- Proactive approach to identifying problems and implementing effective solutions.
- Computer knowledge: Great Plains; ASK MANMAN; MS Word & Excel.

PROFESSIONAL EXPERIENCE:

ACCOUNTING MANAGER, Lightning, Inc., Fremont, CA   XXXX-Present

Manage accounting responsibilities required for company operation and growth. Hired and presently supervise a staff accountant, junior staff accountant and accounting assistant. Play a key financial role in supporting the company's partnership with Fielding Creations. Perform analysis and develop plans to facilitate system conversions. Accomplishments include:

- Currently setting up general ledger and accounts payable for conversion from Great Plains to Oracle, which includes a payroll change from ADP to Ceridian. Interact with Fielding Creations' accounting and IT staff to ensure achieving a consistent Chart of Accounts.
- Created current-year corporate budget independently, from initial phase to completion.
- Set up books for joint company, which included a change from incorporated to LLC structure.
- Collaborated with Fielding Creations' accounting manager to devise a simplified allocation method for overhead billing that resolved conflicts and ensured smooth flow of funding.
- Developed job cost reports to show financial performance of individual jobs and the production division as a whole.
- Provided an effective means to monitor cash flow through weekly forecasts; prepared 3-month forecasts for Lightning, Inc., and Fielding Creations' management to use as a planning tool.
- Assisted conversion from one main payroll into two and from semimonthly to biweekly.
- Spearheaded reconstruction of general ledger records from backups and other documentation following massive destruction of records by winter flooding.
- Served as focal point for company's first external audit, which produced satisfactory results.
- Joined company as an accountant and received a promotion after 7 months.

ACCOUNTING SUPERVISOR, Toyoma, Inc., San Francisco, CA   XXXX-XXXX
ACCOUNTING SUPPORT III, Toyoma, Inc., San Francisco, CA   XXXX-XXXX

EDUCATION:

- Bachelor of Science in Business Administration, University of California, Davis, CA, XXXX

REFERENCES: Available upon request

28

Combination. *Georgia Adamson, Campbell, California*
This individual had been an Accounting Manager for only four years at a company with fewer than 100 employees. To move up, she needed to move out. See Cover Letter 16.

BARBARA B. BATEMANN

(555) **333-5555** home
(555) **555-3333** cellular

e-mail: bbb@aol.com

333-C Bolder Hill Blvd.
Draper, UT 55555

PROFESSIONAL HIGHLIGHTS

- Significant practical background working with all aspects of accounting and budget planning.
- Hands-on accounting activity with a mix of commercial, retail, and service-oriented businesses.
- Considerable expertise with computer systems, especially for accounting, and inventory control.
- Experienced with training accounting personnel in manual and computerized accounting practices.

PROFESSIONAL EXPERIENCE

<u>ACCOUNTING MANAGER</u> - *Universal Printing Services*...Salt Lake City, Utah   xxxx to present

- Manage a 4-person accounting team and report directly to the controller of this worldwide business.
- Coordinated with ADP for installing and debugging a new computerized accounting system, that proved to be highly successful.
- Established a systematic method for improving control of the budget and accounting processes.
- Maintain all of this company's accounting plus reimbursable orders, and special accounting needs.
- Received a *"Special Recognition"* award—and a substantial cash bonus—for creating the MTP.
- Interact directly with the department managers for analyzing their budget needs and usage, and for guiding them in developing short-term and long-term financial forecasts and objectives.
- Produce monthly and annual budgets—for special project plans—and prepare reports on variances.

<u>BOOKKEEPER</u> - *Bigalow Distributing Company*...Salt Lake City, Utah   xxxx - xxxx

- Managed an accounting team for accounts payable, payroll and banking for this $4 million (+) co.
- Performed all accounts payable responsibilities for more than 125 vendor/supplier accounts.
- Calculated and maintained a biweekly payroll for nearly 100 employees.
- Trained a new Assistant Bookkeeper for using the sophisticated computerized accounting system.
- Maintained a bar-coded system to provide minimum—maximum reports for inventory control.
- Balanced daily receipts, prepared deposits, reconciled bank statements and produced tax reports.

<u>BOOKKEEPER</u> - *Figuroa's Department Store*...Bountiful, Utah   xxxx - xxxx

- Reported directly to the Accounting Manager, at the "Parent" store, but managed the daily sales receipts, balanced the registers, and did the daily bank deposits.
- Developed a keen interest in accounting—as a vocation—from this experience; and was prompted to terminated this position to pursue an advanced accounting degree, which was completed in xxxx.

<u>BANK TELLER</u> - *First Security Bank*...Ogden, Utah   xxxx - xxxx

- Praised by management for consistently achieving zero errors on daily cash balances, and for attention to detail in other accounting processes.

EDUCATION & CERTIFICATIONS

<u>B.S. DEGREE</u> - *Major: Accounting & Finance* - University of Utah, Salt Lake City, Utah   xxxx

<u>A.A. DEGREE</u> - *Major: Accounting* - Morgan Community College - Morgan, Pennsylvania

<u>CERTIFICATIONS</u> • 2-years study...Computer Applications Technology, Ryerson Poly. Institute

---

COMPUTER SKILLS

- Experienced with PCs using Windows 3.1 & 95, MS Word, WordPerfect, Excel, Lotus 1-2-3, ACT a sales management database, and considerable business research on the Internet.

29

Combination. *Carl L. Bascom, Fremont, California*
Lines between sections make them visible at a glance. Italic is used for section headings, company names, an award, and academic majors. Positions stand out with underlining.

NIKKI R. RENFRO

4318 Oak Dale Ct.
Sugar Land, Texas 77000
(555) 555-5555
renfro@abc123.com

CAREER PROFILE

Accounting Professional / Accounting Manager with over 16 years of progressively responsible experience. Qualifications include:

- Financial Analysis / Reporting
- Budget Preparation
- Account Reconciliation
- General Ledger

- Cash Flow Forecasting
- Staff Hiring / Training
- Accounts Receivable
- Accounts Payable

MBA in Accounting and MA in Economics. Excellent analytical, problem-solving and project management skills. Fluent in Spanish and Thai. Extensive experience dealing with foreign subsidiaries. Proficient in MS Excel, Oracle and SQL.

PROFESSIONAL EXPERIENCE

CSS AMERICAN INC., Houston, Texas   1985 - Present
> *Accounting Manager* (Land Acquisition & Non-Exclusive Surveys Dept.)
> Work closely with managers of two divisions; recognized for creating internal reports which assist managers in effectively operating their departments

Land Seismic Division:
- Manage accounting functions of land crews
- Verify, control and analyze crew expenses
- Prepare monthly forecast for management in France
- Perform month-end closing
- Generate invoices
- Maintain and reconcile fixed assets
- Prepare and revise annual budget in domestic and foreign currencies
- Organized and streamlined accounts payable

Logistics Division:
- Prepare financial statements, audit work papers and various internal reports for management
- Prepare cash flow forecast and budget

30

Combination. *Kelley Smith, Sugar Land, Texas*
A resume that displays the writer's favorite font (Lapidary333 BT) for a "professional look." The resume could have been squeezed onto one page if she had used narrow margins, small

PROFESSIONAL EXPERIENCE (continued)

CSS AMERICAN INC. *(cont.)*
- Perform month-end closing and reconcile general ledger accounts
- Supervise accounts payable and accounts receivable functions
- Prepare consolidation reports with other international affiliates
- Oversaw successful conversion from manual to computerized accounting system
- Hired, supervised and trained 10 accounts receivable / payable clerks

SHERMAN LIGHTS COMPANY, Houston, Texas   1982 - 1985
Assistant Controller
- Maintained general ledger
- Prepared financial statements, tax reports, audit work papers and internal financial reports
- Reviewed accounts payable, accounts receivable and payroll
- Completed various projects in other departments as needed
- Hired and trained office personnel

EDUCATION

UNIVERSITY OF HOUSTON, Houston, Texas
MBA / Accounting
MA / Economics

VICTORIA UNIVERSITY, Wellington, New Zealand
BA / Economics

References and letters of recommendation provided on request

print, and reduced line spacing, but the trade-off would have been a loss of white space, readability, and friendliness. Those who insist on keeping a resume to one page should consider what traits are lost. Small caps are used for the person's name, section headings, and company and university names.

JOAN CUMMINGS

555 E. 55th Street • New York, NY 55555 • (555) 555-5555

QUALIFICATIONS SUMMARY: Hands-on Accounting Manager with an extensive background in all facets of accounting, office management and staff supervision. Proven track record of mastering and employing computerized accounting software and systems. Excellent customer relations capabilities with demonstrated judgment in decision making. Highly conscientious and detail-oriented professional with strong problem-solving capabilities. *Areas of proficiency include:*

• **Accounts Receivable**	• **Accounts Payable**	• **Computerized Billing**
• **Collections**	• **Bank Reconciliations**	• **General Ledger/Journals**
• **Financial Forecasts**	• **Budgeting**	• **Incentive/Commission Statements**

▸ **Accounting Manager,** John Smith Corporation, 2/97-xxxx

- Played a key role in managing all accounting operations for fine jewelry manufacturer with annual revenues of $8 million.
- Facilitated conversion of the computerized accounting system to Peachtree software. *Independently developed mastery of program without training.*
- Generated and maintained excellent client relations with numerous jewelry companies nationwide.
- Employed accounting/bookkeeping proficiency to successfully obtain the services of a new merchant bank. *This resulted in an expediting of cash flow and additional financing.*
- Consistently achieved 100% balancing on all end-of-month closings.
- Reduced company expenses through meticulous cost-cutting initiatives.

▸ **Accounting/Office Manager,** Stevens Import Corporation, 1994-1996

- Managed diversified accounting and office management functions for importer of fine jewelry.
- Meticulously handled accounts receivable/payable through customized computer application.
- Successfully resolved 50% of outstanding balances through aggressive collections.
- Meticulously prepared financial statements and all ledgers. Reconciled bank statements. Managed ADP payroll.
- Organized and compiled information for bank audits.
- Interacted extensively with clients and vendors.
- Controlled office inventory; negotiated new equipment purchases, maintainence and repair contracts.

▸ **Bookkeeper,** Hegel & Associates, 1989-1994

- Managed computerized client billing, accounts receivable and general ledger.
- Organized and processed monthly financial statements and ADP payroll.
- Formulated cash forecasts, budgets, incentive and commission statements.

▸ **Accounting Administrator,** Mailing Corporation, 1987-1989

- Devised and implemented accounting system for newly established company.
- Supervised conversion of manual to computerized system.

▸ **Bookkeeper,** Summings International, 1983-1987

- Managed all bookkeeping functions including A/R, A/P, payroll, journals, monthly financial statements, cash forecasts and client billing.

▸ **Assistant to Controller,** E.G.E. Associates, 1979-1983

- Supervised a staff of five in various accounting functions.

EDUCATION/SKILLS

New York Community College, New York, NY
A.A.S. in Accounting, 1977

Peachtree; DacEasy 3.1

31

Combination. *Etta R. Barmann, New York, New York*
A box around the Qualifications Summary helps to ensure that it will be seen if not read in full. Because the Summary is in a box, it is more likely to be read than ignored.

ALICE K. RAMEY   2343 TUCKAHOE LANE • FALL MEADOW , MD 21000 • (410) 678-4567

CAREER OBJECTIVE	*A management-level position affording the best opportunity for continued professional career growth in the accounting field.*

HIGHLIGHTS OF QUALIFICATIONS

- Bachelor of Arts degree in accounting (Earned while working full-time in the accounting field)
- Over six years of working experience in accounting
- Knowledge of accounting cycles for corporations, sole proprietorships, partnerships, and limited partnerships
- Knowledge of DacEasy and Peachtree computer accounting systems
- Experience in both corporate and individual tax return preparation
- Ability to prepare budgets and financial statements
- Knowledge of Lotus 1-2-3; WordPerfect; Windows 95, Corel Suite 7, Quattro Pro, SBI, and Macintosh applications

EXPERIENCE

ACCOUNTS PAYABLE/PURCHASING
Smith County Board of Education, Vickers, MD   *8/98 to present*
Duties include working with vendors and administrative staff. Responsible for paying all school system bills.

ACCOUNTING MANAGER
Green Thurm Nurseries, Rockville, MD   *6/97 to 7/98*
Responsibilities included overseeing daily operations of accounting department, including Accounts Receivable. Served as Credit Manager in charge of customer accounts, terms and limits. Prepared all financial statements, sales reports, and quarterly sales reports.

FULL CHARGE ACCOUNTANT
Jack's Clam Shells, Dover, DE   *2/96 to 6/97*
Was instrumental in setting up a new, in-house accounting system. This eliminated the need for more costly outside contract services and yielded more accurate and efficient accounting practices. Other duties included compiling weekly trucking reports, quarterly fuel and mileage reports, bank reconciliations, and weekly payroll.

JUNIOR ACCOUNTANT
Pro Line Accounting, Winston, MD   *10/94 to 2/96*
Duties included processing weekly payroll and quarterly reports, as well as assisting in the preparation of tax returns. Monthly client work included bank reconciliations, financial statements and the calculation of employee tax liability.

STAFF ACCOUNTANT
Winston Broiler Co., Rockville, MD   *11/92 to 12/93*
Was instrumental in setting up a decentralized, in-house payroll system for the Queenstown plant which employed 250 workers. This increased operating efficiency at the plant and helped reduce administrative payroll costs. Was commended by supervisor for designing new Lotus-based operating reports. Custom designed new reports to help line supervisors measure production efficiency. Other duties included accounts payable, posting and reconciling the general ledger, and assisting in the preparation of weekly financial statements.

CASHIER/STOCKER
Winn City Inc., Preston, MD   *1/91 to 1/92*
FRONT LINE MANAGER/AREA SUPERVISOR
Walmart Inc., Denton, MD   *9/87 to 1/91*

EDUCATION & PROFESSIONAL AFFILIATIONS

BACHELOR OF SCIENCE, ACCOUNTING, 1997
Old Line College, Dover, DE

ASSOCIATE OF ARTS, BUSINESS ADMINISTRATION, (CERTIFICATE IN ACCOUNTING), 1993
Tuckahoe College, Wye Mills, MD

NORTH TALBOT HIGH SCHOOL, TALBOT, MD
Graduated, 1988, with college preparatory diploma and two years of accounting and computer classes. Member of the Student Council and the National Honor Society.
MARYLAND SOCIETY OF ACCOUNTANTS, MEMBER

32

Combination. *Thomas E. Spann, Easton, Maryland*
Hanging indentation, small caps, and boldfacing in this Experience section make it easy to see the various positions. The writer downplays firm names through small, italic type.

BARBRA L. WALKER

12831 Mara Drive
Woodbridge, VA 22192
(703) 492-1212

OBJECTIVE

A challenging position in **Payroll/Accounts Payable** which will utilize my successful track record, strong technical skills, outstanding accuracy, and effective organizational abilities in order to maximize productivity.

PERSONAL QUALIFICATIONS

✓ *Enthusiastic*, *dependable*, and self-motivated; assume responsibility necessary to *get the job done.*
✓ Work cooperatively with a wide range of personalities.
✓ Excellent skills in *organizing workflow*, ideas, materials, and personnel.
✓ Possess strong quantitative, analytical and organizational skills; excellent figure aptitude; good records management abilities.

PROFILE

✦ *Organized*, take-charge finance professional with *exceptional follow-through* abilities and *detail-orientation*; able to plan and oversee projects from concept to successful conclusion.
✦ *Analytical problem solver*; proven expertise in assembling and organizing information to accelerate productivity.
✦ Demonstrated ability to *efficiently prioritize* a broad range of responsibilities in order to *achieve maximum level* of *operating effectiveness*.
✦ A *resource person*, *problem solver*, troubleshooter and creative project manager.
✦ Demonstrated strength in *resolving problems swiftly and independently*.
✦ Demonstrated ability to *learn quickly*, *work productively*, and *turn out high-quality results on challenging, time-critical assignments*.
✦ *Versatile*; proven ability to manage multiple projects.
✦ Possess excellent interpersonal skills; proven ability to work well with individuals on all levels.
✦ Computer literate; possess hands-on capabilities with state-of-the-art software packages.

AREAS OF EFFECTIVENESS

✦ *Launching* organizational development initiatives for *productivity/quality improvement*.
✦ *Providing vision and direction* in converting company finances from manual to PC-based operation *yielding substantial cost savings and significant efficiency improvement*.
✦ *Orchestrating* procedural changes *to improve company cash flow* situation.

PROFESSIONAL EXPERIENCE
June 1997 -
Present

EVANS ROOFING, INC., Fairfax Station, VA
Office Manager
✦ Schedule projects and estimates.
✦ Prepare all job proposals.
✦ Analyze accounting data for managerial purposes, including balance sheet and income /expense items.
✦ *Developed* computerized system, which *decreased* project proposal *development time by 80%.*
✦ *Innovated* electronic payroll process *reducing turnaround time by 77%.*
✦ Instituted procedural changes to accelerate billing/invoice process to improve timely customer payments.
✦ Achieved the *first-ever* on time filing of yearly taxes in company's six-year history, *eliminating all penalty charges*.

33

Combination. *Mark D. Berkowitz, Yorktown Heights, New York*
The lines used with the contact information are not only staggered but also partial in not reaching the right margin. This resume below the contact information can be made as a

Barbra L. Walker

PROFESSIONAL
EXPERIENCE
continued
June xxxx –
June xxxx

GES EXPOSITION SERVICES, Lorton, VA
Service Kit Coordinator   June xxxx – June xxxx
✦   Utilized PageMaker to produce service manuals for over 100 trade shows/year involving up to 350 exhibitors/vendors.
✦   Served as liaison between GES and convention managers to ensure optimal service delivery.
✦   Began personally producing service guides in-house, decreasing project turnaround time from 2 to 4 weeks to one week or less.
✦   Computerized pricing sheets to ensure account executives had most current pricing, eliminating situations where GES was previously obligated to honor quotes from outdated pricing sheets. This improvement not only saved outside typesetting costs but also helped increase revenues.
✦   Innovated incorporation of logos on manuals, pricing sheets and name badges to enhance company's professional image.
✦   Supervised one assistant.

Cashier   June xxxx – June xxxx
✦   Received all incoming Account Receivables and applied monies to appropriate accounts.
✦   Processed credit card transactions and refunds, as necessary.
✦   Maintained petty cash.
✦   Prepared all cash boxes and credit card machines for show site.
✦   Provided input to yearly budget.
✦   Developed and implemented procedures yielding significant time savings allowing the opportunity to take on additional responsibilities.
✦   Consistently praised by corporate head office for accuracy, neatness and thoroughness of transaction posting.

December xxxx –
June xxxx

REICO DISTRIBUTORS, Springfield, VA
Accounts Receivable Representative
✦   Analyzed accounts to update A/R records.
✦   Researched discrepancies and contacted clients to resolve billing problems.

April xxxx –
November xxxx

AMERICAN COUNSELING ASSOCIATION, Alexandria, VA
Accounts Payable Coordinator
✦   Was instrumental in converting system from ADT to Cerdian, *realizing a substantial per check savings*.
✦   Implemented use of spreadsheets to track financial information, yielding a significant time saving.

August xxxx –
March xxxx

THE MOSAIC TILE COMPANY OF VIRGINIA, Springfield, VA
Accounts Receivable Representative
✦   *Recognized* for producing volume of work previously done by 3 separate staff thereby allowing for a *30% staffing reduction* in the department.

EDUCATION

STRAYER UNIVERSITY, Woodbridge, VA
Bachelor of Arts: Accounting   *In progress*

REFERENCES

Excellent References Will Be Furnished on Request

three-column table with the lines hidden. The current vertical line can be made as a centered vertical line in the second column (the narrow, 3/16-inch column between the headings column on the left and information column on the right), or the vertical line might be a column side left visible. Note again the use of boldface.

25 Oaktree Circle
Excalibur, MO 00000

Pauline Dempsey

Phone: (555) 555-5555
Fax: (555) 555-5555

Objective: Seeking to broaden scope of accounting skills and contribute to a company's profitability/loss control in areas that include:
- »» Financial statement preparation and analysis
- »» Operational and financial auditing
- »» Project management to restructure or streamline processes for increased cost savings and efficiency

Career Profile:
- » Progressive experience with general accounting functions for manufacturing and retail organizations. Exposure has included:
  - »» Management of income and expense functions
  - »» Liaison for new electronic data processing systems
  - »» Profit planning and forecasting
  - »» Consolidated reporting
  - »» Inventory control
- » Proactive problem solver with an understanding of the various interdependent factors that affect consequences on the total operation.
- » Highly motivated and skilled in envisioning plans, influencing their acceptance, then marshalling the resources to bring them to successful fruition.
- » Recognized expertise in establishing collaborative internal and external working relationships to provide accurate and prompt handling of all account services.
- » Teaching background, enabling insight into how individuals approach tasks and the learning styles best suited to optimize their comprehension.

Experience: PACIFIC RIM ELECTRONICS CORPORATION, ST. LOUIS, MO   19XX–PRESENT

Corporate Accounts Payable Manager
- »» Recruited by this large consumer electronics manufacturer to consolidate the accounts payable system and eventually centralize the function to include the company's eight U.S. divisions and headquarters. Supervise a continually growing staff, currently at six direct reports.
- »» Evaluated existing controls and made recommendations for procedural improvements that have become policy.
- »» Created structure in which to accommodate the different formats of each division during the change implementation process.
- »» Set up a rush desk to accelerate payment turnaround as needed, take better advantage of discounts, and maintain good relationships with suppliers.
- »» Streamlined the payment approval process which eliminated signature redundancy and possibility of paperwork loss.
- »» Participated in a pilot project to implement electronic funds transfer (EFT) for payment of employee expenses, and was instrumental in expanding this process to include vendors.
- »» Identified weaknesses in the initial rollout phase causing out-of-balance situations. Created a framework tied into consolidation operations, which involved the cooperation of various disciplines within the organization. Presented action steps logically, thereby overcoming their resistance to change and making the system workable within two months.
- »» Developed a training program in the use of the accounts payable segment of the system and conducted seminars at regional offices nationwide to all levels of the workforce.

»»» Continued

34

Functional. *Melanie A. Noonan, West Paterson, New Jersey*
A distinctive touch in this resume is the use of chevrons for bullets: one chevron for the first level of bulleted information, and two chevrons for the second level. Three chevrons are used

PAULINE DEMPSEY
Continued »»»

TRENDSETTER SHOPS, INC. (SUBSIDIARY OF DIAMOND RETAIL CORP.) GLENDALE, MO   19XX–19XX

Accounts Payable Supervisor
» Having prior familiarity with this company coming from their headquarters, requested transfer to challenging position which required resolving serious balancing problems with their accounts.
» Entered a dynamic environment that had been neglected for almost six months, completely lacking in a control system, and further complicated by company's rapid growth.
» Designed and implemented a tracking mechanism to monitor disbursements through accounts payable for inventory that was frequently drop-shipped to their various store locations. Brought all backlog up to date within two months.
» Worked with warehouse manager to devise receiving logs at all stores, which saved considerable manual verification time and avoided payment delays.
» Developed and trained a cohesive accounts payable team of nine, responsible not only for merchandise vendor payments but also for construction and fixed asset expenses in various progressive stages for 29 new store openings during the year. Total stores numbered approximately 65 in 19XX.

DIAMOND RETAIL CORPORATION, CORPORATE OFFICE, GLENDALE, MO   19XX–19XX

Disbursements Accountant (19XX–XX). Promoted from **Accounts Payable Clerk** (19XX–XX)
» Held lead position responsible for balancing and maintaining control of accounts payable input for this corporation operating seven diversified retail companies which included Trendsetter Shops, Glamour-Eyes, Trinkets & Gadgets, and other specialty stores.
» Audited, processed and controlled corporate expenses. Assigned to projects which included 1099 preparation, relocation expenses and director's payments to comply with IRS regulations.
» Acted as backup for corporate payroll functions.
» Prepared monthly sales reports and flash forecasts. Designed Lotus spreadsheets that cut manual processing time in half and enhanced accuracy.
» Performed thorough physical inventories that uncovered reasons for excessive shrinkage.

Education: BACHELOR OF BUSINESS ADMINISTRATION IN ACCOUNTING, 19XX
     Central State University

     BACHELOR OF SCIENCE IN EDUCATION, 19XX
     Missouri Valley College

     CAREER DEVELOPMENT PROGRAM
     Case Western University, Center for Management Development and Research

     SUPERVISION SERIES SEMINARS INCLUDING BEHAVIOR MODIFICATION, MOTIVATION AND COMMUNICATION
     Jackson University, Office of Continuing Education

Membership: International Association of Accounts Payable Professionals

Volunteer Work:
     » Participated in annual company-sponsored charity events.
     » Coordinated "Bright Ideas" incentive program and "Mega Events" employee morale booster activities.
     » Initiated corporate fitness program and served as its instructor.

for "Continued" at the end of page 1 and the beginning of page 2. Distinctive also is the font for the individual's name in the contact information and for the section headings. Company names and academic degrees and programs are in small caps in the Experience section and Education section, respectively.

ANN BOUCHARD

1111 – 11th Avenue East ♦ Madison, WI 00000 ♦ 425/379-8174 (Home) ♦ 425/481-1155 (Office)
annieb@jetsen.com

PAYROLL ACCOUNTING / AUDITING MANAGER
*Combining excellence in supervision, accounting, payroll, and personnel records to
accurately track costs and expenses*

A highly adaptable financial professional with extensive experience managing accounting and human resources functions in private industry and the military. Possess well-developed analytical skills, a commitment to accuracy, and a particular talent for payroll. Team player with excellent communication skills and the ability to develop solid internal and external client relations. Established reputation as a "by the book" administrator, yet comfortable with flexibility and compromise. Completed B.S. degree during Marine Corps duty. Served in Desert Storm. Recipient of Navy Achievement Medal for exemplary service. Computer literate (Excel, Word).

Notable proficiencies include:

♦ Multistate Payroll	♦ Financial Statements	♦ Union Contracts
♦ GAAP & GAAS	♦ Collections	♦ Unemployment Claims
♦ Audits	♦ Budget Development	♦ Office Management
♦ AR / AP	♦ Cash Management	♦ Supervision & Training
♦ Garnishment Processing	♦ Financial Tracking	♦ HR Administration
♦ Accounts Reconciliation	♦ General Ledger	♦ Employment Verification

EDUCATION & TRAINING

B. S., Business Administration & Accounting, Madison College, December XXXX

"Advanced Course, Administrative Chief," XXXX
An 8-week course at the Non-Commissioned Officer's Academy, United States Marine Corps

"Personnel Records," XXXX
A 4-week course at the Non-Commissioned Officer's Academy, United States Marine Corps

EXPERIENCE

MILLER & BOWEN ELECTRIC, INC., Madison, Wisconsin   XXXX to Present
Payroll Manager / Human Resources Manager
♦ Prepare weekly payroll for up to 450 employees in 9 offices in Wisconsin and Illinois and a second payroll for subsidiary company of 140 employees, consistently meeting on-time, tight deadlines.
   ◊ Work with two union contracts with widely varying rules.
♦ Manage all financial operations:

◊ Union dues tracking	◊ Reconcile accounts
◊ Garnishments, child support, and advances	◊ General ledger
◊ Electronic funds transfer for employee taxes	◊ Weekly state tax filings
◊ Employment Security payroll tax reports	◊ Quarterly 941 tax reports

♦ Instituted practice of calculating prevailing wages on contacted jobs, resulting in significant savings for company and stronger relationships with unions.
♦ Track and balance equipment costing.
♦ Established Human Resources department and perform all functions, including personnel records, unemployment claims, verification of employment, and preparation of monthly Bureau of Labor report.
♦ Created new personnel records system, including updating badly outdated records and ensuring adherence to legal standards.

U.S. MARINE CORPS RESERVE, Madison, Wisconsin, XXXX to Present   *Administrative Chief*
♦ Inspect active duty units throughout the United States, conducting both physical and personnel testing, to prepare for mobilization in times of war within 24-hour notice.
   ◊ Provide remedial measures and standards when unit inspections fail.
♦ Serve on multistate inspection team, inspecting units of from 150 to 350 staff.
♦ Recruited by Pentagon to manage new office setup for Housing Revitalization.
   ◊ Set up physical site, files, and office procedures.
   ◊ Served as office manager and managed staff of 14.

U.S. MARINE CORPS, Georgia, Louisiana, Texas, XXXX to XXXX   *Administrative Chief*
♦ Managed payroll and maintained personnel records.

35

Combination. *Carole S. Barns, Woodinville, Washington*
This person got her accounting degree in the Marines, worked in HR administration and payroll, and is now active in the Marine Corps Reserve. A substantial resume with many interest areas.

JANET D. MOORE
5555 Sutton Place, #307 • Atlanta, GA 00000
555-555-5555

ACCOUNTING ADMINISTRATOR

SUMMARY *of* QUALIFICATIONS
- Experienced in all aspects of *accounting* functions.
- Expertise in the setup of departmental procedures for start-up companies.
- Effective in research and analysis of procedural discrepancies.
- Tenacious in reconciliation of accounts.
- Work well in high-growth environments: quick learner, able to handle new and increased accountabilities.

PROFESSIONAL HIGHLIGHTS

Payroll
- Managed all aspects of Payroll Department including insurance and benefits administration, workman's compensation administration, weekly salary and hourly 82-person payroll.
- Administered payroll for two companies simultaneously.
- Prepared quarterly payroll tax reports.
- Created personnel file system that resulted in increased organization and efficiency.

Bookkeeping
- Managed all aspects of Accounts Payable and Accounts Receivable Departments.
- Assisted in the preparation of monthly financial statements and budget reports.
- Prepared monthly Sales and Use Tax Report.
- Accountable for cash receipts, deposits, collection, and reconciliation of company receivables.

Administration
- Liaison between Accounting Department and the Sales and Warehousing Departments.
- Experienced in hiring and training office personnel.
- Aided Office Manager in restructuring accounting system.
- General office duties included maintaining office supplies, invoicing, correspondence, data entry.

EMPLOYMENT HISTORY

Accounting Administrator	1997 to Present	Digital Design Communications-Norcross, GA
Accounts Receivable Manager	1996-1997	Pride of Southern Building Materials-Lithonia, GA
Accounting Assistant	1996-1996	Pride of Southern Building Materials-Lithonia, GA
Administrative Assistant	1994-1995	Decatur Machinery Company-Decatur, GA
Office Manager	1992-1994	Chamblee Chiropractic Clinic-Chamblee, GA

EDUCATION
Bachelor of Arts in Business Administration - Furman University, Greenville, SC 1996

SKILLS
10 Key by Touch
Great Plains Accounting • Excel • Lotus 1-2-3 • Microsoft Word

36

Functional. *Karen D. Wrigley, Round Rock, Texas*
The grouping of Highlights according to categories—in this instance, the three side headings
Payroll, Bookkeeping, and Administration—makes it easier to comprehend the Highlights.

Mary Marketer

58 Village Park Way
Anywhere, CA 55555

(555) 555-5555

CAREER PROFILE

Accounting/Marketing/Operations Management

Management professional with fifteen years of demonstrated achievement in both front and back office accounting and marketing procedures. Negotiation and cost-cutting skills which translate to success in business planning and development. A team player, articulate communicator and proactive problem solver with a high level of personal and professional integrity. Entrepreneurial spirit with commitment to operational excellence. Diverse areas of accomplishment include:

- Strategic Financial Planning
- Equipment Leasing, Purchasing, and Vendor Negotiation
- Profit and Loss Management
- Marketing and New Business Development
- Multilocation Site Planning and Facilities Expansion
- Personnel Recruitment, Training and Development, EEO Compliance
- Project Planning and Work Flow Coordination
- Customer Relations, Service and Satisfaction
- Payroll Administration, Banking and Credit
- Traffic/Inventory Control

PROFESSIONAL EXPERIENCE

Senior Accountant/Credit and Collections Manager

California Here I Come, Anywhere, CA   XXXX - Present

Catalyst for designing and delivering solutions "collection" strategies to enhance revenue performance, resulting in increased state and federal funding. Coordinate statewide branch office reporting procedures. Accomplishments include:

- 400% increase in collections over 4-month period
- continuing record-setting collections - $6 million and climbing
- 40% increase in billings with no increase in personnel costs
- establishment of definitive reporting standards
- measurable increase in customer service and satisfaction
- analysis and restructuring of contract procedures

Controller

On-The-Run Promotions, Anywhere, CA   XXXX -XXXX

Recruited to provide direction, energy, strategy, and seasoned business acumen to launch fledgling advertising agency. Worked cooperatively with partners to plan long-term operating, administrative, financial and marketing strategies from conception to multi-location expansion.

37

Combination. *Sonja A. Wittich, Santa Monica, California*
The individual was "underemployed" in her current job. In her preceding position, "she had been the catalyst for launching and growing a fledgling agency into a multisite operation."

Mary Marketer   Page 2

Defined immediate and long-term operational goals to accomplish the following objectives:

- design flexible administrative and accounting systems to meet growth and expansion demands
- negotiate "win-win" contracts to attract top vendors
- develop and lead promotional activities to position company as industry leader
- introduce internship program for training and supervision of student workers
- coordinate work flow for daily operations
- initiate leasing, purchasing, and vendor control procedures
- launch customer service plans, interfacing with all levels of clientele

Director, Sales and Marketing Services

Be Well Foods, Anywhere, CA   XXXX -XXXX

Hired to oversee traffic, inventory control, product complaints and all phases of sales and marketing.

- slashed freight costs 35%
- developed distributor, customer, and broker relationships throughout U.S.
- tracked promotions, P.O.S. materials and price changes to keep brokers current
- successfully managed collections and billing inquiries
- spearheaded program to improve client retention and maintain customer loyalty

Manager, Customer Relations/Order Department

True to You, Inc., Anywhere, CA   XXXX - XXXX

Challenged to reduce operating costs while ensuring productivity and efficiency. Designed programs to provide:

- efficient processing of billing and credits
- timely resolution of customer complaints
- personnel training in streamlining of duties to effect staff reduction

EDUCATION

- University of California - Business Administration Major
- Prestigious University - Certificate in Personnel and Industrial Relations
- Continuing Education - Dun & Bradstreet Collection Seminar; computer applications (including Excel)

COMMUNITY INVOLVEMENT

Children's Home Society Project Coordination and Advocacy
Junior Chamber of Commerce Fund-Raising Chairperson

She now wanted to move on, and the writer needed "to bring the past into the present." Her twofold strategy was (1) to use a career summary to impress readers with the person's accomplishments, and (2) to "quantify some very impressive achievements in her present job to encourage the reader to read on."

Carol S. Lawson

100 North Phillips Lane
Valley, ND 58100
(701) 383-8325

Accountant

Profile

❖ **PROFIT-FOCUSED TEAM PLAYER WITH EXTENSIVE ACCOUNTING EXPERIENCE.**

❖ Knowledgeable and experienced in all facets of accounting functions, including:

Accounts Receivable	Credit Management	Correspondence
Accounts Payable	Sales Tax Reporting	Collections
Payroll & Reporting	Employee Benefits Administration	Management Reports

❖ Well versed in IBM computer operations: Windows, Lotus SmartSuite, and Excel.

❖ Trusted by management to handle highly confidential and sensitive company information.

❖ Enjoy challenge of learning new technology, systems, and skills.

❖ Demonstrated ability to interact well with peers, customers, and supervisors.

Achievements

- Decreased bad debts expense significantly when sales and accounts receivables doubled.
- Converted manual accounting system to computerized, utilizing spreadsheets for reporting.
- Customized payment programs for sluggish accounts receivables, reducing attorneys' fees.
- Handled disgruntled customers effectively to retain their business.
- Gained in-depth knowledge of credit administration.
- Developed new computer forms to achieve higher level of efficiency and lower overhead.
- Volunteered for major computer operation duties and retained ongoing daily responsibilities.
- Cooperated and communicated with sales staff regarding credit arrangements.

Relevant Experience

Major Wood Company, Valley, ND   1980–12/98
[Wholesale lumber company with 95 employees, serving Minnesota, North Dakota, and South Dakota area.]

Accountant/Credit Manager, 1990–12/98
Responsible for collection of accounts receivable, accounts payable, payroll, credit administration, management reports, and human resource functions. Worked closely with Controller.

Accountant/Assistant Credit Manager/Payroll, 1980–90
Assisted Credit Manager and Controller. Responsible for daily/monthly/yearly processing and computer operations.

Valley Public Schools PTA, Valley, ND   1996–98
Volunteer Auditor

Education

Bachelor of Science - Accounting, University of North Dakota, Grand Forks, ND

Dun & Bradstreet Credit and Collections Training

38

Combination. *Mary Laske, Fargo, North Dakota*
Just two, short vertical bars enclosing the contact information make this resume stand out from many other resumes. Decorative bullets in the Profile also make this resume unique.

KAREN R. ANDERSON, CPA

221 - 20th Avenue West ▪ Fargo, ND 58102
(701) 281-0202

PROFILE

- **Certified Public Accountant** since 1994.
- More than five years of advanced accounting experience in a banking environment.
- Strong work ethic which resulted in promotions to positions of increasing responsibility.
- Very accurate and detail-oriented individual with excellent communication skills.
- Nominated for and received company awards for increasing efficiencies and decreasing expenses.
- Proficient with Windows, Lotus 1-2-3, Excel, MS Word, Access, WordPerfect, and Monarch.

"Karen approaches her responsibilities with a high degree of enthusiasm. She is always willing to accept new and more complex challenges, determined to improve upon her contribution to the company . . . Karen demonstrates strong interpersonal skills which enable her to develop and continue a positive rapport with customer banks, management, co-workers, and external accountants." Janet Jackson, VP-Accounting, Midwest Territory Bank, Fargo, ND

SUMMARY OF RESPONSIBILITIES

General journal entries / Financial statement preparation / Financial analysis / Cash flow analysis
Acquisition accounting / Equity accounting / Holding company accounting

- Compile numbers from numerous reports and summarize data into accurate reports.
- Reconcile intercompany accounts payable and accounts receivable records.
- Maintain company and affiliate subsidiary equity records, including entity capital stock records and company common/preferred stock warrants and options.
- Monitor company stock trading activity.
- Provide support in preparation of company's annual reports.
- Assist in preparation of financial statements and supporting data to ensure compliance with SEC and GAAP guidelines in completion of 10-Q and annual 10-K reports.
- Prepare regulatory reports, including FR Y-9C, FR Y-111, FR Y-11Q, FR Y-6A, FR Y-6, and FR Y-8.
- Assist in preparation and analysis of financial data related to merger and acquisition of financial institutions and the resultant regulatory applications and SEC registration statements.
- Involved in preparation of financial statements and supporting data for company's 401(k) and ESOP retirement plans.

RELATED EXPERIENCE

MIDWEST TERRITORY BANK, INC., Fargo, ND	1/92 - Present
Accounting Officer, 3/95 - Present	
Accountant, 10/92 - 2/95	
Accounting Assistant, 1/92 - 9/92	
NUTRITION PLUS, Fargo, ND	9/91 - 12/91
Bookkeeper	
JOHN JOHNSON LEASING, Fargo, ND	1/90 - 12/90
Bookkeeper	

EDUCATION

MOORHEAD STATE UNIVERSITY, Moorhead, MN, 5/91
B.S. Accounting

39

Functional. *Mary Laske, Fargo, North Dakota*
Horizontal lines appear below the individual's name, the phone number, and each section heading. The Profile ends with a testimonial, which builds trust in a functional resume.

ELIZABETH K. PARKER

**1020 First Avenue
New York, 00000
(555) 555-5555**

PROFILE

*"…you have proved to be conscientious, hard-working and professional … your reputation is well deserved."
—L.M. Rodine, VP & CFO*

Award-winning accounting professional with more than 20 years' continuous experience in major corporate environments, demonstrating strong capacity for **financial analysis** and **account reconciliation** skills. Consistent, exemplary record of performance encompasses promotions to increasingly responsible positions.

- Employ high energy level, attention to detail and persistence to track down errors.
- Effective team contributor; known as catalyst for achieving goals in timely fashion.
- Self-directed work style, with ability to anticipate department demands and needs.
- Solid record of identifying shortcuts and designing strategies to streamline operations.
- Recognized for initiative and commitment in performing multiple tasks concurrently.

EXPERTISE

- Financial Analysis
- Spreadsheets
- International Accounting
- General Ledgers
- Training/Cross-training
- System Conversions
- Account Reconciliation
- PC tracking systems
- Payroll

CAREER HIGHLIGHTS

"…enthusiastically dedicated yourself to the ADP project, and your efforts … patience, perseverance and dedication resulted in the successful implementation of the new payroll system."—J.T. King, Financial Information Management

"Cost-cutting suggestions like yours benefit our customers and our company … keep up the good work."—K. Doyle, Chief Accountant

"…managed the department in a proactive, professional and efficient manner … she has been a real asset and helped make a difficult transition for the staff into a team effort resulting in improved morale."—B.J. Madison, SVP, Systems Analysis

- **Improved tracking of company expenses and liabilities by streamlining lump-sum process** and testing multiple conversions of the general ledger system. Collaborated with programmers to break down expenses by code. Minimized internal questions and decreased time spent on reconciling accounts.
- **Spearheaded project to convert from ADP to internal accounting system.** Led team through entire process and identified specifications for interface and data conversion.
- **Detected $500,000 deficit in Social Security account through systematic review and reconciliation** of payroll balance sheets. Ensured accuracy of data on monthly, quarterly and annual financial statements and monitored outsource provider.
- **Cross-trained payroll specialists**, delegated payroll functions and established and communicated important daily routines to guarantee smooth operations.
- **Reduced by 50% time spent by managers** reconciling budgeted versus actual expenses, consulting with department heads and applying well-developed analytical skills.
- **Designed PC tracking system utilizing Excel**, integrating key payroll/benefit data on all global employees. Reduced time balancing expatriate/impatriate records and ensured that records balanced gross to net.
- **Planned and wrote 200-page accounting manual and reduced repeatable, linked errors** on accounting activity posted to general ledgers. Incorporated explanations of transactions and sample print screens to facilitate staff training.
- **Provided timely and accurate product-line figures to Controller and CFO.** Detailed discrepancies between budgeted amounts and actuals on monthly basis.
- **Managed conversion from manual to PC system**; streamlined data-gathering operations by creating new financial formulas with Lotus 1-2-3 and consolidated financial statements for domestic subsidiaries.
- **Expedited data flow and reduced chaos by devising new reporting schedule** for marketing/billing departments and outside companies. Retrieved missing and incorrect data and methodically reviewed reports on bank lockboxes.
- **Assisted conversion from mainframe to PC system** by reconciling numerical and alpha character differences. Analyzed and compared accounting reports from both systems.

40

Functional. *Phyllis B. Shabad, Ossining, New York*
A powerful resume design. Testimonials in the left column from superiors are appealing to readers who don't like functional resumes because they lack the information commonly used to

ELIZABETH K. PARKER

EMPLOYMENT HISTORY

"...successfully supervised general ledger conversions ... and sacrificed many hours of her personal time in order to meet deadlines."

Major Snack Foods, Upscale, NY, Accounting Auditor — **xxxx to present**

Newton-Wells Corp., Upscale, NY, International Accounting — **xxxx**

Business Readers' Magazine, Princeton, NJ — **xxxx to xxxx**
    Assistant Manager and Accounting Analyst — xxxx to xxxx
    Accounting Supervisor; Assistant Accounting Supervisor — xxxx to xxxx
    Senior Accounting Bookkeeper — xxxx to xxxx
Prior related positions in Accounting/Payroll — **xxxx to xxxx**

EDUCATION

Business University, Princeton, NJ
Certificate in Financial Accounting — **xxxx**

SUNJ, Financial Community College, Princeton, NJ
Associate in Science, Business–Accounting — **xxxx**
Honors Student

Current**:** Working on **Bachelor of Science in Accounting,**
SUNJ, Garden State College, Freehold, NJ

PROFESSIONAL DEVELOPMENT

TRAINING & COURSEWORK

Business/Accounting:	**Management/Technical:**
Principles of Accounting	Role of the Supervisor
Analyzing Financial Statements	Role of the Manager
Reconciliation	Problem Analysis & Decision-Making
General Ledgers	Managing for Productivity
Law for Business	Performance Appraisal & Planning
	Lotus Macros Advanced Functions
	TSO/SPF

"You have been able to reconcile accounts that have been out of balance for at least a year ... trained specialists in this task ... done a wonderful job in streamlining ... and created an orderly procedure for tracking compensation."—S.J. Gates, Accounting Manager

AWARDS

Excellence Award–xxxx, xxxx ▸ For top-level performance while taking on additional responsibilities

Outstanding Award–xxxx ▸ For suggesting change in paying out travel and entertainment expenses

SPECIALIZED SKILLS

Computer Literate:
IBM PC platform; Windows environment.
Software: Microsoft Word, Excel; Lotus 1-2-3
Specialized Software:
TSO/SPF; CICS/Masterpiece; SAP;
McCormack-Dodge
Languages:
Bilingual–Fluent in written and spoken
English and French

screen out candidates (gaps in employment, the appearance of job hopping, unrelated jobs, and so forth). Testimonials can be excerpted from reference letters. Ellipses replace phrases omitted to keep a testimonial short. Testimonials are also great confidence builders for those unemployed from downsizing.

Vacancy No.: 00-XXX-00-0000, Auditor, GS-XXXX-XX

TERRY MATTHEWS

12345 Spirit Road NE ◆ Appletown, VA 99999-9999
555/123-4567, Extension 123 (Office) ◆ 555/123-9876 (Home) ◆ 555/123-1234 (Fax)

AUDITOR, GS 13 — OFFICE OF INSPECTOR GENERAL / HUD
Utilizing financial management and auditor skills combined with excellence in research, problem solving, communications, and computers

Social Security Number: XXX-XX-XXXX
Citizenship: United States

Veteran's Status: None
Federal Status: GS-0511-12, Auditor

Detail-oriented, research-minded financial professional with 17 years' experience, including 6 years with the Department of Navy and 6 years in mortgage lending. One of 8 hired out of 2,200 applicants for the Federal Financial Management Program for accelerated, fast-track promotion from GS 7 through GS 12. Skilled problem solver who has a passion for analyzing and investigating a puzzle to discover the facts for the best decision. Excellent communicator who can clearly and concisely provide data, information, and training to all levels and cultures in verbal and written form. Solid, adaptable team member. Possess a natural ability to understand, use, troubleshoot, and train others on computer hardware and software. Serve as Beta Tester for Intuit, with several suggestions relating to mortgages and mortgage banking implemented into current versions of Quicken and QuickBooks. Scheduled to sit for CPA.

Notable areas of expertise include:

- Accounting & Auditing
- Operational & Financial Audits
- Problem Analysis & Resolution
- Research
- LAN Administration
- Mortgage Pool Reconciliation
- GNMA Pools & FHA Loans
- Fraud & Forensic Accounting
- Credit Analysis & Credit Card Audits
- Congressional Requirements & Briefings
- Foreclosures & Bankruptcies
- Financial Reconciliation

Computer expertise includes:

- PCs, Macintoshes, Windows 95
- Word
- PowerPoint
- Databases, particularly Access
- Excel Lotus & Quattro Pro
- Quicken, QuickBooks
- Web Browsers
- CorelDraw, including 3D components
- PageMaker, Publisher
- Computer-Generated Video Editing
- Ventura
- High-End Proprietary Software

EXPERIENCE

DEPARTMENT OF THE NAVY, NAVAL AUDIT SERVICES, Virginia and West Virginia   XXXX to Present
Auditor, GS-12, Step 4, Vienna (40+ hours/week)
May contact Tommy Lee Jones, Supervisor, 555/123-4567, extension 111 or Jeff Black, ADP Specialist, 555/123-4567
Auditor, GS-11, Vienna
Auditor, GS-9 Vienna and Henryville
Auditor, GS-7, Henryville

- Audited Eastern Region acquisition and purchase credit cards, working with banks to acquire reports, download information, prioritize data by established criteria, and investigate problems.
  - ➤ Developed process to establish reconciliation between credit cards and their function, enabling creation of an audit report with meaningful data for future card use and financial tracking.
- Regularly validate a portion of the 35 different activities in Vienna that fall into the Chief Financial Officers Act financial statements for Navy annual budgets.
- Audited the fixed assets section of CFO Act report, verifying the 300 buildings of the physical property at Newport Naval Shipyard.

Continued

41

Combination. *Carole S. Barns, Woodinville, Washington*
A long-time civil employee, this individual "wanted to combine her auditing skills with her earlier experiences in mortgage lending in a job with HUD. The resume follows the guidelines

TERRY MATTHEWS / Page 2

- ◆ Determine what assets are not on record and ascertain the reasons why.
- ◆ Write an audit program and determine the components necessary for the program and what outside forces (for example, a congressional order) can impact it.
- ◆ Received the highest rating of "5" on annual Performance Appraisal.
- ◆ Serve as LAN Administrator for the office, working closely with the agency computer specialist to spot trouble before it surfaces and resolve hardware and software problems when they occur.
- ◆ Initiate the creation of computer-generated templates and standard forms to more efficiently and effectively expedite processes. Receive frequent requests from coworkers, superiors, and subordinates for copies of templates or for development of new ones.
- ◆ Currently developing electronic bulletin board of computer tips to help staff members intimidated by computers and software.
- ◆ Determined the validity of Military Sealift Command, Pacific Materials and Supplies, and Maintenance and Repair of Ships accounts while based in Virginia.
- ◆ Concluded following an audit that invalid accruals of $1.3 million occurred in the Maintenance and Repair of Ships account and that the established internal controls were not adequate because of lack of reconciliation of the subsidiary ledger to the general ledger.
- ◆ Independently obtained the necessary hardware and software to transfer accrual data into a workable database format.
- ◆ Learned database programs on own to allow smoothly coordinated download of Cargo and Maintenance and Repair Accrual raw data from programmers.

NATIONAL MORTGAGE, Glenwood, California   XXXX to XXXX
Loan Funding Officer

- ◆ Completed all legal and miscellaneous paperwork involved in finalizing loan packages, editing for accuracy and conformation to investor specifications.
- ◆ Coordinated closings with title company and drew the loan disbursements.

HOME LOANS, INC., Los Angeles, California   XXXX to XXXX
Loan Servicing Manager

- ◆ Hired a staff to man the West Coast office and defined procedures for cash flow, bank accounts, investor accounting, payoffs, taxes, insurance, and customer service.
- ◆ Researched and purchased a loan-servicing computer package and supervised the conversion.

AETNA MORTGAGE, Sacramento, California   XXXX to XXXX
Financial Examiner

- ◆ Prepared foreclosure, payoff, sale bids, and bankruptcy figures on agricultural and urban loans.

NATIONAL MORTGAGE CORP., San Diego, California   XXXX to XXXX
Investor Accountant

- ◆ Reconciled bank and general ledger accounts and executed investor requirements.

WELLER, TYLER & BANKS, San Diego, California   XXXX to XXXX
GNMA Specialist

- ◆ Maintained and reconciled 265 GNMA pools, processed 3,000 monthly investor payments, and established GNMA portfolio procedures.
- ◆ Recognized as the office expert on reconciliation of mortgage pools, ensuring money and funds were always properly applied.

EDUCATION & TRAINING

B.S., Accounting & Computer Information Services, *XXXX, Western State College, Los Angeles, 99999*
Diploma, Hale High School, *XXXX, Los Angeles, California 99999*
Graduate, Centralized Financial Management Trainee Program, *Department of the Navy, XXXX*
NAVSUP Simplified Acquisition Procedures Course, *XXXX*

for federal application." The first page is impressive in detailing at length the person's areas of expertise, including computer skills. Even more impressive is the Experience section, which extends almost to the end of page 2. Near the bottom of page 1, a single arrow tip points to a significant innovation.

1234 Any Street
City, IN 55555

24-Hour Voice Mail: 555.555.5555
E-Mail: 0000@xxx.com

RESUMÉ OF

John A. Doe

+ Skilled in creation of new spreadsheets

+ Qualified to implement internal auditing policies and procedures

+ Experienced in accounts payable, accounts receivable, and payroll

+ Focused on obtaining highest return on investment of financial systems

+ Trained in aspects of business law

+ Attuned to importance of working as a team player

+ Well versed in accounting, word processing and database software

---

FOR AMPLIFICATION, PLEASE SEE THE FOLLOWING PAGE

42

Functional. *Tina Merwin, Milwaukee, Wisconsin*
This unusual format has lots of white space. Only a profile (not so named) appears on the first page, together with contact information, a resume title, and an invitation to see the next page.

John A. Doe

1234 Any Street
City, IN 55555

24-Hour Voice Mail: 555.555.5555
E-Mail: 0000@xxx.com

Skills & Accomplishments:

Jones Consulting LLP - Suburb, IN
Internal Auditor

+ Reviewed financial records
+ Compiled reports to serve as reliability studies
+ Evaluated financial systems
+ Streamlined management control procedures

ABC, Ltd. - Metropolis, IN
Account Analyst

+ Audited expense reports for 100 or more employees
+ Developed form for reporting travel expenses
+ Reduced inventory control process time by up to 65%
  through implementation of new spreadsheet
+ Updated departmental policies and procedures manual

Doe's Hometown Hardware - Smalltown, IN
Bookkeeper

+ Balanced accounts payable and accounts receivable
+ Handled bank transactions
+ Installed computer hardware and accounting program
+ Trained proprietor in use of computer systems

Education:

City College - A.S. in Accounting

Computer Experience:

Spreadsheets:

+ Simply Accounting
+ Quattro Pro

Word Processing:

+ WordPerfect
+ Microsoft Word

LAN:

+ Personal Access Records
+ E-Mail

Programming:

+ dBASE

Contact information is repeated on the second page. No dates are supplied with work experience, which is listed in the Skills & Accomplishments section. Computer experience is grouped by application or function. Plus signs are used for "positive" bullets.

Mary M. Jeffers

P. O. Box 18
Raleigh, North Carolina 00000
Home: (000) 000-0000 ◆ Office: (000) 000-0000

Profile

MAY XXXX CPA CANDIDATE INTERESTED IN A MOVE FROM PUBLIC TO PRIVATE ACCOUNTING.
Experienced in the development and documentation of internal controls and the establishment
of policies and procedures. Strong supervisory, interpersonal, verbal and written
communication skills. Analytical and thorough; excellent track record of attention to detail.
Proficient in WordPerfect, Microsoft Word, Lotus, and Excel.

Experience

BUSINESS MANAGER, Office of Emergency Medical Services   XXXX-present
Department of Health, State of North Carolina, Raleigh, North Carolina

*Recruited by current Director. Charged with regulation compliance, budget preparation and
monitoring, purchasing, personnel, time-keeping, and contract development. Manage accounts
payable up to $11½ M annually. 6 direct reports.*

- Ensured department's compliance with state regulations by developing and implementing
  internal controls; department had no controls when took over position.
- Developed cash and expense reconciliation procedures as well as voucher processing.
- Provided internal guidance for an automated system to track $3½ M in annual grants.

STAFF AUDITOR, Public Accounts   XXXX-XXXX
State of North Carolina, Raleigh, North Carolina

Reported to Senior Auditor. Developed and implemented portions of auditing programs.

- Member of auditing team that investigated and compiled support documentation for
  $870,000 embezzlement in Department of Health.
- Received above-average evaluations on a consistent basis; often complimented for
  interpersonal and technical skills.
- Acquired solid knowledge of auditing and documentation.

UNITED STATES AIR FORCE   XXXX-XXXX

Education

B.S. IN BUSINESS ADMINISTRATION, CONCENTRATION: ACCOUNTING   XXXX-XXXX
University of Denver, Denver, Colorado

- Completed degree in 3 years.
- Financed own education.

43

Combination. *Betty H. Williams, Richmond, Virginia*
The Profile for this C.P.A. candidate mentions succinctly work-related experience and skills,
adaptive skills, and computer skills. Bullets point to accomplishments under Experience.

Tax-Related
Resumes

DEBORAH AKINS

555 Second Avenue
New York, New York 11111
(212) 666-6666

PROFILE

Auditing/Paralegal professional presenting extensive expertise in **real estate tax compliance.** Proven ability in coordinating and managing high-volume caseload. Maintain ongoing familiarity with changes in tax codes and structures. Utilize excellent interpersonal and communication skills to interact effectively with executives, professional and paraprofessional staff, regulatory agencies and clients.

PROFESSIONAL EXPERIENCE

Jamison, Kurtz & McFarland, New York, New York   19XX - Present
Real Estate Tax Auditor / Paralegal

- Personally manage over 80 cases at a given time. Evaluate financial records of income and non-income-producing properties, abstract commercial leases and reconcile with rental income.

- Assure timely and accurate responses to inquiries from clients, regarding income and expenses, during various (tax) filing seasons.

- Coordinate, schedule and attend audits.

- Attend audit conferences with representatives of the City of New York Law Department to keep abreast of changing real estate tax laws, and ensure conformity of real estate tax audit forms.

- Interface with the City of New York Department of Finance when filing documents for real estate tax protests. Process involves compiling and submitting analysis of income and expenses, fixed assets accounts, mortgage, insurance, payroll and rental information for tax years under review.

- Maintain ongoing contact with clients, to keep them appraised on case status.

Colson Displays, Inc., New York, New York   1996 - 19XX
Senior Accounting Assistant

- Maintained accounts payable processes; responded to inquiries and resolved customer-related problems; trained and supervised new employees.

- Evaluated and established new filing system and procedures, which resulted in 50 percent improvement in overall productivity and efficiency.

EDUCATION

Hunter College, C.U.N.Y., New York, New York
B.S. in Accounting

Paralegal Institute, New York, New York
Certificate in Paralegal Studies
Coursework: Contracts, Torts, Uniformed Commercial Code,
Corporate, Commercial and Real Estate Law

SKILLS

IBM AS/400, Microsoft Word 6.0, Microsoft Excel 5.0, WordPerfect 5.11,
Nexus / Lexis, AS/400 Office Vision

44

Combination. *Judith Friedler, New York, New York*
A paralegal who is also a real estate tax auditor. Lines between resume sections make them easy to see at a glance. Positions, degree, and certification stand out in bold italic.

JACK T. SMITH, CPA

550 Harris Street • Anytown, ST 55555 • (555) 555-5555

PROFILE

Over ten years of experience in *general accounting*, *auditing*, *taxation*, and *finance*. Able to learn custom accounting software programs and spreadsheets quickly and thoroughly. Extensive analysis of diverse computerized accounting and financial information systems and financial operations. Persistent and thorough in completing projects while dealing with pressure deadlines.

PROFESSIONAL HIGHLIGHTS and ACCOMPLISHMENTS

Accounting Research, Analysis, and Auditing

- Extensive experience in analyzing business accounting practices and records including the following areas:

Accounts Payable	General Ledger	General Journal
Accounts Receivable	Balance Sheet	Bank Records

- Determined tax liabilities utilizing extensive knowledge of state and federal tax laws, IRS rulings, court decisions, policies, regulations and practices.
- Gained working knowledge of specialized accounting practices of varying trades and industries.
- Examined companies of diverse complexities including reorganizations, mergers, and leveraged buyouts.
- Identified questionable and fraudulent activities and made appropriate referrals.

Project Coordination and Management

- Planned and conducted detailed audits and investigations of business and individual tax returns.
- ***Reduced A/R by $2.1M*** during employment with the IRS.
- Managed the collection of tax deficiencies including analyzing collectibility, soliciting payments, arranging installment agreements, and referrals to other collection agencies.
- Prepared accurate and timely detailed reports and documents.
- Compiled research to support interpretation of tax laws and unprecedented judgments of cases.
- Utilized negotiating and diplomacy skills in cases with sensitive and controversial issues.
- Received the Special Managers Award in XXXX and XXXX while employed with the IRS.

EMPLOYMENT HISTORY

Revenue Agent	XXXX-XXXX	Internal Revenue Service	Anytown, State
Collections Agent*	XXXX-XXXX	Midtown Agency	Anytown, State
Regional Manager	XXXX-XXXX	Major Insurance Company	Anytown, State
Sales Representative	XXXX-XXXX	American Company	Anytown, State
Transfer Agent	XXXX-XXXX	ABF	Anytown, State

*Part-time, concurrent with Internal Revenue Service employment.

CERTIFICATIONS

Certified Public Accountant 1995 - Somewhere State Board of Accountancy

EDUCATION

Bachelor of Science - Business Administration - Minor: **Accounting** 1993
Somewhere State University, Somewhere, State

45

Functional. *Karen D. Wrigley, Round Rock, Texas*
A functional format detailing highlights and accomplishments eclipses less relevant experience in the Employment History. Important information is in boldface. See Cover Letter 8.

RICHARD ALAN MANN

5555 North University Avenue
Daly City, CA 95555
(555) 555-5555

PROFESSIONAL GOAL

Staff accountant position with a public accounting firm where my graduate studies in taxation, experience as an IRS revenue agent, and strengths in business development will be of value.

EDUCATION

UNIVERSITY OF CALIFORNIA, BERKELEY
Program: Master of Science in Taxation (in progress)

PEPPERDINE UNIVERSITY, Malibu, CA
Program: Master of Science in Taxation
(satisfied 2/3 of degree requirements with 3.8 GPA prior to relocating to Daly City)

ST. MARY'S COLLEGE OF CALIFORNIA, Moraga, CA
Degree: Bachelor of Science in Business Administration
Major: Accounting

PROFESSIONAL EXPERIENCE

REVENUE AGENT, Department of the Treasury, Internal Revenue Service, San Jose, CA   19xx–Present
Results: Completed 770 hours of classroom training in individual, sole proprietorship, partnership, and corporate tax law, followed by field audit experiences. Was assigned to complex cases, such as audits of tax shelters, returns under the tax compliance measurement program, and TEFRA partnerships. Frequently identified issues overlooked by previous agents, capturing "lost revenue" prior to statute of limitations. Earned the respect and trust of IRS supervisors, who commended me for having no cases advance to appeals stage during tenure, and CPAs, who recognized my thorough research and fair settlement of cases.

FINANCE MANAGER, Toyota Automotive Dealership, Daly City, CA   1996–1997
Results: Negotiated retail contracts and leases, capturing aftermarket sales penetration above Toyota's national average and above that of more experienced finance managers in the dealership. Designed internal controls that reduced employee errors on DMV documentation and expedited processing time for vehicle contracts and leases.

FINANCIAL PLANNER & TAX CONSULTANT, Secure Financial Advisors, Los Angeles, CA   1994–1996
Results: Earned securities license, scoring in the top 10 percentile in the nation (hold Series 7, State Securities License, Disability and Insurance License, and Variable Annuities License). Trained telemarketers in program that generated a steady stream of new, prequalified clients. Sourced new business clients for tax department and assisted with tax preparation for corporations, partnerships, and sole proprietorships. Implemented client-specific financial plans that met the needs of high net-worth individuals.

COMMODITIES BROKER, Commodity Traders International, San Francisco, CA   1992–1994
Results: Sourced domestic and international buyers and sellers for sophisticated investor transactions involving currency contracts and commodities contracts.

46

Chronological. *Susan Britton Whitcomb, Fresno, California*
Placement of the Education section in the resume's "sweet spot" calls attention to the individual's persistence in completing an M.S. degree in Taxation.

DORIS SILVER
5000 Northwest 9th Street
Sunrise, Florida 33024
(954) 000-0000

ANALYST / REVENUE-FINANCE / ADMINISTRATION

<u>Skills Summary</u>

Financial Analysis…Research…Analysis…Investigation…Collections…Customer Relations…
Credit Analysis…Case Management…Special Procedures…Asset Location… Compliance…
Tax Laws…Tax Returns…Code Enforcement…Writs of Entry…Net Worth Determination…
Judicial Process…Accounts Maintenance…Administration…Crisis Management…Time
Management…Decision Making…Negotiations…Presentations… Management…Public
Contact…Problem Solving…Communication…Interviewing…Counseling…Flexible…
Organized…Resourceful…People Skills

- Proficient in managing multiple tasks or large caseload simultaneously
- Analyze operations, financial condition and profitability of individuals and businesses
- Knowledge of business laws and practices; ability to understand contents and effects of various legal documents, such as wills, leases, deeds, trusts
- Knowledge of modern collection techniques, including laws concerning rights of creditors, bankruptcy, lien priorities
- Extensive interaction with all levels of management, Power of Attorneys, and general public
- Handle sensitive issues with tact and diplomacy, courtesy and empathy
- Bilingual, English/Spanish
- Computer proficient in Windows 97, Microsoft Word, Excel, Lotus 1-2-3

<u>Awards/Recognition</u>

- Certificate of Appreciation for VITA Program
- Outstanding Customer Service Awards from bank president
- "Customer Service Rep of the Month" for consistently handling large volume of calls
- Letters of commendation from taxpayers for assisting them with tax problems in a professional manner
- Excellent reviews for proficiency, speed and courtesy in resolving problems

<u>Experience</u>

INTERNAL REVENUE SERVICE, Plantation, FL   1991 to Present

Tax Examiner Assistant (7/97 to present)
- Research internal and external sources to locate taxpayers and their assets
- Ensure full compliance regarding tax deposits and timely filing of returns
- Analyze and evaluate research data, and use sound judgment to make case decisions

Revenue Officer (1/91-7/97)
- Coordinate and manage ongoing, simultaneous caseload of 79
- Conduct client interviews and business counseling to assist taxpayers in complying with tax laws and preventing future delinquencies
- Collect 50% of outstanding individual, employment, corporate and 1040 taxes
- Investigate and analyze information that will lead to prompt and proper case resolution
- Secure basic asset information, including banks, income sources, real and personal property; determine filing and depositing requirements; verify and document compliance
- Secure information for 100% penalty determinations on trust funds
- Determine collectibility of accounts and develop installment agreements for repayment

47

Combination. *Shelley Nachum, Ft. Lauderdale, Florida*
A list of keywords at the top of the first page makes the resume scannable for storage in online resume databases. Achievements appear in the Awards/Recognition section. Bullets on both

Doris Silver   page two

- Determine ownership of property and execute notices of levy; release property rights seized under levy
- Involved in auctions to liquidate assets, including mailing of bidders list to public, advertising, and participation in actual auction
- Conduct seizures and sales of real and personal property after lien rights have been determined; determine value of real property based on comparable sales
- Communicate orally and in writing with clients and employees, demonstrating accurate knowledge of procedural and statutory guidelines.

CITICORP SAVINGS OF FLORIDA (now Citibank), Miami, FL   1985 to 1990

Customer Service Representative/Team Leader

- Serviced volume of 150-200 calls daily, resolving disputes, problems, and billing questions of personal bank account and credit card account holders
- Chosen as "Team Leader" to handle difficult cases and adverse customer situations

Volunteer

Volunteer Income Tax Assistance (VITA) Program. Managed program for Dade County. Trained volunteers in basic tax return preparation; setup, scheduling, staffing, advertising and marketing of 27 sites; managed 110 volunteers; also personally prepared tax returns in addition to regular job caseload.

Federal Emergency Management Association (FEMA). Assisted taxpayer hurricane victims in applying for aid; prepared tax returns from previous years for catastrophic loss credits.

Small Business Administration (SBA). Assisted agency in prescreening hurricane victims for loan approval.

Education & Training

ASSOCIATE OF ARTS DEGREE, Miami-Dade Community College

IRS Training: business law, tax law, financial statement analysis, investigative techniques, collection enforcement

pages tie the two pages together. The Volunteer section at the end shows that this efficient, dutiful IRS Revenue Officer donates some of her time in training other volunteers to help people prepare their tax returns, and in helping hurricane victims apply for aid, credits, and loans.

KAREN SCHWIMMER

4321 Nehalem Lane • Portland, Oregon 97229 • (503) 675-4532

BACKGROUND SUMMARY

Licensed tax preparer with strong customer service background and extensive experience communicating with the Hispanic population. Able to deal effectively with the public, resolve problems and project a professional image. Bilingual (English and Spanish).

- Dependable, adaptable employee with ability to handle a variety of job duties and provide backup in all areas of office operations.
- Computer literate; familiar with a variety of tax programs, including LACERTE and TurboTax.
- Previous experience in bookkeeping, records management and paperwork processing.
- Licensed Oregon Tax Preparer.

EXPERIENCE

BEAVERTON BUSINESS SERVICE – Beaverton, Oregon
Tax Preparer (1998-Present, intermittently)
Meet with clients, prepare tax returns and perform data entry. Handle telephone inquiries and conduct research on tax issues.

H&R BLOCK – Tigard, Oregon
Tax Preparer (1997-1998)
Interviewed clients and prepared all kinds of individual tax returns.

PORTLAND TRANSPORT COMPANY – Portland, Oregon
Dispatcher / Bookkeeper (1988-1997)
Dispatched trucks nationwide and prepared fuel tax and mileage reports for several different states. Coordinated payroll and bookkeeping duties.

CITY OF BEAVERTON / BUSINESS LICENSE DIVISION – Beaverton, Oregon
Supervising Clerk (1985-1988)
Assisted the public with the preparation of business licenses. Interviewed license applicants and processed applications. Worked with data processing staff to implement the department's first-ever computer system.

OTHER RELATED EXPERIENCE:
Personal Estate Representative (Five Years)
Managed two personal estates. Maintained records, prepared fiduciary returns and monitored investment activity.

EDUCATION

H&R BLOCK – Portland, Oregon
Tax Preparation (1996)

PORTLAND COMMUNITY COLLEGE – Portland, Oregon
Estate Planning (1993)
Spanish (1990-1993)

AFFILIATIONS

Treasurer, Oregon Association of Tax Consultants

48

Combination. *Pat Kendall, Aloha, Oregon*
Boldface for the occupations makes it easy to see the sequence of positions down the page from the present to the least recent, or up the page from the least recent to the present.

ANNE M. BELSON

1234 – 100th Boulevard North ♦ Anytown, AK 99999 ♦ 555 / 123-1234

ACCOUNTANT / BOOKKEEPER
Combining excellence in accounting, taxes, collections, and computers to accurately track costs and expenses and increase cash flow

A highly adaptable financial professional with extensive experience managing accounting functions in profit and nonprofit arenas and the construction industry. Possess well-developed analytical skills and a particular talent for cost accounting. Strong computer and accounting software knowledge, especially MIP, Quicken, Peachtree. Team player with excellent communication skills and the ability to develop solid internal and external client relations. Familiar with requirements of the Canadian Department of Revenue and U.S. and Canadian Customs.

Notable proficiencies include:

♦ Cost Accounting	♦ Financial Statements	♦ Cash Management
♦ GAAP & GAAS	♦ Collections	♦ State & Federal Taxes
♦ Audits	♦ Budget Development	♦ Financial Conversions
♦ AR / AP	♦ Supervision & Training	♦ Real Estate Finance
♦ Multistate Payroll	♦ Construction Accounting	♦ Financial Tracking
♦ Accounting Software	♦ Office Management	♦ International Business

EXPERIENCE

CONTRACT ACCOUNTING / BELSON ENTERPRISES-H&R BLOCK, Anytown XXXX to Present
Accountant / Bookkeeper / Tax Preparer
♦ Prepare taxes and manage accounting functions for individuals.

ST. ANTHONY'S CATHEDRAL, Anytown XXXX to XXXX
Financial Secretary
♦ Installed and implemented the first computer system fully integrated accounting software program (MIP) to track and administer parishioners' contributions and pledges.
   ◊ Adapted monthly financial statements sent to parishioners to fit MIP program.
   ◊ Dramatically improved efficiency of financial tracking and reduced contributor contact redundancies.
   ◊ Enabled enhanced monitoring and scheduling of cathedral facilities usage, increasing utilization and rental fees.
♦ Managed payroll, bill paying, and all other financial responsibilities.
♦ Tracked cost and paid bills for $4 million cathedral and $1 million roof renovations.

JACKSON CONSTRUCTION CO., Anytown XXXX to XXXX
Controller / Administrative Manager
♦ Managed all accounting activities for a large residential and commercial construction company.
   ◊ Oversaw costing activities, posted daily Accounts Receivable and Accounts Payable.
   ◊ Prepared financial statements, budgets, earnest money agreements, and cash projections.
♦ Hired, trained, and managed accounting and general office personnel.

LOG HOME BUILDERS, INC., Anytown XXXX to XXXX
Cost Accounting Supervisor
♦ Helped introduce and implement computerized accounting processing to HBI, the world's largest manufacturer of precut log homes.
♦ Performed all accounting functions, including payroll for the U.S. and Canada, interfacing with government officials during tax audits, collections, and cost justifications for shipments to Canada.

EDUCATION
B. A., Accounting, *Anystate University*

49

Combination. *Carole S. Barns, Woodinville, Washington*
This individual, a retiree, thought she wanted a part-time job but really wanted a full-time, cost-accounting position with less responsibility than she had in the prime of her career.

Monica Dillard

0000 Trundle Drive • Clarksville, Tennessee 00000   (000) 000-0000

Career Focus • Capabilities

A career-oriented position as a **STAFF ACCOUNTANT** OR **TAX ACCOUNTANT**. Offer well-developed analytical skills with education and experience in **tax return preparation, auditing,** and **financial statement preparation**. Strong ability to learn new software and procedures quickly, emphasizing thoroughness, accuracy, and attention to detail.

Education

Computer Experience

Platinum

Real World

Peachtree

Lawson

RPM

Microsoft Excel

Lotus 1-2-3

Microsoft Word

WordPerfect

FastTax

Plus other customized tax programs

MASTER OF ARTS - ECONOMICS..XXXX
San Jose State University • 4.0 GPA

BACHELOR OF ARTS - ECONOMICS..XXXX
University of California at Los Angeles • 4.0 GPA

Work Experience

TAX ACCOUNTANT / ACCOUNTS PAYABLE......................1996 - XXXX
San Jose & Palo Alto, California

- Full-time, long-term assignments through **Accountants Plus** and **Accountants on Call.** Clients included a nonprofit agency, a software developer, an Internet networking company, and a paint manufacturer.

- Computed sales tax and prepared returns for transactions conducted in 47 states, as well as local sales and use taxes. Processed a high volume of accounts payable invoices.

TEST DATA COLLECTOR......................................Summers 1994 - 1995
Fort Bragg, North Carolina

- Gathered information on military vehicles for the **U.S. Dept. of Defense**.

TAX PREPARER / ACCOUNTANT...1993 - 1995
Fayetteville, North Carolina

- Prepared federal and state tax returns for clients of two income tax services and a CPA firm. Worked closely with clients to accurately compute their returns and transfer data to computer. Positions required a high degree of client contact and attention to detail.

FINANCIAL PLANNING INTERN..1990
Santa Monica, California

- A 3-month student internship with the **Potter Financial Group**.

Affiliations

Volunteer Income Tax Assistance (VITA)...1995
- Prepared income tax returns for members of the military. Received special tax training from the Internal Revenue Service.

Member of *Toastmasters International*..1997

50

Combination. *Carolyn S. Braden, Hendersonville, Tennessee*
To prevent a judgment of "job hopping," the writer used bold uppercase letters to emphasize positions. The left column displays the individual's considerable software knowledge.

LEAH SAN CARLOS
6334 Ressler Avenue
El Paso, TX 79912
(915) 581-1234
lscarlos@worldnet.att.com

A disciplined and detail-oriented professional offering over eight years of experience as an accounting specialist. Thorough knowledge of accounting principles, accounts payable, disbursing, budget, and internal control. Trained in tax preparation. Demonstrated supervisory and management skills. Proven ability to generate quality results under tight time constraints.

"Specialist San Carlos is a true performer who has consistently demonstrated the highest standards of excellence. I am convinced she would be an asset to any organization which has the foresight to use her skills." L. Major, SGT.

CAREER HIGHLIGHTS

Accounting Specialist

Maintained records of financial transactions. Verified and posted details of business transactions to subsidiary accounts. Handled ledgers and general files, transferring data to general ledger as necessary. Reconciled and balanced accounts. Compiled reports to show statistics, such as cash receipts and expenditures, accounts payable/receivable, as well as profit and loss statements. Consistently monitored records for accuracy and efficiently corrected any errors. Generated office reports and memos using customized computer programs, word processing, and spreadsheet programs.

Supervised two other employees. Verbally evaluated job performance and delivered personnel evaluations to management. Trained new employees in office procedures. Researched and reorganized financial documents in order to facilitate the conversion of a manual payroll system to a computer system.

Tax Specialist

Performed yearly tax preparation for a wide variety of clients. Assessed and evaluated client information and prepared accurate returns. Maintained a rapport with customers that resulted in a high customer satisfaction rate and assured return business.

EMPLOYMENT HISTORY

U.S. Army Fort Bliss, TX, Fort Carson, CO	1990 – 1998
H & R Block El Paso, TX	1995 – 1998 (concurrent)
Julian Dyer, CPA Sacramento, CA	1989 – 1990

EDUCATION

A.A. General Accounting	Vista College, Sacramento, CA	1990
Income Tax Preparation	H&R Block, El Paso, TX	1995

EXCELLENT PROFESSIONAL REFERENCES AVAILABLE UPON REQUEST

51

Functional. *Shari Favela, El Paso, Texas*
Some prospective employers dislike resumes that contain little information about past employment. A choice quotation about the individual as a worker helps to build respect.

DELON WILLIAMS, CPA

One Cypress Circle
Seattle, Washington 97345
603-789-9065

Professional Profile

Financial / Tax Expert with broad experience in management, team building, training, budgeting, and creative problem solving. Proven ability to define and achieve operational goals for companies in diverse industries. Extensive knowledge of income tax laws and GAAP financial reporting requirements. Computer literate with solid understanding of business technology and accounting applications.

Experience

DEVILLE & COMPANY, P.C. – Seattle, Washington
Manager, Tax Services Group (1993-1998)
Managed 16-person tax services group for fast-growing CPA firm that grew from 10 to 100 employees in four years. Supervised the delivery of consulting services provided to owners of closely held businesses with annual sales of $100,000-$100,000,000 (i.e., manufacturing, construction, real estate, distribution and service industries). Provided detailed financial analysis, budgeting and cash flow analysis.

- Conducted final reviews of corporate, partnership, individual and estate planning returns, tax accrual reviews for financial statements and corporate succession and estate planning services.
- Played key role in retaining one of the firm's largest clients.
- Coordinated transactions, preparation and review of over 800 trust tax returns for the Trust Department of a major local bank.

HELM & COMPANY, P.C. – St. Louis, Missouri
Manager (1989-1993)
Supervised staff of six and oversaw the completion of corporate, individual, partnership and fiduciary tax returns. Coordinated tax accrual reviews with the Audit Department. Worked closely with principals and client staff to provide strategic business and tax planning for closely held businesses.

- Personally coordinated estate planning services; evaluated retirement plans and researched multistate taxation issues.
- Facilitated smooth transition of merger between Howard, Risso and Company and Helm and Company; assisted in developing *Tax Procedures Manual* to ensure uniformity and quality control within the new firm.

ARTHUR ANDERS & COMPANY – Chicago, Illinois
Manager, Entrepreneurial Services (1986-1989)
Oversaw audit, tax planning and advisory services for financial institutions, high-tech businesses, distribution and service companies.

Managed various special projects:

- Closed and liquidated a large ship repair company.
- Evaluated productivity pay plan for manufacturing business.
- Completed due diligence work with the Merger and Acquisition Group.

Education

UNIVERSITY OF CHICAGO – Chicago, Illinois
B.S. Business Administration (1986)

■ ■ ■

52

Combination. *Pat Kendall, Aloha, Oregon*
Adequate white space, positions in boldface, and bullets make this resume easy to size up at a glance. This resume could be made easily as a three-column table with lines hidden.

JANE E. SIMMONS, C.P.A.

18015 Prestwick Drive
Tampa, Florida 36300
(813) 000-0000

Professional Summary

Senior-Level, Accounting Professional with notable record of advancement and excellent qualifications in accounting, client relationship management, and financial/tax reporting. Well-developed knowledge of federal and state tax guidelines in areas such as income, estate, gift, payroll, sales, intangible and tangible taxes. Experienced in managing diverse client base consisting of *Professional Associations, Corporations, S-Corporations, Partnerships, Sole Proprietors, Nonprofit Organizations, Banks, Trusts, and Individuals*. Well-honed skills in analyzing/interpreting/summarizing data, problem-solving, building client rapport, and organizational management. Able to work well under pressure, with attention to details and meeting time constraints. Equal talents in business management, start-up operations, upholding fiscal efficiency, and staff supervision. Self-directed and service-oriented; offer proactive attitude, strong communication and interpersonal skills, and professional work ethic.

Areas of Expertise

- Public / Corporate Accounting
- Research & Analysis
- State / Federal Income Tax Preparation
- Quality Control Standards
- Strategical & Tactical Tax Planning
- P&L Evaluation / Financial Projections
- IRS Audit Policies & Procedures
- Financial Statement Compilation & Review

Computer Skills

Conversant with numerous specialized and over-the-counter accounting software programs for DOS and Windows 95.

BNA Income Tax Planner ... Creative Solutions ... Field Audit Systems Technology (FAST) ... Lotus 1-2-3 ... RIA On Point Tax Research System ... TValue-Amortization Program ... ProSystem FX ... MAS 90 ... Quicken and QuickBooks ... Safeguard System ... Excel

Professional Experience

SMYTH & ASSOCIATES, P.A. - Tampa, FL   1986 - Present
Manager (1996 - Present)
Senior Accountant (1990 - 1996)
Staff Accountant (1987 - 1990)
Paraprofessional/Firm Bookkeeper (1986 - 1987)

(High standards of integrity, meticulous skills and providing top-notch, quality work led to successive promotions initiating from entry-level to positions of increased responsibilities.)

Pivotal role in providing a broad scope of consultative and accounting services to a diverse client base in areas such as general and complex financial concerns; preparation of state/federal taxes; developing stratagems focused on augmenting P&L performance; preparing financial and tax reports, and IRS audit representation. Administrative duties include supervision of two support staff, active participation as a member of internal quality control inspection team, and serving as United Way Coordinator.

Education / Licensure

UNIVERSITY OF SOUTH FLORIDA (1985-1988)
MBA Program / 5th-year accounting requirement for CPA Examination

State of Florida C.P.A. (1988)
(First time candidate)

UNIVERSITY OF SOUTH FLORIDA (1980-1984)
B. A. - Accounting

Professional Affiliations

Florida Institute of CPA's (FICPA)
American Institute of CPA's (AICPA)

53

Functional. *Diane McGoldrick, Tampa, Florida*
This resume features a thick horizontal line under the contact information, horizontal lines interrupted by centered headings in bold italic, and small print. See Cover Letter 1.

Linda K. Jennings

555 Maple Avenue • Belmont, CA 99999 • (650) 999-9999

PROFILE:

- CPA with 15+ years of diversified Tax Preparation and Compliance experience.
- Accomplished in accounting for small businesses and start-ups.
- Strong communication and human relations skills; responsive to client needs.
- Able researcher who quickly identifies issues and knows how to find answers.
- Demonstrated ability to work well independently and as part of a team.

PROFESSIONAL EXPERIENCE:

XXXX to XXXX   COOPER JONES COLLINS, Redfield CA
Manager

Perform full range of compliance work: individual, partnership, corporation, fiduciary, estate and gift taxes. Conduct staff and peer reviews. Oversee the library, including CD-ROMs.

Client Base: Professional service, software/multimedia development, and manufacturing companies.

19XX to 19XX   DUNN & STURGIS, CPAs, San Francisco, CA
Tax Manager

Reviewed individual, corporate and fiduciary compliance work. Performed tax planning related to estate and gift tax issues.

Client Base: Primarily construction and apparel companies.

19XX to 19XX   CUMMINGS, MILLER & BOSCOW, Santa Bella, CA
Senior Tax Accountant and Acting Manager

In addition to compliance work, performed tax research, prepared client billings, and administered off-site tax return processing.

Client Base: High-tech, bio-tech, and foreign sales corporations; real estate partnerships, manufacturing companies, trusts and individuals.

19XX to 19XX   GOODWIN, PETERS & NAFTALLY, CPAs, Deerfield, CA
Supervisor

Prepared individual, corporate, partnership, and fiduciary income tax returns. Compiled financial statements and designed manual and electronic general ledger accounting systems.

EDUCATION & CERTIFICATION:

Certified Public Accountant - State of California

Master of Taxation Program, State College University - San Francisco, CA

B.S. Business Management, Cornell University - Ithaca, NY

Software: Lotus, Word, AccuPlan, CCH, BNA, IRA, and CD-ROM research products

54

Combination. *Sydney J. Reuben, Menlo Park, California*
This person had followed an "ideal career path," moving to a higher position every three or four years. The Client Base statements show her broad experience. An easy-to-read resume.

Vickie M. Watson

CERTIFIED PUBLIC ACCOUNTANT

2222 North Main
Dallas, Texas 00000-0000

(555) 555-5555
e-mail: vickcpa@www.com

PROFILE

Competent professional with more than fifteen years' diversified accounting experience. Expertise in income tax preparation specializing in small business and individual tax returns. Extensive experience in general ledger maintenance, payroll, accounts payable, accounts receivable, and all tax reporting. Strong technical skills with the ability to stay abreast of current developments. Excellent management and organizational skills to handle all levels of responsibility.

- Computer proficiency: Peachtree, QuickBooks, Quicken, Windows 95, Lotus 1-2-3, various tax programs, spreadsheets, and database applications.
- Extremely detail- and task-oriented with emphasis on accuracy and timeliness.
- Effective communicator who interacts well with people.
- Honest, dependable, noncompromising individual with a strong work ethic.

EDUCATION

University of North Texas, Denton, Texas
Bachelor of Science in Business Controls
August, 1986

12 hours Graduate Studies in Accounting

PROFESSIONAL EXPERIENCE

Owner / Manager
Vickie M. Watson, CPA - Dallas, Texas
1990 - Present

Responsible for start-up and successful operation of business specializing in professional income tax preparation for small businesses and individuals.

Accountant
First Federal Savings Bank - Dallas, Texas
1986 - 1994

Assisted the Comptroller in all accounting functions including general ledger maintenance, payroll, suspense audits, tax reporting, and month-end closings. Managed a $42 million portfolio and worked with mortgage loan accruals. Responsible for governmental reporting and communication with the Board of Directors.

Cost Accounting / Accounts Payable
Andrew Corporation - Fort Worth, Texas
1984 - 1985

Bookkeeper
Bob McCombs CPA - Bedford, Texas
1982 - 1984

AFFILIATIONS

- Member, Texas Society of CPA's
- Member, Dallas Chamber of Commerce
- Past President, Soroptimist International (held numerous other offices)
- Past Co-Chair of Environmental Committee, Dallas Chamber of Commerce

55

Combination. *Dorothy E. Smith, Denton, Texas*
Here is a pleasing mix of centered, balanced, fully justified, and indented left-justified text. Italic helps positions to stand out. The name, headings, and degree are in boldface.

KNOX BRADFORD, CPA

555 Pepperdine Lane
Clovis, CA 93611   Relocating to Sacramento

Residence: (559) 555-5555
Work *(confidential)*: (559) 555-5444

QUALIFICATIONS

EXPERIENCED CPA with comprehensive skills in taxation, audit, and accounting. Firm resource for tax research, analysis of complex tax issues, and preparation of multistate income tax returns. Management consultant qualified to provide business advisory, financial consulting, and negotiation services. MIS expert in both IBM and Macintosh platforms; in-depth knowledge of Windows 98, Excel, Word, Lotus, and numerous tax and accounting programs.

PROFESSIONAL EXPERIENCE

MANAGER & ACCOUNTANT—Miller & Miller, Certified Public Accountants, Clovis, CA   9/90–Present

Provide tax, audit, and financial accounting services for varied client base. Conduct tax planning, reporting, and compliance for complex corporate, individual, partnership, fiduciary, and nonprofit entities. Plan and execute audit engagements with full responsibility for accounting practices and client interaction. Provide technical and theory review as in-house quality control reviewer. Train and supervise staff accountants.

Consult clients on strategic business planning, taxation, finance, and technology applications. Clients range from start-ups to multimillion-dollar diversified entities representing the following industries: manufacturing, agribusiness, retail, nonprofit, government, and service businesses.

Manage IS functions, including hardware and software selection, purchase, installation, maintenance, user training, software interface for 10+ software programs, and ongoing technical troubleshooting. Serve as network administrator for Novell LAN. Contribute to strategic planning, operational enhancements, and directional focus for firm.

Selected Contributions:

+   Generated highest billable production in a seven-member firm and attracted 20+ new clients to firm.

+   Reduced total audit engagement hours 25%, increasing net collection rate through evaluation and updates of audit programs. Wrote random-number computer program for audit engagements.

+   Saved company thousands in computer outsourcing, personally converting antiquated processes and software to state-of-art systems (presently Windows 98 operating system).

+   Represent clients before IRS, lending institutions, and regulatory entities. Sample cases: negotiated loan reduction of 25% for client, saving 2,400 acres of prime farmland; presented IRS Offer in Compromise that eliminated 95% of client's federal tax liability.

EDUCATION

FRESNO PACIFIC UNIVERSITY, Fresno, California

Cum Laude Graduate with **Bachelor of Arts degree in Accounting**
Other Honors: Top Scholar Athlete (Men's Soccer Team, 4 years); Top Accountant Graduate; Top Senior Project; Top Junior Student in Social Sciences Department; Excellence in Business Award

AFFILIATIONS

American Institute of Certified Public Accountants
California Society of Certified Public Accountants

INTERESTS

In spare time, avid reader of finance, accounting, and computer material (*Journal of Accountancy, Accounting Today, Kiplinger's Tax Letter*, accounting technology publications, etc.). Enjoy golf, soccer, and other outdoor recreation.

References on Request

56

Combination. *Susan Britton Whitcomb, Fresno, California*
Thick-thin horizontal lines (reading from the bottom up) separate the contact information from the rest of the resume. Indented information makes the section headings stand out.

IRIS BERRING
876 E. Main Street
Ridgewood, NY 11746
(718) 555-1212

Certified Public Accountant-Taxation Specialist

PROFILE

- *Accomplished tax professional with strong financial and accounting experience with a leading international organization.*
- *Strong expertise in complex domestic and international taxation issues for multiple legal entities, including partnerships and corporate entities.*
- *Candidate for Master's degree in Taxation.*
- *Serve as liaison with all federal, state, and municipal tax authorities.*
- *Public accounting background with general taxation experience.*

EXPERIENCE

A MAJOR LAW FIRM, 1992-xxxx   New York, NY
International law firm headquartered in New York with 4 domestic offices and 32 international offices in Europe, Africa, Asia, and the Middle East. The firm generates $300 million in billings annually. It employs 800 attorneys, including 180 partners, 800 administrative and support staff.

Tax Manager
- Recruited to manage all tax responsibilities for Accounting Department.
- Responsible for recruiting, directing and managing staff for preparation and timely filing of all federal and state tax returns, including partnership, corporate, multistate, expatriate, pension and health and welfare plans, and trusts and estates.
- Member of tax team along with firm partners in developing and implementing domestic and international tax strategies and tax season planning.
- Responsible for preparation of all partner K-1 forms as well as reporting for expatriates in foreign nations.
- Prepare and review a high volume of federal and state tax returns and related schedules for the firm's LLPs, LLCs, and C corporation returns for all of its domestic offices.
- Responsible for all governmental filings for 401(k) and two defined benefit plans.
- Supervised and troubleshooted IRS audit of the firm's defined benefit plan. Compiled and organized key data which resulted in a successful audit.

T.E.D. CORPORATION LTD., 1988-1991   New York, NY
Corporate Accountant
- Supervised staff for preparation and review of annual audited financial statements, governmental filings, and employees' benefit statements for Fortune 100 company with over 10,000 employees.

EASTERN PUBLISHING CORP., 1987-1988   New York, NY
Benefits Director
- Responsible for administration and accounting of defined benefit/contribution plans, 401(k) and stock option plans for multidivisional Fortune 500 company with over 6,000 employees.

ANOTHER MAJOR LAW FIRM, 1986-1987   New York, NY
Benefits Manager
- Managed and administered defined benefit/contribution plans for prestigious New York law firm.

THOMAS & FORMAN, P.C., 1984-1986   New York, NY
PISCATELLO AND COMPANY, P.C., 1977-1984 & 1991-1992
Staff Accountant
- Performed all accounting functions for two public accounting firms.

EDUCATION/PROFESSIONAL AFFILIATIONS

New York University
M.S. Taxation (expected) xxxx
B.S. Accounting (Magna cum Laude)
American Institute of Certified Public Accountants
New York State Society of CPA's

57

Combination. *Etta R. Barmann, New York, New York*
Italic calls attention to important information about the individual, her occupational positions, her academic degrees, and the section headings. Names of firms are all uppercase.

JOSEPH R. HEARNS
5802 Miller Road
Madison, WI 55123   (920) 555-9889

HIGHLIGHTS OF EXPERIENCE AND ACHIEVEMENTS
- Chosen for seven-week special assignment to audit state agency bank statements from 139 banks across the state. Reconciled appropriate statements and reports with Wisconsin Automated Information Network (WAIN) system prior to end of fiscal year.
- Perform annual reviews of financial statements for gasoline and cigarette tax accounts to determine bonding requirements for licensure.
- Named to committee which facilitated Wisconsin's implementation of the International Fuel Tax Agreement (IFTA). Performed internal audits on IFTA procedures to ensure adherence to IFTA Articles of Agreement. Educated employees of applicable tax-paying companies about IFTA procedures and benefits.
- Review and revise Wisconsin tax forms, returns and schedules for conformity with current statutes and department rules. Assist in drafting wording for proposed legislation for letter rulings and revenue administrative bulletins.
- Monitor specified motor fuel accounts; prepare requests to Receipts Processing unit to redistribute funds among five accounts.
- Gather and interpret data from multiple sources to generate monthly reports summarizing activity with respect to revenue, gallonage and aviation fuel.
- Conducted trust fund audits of cemeteries, collection agencies, real estate brokers and builders. Obtained documentary evidence to support administrative action or criminal prosecution. Gave supporting testimony at administrative and court hearings.
- Researched and interpreted laws relative to areas of audits.

EMPLOYMENT HISTORY
State of Wisconsin • Madison, WI   1990-1994 & 1995-Present
Auditor P11 - Department of Treasury
Auditor P11 - Department of Commerce

*Additional employment as **Accountant** in several temporary positions*   1994-1995

COMPUTER EXPERIENCE
• Wisconsin Automated Information (WAIN)	• State Treasury Accounts Receivable System (STARS)	• Tax Audit Collection System (TACS)
• Windows	• Quattro Pro	• EasyAccount
• Excel	• Paradox	• dBASE
• Lotus 1-2-3	• Access	• Tax Accounting
• WordPerfect	• Word	• Bidtek

EDUCATION
Madison College of Business • Madison, WI
Bachelor of Business Administration   1989
Associate Degree in Accounting   1987
Concentrations: Accounting, Computer Information Systems

References furnished on request

58

Functional. *Janet L. Beckstrom, Flint, Michigan*
The individual was "applying for internal jobs within the state," so the writer "used a lot of jargon and acronyms." Achievements are integrated with responsibilities in the Highlights.

NESTER L. ARMISTON
30 E. Main Street
Belleville, Illinois 62223
(618) 555-7020

PROFESSIONAL PROFILE

- More than 15 years' experience as a Tax Auditor for the Internal Revenue Service, with additional duties involving quality control, staff training, audit selection and direct taxpayer assistance in person and via telephone.

- Experienced with Illinois and Missouri State Income Tax, Illinois State Retailer's Occupation & Use Tax, and Illinois Circuit Breaker returns.

- Proficient with database, spreadsheet, word processing, and automated tax preparation software applications. Recently completed the accredited National Tax Training School to maintain up-to-date knowledge of audit techniques, accounting methods, and IRS codes, rules and regulations.

- Able to distinguish between problems caused by computer errors as well as erroneous input. Can perform computations and other job tasks without being totally reliant on automated systems.

SELECTED TAX KNOWLEDGE AND SKILLS

Federal Taxation	Exemptions and Filing Status
Tax Computations	Gross Income Inclusions/Exclusions
Gain/Loss on Sale/Exchange of Property	Capital Gains and Losses
Business Deductions	Depreciation
Accelerated Cost Recovery	Depletion
Amortization	Business/Casualty Losses
Self-Employment Tax	Estimated Tax
Income Tax Withholding	Payroll Tax
Tax Credits	Gain on Sale of Residence

EXPERIENCE

TAX AUDITOR, Internal Revenue Service
- Inspected books and records to determine and adjust taxpayer liability.
- Reviewed and corrected other tax auditor's work.
- Trained new staff members on all self-employed and non-self-employed income, deductions, credits, and audit techniques; provided instruction on indirect methods of determining income including bank deposit analysis, net worth, source and application of funds, and cash analysis.
- Selected which returns would be audited.

Additional experience:
Successful small business owner responsible for all bookkeeping, accounting, sales, and financial management functions.

EDUCATION/SPECIALIZED TRAINING

- B.A. degree, Business Education/Psychology, McKendree College, Lebanon, Illinois
- Accounting/Federal Taxation Courses, Southern Illinois University at Edwardsville
- Advanced Tax Auditor Training, Internal Revenue Service
- National Tax Training School, Monsey, New York

REFERENCES AVAILABLE UPON REQUEST

59

Functional. *John A. Suarez, Troy, Illinois*
Horizontal lines enclosing each heading are a distinctive feature. The Profile section indicates experience and skills. What follows is a two-column list of keywords and key phrases.

JOHN CHANCE
Licensed Public Accountant
10 Ivy Lane • Montvalle, New Jersey xxxxx
(xxx) xxx-xxxx or (xxx) xxx-xxxx

ACCOUNTING/FINANCE PROFESSIONAL

A highly experienced professional with a proven record of consistently increasing business performance. A bottom-line, results-oriented individual who understands the importance of implementing effective strategies to accomplish organizational goals. Excellent analytical skills with the ability to devise and implement effective programs. Reputation as a team builder and facilitator.

DEMONSTRATED STRENGTHS

BUSINESS PLANNING/BUDGETING	INVESTMENT ANALYSIS	TAX/FINANCIAL PLANNING
ORGANIZATIONAL DEVELOPMENT	STAFF MANAGEMENT	LEADERSHIP
PROACTIVE APPROACH	INNOVATIVE	DECISIVENESS

CAREER HIGHLIGHTS

♦ *Installed an insurance safety and savings program for liability and compensation, with annual savings of $300,000.*
♦ *Managed corporate retirement plan investments, increasing annual return from 6% to 10%.*
♦ *Reduced annual expenditures by $10,000 while increasing coverage, by managing company benefits plan.*
♦ *Comanaged realty properties and instituted cost, budgeting and cash management systems with annual savings of $25,000.*

PROFESSIONAL EXPERIENCE

Financial/Investment Consultant (Private Practice)   1991 - Present
- Advise clientele comprising corporate, trusts and individual accounts in all functions pertaining to accounting, finance and tax matters.
- Generate long-/short-term corporate and individual business plans and assist in implementation/execution for maximum profitability.

LA SALA ORGANIZATION • New Rochelle, New York   1979 - 1991

COMPTROLLER (1984 - 1991)

- Directed all financial functions pertaining to a $50 million real estate and construction organization.
- Conceptualized, administered and managed tax planning and preparation, cash management/investing, payroll and cost system management.
- Oversaw insurance programs, risk management, banking functions and financial reporting.
- Developed and controlled annual budgets.
- Implemented IBM System 34/36 computerized accounting system for each division.
- Utilized PC's and Lotus 1-2-3 for tax/investment planning and preparation of spreadsheets.
- Hired, trained and supervised a staff of 15 accounting professionals.

60

Combination. *Alesia Benedict, Rochelle Park, New Jersey*
Page borders and bold, underlined, all-uppercase, centered section headings help to tie together the two pages. Italic links the opening profile, the Career Highlights section, and the

JOHN CHANCE   -Page Two-

LA SALA ORGANIZATION experience continued...

ACCOUNTING MANAGER (1979 - 1984)

- Managed all accounting activities and supervised departmental staff to peak levels of productivity.
- Accountable for financial report and corporate tax preparation.
- Assessed requisitions and made recommendations to upper management.
- Reviewed capital expenditures.

M. STERNLIEB and COMPANY, CPA's - Hackensack, NJ   1971 - 1979

SENIOR MANAGER (1975 - 1979)

- Supervised daily operations pertaining to the small business department, including accounting and bookkeeping functions, daily tax preparation and staff management.
- Reviewed accountants in performing audit services for corporations, trusts, foundations, private businesses and estates.

STAFF ACCOUNTANT (1971 - 1975)

- Performed all accounting and auditing functions for clientele comprising various small businesses.

EDUCATION

Fairleigh Dickinson University • Rutherford, New Jersey
Bachelor of Science: Accounting

PROFESSIONAL AFFILIATIONS

National Society of Public Accountants
National Association of Public Accountants
Institute of Management Accountants

job positions. Bold small caps enhance demonstrated strengths, and filled diamond bullets—possibly the strongest kind of bullet—point to career highlights, also in boldface. The writer thus uses a variety of font enhancements to draw the eye to key information. The resume begins and ends with center-justification.

DANA NORRIS

1234 Sixth Avenue • Miami, Florida 00000 • (555) 555-5555 dana@bellsouth.net

Visionary professional with significant level of experience in all types of financial, business and technical environments acquired as a public accountant, auditor, independent tax consultant and financial advisor. Analytical problem solver bringing excellent technical expertise, systems knowledge, and applications development experience to hand. Talented and self-directed; dynamic leader, facilitator, instructor and manager.

Able to:
→ **Analyze all financial and business operations to develop and implement effective applications solutions**
→ **Apply prior knowledge and technical skills in learning new technologies**
→ **Provide powerful leadership and direction in financial, business, and accounting issues**
→ **Develop technical applications for task performance and project completion**
→ **Instruct individuals and groups on financial/business issues, applications and end-user processes**

TECHNOLOGY SKILLS

VisualBasic • C++ • EasyTrieve • SQL • Oracle and Hyperion Environments
Software and Hardware Configuration • Application Development
Database Design and Management • Mac and PC platforms • Lotus 1-2-3
MS Access • MS Excel • MS Word • WordPerfect Suite • Workpapers Plus
Peachtree • QuickBooks • Adobe PageMaker • dBASE • DOS • Windows NT, 98, 95, 3.11
Numerous Commercial Tax Accounting Software Packages

- **Teamed on tax software application design/development within Microsoft Access Developer Tools for Arthur Andersen**
- **Designed software applications to track mutual fund time performance, daily interest rate activity, and investment administration for an independent broker-dealership**
- **Created investment analysis software for real estate limited partnership evaluation**
- **Administered system conversions**
- **Designed and implemented microcomputer databases**

BUSINESS ACUMEN

Executive Management • Start-up Issues • Incorporation • Business Analysis
Cost Reduction Actions • Business Planning • Marketing • Visionary Strategies

FINANCIAL EXPERTISE

Business Analyst/Financial Consulting

Investment Research/Analysis	Nonprofit Organizations
Cost Analysis	Financial/Legal Coordination
Corporate Tax Analysis	Systems Analysis

Public Accountant - Auditor and Financial Advisor

Senior Level: Tax, Auditor	Tax Consulting and Preparation
Financial Consulting	Brokerage
Securities and Investments	Public Seminars

61

Functional. *Tracy A. Bumpus, Austin, Texas*
This individual "had a long career as Public Accountant/Financial Counselor and desired a career change into Applications Development for financial operations." The writer emphasized

EMPLOYMENT RECORD

→ *Planned, presented and taught public seminars and classes on financial and business issues; pioneered public financial seminars concept establishing national reputation*

→ *Teamed on design/development tax software applications for Arthur Andersen*

→ *Served as Chief Financial Officer of largest HVAC contractor on Florida East Coast*

→ *Performed public accounting and senior/manager level tax and auditing services*

→ *Expertise in nonprofit organizations, government regulatory reporting, and financial requirements under FASB 116 & 117m INB-133, GAAP, GAGAS*

→ *Conceptualized and initiated first investment trust as an issuer of federally insured secondary market mortgage securities for credit union super service organizations*

→ *Fostered changes and improvements of Credit Union laws through direct lobbying efforts and coordination with Federal and State Regulatory officials*

Independent Financial Consultant and Contractor for: continuing operations since 1980

Norris Tax Consultants	Jones, Doe & Smith, CPA's
Romac International	Times Publishing, Inc.
Eckerd Corporation	Gordon & George, CPA's
Arthur Andersen	Tim White, Jr. CPA, PA
Equifunding/First National	
Acceptance Co.	

Chief Executive Officer - AccuMed Claims Corp., AMCC AccuTax
Chief Financial Officer - Air Control Systems Tampa Bay, Inc.
Public Accountant - CPA Firms: Thomas, Andrews & Co; Nelson, Cole & Murray; Ralph Matthews
Ownership/Management of Financial Consulting Conglomerate:
Norris & Associates *(Securities Sales and Financial Planning)*
Norris Financial Strategies Corporation *(Public Financial Seminars)*
Norris Investment Advisory Corporation *(fee-based financial planning firm)*
Midwestern Securities Corporation *(Brokerage/Dealership)*
CISCU Development Corporation *(Credit Union Service Organization)*
LIH Investment Group *(HUD and low-income real estate rehab property investment)*
Neighborhood Development Partnerships *(Rehab Real Estate Investments)*
Neighborhood Management & Development Co. *(Rehab Contractor and Property Management)*

EDUCATION AND TRAINING

Bachelor of Arts - Accounting
Southern State University
Becker CPA Exam Review
Wall Street Training Institute - Series 24 - General Principal NASD Securities Brokerage Firm
Series 7 - Full Securities Broker, Registered Investment Advisor
Hansen Insurance & A.L. Williams Insurance Exam Reviews; Life and Health
Currently enrolled in Microsoft Solutions Developer (MSCD) Certificate Program
Smalltown Junior College

the person's "technical skills and experience in applications development for large corporations." The writer also displayed the individual's "very high level background in management in order to assist her hire-in level in her new career." The resume contains only one date (1980) to mask the individual's age.

REESE TALBOT
CERTIFIED PUBLIC ACCOUNTANT

89 Luna Court ◆ St. Paul, MN 00000 ◆ (555) 555-5555

— *Objective* —

Controllership or Financial Consulting position requiring a proven team leader and problem solver with highly developed analytical, organizational, communication, and strategic planning skills.

— *Summary* —

- ◆ Solid background of more than eight years, providing professional accounting, tax and consulting services to individuals and various business entities. Additionally knowledgeable of FASB standards implementation/updating for both nonprofit and for-profit concerns.
- ◆ Take great pride in supplying clients with timely and responsive services, thereby establishing trust relationships, generating repeat/referral business and enhancing the reputation of the company.
- ◆ Strong quantitative and analytical orientation, and proficiency with sophisticated computerized accounting and tax-related programs (SAP FI/CO, Hyperion, Fast Tax, and others) as well as Microsoft Word and Excel software.
- ◆ Accustomed to working long hours to meet demands and deadlines; willing to relocate.

— *Areas of Expertise and Career Interest* —

- ◇ Financial statement audit/review/compilation
- ◇ Tax planning
- ◇ Operational and financial auditing
- ◇ Policy and procedure development
- ◇ Acquisitions and consolidations

- ◇ Business growth strategies
- ◇ Investment analysis
- ◇ Financing procurement
- ◇ Start-up and turnaround situations
- ◇ Regulatory compliance

— *Experience* —

FINANCIAL PLANNING, AUDITING AND CONSULTING

- ◆ Reviewed and prepared consolidated and comparative financial statements to implement the adoption of current financial accounting standards for compliance with individual requests.
- ◆ Interfaced with top management at client companies and their financial advisors to develop and maintain prudent investment policies, tax avoidance strategies, and proposals for improving profitability.
- ◆ Prepared analytical reviews and trend analyses to develop suggestions to aid management in reducing expenses and expanding revenue.
- ◆ Performed attestation engagements relating to elements embodied in financial statements.
- ◆ Determined client organizations' goals, reviewed their operations, assessed/made recommendations on weak areas, and proposed extended services to address their needs.
- ◆ Developed projections and forecasts of cash flows to ascertain feasibility of planned growth. Implemented alternative financing options when necessary.
- ◆ Assisted clients with procedures related to the commencement of new business ventures and preparation of dissolution filings of terminated corporate structures.
- ◆ As consultant to elder law attorneys, provided financial planning guidance within framework of state laws to preserve assets of older adults while addressing the eventuality of long-term care.
- ◆ Over the past year, promoted business relationships resulting in 350 additional billable hours beyond standard for the firm.

62

Functional. *Melanie A. Noonan, West Paterson, New Jersey*
Short horizontal lines enclose bold, italic, centered section headings, which are visible at a glance. For variety, the writer used unfilled diamond bullets in the Areas of Expertise and

REESE TALBOT, CPA
Page 2

TAX ACCOUNTING

◆ Prepared and reviewed corporate, partnership and individual federal and state tax returns, as well as fiduciary, gifting, payroll, and sales and use taxes.

◆ Kept investment activities current, monitoring capital gains that would trigger a tax effect. Established tax payment schedules.

◆ Interpreted tax law changes relative to different client situations and assisted them with year-end and estate planning matters.

◆ Led project to plan and recommend tax avoidance strategies for retiring owners of a large restaurant business and associated real estate, whereby heirs could reduce their personal tax liabilities going forward while the corporation would also receive a tax benefit.

TEAM LEADERSHIP AND COLLABORATION

◆ Supervised other professionals and administrative personnel as well as participated in concurrent audit engagements for a diversified client base that included service companies, health care providers, and nonprofit organizations.

◆ Allocated proper mix of staff through a cost/benefit equation, setting the level of expertise needed for the project while staying with budgetary framework.

◆ Motivated and shaped the technical endeavors of newer staff members.

◆ Contributed to audit services requested by Big 6 accounting firms in areas not feasible for them. As an example, worked on system narrative for a major hospital experiencing revenue decline due to improper billing for services. Ensured effective personnel training and thorough coding of chargeable items to curtail losses.

— *Employment* —

19XX - Present **Audit Supervisor** Wells, Dexter & Company, Certified Public Accountants, Rochester, MN
19XX - 19XX **Senior Accountant** Lindstrom & Company, Certified Public Accountants, Minneapolis, MN

— *Education* —

Notre Dame University — Bachelor of Science in Accounting, 19XX

— *Professional Memberships* —

Minnesota State Society of Certified Public Accountants
American Institute of Certified Public Accountants

Consistently attended approximately 10 continuing professional education seminars per year conducted by the AICPA, MSCPA, IRS, and the State of Minnesota. Keep up to date in matters such as auditing and consulting procedures, preparation and presentation of financial statements, and new legislation regarding taxes and retirement plans.

Career Interest sections. Bold small caps link the contact information at the top of the first page with the side headings in the Experience section across the two pages. The earlier position listed in the Employment section is a senior position, so the resume is silent about all of the individual's previous employment.

JOHN M. BOLLES
BOLLES & BOLLES, INC.
5555 MAIN STREET
TAMPA, FLORIDA 33600
(555) 555-5555

PROFESSIONAL PROFILE

- More than 27 years' experience in real estate appraisal and property tax assessments field.
- A dedicated specialist focusing on excellence, quality, and professionalism.
- Results-oriented – primary goal: client satisfaction.
- Active participant in real estate appraisal and related real estate organizations.
- Effective negotiator achieving the highest and best conclusions.

EXPERIENCE

Bolles & Bolles, Inc.	President / Real Estate Appraiser	1995 - Present
Mayer-Bolles Associates	Vice President/Real Estate Tax Consultant	1990 - 1995
Real Estate Tax Services	Real Estate Tax Consultant	1988 - 1990
Southern Computer Corp.	Consultant-Appraisal Specialist	1981 - 1988
John M. Bolles Consulting	Registered State Consultant	1979 - 1981
Flag County Property Appraiser	Deputy Property Appraiser	1973 - 1979
Howze & Associates, Inc.	Appraisal/Administration Supervisor	1971 - 1973

LICENSES / CERTIFICATIONS

- Florida State Certified General Appraiser #0000000
- ASA - Accredited Senior Appraiser, American Society of Appraisers
- Licensed Real Estate Broker - Florida
- Registered Tax Agent - Tennessee

EDUCATION

University of South Florida - Tampa, Florida
Bachelor of Arts - Business Administration

PROFESSIONAL AFFILIATIONS

American Society of Appraisers (ASA)
International Association of Assessing Officers (IAAO)
Florida Chapter of International Association of Assessing Officers (FLIAAO)
Florida Association of Property Tax Professionals (FAPTP)
National Association of Realtors (NAR)
Florida Association of Realtors (FAR)
Florida Gulfcoast Commercial Association of Realtors (FGCAR)
Institute of Real Estate Management (IREM)

63

Combination. *Anita L. Babcock, St. Petersburg, Florida*
A bold horizontal line connected to a bold vertical line, together with a framed initial balancing the contact information, is a distinctive design that draws you into this resume.

KATHLEEN SMITHERS

7870 134th Loop	Beaverton, Oregon 97007	(503) 642-3455

OBJECTIVE

Position in public accounting.

PROFESSIONAL PROFILE

Highly motivated accounting professional with well-developed analytical skills and broad experience in auditing, tax return preparation and financial statement preparation.

- Detail-oriented with strong planning and organizational abilities.
- Enthusiastic team player; able to communicate effectively with colleagues, supervisors and clients.
- Solid educational background, including degrees in accounting and business management.

PROFESSIONAL EXPERIENCE

SAMFORD & DILLON, CPAs, Tigard, Oregon (11/94-X/XX)
Accountant – Administered pension plans and assumed responsibility for participant reporting, contribution allocation and preparation of form 5500.
- Conducted audit on defined contribution pension plan; prepared all related financial statements.
- Assisted corporate clients with year-end tax planning.
- Prepared corporate and complex individual tax returns.
- Involved in all phases of financial statement preparation.

STAFFORD & STAFFORD, CPAs, Portland, Oregon (1/92-11/94)
Staff / Senior Accountant – Prepared and reviewed financial statements. Completed tax returns for pension and profit sharing plans. Assisted manufacturing clients with preparation of monthly financial statements.
- Participated in the firm's largest financial audit for three year-end engagements.
- Prepared corporate and individual tax returns.
- Conducted comprehensive pension/profit sharing plan audit.

HOFFMAN, BAUM & CO., CPAs, Portland, Oregon (2/91-12/91)
Staff Accountant – Responsible for tax return preparation, payroll and quarterly payroll tax reports. Prepared month- and quarter-end financial statements.

EDUCATION

B.S. Accounting, Portland State University, Portland, Oregon (1995)
B.A. Business Management, Whitworth College, Spokane, Washington (1991)

AFFILIATIONS

OSCPA – Member, Accounting Careers Committee

64

Combination. *Pat Kendall, Aloha, Oregon*
This individual has *two* bachelor's degrees, each from a different institution, and tax experience in each of the positions held. Plenty of "white space" makes the resume easy to read.

ROBERT I. BRIGHT

555 South Street
Phoenix, AZ 00000
(000) 000-000

AREAS OF EXPERTISE

Broad Knowledge of Federal Income Tax and Employee Benefit Laws • Investment Products • Trust Operating Systems & Procedures • Participant Recordkeeping Systems & Procedures • Highly Successful in Establishing Rapport with Clients and Accurately Determining Needs /Requirements • Outstanding Multilevel Communication Skills • Proven Ability to Achieve Revenue Goals & Objectives • Leadership & Team-Building Skills • CEBS Program [Partial Completion] • Successful Completion of CPA Examination

PROFESSIONAL HIGHLIGHTS

US CORPORATION
Birmingham, AZ

Employee Benefit Trust Officer
1994 - 1999

Administrative / Management	• Participated in the centralization of all Arizona Employee Benefits Administration facilities into the Birmingham location. Specifically concentrated on Ann Arbor region consisting of 70 account relationships which generated in excess of $600,000 in annual revenue • Coordinated and managed organizational phases • Analysis & Development of Procedures • Vendor Management • Solely assumed responsibilities for all Ann Arbor account relationships upon retirement of employee benefit trust officer • Recognized for exceptional ability to coordinate diversified phases of centralization
401(k) Participant Recordkeeping / Education	• Designed computer spreadsheet application to compile participant data during transition period • Redefined services provided by third-party recordkeeper • Negotiated new pricing structure based upon redefined level of service • Created and presented participant education programs
Leadership & Supervision	• Trained, monitored performance, and conducted evaluations of support staff • Provided leadership and training to support staff • Participated in the interview process of other officers and support personnel
Computer Knowledge	• Trust Operating Systems • Lotus 1-2-3 • Participant Recordkeeping Systems • E-mail

NATIONAL BANK
Hottland, AZ

Employee Benefit Trust Officer
1986 - 1994

Administrative / Management	• Administered 100 employee benefit accounts exceeding $150 million in trust assets which generated approximately $900,000 in annual revenue • Coordinated and managed administrative processes • Analysis & Development of Procedures
401(k) Participant Recordkeeping / Education	• Interfaced with in-house Participant Recordkeeping Department • Designed computer spreadsheet applications to supplement formal recordkeeping system in specialized situations • Created and presented participant education programs
Leadership & Supervision	• Trained, monitored performance, and conducted evaluations of support staff • Provided leadership and training to support staff • Acted as liaison between support staff and management • Participated in the interview process of officers and support personnel

65

Combination. *Betty Callahan, Vicksburg, Michigan*
A resume for an individual who has been on both sides—as a Revenue Agent and as an Employee Benefit Trust Officer. In the Areas of Expertise section, knowledge and skills are

ROBERT I. BRIGHT

SAVINGS BANK

Hollywood, CA

Assistant Trust Officer / Pension Administrator

1985 - 1986

- Administered 200 retirement plans with over $35 million in trust assets
- Gained and maintained the confidence of assigned customer base
- Utilized knowledge of Federal tax laws respectful of compliance with law
- Collaborated with investment portfolio manager to develop client investment strategies
- Designed and implemented computerized database for monitoring work flow of accounting department
- Made significant improvements in accounting procedures generating an improved / more clearly defined product and increased management controls
- Assigned on a temporary basis to assist in the training and supervision of accounting/recordkeeping staff

INTERNAL REVENUE SERVICE - EXAMINATION DIVISION

Chicago, IL

Revenue Agent

1984 - 1985

- Independently planned and implemented on-site audits of complex business tax returns
- Utilized sophisticated analytical methods and knowledge of accounting principals, auditing procedures, and tax law to determine correct tax liability
- Implemented package audit concept by expanding audit where applicable to include related employment and excise tax returns
- Contributed to Tax Shelter Program
- Served on a temporary assignment to Regional Classification Group

Journeyman Tax Auditor

1981 - 1984

- Performed limited scope audit of business / nonbusiness income tax returns
- Applied analytical abilities, accounting skills and knowledge of income tax laws to determine correct tax liability
- Developed numerous cases for referral to Criminal Investigation Division
- Worked in Tax Protestor Program
- Served as local coordinator of Form W-4 Tax Protestor Program
- Chosen twice for temporary assignment to District Quality Review Staff
- Was selected as an instructor for newly hired auditors

Entry Level Tax Auditor

1979 - 1981

- Performed limited scope audit of nonbusiness income tax returns
- Applied analytical abilities and knowledge of income tax law to determine correct tax liability
- Effectively utilized written and verbal communication skills

---

CONTINUING PROFESSIONAL EDUCATION

CEBS Program	Certified Employee Benefit Specialist Program [Partial Completion] Basis Features & Defined Contribution Approaches • Accounting & Finance Defined Benefit Approaches & Plan Administration • Asset Management Employee Benefit Plans & The Economy
CPA	Successful Completion • State of Illinois • Springfield, IL
Bachelor's Degree	The University of Iowa • Des Moines, IA
Seminars / Expos	Benefits Management Forum & Expo 3-Day Seminar by Employee Benefits Magazine • Milwaukee, WI • 1996
	Legal Issues 3-Day Seminar • J. McKay Seminars • 1995

---

presented as phrases separated by bullets in a centered, doubly indented paragraph. Responsibilities and achievements for each of the last two positions are clustered according to the same sub-subheadings in italic at the left margin. Subheadings and sub-subheadings are in italic throughout the resume.

— *Peter F. Corman* —
4778 Mullhaven Drive
Yorktown Heights, New York 00000
(555) 555-5555

— *Management Profile* —

More than 15 years of experience managing corporate payroll and relocation functions for global corporation. Initiated and led conversion to automated systems, increasing efficiency while streamlining functions and expenses. Demonstrated ability to build team work/morale, improve productivity and enhance customer service. Expertise includes:

Payroll Taxes & Reporting • Stock Benefits Administration
Expense Auditing • Accounting & Tax Preparation • Employee Relocation Management
Development of Policy & Procedures • Financial Analysis & Reporting

— *Professional Experience* —

REXNARD CORPORATION, Boston, Massachusetts
Promoted through series of increasingly responsible positions in payroll/finance department at multi-billion-dollar global consumer products corporation. Career highlights include:

Director, Payroll and Relocation (1988-XXXX)

- Managed staff of 19 in day-to-day operations of corporate Payroll Department which included preparation, disbursement and reporting of $780M in gross payroll and pension funds to 25,000 employees/retirees globally. Concurrent accountability for entire relocation program involving 400 employees worldwide each year.

Accomplishments

➤ **Turned around employee morale and dramatically reduced turnover rate from 20% to less than 5% within first year after assuming management of department.**
➤ **Led conversion and flawless implementation of $15M annual executive bonus program for 1,400 employees from a manual to an automated system, substantially saving time and labor costs and enhancing customer service.**
➤ **Streamlined and cut costs while maintaining peak customer service and high employee morale.**
➤ **Instituted enhancements and improved work flow processes that saved costs and increased efficiency, accuracy and productivity.**
➤ **Developed and implemented corporate-wide relocation policy and procedures.**
➤ **Collaborated with systems personnel to automate direct tax gross-up process between relocation and payroll areas, reducing processing time from 7 days to 1.**

Manager, Stock Benefits Administration and Expense Reporting (1987-1988)

- Administered various corporate stock benefit plans including stock options, SARs, restricted stock and long-term performance. Developed and implemented PC-based application in Lotus to record and track all stock benefit transactions on daily basis. Managed the audit operation of 400 travel expense accounts, ensuring compliance with IRS and comptroller's policies.

66

Combination. *Louise Garver, Enfield, Connecticut*
The individual's original resume was only "a series of job descriptions that did not reflect the full scope of his responsibilities or achievements. He was in a highly competitive market with few

Supervisor, Payroll (1982-1988)

- Supervised staff in preparation and disbursement of multistate and multinational payrolls for approximately 1,500 employees and all U.S. expatriates. Directed payroll processing, tax reporting, payroll accounting, and data processing activities.

Supervisor, Expense Voucher Auditing (1980-1982)

- Supervised and controlled 700+ employee travel expense accounts. Developed and implemented policies/procedures. Instituted new guidelines reducing travel expense balance from $1M to $200K within first 15 months. Promoted from financial analyst.

— Education —

M.B.A. (Finance Concentration)
St. John's University Graduate School of Business, Jamaica, New York

B.S. (Marketing)
Fordham University, New York, New York

positions available at this level in the area." The writer made a chronological Professional Experience section that "pulled out his achievements [and] eliminated irrelevant experience that dated him." The individual was offered "a great position at his level within six weeks." Special bullets point to achievements.

DEAN WONG, CPA

237 Manoa Drive	Portland, Oregon 98654	(503) 244-9076

PROFESSIONAL PROFILE

FINANCE / TAX EXPERT with broad background in diverse organizational environments and 18 years of combined experience in finance management, budgeting, public accounting, tax planning, department administration, compliance management and auditing.

- Skilled in developing policies and procedures to support accounting, finance and internal control systems.
- Thoroughly familiar with GAAP and related tax laws and regulations.
- Effective team leader with well-developed supervisory skills and ability to communicate with staff at all levels.

Solid knowledge of computer technology and applications for finance management, tax processing and research. Experienced in using Windows, Word, Excel, Quattro Pro, Lotus 1-2-3, and QuickBooks.

EXPERIENCE

OREGON SPECIAL OLYMPICS – Portland, Oregon   10/96-Present

Financial Director

Coordinate financial operations and oversee accounting, budgeting, payroll, cash management, treasury functions, retirement plan administration, annual audit, tax compliance, and management reporting. Supervise accounting staff of four. Foster interdepartmental communication and teamwork to ensure a positive and productive work environment.

- Develop initial draft of $2 million annual budget. Work with managers to refine and finalize final version for Board of Directors.
- Prepare the organization's annual income tax returns.
- Facilitate accurate budget planning by expanding financial reports and budget documents to include comparative data and trend analysis.
- Review government and foundation grants to ensure compliance.
- Negotiate casualty insurance and employee medical benefits package. Expand available investment options and prepare related income tax returns.
- Redesigned internal control policies and financial management reporting system.
- Totally revamped accounting systems to ensure Y2K compliance.
- Developed new *Employee Policies and Procedures Manual* and *Employee Benefits Guide*.

SYMONDS MANSON, P.C. – Portland, Oregon   5/93-10/96

Senior Manager

Managed Tax Department for full-service accounting firm. Supervised staff of three and ensured that all projects were completed in a timely manner. Assisted clients with business planning and prepared tax returns for individuals and companies.

- Implemented new billing controls that improved efficiency by 32%.
- Conducted research on obscure tax laws.

(Continued)

67

Combination. *Pat Kendall, Aloha, Oregon*
As a Finance/Tax Expert, this individual applies tax-compliance knowledge gained as the Manager of the Tax Department of different accounting firms. The Profile summarizes the

DEAN WONG, CPA

Page Two

EXPERIENCE *(Continued)*

TIMOTHY HAUTON, CPA – Portland, Oregon   3/88-5/93

Manager

Directed the preparation of compilations, reviews and tax returns. Assisted client attorneys by providing "expert witness" testimony.

- Played a key role in creating the firm's *Financial Statement Preparation Manual.*
- Developed comprehensive employee policy/procedure manual.

Assistant Controller *(for family-owned business)*

Oversaw accounting and general office operations. Completed financial statements for corporations with combined assets of $7.9 million.

- Assisted with administration of $29 million budget.
- Hired and supervised accounting staff of three.

MILLENNIUM HEALTH CORPORATION – Portland, Oregon   6/85-3/88

Accounting Manager

Managed Accounting Department and prepared financial statements for seven hospitals with $17 million in combined assets. Supervised regional accounting staff of seven.

- Streamlined the GL month-end closing process and cut staff overtime by 23%.
- Developed and implemented internal controls.

ARTHUR YOUNG AND COMPANY – Seattle, Washington   9/81-6/85

Manager, Tax Department

Supervised staff and oversaw the preparation of tax returns for corporations and individual clients. Prepared and monitored engagement budgets and client billings. Supervised and evaluated staff.

- Researched alternative tax decisions for clients.
- Provided computer-facilitated tax planning services.

Senior Accountant, Audit Department

Planned audits for various types of clients (i.e., manufacturing, banking, real estate and nonprofit).

EDUCATION

CERTIFIED PUBLIC ACCOUNTANT   1983

UNIVERSITY OF WASHINGTON – Seattle, Washington   1981
B.S. Business Administration / Accounting

AFFILIATIONS

American Institute of Certified Public Accountants

Oregon Society of Certified Public Accountants

---

person's experience, skills, and knowledge. In the Experience section, the paragraph under the job position indicates mainly the individual's duties and responsibilities. Each bulleted list shows achievements. This sequence—of duties in a paragraph, then achievements in a bulleted list—is a popular resume pattern.

PAMELA SUE HANSON

1 Anywhere Drive • Anytown, ST 00000 • (000) 555-5555

PIONEERING BANKING & STATE GOVERNMENT EXECUTIVE

Leader in establishing women as viable professionals in the business community.
Career in business . . . Service in state government

Organizational Management & Development • Tax Law Administration & Compliance
Taxpayer Needs & Concerns • Customer Service • Strategic & Operational Planning
Crisis & Merger Management

Experience . . . Expertise . . . Enthusiasm

SPECIAL RECOGNITION & ACHIEVEMENTS

- Recognized nationally as leading woman banker in state and pioneer in the banking industry:
  - 1st woman Secretary of Revenue in State of Xxxxx (as a Democrat in a Republican administration!).
  - 1st woman senior vice president in Xxxxx State banking.
  - 1st female executive and woman director for Bank of Anytown.
  - 1st woman in United States to graduate from both University of Anywhere School of Bank Administration and Rutgers University Stonier Graduate School of Banking.
- Awarded *19XX Distinguished Woman of Xxxxx State* by Governor James Jones.
- Upon retirement in 19XX, received first and only "Resolution of Appreciation" ever given to a Cabinet Secretary by the Xxxxx Council of State, recognizing major achievements as Secretary of the Xxxxx Department of Revenue.
- Cochaired Xxxxx State Government Performance Audit, a $3-million project authorized by the 19XX state legislature to study and recommend improvements on all aspects of state government operations. Resulting recommendations captured $275 million in initial savings (although not all were implemented).
- Conducted first and only Tax Amnesty Program ever held in Xxxxx State, resulting in more than $38 million collected against a budgeted figure of $20,000,000.
- Newly created women's health center designated Pamela S. Hanson Women's Regional Health Center at Memorial Hospital, Anywhere, ST, in 19XX in recognition of advocacy for women's health issues in western Xxxxx State and for philanthropic endeavors. Regional Bank donated a $200,000 gift in honor of this event.

HIGHLIGHTS OF PROFESSIONAL EXPERIENCE

State Secretary of Revenue • STATE OF XXXXX   XXXX-XXXX
$50 million annual budget; over 1200 employees, with 400 located in 66 field offices.
- Initiated and implemented major departmental reorganization; significantly enhanced computer capabilities and efficiency.
- Initiated/Implemented outreach program, assisting Xxxxxians in better understanding their tax system—thereby increasing collections.
- Improved/Enlarged department's tax research efforts, providing enhanced information for State departments and General Assembly and better understanding of the Xxxxx tax system.
- Initiated and obtained $36-million funding for new Revenue Building.

Securities Representative/Financial Consultant • ANSON-EVERS, Anytown, ST   19XX-XXXX
Specialized in municipal bonds, fixed income securities, Xxxxx bank stocks.

Senior Vice President • XXXXX NATIONAL BANK   19XX-19XX
- Following merger of Xxxxx National Bank and The Bank of Anytown, directed all operations and administrative functions in 5th largest Xxxxx National Bank city office. Retired to pursue other interests, under terms of merger contract (golden parachute).

Senior Vice President ~ Cashier ~ Director • BANK OF ANYTOWN   19XX-19XX
- Directed all corporate accounting, tax planning and reporting, financial reporting (external and internal), customer accounting, electronic data processing, administration of 9 branch offices, personnel administration, purchasing, legal problems and contacts, corporate insurance management, audit and control, bank security, construction planning, and maintenance at all facilities for $100-million leading community bank.
- Responsible for 80% of institution's workforce, including 5 direct executive reports.
- Corporate Secretary and principal administrative officer to Board of Directors.

68

Combination. *Dayna J. Feist, Asheville, North Carolina*
This individual is "an older woman who was being considered for a position on the Oversight Board of the Internal Revenue Service." She worked her way up before feminism had become

PAMELA SUE HANSON

- Director of Management Committee, participating in formulation of bankwide policies in all areas (e.g., lending, investment management, Trust administration). Directed Board Audit Committee.
- Crisis Manager. Directed insurance, construction, operations, and customer service during 3-year rebuilding process after Bank of Anytown burned to ground in 19XX. (Within 36 hours, bank reopened in nearby temporary location.) Opened newly constructed main office in 19XX.

Administrative Assistant to Plant Manager • AMERICAN COMPANY, Anytown, ST   19XX-19XX
Subsidiary of AllAmerican Inc.; at time County's largest employer.
- 1st woman to rise above traditional secretarial role at one of state's largest manufacturing plants.

EDUCATION

Graduate, School of Bank Administration, University of Anywhere, 19XX
Graduate, Stonier Graduate School of Banking, Rutgers University, 19XX
- Thesis at Stonier on Risk & Insurance Management in the Commercial Bank established authority in these fields and gained recognition with ABA.

Undergraduate Work, Western University, Elsewhere, ST

PROFESSIONAL & COMMUNITY SERVICE

Xxxxx Banking Commission
Twice Appointed by Governor James Jones (19XX-19XX, XXXX-Present)

Memorial Foundation
Board of Directors (Major Gifts Committee), XXXX-Present

Memorial Medical Center
Board of Directors (Finance Committee), XXXX-Present

Where Else College
Chairman, Business & Finance Committee, XXXX-Present

Xxxxx Capital Management Trust
(an open-end investment fund for Xxxxx municipalities and public entities), XXXX-Present

Xxxxx Community Foundation (an Anytown-based philanthropy), XXXX-Present

American Bankers Association
Government Relations Council (19XX-19XX), a top-level policy group
Insurance & Protection Committee (19XX-19XX)
Special ABA Task Force to study insurance problems facing banking industry

Xxxxx Bankers Association
Director (19XX-19XX)
Insurance Committee . . . Bank Management Committee . . . Education Committee . . .
Financial Structure & Regulations Committee

popular, and she "did it by and large alone." This resume has characteristics of many resumes for top executives: narrower margins, longer lines, and smaller print, making it possible to present much information on one or two pages. The three-keyword slogan in italic with ellipses is a nice touch.

ADRIENNE MIDDLEBURY

555 East Cornelia
Santa Clarita, CA 95555   Available for Relocation   (213) 555-5555
ajmid@compuserve.com

QUALIFICATIONS

EXPERIENCED FINANCE PROFESSIONAL offering:

➤ **Expertise in taxation:** Well versed in tax compliance, planning, research, audits, and appeals; resolved complex tax issues for multientity organizations; provided legal support; served as liaison with federal and state taxing authorities.

➤ **Comprehensive accounting skills:** Experienced in budgeting, financial reporting, GAAP, cost accounting, cash management, asset management, payroll, accounts payable, accounts receivable, and credit and collections.

➤ **Advanced computer skills:** Knowledgeable in technology forecasts, installations, enhancements, and user instruction for accounting, tax, finance, inventory, human resources, and other business applications.

EDUCATION

Master of Science degree, Taxation—California State University, Long Beach   1999
Bachelor of Science degree, Business Administration—University of Washington, Seattle   1996

PROFESSIONAL EXPERIENCE

EXCHANGE TECHNOLOGIES, INC., Los Angeles, CA   1994–19xx
(Diversified investment firm with $35 million in annual sales)

➤ **V.P., Finance (Controller):** Challenged with managing SEC and Canadian stock exchange audits. Successfully answered and resolved disputes with IRS, Canadian tax agencies, and multiple state taxing agencies. Conducted seven-year financial audit; revised and resubmitted financial statements with approval of governmental agencies. Negotiated settlements resulting in substantial savings to firm.

BOXPLUS MANUFACTURING COMPANY, Corona, CA   1990–1994
(Multidivision manufacturing company)

➤ **Controller / Chief Financial Officer:** Managed accounting staff in four divisions, with payroll at each location ranging from 75 to 325 workers. Established cost accounting systems for standard and automated jobs. Primarily involved in credit and collections, cash flow, and risk management. Devised financial strategies for division in jeopardy of receivership, enabling turnaround of division to a financially solvent position.

GOLDEN STATE HYDRAULICS, INC., Whittier, CA   1989–1990
(Start-up venture)

➤ **Office Manager & Accountant:** Designed operational infrastructure and accounting systems that led start-up company to sales of $5.6 million in less than one year. Established sales order system, purchasing policies, and dual costing systems.

B. B. B. EQUIPMENT COMPANY, San Bernardino, CA   1982–1989
(Leading national multiline equipment dealership)

➤ **Administrative Manager & Chief Financial Officer:** Provided administrative and financial leadership for Fortune 250 company. Converted multilocation organization from manual to fully integrated, computerized system. Served as credit manager with assistance on some 10,000 active accounts. Met audit and reporting needs for division of a NYSE-listed firm, with a 100% record for deadline compliance on financial flash reports and 20-page monthly financial statements. Management buyout of company altered accounting needs to local, quick reports. Provided new direction for cash flow, loans, cost controls, and risk management.

◆ ◆ ◆

69

Combination. *Susan Britton Whitcomb, Fresno, California*
An easy-to-read resume. Information in italic explains lesser-known companies. Boldfacing enhances skills, degrees, positions, headings, and the individual's name.

Finance-Related
Resumes

ROSE J. FURILLO, CLU
441 East Main Street
City, State 00000
(555) 555-5555

SUMMARY: *Financial Planning professional with 16 years' experience providing investment/insurance counseling and advice to individual and small business clients. Excellent capabilities to maintain and service existing account base and develop new accounts. Hold NASD Series 6 and NYS Life, Accident, and Health licenses.*

PROFESSIONAL EXPERIENCE:

1982 - Present   **Financial Planner / Insurance Agent, Mutual Insurance Company; City, State.**
Provide insurance and investment solutions to a diverse client base in areas of retirement planning, disability insurance, and life insurance. Service over 500 individual and small business clients.
- Confer with clients and develop investment plans to meet individual client's needs.
- Design investment programs to meet retirement and education goals.
- Recommend mutual funds and insurance products consistent with clients' overall plan.
- Develop new clients through referrals and prospecting.
- Consistently produce annual mutual funds sales of $300,000 to $500,000.
- Generate $45,000 to $50,000 in first-year insurance premiums annually.
- **Named to Honor Club eight times for outstanding performance.**
- **Selected G.A.M.A. Agency Leader five times.**
- **Achieved numerous additional awards for superior performance.**

1978 - 1982   **Manager, Mall Shoe Stores; City, State.**
Accountable for management and operations of retail shoe store grossing $800,000 annually. Hired, trained and supervised employees, and fulfilled all administrative and customer relations functions.

1970 - 1978   **Buyer / Management Trainee, SLC Department Stores; City, State.**
Purchased footwear product lines for nine large retail department stores in City and Othercity. Completed retail management training program.

LICENSURE / PROFESSIONAL ENRICHMENT:

State Master's License - Life, Accident and Health, and Variable Annuity.
NASD - Series 6; Pursuing Series 7.
Certified Life Underwriter (CLU).

Continuing Education in the Insurance field.

EDUCATION:

County Community College; City, State.
Coursework in Business Administration.

COMMUNITY INVOLVEMENT:

Habitat for Humanity Annual Golf Tournament.

70

Combination. *Arnold G. Boldt, Rochester, New York*
Italic is used in the Summary of the individual's financial planning experience, under each job position to describe the position, and in the Education section to show the field of study.

PATRICK M. MAGUIRE

12345 North Avenue
Any Town, USA 99999
999.999.9999

FINANCIAL SERVICES EXECUTIVE

*Personal reputation and solid ability to build profitable relationships with high-profile investors
on national levels and in diversified markets.*

SUMMARY

Dynamic **Banking Executive** with a distinguished financial career in the highly competitive banking industry. Proven business development and portfolio management expertise underscored by sound knowledge of credit analysis/loan structuring, integrated financial planning process, cross-selling techniques, cash management and client relations. Specialized expertise in structuring credit to alternative investment funds. Skilled salesperson, negotiator and communicator with keen problem-solving, analytical and organizational abilities.

Licensed Certified Financial Planner.

PROFESSIONAL EXPERIENCE

PRIME TRUST & SAVINGS BANK, City, USA   1985 to Present

**Vice President / Senior Relationship Manager - Banking Division
Member, Wealth Management Team**

August 1992 to Present:

Joined Wealth Management Team's banking group with core mission to provide expert financial advice to affluent national client base comprising wealthy families and individuals (cumulative family net worth: $35 million+). Territory encompasses East Coast (including New York) and Midwest regions.

- Grow loan portfolio from $75 million to $225 million and manage $50 million in deposit accounts; portfolio generates over $3 million in revenue.
- Develop profitable relationships based on exemplary client service, plus adept understanding and assessing of a client's credit needs for working capital, acquisition and investment purposes.
- Consistently rank in top sales tier; earned award for largest loan fees in 1996.
- Introduce full suite of bank offerings (Trust Administration, Investment Management, Family Office Services) to meet financial objectives of clients
- Work closely with Bank's investment arm to offer clients a wider range of services (e.g., private placements, capital market products, derivatives and interest rate products).
- Coordinate details (e.g., venue, speakers) and promote highly acclaimed Wealth Management Conferences.

Within the Wealth Management Team, loan portfolio includes a specialized niche market that encompasses lending to hedge funds and other alternative investment entities.

- Underwrite credit facilities for working capital, liquidity and leverage, commanding extensive knowledge of a particular fund's trading strategies, portfolio concentration and market performance.
- Evaluate a fund's core operating businesses, including technology systems and management experience.
- Structure syndicated deals and act as an agent in organizing transactions.

71

Combination. *Cathleen M. Hunt, Chicago, Illinois*
As banks acquire the right to market investments, there is a need for bank executives to be savvy about securities. This resume is for an individual who is not just "a banker" but also

PATRICK M. MAGUIRE

Page Two

Vice President / Relationship Manager - Banking Division

May 1990 to August 1992:

Selected for two-person team to lead startup and development of new initiative, *"Women in Business."*

- Integral in successful launch of program that merited numerous awards since its inception; set into motion aggressive marketing campaign; conducted educational speeches and presentations to various women focus groups; consulted with women business owners on financial issues (e.g., business loans).

Capitalized on opportunity to establish new entrepreneurial team targeting high-net-worth individuals and corporations. This venture expanded own professional growth by branching into new areas of banking, from cash management to commercial lending.

- Advised owners of closely held businesses on corporate and personal financial strategies, including credit needs, retirement, estate planning, and capital market opportunities.
- Managed a $65 million loan portfolio and $20 million in deposit accounts.

January 1985 to May 1990:

Stationed at Bank's downtown facility in role that dealt extensively with traders and brokers operating on Stock, Options and Mercantile Exchanges. Conferred with individuals and addressed their specific financial needs.

- Procured and maintained a strong account portfolio comprising primarily trader seat loans and margin loans.

NATIONAL BANK & TRUST COMPANY, Chicago, IL

1982 to 1985

Commercial Banking Officer

Managed a $15 million loan portfolio and serviced 37 commercial banking relationships. Developed new account relationships and expanded existing business through cross-selling of Bank's products and services.

MAJOR CORPORATION, Oak Brook, IL

1980 to 1982

Sales Representative

EDUCATIONAL BACKGROUND

COLLEGE FOR CERTIFIED FINANCIAL PLANNING, Denver, CO
Certified Financial Planning License; XXXX

NORTHWESTERN UNIVERSITY, Evanston, IL
Master of Management, Finance / Marketing; XXXX
Kellogg Graduate School of Management

UNIVERSITY OF MICHIGAN, Ann Arbor, MI
B.B.A., Finance / Marketing; XXXX
School of Business Administration

COMMUNITY ACTIVITIES

Volunteer, Junior League
Volunteer, Mentor Program, Scholarship Foundation
Coach, U.S. Olympic Development Camp
Member, Illinois High School Athletic Association

someone with a prestigious master's degree and certification from the College for Certified Financial Planning in Denver. The capsule profile enclosed within two horizontal lines is a confidence builder for the reader. The Summary shows skills that will easily transfer to other activities like fund management.

SUSAN O. KEMPNER

12345 Sandy Spring Court   •   Columbia, MD 00000   •   (xxx) xxx-xxxx

SUMMARY OF QUALIFICATIONS

A Certified Financial Planner experienced in sales, retirement, administrative aspects, and products of the investment industry. Experienced in evaluating entire portfolios, including stocks, bonds, and insurance products. Use superb interpersonal, communication and presentation skills to develop and maintain strong relationships. Possess excellent analytical and problem-solving skills.

PROFESSIONAL EXPERIENCE

<u>Registered Representative</u>   ***Aetna, Life Insurance & Annuity Co.***   **XXXX - Present**
- *Retirement & Investment Services* - Promote Retirement 403B - Tax Deferred, fixed and variable annuity products to nonprofit organizations.
- Clientele includes *University of Maryland Schools* (Towson State), *Community Colleges (*Harford & Carroll), *County Public Schools* (Harford, Howard & Carroll) and the *Red Cross* (both the National and Greater Chesapeake & Potomac Chapters).
- Open Individual IRA accounts.
- Utilize computer analysis to monitor market trends and performances to assist with the development closely of investment strategies.
- Conduct in-depth consultations with prospective clients to assess needs and suggest appropriate financial products. Maintain ongoing knowledge of more than twenty-eight funds to properly service account base.
- Educate prospective clients on tax advantages, legal requirements, and IRS policies.

<u>Teacher</u>   ***Maryland Board of Education***   **XXXX - XXXX**
- *Howard County* - Served as a substitute teacher for various classes and subjects.
- *Prince George's County* - Full-time social studies instructor, prior to 1986.

<u>Assistant Broker</u>   ***Stuart James Investment Bankers, Columbia, MD***   **XXXX - XXXX**
- Recorded and tracked client investments and transactions.
- Assisted in preparation of profit and loss statements for clients' income tax computations.
- Opened trading accounts and recommended buy and sell trades.
- Researched and analyzed public companies to determine financial health and investment potential.
- Used Quotron, ADP, telemarketing and direct mailings.

<u>Financial Planner Assistant</u>   ***Harvest Financial Group, Baltimore, MD***   **XXXX - XXXX**
- Assisted financial planner in analyzing and reviewing clients' financial portfolios.
- Made insurance (life and health), stock, and mutual fund recommendations.
- Extensively used Quotron and financial planning software.

EDUCATION
Certified Financial Planner, *College Financial Planning, Denver, Colorado*
Master of Modern Studies, *Loyola College, Baltimore, Maryland*
Bachelor of Arts, Secondary Education, *University of Maryland, College Park, Maryland*

COMPUTER SKILLS
Experienced in the use of IBM computers and compatibles.

LICENSES & ORGANIZATIONS
NASD Series 7   •   Licensed Health & Life Insurance Agent (MD, VA, & DC)
Certified Teacher, *State of Maryland • **Member, IBCFP***

REFERENCES AVAILABLE UPON REQUEST

72

Combination. *Audrey A. Boatwright, Columbia, Maryland*
Bold, italic, and underlined positions are easily spotted. Contact information, headings, and sections from Education to the end of the resume are center-justified. Dates are right-aligned.

LIZA JANE CALDERWOOD
55 Elm Street, Apt. 55-A • New York, NY • 55555 • (555) 555-5555

CAREER PROFILE

FINANCIAL ANALYST / FINANCIAL ADVISOR

- Top-producing financial analyst/advisor with 10 years of professional experience.
- Able to generate new business, service and maintain existing accounts, and earn profits for investors and management. Effectively prioritize tasks and meet deadlines.
- Keep up-to-date on market trends; recommend financial instruments based on client needs.
- Public speaker, with the ability to comfortably deliver presentations to small and large groups.
- Excellent communication and interpersonal skills. Highly organized and a fast learner.
- Computer literate...Windows 95/NT/3.1, Lotus Notes, MS Exchange, Word, WordPerfect.

EDUCATION, TRAINING & LICENSURE

BROOKLYN COLLEGE - Brooklyn, NY
Bachelor of Arts, Political Science, XXXX
- Pre-Law Society, XXXX to XXXX

ABC SECURITIES COMPANY - New York, NY
Series 7 & Series 63 Licenses, XXXX

NATIONAL ASSOCIATION OF INVESTMENT COUNSELORS (NAIC)
- Investment Techniques course completed, XXXX

PROFESSIONAL EXPERIENCE

MORGENSTERN, ROBERTS, & HORN, INC. - New York, NY
Financial Consultant/Advisor, XXXX to present
Open new retail accounts for full-service brokerage firm. Manage approximately 20 large accounts with $.5 million in assets. Monitor market trends and review portfolios to provide clients with sound financial information and advice. Listen carefully to the needs of clients, mostly individuals and investment clubs, to develop appropriate strategies. Prepare financial plans for beginner and sophisticated investors.
- Assisted clients with achieving a growth rate of 25%-30%, a higher return than market levels.
- Selected from a group of 15 colleagues to teach a 7-week NAIC course for new investors.
- Guest speaker in public schools on how to diversify and enhance TIAA/CREF portfolios.

MARTIN D. ROGERS CO. - New York, NY
Stockbroker/New Account Representative, XXXX to XXXX
Opened new accounts for a venture-capital firm specializing in small-cap stocks and IPO's. Dealt with high-profile and affluent clientele with $500,000 minimum in common stock.
- Consistently met company expectations by generating 10 leads per day.
- Opened $100,000 account as a Rookie Broker.

RICHMOND SECURITIES - New York, NY
Stockbroker Trainee, XXXX
Developed new account leads and effectively handled business inquiries. Worked on trading desk and produced daily market newsletter.

PRESENTATIONS DELIVERED

- Investment Techniques for TIAA/CREF Portfolios (100 in attendance), XXXX.
- Investment Strategies for Beginners Using NAIC Investment Tools (65 in attendance), XXXX.
- How to Get Rich by Investing $25 a Month (50 in attendance), XXXX.

73

Combination. *Kim Isaacs, Jackson Heights, New York*
Except for the line after the contact information, a thin horizontal line appears below each section heading. Boldface calls attention to the degree, licensure, and job positions.

JOHN PAUL
5555 Street #111
Anaheim, California 90000
Res. (555) 000-0000 ● Bus. (555) 000-0000

Certified Financial Analyst

General Securities Executive who possesses excellent market insight. Precise, detail-oriented and analytical.
- Licensed General Securities Sales Supervisor NASD Series 8
- Licensed General Securities Sales Representative NASD Series 7
- Chartered Financial Analyst
- Certified Market Technician

CAREER HISTORY

xxxx - Present   **MAJOR STOCK & INVESTMENT COMPANY**, Anaheim, California
Senior Registered Representative
- Accurately place stock, bond, mutual fund and option orders as branch trader.
- Review all orders for branch customers for accuracy and risk to the firm.
- Successfully control risk to the firm as Branch Margin Clerk.
- Maintain high level of customer service as evidenced by satisfaction surveys.
- As Mutual Fund Coordinator, created a dynamic training program for branch personnel in mutual fund order entry.

xxxx-xxxx   **MAJOR STOCK & INVESTMENT COMPANY**, Anaheim, California
Account Executive/Education Director
- Sold investment products including options, stocks, bonds and mutual funds.
- Spearheaded recruitment and new broker training program for the branch.

xxxx-xxxx   **JONES INTERNATIONAL ADVISORY**, Anaheim, California
Investment Analyst
- Edited and published the newsletters, "International Capital Outlook" and "The Raymond Stock Forecaster."

PUBLICATIONS
- "Ten Rules for Picking Winning Growth Stocks," *Personal Investing News*, October xxxx.
- Letter to the Editor, *Barrons*, January xxxx.
- Analyst Summary, *Coin World*, December xxxx.
- Analyst Summary, *Coin World*, October xxxx.

AFFILIATIONS
- Association for Investment Management and Research.
- International Society of Financial Analysts.
- Los Angeles Society of Financial Analysts.
- Market Technicians Association.

EDUCATION
CHARTERED FINANCIAL ANALYST PROGRAM

CERTIFIED MARKET TECHNICIAN PROGRAM

BACHELOR OF ARTS IN BUSINESS ADMINISTRATION
California State University at Fullerton, xxxx
- Concentration in Finance.
- Specialized in Securities and Investing.
- Minor in Economics.

LICENSES
- NASD Series 8 - General Securities Sales Supervisor
- NASD Series 7 - General Securities Sales Representative

74

Combination. *Christine Edick, Orange, California*
The original resume was printed on decorative paper with a color border. That is why most of the information is to the right. Larger bullets direct attention to the listed information.

TROY MELVIN
5 Plumcrest Court • Orangeburg, NJ 55555 • (000) 000-0000

SUMMARY OF QUALIFICATIONS
- Over 10 years' experience in the financial arena.
- Outstanding communication, analytical and presentation skills.
- Equally effective working in self-managed projects and as member of a team.
- Strong interpersonal skills; diplomatic and effective with customer relations.
- Strength in analyzing, researching, organizing, and problem solving.
- Knowledgeable of Treasury policy, Federal and State law and regulations about securities.

PROFESSIONAL EXPERIENCE

Financial Analyst   **_U.S. Department of HUD, Newark, N.J._**   **_XXXX - Present_**
- Researched, analyzed and solved discrepancies in HUD billing notices sent to mortgage companies.
- Responded to letters and telephone inquiries from mortgage companies.
- Authorized to correct and delete interest and late fees for late payment of insurance premiums.
- Knowledgeable of HUD policy and procedures, regulations, insurance and mortgage rates.

U.S. Department of Treasury, Washington, D.C., XXXX - XXXX

Securities Transactions Analyst   **_U.S. Department of Treasury_**   **_XXXX - XXXX_**
- Researched and analyzed evidence and documents involving the issuance, maintenance and disposition of all treasury securities. Modified, approved and disapproved security transactions.
- Handled purchasing, transferring over of securities, and replacing stolen securities for individuals.

Program Analyst   **_Accounts Maintenance Branch_**   **_XXXX - XXXX_**
- Analyzed, evaluated and prepared studies, surveys and data analysis of Treasury programs.
- Team member assisted and handled special projects. Located overdue security payments for personnel.
- Computerized case payment reports daily, weekly and monthly and submitted to management.

Securities Transactions Analyst   **_Payment Certification Branch, Claims Sections_**   **_XXXX - XXXX_**
- Supervised three accounting technicians. Prepared input for employees' performance evaluations.
- Researched and analyzed accounts receivable and accounts payable for all Treasury payments.
- Evaluated legal evidence and documents to ensure claim payments were in compliance with regulations.
- Authorized or disapproved payments of all claims made to the Department of Treasury.

Securities Transactions Analyst   **_Review and Rulings Branch_**   **_XXXX - XXXX_**
- Supervised five accounting clerks who processed security transactions.
- Counseled employees on job performance and prepared employees' performance appraisals.
- Researched and analyzed information involving transactions of bills, notes and bonds.
- Prepared and made oral presentations to managers on duties of Securities Transactions Analysts.

EDUCATION
B.S., Business Administration, _University of the District of Columbia,_ Washington, D.C.

PROFESSIONAL TRAINING AND DEVELOPMENT
• Elements of Management Analysis	• Management Analysis and Review
• Introduction to Financial Management	• The Federal Budget Process

PROFESSIONAL ORGANIZATION
Vice President, Prince Georges County Largo Civic Association, XXXX

TECHNICAL SKILLS
IBM Computer Compatibles **_Software:_** • Microsoft Windows • WordPerfect • Lotus 1-2-3

75

Combination. *Ms. Earl M. Melvin, Columbia, Maryland*
The person had a diverse background in securities, claims, mortgages, and insurance in relation to the U.S. Departments of the Treasury and of HUD. Bold italic is used effectively.

JOHN B. ANDERSON

700 North Street
Chicago, IL 60000

Residence: 312.555.1212
Office: 847.555.1212
E-mail: xxxxxxx@xxxx.xxx

CAREER FOCUS   *Management position in finance or accounting within a dynamic, growth-oriented company.*

SUMMARY

Diversified and successful 16-year business career within accounting, finance, information systems and project management disciplines, highlighted by 5 years of experience in cellular wireless telecommunications industry and 3 years with *Corporate-Wide* financial accounting system. Adept in fast-paced work environments demanding increasing responsibility and solid team leadership. Well-honed analytical and problem-solving skills enhanced by high-level organizational and planning abilities. Excellent group and interpersonal communications.

Proficient in various computer software applications and platforms. Strong academic and professional career development background with advanced degrees in *MIS*, *Finance* and *Accounting*.

PROFESSIONAL EXPERIENCE

TELECOMMUNICATIONS, INC., Chicago, IL   August 1994 to Present
(Provider of wireless personal communication services)

Financial Analyst - Engineering & Operations Group   (October 1995 to Present)
Maintain key financial operations support for company's full-scale construction of a new personal communications system, including preparation of a $175 million annual capital and operating budget. Analyze variances in key financial and operating measures. Manage seven accounting temporaries in handling day-to-day activities.

- Introduced new policies and methods that streamlined and ensured more control over accounting processes.
- Performed project costs tracking and progress reporting utilizing an innovative program management tool.
- Developed custom financial reports via online analytical processing software to support key business decisions.

Project Engineer - Wireless Implementation Group   (January 1995 to October 1995)
Served on construction project management team for build-out of a new personal communications system, with oversight responsibility for $22 million in total construction costs. Approved all purchase orders, vendor invoices and work change orders.

- Completed on-time construction of 52 new wireless communication sites, within budget and quality constraints.
- Demonstrated keen management skills in supervising general contractors, field engineers and subcontractors.
- Worked under pressure to control site plans, costs and schedules while placing safety and quality in forefront; direct involvement in site preparations, including property assessments, zoning, regulatory filings, engineering designs, procurement of towers, materials, equipment, utility orders and solicitation/awarding of bids.
- Implemented project management methods and procedures for better department practices.

Staff Analyst - Company Startup Operations, Big City   (August 1994 to January 1995)
Completed special projects for startup of new nationwide personal communications service company. Solicited and evaluated vendor proposals. Documented recommendations for management.

- Developed financial models and business cases to forecast future capital requirements for a national wireless service network based on different digital technology platforms.
- Defined business requirements for a new project management system and a new customer billing system.
- Evaluated vendor proposals for different network build-out support services, including property acquisition, architectural, engineering and construction management.

CELLULAR GROUP, Big City, IL   December 1988 to August 1994
(Regional cellular service provider)

Systems Analyst, Information Technology - Development Group   (November 1993 to August 1994)
Managed software testing project for acceptance of a new customer information billing system.

76

Combination. *Cathleen M. Hunt, Chicago, Illinois*
A well-crafted, two-page resume with much information but enough white space to avoid a crowded look. The trick is to use two blank lines between main sections and at least one blank

JOHN B. ANDERSON   Page Two

Systems Analyst, Information Technology - Development Group (Continued)

- Recruited and managed team of four software testers.
- Developed structural testing methodology and techniques (defined test plans, specifications and reports).
- Outlined acceptance criteria; designed and constructed comprehensive functional test cases; performed regression, integration and stress software testing.
- Implemented an automated software testing tool.
- Set up a new software testing laboratory facility.

Financial Systems Analyst - Financial Systems & Controls (December 1988 to November 1993)
Provided user support and technical maintenance for a large corporate financial accounting system on midrange computer. Scope of responsibility was diverse and included user training and instruction, internal controls and procedures, system upgrades, troubleshooting and special projects. Supervised two accounting associates.

- Assisted in successful installation and conversion of *Corporate-Wide* accounting system on an IBM AS/400.
- Established and effectively managed help desk operations to support 225 corporate users.
- Named *Lead Software Technical Expert* upon completion of extensive vendor training.
- Received honorary *Leadership Award* in 1992, as chairperson of Midwest Users Group.

BIG ACCOUNTING, City, IL   May 1985 to December 1988
(Public accounting firm)

Staff Analyst - Tax Computer Services
Maintained company's microcomputer tax software products for tax offices and clients worldwide.

- Designed, implemented and maintained software for tax planning and compliance applications.
- Provided key user support for firm's tax practice professionals and clients.
- Attended *Big Accounting Center for Professional Education* for computer and tax training.

EARLIER EXPERIENCE in general accounting and financial management positions within distinct industry environments includes the manufacturing, retail and not-for-profit sectors.

EDUCATION / PROFESSIONAL DEVELOPMENT

GRADUATE SCHOOL OF MANAGEMENT, Big City, IL
Master's degree in Accounting & Financial Management (target date of completion: December XXXX)

UNIVERSITY, Big City, IL
M.B.A., Management Information Systems & Finance, with Distinction; XXXX
B.S. degree, Accountancy, with Honors; XXXX

University Telecommunications Certificate Program; XXXX
Dale Carnegie - Management Training Program; XXXX
Effective Speaking & Human Relations Program; XXXX

COMPUTER PROFICIENCIES

Knowledge of various financial accounting, billing and project management applications.
Well-versed in several PC-based general and specific software programs.

AFFILIATIONS

Member, Honor Society for AACSB Accredited Business Programs; XXXX to Present
Member, Project Management Institute; XXXX to Present
Director, Board of Directors, Management Institute - Midwest Chapter; XXXX

line before and after subsections and clustered information. If blank lines aren't there, it becomes more difficult to recognize groups of related items. The shadowed box for the Career Focus at the top of page 1 is an inviting open door at the resume's threshold. Company names are explained in italic.

DARLYN B. WILLIAMSON

1234 Harrison Avenue ◆ Anytown, WA 98000 ◆ (555) 123-4567

FINANCIAL ANALYST

Data Analysis / Resource Management / Financial Reporting
Retirement Financial & Healthcare Expense Planning / Accounting

---

A data-savvy financial professional with extensive experience analyzing fiscal information in the healthcare and academic environments. An analytical thinker who understands details as well as the broader opportunities and implications. Capable of seeing shades of gray to creatively solve problems. Particularly skilled at unearthing data and translating complex information into clearly understandable language. Demonstrated ability to interpret and summarize vast qualities of data into meaningful information and relevant statistics. Proven talents in working with all ages and diversity of clientele. Skilled in the development of customized products to meet customer needs. Energized by challenges, steep learning curves, and high-pressure deadlines. Solid team member. Strong communicator – listening, verbal, written.

Notable areas of expertise include:

- Financial Analyst & Management Reporting
- Systems Design & Development
- Interdepartmental Coordination & Collaboration
- Long-Range Asset & Resource Utilization
- Short- & Long-Range Budgeting
- General Accounting Procedures
- Capital Equipment Analysis

- Managed Care
- Applications Development
- Productivity Analysis
- Client & Contract Relations
- Forecasting
- Project Management
- Total Quality Management

Computer expertise includes:

- Database Mainframe Application (FOCUS 4GL)
- Word
- Access

- Windows 95
- Excel
- PowerPoint

EXPERIENCE

ANYSTATE UNIVERSITY MEDICAL CENTER, Anycity   XXXX to XXXX

Senior Financial Analyst / Computer Specialist, Surgical Services (XXXX to XXXX)
Senior Financial Analyst, Finance Division (XXXX)
Budget Analyst III, Finance Division (XXXX to XXXX)
Budget Analyst III, Accounting Division (XXXX to XXXX)
Accountant III, Accountant II, Accountant I, Accounting Division (XXXX to XXXX)

- Created concept of "prime time" reports to determine best utilization of AUMC resources, including 19 operating rooms, 11 surgical units, and more than 125 physicians handling over 10,000 patients annually.
  - ➤ Matched availability of surgeons, patients, anesthesiologists, and nursing staff during 8 a.m. to 3:30 p.m. "prime time."
  - ➤ Determined 80% utilization represented most effective and efficient use of resources, generating procedural changes to improve productivity of surgical services, which generate 60% of AUMC total revenues.
- Developed reports reflecting statistical and information needs to improve surgical services:
  - ➤ Compared volume of surgical cases versus availability of surgical minutes.
  - ➤ Sorted data by 10 divisions and patient type, accurately capturing a true portrayal of surgical services and enabling AUMC to track trends and project future needs.
- Prepared operating room utilization analysis comparing actual vs. budgeted usage, providing hard data to adjust facility use in accordance with need.   *Continued*

77

Combination. *Carole S. Barns, Woodinville, Washington*
After legislative budget cuts, the medical center asked all management employees "to justify their existence." The individual used this resume "as part of her presentation package to

- Provided the Contracting/Payor Relations Director with modeling for numerous contract proposal arrangements and "what if" analysis.
  - Directed and established the financial performance reporting on all contracts.
  - Created an information system to maintain a database of managed care contracts, provider utilization patterns, and financial modeling and analysis capability.
- Maintained the day-to-day operations and integrity of managed care enrollment/claims databases.
- Developed method of tracking and driving reports showing financial performance by surgeon to determine actual bottom line contribution and to monitor frequency of service delivery which was nonrevenue producing.
- Generated reports that showed for the first time the payor mix of revenues.
- Served as the financial analyst on various surgical quality action teams that reviewed surgical procedures for ways to improve efficiency and to justify purchase of new equipment.
  - Team revised resource mix for an orthopedic surgeon, doubling his output from 3 to 6 operations/day.
- Performed overall trend analysis, market share, long-range planning, and strategic planning projections for the AUMC's Associate Administrators in Finance, Marketing, Nursing, and Planning.
- Provided financial consulting services to AUMC directors and heads of medical services, including business plans and marketing studies.
- Reviewed budget requests, determined capital and expense items, and prepared capital budget report.
- Managed accounting responsibilities for $70 million expansion project, including construction in progress accounting, requirements to close construction in progress to proper fixed asset account, and determination of depreciation period for new assets.
- Ensured ongoing compliance with Medicare and AnyState Hospital Commission regulations.

DEACONESS HOSPITAL & MEDICAL CENTER, Anycity   XXXX to XXXX

Accountant

- Reconciled General Ledger accounts for both hospital and medical center prior to merger.
- Collected and analyzed data for Medicare/Medicaid reports.
- Assisted Payroll Department with payroll of more than 1,400 employees.
- Developed salary expense estimates according to expected wage increases and volume forecasts in patient care areas.
- Served as member of 3-person team to prepare annual budget, including historical data collection, capital equipment and expense determination, and allocation of revenue deductions for rate setting by contractual allowance and bad debt/free care categories.
- Assisted auditor in preaudit work and other special projects.

EDUCATION

- B.A., Accounting
  Western Anystate University

- A.A., Accounting
  Anycity South Community College

ensure continuation of her position." A resume can thus be a means for keeping a job. The individual wanted an impressive description of her experience, areas of expertise, and computer skills. Her work experience displays her career growth. Bulleted statements indicate the scope of her duties and achievements.

Clarissa A. Counting

55555 Tables Street
La Belle, CA 99999
(999) 999-9999

PROFILE:

Experience: 15 years in Accounting: receivables, payables, credit, collections, financial analysis.

Communication: By asking intelligent questions and giving clear explanations, keep myself, my staff, and upper management well-informed.

Supervision: Encourage individual responsibility through fair and consistent treatment.

Follow-Through: Whether following up on a customer's product shortage or keeping an eye on the credit balance, I stay on top of my accounts.

BIOTECHNIQUES, INC., Redfield, CA

Served as key member of accounting team during the growth of this biotechnology research and manufacturing pioneer, from 350 employees and no product sales when I started to its current 3,000 employees and $635 million in product sales.

Customer Finance Manager   XXXX-Present

As department comanager, jointly oversee credit and collections for customer base of 500 and average monthly A/R balance of $90M. Prepare month-end closes and quarterly reserve analysis. Read and interpret contracts that impact reserves against sales. Work with multiple customer payment programs for wholesalers, hospitals, HMOs and government.

- Directly responsible for $50M A/R balance of which 95% is current or better.
- Reduced day's sales outstanding (DSO) by 10% through attentive account maintenance, periodic credit review, analysis of customers, and proactive collection operations.
- Participated on teams for the following: assessing banks as potential vendors for EFT, electronically invoicing major accounts, and implementing innovative distribution channel.
- Received recognition awards from Marketing and Accounting Departments.

Customer Finance Representative   19XX-19XX

Played integral part in developing the Customer Finance Department.

- Helped establish credit lines, cash application, and monthly management reports.
- Worked closely with Customer Service to establish procedures for smooth interactions between the two departments.
- Was intrumental in implementing A/R software system.

Accounts Payable Supervisor   19XX-19XX

Supervised team of 8 for daily A/P functions during company's greatest growth spurt, regularly interfacing with other departments and vendors.

- Assisted in implementing two A/P software systems, successfully maintaining department operations while working out innumerable bugs.
- Jointly developed standards for future software system linking A/P and Purchasing.

EDUCATION & AFFILIATIONS:

B.S., Accounting, University of San Francisco

National Association of Credit Managers, Health Care Division
Health and Beauty Care, Division of the National Management Group
Credit Research Foundation

78

Combination. *Sydney J. Reuben, Menlo Park, California*
To enliven this resume, the writer chose a nontraditional Profile format, put years closer to job titles to mask work for the same company, and used personal pronouns (I, my, etc.).

BRANDON C. DAVID

(555) 444-4444
333 Proctor Avenue • Los Angeles, CA 55555

PROFESSIONAL EXPERIENCE

McMurphy & Donald Corporation...Northridge, California

SENIOR BUDGET ANALYST & STRATEGIC PLANNER   xxxx to present
- Manage a team of 6 Budget Analysts, working as liaisons 8 manufacturing departments.
- Spearheaded a plantwide, cost-reduction strategic planning process that is proving to be highly successful, and has full support of the executive management team.
- Created a unique, new technique for developing semiannual budgets for 8 manufacturing depts.
- Organize & oversee special projects such as VIP programs and Public Relations presentations.

FINANCE MANAGER - Budgets, Planning & Cost Reduction   xxxx - xxxx
- Managed 12 finance analysts developing budget and cost mgmt. systems for this $35 billion (+) co.
- Met annually with the Board of Directors to present future budget and current-year actual.
- Developed new procedures like a major, innovative, computerized "Budget Commitment System" to ensure departments have budget before spending occurs.
- Achieved significant $30 million cost savings in 2 years by developing and implementing plant-wide cost-reduction campaigns through new policies.

FINANCE MANAGER - General Accounting & Taxation   xxxx - xxxx
- Supervised a staff of 13 accountants in general accounting and taxation for the corporation
- Consolidated into Allied and Gentec results, including 10K and 10Q activities.
- Developed and instituted a new "Flash" profit and loss report for use by senior management.
- Worked in-depth on audits by the IRS and the County Assessors. Each audit lasted more than one year, yet resulted in no penalties being assessed, a credit to the quality of the financial details.

FINANCE MANAGER - Cost Accounting, Pricing & Future Models   xxxx - xxxx
- Managed a team of 10 finance professionals doing cost accounting and cost planning.
- Responsible also for managing the Product-Pricing Group, a significant challenge in this industry.
- Promoted in xxxx, from Assistant Finance Manager to Finance Manager.

Montague Peripheral Systems...Costa Mesa, California

CONTROLLER   xxxx - xxxx
- This was a small leading-edge, computer research and development startup business initially with 50 employees...Performed such Controller functions as budgeting/forecasting, cost accounting, cash, reporting (10K & 10Q), accounts payable/receivable, payroll, and more.

Pierpoint Project Management...Santa Ana, California

SENIOR. FINANCIAL ANALYST   xxxx - xxxx
- Promoted 2 times...from Cost Accounting and Pricing...to Financial Analysis and Reporting.
- Activities: cost accounting, parts pricing, strategic forecasting and consolidation of world entities.

Finlayison Corp...Monrovia, California

ACCOUNTANT   xxxx - xxxx
- Received 2 promotions and excellent training in numerous general accounting operations.

EDUCATION

M.B.A. DEGREE • *Major: Finance* ...Stanford University - Stanford, California   xxxx
B.S. DEGREE • *Major: Accounting*...University of Southern California - Los Angeles   xxxx

79

Chronological. *Carl L. Bascom, Fremont, California*
A two-section resume in which experience and education are everything. Hanging indentation makes the company names stand out. Bold, underlined caps highlight jobs and degrees.

MARGARET C. YOUNG

251 Whispering Pine Court • Smithfield, Rhode Island 12345 • (555) 555-5555

PROFESSIONAL PROFILE

Dynamic Financial Manager with over 15 years' experience in the banking industry. Outstanding analytical skills; demonstrated ability to interpret and summarize data into meaningful information. Extensive background in FDIC and SEC reporting, internal reporting, trusts, and accounting procedures. Excellent interpersonal, management, and supervisory skills.

PROFESSIONAL EXPERIENCE

GIBSON BANK - Providence, Rhode Island

Trust Officer / Financial Manager   XXXX to present
Manage financial reporting of Trust Department with assets of $5 billion; prepare SEC filings, FDIC filings and state reports. Prepare monthly income, asset liability, and income statement reports. Supervise staff of five whose duties include reconciliations, Common Trust Fund processing, and records retention. Responsible for hiring, training and drafting job evaluations for supervised employees.

- Created test scripts and tested Y2K compliance of Trust Accounting System
- Currently writing the business resumption plan for the Trust Operations Department
- Designed and implemented charge-off policy to tighten control of losses within the department
- Automated demand deposit accounts to achieve higher accuracy and efficiency
- Successfully researched, reconciled and cleared all variances in Trust Department accounts

Accounting Officer   XXXX to XXXX
Supervised staff of four in Accounting Department. Adjusted general ledger month-end entries. Maintained fixed asset accounts, ran reports and depreciation schedules.

- Revised and implemented standard operating procedures resulting in a more efficient operation
- Managed special projects for department
- Converted fixed assets of two bank acquisitions to Gibson's Millenium system

Assistant Manager   XXXX to XXXX
Supervised staff of 15. Reviewed general ledger proofs for accuracy. Released and extracted journal entries into general ledger database. Adjusted Trust Department income to actual figures quarterly.

- Performed analysis of financial statements
- Calculated and prepared various branch reports
- Successfully reconciled all variances in statements and accounts

Supervisor   XXXX to XXXX
Balanced general ledger and prepared month-end journal entries. Responsible for accounting in Property Management Partnership; balanced general ledger and tracked down out of balance variances. Reconciled Federal Reserve and demand deposit accounts. Supervised staff of two.

80

Combination. *Mary Sward Hurley, Smithfield, Rhode Island*
After reading her own resume, the applicant "realized how much she had accomplished in her career." This realization "did wonders for her self-esteem." That has been the experience of

FIRST FIDELITY BANK - Providence, Rhode Island

Staff Accountant   XXXX to XXXX

Performed accounting procedures for VISA Department and Installment Loan Department. Responsible for intercompany expense verification. Analyzed monthly financial statements for variances.

- Performed accounting procedures for investment portfolios
- Calculated monthly yields for savings deposits, federal funds, and loans
- Analyzed monthly noninterest income and expense accounts
- Prepared written explanations of variances for Corporate Finance Department
- Achieved merit raises every year

Accounting Clerk   XXXX to XXXX

Reconciled interbank settlements daily. Reviewed and reconciled proofs for branch accounts. Performed general ledger reconciliation. Set up and maintained all amortization schedules for FDIC assessments, and Comptroller of the Currency Assessments.

Head Teller   XXXX to XXXX

Opened and closed accounts. Handled deposits and withdrawals. Successfully resolved customer problems.

- Supervised staff of three
- Balanced drawer to the penny every day for duration of employment

EDUCATION

BRYANT COLLEGE, Smithfield, Rhode Island
Bachelor of Science degree in **Accounting** (1992)

- Graduated **magna cum laude**
- Achieved GPA of 3.78

Additional Training

1998 - How to Develop and Administer a Budget	Fred Pryor Seminars
1997 - Access Database Management	New Horizons
1997 - Time Management Seminar	Franklin Day Planner
1995 - Habits of Successful Supervisors	Dun & Bradstreet
1995 - Effective Supervision of People	Dun & Bradstreet

COMPUTER SKILLS

PROFICIENT IN:

- Access
- Excel
- Lotus 1-2-3
- TrustWare II
- Word / WordPerfect
- Windows 95

REFERENCES AVAILABLE ON REQUEST

many whose jobs have ended because of restructuring. A new resume helps them see themselves with new perspective. A Profile helps them see their range of skills. Paragraphs and lists about responsibilities and achievements help the unemployed see how much they have done—and may yet do—for a company.

Samuel Thomas

113 Bog Lake Road
Northville, Maine 00000
Residence (Northville): (207) 555-5555
Business (Machias): (207) 555-5555

Profile

Finance Director with a proven record of success in business office operations, budgeting, financial planning, and human resource management seeking position with challenge and potential for growth. Strong analytical and financial decision-making abilities with budgets ranging from $2MM to $23MM. B.S. in Business Administration and Management from the St. Joseph University. Solid communication, organizational, and management skills. Expertise in the following areas:

- Business Management
- Employee Supervision
- Staff Training & Development
- Accounting & Cash Flow Management

- Payroll Management
- Computer Technology
- Financial Planning & Budgeting
- Human Resource Management

Professional Experience

Downeast Social Services, Machias, Maine   19xx - Present
Finance Director

- Overall responsibility for all aspects of financial management including the supervision and management of all accounting and administrative personnel. Responsible for all human resource management and benefits administration for staff of 60.

- Prepare annual budgets for fourteen separate programs. Also prepare monthly financial statements with computerized accounting software. Act as audit liaison. Responsible for payroll tax requirements including 940, 941 and SUTA. Attend all Board of Directors' meetings.

- Conduct workshops for management and direct service personnel on benefits administration, budget management, hiring procedures, and form processing. Conduct all new employee orientations.

  Key Accomplishments:

  - Developed internal control procedures for financial and human resource management systems to bring company into compliance with State and Federal regulations. Ensured that financial statements were accurate in order to complete Medicare/Medicaid cost reports.

  - Trained managers to make better budget and financial management decisions within their program areas.

  - Created Personnel Policies & Procedures Manual and Accounting Procedures Manual.

Washington County Health Services, Machias, Maine   19xx -19xx
Accountant

- Supervised payroll and accounts payable functions. Responsible for the agency cost centers financial records. Provided oversight for cash flow and automated accounting system.

  Key Accomplishments:

  - Assisted in the conversion of $13MM payroll from two systems to one while also integrating Human Resources with Payroll. Designed the payroll system and assisted consultants in programming new system. Managed operating budget of $23MM with 600 employees.

  - Assisted in the design of accounting and financial reporting manuals. Served as audit liaison for finance department.

81

Combination. *Joan M. Roberts, Bangor, Maine*
This individual "was working for a nonprofit organization and wanted greater challenges and opportunities." Because the market was very competitive, he wanted to stand out in the

Jonesboro Manufacturing Company, Jonesboro, Maine   **19xx - 19xx**
Payroll and Personnel Manager

- Supervised weekly payroll for 350 - 400 employees. Administered employee benefits program.
  Prepared and issued all tax reports. Responsible for inventory control and accounts payable.

- Successfully upgraded computerized payroll system. Assisted Executive Vice President with
  administration of the cash management system.

Town of Northville, Northville, Maine   **19xx - 19xx**
Accounting and Payroll Clerk

- Overall responsibility for the preparation of the annual budget; complete computerization of the Town
  of Northville payroll; purchasing and inventory control; and tax collection and taxes receivable record
  management.

Education & Professional Development _____

St. Joseph University, Machias, Maine   **19xx**
B.S. Business Administration and Management

<u>Professional Development</u>:

- Excel, Windows 95, Networking, and Spreadsheets
- Managed Care Conference - San Francisco
- Technology Consideration for Communicating Effectively

References Available upon Request

crowd. By creating a Profile and bulleting the person's skills at the top of the resume, the writer was able to "highlight the value the individual would potentially offer an organization." He was offered and accepted a State position. Afterward he wrote, "I feel that my great resume was the extra help I needed."

JEFFREY A. GELLER

000 West New Street
Elmira, NY 00000
(000) 555-5555

SUMMARY OF QUALIFICATIONS:

♦ Proven administrative, management, supervisory and training abilities.
♦ Extensive experience in budgeting and general accounting procedures.
♦ Background in sales, marketing, promotion and public relations.
♦ Strong organizational, interpersonal and communication skills.

PROFESSIONAL EXPERIENCE:

April 1994 - Present

Director of Financial Services, State University of New York at Anytown, Anytown, NY
In addition to the responsibilities as Assistant University Financial Analyst (see January 1991 below), oversee the operations of the Student Billing Office. Regular duties include the supervision of the collections and distribution of all revenues for the College, oversee the distribution of EOP funds and the Book Credit Program, maintain and review records of all student receivables, supervise the recording and distribution of all financial aid programs, review and approval all disbursements of refunds to students, supervise and train office staff.

January 1991 - Present

Assistant University Financial Analyst, State University of New York at Anytown
Responsible for the reestablishment of accuracy and validity of all financial reporting of the Revenue Accounting Department and for the development and installation of the BANNER General Ledger. Also, responsible for the daily balancing and reconciliation of all financial accounts and reports, all revenue budgeting, and overseeing the implementation of the Internal Control Program on campus.

1985 - 1990

Regional Commercial Loan Officer, Community Bank, NA, Anytown, NY
Oversaw nine offices handling commercial loans including supervision of branch managers, assistants and clerical staff. Responsible for financial analysis and loan presentation. Utilized computer system on a range of applications. Promoted from Management Trainee Program (New York Office), Assistant Manager (Pennsylvania Office), Assistant Manager (New York Office).

1981 - 1984

Insurance Agent/Claims Clerk, Good Name Corporation, Anytown, NY
Responsible for the sales of insurance policies. Also, served as a rater for commercial and personal policies and claims clerk.

EDUCATION:

M.B.A. (In Process) - Anytown University
B.S. Accounting (December 1985) - New York State College of Business and Administration at Anytown University
Insurance License (March 1983) - Anytown Institute of Technology
A.A.S. Accounting (May 1981) - SUNY Agricultural & Technical College at Anytown

TRAINING CERTIFICATES:

Managing the Financial Sales Team - Community Bank, NA
Quality Management Skills - Community Bank, NA
Understanding Business Cash Flow - American Institute of Banking

82

Chronological. *Betty Geller, Elmira, New York*
A chronological resume with a Summary of Qualifications at the top. The individual wanted to stay in a college environment. A strong thin-thick page border is used on both pages. The

HONORS/
AWARDS:

♦ Outstanding 4-H Boy of the Year (1977-78)
♦ President of Student Council
♦ Boys' State Member
♦ National Honor Society
♦ Member of Community College Pacioli Club
♦ Anytown University - Cum Laude and Dean's List

ACTIVITIES/
INTERESTS:
Work Related

Notary Public
Member of SUNY Accounting and Bursars Subcommittees
Member of related Subcommittee Task Groups
Member of BANNER G/L Committee
Member of Student Conduct Committee
Member of Student Health Advisory Committee

Other

Member of Anytown Volunteer Fire Company
     (Former Treasurer and Budget Officer)
Emergency Medical Technician (EMT)
Member of the F&AM Sentinel Lodge #000
College and High School Volleyball Official
ASBOGWS Officer
Member of Anytown Central School Board
Member of GCS Teachers' Negotiation Team
Member of GCS Building Renovation Task Group
Past President of GCS Alumni Association
Boy Scouts of America - Cub Master

References Provided Upon Request

program name for this kind of border (thin-thick) is derived from the left side or top of the border. You see first the thin line and then the thick line. The *bottom* of this border, however, is used for a horizontal line. There you see first a thick line and then a thin line. Calling *that* line thin-thick can be confusing.

MATT S. PETERS, M.B.A.

222 Swed Circle
Yorktown Heights, NY 10598
(914) 962-1212

CORPORATE FINANCE EXECUTIVE

Financial Executive with 10+ years of operating, project management, and strategic financial analysis experience. Fast-track, forward-thinking professional with proven ability to operate effectively under pressure in time-sensitive environments. Areas of expertise include:

- Strategic Planning
- Capital Budgeting
- Cost Containment & Profit Improvement
- Database Design
- Financial Analysis & Reporting

- Expense Planning
- Staffing & Management Development
- Acquisition & Divestiture Transactions
- Policy & Procedures
- Real Estate Management

EXECUTIVE PROFILE

- Achieved reputation for having "… a knack for *managing people* and *priorities achieving on-time, accurate results*."
- *Catalyst* for establishing cross-functional team which streamlined the new store planning, design, and construction process.
- Recognized by superiors for being " **a very good leader... extremely organized and second to none with his attention to detail... accomplishing multiple objectives and achieving quality results.**"
- Demonstrated foresight in designing and implementing organization's first-ever Executive Training program for finance professionals.
- Substantial hands-on experience in the implementation and management of state-of-the-art information systems, supporting major business initiatives.

EXPERIENCE
December xxxx -
Present

SAKS FIFTH AVENUE, New York, NY
Director of Strategic Planning & MIS Control
- Control SFA's five-year strategic plan forecasting Sales, EBITDA, Net Income and EPS contribution from the company's Capital Investment Plan.
- Provide significant input to the strategic decision-making process. Heavy involvement in sales planning, gross margin forecasting, real estate negotiations, staffing and non-payroll target setting.
- Prepare/compile pro-forma analysis, store merchandising plans, strategic rationale, and market demographics for submittal to Board of Directors for approval. Five new stores, one replacement store, and twelve renovations were submitted and approved.
- Spearhead the post audit store evaluation process, identifying key drivers of the successes and shortfalls. Recommended store format, merchandising, and staffing changes yielding significant EBITDA improvement.
- Perform various acquisition and joint venture analyses for CEO, COO, and CFO. Structured a $30MM joint venture with prominent Saudi Arabian Investor. Financially evaluated the buyout of a $20MM catalog business.
- Administer company's $25 MM MIS expense budget and $18MM capital expenditure plan and developed PC procurement and rotation program maximizing asset value.
- Innovated an MIS contract database containing all equipment and software leases and maintenance contacts leading to *recovery* of *$1MM* in contract payments.
- Manage company's $300MM Capital Expenditure Plan. Directed all activities from target setting, budgetary review, financial justification, approval authorization, monthly reporting as well as policy & procedures.
- Direct three departments with staff of 12 and payroll budget of $600K.

83

Combination. *Mark D. Berkowitz, Yorktown Heights, New York*

For a similar format for contact information, see Resume 33. On page 1, an opening profile (not so named) ends with a two-column list of areas of expertise. Beginning with the Executive

Matt S. Peters, M.B.A. *page 2*

May xxxx –
December xxxx

PERRIER GROUP OF AMERICA, Greenwich, CT
Manager: Capital Planning & Analysis
- Managed Perrier's Capital Expenditure Program (1995 Plan $144MM): authorization and monthly tracking and reporting of Technical Depreciation ($50M annually).
- Oversaw Perrier's Fixed Asset Investment Base (NAB $340M): including 58 Route Branches, 115 Manufacturing Facilities, 4 Reconditioning Centers and various warehouses.
- Was instrumental in Perrier's 1995 Cooler Inventory Team implementing new inventory procedures to track all customer equipment movement throughout the company thereby reducing unreported write-offs.
- Performed capital investment analysis: cash flow analyses, Lease vs. Buy scenarios, Technical Depreciation estimates, LTP projections, ROI projections, write-off analyses, and standard costing analyses related to customer equipment.

April xxxx –
April xxxx

KRAFT GENERAL FOODS USA, OPERATIONS AND TECHNOLOGY DIV., White Plains, NY
Assistant Manager: Capital & Productivity Group   August xxxx – April xxxx
- Managed $76M Capital Expenditure budget for four divisions. Developed, prioritized, and evaluated capital programs.
- Controlled $15M of P&L impacts of capital (start-up costs EPOC, disposals, and first-year depreciation).
- Redesigned capital authorization process from six weeks to two.
- Instrumental in the TQM development of a greatly improved productivity tracking system.

Financial Associate: Manufacturing Cost Group   September xxxx – August xxxx
- Served as Plant Analyst for two manufacturing facilities, developing O.B.'s and revised forecasts concerning variable, fixed, raw and packaging material estimates.

Senior Financial Analyst: Planning & Reporting   February xxxx – September xxxx
- Developed time tables and standardized reporting requirements for HQ units and plans.

Financial Analyst: Overhead Budgeting Analysis   April xxxx –February xxxx
- Developed operating budgets; tracked head count and productivity

May xxxx –
April xxxx

KRAFT GENERAL FOODS INTERNATIONAL, CORPORATE ACCOUNTING, Rye Brook, NY
Senior Accounting Analyst: World Trade/Latin American Group   September xxxx – April xxxx
Accounting Analyst: Consolidations   May xxxx – September xxxx

EDUCATION

PACE UNIVERSITY – LUBIN SCHOOL, White Plains, NY
Master of Business Administration   xxxx
Major: *Finance*

IONA COLLEGE, New Rochelle, NY
Bachelor of Business Administration   xxxx
Major: *Finance*

COMPUTER SKILLS

Computer Literate; significant hands-on expertise using the following information Systems: Lotus 1-2-3, Harvard Graphics, Micro Control (LAN), M&D F/A System, System W, Masterpiece G/L System, Microsoft: Word, Excel, PowerPoint & Access, WordPerfect, Commander Prism, dBASE, and Paradox.

Profile, the design changes to two-column format, and bold italic calls attention to key concepts. On page 2, dates in the left column indicate years when the person worked for the company. Right-aligned dates show years worked at each position. Small diamond bullets are used throughout the resume.

FRED E. FINANCIAL
0000 Anytowne Street • Anytowne, AL 55555
(555) 555-5555

CONSUMER FINANCE
Team Building / Account Maintenance / Relationship Building / Problem Resolution

Market-driven consumer finance professional with excellent understanding of lending, collections, and business relationships. Exceptionally effective in undertaking a project, building a team, and bringing project to successful completion. Exceptional combination of detail and overall skills; work well under stress. Team player; goal-oriented with superior problem-solving skills. Computer literate: hardware/software.

PROFESSIONAL EXPERIENCE

ANYTOWNE BANK (Consumer Lending Unit), Anytowne, AL

Global financial institution comprising 5 divisions: Collections, Consumer Lending Unit, Account Cards, Investment Banking, and Retail Banking. Consumer Lending Unit combines CLU I (initial approval for credit), CLU II (housing of receivables for retail purchases), and CLU III (credit card division), accounting for 10% of assets and 28% of profit.

Director / Consumer Lending Unit, Anytowne, AL   August 0000 - Present
Oversee CLU activities including implementing policies, procedures, and practices to extend consumer lines of credit to key retail accounts such as The Best Company, The Better Company and The Greatest Company. Evaluate and process loan applications; prepare financial and regulatory reports required by law; direct and coordinate a staff of 152 managers and administrative personnel.
- *Recruited to set up CLU infrastructure and operations in Anytowne, including training, purchasing, and final evaluations; direct responsibility for resolving problems and instituting workable solutions*
- *Increased receivables from $40,000 to $55 million in 3 years*
- *Reengineered invoicing system to reduce processing time*
- *Key member of intense training sessions for new development*
- *Maintained strong business and community relationships*
- *Reduced delinquent accounts from 63% to 54% in 6 months*
- *Significant knowledge of bankruptcies, garnishments, and other legal actions*

Manager Trainee, Anytowne, AL   October 0000 - July 0000
Recruited for 2-year manager trainee program. Involved in all aspects of operations, including sales, collections, consumer lending, interviewing trainees, and marketing.
- *Set up new accounts for participation in financing program*
- *Assumed managerial duties in absence of manager*
- *Consistently recognized for best business relationships and superior loan judgment*
- *Office named Most Improved (0000-0000)*
- *Completed program in less than 2 years*

EDUCATION

ANYTOWNE UNIVERSITY, Anytowne, AL
Bachelor of Science
Double Major: Marketing and International Business   December 0000

Honors: Dean's List, High School Valedictorian

84

Combination. *Cathleen Fahrman, Tampa, Florida*
The individual was an aggressive professional with a short work history. For this person, the writer made a strong resume with shaded lines and varied use of italic. See the italic bullets.

HAROLD A. HANSON II

500 Edgewood Lane • Anytown, ST 00000 • (000) 555-5555

. . .seeking financial position with opportunity to work directly with customers.

"...outstanding professional skill and initiative."
US Air Force Commendation

Financial Management • Customer Service • Business Management
Investment & Retirement Planning • Computer Models
Operations & Administrative Management • Margin Analysis
Personnel Development & Training • Report Preparation & Management

17+ years' experience in Financial Services . . .
Liaison, organizational, and troubleshooting skills . . .
Computer literate on wide variety of financial software . . .
Work very well with all levels of individuals . . .
Team member who strives to make a positive difference.

"...consistently demonstrates superior ability in all phases of operations."
Merrill Lynch Vice President

Highlights of Professional Experience

LAW ANSON SMITH JONES INC. • Anytown, FL • XXXX - XXXX
Branch Office Coordinator
Comprehensive responsibility for administrative, physical, and personnel (support and sales) functions.
• Slashed postage costs by over 50% by identifying and eliminating abuse.

"...reinforces the notion that we are all on the same team."
Merrill Lynch Insurance Administrator

BRADFORD SECURITIES INC. • Anytown, FL • 19XX - XXXX
Margins Analyst, Operations Department
Computed margin requirements; troubleshooting accounts; margin trading theories; trained personnel in every aspect of investment operations.
• Position was created for me—elected Employee of the Year at end of first year amid strong competition.

"...good work and good sense...kind and excellent attention...Thanks to him my sanity and my money were saved."
Merrill Lynch Customer

MERRILL LYNCH PIERCE FENNER & SMITH • 19XX - 19XX
Customer Service Representative/Retail Bookkeeper Supervisor/ IRA Department Supervisor, Customer Accounting, Anytown, GA
Field Service Representative, Liaison Department, Anytown, GA
Administrative/Operations Manager, Sales Office, Anytown, AK
Operations Manager, Sales Office, Anytown, FL
• Within 6 months of assuming leadership of troubled IRA Department, won most awards of any department.
• First Place performance in Southern States Area Operations Contest (monetary award).
• Lead unit to Winners Circle in 19XX Performance Contest/Customer Accounting.
• Planning and monitoring efforts led Georgia office to company-wide recognition as "Most Organized" despite severely reduced staff.

"...solved a highly complex problem under severe time constraints."
Merrill Lynch Atlanta Center Manager

"Good job!"
Merrill Lynch Southeast Regional Director

MERRILL LYNCH TRAINING INSTITUTE, Princeton, NJ
• Supervisor School, 19XX
• Operations Manager School, 19XX
• DMT-II Advanced Managerial Strategies, 19XX
Continuing Education:
• Series 7 - License to Sell Stocks, 19XX
• Series 8 - Supervisory License, 19XX
• Series S101 Continuing Education Requirement, 19XX

"Are you going to part the Red Sea next??"
Merrill Lynch Asst. VP/Operations, Systems & Telecommunications

UNITED STATES AIR FORCE • 19XX - 19XX
Administrative Specialist
• Air Force Commendation Medal and Airman of the Month.

85

Combination. *Dayna J. Feist, Asheville, North Carolina*
The person handed the writer letters of reference and job reviews. Creating the resume with quotes down the left column was the way to proceed. Be sure to see the last quote.

LORAINE SCHMIDT

1234 – 6th Street NW ▪ Portland, OR 99999 ▪ 555 / 123-4567

FINANCIAL MANAGEMENT SERVICES

Utilizing strong interpersonal relationship and communication skills coupled with comprehensive financial management abilities and international experience

Highly organized management professional with a particular talent for building strong relationships to grow the business. In-depth knowledge of financial administration techniques gained through a career in mortgage banking, consumer financial consulting, and business management in the profit and not-for-profit sectors both domestically and internationally. Known for strength and ability in dealing with cross-cultural issues. Skilled in leading and working with all ages and levels. Able to see shades of gray and creatively solve problems. Demonstrated ability to interpret and summarize data into meaningful information. Generated more than $100 million in loan production, turned around a failing company, and established 2 profitable organizations. Currently studying Spanish. Proficiencies include:

- Financial Statements
- P & L Responsibilities
- Business & Financial Planning
- Resource Utilization
- Asset, Liability & Credit Analysis
- FHA & VA Loan Regulations
- Project Management

- Feasibility Studies
- Budgeting
- Cash Management
- Corporate Client Relations
- Customer Service
- Human Resource Planning
- Supervision & Training

Demonstrated expertise in growing portfolios and business

EXPERIENCE

WORLDWIDE MORTGAGE CO., *Spokane and Seattle, Washington, XXXX to XXXX*
Branch Manager - Spokane *(XXXX to XXXX)*
Consumer Financial Consultant - Seattle *(XXXX to XXXX)*

- Organized and directed the establishment of a new branch office in Western Washington, including hiring and training of personnel.
- Managed the production of more than $45 million in loans.
- Established relationships with local and regional companies and organizations to solicit and generate new business.
- Streamlined recording techniques and developed procedural changes to enhance productivity.
- Developed new markets for residential loan products.
- Created new marketing strategies to promote Federal Housing Authority and Veteran's Administration loan products, resulting in increased market share.

FIRST BANK MORTGAGE CORP., *Seattle, Washington, XXXX to XXXX*
Senior Loan Officer

- Marketed residential loan products, generating more than $30 million in loan production in the high-end mortgage market.
- Consistently ranked in top 5% of loan officer output.

U.S. NATIONWIDE MORTGAGE, INC., *Albany, New York, XXXX to XXXX*
Loan Consultant

- Developed marketing strategies directed at high-end clients in New York and New Jersey.
- Achieved #1 ranking among 17 loan officers within 5 months.
- Ranked top loan producer out of 38 loan officers in 17 out of 26 months.
- Trained all marketing personnel.

Continued

86

Combination. *Carole S. Barns, Woodinville, Washington*
This individual lacked a college degree but had a great deal of financial experience. The writer emphasized the person's skills, knowledge, and experience but de-emphasized her lack of

THE TREASURE COMPANY, *New York, New York, XXXX*

General Manager

- Recruited to lead the start-up operation of a multimillion-dollar heavy equipment trading enterprise that took over management of a Liberia, Africa, logging company.
- Negotiated pricing and terms with U.S. suppliers and established all initial trade logistics, including shipping.
- Supervised staff of 7.
- Coordinated all export functions, including applications to and negotiations with appropriate U.S. and African agencies.

GREEN TREES, *Rhodesia, Africa, XXXX to XXXX*

Vice President - General Manager

- Successfully assumed leadership of a failing logging company that cut and exported logs and lumber to several European countries.
- Restructured all operations to increase efficiency and decrease costs, resulting in significant improvements in manpower planning, production, sales, budgets, equipment selection, and purchase and created process to share resources with other start-up, small, or failing African companies.
- Supervised 300 employees, including 20 direct reports.
- Established a subdivision to purchase $2.5 million in heavy equipment from the U.S. for use by Universal and other African companies.
- Generated a turnaround in profitability, achieving more than $1 million in sales after 1 year and sales of $3 million within 2 years.

REACH HIGH CORPORATION, *New York, New York, XXXX to XXXX*

General Manager

- Established videotape duplication company, now second largest in the U.S., to amortize large capital equipment purchases of parent organization.
- Expanded operations to include an international commodity brokerage trading in coffee, cocoa, coal, metals, and other products.
- Produced a $250,000 profit within 9 months.

THE MULTICULTURE GROUP, *Boston, Massachusetts, XXXX to XXXX*

Project Manager

- Managed the development, packaging, and distribution throughout the United States of 300,000 sets of written and videotaped educational and promotional materials.
- Supervised a multicultural, non-English-speaking staff of 90 individuals.

FUTURE LEADERS OF THE WORLD, *New York, New York, XXXX to XXXX*

Program Coordinator

- Coordinated the planning and presentation of leadership training programs for participants representing 60 countries.
- Solicited and signed instructors and guest lecturers from throughout the world.

EDUCATION

Completed education and licensing requirements for Property, Casualty, Life, Disability Insurance

formal training. The first half of page 1 makes it clear that this person is a competent manager with diversified experience and the accumulation of many areas of expertise. The rest of the resume details her varied career experience. Bulleted items display quantified accomplishments in each job for every company.

ROGER S. GRAHAM

445 East 83rd Street
New York, NY 00000
(555) 555-5555

BUSINESS EXPERTISE

"Financial wizard" ... *"complete commitment to the job"* ...
"Mr. Investment"...
Team Leadership
Organization
Communication
Sales

FINANCE

Trade Execution
International Money Brokering
Spot Currencies
Currency Options
Telecommunications
Banking
Investment Houses
Japanese Institutions

HUMAN RESOURCES

Recruitment
Hiring
Scheduling
Training & Development
Coaching
Mentoring
Team Building

NEW BUSINESS DEVELOPMENT

Business Planning
Capitalization
Budgeting
Advertising
Marketing
Purchasing
Vendor Relationships
Staff Administration
Site Operations/Renovations
Industry Networking

SENIOR RELATIONSHIP MANAGER ▪ ENTREPRENEUR

Decisive, market-driven professional with 15 years of combined experience managing key account relationships and developing business operations in the financial services and hospitality industries. Utilize widely respected leadership and negotiation skills to achieve bottom-line results. Motivated self-starter who thrives in fast-paced environments.

- Blend management skill and business strategy to ensure that short- and long-range goals are met.

- Retain and expand solid client base by directing 15-member team to resolve problems rapidly, outpacing the competition.

- Deliver exceptional customer service, consistently improve public relations and bridge the gap effortlessly by identifying cross-cultural business practices.

SELECTED ACCOMPLISHMENTS

CLIENT SERVICE

- Generate repeat business, expand client base and increase brokerage revenue through well-nurtured relationships, achieving strong track record in sales and service.

- Devised and implemented strategies of matching broker to client by observing and assessing competition, capturing dominant market share.

- Managed fast and accurate service on multimillion-dollar trade executions to retain major Japanese banks as clients.

- Negotiate daily with top players to consummate deals. Meet directly with banking executives in group and one-on-one presentations to provide professional image of company.

- Recruit, hire and motivate key personnel to function cooperatively as team members. Train staff to execute trades accurately. Mentor "rookies" and develop their acclimation to business environment and culture.

HOSPITALITY

- Conceived, managed and developed American/Continental restaurant and bar achieving annual sales in excess of $500K.

- Directed food and beverage operations with full P&L responsibility. Oversaw menu planning, advertising campaigns, payroll, accounting and staff development.

- Managed daily operations of world-class, landmark restaurant in the Wall Street area catering to high net worth executives. Ensured top-quality service with personal approach, utilizing well-developed communication and problem-resolution skills.

87

Functional. *Phyllis B. Shabad, Ossining, New York*
A resume for an individual who wanted "to integrate financial and entrepreneurial skills for more challenging career growth." The first page starts off with a bang: three brief quotes that

ROGER S. GRAHAM

PROFESSIONAL EXPERIENCE	**Pacific Rim Investments**, New York, NY *Manager/International Money Broker:* *OTC Currency Options; Spot* *International Currency Broker: xxxx–xxxx*	xxxx–present
	Claude Martine Brokerage, New York, NY *International Currency Broker*	xxxx–xxxx
	Lord & Kingsley, New York, NY *Manager Training Program* *Manager & Currency Broker*	xxxx
	Graham Wilson International, New York, NY *Owner and General Manager*	xxxx–xxxx
	Wall Street Restaurant, New York, NY *Manager*	xxxx–xxxx
EDUCATION	**University of Chicago**, Chicago, Illinois **Bachelor of Science in Business Administration** Major: Financial Management Dean's List Major GPA: 3.6–4.0	December, xxxx
ACTIVITIES	**American Society of Finance Administrators**, *Chapter Public Relations Coordinator and* *Treasurer*	
TECHNOLOGY	**Specialized Financial Software:** Expertise in using Derivatech Pricing System for OTC currency options	

awaken interest. The left column displays a novel way to list keywords, which are grouped according to four main categories. This kind of grouping helps to ensure that competencies in a main area of interest will not be overlooked. The two-column format is carried over to page 2. Vertical lines provide design interest.

FINANCIAL MANAGER

555 Maple Street
Anytown, Anystate 55555
(555) 555-5555

--Finance Management position--

SUMMARY:

- Results-oriented Financial Manager with demonstrated leadership and effective communication skills.

- Proven ability to develop efficient operations, allocate materials, and manage staff to ensure high productivity and low cost. Aggressive cost reduction and unique problem-solving capabilities.

- Expertise includes administration of sales, personnel, production controls and scheduling, inventory control, payroll, order processing, and purchasing.

EXPERIENCE:

Rolling Hill Children's Home   Anytown, AS
BUSINESS MANAGER (Report to CEO), 1989 to Present

- Develop annual budgets along with CEO and Board of Directors and present budget to County. Develop long-range financial goals with Board of Directors. Develop cost studies as requested. Monitor budget closely and maintain control of line items.

- Supervise all accounting activity in financial area. Facilitate annual audit and coordinate report to Board of Directors. File all state and federal reports and documents on time.

- Write numerous grants for facility.

- Obtain bids, purchase items, and handle accounts payable. Maintain inventories. Cooperate with Administration and staff teams regarding purchase and program needs. Report on property needs as necessary.

- Maintain professional relationships with county administrators.

- Maintain computer systems for business and main office.

- Educate self on program issues to meet team needs more effectively.

- Supervise maintenance, kitchen, and housekeeping personnel.

Accomplishments

- Most outstanding financial years of 1996 and 1997.

- 1996 audit stated excellent handling of additional funds. Improved reporting of financial data monthly because of complete computer network with business office.

- Maintained below budget expenses overall throughout 1997.

- Ongoing excellent audit results in various state and city grants for NYS.

- Enhanced tracking of all grant monies and provided on-time deadlines.

- Reduced food costs while still providing quality meals.

- Handled difficult neighborhood questioning through Anytown officials and City

88

Combination. *Linda Wunner, Duluth, Minnesota*
The individual needed a readable, professional-looking resume that stressed skills, accomplishments, and results. This resume fulfills these needs. Skills are evident in the Summary and in the

Council member to resolve landfill issues. Helped secure finance of NYS funding through CDGB.

- Secured purchase of Cobb School to assist in the development of future educational needs for Rolling Hill's programs and expansion.

Signa-Minor Company   Anytown, AS
MANAGER OF TRAFFIC AND PURCHASING/ASSISTANT SALES MANAGER (SALT DIVISION), 1978 to 1989
Reported to VP of lime manufacturer and salt distributor for a $750,000 truck fleet operation. Responsibilities included purchasing, hiring, training, dispatching, negotiating labor contracts, and managerial control. Reported to sales manager on supply, distribution, and logistics of salt marketing. Conducted product and vendor research to ensure pricing, delivery, and quality standards. Purchased all additive ingredients. Reviewed all customer issues and expedited orders.

Accomplishments:

- Reassessed and developed a computerized sales system that tracked pricing and inventory controls and RESULTED in better customer telecommunications and services as well as reduced costs and increased operational efficiency.
- Designed and implemented a purchasing control system for tracking additive ingredients and packaging which ENABLED efficient expediting and forecasting of future price increases and ensured pricing, delivery, and quality standards.
- Defined and implemented FDA requirements and standards RESULTING in conformation of rules, regulations, and needs of industry.
- Successfully negotiated trucking contracts with Teamster Local RESULTING in no downtime and turned a truck fleet operation into positive revenue flows.
- Created and implemented an innovative trucking program RESULTING in more efficient operations and reduced costs on deliveries.
- Recommended and implemented responsibilities for packaging RESULTING in increased sales and revenues.
- Managed pricing of salt and contracts RESULTING in an approximate 25% increase in sales over an 18-month period.

EDUCATION:

University of Any State, Anytown   Anytown, AS
COURSEWORK TOWARD MBA, 1975 to 1976

University of Toledo   Toledo, OH
BACHELOR OF BUSINESS SCIENCE, 1974

MEMBERSHIPS:

Steering Committee of Capital Campaign
Corporation Committee of Capital Campaign
Risk Management Team

bulleted items and paragraph after the job titles in the Experience section. Results are visible in the two Accomplishments subsections—especially the second subsection, where the uppercase words RESULTED, ENABLED, and RESULTING make consequences explicit. These offset the unfinished M.B.A.

Cynthia P. Mills

00 Park Avenue
Monopoly, MN
(000) 000-0000

SUMMARY

- Over fifteen years of progressive, professional accounting and supervisory experience.
- Computer skills include Lotus 1-2-3, Excel, WordPerfect, and AS400.
- Self-motivated; able to set effective priorities and implement decisions to achieve immediate and long-term goals and meet operational deadlines.
- Taught Accounting I, Intermediate Accounting, and Computerized Accounting at Davenport College evening classes, Kalamazoo, MI.

EDUCATION

Messers College, Birmingham, AL
Master of Management, XXXX (Emphasis on Analytical Accounting)

Hinesville College, Birmingham, AL
Bachelor of Accounting, XXXX

Birmingham Community College, Birmingham, AL
Associate of Applied Science, XXXX (Emphasis on computers)

EXPERIENCE

XXXX - Present
Credit Manager / Assistant Controller
TEAM, Inc., Birmingham, AL

- Research, consolidate, compile, and print month-end and year-end reports and tax information.
- Inventory cost and other accounting functions as necessary.
- Perform Credit Manager functions of controlling credit and collecting monies owed.
- Involved in the formation and disbursement of budget.

XXXX - XXXX
Perigo Gas, Inc., Huntsville, AL
Regional Administrator

- Supervised all of the region's Branch Administrators (10) in the accounting procedures and practices as determined by Corporate office.
- Performed auditing functions at branch to ensure policies were followed.

89

Combination. *Peggy M. Weeks, Battle Creek, Michigan*
With 15 years of supervisory accounting experience, a master's degree, and college teaching experience, this person wanted a new job for advancement. An easy-to-read resume.

JENNIFER G. HARRIS, CPA

100 Buttonhook Drive • Cortland, New York 10706 • 914-111-0000

More than 10 years of experience as **Controller/Accounting Manager** in not-for-profit and health care fields with background in business analysis and **cost-conscious financial management**. MPA, with strengths in:

- Financial Statements & Analysis
- General Accounting Administration
- Fund Accounting / FASB 116,117
- Budgeting / Financial Forecasting
- Accounting Information Systems
- Internal Controls / Auditing

Organized, straightforward, persevering, results- and goal-oriented professional, with expertise in financial reporting and accounting software, including Excel and FundEZ.

PROFESSIONAL EXPERIENCE

AMERICAN JEWISH WORLD SERVICE, New York, NY   xxxx-xxxx
Controller
Responsible for financial operations of international development organization, including financial statements, cash management, financial analysis, investment accounting, tax reporting, internal controls.
- Prepared year-end and monthly financial statements, operating and cash budgets.
- Monitored financial performance, reporting to President.
- Coordinated audits, benefits and insurance administration.
- Improved cash reporting system and internal control procedures.
- Evaluated, selected and implemented accounting software package.
- Supervised accounts payable and payroll functions.

MANHATTAN & SOUTH BRONX KIDNEY CENTERS, New York, NY   xxxx-xxxx
Controller
Responsible for accounting operations for two dialysis centers.
- Managed G/L, A/P and payroll tax filings.
- Improved timeliness of monthly financial statements.
- Set up accounts receivable system, reducing receivables by 20% within a year.
- Prepared Medicare cost report.

METROPOLITAN JEWISH GERIATRIC CENTER, Brooklyn, NY   xxxx-xxxx
Accounting Manager
- Prepared monthly financial statements and Medicaid cost reports. Analyzed accounts.
- Implemented controls for newly installed billing system. Worked with mainframe computer.

NEWARK BETH ISRAEL MEDICAL CENTER, Newark, NJ   xxxx-xxxx
Accounting Manager / Internal Auditor / Budget Analyst
- Promoted through a series of increasingly responsible financial positions.
- Supervised General Accounting Department for $100M teaching hospital.
- Oversaw monthly financial statement preparation and worked with public accounting firm for audits.
- Conducted operational and financial audits, identified deficiencies and made recommendations.
- Appointed first Budget Analyst for Nursing Department.
- Prepared annual operating budget and monitored performance.

RESEARCH FOUNDATION, CITY UNIVERSITY OF NEW YORK, New York, NY   xxxx-xxxx
Fiscal Administrator
- Monitored expenditures and prepared financial reports for sponsoring agencies for 40 grants.
- Effected full funding during city's fiscal crisis.

EDUCATION

NEW YORK UNIVERSITY, New York, NY   **Master of Public Administration**, Health Policy & Management
UNIVERSITY OF PENNSYLVANIA, **Wharton School**, Philadelphia, PA   **Bachelor of Science** in Economics

PROFESSIONAL ASSOCIATIONS

Certified Public Accountant, New Jersey, 1986
New Jersey Society of Certified Public Accountants   •   Healthcare Financial Management Association

90

Combination. *Linsey Levine, Chappaqua, New York*
Visual aids are important in resumes. In this resume, italic is used only for job titles. Once you recognize this fact, you can look just for italic and spot any job title quickly.

TONI R. ALICKSTEN, CPA

555 Joliette Lane
Dallas, TX 75555

(214) 555-5555
talick@lightspeed.net

PROFESSIONAL QUALIFICATIONS

EXPERIENCED ACCOUNTING PROFESSIONAL with strong combination of public accounting and private sector experiences. Comprehensive skills in budgeting, reporting, auditing, tax, and MIS systems. Consistently successful in linking accounting with multidisciplinary operations to provide business-driven focus. Excellent analytical, communication, and problem-solving skills. Fully literate in financial technology tools and software applications.

PROFESSIONAL EXPERIENCE

NATION'S INSURANCE SERVICES, Dallas, Texas   1994–Present

CONTROLLER: Plan, manage, and administer accounting systems for multientity insurance organization. Directly accountable for compliance, managerial financial reporting, internal controls, general ledger maintenance, financial statements, and audits. Prepare, review, analyze, and administer budgets for ten departments. Supervise accounting staff in accounts payable, accounts receivable, payroll, broker commissions, and asset management functions. Report to CFO; maintain extensive verbal and e-mail communications with internal departments, San Francisco division office, and New York corporate office.

Contributions:

➤ **Profit Performance:** Identified and implemented methods to reduce operating expenses and improve profit performance; converted fixed assets from bookkeeping to tracking system with resultant decrease in property tax; implemented purchase controls that accounted for a 60% reduction in budget items.

➤ **Audit Compliance:** Received unprecedented high marks for compliance on internal financial audits and fiduciary compliance audits by various insurance carriers.

➤ **Change Agent:** Facilitated change environment with sale of company in 1995—converted financial data to new accounting method, transitioned employees to new payroll cycle, and coordinated assumption/assignment of contracts.

➤ **Business Process Reengineering:** Accommodated a 50% reduction in accounting staff (with increase in work volume) without compromising internal controls through business process reengineering and staff cross-training.

➤ **Business Analysis:** Conducted in-depth examination of systems, providing management with financial and operational analyses and recommendations. Researched and resolved inquiries regarding complex tax issues.

PERRY & HAMBOURIAN, CPAs, Dallas, Texas   1990–1993

STAFF ACCOUNTANT: Directed and supervised audit teams for key healthcare and retail clients. Prepared corporate, partnership, fiduciary, and individual tax returns. Prepared financial statements for nonprofit organizations, corporations, partnerships, and high-net-worth individuals.

EDUCATION, LICENSURE

SOUTHERN METHODIST UNIVERSITY, Dallas, Texas   1991

➤ **Bachelor of Science degree, Business Administration ◆ Accountancy Option (Magna cum Laude)**

LICENSURE, AFFILIATIONS

Certified Public Accountant (1993), American Institute of Certified Public Accountants, Texas Society of Certified Public Accountants, American Society of Women Accountants

References on Request

91

Combination. *Susan Britton Whitcomb, Fresno, California*
A resume with the executive look. Because of small print, much information fits on the page.
With many blank lines, however, the resume has plenty of white space—and class.

Lady O. Finance

1234 Some Street • Anytown, State 00000 • (122) 555-1234

PROFILE

Efficient, detail-oriented individual with excellent accounting experience seeking controller position with a business that offers opportunities to learn and advance. Experience includes:
- General ledger administration; financial statements and tax reporting
- Payroll administration in two states including 401(k) distributions and contribution verification; compilation and payment of payroll taxes
- Management of multimillion-dollar budget; terms negotiation
- Forecasting; budget preparation; cash flow analysis
- Knowledge of EOE requirements for various municipalities, two states

PROFESSIONAL EXPERIENCE

DISTRIBUTION COMPANY, Anytown, State (1991-XXXX)
Controller
Maintained full-charge financial responsibility for a multistate equipment distributor including general ledger, monthly financial statements, payroll, AP and AR, 401(k) administration, budgeting, tax reporting and collections. Supervised four assistants. Served as treasurer of the board and Equal Opportunity Officer.
Achievements:
- Restructured payroll and benefits package to produce $90,000 savings in 1994
- Proposed and implemented reductions in advertising and marketing expenses without sacrificing company visibility
- Produced 15% savings through careful analysis of business insurance packages
- Wrote EOE program and company employee manual

LEASES, LEASES, Metro City, State (1990)
Commissioned Sales Representative
Promoted and leased apartment space in Kansas City metro area on straight commission basis. Verified credit and approved prospects.

SOME FINANCE COMPANY, Metro City, State (1989-1990)
Management Trainee

EDUCATION

B.S. Business Administration (August 1989)
STATE UNIVERSITY, Someplace, State
- 100% financial responsibility for college expenses

POSTGRADUATE EDUCATION

9 hours completed toward qualification for CPA examination, anticipated Fall 1996

COMPUTER SKILLS

Real World Accounting 6.0	PFS
Q&A	Quattro Pro

92

Combination. *Linda Morton, Lawrence, Kansas*
The person had "excellent accounting experience but not an accounting degree." The writer shows the person's professionalism and broad experience gained in a short time.

DANIEL L. HILGER

115 Round Top Road
Sunningdale, PA 11111
000-000-0000 (H)
555-555-5555 (W)

QUALIFICATIONS PROFILE

Finance Director with eight years' experience in not-for-profit organizations. Deliver strong operating results through efficiency improvement and cost reductions. Scope of expertise includes:

- Finance, Budgeting & Banking
- Auditing
- Fixed Asset Details
- Cash Flow Analysis

- Resident & Agency Inventory
- Grant Writing & Funding Procurement
- Contract Bidding & Negotiations
- Employee Benefits Administration

Technical skills and systems troubleshooting include Microbudget, Great Plains, and EDS (Electronic Data Systems for Medicaid billing) automated accounting applications; Lotus 1-2-3; and DOS and Microsoft Windows operating systems.

PROFESSIONAL EXPERIENCE

SUNCORP INDUSTRIES, INC., Sunderland, PA   1997 to Present
Comptroller

A vocational rehabilitation organization.

Supervise 4 employees in day-to-day operations of the finance office. Maintain financial records of expenses and revenue to meet the needs of the organization and auditor. Prepare annual budget and monitor expenses and revenue to budget projections. Monitor fringe benefits enrollment for staff. Implement and develop electronic spreadsheets and database management programs to effectively track and report information. Also handle A/R, purchasing, cost accounting, payroll and banking.

RESIDENTIAL SERVICES, INC., Carrington, SC   1993 to 1997
Finance Director

A not-for-profit long-term care facility serving developmentally disabled individuals. Organization experienced dramatic growth during term of employment, doubling its annual budget from $2 million to $4 million and increasing employees from 100 to 150. During this time 5 group homes were added for a total of 12 homes.

Accounting Activities: Oversaw corporation's financial records, payroll records, multiple bank accounts, and depreciation schedules. Directed activities of 2 employees through A/P, A/R, and bank reconciliations. Recorded journal entries and prepared month-end reports. Analyzed cash flow, handled fixed asset details, oversaw resident / agency inventory, and performed audits. Managed state and federal reporting related to funding. Maintained contact with auditors and state division of medical assistance.

Human Resources Activities: Involved in the selection process for corporation's new employees. Administered employee benefits package which included medical and hospitalization insurance, vacation, holiday and personal leave, profit sharing, and retirement.

93

Combination. *Deborah S. Edwards, Wellsboro, Pennsylvania*
The individual "felt that not having a degree in accounting was limiting his options." The writer's focus was "on presenting his 'hands-on' experience and what he had accomplished."

Highlights:
- Improved overall accounting system efficiencies to streamline functions, resulting in a reduction of processing time and a decrease of outstanding receivables.
- Cut workers compensation costs 50% from $40,000 to $20,000 by implementing claims and risk management.
- Successfully procured additional funds for the care, maintenance, and well-being of residents.
- Instrumental in writing a grant which won an award from The United Way for computers provided by IBM.

ACCOUNTEMPS, Raleigh, NC   1992 to 1993
Accountant

Nine month assignment with the southeast regional office of a national auto parts distributor.

Assisted in all daily accounting activities.

HUMAN SERVICE PROVIDERS, INC., Mannington, PA   1989 to 1992

A not-for-profit, long-term-care facility with an annual budget of $3 million serving developmentally disabled individuals. Services covered 10 group homes throughout a 2-county area in North Central Pennsylvania. Experienced fast-track promotion within two years to final position as Fiscal Director.

Fiscal Director (4/91 to 6/92)

Directly reported to the chief executive officer for all accounting activities. Prepared and maintained budgets for multiple operating locations. Supervised 2 employees in A/R, Medicaid billing, A/P, and administration of client / resident accounts. Involved in hiring new employees. Administered corporate benefits plan for 75 employees. Coordinated accounting process from purchasing to report generation.

Highlights:
- Prepared bid package and was awarded service contract for group home funding through the county government.
- Controlled spending without sacrificing quality of services provided to clients, which enabled one of the counties to utilize the cost savings for other projects.
- Solicited bids and negotiated outsourcing contracts for transportation, day care and workshop services, and facility maintenance.

Fiscal Technical (11/89 to 4/91)

Maintained 41 client accounts in a single account. Assisted in budget development and implementation; allocated costs to specific projects. Processed A/P and A/R according to established procedures.

EDUCATION & PROFESSIONAL DEVELOPMENT

B. S. DEGREE • BUSINESS ADMINISTRATION, Mannington University, Mannington, PA   1988
Coursework included 18 credit hours in Accounting

PROFESSIONAL DEVELOPMENT • Successfully completed various accounting-related seminars including "Sources of Funding" and "Cost Reporting."

ACTIVITIES

Special Olympics Swimming Coach for 10 individuals - Summers 1995 & 1996

Hanging indentation makes the section headings stand out, and other indentation is well controlled. Generous line spacing provides white space. Italic explanations are given not only for companies but also for job titles. At the end of page 1 are "embedded headings" in paragraphs.

MICHAEL WEST
2000 Southwest 25 Street
Ft. Lauderdale, Florida 33301
Phone: (954) 000-0000   E-mail: CASIOWIN@aol.com

ACCOUNTING/FINANCE

Financial Statements...Financial Tracking & Reporting...Cash Management...Accounting Systems... Internal Auditing...Internal Controls...P&L...Budget Preparation...Forecasting... Projections...Financial Integrity...Cost/Benefit Analysis.....Policies & Procedures... Interviewing, Hiring, Training...Supervision...Lotus 1-2-3...Quattro Pro...Ami Pro...Microsoft Word...Excel...Peachtree...Quicken...QuickBooks...Platinum...Tech 7...MACOLA...Novell LAN Server administrator...J.D. Edwards...Integral.

Scope of Responsibilities

- Established, implemented, and reviewed internal controls
- Established and managed Cashiering and Accounting Departments for start-up and existing ventures
- Prepared and reviewed budgets and projections on a monthly basis
- Established effective cash management procedures for a multilocation operation
- Restructured general ledger and financial statements for consolidation purposes
- Supervised and trained staff to oversee all daily finance, accounting and income audit functions
- Installed computerized accounting system
- Management control of general ledger, balance sheet, accounts payable, collections, payroll and human resources
- Prepared Internal Control System for submission to Nevada Gaming Control Board, which was then used for all domestic and foreign gaming operations
- Directed staff to maintain consistent accounting policies & procedures
- Designed underlying accounting documentation to ensure proper reporting of gaming revenue
- Produced standard policies & procedures manual for consistent shipboard operation
- Designed management tools to track and report continuing casino operation
- Coordinated production and review of each financial statement through P&L and balance sheet
- Reviewed monthly financial statements and performed variance analyses on significant fluctuations

Employment

GAMING CONSULTANT/CONTROLLER   2/97 to Present
Blue Moon International, Coconut Grove, FL

- Gained control of corporate accounting function of two gaming vessel concessions and a vessel management contract

CONTROLLER/ASSISTANT GENERAL MANAGER   7/96 to 3/97
Casino Play Miami, Miami, FL

- Oversaw the opening and continued operation of casino's Accounting Department, as well as acted in management capacity for start-up of the business

94

Combination. *Shelley Nachum, Ft. Lauderdale, Florida*
The individual's 10-year accounting/finance career in the gaming industry had been "unique, interesting, and unparalleled," but he was now looking for a position in the hospitality industry.

Michael West   2

CONTROLLER   9/95 to 7/96
Hollywood/Holiday Casino Cruises, Ft. Lauderdale; Key Largo, FL

- Established fully functioning accounting environment for two independently operating casino vessels and one leased vessel

CONTROLLER   10/94 to 9/95
Crystal Vacations, Nassau Marriott Resort & Crystal Palace Casino
Ft. Lauderdale, FL

DIRECTOR OF CASINO ADMINISTRATION   10/93 to 10/94
Carnival's Crystal Palace, Miami, FL

- Promoted to oversee financial analysis of casino's Sales and Marketing area, as well as performed special projects for the Executive Vice President of Marketing. Liaison with MIS and Financial Analyses Departments on property in the Bahamas

SENIOR INTERNAL AUDITOR   10/92 to 10/93
Carnival Cruise Line, Miami, FL

- Reviewed internal controls for many casino operations, both shipboard and shoreside. Reviewed casino management and operational structures, accounting systems, gaming audit and internal controls of slot machine and table game operations

GAMING CONSULTANT   3/92 to 6/92
Blackburn International Casino, KFT, Budapest Hungary

- Oversaw opening and continued operation of casino's financial affairs, as well as provided status reporting to owners and senior management located in the United States. Ensured adequate casino controls were in place and operating to conform to Hungarian gaming regulations.

MANAGER, CASINO INCOME CONTROL   10/89 to 3/92
Royal Caribbean Cruises Ltd., Miami, FL

- Responsible for internal control and financial reporting of shipboard Casino Operation Division, which consisted of 10 vessels accounting for $30+ million in revenue

INTERNAL AUDITOR; STAFF AUDITOR   1/88 to 10/89

Education

BACHELOR OF BUSINESS ADMINISTRATION IN ACCOUNTING
University of Nevada, Reno, NV

Accounting/Finance keywords are separated by ellipses. Duties are clustered under Scope of Responsibilities to avoid repetition under all of the job positions. Special responsibilities or achievements are then given for each of the jobs held. Consistent use of blank lines provides adequate white space.

EDWARD WINSTON
319 Allendale Drive ▪ Los Gatos CA 95000
(408) 555-5555   E-mail: winstone@aol.com

OBJECTIVE: Position as a Financial Controller.

KEY QUALIFICATIONS:

- Over 16 years of responsible financial experience, including 6 years as a Controller.
- M.S. in Finance; B.S. in Accountancy; Certified Public Accountant.
- Proven ability to identify critical issues and implement or recommend effective remedial action.
- Experience in both international and domestic financial operations.
- Team player with effective combination of profit-oriented and interpersonal strengths.

PROFESSIONAL EXPERIENCE:

Heraux Corporation   May 1989-Present

Heraux Textron, Mountain View, CA, Sept. 1997-Present
CONTROLLER

Supervise staff of 7. Responsible for internal and division financial reporting. Prepare division budgets and financials for the upcoming year. Coordinate accounting activities between U.S. operations and France. Brought in to identify and resolve deficiencies related to inventory, contract accounting and government contract issues.

Actions and accomplishments include:

- Within 30 days, identified several critical issues for inclusion in the quarterly management letter to Corporate and developed monthly internal financial reports to assist senior managers in evaluating results against the annual plan.
- Reorganized accounting department structure, which included personnel recruitment, reassignment and termination, to improve communications and enhance quality of service.
- Recruited individuals to focus on implementation of a fixed asset subsidiary ledger and to rebuild the cost accounting structure.
- Instituted new cost accounting and inventory procedures for month-end closing.
- Facilitated resolution of outstanding 1993-1994 DCAA audit issues.
- Spearheaded drive to upgrade seriously lagging technology by obtaining budget approval for over $100,000 of equipment, including a major computer upgrade and a new phone system.

Heraux Francais, Paris, France, Oct. 1993-Oct. 1995
CONTROLLER

Supervised staff of 8. Responsible for internal and division financial reporting, insurance matters, banking relations, and external audit requirements. Prepared division plans and developed separate plans for 2 businesses consolidated with divisions in Italy and California.

Actions and accomplishments include:

- Coordinated efforts with Division Manager to assist in divestiture and sale of a business unit.
- Instituted policies and procedures that reduced accounts receivable balance by $1,700K and bad debt reserve by $300K, leading to increased profits for 1994.
- Assisted in integration of this acquisition to be compliant with the financial reporting policies and procedures of Heraux Corporation.

95

Combination. *Georgia Adamson, Campbell, California*
An interesting resume because the Experience section appears to be chronological but is actually topical to aid the individual in his search for a new Controller position. If you examine

EDWARD WINSTON   **PAGE TWO**

HERAUX CORPORATION, Needham, MA
SUPERVISOR OF OPERATIONS ANALYSIS, Nov. 1995 to Aug. 1997
SENIOR OPERATIONS ANALYST, May 1989 to Sept. 1993

- Performed international and domestic financial and operational audits for this Fortune 1000 company. Prepared management reports identifying financial exposures, compliance problems and internal control weaknesses; recommended improvements to senior management.
- Participated in acquisition review teams, as part of due diligence, to establish existence and value of company assets and determine the potential of unrecorded and contingent liabilities.
- Discovered and advised management of a significant export control problem, which enabled the company to avert potential liability and penalty issues by submitting a government report.

Jefferson & Allen, Boston, MA   Dec. 1987-Apr. 1989
SENIOR/SUPERVISOR AUDITOR

- Identified potential risk areas; participated in planning, scheduling and conducting audits. Prepared audit reports and presented findings to client management.
- Trained, supervised and reviewed audit staff.
- Performed special 3-month project in the corporate trust department of a bank: inventoried and reconciled securities, reviewed procedures and set up temporary controls pending establishment of permanent controls and procedures.
- Performed an extensive IPO audit of a software development company.

Previous Experience:
Daley Research Center, Inc., CONTROLLER (2+ years)
Petrie & Clarke, Public Accountants, SENIOR AUDITOR (3+ years)

EDUCATION:
- Master of Science in Finance, Boston College, Boston, MA, 1986
- Bachelor of Science in Accountancy, Boston College, Boston, MA, 1980

AFFILIATIONS & CERTIFICATIONS:
- Certified Public Accountant, Commonwealth of Massachusetts (1983)
- APIC Certification, Production Activity Control
- American Institute of Certified Public Accountants
- Massachusetts Society of Certified Public Accountants

the dates for the positions the person has held for the same company, you can see that they are not listed in chronological order. Instead, the Controller positions are grouped together and put first. All of the person's Controller experience can then be seen on page 1. Note the use of italic for showing responsibilities.

Jim Braden

0000 Lakeside Drive
Hendersonville, TN 00000

Home • (000) 000-0000
Office • (000) 000-0000 ext. 00

Experience Summary

Hospitality Management Accounting professional with 20 years' experience in financial and operational management, budgeting, forecasting, accounting, and auditing. Diverse background in full-service convention / medical center / university hotels and multiple properties, up to 477 rooms.

- Complete P&L and Balance Sheet
- A/P, A/R, Payroll, and Purchasing
- Computer Systems and Operations
- Front and Back Office Setup

- Night Audit and Internal Audit
- Staff Training, Supervision, and Motivation
- Human Resources and Benefits
- Hotel Openings, Renovations

Thoroughly familiar with "GAAP" procedures customized to the unique requirements of the hospitality industry. Highly successful in installing, streamlining, and automating accounting systems design and setup. *Hospitality and positive guest relations a priority!*

Computer Operations

Installation, programming, training, and hands-on experience with:

- Encore Worldwide Hotel Systems
- Logistics Property Management System
- Peachtree III Complete Accounting System

- Microsoft Office 97
- Lotus 1-2-3 for Windows
- Micros 470 HMS & 451 MHM

Professional Experience

MASTERSON HOTEL COMPANY • 1995 - Present

Holiday Inn Lakeside (208 rooms) • Nashville, Tennessee
Controller • XXXX - Present

Scope of responsibility includes daily deposits, A/P, A/R, biweekly payroll, human resources, insurance, labor forecasts, weekly operational forecasts, and review of P&L statements. Prepare annual operating budget.

- Reduced A/R and collected 100% of outstanding accounts over 60 days. Maintain all accounts each month under 60 days.
- Reestablished purchase order system for all departments.
- Initiated sending A/R statements on a daily basis, thus contributing to increased percentage of collections.
- Reviewed past internal audits and reestablished accounting procedures that had lapsed.

Crowne Plaza Hotel (477 rooms) • Nashville, Tennessee
Assistant Controller • 1995 - XXXX / *Night Audit Manager* • 1995

Oversaw and handled A/P and A/R. Prepared Manager's Monthly Recap (MMR), weekly updates of monthly forecasts, and weekly labor progress reports. Personally executed billing of special group accounts, such as XYZ Corporation (100-150 rooms per night, 7 days a week). Directed and reviewed all night audit and general cashier operations.

- Reduced A/R by 66% from $1.5 million to $500,000 within a 3-month period.
- Developed and implemented night audit procedures manual.
- Reorganized Human Resources department and updated all employee files.
- Organized A/P procedures and trained Accounts Payable Clerk.

96

Combination. *Carolyn S. Braden, Hendersonville, Tennessee*
This resume highlights the financial and operational management experience, computer abilities, and accomplishments of an individual with over 20 years of experience in hotel

Jim Braden   Page 2

Professional Experience (continued)

MEDICAL PROPERTIES, INC. • Nashville, Tennessee
Corporate Controller / Operations Manager • 1991 - 1995

Corporate management and financial responsibility for three properties adjacent to major university medical centers: Nashville CareCenter Inn (107 rooms); Cornerstone CareCenter Inn (156 rooms), Durham, NC; The University Inn (185 rooms), Birmingham, AL.

- Advised and assisted General Managers in controlling expenses, setting up budgets, and making day-to-day management decisions.
- Developed and implemented guidelines for employee handbooks, staffing guides, position descriptions, and employment / termination practices.

THE HERMITAGE (132 suites) • Nashville, Tennessee
Acting General Manager • 1990 - 1991 / *Controller* • 1989 - 1990

- Managed and oversaw operation of property including budget, profit and loss, expenses, staffing (e.g., food and beverage, accounting, sales, catering, housekeeping, maintenance, front desk, and security).
- As Controller, directed daily financial and accounting operations (bank deposits, audit reports, A/P and A/R, general ledger). Prepared annual budget.

HOLIDAY INN WEST HOTEL & CONFERENCE CENTRE (269 rooms) • Fort Lauderdale, Florida
Controller • 1983 - 1989

- Performed all A/P and A/R operations. Handled payroll, general accounting, cashier operations, vendor contracts, and insurance benefits. Supervised night audit. Prepared annual operating budget.

Education and Professional Development

Have earned 100+ points required for the **CHAE designation** offered by the **International Association of Hospitality Accountants (IAHA)**.

HOLIDAY INN UNIVERSITY • Olive Branch, Mississippi • *Food and Beverage Management*

Volunteer State Community College • Gallatin, Tennessee • *Accounting*

Broward Community College • Coconut Creek, Florida • *Accounting*

Professional Membership

International Association of Hospitality Accountants • Member since 1980
Currently serving a second 1-year elected term as *Treasurer* of the Nashville Chapter.

accounting. Inquiries from recruiters and hotel management companies prompted the resume. In the Experience section, responsibilities are indicated in the paragraph after the job title for the first three positions mentioned. Achievements are then bulleted. For the earliest two jobs, duties are bulleted.

DONALD P. ROWING

15 Church Street
East-West, PA 11111
(123) 456-7890

PROFESSIONAL PROFILE

Dedicated performer with 12-year track record of improving cash management systems, developing information systems, and establishing key analytical tools for management team within a manufacturing environment. Scope of experience includes:

- General & Cost Accounting
- Foreign Subsidiary Conversion & Consolidation
- Procedures & Policies Development
- Strategic Planning
- Leveraged Buyout Accounting
- Forecasts & Financial Analysis

HIGHLIGHTS OF EXPERIENCE

- Identified and developed key manufacturing ratios which enabled plant management to think in terms of bottom-line improvement. Sold concept to management who implemented concept resulting in improved margins.

- Implemented cost reduction program. Developed detailed annual budget for every expense and line item. Developed monthly forecast and built financial analysis models, making department heads accountable for cost reductions.

- Reduced fixed operating expenses that contributed four percentage points to bottom line through the development of chart of accounts to measure and inform users of the dollar value of activities. Extended to detail reporting by department so that every expense category had accountability by one person.

- Identified inefficiencies in external reports required to collect data for workers compensation. Made recommendations to reclass staff and facilitated measurement systems which substantially decreased costs.

- Contributed to record-breaking annual income in 1993 of $1.4 million by saving $200,000 through the development of new accounting systems.

- Effectively interfaced with other departments to develop and design financial and forecasting models which included personnel requirements and needs.

- Recognized by company president as line of defense in reference to cost capital projects, natural expense items, cost overruns, inefficiencies, and holding staff to budget.

- Key proponent for top management in leveraged buyout. Acted as liaison between top management and the seller, interfacing with consulting team. Prepared all financial elements of the prospectus including one- and five-year pro-forma forecasts for all potential investors.

- Developed and improved financial statements which includes labor and overhead inventory valuation, detailed variance reporting, product segmentation reporting, statistical ratios, and trend reporting.

97

Combination. *Deborah S. Edwards, Wellsboro, Pennsylvania*
A challenge for this resume was to help the individual recognize his strengths and eligibility for competition in the employment market. The Profile indicates breadth of experience by

EXPERIENCE

Controller   XXXX to Present
MANUFACTURING, INC., East-West, PA
  Supervise accounting department of five plus hold responsibility for $15 million annual budget for
  this 170 person facility. Maintain integrity of all company financial and reporting systems. Assist
  all department heads in reporting concerns. Prepare short- and long-term budgets and forecasts,
  and monthly financial statements.
  - Developed accounting structure for entire company.
  - Developed closing schedule. Cut publication time of monthly statements by two weeks. Lead
    all divisions in timeliness and accuracy.
  - Developed and improved financial statements which include labor and overhead inventory
    valuation, detailed variance reporting, product segmentation reporting, statistical ratios, and
    trend reporting.
  - Implemented monthly and three-month forecasting program by department head for revenue
    and expenses.
  - Spearheaded cost reduction program where each expense line item is assigned to an individual
    for accountability.

Consultant   1987 to 1991
East-West, PA
  Provided expertise to small businesses as adjunct to full-time MBA pursuits.

Supervisor of General Accounting   1981 to 1987
FOUNDRIES, Bloss, PA
  Maintained general ledger of Ward and its foreign subsidiary. Supervised Accounts Receivable,
  Accounts Payable, and General Accounting areas. Prepared monthly financial statements.
  - Computer Systems: Selected and installed hardware/software for general ledger systems
    including over 300 accounts, general ledger, and Canadian division's general ledger.
    Introduced Lotus 1-2-3 to organization.
  - Month-end closing / financial reporting: Developed a month-end closing schedule coordinating
    document flow from all departments to MIS and Accounting, resulting in the closing of many
    reporting gaps and reducing closing time 1-2 weeks.
  - Foreign Subsidiary - Canadian Division: Held full accountability for operation's financial activity.
    Identified general ledger discrepancies with supporting detail and resolved problems. Identified
    and corrected all procedural items. Handled foreign conversion and consolidation.

Credit and Collection Manager   1980 to 1981
COMMUNITY HOSPITAL, Tray, PA
  Managed seven employees involved in billing and collection systems.
  - Established the department and set up policies and procedures.

EDUCATION & PROFESSIONAL DEVELOPMENT

Master of Business Administration   Present
SYRACUSE UNIVERSITY GRADUATE SCHOOL OF BUSINESS, NY
  Concentration: Accounting and Management Information Systems.
  MBA Paper: "Spirituality In the Work Place"
  Four courses remaining in a 52-credit-hour program.

BACHELOR OF BUSINESS ADMINISTRATION   1980
ST. BONAVENTURE UNIVERSITY, NY
  Major: Accounting GPA 3.75 Sigma Tau Epsilon Honor Society Member

accounting categories. The Highlights show in depth some significant tasks the individual performed on the
job, major accomplishments, and achievements for which the person received special recognition. In the
Experience section, square bullets point mostly to important accomplishments. See Cover Letter 2.

DANIEL JAMES OLSON, CPA

60 Johnson Court
Stamford, Connecticut 55555

Home: (555) 555-5555   E-mail: DJOlson@prnl.com   Office: (555) 555-5555

CORPORATE FINANCE, ADMINISTRATION & OPERATIONS

Senior Finance Manager with 15+ years of experience in the planning, management and leadership of diverse finance functions. Resolved complex business issues in a fast-paced, dynamic business environment. Delivered strong and sustainable financial gains through cost reduction, cash flow improvement and asset management. Solid general accounting, corporate banking, strategic planning, project management and corporate administration qualifications. Outstanding analytical, problem-solving, leadership, technology and communication skills. PC-proficient. Broad-based industry experience with privately held companies and SEC corporations. Certified Public Accountant.

PROFESSIONAL EXPERIENCE:

Director of Finance / Controller   1993 to Present
TOWN MUSIC GROUP, INC. AND SUBSIDIARIES, New York, New York

Recruited to this $30 million entertainment company and promoted through several increasingly responsible finance and administrative positions. Challenged to identify organizational needs and lead the design, development and implementation of improved business/financial systems, processes and technologies to meet ever-changing operational demands.

Scope of responsibility expands beyond finance and accounting to include banking, credit, treasury, tax, MIS, benefits, insurance, recruitment, training and leadership. Provide finance and management guidance to Operations Managers in geographically-dispersed locations. Participated in corporate development and long-range planning initiatives. Career highlights and achievements include:

- *Accounting, Finance & Budget Management*. Directed accounting, billing/collections, budget development, forecasting, cash management, and financial planning/reporting functions. Partnered finance with core operations to improve communications and provide critical key information to management team. **RESULTS:** Enhanced communications throughout the organization. Revitalized banking relationship and was instrumental in securing improved terms on $3.75 million line of credit.

- *Technology Acquisition*. Managed technology reviews, contract negotiations and internal development projects to automate all accounting, finance and administration functions. Implemented advanced networking systems including automated cash flow forecasting, cash management, payroll and data processing. **RESULTS:** Reduced payroll processing costs by 40%, increased float on cash by $300,000 annually and reduced interest/bank fees by 30%.

- *Operations Management*. Created a cohesive support organization through the introduction of streamlined processes and standardized operating policies/procedures. Maintained positive relations with union leaders and employees. **RESULTS:** Saved $40,000 in payroll expenses and developed comprehensive employee policy manual.

- *Corporate Tax & Reporting*. Conducted a comprehensive evaluation of all corporate payroll, property and income tax filings. Worked with multiple state and federal regulatory agencies and tax authorities to resolve discrepancies. **RESULTS:** Identified and reversed over $200,000 of various state and local tax assessments. Implemented new corporate filing methodologies and saved $50,000 in corporate taxes.

- *Internal & External Communications*. Acted as the liaison between the corporation and outsourced service agencies (legal counsel, outside accountants, and credit card processors). **RESULTS:** Reduced credit card processing fees by $40,000 annually and lowered workers compensation premiums by 25%.

- *Human Resources & Administration*. Recruited, trained and led a cross-functional accounting and administrative staff. Maintained internal HR record keeping systems for more than 600 employees. Managed relations with outsourced payroll service and benefits administrators. **RESULTS:** Improved cash flow by $200,000 through redesign of corporate pension plan.

98

Combination. *Rebecca Stokes, Lynchburg, Virginia*
"The individual had been with a small company for several years and wanted more accountability in a senior-level role." The writer highlights areas of expertise so that a reader can see

DANIEL JAMES OLSON, CPA   **Page Two**

Audit Supervisor   1988 to 1993
OSKAR & COMPANY LTD., New York, New York

Joined this 90-person public accounting practice and given full autonomy for directing multiple audit engagements on behalf of privately held and SEC clients in the real estate, service, distribution and non-profit industries. Assessed audit engagements, delegated specific tasks to team members, compiled data and presented findings to senior partners. Led a staff of six and had direct management oversight for research, quality, training and billing. Member of quality control and internal review committee.

- Identified key areas for improvement throughout the audit department. Designed new systems, processes and tools to expedite audit engagements, and improve the quality, reliability and accuracy of key financial data.

- Developed innovative cash management system to ensure adequate cash flow for client and reduce number of bank overdrafts. Coordinated multiparty communications between the client and its banking institution.

- Facilitated due diligence on behalf of client and major law firm. Outlined key areas in dispute and assisted in the favorable settlement. Participated in the sale of $20 million privately held company to publicly held corporation.

Audit Supervisor   1984 to 1988
MARTIN L. STEVENS & COMPANY, New York, New York

Held full responsibility for the planning/execution of financial audit engagements in the manufacturing, service, distribution and nonprofit industries. Led a cross-functional team of up to six professionals.

- Appointed to the due diligence team for the sale of $12 million company.

- Edited/Enhanced the corporation's audit manual to streamline processes and improve efficiency.

Staff Accountant   1982 to 1984
WOOD PETERSEN STONE & LAWTON, CPAs, Newark, New Jersey

Gained extensive experience in all general accounting practices. Specialized in the research, analysis and preparation of financial statements, corporate and individual tax returns and other financial documentation for a diverse clientele in the entrepreneurial, professional services and manufacturing business segments.

EDUCATION & CERTIFICATION:

B.S., Accounting, 1982
UNIVERSITY OF CONNECTICUT

Certified Public Accountant, 1983

PROFESSIONAL AFFILIATION:

Treasurer, Director & Board Member, Advanced Resources, Inc. (1995 to Present) – Active role in developing the financial infrastructure to support rapid growth and market expansion for this start-up recruitment, staffing and outsourcing business. Automated all finance and accounting systems, established internal controls, and currently manage all corporate tax/financial planning affairs.

the diversity of the person's background with quantifiable results. To see them, look for the RESULTS statement in each of the bulleted statements in the bottom half of page 1. Note the thick bar under each of the section headings. Each bar is a thick line of a specified length determined by the text above it.

JAMES BENNETT CPA / MBA
555 Linwood Avenue, White House, NJ 00000
(000) 000-0000   email-James Bennett@555-net.com   000-00-000-000-000

VICE PRESIDENT FINANCE / CONTROLLER

Evaluating Business Ventures — Improving Profitability — Applying Cost Controls

Highly qualified executive offers broad financial, accounting and business planning background, including both corporate and operations experience.... Proven ability to direct start-up ventures designed to meet corporate objectives.... A team player accustomed to collaborating with sales, marketing and all operating departments.... Experienced in international business operations.

CAREER EXPERIENCE:
INTERNATIONAL MEDIA CORPORATION, London, UK   XXXX-Present
Group Controller/Director of Corporate Finance
Manage financial operations, including corporate accounting and full P&L, of media concerns in eight Central and Eastern European countries. Evaluate new business ventures. Supervise nine direct reports.

Business Ventures
- Monitor and adjust business plans of 18 fledgling enterprises to increase profitability. Work closely with General Managers and Financial Directors, formulating new approaches and identifying new markets. Brought combined operations in two countries into profitability.

Budgets
- Prepare operating budget for entire corporation based on revenues of $275 million. Improved bottom line by $23 million through identifying cost savings and expanding revenue objectives.

Tax Planning
- Lead management in strategically structuring business transactions utilizing tax research. Reduced tax liability by $4 million by proposing realignment of certain entities.

SEC Reporting/Investor Relations
- Direct preparation of all financial aspects of SEC reports. Developed corporate message for investors in conjunction with management team.

MAJOR NETWORK BROADCASTING, US   XXXX-XXXX
(Break in employment while with the National Corps (xxxx-xxxx) is noted in Supplemental Experience section.)
Progressed to senior management level during 13-year tenure with this industry leader with annual billings of $2 billion for Television Station Group division. Scope of positions covered both corporate and operations financial planning/accounting. Promoted seven times.

Strategic Planning
- Developed five-year plans for divisions, including capital budgets. Evaluated acquisitions and divestitures, maximizing returns of business operations and improving cash flow.

Financial Management
- Implemented new approach to evaluating financial data based on principles of "cost drivers" and "benchmarking." Reduced operating and staffing costs by 20% in year-one of use.
- Utilized balance sheet analysis along with P&L to supplement budgeting and forecasting process. Enabled treasurer's office to better manage investment and cash needs.
- Developed a computerized reporting system for senior management in collaboration with internal/external IT consultants. Enhanced decision making through varied data sorts.

Continued....

99

Functional. *Vivian Belen, Fair Lawn, New Jersey*
The resume emphasizes accomplishments in the most marketable areas for an individual who had 15 years with a national network and held nine different job titles during that time. In the

JAMES BENNETT CPA / MBA   Page 2
(201) 000-0000

CAREER EXPERIENCE: (continued)
MAJOR NETWORK BROADCASTING   XXXX-XXXX

Forecasting/Budgeting

- Initiated forecasting function for new ventures and acquisitions. Allowed companies to compete more aggressively for business opportunities, resulting in significant savings such as 37% in equipment leases in one instance.

Accounting Practices

- Spearheaded development and implementation of division-wide accounting policies and internal controls to integrate two diverse corporate organizations (XYZ & Major Network). Produced new policy manual and monitored transition to ensure compliance.

- Improved accounting processes allowing for more timely and accurate closing cycles.

Labor Negotiations

- Part of management team which negotiated union contracts in two major metropolitan areas. Resulted in substantial cost savings and operational effectiveness.

Staff Development/Productivity

- Managed and trained a diverse staff in every position held. Emphasized quality of output and workflow efficiency. Reduced accounting staff by 25% in Red River City operation while improving A/R collections by 15 days.

POSITION TITLES AT MAJOR NETWORK BROADCASTING

Director of Financial Planning, Television Station Group, NY	Assistant Controller, WXX-AM/TV, Boston
Controller, KBTV L.P., Red River City, TX	Business Manager, GWCC/Superchannel, Fresno
Assistant Controller, Radio/Television Group, NY	Manager of Financial Planning, Corporate Headquarters
Financial Manager of Production, Group Y Productions, LA	Accounting Supervisor, Corporate Headquarters
Business Operations Manager, WXX-TV News, Boston	

PREVIOUS EXPERIENCE includes senior-level auditing responsibilities at big six public accounting firm of **Coopers & Lybrand**.

SUPPLEMENTAL EXPERIENCE:
FOUNDATION COLLEGE OF BUSINESS ADMINISTRATION, Warsaw, Poland   XXXX-XXXX
National Corps Business Advisor
Brought on board as advisor to management of a newly formed private business school modeled after American higher education system.

Business Consulting

- Guided development of Foundation's first business plan.
- Trained staff in accounting systems and mentored local businesses in managerial accounting.

EDUCATION/PROFESSIONAL:

Columbia University School of Business -- MBA Degree/Finance
  - Member of Beta Gamma Sigma National Scholastic Honor Society

University of Delaware -- BS Degree/Business Administration & Accounting
  - Magna cum Laude Graduate

Licensed Certified Public Accountant in State of New York

COMPUTER SKILLS:

SAP	Excel	Lotus	Paradox
Word	PowerPoint	Oracle	Hyperion

Career Experience section, underlined subheadings are categories for indicating areas of activity. On page 2, the Position Titles section in small print is like a Work History but without dates. A glance at the entire resume reveals a carefully constructed document with much information that is easily accessed.

RAYMOND MONROE
12 Main Street
New York, New York 00000
(555) 555-5555

SENIOR FINANCE EXECUTIVE

Finance & Accounting Management ... Banking & Cash Management ... Budgeting
Insurance & Risk Management ... Tax & Regulatory Compliance ... Information Systems

Senior-level executive with extensive finance, administration and public accounting experience in diverse industries including retail/wholesale distribution, financial services and manufacturing. Proven ability to improve operations, impact business growth and maximize profits through achievements in finance management, cost reductions, internal controls, and productivity/ efficiency improvements. Strong qualifications in general management, business planning, systems technology design and implementation, and staff development/leadership.

PROFESSIONAL EXPERIENCE

SOUTHINGTON COMPANY • New York, New York • 1991-XXXX
Treasurer/Senior Controller • 1993-XXXX
Corporate Controller • 1991-1993

Chief financial officer appointed to treasurer and Executive Committee member directing $500M international consumer products company. Accountable for strategic planning, development and leadership of entire finance function as well as day-to-day operations management of company's largest domestic division. Recruited, developed and managed team of finance professionals, managers and support staff.

Operations Achievements

♦ Instrumental in improving operating profits from less than $400K to over $4M, equity from $8.6M to $13.6M and assets from $29.7M to $44.4M.
♦ Boosted market penetration by 27% which increased gross sales 32% through acquisition of 25 operating units as key member of due diligence team.
♦ Initiated strategies to redeploy company resources, resulting in 54% increase in gross margin by partial withdrawal from high-risk/low-margin product lines.
♦ Directed annual plan review process and strengthened accountability by partnering with senior-level department and district managers in all business units.

Financial Achievements

♦ Cut receivable write-offs $440K by developing credit policies, instituting aggressive collection strategies and establishing constructive dialogue with delinquent accounts.
♦ Negotiated and structured financing agreements, resulting in basis point reductions, easing/more favorable covenant restrictions and simplification of borrowing process.
♦ Saved over $2M through self-insurance strategy and an estimated $200K annually by positioning company to qualify to self-insure future workers' compensation claims.
♦ Designed executive and management reporting systems and tailored financial and operating reporting system to meet requirements of 100+ business units.

100

Combination. *Louise Garver, Enfield, Connecticut*
[Winning resume of the 1998 PARW Convention Best Resume Contest – Finance Category] This individual had been unemployed for a year and had mailed over 1,000 of his own resume

Southington Company continued...

Technology Achievements

♦ Turned around organization-wide resistance toward automation and streamlined procedures that significantly improved efficiency while reducing costs.

♦ Championed installation of leading-edge systems technology resolving long-standing profit measurement problems and created infrastructure to support corporate growth.

♦ Implemented automated cash management system in over 100 business unit locations and reduced daily idle cash by 50% ($750K).

♦ Recognized critical need and upgraded automated systems to track long-term assets which had increased from $28M to $48.8M in 5 years.

HAMDEN COMPANY • New York, New York • 1987-1991
Chief Financial Officer

Recruited for 3-year executive assignment to assume key role in building solid management infrastructure and positioning $15M company for its profitable sale in 1991. Directed general accounting, cash management, financial and tax reporting, banking relations, credit and collections, data processing, employee benefits, and administration. Managed and developed staff.

♦ Converted company to small business corporation saving $450K in taxes over 3-year period.

♦ Realized $195K in accumulated tax savings through strategies adopting LIFO inventory method, minimizing taxes on a continual basis.

♦ Secured 25% of company's major client base (50% of total sales volume) by leading design, installation and administration of computer-based EDI program.

♦ Reduced collection period from 3 weeks to 5 days by initiating new policies and procedures.

MADISON COMPANY • New York, New York • 1981-1987
Partner

Jointly acquired and managed public accounting firm serving privately held companies (up to $200M in revenues) in wholesale distribution, financial services and manufacturing industries. Concurrent responsibility for practice administration and providing accounting, business and MIS consulting services to corporate clients.

EDUCATION

B.S. in Accounting
New York University • New York, New York

Certified Public Accountant - New York

creations with no response. This writer helped him showcase his achievements in operations, finance, and technology management for a senior-level position as Vice President of Finance. He began interviewing immediately and became "happily employed" as CFO of a large company. See Cover Letter 11.

JOHN HARRIS
555 E. 55st Street
New York, NY 55555
(555) 555-5555

SUMMARY:

- *10 years of senior-level financial management with an established import-export company.*
- *Exceptionally well organized and resourceful with a wide range of financial and accounting expertise.*
- *Successful experience with international transactions.*
- *Ability to work independently and under pressure to meet deadlines.*
- *Proven reliability, stability and honesty in all aspects of performance.*

EXPERIENCE:
11/87-xxxx

FAR EASTERN TRADING, INC.   New York, NY
<u>VP Finance</u> (1/95-xxxx)
<u>Accountant/Controller</u> (6/87-12/94)

- Oversee all financial functions for rapidly expanding, $30 million international trading company (industrial hardware and materials), which includes 3 subsidiaries. The company consists of three offices in the U.S., as well as locations in Hong Kong and China.
- Report directly to President of company and operate independently.
- Control cash and financial management of more than 10 accounts in 4 banks.
- Supervise all bookkeeping functions, preparation of payroll and payroll taxes.
- Authorize payments with full signatory authority.
- In charge of annual and quarterly financial statements.
- Responsible for A/R and A/P reports, departmental performance report, and projection report for the firm.
- Control multimillion dollar operating budgets and analyze variances.
- Supervise, train and evaluate accounting staff.
- Interface with outside CPA firm for annual audit and corporate tax returns.

<u>Accomplishments:</u>

- **Negotiated and secured over $6 million in credit facilities from major banking institutions to finance company expansion.**

- **Cultivated and maintained productive working relationships with banks to facilitate opening and negotiation of L/C's and collection of payments.**

- **Provided key financial advice to President which optimized company resources.**

EDUCATION:

City College, City University of New York, Brooklyn, NY
Bachelor of Science Degree in Accounting, June 1987
Overall GPA: 3.8/4.0, Honors: Dean's List
Grade Point Average (Major): 3.7

SKILLS:

- Microsoft Word, Excel, Lotus 1-2-3

101

Combination. *Etta R. Barmann, New York, New York*
A resume that does not fill a page—that is, does not reach the bottom of it—appears weak.
One way to make information reach the bottom is to widen the left margin—a useful trick.

JOHN HENRY

555 E. Main Street, New York, NY 10017 • (555) 555-5555

PROFESSIONAL PROFILE

Top-producing broker/vice president with strong experience in the financial industry and 12 years of successful background in sales. Proven track record of cultivating and servicing high net worth accounts. Persistent prospector and consultant ranked in the top 10% of current full-service investment firm. Outstanding interpersonal skills with ability to generate a high degree of client satisfaction.

FINANCIAL INDUSTRY EXPERIENCE

Senior Financial Advisor/Vice President-Investments
xxxx-xxxx

John Smith & Co.   New York, NY

- Develop and service high net worth accounts for full-service investment firm with 120 brokers and member of Philadelphia Stock Exchange.
- The firm specializes in IPO's, secondary offerings, and private placements.
- Aggressively prospect for new clients via cold calling, mailings, repeat and referral business.
- Interact with new clients and service existing accounts for a wide range of financial products, including blue chip and OTC stocks, corporate bonds, IRA accounts, options and other investment vehicles.
- Analyze and manage client portfolios based upon investment goals and risk tolerance.
- Research and consult with clients daily regarding new investment opportunities.
- Work closely with in-house analyst on investment recommendations and technical factors.
- Manage all trading functions for discretionary accounts.
- Train and orient new hires in aggressive account development/management.

Highlights

$ Rapidly promoted to Vice President of Investments.
$ Generated a total client portfolio of over $3 million under management.
$ Ranked in the top 10% of brokers for the firm.
$ Generated an average annual return of 45%-55%.

Financial Advisor
xxxx-xxxx

Heller Financial   New York, NY
- Aggressively prospected for clients through cold calling and mailings.
- Developed and serviced clients for the sale of over-the-counter equities.

ADDITIONAL EXPERIENCE

- Previously worked in sales positions in direct mail, radio advertising, and copier equipment sales.
- Have always done exceptionally well with various awards and bonuses.
- Awarded "Sales Rep of the Month" at Garden State Copiers.
- Received Awards at WLCW Radio Station for sales.

LICENSES

Series 7 and Series 63

EDUCATION

Brooklyn College, Brooklyn, NY
B.A. in Business Administration, 1984

102

Combination. *Etta R. Barmann, New York, New York*
Centered headings make it possible for a reader to size up the resume by reading down the middle of the page. A unique feature is the use of dollar signs as bullets for Highlights.

BEVERLY BARRINGER

**222 Anthem Drive
Hancock, NH
55555**

**Telephone:
(555) 555-5555**

**Fax:
(000) 000-0000**

OBJECTIVE:

Financial

Analyst

Series #6 License:

Mutual Bond

Broker

SUMMARY OF QUALIFICATIONS

♦ Competent and experienced financial professional with extensive knowledge of capital markets and investment instruments.

♦ Successful in translating long-range organizational objectives into effective financial plans; sharp analytic, problem-solving and presentation skills.

♦ Involved for eight years in all operations of a start-up company from financing to marketing to production setup.

♦ Language proficiency in Russian, Ukrainian and formerly Portuguese. Computer literate.

PROFESSIONAL EXPERIENCE

**XXXX -   Vice President of Finance / Investments
present   ACME ARMS, Inc.,** Hancock, NH

- Instrumental in the start-up, business plan development for venture capital, financing and production setup for this company
- Conducted proprietary research and analyzed research ideas for various investment instruments, patents and seeking government funding contracts involved in positioning this company to go public
- Develop strategic planning, pricing, marketing, troubleshooting, supervising and ensuring subcontractors meet their obligations
- Perform accounting functions from posting to preparing balance sheet as well as other financial statements and reports

**19XX-XX   Treasurer on the Board of Directors
ST. BARTHOLOMEW'S CREDIT UNION,** South Central, NY

- Prepared and analyzed monthly statements and reports for this credit union with total assets of $21M and 50,000 members
- Developed and implemented mortgage policy incorporating FNMA guidelines; dealt directly with membership in refinancing loans and financial counseling
- Collaborated with attorney and collection manager in developing a successful collection policy and procedures

**19XX-XX   CMA / Coordinator
MERCURY CAPITAL MARKETS,** Lexington, VA

- Developed standard operating procedures to ensure that cash or securities were deposited in clients' accounts; bonded and trusted with funds
- Used the Quotron and computer terminals to perform financial functions

EDUCATION

MBA, Finance, International Finance
Post University, New York, NY

MA, Russian Language, Central State University
BA, Slavic Languages & Science, Central State University, Burdock, VA

PROFESSIONAL MEMBERSHIPS

Association of MBA Professionals, Inc.
Post University Alumni Association
Central State University Alumni Association

References furnished upon establishment of mutual interest

103

Combination. *Susan Guarneri, Lawrenceville, New Jersey*
The column with a border for the contact information, Objective, and Profile is unique. The person's education and multiple language skills are impressive. See Cover Letter 7.

JAMES W. MANCHESTER
55 Jamison Drive · East Carlton, New York 55555
(555) · 555-5555

SENIOR MANAGEMENT EXECUTIVE
General Management · Business Planning & Development · Financial Management
Marketing · Staffing · Training · Team Building · Customer Relations

PROFILE

Accomplished, results-oriented professional with over 20 years of senior level management, marketing and public relations experience in the financial services/insurance industries. Extensive knowledge of finance, insurance products and operations. Strategic and tactical planning, decision-making, communication, and problem-solving abilities. Expertise in introducing the systems and processes that build revenues, boost productivity, enhance customer service and strengthen employee performance/satisfaction. Bottom-line-oriented with a consistent record of exceeding standards and expectations – delivered strong operating and financial results in highly competitive markets. Computer capabilities include Windows, MS Word, MS Excel, Lotus 1-2-3, E-mail, Internet.

Allied Insurance Group, Syracuse, NY · **July 1993 - present**
VICE PRESIDENT MARKETING (East Division)
· Directed marketing operations for a territory covering 11 northeast states.
· Managed all activities related to the marketing of specialty insurance programs to independent, general, lender and point-of-sale agents for Allied Insurance Group (a specialty insurance company).
· Managed two division marketing representatives.

Stanley Funding Corp., Syracuse, NY · **November 1992 - July 1993**
MANAGER (Manufactured Housing Division)
· Managed all activities associated with origination of manufactured housing loans from manufactured housing dealers and private sales.
· Managed staff, whose duties included marketing, credit, loan document preparation, closings, and collection activities through to repossession.
· Served as insurance agent for individuals purchasing homeowners insurance.

United Financial Services, Inc., Syracuse, NY · **January 1987 - November 1992**
PRESIDENT
· Total operations management responsibility for UFSI, a company involved with originating and servicing manufactured housing loans for various banks, located in New York and several New England states.
· Coordinated all activities involved with originating and servicing loans including marketing, credit, loan document preparation, closings, and collection activities through to repossession.
· Served as insurance agent for individuals purchasing homeowners insurance.

National Manufactured Housing Credit Corp., Syracuse, NY · **June 1969 - January 1987**
REGIONAL VICE PRESIDENT (Albany Office)
· Directed all duties and activities of a staff of 30 employees including marketing, credit, loan document preparation, closings, and collection activities including repossession.
· Facilitated the purchasing/servicing of two large portfolios of manufactured housing loans throughout 30 states.

EDUCATION
A.A.S., Accounting, Hudson Valley Community College, Troy, NY

Business Administration (1 year), Russell Sage College, Albany, NY

LICENSES
New York State Insurance Brokers License · 1972 - present

PROFESSIONAL AFFILIATIONS
Director, New York State Manufactured Housing Association · 1996 - present

104

Combination. *Barbara M. Beaulieu, Scotia, New York*
A resume for a high achiever who earned a two-year degree and attended college for a third year. Boldfacing makes evident his impressive career path of successful marketing.

Michael Davidson

72 Longfellow Road
East Anyplace, MA 00000

(555) 555-5555
E-mail: xxx@123.com

SUMMARY

Senior Financial Executive with 20 years of experience in finance and strategic management. Diverse background in large and small, national and multinational, and public and private companies. Outstanding record formulating and implementing long-range financial strategies. Leadership role in driving information technology systems. Demonstrated ability in streamlining presentation of financial data. Extensive experience with restructuring and mergers and acquisitions.

PROFESSIONAL EXPERIENCE

PUBLISHING COMPANY, Boston, MA   1996–present
A $75 million NASDAQ multinational publishing company.

Vice President, Treasurer & CFO
- Reengineered company's finance function including policies, procedures, and personnel.
- Restructured company's IT function, including new hardware platform and business system.
- Built relationships with investor constituents through presentations, conference calls, and shareholder meetings.
- Redesigned $7 million retirement fund, generating 25 percent increase in returns.
- Initiated and designed company-wide commission and incentive plans based on performance.
- Achieved $250,000 in savings by outsourcing key functions.

PRINTING COMPANY, Worcester, MA   1994–1995
A $10 million printing company.

Executive Vice-President – CFO/COO
- Developed cash management funding process covering receipts, disbursement, and capital.
- Initiated and facilitated design, search, and implementation of company's outsourcing strategy.
- Negotiated credit lines with key vendors.
- Negotiated new working capital revolving credit facility.
- Participated in $5 million private equity placement.

FOOD AND BEVERAGE COMPANY, Waltham, MA   1991–1994
A $500 million food and beverage company.

Senior Vice President – CFO
- Restructured Finance function into peak performing team with improved internal controls, reporting, budgeting, and strategic planning processes.
- Right-sized strategic business units resulting in annual savings of $15 million.
- Redesigned working capital strategy generating an improvement of $8 million in annual cash flow.
- Negotiated $30 million credit arrangement with new lenders reducing annual fees by $450,000 and improving cash availability by $6 million.
- Directed the design and implementation of an information technology strategy including the development of a technology center-based integrated desktop and data center technologies incorporating the use of Local Area and Wide Area Networks.
- Restructured balance sheet including $50 million in subordinated debt.
- Authored and implemented performance-based management incentive programs consistent with the company's strategic imperatives.

105

Combination. *Wendy Gelberg, Needham, Massachusetts*
The challenge of this resume is "to turn two potential liabilities—a diverse rather than a specialized background and several relatively short jobs—into advantages." The Summary section

Michael Davidson   **Page 2**

HIGH TECH COMPANY, Hudson, MA   1975–1990
A $1 billion multinational NYSE high-tech company.

Corporate Controller (1987–1990)
- Reorganized the company's financial control functions to improve the flow and organization of management information.
- Established a Financial Systems Planning Group to identify, develop, and implement management information strategies.
- Led the corporate downsizing effort resulting in $10 million in annual savings as well as the adoption of outsourcing for a benchmarking program.
- Managed the selection and installation of state-of-the-art general ledger, accounts payable, and report writer systems.
- Formulated and implemented an Activity-Based-Cost approach for the company's central services functions, totaling over $75 million of expenses per year.
- Revised company-wide policies and procedures for initiating, justifying, and approving capital expenditures.

Assistant Corporate Controller (1983–1987)
- Led the installation of financial reporting system within the company's domestic divisions with sales in excess of $500 million.
- Managed the design and implementation of a cost-management system for the company's domestic operating divisions, resulting in savings of $75 million.
- Improved the annual operating budget process to focus on shareholder value generated by cash flow, as well as to provide a forum for participation by business-unit management.
- Formulated strategy for transfer-pricing activities resulting in the adoption of corporate policies governing all foreign and domestic intercompany product transactions.
- Managed the company's management development program for the finance function.

Controller (1981–1983)
- Integrated new acquisition into the finance function of the parent company. Reorganized the control function. Initiated and formulated product-line and customer-profitability reporting. Introduced PC-based contingency planning/budgeting process.

Controller (1975–1981)
- Introduced product-line and geographical profitability reporting. Modified sales and marketing personnel incentive programs to include expense control and working capital factors. Executed due-diligence and financial justification efforts on acquisition candidates. Designed financial strategy to revise and expand telemarketing program. Installed products cost controls eliminating annual inventory shrinkage.

EDUCATION

MBA Harvard Business School, Boston, MA
BS Williams College, Williamstown, MA

PROFESSIONAL AFFILIATIONS

Financial Executives Institute, Institute of Management Accountants, Treasurers' Club/Boston

emphasizes the breadth of his experience "to broaden his marketability." His leadership in companies in transition increases "his marketability in the current economy." Noteworthy are the italic explanations of company names, the many quantified achievements, his education, and the professional look of the resume.

WILLIAM ANDERSON

1044 Causey Road
Poughkeepsie, NY 00000
(555) 555-5555

WILLING TO RELOCATE

SENIOR FINANCE & ADMINISTRATION EXECUTIVE

Mortgage Banking / International - Commercial Banking / Savings & Loan / Consulting
Financial & Operations Analysis / Information Technology / Team Building & Organizational Leadership

Results-oriented professional with strong managerial, administrative, and problem-solving skills and over 20 years' experience directing domestic and international finance for challenging and complex operations. Accomplished in strategic planning, negotiating, and legal analysis. Combine cross-functional performance success to improve operations and maximize profits. MBA degree. Functional areas include:

- Financial Accounting
- Change Management
- Risk Management
- Banking Relations

- Treasury
- Credit / Collection
- Audit / Compliance
- Taxation

- Servicing Portfolio Management
- Pension & Benefits Administration
- Property Management
- Contract Administration

CAREER HISTORY

SENIOR VICE PRESIDENT, *National Bank, New York, NY*　　　　　　　　　**xxxx to Present**

Develop and lead the complete finance function for this full-service residential and multifamily mortgage banking company. Management accountability includes: strategic planning, loan administration, treasury operations, human resources, and regulatory affairs. Serve as Chief Financial Officer, Corporate Secretary, Treasurer, Compliance Officer, and Legal Liaison. Quality Control Management Committee member.

- Introduced strategic plans, financial controls, and information technologies to reduce operating costs and strengthen administrative processes, representing over $1 million in annual savings.

- Served as the coordinator of a quality control task force to ensure policy protocol which virtually eliminated buy-back demands, conserved capital, and avoided $250,000 in potential loan losses.

- Led the conversion of a mortgage servicing system from a service bureau to a fully operational in-house system, realizing over $200,000 in annual savings.

- Directed the selection and implementation of a networked mortgage processing and loan tracking system which increased processor efficiency by 100%.

- Excellent working rapport with NYS & NJ Banking Departments, Fannie Mae, Freddie Mac, Ginnie Mae, RFC/GMAC & other lenders.

- Increased servicing fee income over $50,000 annually by instituting a proactive collection process, mitigating losses by negotiating alternatives to foreclosure, and effectively managing REO property.

- Served as the sole company representative in annual review and negotiations for a $10 million mortgage warehousing credit facility. Utilized escrow balances to reduce interest borrowing costs and bank service charges by over $225,000 annually.

- Maintained health insurance premium costs significantly below industry averages for the past 9 years by annually evaluating cost structures of comparable providers and switching plans as dictated.

- Negotiated financial, legal and contractual terms for a 5-year office lease renewal saving $1 million.

106

Combination. *Kristin Mroz Coleman, Poughkeepsie, New York*
This individual too had dual interests in finance and business administration, experience in many fields, and multiple areas of expertise. The headline makes clear the two chief interests, and the

WILLIAM ANDERSON - Page Two

CAREER HISTORY cont.

VICE PRESIDENT/CONTROLLER, *International Bank, New York, NY*   **xxxx to xxxx**

Led the Bank's entry into the US market. Established the strategic plan, operational objectives, organizational structure, and facilities layout. Managed the accounting, operating and administrative functions of the Branch including: human resource administration, tax planning, regulatory and management reporting, operations analysis, and investment analysis.

- Acted as the Branch liaison with all regulatory authorities, external auditors, tax and legal counsel.
- Developed the Branch operating policies and procedures.
- Monitored the money market trading and money transfer operations.
- Developed and implemented strategies to maximize the benefits of the Branch's IBF.

INDEPENDENT MANAGEMENT CONSULTANT, *New York, NY*   **xxxx to xxxx**

Consulted for savings and loan association, identifying and resolving internal control problems concerning correspondent transactions with other financial institutions.

- Recovered in excess of $500,000 in funds not received.
- Recorded over $150,000 of income not booked.
- Developed procedures to enhance internal control in paying & receiving, branch proof settlements, bank reconciliations and abandoned property.

SENIOR VICE PRESIDENT/FINANCE, *Savings & Loan, New York, NY*   **xxxx to xxxx**

Managed the accounting and treasury activities and strategic planning of asset and liability structure in different interest rate environments. Accountable for funding the Association through money markets and the Federal Home Loan Bank for investment and liquidity needs. Served as Reporting Officer on the Board of Directors' Investment, Budget, and Salary Committees. Member of the Loan Committee.

- Implemented cost reduction programs to minimize the effect of operating expenses on profitability.
- Evaluated the impact and coordinated the sale and leaseback of bank-owned buildings.
- Successfully restructured nonperforming commercial loans to create earning assets.

SENIOR CONSULTANT, *Investment Company, Inc., New York, NY*   **xxxx to xxxx**

Developed and conducted consulting assignments for domestic and international financial institutions.

- Designed and implemented an integrated planning and reporting master plan for a major international bank in Sydney, Australia.
- Evaluated the feasibility for a leading credit card association's proposed entrance into the travelers cheque market.
- Assisted a major New York bank in establishing a branch operation in Madrid, Spain.
- Assisted foreign banks in establishing operations in New York.

EDUCATION

MBA - Finance, New York University, New York, NY

BS - Finance, State University of New York at Albany

fields and areas of expertise are indicated within the two horizontal lines. Paragraphs after job titles describe responsibilities, and bullets point to accomplishments—many of them quantified. The placement of "WILLING TO RELOCATE" centered in the contact information is a good indication that he *is* willing.

Jennifer Trevalian

150 Spring St., 2A, New York, NY 10003   voice/fax 212-555-5555   e-mail Jtre@aol.com

---

Investment Banking ▪ Telecommunications ▪ Media

- Fast-track and comprehensive career path to Vice President in Investment Banking for IBIS Securities, Inc., the world's largest financial institution. Wide experience in media and telecommunications industries with IBIS; Merril Lynch; Entertainment, Inc.; and Trade Publishing Group. Hold M.B.A. and Certificate in Investment Banking from New York University.

- Originate, execute, and close deals representing a career total of $5.6 billion. Author and deliver dynamic Board of Director-level presentations, achieving bottom-line results through a blending of financial acuity, industry knowledge and humor. Proactively originated and managed 18 months of VP-level projects as an associate. Accomplished in M&A cost analysis, valuation and due diligence.

Areas of Knowledge and Experience

▪ Telecommunications	▪ IPOs and Secondaries	▪ Origination	▪ Client Presentations
▪ Media / Entertainment	▪ Mergers / Acquisitions	▪ Fairness Opinions	▪ Team Building
▪ Equity	▪ Private Placements	▪ M&A Cost Analysis	▪ Research
▪ Equity-Linked	▪ Debt Financing	▪ Valuation	▪ Internet
▪ Fixed Income	▪ Corporate Finance	▪ Due Diligence	▪ MS Office Suite

---

Career Highlights

- **Originated and closed a $15 mm convertible mandate for TELEX (revenue: $4 mm).** Managed origination effort, wrote and led all presentations, partnered with team to execute transaction, and coordinated with CEO of investment banking. Created road show slides, wrote valuation, and performed due diligence.

- **Originated and currently executing a $10 mm private placement mandate for an Internet retailer of entertainment collectibles (anticipated revenue: $700,000).** Created and coled all presentations. Currently working with team to execute transaction. Presently writing valuation and projections.

- **Originated research relationship with Seattle Tech Group (revenue: $50,000).** Persistently contacted client to originate relationship. Authored and led all presentations. Officially commended for presentation's hard facts, energy, and humor.

- **Originated $100 mm IPO mandate for UHC Japan.** Managed origination effort with head of global equity underwriting. Wrote and delivered all presentations and valuation, and performed due diligence. Effort established quality of presentation skills and precipitated IBIS fast-track career path.

- **Assisted origination and closing of $100 mm sell-side M&A mandate for Blueside N.A. (revenue: $1 mm).** Participated in strategic buyer solicitation and closing while an associate (winning bidder: CATR Telecommunications). Performed all valuation work, conducted due diligence in Argentina, and coauthored selling memorandum.

- **Assisted closing of $275 mm buy-side M&A mandate for NA Communications, Inc. (revenue: $1 mm).** Represented buy-side as member of the telco M&A team and cowrote fairness opinion. While an associate, entrusted with sole responsibility for valuation, projections and due diligence

- **Assisted origination of $320 mm IPO mandate for CRT International, Inc.** Performed all valuation work. Cowrote and attended presentations.

107

Combination. *Deborah Wile Dib, Medford, New York*
This investment banker wanted to move to "a larger firm with more growth potential." When a line above text and a line below it appear to be the same distance away from it, the two lines

Jennifer Trevalian

Career Development

IBIS Investment Banking, New York, NY   1995 to present
Vice President in Investment Banking 1998 to present
Senior Associate in Investment Banking 1995 to 1997

■ Corporate finance and M&A advisory services in Media and Telecommunications

Developed relationship and led team effort that won and closed a lead-managed, $15 mm convertible issue for SmallCap telco (TELEX). Currently executing a personally originated $10 mm private placement mandate for Internet retailer of entertainment collectibles. Originated comanaged mandate for $100 mm IPO of cable television operator (UHC Japan). Originated research relationship with wireless telco operator (Seattle Tech Group). Advised privately held Argentine telco on $100 mm strategic sale (Blueside N.A.). Advised Techcast UK on $600 mm strategic sale. Keynote speaker at Cambridge Telecommunications Association.

Entertainment, Inc. (a subsidiary of Doubleday), New York, NY   1995
Corporate Development Consultant

■ Corporate development in Media / Entertainment

Assisted in evaluation of offering memoranda and investment banking proposals. Advised United Media on entry options into comic book publishing, focusing on strategic fit, cross-licensing opportunities, and return on invested capital.

Merril Lynch, Inc., New York, NY   1994 to 1995
Senior Associate in Investment Banking

■ Corporate finance and M&A advisory services in Media and Telecommunications

Won $320 mm IPO mandate for global cable system operator (CRT International). Delivered fairness opinions for $275 mm sale of cable system operators (NA Communications, Inc.). Executed $95 mm collared preferred for News Corp. Co-originated and executed $50 mm IPO of Peruvian telco (Grupo Pantel).

Trade Publishing Group, New York, NY   1993 to 1994
Senior Analyst in Corporate Development

■ Analysis for new business opportunities via acquisition and start-up

Evaluated acquisition candidates in the apparel, trading card and comic book industries for investment banker. Assisted in acquisition of Trade Mag International. Cowrote the "Comic Publishing Retail" business plan. Performed valuation and wrote projections.

Chemical Bank, New York, NY   1992 to 1993
Associate in Investment Banking

■ Corporate finance, corporate restructuring and advisory services

Assisted in start-to-finish origination and closing of buy-side mandate for US Bankers Insurance Group (revenue: $1 mm). Cowrote fairness opinion. Coauthored valuation models and performed due diligence. Involved in capital markets transactions for large cap clients. Total capital raised: $475 mm.

Education, Certification and Registrations

M.B.A.	New York University, New York, NY	1992
B.A.	Fordham University, New York, NY (magna cum laude)	1987
Certificate	Investment Banking (12 credits), New York University, New York, NY	1997
Series 63	Registered under Uniform State Law (Blue Sky)	1996
Series 7	General Securities Registered Representative	1992

appear to enclose that text instead of separating resume sections. The two lines at the top of the page therefore appear to enclose the headline, and the two lines near the middle of the page seem to enclose the Areas of Knowledge and Experience. Quantified achievements stand out. See Cover Letter 21.

SALLY J. LAWRENCE
53 Belvedere Court
Lynchburg, Virginia 55555

Phone: (555) 555-5555   Fax: (555) 555-5555

SENIOR FINANCE & ADMINISTRATION EXECUTIVE
Start-Up, Turnaround, High-Growth & Multinational Operations

Distinguished management career building and leading performance-driven domestic and international finance organizations. Partnered finance with core business operations to achieve sustainable cost reductions, process redesign, revenue growth and profit improvement. Combines expert strategic planning and financial qualifications with strong business management, negotiation and leadership skills. Extensive experience in merger, acquisition, joint venture and divestiture activities worldwide.

- Financial Planning & Budgeting
- Cash & Asset Management
- Tax Planning & Compliance
- General Accounting & Reporting
- Banking & Credit Management

- Multisite Operations Management
- Merger & Acquisition Integration
- Business & Organizational Development
- Cost Reduction & Process Improvement
- Technology & Systems Integration

PROFESSIONAL EXPERIENCE:

ROV OIL TOOLS, INC., Lynchburg, Virginia   1996 to 1998

Vice President of Finance & Administration
Recruited to this $700 million international manufacturing and distribution company formed through consolidation of two U.S. and one Canadian business units. Challenged to facilitate the merger and integration of the entire finance and operating infrastructure to support aggressive growth and market expansion. Held full P&L and accountability for all financial, legal, operations, purchasing, human resources, IS and administrative functions. Recruited, trained and directed a 130+ person finance and administrative staff.

- Played a critical role in the tremendous growth of this global manufacturing organization from revenues of $130 million to more than $700 million in two years.
- Appointed the Senior Financial Advisor to due diligence team. Participated in the identification, negotiation and structuring of 23 individual acquisitions valued in excess of $475 million cumulatively.
- Developed worldwide cash and asset management policies, procedures and reporting systems to control numerous lines of credit, minimize currency fluctuations and ensure compliance with required in-country debt to equity ratios. Provided maximum availability of cash for use in acquisition initiatives.
- Spearheaded the reorganization and integration of 26 distinct operations with multiple manufacturing and distribution facilities. Established the systems, processes and methodologies to create one cohesive operating environment.
- Restructured underutilized manufacturing/distribution facilities to maximize productivity and profitability. Delivered $7 million in operating cost savings within one year.

PROGRESSIVE CONSULTING SERVICES, Lynchburg, Virginia   1993 to 1996

Senior Finance & Operations Consultant
Partnered with executive staff of diversified high-tech and manufacturing organizations to create the vision, strategy and action plans to improve revenue, profit and market performance. Developed comprehensive financial analysis/reporting systems, cost reduction initiatives and technology automation programs.

- **Sterling Graphics** (*$175 million multinational software developer*). Restructured international reporting systems to streamline flow of information and enhance decision-making capabilities.
- **K&L Marwick** (*$50 million plastic extrusion manufacturer*). Appointed Interim CFO. Identified several key areas for operational and process improvement throughout the manufacturing, distribution and administrative functions. Positioned business for profitable sale for higher return than originally anticipated.
- **Camden** (*$40 million oilfield equipment manufacturer*). Redesigned the entire manufacturing and product line reporting system. Led cost accounting training for all senior managers.

108

Combination. *Rebecca Stokes, Lynchburg, Virginia*
This Senior Finance Executive had a long-term career with one company, became a consultant
for a while, and then returned to the corporate environment. The resume has the look of an

SALLY J. LAWRENCE Page Two

MYSTIC CORPORATION, Forest, Virginia 1979 to 1993

Advanced through several increasingly responsible assignments at the plant, division and corporate level for this $4 billion diversified manufacturer with operations throughout North America, South America, Europe, the Middle East and Asia. Provided key financial, administrative and operating leadership through rapid expansion, diversification and consolidation.

Controller – Westbury, Inc. (1989 to 1993)

Promoted to Senior Finance position of this $90 million global business unit following major corporate reorganization. Given full management oversight for all finance, accounting, treasury, MIS and administration functions. Challenged to create a cohesive finance organization, implement new technologies, streamline processes and improve reporting capabilities. Led a staff of 15.

- Championed the introduction of PC automation to transition from antiquated mainframe systems. Implemented new operating, costing and reporting processes which significantly enhanced the quality, reliability and accuracy of key financial data.
- Instituted sophisticated financial planning, analysis and modeling processes to guide executive staff in long-range corporate development and strategic planning.
- Participated in the sale of Westbury to leading industry competitor in 1992.

Manager of Business Development – Corporate Headquarters (1987 to 1989)

Selected by CEO to participate in the development of strategic business plans to redeploy $1.5 billion in corporate assets in the U.S. and abroad following hostile takeover and severe decline in market performance. Conducted a complete financial assessment of eight core business units and more than 20 core product lines to identify areas for consolidation, divestiture and/or reengineering.

- Instrumental in the divestiture of four nonstrategic business operations. Increased cash flow by $120 million and provided critical capital needed to pay off debt and increase corporate value.
- Completed a six-month, on-site project in Germany to facilitate the liquidation of all corporate assets following divestiture of subsidiary operation. Thwarted potential labor disputes and successfully transferred $7 million in tax savings to sister operation.

Controller – RSG Division (1984 to 1987)

Key member of two-person due diligence team. Subsequent to acquisition, was promoted and charged with orchestrating the restructuring and complete integration of all personnel, facilities and assets into the existing corporate business culture. Held full responsibility for finance, human resources and administrative functions of this $7 million niche product subsidiary.

Controller – Seacrest Division (1982 to 1984)

Promoted to newly created, high-tech division. Established the systems, processes and methodologies critical to market success of the operation which now generates $250 million in annual revenues.

Plant Controller – Sutter Division (1979 to 1982)

Prepared justification, investment program and participated in the start-up of a greenfield manufacturing facility which grew to $60 million in annual revenues within two years.

STONE COMPANY, Forest, Virginia 1972 to 1979

Product / Cost Accounting Manager – Various Locations

Tenure was distinguished by rapid promotion subsequent to an intensive 18-month management training program. Held full responsibility for analyzing key manufacturing processes and product lines for 20 facilities (U.S. and Puerto Rico) to determine most efficient and profitable means of production for the $1 billion beverage division. Contributed to significant cost reductions through the transfer of manufacturing processes between facilities to maximize plant capacity and enhance cost effectiveness.

EDUCATION:

BBA – Business & Accounting, University of Virginia, 1972

executive resume. This look is achieved by smaller point sizes, narrower margins making wider lines, tasteful horizontal lines, restrained use of font enhancements, and many single blank lines for white space. Her degree was in business and accounting; her career displays this double focus.

THOMAS L. JONES
2482 Rainbow Street
Somewhere, USA

xxx/xxx-xxxx
xxxxxxx@aol.com

CAREER PROFILE

Senior Financial Executive/Certified Public Accountant with 18 years' experience in corporate accounting and 10 years' experience in operations management. Precise, detail-oriented, and analytical. Areas of expertise include:

- Operations Management
- Financial Planning/Analysis
- Bankruptcy and Corporate Restructuring
- Cost Accounting
- Public Speaking & Presentation

- Mergers & Acquisitions
- Strategic Planning/Budgeting
- Asset Liquidation
- Credit Lines/Administration
- Customer Management

PROFESSIONAL EXPERIENCE

Nationwide Company, City, USA   1995 - Present
Chief Financial Officer
Direct all corporate accounting, cash management, and finance functions within a $227 million budget. Manage general accounting services AP/AR, MIS, data processing and budgeting departments. Liaison between customers, management, and Board of Directors.
- Renegotiated $16 million bank line of credit
- Developed criteria and bid proposal for new accounting hardware and software, resulting in a 10% cost savings and more efficient processing
- Led corporation through bankruptcy proceedings; successfully liquidated $32 million in assets during reorganization
- Negotiated and executed transaction for the Affiliated of Florida/Associated Grocers merger

Certified Public Accounting Firm, City, USA   1994 - 1995
Manager
Handled accounting services for a variety of corporations and small businesses. Prepared monthly general ledgers, bank reconciliations, financial statements, trial balances, monthly payroll and sales taxes, quarterly reports, and corporate and federal income taxes. Processed payroll and payroll summary reports.
- Took business from ground zero to $50,000 in less than one year

National Telecommunications Company, City, USA   1984 - 1994
Director of Finance
Recruited to serve as Interim Western Region Operations Manager. Performed all divisional accounting and finance functions within a $100 million budget. Selected to join Mergers and Acquisitions team. Handled all financing, maintenance, accounting and sale of corporate fleet of over 500 vehicles and equipment.
- Lead M&A team on four successful mergers ranging from $50,000 to $5 million
- Appointed as Project Manager on a troubled $3.5 million project; successfully resolved client issues resulting in full payment from a satisfied client
- Implemented cost accounting programs in 25 national and 5 international field offices resulting in greater reporting efficiency
- Restructured operations resulting in net profit of $60,000 per month

Certified Public Accounting Firm, City, USA   1981 - 1984
Certified Public Accountant
Performed client auditing; tax compliance, preparation and planning; and bankruptcy and corporate restructuring services.

109

Combination. *Cynthia Kraft, Valrico, Florida*
Horizontal lines enclosing the Career Profile ensure that it will be seen. In the Professional Experience section, boldfacing of the job titles makes them readily seen if you look down

THOMAS L. JONES   Page 2

EDUCATION

Minimum 40 Hours Annual Continuing Education including updates on Accounting & Auditing, Tax, Bankruptcy, and Small Business Finance

Certified Public Accountant - Florida State Board of Accountancy, 1992

Certified Public Accountant, South Carolina State Board of Accountancy, 1982

B.A., Accounting, minor in Finance, 1979
University of Florida, Gainesville, Florida

PROFESSIONAL AND CIVIC AFFILIATIONS

Florida and American Institute of CPA's
Member, Tampa Chamber of Commerce
Past President, Local Chamber of Commerce

the left margin. Each paragraph after a job title shows the person's responsibilities. Bulleted items after the paragraph point to quantified accomplishments. The rhythm of responsibilities paragraph, bulleted accomplishments, responsibilities paragraph, bulleted accomplishments, is sustained throughout the section.

Joseph Financial, CPA

10 Money Terrace
Cash, New Jersey 07040

Home: (201) 555-5555
Office: (212) 444-4444

PROFILE

Chief Financial Officer with a proven record of accomplishment and growth within Financial Services, Manufacturing and Services industries. Areas of expertise include, but are not limited to:

- Financial Operations
- General & Futures Accounting
- Budget Preparation & Management
- Consolidated Financial Statements

- Purchasing & Inventory Control
- Corporate Taxation
- Auditing & Compliance
- Systems Development & Conversions

EDUCATION & CERTIFICATION

M.B.A., Financial Management, Rutgers University

B.S., Accounting, New York University

Certified Public Accountant, State of New Jersey

PROFESSIONAL EXPERIENCE

A MAJOR COMMODITY EXCHANGE, New York, New York   March xxxx - Present

Controller

Maintain full oversight for General Accounting. Budget, Financial Operations and Purchasing areas, directing the activities of 17 professional and support personnel. Delegated with the responsibility to maximize the financial performance of the Exchange by designing and implementing procedures and Systems that strengthen and improve Internal Controls, enhance Financial Reporting and facilitate smooth operation through automation and process reengineering.

Accomplishments:

- Effected a seamless transition during merger with COMEX. Fully absorbed operations and accounting systems, with little or no downtime, while significantly reducing labor costs.

- Instrumental in the functional design of newly implemented client-server-based Accounting software application (Computron) for general ledger, accounts payable / receivable, purchasing and fixed assets.

- Linked control systems for capital expenditures and contracts to the accounting system via purchasing module.

- Developed approach to implement and enhance data storage and work flow software.

- Skilled in accounting software systems, security administration functions and system setup.

- Identified error in previous corporate tax filings resulting in an $80,000 refund upon amended filing.

- Integrated and authored a comprehensive Policies and Procedures Manual.

- continued -

Combination. *Judith Friedler, New York, New York*
"A straightforward resume." Its uncluttered look is achieved through ample white space (many blank lines). The distinctive set of horizontal lines under the contact information is repeated as

Joseph Financial, CPA
Page Two

PROFESSIONAL EXPERIENCE (cont...)

XYZ TRADING CORPORATION, Livingston, New Jersey   August xxxx - March xxxx

Controller / Chief Financial Officer

Directed fiscal operations of XYZ Trading Corporation and its subsidiaries, U.S. Trading, Nassau Films. Nassau Films International and Supro Trading. Responsible for developing strong relationships with banks and other financial institutions. Negotiated bank financing and foreign/domestic letter of credit arrangements. Analyzed potential acquisitions.

Accomplishments:

- Established credit and collection policies and procedures, ultimately improving cash flow and reducing delinquencies.
- Directed computer conversion of software on a PC network.
- Instituted controls and reporting procedures to facilitate multiplant operations.

CS&C COMMODITY EXCHANGE, New York, New York   May xxxx - August xxxx

Controller

Managed general accounting, financial statement preparation, budgeting, corporate tax returns, accounts payable/receivable, fee auditing, payroll and benefits administration functions for the Commodity Futures Exchange. Wholly involved in corporate strategic planning processes.

Accomplishments:

- Implemented fixed asset software program.
- Redesigned and standardized monthly closing procedures.
- Improved monthly and quarterly reports by greater utilization of general ledger software package and Lotus 1-2-3.
- Adapted accounts receivable software program.

GLOBAL PUBLISHING INC., Summit, New Jersey   September xxxx - May xxxx

Assistant Treasurer / Controller

Performed financial control functions for $45 million international publishing company, including financial statement consolidation, general accounting, cash management and forecasting, budgeting, federal and multistate tax returns, accounts receivable/payable, payroll/ benefits administration, cost and acquisition analysis.

SKILLS

- Proficient in numerous Accounting systems and software, including Computron, Solomon, Real World, SBT, MCBA, Excel and Lotus 1-2-3.

part of a header on page 2. The Profile concludes with a two-column list of bulleted areas of expertise. Education is put second to display the M.B.A and the person's certification as a C.P.A. An "Accomplishments" subhead precedes each list of bulleted achievements.

THOMAS FRIEDMAN

3739 Woodcrest Drive
Akron, Ohio 55555
(555) 555-5555

CORPORATE FINANCE / ADMINISTRATION / ACCOUNTING / MIS EXECUTIVE
Strategic Planning / Financial Analysis / P&L Management / Performance Improvement
Corporate Banking & Lending / Debt Management / Cash Flow / Auditing / Budgeting / Forecasting

Well-qualified Controller / CFO with 15+ years experience building and directing corporate finance organizations. Contributed to significant cost reductions and revenue/profit improvements through reengineering, team building and leadership expertise. Skilled negotiator and analyst. IPO experience.

PROFESSIONAL EXPERIENCE:

Controller/CFO   1998 to Present
JONES REFRIGERATION INC., Akron, Ohio
(100-year-old manufacturer with two U.S. locations and affiliated companies in Puerto Rico and Central America)

Recruited to corporate headquarters to provide strategic/tactical financial leadership. Primarily focused on reducing overhead costs, modernizing/enhancing organizational capabilities, and introducing new processes through technology automation. Conduct ongoing analyses of individual departments to maximize operational efficiencies, increase autonomy and ensure accountability through establishment of internal controls.

- Initiated the upgrade of leading edge technologies to automate processes, expedite workflow, and accommodate business growth. System will provide the groundwork for MRPII Manufacturing System, and introduce state-of-the-art software in all departments.
- Directed cross-functional project team efforts (engineering, marketing, finance departments) to create an effective job cost system. Utilized a more efficient process of checking and reviewing contract compliance and delivered 10-15% cash flow increase on all projects.
- Implemented improved sales processing system capable of tracking orders from start to finish. Resulted in a more efficient and expedient billing/collection process.
- Designed/Implemented departmental budget/goals, partnering finance with core operations. Established capital needs assessment program to provide key data for use in long-range corporate planning.

Controller/CFO   1989 to 1998
WESTOVER MANUFACTURING INC, Akron, Ohio
(140-year-old, multicompany building materials distributor)

Member of the Senior Executive Team with full responsibility for the strategic planning and leadership of all financial, treasury, accounting, budgeting, administrative and MIS operations for the corporation. Recruited by President/CEO to reengineer the entire finance/administrative function, upgrade reporting capabilities, improve cash availability and manage financial resources for sustained market growth.

- Designed and implemented a comprehensive program of internal controls for A/R, A/P, cash flow and purchasing to ensure the complete and accurate documentation of all transactions.
- Selected hardware/software and directed installation of PC technology for general accounting, financial reporting, financial analysis, purchasing and materials management functions. Facilitated development of customized applications for perpetual inventory and customer margins. System improved cash flow by increasing inventory turns by 10 per year and enhancing the operational efficiency of the corporate purchasing function.
- Established a credit and collection policy which reduced A/R days outstanding by an average of 7-10 days through a system of standardized weekly reporting and customer follow-up.
- Replaced debt with other institutions for more favorable financing, better payment terms and interest reductions averaging 2%-3%.
- Revised risk management function for the entire company, reducing custody 10-15%.
- Developed new health/welfare system which increased benefits and saved more than $40,000.
- Initiated a 401K program for personnel, resulting in a savings of 15-20% in pension benefits.

111

Combination. *Rebecca Stokes, Lynchburg, Virginia*
An executive resume displaying small type, narrow margins, wide lines, and therefore much information representing considerable experience. The reader is more apt to see the opening

THOMAS FRIEDMAN   *Page Two*

PROFESSIONAL EXPERIENCE *(Continued):*

Subsidiary Controller   1985 to 1989
LGI SERVICES CO. / JOHNSON SYSTEMS, INC.
(Turnkey waste management subsidiaries of B&G International, Inc.)

Recruited as a Financial Analyst/Planner with Johnson Systems, Inc. (Akron, Ohio). Accountable for monthly summaries, year-end closing schedules, and monthly financial analyses for Board of Directors and executive management. Created financial reports (Lotus 1-2-3, Report Writer), and maintained computerized project management system.

Transferred to sister company, LGI Services Co. (Cleveland) in 1986. Promoted from Financial Analyst to Accounting Manager to Controller. Held full responsibility for all financial affairs for a subsidiary of this $50 million public company. Directed receipt and disbursement of all funds, maintained standard accounting practice and published all financial reports.

- Designed a leading edge job cost system to track project costs, identify overrides and ensure adequate profit margins.
- Worked cooperatively with CEO, Board of Directors, and outside legal and financial counsel to prepare IPO documentation for the SEC.
- Provided financial guidance for multimillion-dollar projects with Alpha Corporation and other key national accounts.

Cost & Budget Analyst   1983 to 1985
TRANSPORTATION USA (THE FELLHOELTER COMPANY), Columbus, Ohio
($200 million, German-owned automotive parts and railroad car manufacturer)

Designed a series of operational, budget, variance, productivity, labor, sales and profit analyses to provide senior management with information critical to long-range planning, reengineering and productivity improvement. Prepared monthly job cost reports that compared actual costs to manufacturing projections, identified variances, and recommended actions to control future expenditures.

Controller   1980 to 1981
INTERIOR WORLD, INC., Cleveland, Ohio
($2 million specialty contractor)

Built a formal accounting and finance function, created internal systems and procedures, established operating and project budgets, and designed monthly reporting methods to improve cash flow. Directed all corporate tax and insurance matters. Trained/Supervised bookkeepers and administrative support staff.

Assistant to Controller   1974 to 1979
JAMES T. HERNDON, INC., Cincinnati, Ohio
($35 million international distributor of rope, tape and agricultural baler twine)

Managed an 11-person Accounting Department and all general accounting, monthly reporting, international banking, letters of credit and foreign financial transactions.

Staff Accountant   1973 to 1974
OMEGA SERVICES, INC., Spring Hill, Ohio

Prepared operational statements and general ledger analyses.

EDUCATION:

MBA / Finance, Purdue University, Lafayette, Indiana
BBA / Accounting, Loyola University, Chicago, Illinois
AAS / Business, Community College of Ohio, Cincinnati, Ohio
Graduate, Cardinal Burbank High School, Cincinnati, Ohio

Continuing Professional Education:

Stephen Smith Effective Public Speaking and Human Relations
Variable Report Writer Program, McLaughlin Software Company, Inc.

profile section as within the horizontal lines rather than as one section in a series of sections separated by horizontal lines. For each position, the writer shows "the unique business environment, organizational challenges, and the individual's role in leading change."

ELIZABETH BLANCHETTE

45 Coffee Road
Philadelphia, Pennsylvania 55555

(555) 555-5555
eblanch@phil.net

Strategic Planning / Business & Financial Management / Corporate Development
Internal Growth / Reorganization & Turnaround Management / Market Expansion & Diversification
MBA Degree / Certified Public Accountant

NOTABLE CAREER ACCOMPLISHMENTS

- Leveraged strategic, operational and financial expertise to facilitate corporate culture change and business process reengineering. Demonstrated transferability of skills across diverse products, services and markets.
- Facilitated strong and sustainable revenue, profit and market performance in public, private, for-profit and non-profit organizations with operations throughout the U.S. and international markets.
- Orchestrated creation and implementation of fully integrated strategic business, marketing and corporate development programs. Managed all projects from concept through tactical execution.
- Recognized for expertise in team leadership, consensus building, partner development and relationship management. Outstanding presentation, negotiation and interpersonal skills.

PROFESSIONAL EXPERIENCE

Senior Vice President / Chief Financial Officer   1994 to 1998
Global Research Association, Philadelphia, Pennsylvania

Recruited to this $20 million diversified organization comprising high-tech scientific research operations, off-shore insurance company and sales agency, and nonprofit association representing the $430 billion food products industry. Facilitated development of strategic plans, concepts and initiatives to drive revenue growth and improve financial position. Operated under the direction of the President/CEO and Board. Held full accountability for the performance of seven disparate business operations, and directed 30 personnel.

Strategic Planning & Business Restructuring

- Spearheaded an aggressive reorganization and redeployment of corporate assets to reverse an ever-increasing annual loss to profitable earnings in three years. Increased revenues by 10% annually while reducing costs.
- Facilitated development of the corporation's strategic business plan outlining short-range and long-term goals. Built consensus across business units and won support of Board of Directors for full-scale implementation.
- Pioneered the introduction of standardized systems, processes, technologies and programs resulting in dramatic improvements productivity, cost control and business management. Revitalized Board's confidence in the capabilities of the management team.

Multiunit Operations Management

- Established cost centers and zero-based budgeting to appropriately allocate resources from declining business to market growth areas.
- Initiated interdepartmental communications, led a series of staff development and training programs, and established performance-based incentives.
- Facilitated the migration from antiquated personal computing system to fully integrated, client/server environment. Installed WAN, e-mail and other communications applications linking geographically dispersed offices and satellite locations.

Business Development & Communications

- Justified need for comprehensive marketing and communications plan to enhance the organization's image and retain membership within a mature industry.
- Managed relations with senior executives from Smith's, Lentz, Ford Summer, Sea Mist and several other industry leaders.
- Initiated transition to a team-based enterprise to meet the diverse and changing needs of the client base.

112

Combination. *Rebecca Stokes, Lynchburg, Virginia*
The person was "heavily focused in Finance" but wanted to move away from the day-to-day
financial role. The writer therefore displayed the individual's specialties in strategic planning

ELIZABETH BLANCHETTE – Page Two

Consultant   1990 to 1993
Southeast Insurance, Philadelphia, Pennsylvania

- *Financial & Investment Consulting* – Successfully transitioned broad financial planning and investment management experience into the consulting arena. Identified business opportunities, assessed client needs, developed customized service portfolio and delivered innovative solutions to diverse client base.
  - Built several long-term relationships with high-net worth individuals and small businesses.

Chief Financial Officer   1987 to 1990
RTS Mortgage Group, Philadelphia, Pennsylvania

- *Finance & Operations Reengineering* – Challenged to design and execute a series of internal financial and operating change initiatives for this national trade association representing the $80 billion real estate financing industry. Assessed all core operations, identified key areas for improvement and developed comprehensive program to streamline functions, reduce costs and strengthen internal controls.
  - Delivered cost reductions through elimination of unnecessary operating functions.
  - Created a structured financial management and reporting system, including organization-wide budgeting, accounting and cash management programs.

Director / Manager   1979 to 1987
TLI Corporation, Philadelphia, Pennsylvania.

Fast-track promotion through several increasingly responsible and diversified management positions with this Fortune 500, publicly held organization specializing in the development of high-tech satellite communications technology for commercial and government clients worldwide. Advanced based on proven success in leading cross-functional business teams and managing high-level financially critical projects. Career highlights included:

- *Turnaround Management* – As **Director of Financial & Operational Audit**, orchestrated turnaround of a 10-person business unit plagued with operating, image and morale issues. Established quality standards, operating guidelines and performance measurement tools.
  - Transitioned the department's reputation from "watch dog" function into a strategic business partner and consultant to core operations.

- *Cash & Investment Management* – As **Treasury Manager**, consolidated geographically dispersed banking activities and renegotiated banking relationships. Additionally, implemented innovative programs for cash management, corporate investments and debt financing.
  - Reduced annual banking fees while improving overall level of service.
  - Delivered significant improvement in cash flow necessary for national and international development projects.

- *Accounting & Reporting* – As **Accounting Manager**, restructured fixed asset accounting and financial reporting systems. Improved communications between corporate headquarters and subsidiary operations.
  - Enhanced the quality and reliability of incoming data for use in preparation of consolidated financial statements.

Associate   1977 to 1979
Morris & Freeman CPAs, Pittsburgh, Pennsylvania

Prepared corporate, partnership and individual tax returns and completed financial audits on behalf of clients in the real estate, construction, education and professional services industries.

EDUCATION

MBA – St. Joseph's University, Philadelphia, Pennsylvania, 1983
BS – Temple University, Philadelphia, Pennsylvania, 1974
Certified Public Accountant

and operations in order to broaden the appearance of her skills. The Career Accomplishments section helps to direct the focus away from just the financial area. The shadowed box around the areas of expertise ensures not only that these will be seen but also that the resume will stand out from others.

STEPHEN SCHRADER

6701 Murietta Avenue ▪ Valley Glen, California 91405 ▪ (818) 994-6655

Senior-Level Financial & Administrative Management Executive

Corporate Finance Executive with extensive experience building, leading and advising corporations through complex turnarounds as well as high-growth cycles. Combines expert strategic and tactical financial expertise with strong qualifications in general management, human resources management and transaction structuring/negotiations. Key team member in structuring and negotiating complex public and private financing, mergers, acquisitions and divestitures. Expert qualifications include:

- Financial Planning and Analysis
- Cash Management and Optimization
- Equity and Debt Management
- Cost Reduction
- Systems Development

- Budgeting (Capital and Operating)
- Banking and ALM Treasury Functions
- General Accounting & Reporting
- Mergers and Acquisitions
- Performance/Profit Improvement

KEY ACCOMPLISHMENTS

✔ Instrumental in raising $81 million in stock rights offering for major Southern California financial institution.

✔ Facilitated private placement of $5 million capital infusion for $14 million company.

✔ Key member of expense reduction task force, reducing overhead by 30% in two-year period for $5 billion company.

✔ Restructured and consolidated infrastructure of $500 million company, realizing savings in excess of $150,000/year.

✔ Implemented complex system conversions, including investment accounting and budget/planning.

✔ Supervised Human Resources/Payroll department for company with staff in excess of 300.

✔ Renegotiated group insurance, increasing employee benefits while reducing company costs by 22%.

✔ Implemented IRS Section 125 Cafeteria Plan.

✔ Member of cross-functional team charged with researching and solving underfunded pension plan problem.

PROFESSIONAL EXPERIENCE

MARQUETTE, FIRESTONE & CRANE, L.L.P. Glendale, CA • xxxx to Present
Formerly Zimetti, Garnet & Torronne

Chief Financial Officer / Executive Director

Recruited by independent CPA firm to plan and implement financial turnaround of multioffice law firm. Given full responsibility for redesigning core financial processes, budgeting, cash management, treasury, banking and long-range investment planning.

- Reengineered financial operations and reduced staffing requirements by 15%.
- Initiated company's first outsourcing program, significantly improving billing and accounts receivable capabilities while reducing annual costs by more than $200,000.
- Orchestrated aggressive cash management policies, increasing value of pension and firm investments by 22%.

113

Combination. *Vivian Van Lier, Los Angeles, California*
This individual had been in banking for many years. In an earlier version of this resume, the writer highlighted quantifiable achievements and de-emphasized the concentration in banking.

PROFESSIONAL HISTORY, continued

THEODORE DIXON, DISTRIBUTOR, INC., Carson, CA • xxxx to xxxx

Controller
Recruited by Chief Financial Officer to reengineer $14 million company and successfully position it for acquisition.
- Directed cash management functions, installed fixed assets accounting system; improved accuracy of financial reporting systems and asset accounting procedures.
- Developed business plans, participated in financial strategy and planning, coordinated preparation of financial statements and liquidity analyses.
- Created timelines, labor allocation resource management and weekly status reports for new operating segment of company.

CITY NATIONAL BANK, Beverly Hills, CA • xxxx to xxxx

Senior Vice President/Controller
Vice President/Manager Financial Planning & Budgeting
Assistant Vice President, Financial Reporting
Achieved fast-track promotions to positions of increasing responsibility.
- Key player in successful stock rights offering, raising $81 million in new capital.
- Implemented complex system conversions, including investment accounting and budget/planning.
- Created and implemented budget and forecasting reports; consolidated unit budgets into divisional/corporate budgets; provided management with estimates of future impact of decisions.
- Coordinated effectively with executive management, branch, department and division managers, audit committees, outside auditors and corporate counsel.

EDUCATION

UNIVERSITY OF CALIFORNIA AT LOS ANGELES
Bachelor of Arts Degree

LOYOLA MARYMOUNT UNIVERSITY, Los Angeles, CA
MBA in progress, completion expected xxxx

Additional postgraduate studies include Accounting, Finance, Statistics, Taxation, Organization Behavior, Project Management, Business Law and Marketing at UCLA School of Management, and Golden Gate University.

COMPUTER LITERACY

Windows, Lotus 1-2-3, Excel, WordPerfect, Peachtree Accounting, Solomon, MAS 90, Great Plains and Microsoft Projects. E-mail and Internet proficient.

MEMBERSHIPS

Institute of Management Accountants — Member Controller's Council
American Management Association
CMA Candidate, xxxx

With that approach, the person was able to obtain his current position in a multioffice law firm. Using this updated version of his resume, the individual has been successful in generating "multiple interviews and several offers." Check marks accentuate the list of quantified key accomplishments.

James T. Robertson

300 Hemlock Road
Nashua, NH 03257
603-555-5555

Senior-Level Executive • Financial Management Professional

**Executive
Summary**

Entrepreneurial CFO-level executive with over fifteen years of quantifiable achievement. Direct financial management and company development for profit and not-for-profit enterprises. Turnaround and lead strategic business units. Teach university courses. Hold MBA in Finance and 88 postgraduate credits in Law and the Humanities.

Cross-industry experience creating and increasing productivity, efficiency, and profitability. Consistently employ an energized, can-do management style utilizing financial analysis skills, organizational abilities, vision, and tenacity. Blend motivation, leadership, creative, and analytical abilities to develop and implement innovative ideas that produce bottom-line results.

**Areas of
Knowledge
and
Expertise**

- Company Formation / Start-up Consulting
- Business / Enterprise Turnarounds
- Strategic / Creative Marketing / Planning
- Budgeting and Forecasting
- Credit Management
- Operations and Financial Analysis
- Financial Statement Generation
- Margin Improvement
- Innovative Program Development
- Corporate Accounting and Tax Preparation

- Human Resources Management
- Fund-raising and Grant Writing
- Acquisition Due Diligence
- High-Level Relationship Management
- Bid Research and Generation
- Contract Review and Negotiation
- Customer Retention Strategies
- Relationship and Team Building
- Training and Mentoring
- Presentation Development / Delivery

**Career
Profile**

Experienced CFO, vice president, consultant, and entrepreneurial business owner. Companies have included The Visiting Nurse Association (V.N.A.) Hospice, a New Hampshire not-for-profit organization; Rialto and Sons, a major Long Island-based waste management firm; Robertson Financing, Inc., a privately owned financial consulting firm; and YMCA of Long Island, Inc., a seven-branch chapter of the national organization.

Offer cross-functional financial, management, troubleshooting, and development skills. Experience as consultant for multi-industry client base provided comprehensive background in property / shopping center management, commercial trucking, construction trades, nursery / garden center, retail, healthcare, and service industries. Abilities are transferable to any industry or venture.

Structure innovative programs / businesses that produce strong and sustainable results. Consistently revitalize and restructure problem organizations or organizational business entities. Expert in solving small business tax difficulties — sales, payroll, and corporate, both federal and state.

Directly responsible for multimillion-dollar company growth, contracts, and accounts. Oversee budgets of up to $4 million and staffs of up to 450 persons. Bid and negotiate million-dollar-plus contracts. Administer intricacies of government-regulated programs including Medicare and Medicaid. Motivate teams to excellence.

114

Combination. *Deborah Wile Dib, Medford, New York*
A resume for an entrepreneurial CFO-level financial management professional. The individual had so much experience that the writer took three pages to display that experience to the

James T. Robertson

Executive Highlights

As CFO, was directly responsible for the construction and implementation of a business plan for Rialto & Sons Private Sanitation that built a profitable $5 million gross revenue stream from an original $400 thousand gross, in only eight years.

Overcame bank's initial skepticism regarding doing business with a "carting company." Developed comprehensive business plan that positioned company for major growth. Plan was so thorough that it persuaded bank to change direction and do new business with a waste management company.

Landed profitable contracts ranging from $100 thousand to $1.2 million. Developed all costs and negotiated all bids for contracted work with three Long Island towns. Generated numerous government, municipal, and commercial accounts.

Ensured, through an innovative arrangement, that a $100 thousand+ annual contract with 35 local U.S. Post Offices remained in effect without utilizing a rebid process.

Formulated the business plan that positioned Rialto & Sons to successfully compete in the post Year 2000 waste management industry. Plan made possible the acquisition of a valuable, revenue-generating transfer station license.

Discovered unadvertised opportunity, researched, and arranged "assets only" purchase of major competitor, holding the largest, three-district contract in the area.

As CFO, turned around operations, established consistent and appropriate business practices, and built staff / client morale for New Hampshire V.N.A. Hospice in financial distress.

Interfaced with board of directors to obtain approval for plans to assess and repair V.N.A. financial health. Instituted controls, teamwork, accountability, and open atmosphere. Overhauled administration of Medicaid payments and numerous federal / municipal programs. Secured new $200 thousand line of credit.

Built constructive relationships between clinical and finance departments. After less than one month with organization was told by staff that the business office had established direction, strength, and normalcy for the first time in years.

As Vice President for Business / Controller, created a $100 thousand surplus that reversed a $125 thousand cash flow deficit for YMCA's Long Island Chapter, in only eighteen months.

Designed and implemented an action plan focusing on operational problems and budgetary issues. Organized specific methods for financial oversight that kept a scheduled pulse on all branch functions, a payroll budget of up to $125 thousand and a paid / volunteer staff of 250 that swelled to 450 in summer months.

Steered operations around distinctly different focus / needs of programmatic / social work staff, business office, and executive director / board. Coined the phrase "**Y**ou **M**ust **C**ome **A**cross" to create successful, humorous fund-raising atmosphere.

As President and founder of Robertson Financing, provided cross-industry financial and tax consulting services to 25+ small- to mid-sized businesses.

Reviewed New York / Long Island client business practices and made substantial suggestions to improve financial, tax, contract, account development, and customer care / retention processes. Specialized in resolution of difficult tax problems, as well as commercial equipment financing/leasing.

Dissolved business when offered an unprecedented challenge and financial opportunity for the autonomous development of a client company — Rialto & Sons.

individual's advantage. The writer wisely broke up the Executive Summary into two paragraphs, and the Career Profile into four paragraphs. Each of the paragraphs is preceded by a one-line focusing phrase in boldface. The Executive Highlights section also consists of small paragraphs. They are grouped, and each

James T. Robertson

Career Development

CFO / Regulatory Compliance Officer   **1997 to present**
V.N.A. Hospice of South Carroll County NH, Inc., Wolfsboro, NH

Oversee long-range financial planning and budget requirements for this $2 million not-for-profit healthcare association. Develop and maintain operational systems for financial functions, billing, and collections. Design and implement effective cost controls. Serve as primary relationship manager for business, government, and municipal representatives. Monitor all administrative and regulatory issues, corporate compliance, patient care issues, antitrust, contracts, and employment law.

CFO / Business Operations Director   **1989 to 1997**
Rialto & Sons Private Sanitation, Inc., Long Island, NY

Hired by owners of this highly respected $5 million waste management / carting business after long association as consultant for development and tax issues. As CFO, was given autonomy to guide daily and long-term operations / planning. Created comprehensive business plan and was directly responsible for account development, contract negations and systems creation that took company from $400 thousand gross to $5 million gross in under ten years.

President   **1985 to 1989**
Robertson Financing, Inc., Long Island, NY

Founder and principal of firm specializing in financial accounting and reporting functions for up to 25 small- to mid-sized businesses in a wide range of industries. Firm also engaged in commercial equipment leasing and financing.

Vice President for Business and Controller   **1981 to 1985**
YMCA of Long Island, Inc., Long Island, NY

Directed one of the YMCA's largest metro area chapters, with seven branches and a corporate budget of $4 million. Administered staff responsible for all business, budget, and financial functions. Managed Capital Improvement and Endowment Funds of $4 million.

Employment in Education

Adjunct Professor   **1978 to 1997**
St. John's University, St. Joseph's College, Dowling College

Education

Master of Business Administration in Finance
Bachelor of Arts, *magna cum laude*
C.W. Post College, Greenvale, NY

64 postgraduate credits toward J. D. degree
St. John's University, Jamaica, NY

24 postgraduate credits toward Master's in English Literature
St. John's University, Jamaica, NY

115 nontransferred credits toward Bachelor of Science in Math
Queens College, Flushing, NY

group begins with a multiple-line statement in boldface. In a shorter resume, the Career Development section might have been just a brief Work History, but in this resume some comment about each position held provides balance. The Education section shows a variety of fields. See Cover Letter 15.

Law-Related
Resumes

LINDSAY JUDGE
XXXX Curving Drive
Anytown, Southern State 55555
555-555-5555

Objective: A Paralegal position

HIGHLIGHTS OF QUALIFICATIONS

- More than 12 years' experience in a variety of office settings.
- Proficient in Word, WordPerfect and Works.
- DOS, Windows 3.1 and Windows 95 and 98 operating systems.
- Dependable, loyal, and honest.
- Accurately type more than 70 wpm.
- Tape transcription.

RELEVANT EXPERIENCE

XXXX **Paralegal**
Mall Magic, Anytown, Southern State
- Temporary, long-term position. Assisted contract attorney in matters relating to leasing of major southeastern consumer mall, including lease renewal and litigation. Also provided support for the attorney in her own private personal injury practice.
- Word processed correspondence and legal briefs from handwritten notes as well as tape transcription and immediate dictation.
- Prepared briefs and drafted notices, motions, and orders and proofread documents for consistency and accuracy.
- Maintained files.
- Prepared billing statements for attorney's time.

XXXX-XXXX **Legal Secretary**
Southern State General Contractors' Licensing Board, Anytown, Southern State
- Assisted attorney in dispute resolution between general contractors and the public in matters pertaining to faulty building practices and licensing matters.
- Prepared hearing and litigation documents to bring contractors before the licensing board.
- Updated computer and hard copy files regarding licensing status of contractors.
- Acted as liaison between staff investigators and attorneys. Provided intake from public regarding disputes with contractors.
-

XXXX-XXXX **Legal Secretary**
Solomon, King and Judge, LLC, Anytown, Southern State
- Provided support for two senior-level attorneys with trial practice in business and major environmental issues. Sorted and priortized mail, handled telephone calls, prepared for client meetings, transcribed tapes, prepared correspondence.
- Prepared briefs and drafted notices, motions, and orders.
- Assisted attorneys in preparation for depositions and major litigation.
- Kept attorney time and prepared billing statements.
- Assisted paralegal in abstracting depositions.
- Assisted in document production in major litigation.
- Opened, closed and maintained files.

115

Combination. *Lynda Lowry, Knoxville, Tennessee*
This Paralegal wants to move from long-term temporary work to a full-time position. The Highlights show skills and worker traits. Bullets point mostly to duties.

AMELIA HENDERSON

4 Baywood Boulevard
Phillipsburg, New Jersey 55555
Home: (555) 555-5000

OBJECTIVE: Seeking paralegal position.

CREDENTIALS

- AAS (Legal Assistant) Degree
- Paralegal Certificate

STRENGTHS

- A very organized, fast learner who works well under pressure and completes projects in a timely manner.
- A people person with excellent verbal and written communication skills.
- Self-reliant and able to work with little supervision.
- Familiar with accounts payable and accounts receivable.
- Proficient in operating office equipment including copiers, multiline phones, fax, and adding machines.
- Type 60-65 wpm and skilled in speed writing.

EDUCATION & MEMBERSHIPS

AAS (Legal Assistant) Degree • Easton State College, Easton, Pennsylvania • 3.34 GPA • May XXXX
~Paralegal Major, Criminal Justice Minor
~Paralegal Association Member

LEGAL COURSEWORK

• Legal Research	• Real Estate Law	• Criminal Law
• Family Law	• Health Care Law	• Constitutional Law
• Business Law	• Wills & Estates	• Litigation

- Participated in minitrials in Litigation, Criminal Law, and Constitutional Law. Conducted research and completed paperwork for each case from beginning to end.
- Prepared legal documents for real estate closings, divorces, and wills. Participated in a real estate closing.
- Attended actual court cases, prepared papers summarizing courtroom events, and gave classroom presentations.
- Previously prepared briefs, pleadings, affidavits, appeals, contracts, initial and amended articles of incorporation, and trust instruments.
- Investigated facts and laws of various cases to determine causes of action and appropriate documents to prepare.

COMPUTER SKILLS

• Westlaw (familiar)	• MS Excel	• Access Database
• MS Word	• Windows 95	• DOS
• WordPerfect	• IBM Systems	• Macintosh Systems

OTHER EXPERIENCE

Bartender • Corner Post Inn • Phillipsburg, New Jersey • 1996 - Present (Concurrent with college attendance.)
Complete drink orders, account for accuracy of cash register, interact positively with customers and coworkers, cover other employees' shifts and work overtime as needed.

Prior 3½ years in another bartender position, and 4 years in retail positions.
Learned importance of customer/client satisfaction, detailed paperwork, accuracy in money management, arriving punctually, and helping team members with shift coverage.

116

Functional. *Carol Rossi, Brick, New Jersey*
A resume for "a new graduate seeking an entry-level position." To offset a lack of paralegal-related work, the writer played up strengths and courses.

SUE ANN McKINERNAY
555 N.W. Parot Portway
Melbourne, FL 55555
(555) 555-5555

LEGAL NURSE CONSULTANT / NURSE PARALEGAL
Registered Nurse, Case Management / Assessment, Charting

In training for legal nurse consulting and nurse paralegal program. Classes include Contracts, Wills, Trusts & Estate Planning; Criminal Law Process; Interviewing and Investigations. Studying all facets of legal process with emphasis in tort law, legal research, litigation assistantship and principles and concepts of legal nurse consulting.

- Over ten years in psychiatric nursing; over six years with case management background
- Registered Nurse, State of NY; Certified Psychiatric and Mental Health Nurse
- Extensive public relations with physicians and patients
- Outstanding troubleshooting/problem solving and communication skills
- Basic computer competency skills; knowledge of Internet research and Windows

EDUCATION

Pursuing A.S. in Legal Nurse Consulting, Hartford Community College, NY
M.A. in Mental Health Counseling, NOVA University, Schenectady, NY
B.S. in Nursing, SUNY College, Buffalo, NY

PROFESSIONAL PROFILE

- Implemented first psychiatric program for Buffalo Hospital.
- Patient admissions, counseling, training, monitoring of medications and follow up.
- Case management of psychiatric patients and shared case management of medical patients with medical nurses.
- Psycho social consults and histories completed upon request from doctor and/or nurse.
- Supervise adolescent and adult psychiatric patients in locked facilities.
- Supervise up to seven employees; engage in team meetings for patient plan of care.
- Interpret physician orders, chart on clients and administer medications.
- Assess client coping skills, using appropriate intervention techniques in coordination with team members; knowledge and experience with various restraints.
- Work with multiple personalities, depression, eating disorder diagnoses, anger, rage, schizophrenics, Satanism, head trauma and bipolar patients.
- Assess and report patient's level of acuity and the necessity for hospitalization.
- Coordinate and mediate patient care between insurance company, primary doctor, and hospital.
- Provide generalized public health nursing services, children's physicals, prenatal and postnatal home visits, education classes in health and sex education for elementary students.

WORK HISTORY

Case Manager	Case Management Affiliated, Albany, NY	XXXX-Present
Clinic Director	Sebastian Medical Care Center, Syracuse, NY	XXXX
Psychiatric RN	Master's Hospital, Syracuse, NY	XXXX-XXXX
Psychiatric Consultant	Nurse Care Association, Syracuse, NY	XXXX-XXXX
Utilization Review	Nurse Care Association, Syracuse, NY	XXXX-XXXX

117

Functional. *Laura DeCarlo, Melbourne, Florida*
The challenge was to combine a nursing background with current training for legal nurse consulting. The focus is on courses and experience; Work History is put last.

PARALEGAL

— FOR ATTORNEY, BANK OR TITLE COMPANY

PROFESSIONAL SKILLS AND STRENGTHS

Minnesota State Notary ... assertive leader ... thorough skills in research, drafting, report tracking and document inspection ... language and writing mastery ... strong presenter and speaker ... highly organized, productive professional with ability to manage tight schedules and reprioritize on short notice ... present polished appearance and remain calm and confident in crises ... high degree of accuracy ... decisive ... stickler for detail and follow-through ... read and speak French.

CHALINA

LEGAL EXPERIENCE

Wills ... Powers of Attorney ... corporate law ... domestic law ... civil law ... criminal law ... estate planning ... UCC filings ... real estate sales contracts, closings and title searches ... divorces.

PROFESSIONAL / WORK HISTORY

JOHNSEN

Large Developer, Mytown, MN   10/94 to present

Lease Administrator for large owner, developer and operator of outlet retail properties. Review, abstracting, renewal and notarization of leases for 14 properties in 19 states ... coordination and supervision of co-workers and subordinates during August '96 [team leader] ... involved in staff training ... drafting and processing of legal documents, including lease terminations and amendments ... monthly and quarterly tracking reports for Leasing and Finance Departments.

Plenton Martin, Esq., Attorney at Law, Hart, MN   08/94 to 10/94 and 11/93 to 01/94

An attorney specializing in real estate, probate, criminal and civil law. Promoted to Paralegal from legal assistant and secretary ... substantial research and drafting of legal documents, as well as changes of venue and criminal matters ... assistance with Civil, Criminal and Probate cases ... heavy interaction with attorneys and clients, including involvement in Circuit and Probate Court proceedings and client interviews ... preparation of probate forms and drafting of deeds (warranty, quit claim and land contracts) ... conservatorship and adult guardianships ... updating of legal volumes.

EDUCATION

My State University, Big Town, MN

BS, Business Administration — Minor in Accounting (tax and government accounting)   1994
AAS, Legal Assisting   1994
Current member of Pre-Law Fraternity and past member of Paralegal Association
Chair, University Speaker Committee; Cochair of Rush Committee, Phi Alpha Delta

5321 31ˢᵗ Avenue
Sheltin MN 00000

(555) 555-0000

TECHNOLOGY SKILLS

PC platform, with the following software:

J. D. Edwards Property Management • ACT • dBASE • Windows • Excel • Lotus 1-2-3 • Westlaw • WordPerfect 5.1 • Word 6 • e-mail

118

Combination. *Beverley Drake, Rochester, Minnesota*
"The design of this resume . . . resembles actual legal documents." A simple clipart graphic makes the resume stand out. Ellipses in three of the sections help to increase white space.

MARTHA SAYLES

333 Morrow Lane
Carson, Ohio 00000
(555) 555-5555

OBJECTIVE   Professional seeks to apply paralegal experience along with exceptional communications and organizational skills within a legal environment.

SUMMARY
- Extensive paralegal and administrative support experience in private law practices.
- Outstanding planning and organizational skills with keen attention to detail.
- Effective interpersonal communications with management, judges, court clerks, attorneys and clients.
- Knowledge of bookkeeping and probate accounting.

EDUCATION   Associate of Arts in **Paralegal Studies**
Bay Path College, Carson, Ohio, 1990

EXPERIENCE   PETERSON, MEYERS AND GALLIHAN, P.C.s   Carson, Ohio
Paralegal   1996-XXXX

Performed various paralegal and administrative support functions for several criminal and personal injury attorneys. Ensured smooth office operations and fostered positive client relations in busy practice.

◊ Prepared computerized court documents including summons, complaints, agreements, evictions, and other materials.
◊ Participated in meetings with clients and attorneys in the preparation of legal materials and court appearances.
◊ Interfaced and served as liaison with court clerks, judges, arbitrators, clients, and opposing attorneys.

BARLOW AND WILSON, P.C.s   Carson, Ohio
Paralegal/Office Manager   1990-1996

Performed various paralegal functions and concurrently managed all administrative aspects of general law practice. Hired, trained and supervised support staff. Organized and maintained efficient work flow, earning recognition for productivity.

◊ Managed estates valued up to $500,000 for incapable clients; functions included processing income, paying bills, and hiring personal care attendants.
◊ Prepared all probate court accounting for estate administrators.
◊ Researched information and prepared Last Wills and Testaments for clients.
◊ Prepared selected court documents including summons, complaints and wage executions.
◊ Utilized investigative and research skills to obtain information for serving court papers.

119

Combination. *Louise Garver, Enfield, Connecticut*
The problems: previous experience overshadowed paralegal degree; the possibility of age discrimination. The solutions: focus on degree and paralegal experience; omit prior work.

Lindsey J. Jacobson, CLA

9876 Cheval Drive   ❖   Tampa, Florida 33600   ❖   (813) 000-0000

Professional Summary

Self-directed Real Estate Paralegal with nine years of progressive experience in areas such as *purchase/sale transactions, all aspects of title work, corporate and partnership matters, creditor's rights and bankruptcy, and litigation*. Competent facilitator with keen analytical ability. Exhibit well-honed skills in organizational and time management, performing due diligence and legal research, drafting a broad range of legal documents, and coordinating complex, multimillion-dollar closings. Notable talents in client management highlighting proficiency in building a working rapport with prominent, national and local *Institutional Lenders, Land Developers, Investors, Partnerships, and Corporations*. Team Player, conscientious and hardworking; able to grasp new information quickly and work well under pressure, with minimal supervision and attention to details. Offer a record of top-notch performance and professionalism. Recognized by coworkers and superiors for *"willingness to go the extra mile."*

Technical Skills

Windows 95, WordPerfect, Lexis, Westlaw, West CD Rom Library, LegalEase Auto System, Attorneys' Title Information Display System, Groupwise, Matthew Bender Bankruptcy Program, Dapix Legal Series Billing Program, CompuServe, Various Online Systems

Professional Experience

SMITH, JONES, ET AL, P.A. - Tampa, FL   1993 - Present
Real Estate Paralegal (1995-Present)
Creditor's Rights & Bankruptcy Legal Secretary (1993-1995)
Exceptional performance led to advancement and assuming a pivotal, paralegal role; charged with directly supporting senior partner of the real estate development and finance group. Serve as a liaison between attorney and clients for transactions pertaining to purchase/sale/option agreements, construction/permanent mortgage lending, problem loan workouts, title insurance, restrictive covenants, and owner associations; involvement in contract negotiations. Interact with county authorities pertaining to developing/platting matters.
Core competencies in areas such as:

❖ Handling all title work (searches, commitments, and issuance of policies), analyzing and resolving complex title issues, and reviewing surveys.

❖ Drafting real estate, corporate, and partnership documents such as purchase/sale agreements, easement agreements, leases, and corporate authorization documents.

❖ Managing and organizing all documentation through closing and post-closing phases from preparing detailed checklists to closing statements through follow-up and completion of conveyance/funding details.

LAW OFFICE OF SAMUEL S. BARRISTER - Palm Harbor, FL   1990 - 1993
Legal Assistant/General Law Practitioner
Performed a diverse scope of responsibilities that involved drafting documentation and executing procedural protocol for matters pertaining to family law, personal injury, foreclosure, bankruptcy, civil litigation, wills and trusts, and corporate and real estate transactions. Maintained time sheets and prepared monthly accounting reports.

LAW OFFICE OF LYDIA R. JUDGE - Palm Harbor, FL   1989 - 1990
Legal Secretary/Litigation, Family Law Practice
Managed administrative functions combined with drafting and filing pleadings, coordinating calendar for hearings, organizing docket and filing system, tracking attorney time, and billing clients.

Education/Certification

UNIVERSITY OF TAMPA
B.A. degree - Business Administration/Marketing

ST. PETERSBURG JUNIOR COLLEGE
A.A. degree - Legal Assisting

NALA Certification

Professional Affiliations

Member, Florida Legal Assistants, Inc.
Member, Hillsborough Chapter of Legal Assistants

120

Combination. *Diane McGoldrick, Tampa, Florida*
A resume with narrow margins, wide lines, small type, reduced line spacing to present much information on one page, but with blank lines for white space to avoid a crowded look.

TANYA A. VIOLA
9999 Puritan Road
City, State 44444
(555) 555-5555
E-mail: viola@website.com

SUMMARY: *Skilled office professional with exceptional organizational skills and high level of attention to detail. Strong customer relations, computer, and administrative capabilities. Experience managing projects, exercising independent judgement, and working without supervision to achieve personal and organizational goals.*

PROFESSIONAL EXPERIENCE:

1996 - Present **Office Manager / Legal Assistant, Donald Smith, Attorney-At-Law; Village, State.**
Provide administrative support and supervision of part-time office staff for attorney handling personal injury claims.
- Administer Accounts Payable and Accounts Receivable.
- Purchase office supplies and outside services; administer operating budget.
- Answer incoming phone calls and greet clients.
- Conduct meetings/conferences with clients to assess their cases.
- Schedule client meetings with attorney.
- Request medical reports and other pertinent information on cases.
- Assist attorney in drafting and preparing pleadings and motions.

Accomplishments:
Implemented new filing systems to better organize information and increase office efficiency.

Instituted automated accounting system. Managed the transition of financial data from manual to automated system.

1987 - 1996 **VAGABOND INSURANCE; City, State.**
Claims Representative   **1992 - 1996**
Processed insurance claims involving personal injury, workers' compensation, and property damage.
- Fulfilled customer relations functions with a variety of individuals.
- Interviewed claimants; evaluated claims and coverages.
- Requested medical reports, property appraisals, and other relevant data.
- Negotiated settlements with claimants and attorneys.
- Coordinated salvage sale of vehicles declared "total losses."

Special Project:
Served as Team Leader for implementation of Team Environment for handling liability and property claims. This initiative led to improved service through faster response to customer inquiries.

Administrative Assistant - Auto Appraisal Center   **1989 - 1992**
Supported automotive appraisers in preparing estimates and processing claims for collision damage.
- Greeted customers in person and on the phone; fulfilled other receptionist duties.
- Input data and generated written estimates for collision claims.
- Fulfilled other administrative support functions as necessary.

Accomplishment:
Developed spreadsheet for Manager's use in tracking activities of appraisers.

Data Entry Operator / File Clerk   **1987 - 1989**

PROFESSIONAL ENRICHMENT:

Licensed Notary Public.
Former Licensed Real Estate Salesperson.

Extensive In-House Training with Vagabond Insurance:
- Customer Service   - Telephone Skills   - Dealing with Irate Customers

COMPUTER SKILLS:

Windows 95, MS Word, Excel, MS Money, Quicken, Law Desk.

121

Combination. *Arnold G. Boldt, Rochester, New York*
This individual sought to use her legal experience for a new role as a Proofreader of legal text. Boldface is used for job titles; italic, for important information. See Cover Letter 10.

MarciaWard

385 Grove Street
Freeport, New York 11111
(516) 555-5555

Profile

Legal Assistant offering substantial experience within both **legal and financial services** settings. Maintain the highest standard of professionalism, performance and integrity at all times. Areas of strengths include:

- Drafting agreements, regulatory filings and Blue-Sky registrations.
- Familiarity with SEC, NYSE, AMEX and NASD regulations and compliance issues.
- Ability to communicate effectively with high-profile and high-net-worth clientele, utilizing discretion at all times.
- Attention to detail, follow-through and time management.
- Proficient in Microsoft Word, Excel and PowerPoint; WordPerfect; Lotus 1-2-3; Lexis-Nexis and Westlaw legal research systems; and Time Slips Deluxe client billing system.

Professional Experience

Law Offices of Thomas J. McCabe, New York, New York   **19XX - Present**
Legal Assistant / Paralegal

- Provide legal support at corporate and securities practice, which represents parties in securities arbitration and litigation, formation, structuring and governance of broker-dealer organizations.
- Prepare regulatory filings for broker-dealers, Form U-4s, private placements, SRO applications (AMEX, PCX, PHLX, NASD, NYSE), options applications for the CBOE, and Blue-Sky registrations.
- Draft an array of agreements, including Continuing Education for NASD applications, supervisory procedures and operating agreements.
- Draw up documentation for corporate filings, legal opinions, and sole proprietorships.
- Administrative responsibilities encompass payroll input; monthly billings; maintaining appointment calendars; updating administrative lists; computer backup; inventory control and purchasing of office supplies.

Citibank, N.A., New York, New York   **1990 - 19XX**
Specialist - Commercial Paper Issuance Billing (1994 - 1995)
(Placed by Manpower on long-term assignment)

- Generated daily reports reflecting volume of commercial paper issuances.
- Reconciled in-house Depository Trust Company transactions.
- Maintained relations with commercial paper clients regarding billings and associated problems.

Service Officer - Private Banking Division (1991 - 1993)

- Provided support to two private bankers and assisted in the relationship management of 500 private banking clients. Extensive one-on-one contact with clients.
- Managed client accounts; expedited the transferring of funds; provided mortgage documentation; and initiated investigations as warranted, to resolve account-related problems.

Assistant to Unit Head - Private Banking Division (1990 - 1991)

- Reconciled and paid bills; maintained payroll and personnel records; and updated yearly performance appraisals.
- Managed unit head's calendar, travel arrangements, and organized meetings and special events.

Kimmelman, Sexter, Warmflash & Leitner, New York, New York   **1987 - 1990**
Head Receptionist

Education

St. John's University, Queens, New York
Major: *Liberal Arts*

122

Combination. *Judith Friedler, New York, New York*
The challenge was to display the person's experience and expertise in relating financial services with legal services. Small print makes room for extra information. See Cover Letter 18.

Cynthia M. Lee

874 East River Bend Road • Green Bay, Wisconsin 54303
(414) 469–8077

Paralegal

Talented researcher with excellent communication skills. Resourceful and thorough in gathering information and conducting investigations. Offer a strong combination of legal knowledge, ability to interact effectively with diverse populations, and self-motivation.

Summary of Attributes

- Excellent communication and interpersonal skills; persuasive and tenacious.
- Follow-through on assignments independently or as an interactive team player.
- Highly organized and detail-oriented; efficiently manage time and projects with close attention to deadlines; effective in stressful situations.
- Creative, logical approach to problem solving; high ethical standards.
- Proficient in: Excel, Lotus 1-2-3, Microsoft Word, Quattro Pro, Windows 95, WestLaw Legal Research, Summation for Windows, and Netscape.
- Active member, Paralegal Association of Wisconsin

Experience

Paralegal   1987–Present
Brown, Miller, Stevens & White, S.C., Green Bay, Wisconsin

- Assist attorneys in personal injury litigation cases.
- Interview clients and witnesses; communicate extensively with clients throughout all phases of litigation process.
- Conduct research and draft legal memoranda.
- Assemble and summarize medical records and testimony.
- Abstract depositions, prepare trial exhibits.

Legal Assistant   1985–1987
Wiese, Smith & Sanders, Appleton, Wisconsin

- Assisted attorneys in the areas of probate and family law.
- Interviewed clients and completed investigations to obtain social, financial, and legal information; prepared financial accounting statements.
- Drafted pleadings, court, and tax documents.
- Conducted legal research.

Education

Bachelor of Science: Paralegal Studies   1987
Mankato State University, Mankato, Minnesota

123

Combination. *Kathy Keshemberg, Appleton, Wisconsin*
A full line and partial lines separate the sections. Boldface makes the name, headline, headings, job titles, and degree stand out. The Profile and Summary sell the individual.

Susan J. Pitman

706 Huron Place
Florham Park, New Jersey 07932
(201) 397-0194

Education

Paralegal Studies Program: General Practice, 1991, **Fairleigh Dickinson University,** Madison, NJ; ABA approved.

Relevant Course Work: 42 hours each in Civil Litigation, Estates, Wills & Trusts, Corporate Law, Real Estate and Mortgages. 21 hours each in Matrimonial Law, Criminal Law and Ethics. 30 hours each in Legal Research, Computer Literacy, and Bankruptcy.

Bachelor of Arts, Communications, 1978, **William Paterson College,** Wayne, NJ

Experience

Legal Skills

- Research to identify law and other material relevant to client's case.
- Prepare legal documents and nontechnical correspondence for attorneys; update diary and tickler system. Maintain client files.
- File pleadings and direct delivery of subpoena to witnesses and parties of action.
- Position entails extensive contact with clients; maintain computerized schedules and document files.

Communications Skills

- Formerly marketed and sold accounting systems and other peripherals for computer usage to small- and medium-size companies.
- Generated leads through Certified Public Accountants.
- Maintained client relations to acquire resale business; developed referrals.
- Conducted presentations and seminars on product usage; participated in trade shows.

Financial Services

- As a Shareholder Representative, managed a $50 million corporate account for the Securities Operations Division of Citibank, NA, New York, New York.
- Bought and sold stock for 2,000 shareholders. Handled a reinvestment sum of $70,000.
- Counseled and corresponded directly with shareholders; interfaced with brokers, banks, and corporate clients.
- Managed stock transfers, including accounts receivable for dividend and interest payments. Maintained computerized shareholder files; processed legal documents.

Computers

WordPerfect 5.1 & 6.1, PC Law, MultiMate, Lotus 1-2-3, Westlaw, & Legal Billing.

Business Affiliations

Betz & Warren, P.A., Summit, NJ *Paralegal*	1/95-Present
Garner, Hellmann, Martin & Cohen, P.C., Parsippany, NJ *Legal Secretary*	1993-1994
Rittenhouse, Rittenhouse & Cantor, Florham Park, NJ *Legal Secretary*	1991-1993
Smart Business Systems, Orange, NJ *Field Representative*	1981-1987
Citibank, N.A., New York, NY *Shareholder Service Representative*	1979-1981

References

Furnished upon request

124

Functional. *Beverly Baskin, Marlboro, New Jersey*
The grouping of the Experience section according to four categories—Legal Skills, Communication Skills, and so on—makes it easier to grasp the person's responsibilities.

MADELINE C. PARKER

3406 Davison Highway
Vassar, Michigan 48555

Residence: (517) 555-9883
Office: (810) 555-3512

SUMMARY OF QUALIFICATIONS

❑ Well-developed communication skills with management, peers and the public.
❑ Ability to work well under pressure and against deadlines.
❑ Strong leader who assesses and takes charge of situations, delivering appropriate results.

SUMMARY OF EXPERIENCE

Paralegal
- Participated in cases involving personal injury, civil, family law, criminal and contracts.
- Drafted and assisted clients with answering interrogatories.
- Interviewed clients to obtain pretrial information.
- Composed drafts of complaints and wills.
- Coordinated law library and maintained its viability.
- Performed legal research.
- Negotiated settlements for personal injury cases and processed settlement disbursements.

Office Management
- Trained, supervised and evaluated up to 36 employees; substituted for managers in their absences.
- Supervised training of prelaw and law students.
- Conducted closings of land contracts and mortgage assumptions.
- Coordinated commercial property management.
- Monitored inventory and purchased supplies.
- Assisted clerical staff with receptionist duties.

Accounting
- Utilized specialized computer software to process accounts payable and payroll.
- Performed functions relating to accounts receivable, job costing, and general accounting.
- Processed payments and monitored status of appropriate taxes.
- Prepared financial reports.
- Implemented and utilized pegboard bookkeeping system.

CERTIFICATIONS

Certified Paralegal - American Institute for Paralegal Studies   1983
    Achieved and maintained 92% grade rating while working full-time.

Certificate of Completion - Michigan Real Estate Course   1987

EDUCATION

Baker College • Flint, MI   Ongoing
    Pursuing *Associate degree* in Paralegal/Legal Assistant Program

Delta College • University Center, MI   1983-1984
    Criminal Justice course work

EMPLOYMENT HISTORY

Paralegal/Bookkeeper	Baker, Jones, Tallman & Johnson P.C. • Flint, MI	1990-Present
Office Manager	Century 21 Realty • Davison, MI	1986-1990
Paralegal	Avery & Weinstein, P.C. • Cleveland, OH	1984-1986
Paralegal	Paige, Doan & McKendrick, P.C. • Flint, MI	1979-1984

Excellent professional references available on request.

125

Functional. *Janet L. Beckstrom, Flint, Michigan*
Experience is displayed according to a different set of categories. Clustering information by category enables the reader to look immediately at information of interest to the reader.

SUSAN K. SCHUMM

000 S. County Line Road
Hebron, Indiana 00000
(555) 555-5555

EDUCATION

Valparaiso University School of Law, Indiana
Juris Doctor Candidate, XXXX
> Dinner Chairwoman, International Law Society
> Phi Delta Phi Legal Fraternity
> Midwest Environmental Law Caucus
> Women's Law Student Association
> Equal Justice Alliance

Spring Hill College, Mobile, Alabama
Master of Liberal Arts, Theology, Candidate, XXXX
G.P.A. 3.5/4.0
> Thesis: "Divine Czarinas: A Reflection on Female Theologians"

Auburn University, Montgomery, Alabama
Bachelor of Arts, Liberal Studies, XXXX
G.P.A. 3.3/4.0
> Dean's List, Spring **XXXX**
> Air Force R.O.T.C.
> Director of Operations, Arnold Air Society, **XXXX**
> Recipient of Distinctive Cadet Award, Fall **XXXX**
> Recipient of Order of World Wars Medal, **XXXX**
> Alpha Gamma Delta Fraternity for Women
> Ritual Chairwoman, **XXXX**
> Active Alumnae, **XXXX**-Present
> Archaeological Field Team, Fusihatchee Creek Site, Spring **XXXX**

LANGUAGE SKILLS

Moderate comprehension of French and German.

EXPERIENCE

Front Desk Receptionist   XXXX-Present
Fitness Barn Health Club, Valparaiso, Indiana

Volunteer   Spring XXXX
The Nature Conservatory/Alabama Natural Heritage, Montgomery, Alabama

Consultant/Cashier   Summers XXXX & XXXX
Virginia's Health Foods, Mobile, Alabama
> Representative buyer at the **XXXX** National Natural Foods Convention

INTERESTS

European Travel; Abstract and Portrait Painting; and Archaeological Digs.

126

Combination. *Susan K. Schumm, Hebron, Indiana*
A resume for a law school student. Education, which is the current area of interest and activity, is put first. Experience, which is not related to law, is put near the end.

Joan B. Rogers

1515 Main Street ▸ Ft. Lauderdale, FL ▸ 55555
(555) 555-5555 ▸ joanrogers@yahoo.com

Education   **Florida University** - College of Law - Ft. Lauderdale, FL
Juris Doctor Candidate, May XXXX ...GPA: 3.5

Activities:
- Exchange program, **College of London** - London, England
  - Comparative British Law, Spring XXXX
- Marina Rickman First Year Moot Court Competition
- Student Bar Association, Alumni Liaison - Office of Development and Alumni Relations
- Women's Law Association

New York University - New York, NY
Master of Arts in History, August XXXX ...GPA: 3.6

Brooklyn College - Brooklyn, NY
Bachelor of Arts - Majors in History and Philosophy, May XXXX ...GPA: 3.5
- President, Student Foundation
- Secretary, Order of Omega
- Volunteer, Disabled Student Services
- President, Delta Gamma Sorority
- Representative, Panhellenic Council
- Volunteer, Brooklyn County Adult Literacy Council

Publication   "Analysis of Disciplinary Action and Results of EEOC Policy," in <u>Justice Today</u>, Office of the National Counsel Assistance, Spring, XXXX.

Legal Experience   **British Environmental Law Association** - London, England   Spring XXXX
Volunteer
- Studied impact of political changes on environmental law.
- Devised questionnaire on environmental policy and regulation for regional business survey.
- Researched relevant case law and edited newsletter.

National Counsel Assistance - Miami, FL   Summer XXXX
Legal Intern
- Conducted research on broad legal issues, including:
  - Ethics Regulations and Instructions.
  - Possible policy violations and need for investigative action.
  - Equal Opportunity rights.
  - Exemption 55A, regarding release of information by independent contractors.
- Authored article to be used as the National Counsel Assistance guide for deciding whether to pursue investigations.
- Reviewed Nomination Packages and Public and Confidential Disclosure Forms.
- Reviewed final agency decisions on EEOC claims.

Employment   **A&A Insurance Company** - New York, NY   XXXX to XXXX
Executive Assistant
- Created and maintained computer database with 100,000 entries, which automated office activities and significantly increased operating efficiency.
- Processed accounts payable and receivable; prepared income and expenditure reports.
- Collected delinquent accounts and processed settlement documents.

Computers   - Westlaw, Lexis-Nexis, Microsoft Word, WordPerfect, Quicken, Internet services
- Proficient user of Windows and Macintosh operating systems

Travel   - Extensive international travel, including Asia, Europe, and Australia

127

Combination. *Kim Isaacs, Jackson Heights, New York*
Another resume for a law school student. As in the preceding resume, Education is put first, and Employment unrelated to law is put toward the end, giving way to Legal Experience.

Mary Ann Alleva

428 Cucumber Street ▪ Anytime, New York 00000
Phone ▪ (000) 555-0000

PROFESSIONAL SKILLS:

Highly self-motivated, talented and organized individual with strong educational qualifications in Political Science and Law. Ability to coordinate and manage multiple priorities. Experience includes:

- Strong writing skills.
- Excellent research and analytical abilities.
- Computer literate: WordPerfect, Westlaw, Lexis-Nexus.

EDUCATION:

UNIVERSITY OF CITY SCHOOL OF LAW, Anytown, New York
Juris Doctor candidate ▪ In Process

THE AMERICAN UNIVERSITY, Washington, DC
Bachelor of Arts in Political Science ▪ May 1997
Major in Government

RELATED EXPERIENCE:

LOCAL COUNTY DISTRICT ATTORNEY'S OFFICE, Anytown, New York
Intern ▪ June 1998 to August 1998
Third Judicial Department Appellate Division (Law Intern Appointment). Conduct arraignments, preliminary hearings, bench and jury trials.

LOCAL COUNTY PUBLIC DEFENDER'S OFFICE, Anytown, New York
Intern ▪ June 1997 to August 1997
Screened and interviewed clients to ascertain pertinent information, conducted legal research, and interacted extensively with attorneys.

JFK CENTER FOR THE PERFORMING ARTS, Washington, DC
Intern ▪ August 1996 to December 1996
Assisted in the management of volunteer staff of 500 for the Friends of the Kennedy Center (Volunteer Department). Coordinated with production in implementing Center Honors Program. Responsible for special events planning.

CONGRESSMAN JAMES DOE, District Office, Anytown, New York
Political Science Intern ▪ June 1996 to August 1996
Provided administrative and clerical support. Served as resource/support to constituents.

CONGRESSMAN YOU KNOW WHO HE IS, Washington, DC
Political Science Intern ▪ September 1994 to February 1995
Performed the same duties as aforementioned position.

ADDITIONAL EMPLOYMENT:

Microfiche Department, The American University Library, Washington, DC ▪ 9/95-5/96
Data Entry Clerk, Mail Order Company, Inc., Anytown, NY ▪ 5/95-8/95
Sales Associate, The Express, Washington, DC/Some City, NY ▪ 1/94-8/94
Wait Staff, Four-Star Restaurant, Smaller City, NY ▪ 1/93-8/94

ACTIVITIES:

- Jessup International Moot Court Board (1998)
- University Public Interest Law Program (1997-1998)
- Secretary and Social Chair, Sigma Delta Tau Sorority
- Leadership Program, School of Public Affairs (1993-1994)

128

Combination. *Betty Geller, Elmira, New York*
A third resume for a law school student. The Professional Skills section is put first to sell the individual. The Related Experience section about important internships is given prominence.

Joseph Dons, Attorney at Law

25 West Main Street ♦ East Alton, Illinois 62024

Voice: (618) 555-5000 ♦ Pager: (618) 555-9000 ♦ Fax: (618) 555-9001

Licensed in Illinois, Georgia, and Florida

EDUCATION

Juris Doctor

Southern Methodist University ♦ Dallas, Texas

Moot Court...Mock Trial...Christian Legal Society

Bachelor of Science, Political Science

Southern Illinois University ♦ Edwardsville, Illinois

Student Body President...Dean's College...Dean's List...Student Senator...Who's Who Among College and University Students...Scholastic All-American

EXPERIENCE

The Simmons & Dons Firm, P.C.

A professional corporation and law firm specializing in:

Wills & Trusts	Estate Planning
Probate	General Practice
General Litigation & Appeals	Nonprofit Corporations
Small Business Affairs	Ecclesiastical Agencies

Dale A. Allison, Jr. & Associates

Leaders in legal representation for churches, evangelistic associations, ministries, and Christian schools. Provided legal support involving litigation, governmental compliance, asset management, and organizational structure.

Tax Fraud	RICO
Pastoral Compensation	Sexual Harassment
Church Real Estate Withdrawal	IRS Audits

Clark/Bardes, Inc., Dallas, Texas

Used corporate-owned life Insurance (COLI) to fund projects and cooperate planning. Lobbied state legislatures to pass COLI laws. Clients included American Airlines, Dial Corporation, and Wrigley Corporation.

OTHER

- U.S. Army Combat Engineer, Expert Rifle/Grenade Division
- Hold division record for 21-mile road march
- Earned Soldier of the Quarter honors

129

Functional. *John A. Suarez, Troy, Illinois*
Lines, which mark the beginning of resume sections, are artfully integrated with each section heading and the individual's name in the contact information. No dates are given.

DANIELLE S. VAN LIER

6701 Murietta Avenue ▪ **Valley Glen, California 91405**
(818) 994-6655 ▪ **E-mail: namaenai@aol.com**

Passed California State Bar Exam on First Attempt; February 1998

EDUCATION

WASHINGTON UNIVERSITY SCHOOL OF LAW, St. Louis, MO
Juris Doctor, December 1997
Master of Arts in East Asian Studies
    Honors and Activities
- *Washington University Journal of Urban and Contemporary Law*, Associate Editor
- *Jessup International Moot Court*
- U.S. Congress/Korean National Assembly Intern/Exchange, Summer 1997
- Congressional Clinic, Washington D.C., Spring 1997
- Negotiation Competition; Finalist
- Phi Alpha Delta; Justice (President)
- Student Bar Association; Social Committee Chairperson
- East Asian Law Society; Cofounder/Vice President
- Sports and Entertainment Law Society; Vice President

    Publications
- *Boy, You Possessed My Heart & Soul: a Post-Modern Noh Play*, 3 Washington University Occasional Papers in East Asian Studies (Summer 1998).

UNIVERSITY OF CALIFORNIA, Santa Barbara, CA
Bachelor of Arts, Spring 1994   Major: Japanese
    Activities
- Charter member — Toastmasters International, U.C.S.B. Student Chapter
- "Youth in Action" summer exchange program in Netherlands and Spain, Summer 1991

TOKYO INTERNATIONAL UNIVERSITY, Kawagoe, Japan
Japan Studies Program, Fall Semester 1993
    Activities
- Guest Speaker — English speech contest "Kaneko Trophy"
- Emcee — Japan Studies Program Speech Festival
- Volunteer — Japan Association of Language Teachers 19th International Conference, Ōmiya, Japan

EXPERIENCE

JULIA BUG ENTERTAINMENT, Beverly Hills, CA • March 1998 to August 1998
Legal & Business Affairs Liaison
Worked with outside counsel on corporate and intellectual property issues including trademark registration, corporate reorganization, shareholders and directors meetings, LLC formation and employment and partnership issues. Worked directly with French partner who is exclusive consumer products licensing agent for Universal Studios and Dreamworks, SKG in France and other French-speaking countries. Attended L!censing 98 International Convention in New York City.

UNITED STATES HOUSE OF REPRESENTATIVES, Washington, D.C. • January to August 1997
Representative Howard L. Berman, 26th Congressional District, California
Legislative Fellow
Performed research, drafted memoranda, and provided assistance on diverse subjects including immigration, intellectual property and judicial issues. Attended and summarized congressional committee meetings. Drafted official and constituent correspondence. Interfaced with multiple legislative offices and foreign embassies. Handled constituent calls and monitored pending legislation.

130

Combination. *Vivian Van Lier, Los Angeles, California*
A resume for a new law school graduate who passed a state bar exam a couple of months later.
The Education section reads like a Summary of Qualifications or Skills section because of the

EXPERIENCE, continued

U.S. CONGRESS/KOREAN NATIONAL ASSEMBLY EXCHANGE • Summer 1997
Washington, D.C. / Seoul, South Korea
Intern
One of eight students nominated by Members of U.S. Congress in jointly sponsored government
exchange. Met with representatives of U.S. and Korean political and nongovernmental organizations as
well as members of the Korean National Assembly. Discussed current U.S. and Korean bilateral issues
with elected and appointed officials in Korea. Participated in field trips to P'anmunjŏm (demilitarized
zone) and Kyŏngju (ancient Korean capital).

SCHONBRUN & DE SIMONE, Venice, CA • Summer 1996
Law Clerk
(*Law firm specializing in Civil Rights*)
Performed research; summarized depositions for high-profile civil rights case.

REPRESENTATIVE HOWARD L. BERMAN • Summers 1995, 1996
26th Congressional District, California District Office
Intern
Assisted with immigration and INS casework; handled constituent calls; researched pending legislation.
Performed clerical functions. Contacted community agencies and elected representatives' offices.

FEINBERG, GOTTLIEB & WALLER, Encino, CA • Summer 1996
(*Law firm specializing in Civil Litigation*)
Law Clerk

WASHINGTON UNIVERSITY SCHOOL OF LAW, St. Louis, MO • 1995 to 1996
Computer Lab Assistant
Provided computer assistance, monitored network and coauthored Web page composition.

R&J GRAY INTERNATIONAL LANGUAGE SCHOOL, Ogawa, Japan • November 1993 to April 1994
English Instructor
Taught conversational English to 1st grade through high school students.

LANGUAGES: Japanese

COMPUTER SKILLS

Operating Systems: DOS, Windows, UNIX
Hardware: Built all computers for Washington, D.C. and California offices of Representative Howard L.
   Berman; installed LAN in California district office.
Applications: WordPerfect, Microsoft Word, Microsoft Publisher, CorelDRAW, Corel Flow, PC Tools,
   Japanese word processing programs
Internet: HTML/World Wide Web page composition. Designed and built official Web site for U.S.
   Congressman Howard L. Berman and Washington University School of Law student organizations.
Research Tools: Lexis/Nexis, Westlaw, Internet

COMMUNITY ACTIVITIES

Participated in conference: "Uncommon Women on Common Ground," Long Beach, CA, 1995
Delegate — California State Democratic Convention, 1993
Attended seminar: "Doing Business in Japan," Soka University, Calabasas, CA, 1993
Volunteer — Campaign 1992 including voter registration drive
Volunteer — Encino Chamber of Commerce - Taste of Encino 1991, 1992

listed Honors and Activities. The Experience section is developed because it, too, consists mainly of law-
related activities. The Computer Skills section is law-related because of the person's projects for a Congressional Representative. Main section headings stand out with hanging indentation.

Kory D. Kasler
1 North Lancaster Street
Athens, Ohio 45701   (740) 592-3993

EDUCATION

CLEVELAND MARSHALL COLLEGE OF LAW
Cleveland State University, Cleveland, Ohio
Juris Doctorate degree, 1992

OHIO UNIVERSITY, Athens, Ohio
Bachelor of Arts in Political Science, 1988

PROFILE OF EXPERIENCE

- General practice of law
- Insurance defense
- Domestic relations
- Litigation of all aspects of civil trial and appellate court practice
- Real estate: title search, coordination and completion of loan closings
- Supervision of legal and clerical staff
- Development and institution of new personnel policies
- Personnel management: interviewing, hiring, evaluation and termination

EMPLOYMENT HISTORY

Attorney/Partner   1992-present
RHODES, RHODES & KASLER, CO., L.P.A., Shade, Ohio
- Partner, January 1993

Law Clerk   1992
ATHENS COUNTY PROSECUTOR'S OFFICE, Athens County, Ohio
- Researched criminal, tax and landfill laws
- Authored briefs and memorandums on pending appeals
- Authored motions for pending litigation

Gourmet Food Salesman   1990-1991
CLINE HOUSE FOODS, Medford, New Jersey
- Increased sales from $80,000 to $600,000 during tenure

Gourmet Food Salesman   1988-1989
EDGAR MILLER COMPANY, Youngstown, Ohio
- Increased sales from $200,000 to $400,000 during tenure

PROFESSIONAL AFFILIATIONS

Member, Ohio State Bar Association
Member, Athens County Bar Association
Admitted to Practice, Federal Court for Southern Ohio District

ASSOCIATIONS

Board Member, Athens County Kiwanis Club
Board Member, Hospice of Appalachia

131

Combination. *Melissa L. Kasler, Athens, Ohio*
A resume that is easy to read because of hanging indentation with the headings, partial lines
separating the sections, boldface for degrees and job titles, and minimum information.

Legal Beagle

31 White Bark Place ✦ Austin, Texas 78700 ✦ (819) 555-0000

Talented, results-oriented business professional offering a Bachelor of Science degree in Mechanical Engineering, a Juris Doctor degree and 10 years' experience evaluating and managing new product and technology development within manufacturing environments. Strong analytical, research and project management skills combined with expertise in building and managing strategic business alliances. Skillful negotiator with excellent qualifications analyzing and valuing intellectual property, and structuring contract terms and conditions. Licensed Patent Attorney.

PROFESSIONAL EXPERIENCE

TEXAS CORPORATION, The Woodlands, Texas   1994 - Present
$500 Million Industrial Computer Manufacturer
Product Development Analyst/Patent Attorney
Recruited from law school and challenged to create, build and manage a corporate-wide patent program to support new product and technological advancements. Developed and implemented all policies and procedures, prepared all legal instruments and coordinated R&D functions.
▸ Cultivated and built solid business relationships with outside attorneys and design contractors.
▸ Grew product development portfolio to 65 US patents to date.
▸ Created nine inventions (two software systems) and secured patents to all.
▸ Wrote and executed Company's Incentive and Disclosure Program.
▸ Evaluated competitive patents and advised R&D on new technologies.
▸ Chosen to evaluate the intellectual property of over 20 prospective company acquisitions. Conducted formal presentations to Executive Management and Board of Directors advising them of patent and legal issues, making appropriate recommendations on structuring deals.
▸ Negotiated and secured a two-year, $3.5 million design engineering contract.
▸ Advised senior management on setting the value of intellectual property and structuring R&D write-offs.
▸ Scrutinized all 10K and 10Q filings for technological accuracy and codeveloped SEC reporting documents.

NCR CORPORATION, Decatur, Georgia   1992 - 1993
Manufacturer of Point of Sale Computer Software and Devices
Legal Intern
Selected by a competitive group of candidates for an 18-month internship. Exposed to and provided legal guidance on patent and infringement issues. Conducted extensive legal research and prepared written documentation regarding patentability of bar code scanners, multimedia software and data security systems.

DIAMOND STAR MOTORS CORPORATION, Normal, Illinois   1988 - 1991
Auto Assembly Plant – A Chrysler and Mitsubishi Joint Venture
Manufacturing Engineer
Recruited from college and assigned to design, develop and implement assembly process and process control procedures to maximize efficiencies.
▸ Spearheaded the design and implementation of a fully automatic robotic installation system for interior linings.

EDUCATION

Emory University School of Law, Atlanta, Georgia
J.D., 1994
Admitted to the Georgia Bar 1994

University of Illinois, Urbana, Illinois
B.S., Mechanical Engineering 1988

132

Combination. *Cheryl Ann Harland, The Woodlands, Texas*
This individual wanted "to transfer his skills into a Corporate Business Development environment." Project management, negotiation, and development achievements are stressed.

JOHN TANNER, Esq.
555 Fifth St.
Syosset, NY 5555
(555) 555-5555

PROFESSIONAL PROFILE

15 years of legal experience in corporate and real estate law, with successful experience in high-profile cases.

AREAS OF EXPERTISE

- Expert negotiation skills in mediating difficult and complex legal issues/cases.
- Comprehensive legal research and writing skills.
- 14 years of litigation practice.

HIGHLIGHTS OF ACHIEVEMENTS

- Represented a 600-unit cooperative corporation in New York, New York, that defaulted on a $25 million mortgage held by New York Bank. Brought in as special litigation counsel for defendant corporation. Played a lead role in complex litigation and negotiations which ensued, and the ultimate favorable workout. Worked with Manhattan Borough President and City Council President in bringing parties together in high-profile case.

- Played a major legal role for Resolution Trust Corporation (now F.D.I.C.) with regard to millions of dollars in asset securitization. Managed the disposition of millions of dollars of commercial and residential properties. Conducted foreclosure litigation, defensive litigation involving liability for failed loans, participation agreements, failure to lend, and offensive litigation concerning officer/director liability.

- Performed extensive legal work for major financial institutions, corporations and business entities. Exposed to banking law, credit issues, liability of bank officers.

- Represented union employees in Railway Labor Act dispute in major litigation involving Pan American Airlines.

- Represented plaintiff investor in multimillion dollar lawsuit against multiple defendants for fraudulent representation of outstanding financial assets involving extensive document review and motion practice.

EXPERIENCE

JOHNS, GARRICK, AND HEIGEL, P.C., New York, NY
AV-RATED FIRM, member of the firm since 1993
Associate, 1989-xxxx
Corporate: Litigation and appellate practice in state and federal courts involving dissenter's rights, profit/salary disputes, escrow deposit disputes, commercial contracts, professional liability of bank officers/directors for questionable lending practices under Financial Institutions Reform and Recovery Act (FIRREA), liability of lending institutions for miscalculation of mortgage payments, defense of Resolution Trust Corporation in breach of contract claims for failure to lend and first right of refusal, negotiation of exclusive distribution agreements in Eastern Europe, asset securitization for Resolution Trust Corporation real estate sales, and representation of cooperative corporations in mortgage foreclosure litigation/workouts.

Real Estate: Representation of sponsors in coop/condo conversions; representation of lending institutions in residential and commercial loan closings; representation of sponsors and tenant shareholders in connection with sponsor/board of director disputes.

JOHN W. BLEMARD, Esq., Elmhurst, NY
Associate, 1986-1987
Represented purchasers and sellers of commercial, residential, cooperative and condominium property. Conducted general civil and real estate litigation.

COLLINS & ASSOCIATES, New York, NY
Associate, 1982-1987
Supervised major litigation and appellate projects including Railway Labor Act and Martin Act disputes. Drafted commercial agreements for sale and purchase of businesses and related assets.

EDUCATION

J.D., Columbia University Law School, June 1982

ADMISSIONS

New York State, Appellate Division, Second Department;   U.S. District Court, SDNY
U.S. District Court, EDNY; U.S. Tax Court; U.S. Supreme Court

133

Combination. *Etta R. Barmann, New York, New York*
With narrow top and bottom margins, smaller type, and wide fully justified lines, this resume offers much information. Lines separating sections and blank lines make it readable.

Martha E. Rehnquist
247 Liberty Street
Braintree, MA 02184
781-849-0637

Experience

1994 to Present
(Full time)

1989 to 1993
(Part time)

Madison, Adams & Paine, P.C.
Associate
- Concentrate on insurance defense and personal injury law.
- Practice at Department of Industrial Accidents from conciliation through conference hearing and appeal.
- Handle matters in District and Superior Courts including summary judgment and other motions, trials, and mediation in Superior Court.
- Represent plaintiffs in personal injury cases.
- Bring extensive medical background to bear during discovery to clearly understand the dominant and collateral issues and value of each case.
- Conduct depositions and thorough discovery to secure all information necessary to develop strategies for resolution of the case.

1993 to 1994

Trial Court of the Commonwealth
Clerk
- Served as Law Clerk to the Justices of the Superior Court.
- Performed legal research, drafted memoranda, decisions, and jury instructions.
- Assisted justices in motion sessions and at trial.

1975 to 1993

Boston Hospital
Quality Assurance Coordinator (1986 – 1993)
Research Nurse (1978 – 1986)
Registered Nurse (1975 – 1978)
- Monitored compliance with all applicable state regulations and made recommendations as appropriate.
- Developed close working relationships with medical staff and administrators.
- Assisted in developing Quality Assurance program that met and exceeded administrative expectations.
- Coordinated NIH Study of infertility focusing on compliance issues and reporting requirements.

Education

Suffolk School of Law
Juris Doctor, *magna cum laude*, May 1983
Lead Articles Editor, New England Law Review (1992 – 1993)
Staff Member, New England Law Review (1991 – 1992)
Awarded, New England Scholar, for finishing in the Top 10% of the class (1990 – 1993); AmJur in Family Law, 1992.

Boston University
Master of Public Health, School of Public Health, May 1982
Bachelor of Science, School of Nursing, May 1975

Licensure

Board of Bar Overseers, No. 563974
Massachusetts Board of Registration in Nursing, No. 128221

Publications
(Partial list)

Adam BF, Krache M, Phillippe M, Munoz A, Hutchinson D, Miao L, Schoenbaum SC: *Randomized clinical trial of perioperative cefoxitin in preventing maternal infection after primary cesarean section.* Am J Obstet Gynecol. 1982; 142 (8): 983-987.

Junior S, Walsh B, Evans S, Krache M, Ravnikar V, Schiff I: *The effect of transdermal estradiol on hormone and metabolic dynamics over a six-week period.* Obstet Gynecol. 1988; 71 (5): 671-676.

134

Chronological. *Steven Green, Northboro, Massachusetts*
This individual's career path has been from nursing to law in order to bring her medical background and knowledge to the practice of law. Chronological format shows this path.

ALISA WASHINGTON
Attorney-at-Law
30 Frank Road • Engle, New Jersey 07631
(xxx) xxx-xxxx

AREAS of EXPERTISE . . . .

COMMERCIAL LITIGATION	BANKRUPTCY / FORECLOSURE	QUIET TITLE
LENDER LIABILITY	SPORTS LAW	ENVIRONMENTAL LAW
REAL ESTATE	PUBLIC UTILITIES	WORK OUTS

PROFESSIONAL EXPERIENCE . . . .

KAUFMAN, GELBERT & BERN   Fort Lee, New Jersey
A firm specializing in commercial litigation and diverse real estate matters.

Senior Associate   *1988 - Present*
- Accountable for firm litigation team including overseeing complex matters in state and federal courts.
- Interface with clients which include insurance companies, financial institutions, title insurance companies, real estate developers, professional athletes and marketing companies.
- Conduct discovery, draft briefs and pleadings and successfully try cases.
- Review associates' files, deliberate strategies, review briefs/pleadings and assist associate attorneys in trial preparations.

Selected Achievements:
- ◆ *Successfully tried a novel foreclosure matter where mortgage was outside the chain of title.*
- ◆ *Increased billable hours 30% defending security guard companies.*
- ◆ *Oversaw diversification/expansion of litigation due to real estate market decline.*
- ◆ *Expanded practice regarding sports marketing and generated $130,000 in additional revenues.*
- ◆ *Profitably promoted, developed and sold three multifamily buildings.*

NEW JERSEY ATTORNEY GENERAL'S OFFICE   Newark, New Jersey

Deputy Attorney General   *1987 - 1988*
- Represented Public Utility Commission and agency staff in state and appellate courts.
- Tried major utility rate cases and enforcement actions for gas, electric and solid waste companies.
- Counseled utility commissioners, developed policy and interfaced with division directors.
- Provided legal expertise for the Department of Environmental Protection.

Selected Achievements:
- ◆ *Assigned to special task force regarding investigation and prosecution of organized crime into solid waste industry.*
- ◆ *Counseled commissioners during hearing to debar a solid waste hauler.*
- ◆ *Obtained favorable published opinion pertaining to the allocation of sewerage capacity and antitrust issues.*

(continued...)

135

Combination. *Alesia Benedict, Rochelle Park, New Jersey*
Dot leaders instead of horizontal lines connect the left-aligned section headings with the right margin. As is true for other resumes by this writer, the areas of expertise are in three columns—

ALISA WASHINGTON   (xxx) xxx-xxxx   -Page Two-

PROFESSIONAL EXPERIENCE continued . . . .

STERN, STEIGER, CROLAND & CONWAY   Morristown, New Jersey
A 26-member firm concentrating in commercial litigation and matrimonial law.

Associate   *1985 - 1987*
- Managed 50+ cases for an insurance company involving surety bonds, real estate syndication, RICO, fraud in addition to an active caseload of complex commercial and noncommercial matters.
- Tried cases in state and federal courts.
- Extensively interfaced with clients and prepared complaints, interrogatories, motions and briefs.
- Conducted depositions and researched commercial litigation matters.

Selected Achievements:
- ◆ *Successfully managed all aspects of insurance cases which generated over $100,000 in annual revenue.*
- ◆ *Assisted in a commercial nuisance case that resulted in trial verdict of $383,000 compensatory damages and $100,000 punitive damages.*

EDUCATIONAL BACKGROUND . . . .

RUTGERS SCHOOL of LAW - Camden, New Jersey
Juris Doctor (1985)
- Moot Court Best Oral Argument (Commercial Law, Real Estate, Taxation, Environmental Law)
- Teaching Assistant for Legal Research and Writing Class (Performance rated A+)
- Coordinated tutorial program for affirmative action students
- Dean's List

YALE UNIVERSITY - New Haven, Connecticut
Bachelor of Arts in Economics and Political Science (1981)
- John M. Brodie Memorial Scholar Athlete Award
- Captain of Wrestling Team
- Officer/Charter Member of Black Athletes at Yale Organization

CONTINUING EDUCATION . . . .

Institute of Continuing Legal Education / Practicing Law Institute
- Representing Professional Athletes and Teams
- Revised Business Corporations Act
- Trial Preparation
- Mastering the Art of Direct and Cross Examination
- Entertainment Law
- Mock Trial of a Bankruptcy Case
- Power of the Bankruptcy Court Under Section 105

BAR ADMISSIONS . . . .

State of New Jersey
Federal District Courts of New Jersey and Southern District of New York
State of Connecticut

PROFESSIONAL MEMBERSHIPS . . . .

New Jersey Bar Association
Bergen County Bar Association
Bergen County Bar Arbitration Panel
Garden State Bar Association

the first, left-aligned; the second, center-aligned; and the third, right-aligned—for a symmetrical, balanced look. Job titles stand out in italic. To make selected, quantified achievements stand out even more, the writer used centered subheadings, diamond bullets, and bold italic. A small phrase describes two firms.

TANYA L. SCHWARTZ

15000 Bayshore Drive • Odessa, Florida 33500 • (813) 000-0000

Career Profile

Corporate Attorney offering dynamic career that combines expertise in civil law with core competencies in business management. Fourteen-year tenure consists of diverse legal experience involving a myriad of clients ranging from Fortune 500 and 100 companies to small business owners and individual consumers. Astute in identifying, clarifying, and resolving legal issues pertaining to *employment guidelines, professional licensing, corporate actions, contractual prerequisites, import/export transactions, real estate matters, and estate planning*. Equal talents in legal research/analysis, client management, administrative operations, financial management, staff supervision, and personnel management. Articulate communicator, exhibit well-honed presentation and interpersonal skills. Self-directed and very conscientious; able to work well under pressure. Dedicated lawyer possessing positive attitude, professional work ethic, and high-level integrity.

Technical/PC Skills: Broad-based knowledge of Lexis, Internet Research Services, Windows 95, Microsoft Word, E-mail

Professional Experience Summary

Legal Expertise

• **Employment Law**:	Worker's Compensation, ADA, and EEO issues; state and federal employment guidelines; employee screening and investigation procedures; Fair Credit Reporting Act (FCRA); and compliance mandates.
• **Business Law:**	Negotiate corporate contracts; draft various legal documents; and prepare FCRA documents, Limited/General Power of Attorneys, and Purchase/Sale Agreements.
• **Contract Law:**	Manage due diligence, contract analysis, interpret/structure contractual provisions, and address litigation and compliance issues.
• **Estates/Trusts:**	Wills, Codicils, Trust Amendments, Living Wills, and Health Care Designated Agent documentation.
• **Import/Export Laws:**	U.S. Customs regulations; federal statutes governing international imports/exports; Bureau of Alcohol, Tobacco, and Firearms guidelines; and federal and state licensing requirements.
• **Legal Research:**	Conversant with federal, criminal, civil, and professional licensing investigations; explore legitimacy of educational and employment backgrounds; and examine litigation matters, case law, and judicial decisions.

Corporate Management

• **Administrative Operations:**	Direct multiple divisions, project management, delegate and monitor daily workflow, change management, scheduling, and implement/enforce policies and procedures.
• **Financial Management:**	Cost analysis; active participation in revenue projections; and oversee accounts payable, accounts receivable, general ledger activities, and state excise taxes.
• **Personnel Management:**	Supervise 50 employees; hire, train, evaluate staff, annual merit reviews, reprimands and terminations; strengthen employee relations; team building; motivate staff; and develop staff incentive programs.

Education / Licensure

Juris Doctor (May 1984)
Villanova University Law School - Villanova, Pennsylvania

Bachelor of Arts, Political Science (May 1981)
Muhlenberg College - Allentown, Pennsylvania

Bar Admissions: Florida Bar (February 1993)
New Jersey Bar (December 1985)

Private Investigative Licensure (1995)

136

Combination. *Diane McGoldrick, Tampa, Florida*
An executive resume with narrow margins, wide lines, small print, and white space through blank lines. This Corporate Attorney had a part-time practice and wanted to move into full-

TANYA L. SCHWARTZ

Employment History

CORPORATE SERVICES, INC. - Tampa, Florida
Attorney / Director of Research

1994 - Present

Pivotal role executing a broad scope of responsibilities as in-house counsel and Director of Research for Florida branch location of a Chicago-based business specializing in corporate investigative services for Fortune 500 and 100 companies and small businesses. Spearhead operations of five internal research divisions (federal, criminal, civil, professional license, and education and employment verification) consisting of 50 staff members; sustain client management; and render legal expertise in the areas of employment and contract laws, research and investigative procedures, and drafting documents.

- Analyze and address various legal actions and issues involving ADA, EEO, Workers Compensation, FCRA, and background investigations/screenings.

- Review, interpret, and negotiate contracts in conjunction with Contract Administration. Serve as a liaison to corporate entities to foster information exchange.

- Instrumental in assisting corporate and representative counsel in various legal proceedings; research complaints and litigation issues; and ensure compliance with federal and state laws.

- Direct all related administrative duties necessary to maintain productivity of each division — implement changes in policies and procedures, delegate assignments, manage projects, train staff, scheduling logistics, and personnel management.

- Led development and implementation of incentive programs to bolster employee relations and reward peak-performers.

PRIVATE LAW PRACTICE - Odessa, Florida
Attorney-at-Law

1997 - Present

Solo practitioner specializing in estate/probate. Prepare wills, codicils, power of attorneys, trust amendments, living wills, and health care designated agent documentation for a select client base.

L&K RESEARCH & REPORTING, INC. - Tampa, Florida
Director of Research

1992 - 1994

Presided over daily operations of all research divisions.

COLLECTIBLE GUNS, INC. - Cherry Hill, New Jersey
Assistant Vice President

1984- 1991

Managed company's legal and business affairs pertaining to federal and state licensing requirements, records compliance, and various international import/export transactions. Provided active participation in areas such as upholding fiscal efficiency; cost analyses; revenue projections; and oversaw AR, AP, general ledger activities, and state excise taxes.

CITY PROSECUTOR'S OFFICE - Philadelphia, Pennsylvania
Intake Counselor (*Recruited during second year of law school to work part-time*)

1982 - 1984

Charged with reviewing complaints and rendering appropriate dispositions, drafting criminal warrants and complaints, and presenting Motions for the Night Prosecutor's and Bad Check Programs. Initially started as Mediator for The Night Prosecutor's Program; conducted nonjudicial hearings without court intervention.

Affiliations

American Bar Association
Notary Public, State of Florida

time practice. Usually the flow is from private practice to a corporate position. Her immediate goal was to work first for a law firm. Through networking she got a job offer before the resume was completed. It was still "necessary for Human Resources." A resume worthy of close inspection. Note the use of bold and italic.

Judith S. Sullivan, J.D.

22040 – 65th Pl. S. E. ▪ Snohomish, Washington 98008 ▪ (000) 555-4312
lawyer@mmm.com

Dynamic, Multifaceted Human Resources Lawyer

- Energetic, focused Human Resources lawyer with extensive experience resolving corporate and human resource challenges for major national and Northwest employers.
- Comprehensive grasp of EEOC, ADA, FMLA, and civil rights, and Federal and State regulations as they apply to human resource decisions.
- Perception coupled with strong communication abilities enhance recruiting/placement skills.
- Author of policy and procedure handbooks that also promote awareness of the potential for (and how to avoid) catastrophic lawsuits.
- Creative trainer/developer; create and conduct engaging presentations that incorporate role playing and other dramatic participatory techniques for managers, employees, user groups, and legal industry organizations.
- Profitability analysis expert; in this capacity, earned reputation for delivering "tough news" tactfully and compassionately.
- Designer and beta tester of large, complex databases for tracking and controlling documents and financial data.
- Recognized for coaching, problem-solving, and consensus-building skills.
- Unequaled commitment to customer service and achievement of performance goals.
- Disciplined, organized achiever—*earned law degree while working 50 hours per week.*

Skills Include

Recruiting	Negotiating/Mediating	Team Building
Sourcing/Screening	Budgeting/Forecasting	Training
Hiring	Compensation Analysis	Personnel Development

Professional Experience

Legal Matters, Inc., Snohomish, WA;   XXXX-Present
President / CEO

- Source, recruit, screen, negotiate, and hire employees at all levels for large national and Pacific Northwest companies and law firms.
- Through attention to detail and use of a perceptive, personalized approach, earned a reputation for closely matching candidates with employer's needs and culture—thereby allowing an unprecedented one-year placement guarantee.
- Analyze compensation structures and advise employers on packages that not only meet market standards, but avoid potential legal and/or IRS complexities.
- Analyze expansion/replacement needs, and the economic impact of and options for change.
- As a consultant to large retailer, wrote a complete set of software licensing agreements.

"Ms. Sullivan brings a unique blend of enthusiasm and technical skills to the recruitment arena. Her efforts to thoroughly familiarize herself with our firm's needs and goals gave her a strong base to provide excellent, well-targeted referrals." –*Bill Sewell, Managing Member, Smith Thorne Gibbons, P.L.L.C.*

"Ms. Sullivan is a valuable team player, very attuned to our firm's culture and needs. She provides superior candidates in response to our *highly specific, complex needs. . . .* Her enthusiasm and skill are outstanding." –*Jerry Wright, Executive Director, Athens Lundmark & Crowder*

137

Combination. *Kathy Vargo, Issaquah, Washington*
A dynamic resume for a "dynamo" lawyer who had "done it all"—an attorney who could write software code and was the "consummate professional." This person wanted to reenter

Judith S. Sullivan, J.D.
Page 2

Software Creations, Olympia, WA;   XXXX-XXXX
National Training & Support Manager of Litigation Management Database

- Initially hired as Litigation Support Software Design Consultant to participate in database design for control of large (one million-page plus) cases.
- Because of solution orientation, rapidly promoted to National Litigation Support Manager, overseeing both the client service and technical support teams.
- Wrote/Edited LSS Specifications, System Administrator's Guide, User's Guide, Advanced Report Writer Guide, and Training Manuals.
- Traveled extensively, speaking at seminars and user group meetings; conducted legal continuing education courses, and spoke to legal industry associations.
  - *Promoted to Northwest Regional Sales Manager while continuing Litigation Support Management activities; quickly achieved #2 region in sales in the country.*

Twiddle & Snoreson, Attorneys at Law, Seattle, WA;   XXXX-XXXX
Corporate and Business Transactions Attorney

- Joined firm as an Associate Attorney; effectively handled and resolved complex corporate and business transactions and issues.
- Honed ability to negotiate, using a highly successful analytic, yet perceptive style.
  - *Designed and implemented an automated system to track productivity and accounts receivable. As a direct result, collections increased 25% in one year.*

Ridgemont & Larson, San Francisco, CA;   XXXX-XXXX
In-house Counsel / Director of Sales and Acquisitions for Real Estate Limited Partnerships

- Recruited through the recommendation of one of firm's largest clients.
- In an environment where compensation was heavily incentive-based, charged with the sale and acquisition of properties ranging from $3.5 to $9 million dollars.
- Progressed to acquiring properties nationally; performed financial due diligence and inspections. Astutely negotiated purchase and sale terms, overseeing entire process to ensure closings were accomplished in a timely fashion.
  - *In first six months, sold seven of the historically most troublesome out-of-state commercial properties, earning a colossal bonus.*

SoftWrite Corporation, Santa Ana, CA;   XXXX-XXXX
Senior Software Technical Writer

- Recruited and assigned to OEM Products Groups to write CAD/CAM specifications for a UNIX-based system.
- Selected to work on-site with Mogul Software, Inc., to design and implement a document production plan.
- Persuaded SoftWrite to support tuition reimbursement for law degree studies.

Education & Training

Some State University Law School; *J.D., AmJur Award in Commercial Transactions;*   XXXX
Some State University; *B.S., Economics, Summa cum Laude;*   XXXX

the job market after five years of self-employment and doubted whether anyone would hire her. At a job fair, employers "went nuts." She got six interviews and job offers up to $150,000. The writer's secret was to "soften" the resume with people skills and to project the individual's personality into the resume.

MAUREEN METZGER————————————————————

10 12th Street • Fair, New Jersey XXXXX
(H) xxx/xxx-xxxx • (O) xxx/xxx-xxxx

Summary of Qualifications——————————————————

A dedicated and seasoned professional with an accomplished career spanning 15 years. Excellent interpersonal skills with the ability to develop and build rapport with clientele. Highly organized, with demonstrated strengths in successfully managing large caseloads. Maintains a proactive and results-oriented approach, enhancing both the firm's profitability and client representation. Martindale Hubble rating of BV.

Areas of Expertise————————————————————

FAMILY LAW • REAL ESTATE • CIVIL LITIGATION
WILLS AND ESTATES • SOCIAL SECURITY DISABILITY

Professional Experience————————————————

Self-Employed • Fair Lawn, NJ   **1982 - Present**
Directs all functions pertaining to a successful law practice, including conducting client interviews, research and case preparation.

Matrimonial/Family Law:
- Extensive involvement in all aspects of family law: setting and collecting fees, client intake and analysis of issues, preparation of pleadings, orders to show cause, property settlement agreements and prenuptial agreements.
- Experienced in alimony, child support, visitation, postjudgment applications, domestic violence and child sexual abuse matters.
- Excellent negotiating skills resulting in effective resolution of issues.
- Trial experience in all aspects of matrimonial/family law.

Real Estate Law:
- Proficient in the purchase, sale and refinance of both residential and commercial property.
- Experienced in lease negotiations and preparation/trial of landlord/tenant and wrongful eviction cases.

Civil Litigation:
- Experienced in handling plaintiff/defense cases including automobile collisions, slip and fall practice, contract disputes and trespass actions.
- Responsible for conducting initial client interviews and background investigations, determining legal strategies, preparing pleadings, conducting discovery and preparing for trial.
- Negotiates with claims personnel and prepares letters to carriers illustrating exposure and recommending settlement figures.
- Represents clients at settlement conferences, arbitrations and trials.

(continued...)

138

Combination. *Alesia Benedict, Rochelle Park, New Jersey*
Italic throughout the Summary of Qualifications gives the content the appearance of being special. A topical grouping of areas of law practice is presented as self-employment, which

Maureen Metzger————————————————————————————————

(H) xxx/xxx-xxxx • (O) xxx/xxx-xxxx
-Page Two-

Professional Experience continued————————————————————————

Wills and Estate Matters:
* Experienced in drafting wills, living wills, powers of attorney and insurance trusts.
* Represents Estates in the sale of real estate properties.
* Negotiates with creditors on behalf of the Estate.
* Drafts and files New Jersey Estate Tax Returns.

Social Security Matters:
* Experienced in all aspects of disability cases including conducting hearings to determine disability and litigating appeals in both the U.S. District Court and Court of Appeals.
* Secures medical reports regarding claimant's physical/psychiatric conditions, and evaluates claimant's case pursuant to applicable regulations and case law.

Previous Experience————————————————————————————————

Associate, Edwin Eastwood, Esq. • North Bergen, NJ   1981
* Provided legal representation for clients in a general practice firm.
* Drafted pleadings and motions, participated in discovery, and appeared in court.

Staff Attorney, Somerset/Sussex Legal Services • Somerville, NJ   1979 - 1981
* Managed a heavy and varied caseload.
* Fully accountable for all assigned cases.
* Frequent court appearances.
* Conducted pro se divorce clinics and lectured at community outreach programs.

Associate, Freeman and Bass • Newark, NJ   1978
* Assisted in case preparation for a firm concentrating on social security, workers compensation and personal injury matters.

Education————————————————————————————————————

J.D. Rutgers Law School • Camden, NJ (1978)
B.A. (Political Science), Ohio State University • Columbus, OH (1975) • *Cum Laude*

Bar Admissions————————————————————————————————

State of New Jersey (1978)
U.S. Court of Appeals, 3rd Circuit (1987)

Awards————————————————————————————————————

Bergen County Legal Services Pro Bono Service Award (1985)
Legal Services of New Jersey Equal Justice Medal (1988)

Professional Affiliations————————————————————————————

American Bar Association
New Jersey State Bar Association
Association of Trial Lawyers of America
Bergen County Bar Association

is part of the larger chronology of Experience (Professional and Previous). On page 2, small clusters separated by blank lines ensure adequate white space. The writer's use of a page border on both pages ties together the two pages visually. Years are right-aligned. The partial lines help to separate the main sections.

WILSON P. ALVAREZ

400 Galaxy Boulevard East, Chesapeake Bay, MD 00000   (555) 555-5555

—SUMMARY—

Over fourteen years of extensive involvement in employment law matters, particularly in labor/ industrial relations focused on the avoidance of liabilities. Experience gained in a complex corporate environment undergoing continual restructuring, massive layoffs, and changing technology.

—PROFESSIONAL DEVELOPMENT—

19XX to Date   ASTRA AEROSPACE CORPORATION, Baltimore, MD

Sr. Corporate Counsel/Industrial Relations (Since 19XX)
Sr. Industrial Relations Administrator (19XX to 19XX)
Labor Relations Administrator (19XX to 19XX)

At present, solely responsible for labor relations activities involving two corporate divisions, three union locals, and five collective bargaining agreements covering up to 2,000 employees. Monitor all labor matters to ensure adherence to contracts, corporate policies, and federal/state laws as affected by new legislation, Labor Board decisions, and court or EEOC rulings. Areas of involvement include:

Negotiations/Contract Administration
➤ Negotiated collective bargaining agreements in joint sessions with union locals, as well as other issues affecting production, maintenance, crafts, technical and clerical workers.
➤ Conducted compensation and benefit surveys in preparation for bargaining.
➤ Prepared demographic studies determining factors such as age, sex and length of service of the labor population to develop meaningful bargaining terms.
➤ Drafted new contract language which clearly and fairly interpreted existing articles/sections as well as addressed new issues arising out of problematic situations.
➤ Educated supervisors on provisions and constraints of contracts and the effects of current labor laws.
➤ Advised management in the proper handling of contractual concerns when dealing with employment matters ranging from upgrading/promotion through discipline/discharge.

Litigation/Arbitration/Grievance Handling
➤ Acted as liaison with outside counsel in various labor relations issues.
➤ Negotiated settlement of all final grievance packages in-house, precluding the need for costly trial proceedings.
➤ Investigated causes of labor disputes in their early stages and intervened to prevent their exacerbation and analogous precedent setting actions.
➤ Took depositions in complicated cases involving alleged discrimination and provided witness testimony in court which resulted in favorable rulings.
➤ Monitored records of individuals' actions leading to dismissal to ensure sufficient supporting documentation. Throughout entire tenure was successful in warding off all wrongful discharge suits.
➤ Directed and administered all discipline for bargaining unit employees.
➤ Argued management's position at arbitration and top grievance sessions as well as for those issues brought before outside dispute resolution forums such as the EEOC and Maryland Division on Civil Rights.
➤ Obtained awards of costs and partial attorney's fees in cases that had to be litigated in federal and state courts.

… Continued

139

Functional. *Melanie A. Noonan, West Paterson, New Jersey*
Because of an anticipated closing of an aerospace contractor within a year, this corporate attorney wanted to move to a law firm specializing in labor matters. The two areas of

WILSON P. ALVAREZ

Page 2

Human Resource Administration

➤ Collaborated with supervisors and union officials. Developed appropriate descriptive wording for newly created bargaining unit jobs and determined equitable pay rates.

➤ Consulted with training department to ascertain basic skills requirements for open positions and recommended job-specific testing procedures.

➤ Interviewed and recruited on-campus candidates for engineering or technical positions based on company's selection criteria.

➤ Using computerized Human Resource Information System (MSA software), designed reports which increased productivity and morale of the workforce by facilitating timely data retrieval for management decision making.

➤ Automated the recall expiration tracking system to more efficiently handle a large volume of laid-off employees with varying eligibility dates for rehire.

Personnel Policies and Programs

➤ Carried out company's Affirmative Action plans and monitored compliance. Periodically submitted reports to the EEOC of current and terminated employees by job category, age, sex and minority designation.

➤ Coordinated company-wide Employee Assistance Program offering all employees help in dealing with issues affecting work performance. These included alcohol and drug abuse treatment, family leave, and coping strategies to handle stress from job and personal problems.

➤ Provided for qualified trainers to educate supervisors in detecting possible substance abusers among their work group.

➤ Assisted in the implementation of corporate directives to address current workplace issues such as bloodborne pathogen (HIV) carriers, sexual harassment, designation of no-smoking areas, and structural modifications to accommodate handicapped workers.

—OTHER EMPLOYMENT—

19XX to 19XX	NOVAK & O'MALLEY, Silver Springs, MD *Attorney, general practice*
19XX to 19XX	KALSTEIN, EDWARDS & FURMAN, Newark, NJ *Law Clerk, labor relations (representing management)*

—EDUCATION—

J.D., 19XX	Rutgers University School of Law, Newark, NJ
B.A. *cum laude*, 19XX	Syracuse University School of Business Administration, Syracuse, NY

—PROFESSIONAL ORGANIZATIONS—

American Bar Association
American Society of Association
Maryland State Bar Association
New Jersey State Bar Association

involvement on the first page are more relevant to a private practice; the two on the second page are more geared to a corporate environment. Should the person decide to join a corporation, the two pairs could be switched. "Shaded arrowheads for the bulleted items add a touch of interest without going overboard."

WALTER J. BRADFORD, ESQ.
433 State Highway
City, State 00000
555-555-5555

Admitted to Practice in All State Courts.
Admitted to Practice in US District Court for the Western District of the State.
Member, State Bar Association.

SUMMARY: *Accomplished investigator and litigator with extensive experience supervising criminal investigations, trying cases, and supervising other attorneys. Knowledgeable in all facets of criminal and civil law with experience advising State Supreme Court Justice on matters of law relating to cases tried in his courtroom. Excellent management capabilities, including staff supervision and budgetary accountability.*

PROFESSIONAL EXPERIENCE:

STATE SUPREME COURT; City, State.

1993 - Present   **Principal Law Clerk / Legal Counsel to Justice Carl J. Smith.**
Advise Supreme Court Justice on all legal matters pertaining to cases in litigation before the court.
- Research points of substantive law, evidentiary issues, and procedural issues.
- Respond to the Justice's immediate requests while court is in session.
- Confer with Justice Smith and other Justices on issues before the court.
- Research underlying case law relevant to motions made before the court.
- Draft court opinions for the Justice's review and approval.
- Serve as a Matrimonial Referee as appropriate.

COUNTY DISTRICT ATTORNEY'S OFFICE; City, State.
(1980 - 1993)

1985 - 1993   **Bureau Chief - Investigations / Special Assistant District Attorney**
Supervised Chief Investigator with accountability for ten investigators involved in criminal investigations. Directed the activities of eight attorneys engaged in prosecuting narcotics, organized crime, and conspiracy cases. Served on Executive Staff of District Attorney's Office, participating in the development and administration of $6.5 million operating budget and establishment of departmental policies.
- Directed undercover and informant investigations.
- Reviewed and approved electronic surveillance warrants.
- Served as Chief Legal Advisor to County Drug Enforcement Task Force.
- Litigated major narcotics and conspiracy cases.
- Trained attorneys in felony litigation; assigned cases.
- Participated in interviewing, hiring, and ongoing evaluation of attorneys.
- Administered federally funded grants for narcotics prosecution.

1983 - 1985   **Assistant District Attorney / Appeals Bureau**
1981 - 1982   *Performed appellate and criminal trial work for homicide and other major felony cases.*
- Defended federal and state Habeas Corpus and Coram Nobis actions.
- Prepared trial briefs, trial memoranda, and jury charges for Chief of Homicide and First Assistant District Attorney in major cases.
- Conducted civil forfeiture actions and negotiations.
- Directed Post-Conviction Tracking Team; made recommendations to Department of Corrections regarding parole for incarcerated felons.
- Reviewed Change of Status applications for defendants committed to mental health facilities.
- Argued appeals in State courts at all levels.
- Supervised appellate attorneys and appeals from local courts.

Combination. *Arnold G. Boldt, Rochester, New York*
A resume for a lawyer whose career path over 20+ years has been from Public Defender to Counsel for a State Supreme Court Justice. Boldface, bold italic, or just italic is used for

Walter J. Bradford, Esq.
Résumé - Page Two

PROFESSIONAL EXPERIENCE *(continued):*

COUNTY DISTRICT ATTORNEY'S OFFICE *(continued):*
1982 - 1983   **Assistant District Attorney / Special Criminal Investigations.**
1980 - 1981   **Assistant District Attorney / Grand Jury, Criminal Trials.**
- Conducted felony trials in narcotics and organized crime cases.
- Advised police agencies in narcotics and organized crime investigations.
- Prepared search warrants and electronic surveillance warrants.
- Presented felony cases before Grand Juries.

COUNTY PUBLIC DEFENDER'S OFFICE; City, State.
1977 - 1980   **Public Defender**
Provided legal defense to indigent defendants from arraignment through final disposition.

ADDITIONAL EXPERIENCE:

Guest Lecturer at Regional Police Training Academy.
Instructor, SUNY at Jamestown.
Legal Assistant Internship, City Board of Education.

EDUCATION:

1977   **Juris Doctor**
State University at City; City, State.

1973   **Bachelor of Science, Comparative Religion & Ethics**
State University at City; City, State.
Cum Laude Graduate

References Provided Upon Request.

information the writer wants seen. Hyphens are fainter than bullets and don't compete with italic text under a job title but nevertheless do their job of indicating clearly the first line of a two-line "bulleted" item. The individual was especially active in his various roles in the District Attorney's office. See Cover Letter 20.

ERIC N. LESTER
1234 East Broadway Avenue ♦ Monroe, NY 12345 ♦ 555 / 123-4567 *(Home)* ♦ 555 / 321-7654 *(Office)*
ericnlester@alumni.princetonuniversity.edu

ASSOCIATE ATTORNEY
Labor Law / Employment Law / Discrimination Law / Health Law / Corporate & Business Law

Practicing attorney with excellent qualifications in employment, labor, and health law. Solid track record of reducing legal costs through effective preventive advice. Possess ability to create an atmosphere of approachability to make individuals comfortable, enabling successful gathering of needed information. Skilled in establishing solid relationships with clients (particularly physicians), outside counsel, union officials, and government agencies. Thorough experience in writing responses to complaints of federal, state, and municipal agencies regulating discrimination, harassment, or other workplace issues. Computer literate. Web designer.

Areas of Knowledge & Proficiency Include:

- ♦ EEOC Rules & Regulations
- ♦ Massachusetts Bureau of Labor
- ♦ New York Human Rights Commission
- ♦ Unfair Labor Practice Charges
- ♦ Communications *(Written, Oral, Presentation)*
- ♦ Workshop/Seminar Development

- ♦ Arbitration
- ♦ Negotiations
- ♦ Grievance Complaints
- ♦ Sexual Harassment
- ♦ Family Medical Leave Act
- ♦ Union-Free Workplaces

- ♦ Wage & Hour Laws
- ♦ Union Contracts
- ♦ HR Management
- ♦ Risk Management
- ♦ Employee Relations
- ♦ Medical Staff Peer Review

EDUCATION
J.D., Certificate in Business Law, University of New York School of Law, *XXXX*
M.B.A., Goldstein College of Business, University of New York, *XXXX*
A.B., Political Science, Princeton University, *XXXX*

EXPERIENCE
HEALTH CARE SERVICES, Monroe, New York   *XXXX, XXXX to Present*
Operator of hospitals and healthcare facilities employing 75,000 employees throughout the U.S. Headquartered in Chicago.
Assistant General Counsel – Eastern Region *(XXXX to Present)*
Legal Intern (XXXX)

- ♦ Provide legal counsel, focusing primarily on labor and employment law issues, throughout the 12-state Eastern Region for 18 acute-care hospitals and numerous long-term and skilled nursing facilities employing more than 15,500 and generating gross revenues of $2.3 billion.
- ♦ Acknowledged as reducing labor and employment expenditures by $750,000 since full-time hire through effective caseload management, negotiations, and arbitration.
- ♦ Settled within 16-month period 12 discrimination, wrongful discharge, grievance, sexual harassment, and other cases. Successful in gaining settlements below HCS break-even points.
- ♦ Work with 7 labor unions (Teamsters, Service Employees International, United Food & Commercial Workers, New York State Nurses Association, Massachusetts Nurses Association, IBEW, IUOE) on grievance complaints and arbitration issues.
- ♦ Represent medical staffs during the peer review process, ensuring compliance with the medical staff bylaws, rules, and regulations.
- ♦ Created, implemented, and delivered a series of "Ask the Attorney" workshops for hospital and healthcare facility management teams. Topics ranged from Death with Dignity laws to latex sensitivity.
- ♦ Assumed leadership and delivery of regularly provided seminars on harassment.
- ♦ Created a 100-page management guide on the federal FMLA for corporate-wide distribution.
- ♦ Delivered FMLA presentation to all human resource and risk management staff and authored article on the subject for *Healthy Lives,* a quarterly, in-house publication on healthcare issues.
- ♦ Established and maintained a legal services site on the HCS Internet site.

LICENSURE & PROFESSIONAL AFFILIATIONS
New York State Bar Association, *NYBA #945128,* Manhattan Borough Bar Association
New York State Society of Healthcare Attorneys, American Health Lawyers Association

141

Combination. *Carole S. Barns, Woodinville, Washington*
With outstanding academic credentials and less than two years' experience, this person sought work at a law firm. On the same day the resume was received, he got a great offer.

EDWARD THOMAS DeMORAL

111 Finnigan
Columbus, North Carolina 24200

Residence: (555) 970.9191
Business: (555) 432.1212

PROFESSIONAL EXPERIENCE

MAJORS COMMUNICATIONS, INC., City, State   1994 – Present
Assistant General Counsel
Current responsibilities include: new business development for U.S. and Canada, Office of Public
Affairs (legislative, regulatory, and political matters), intellectual property rights, workmen's
compensation, and litigation oversight.

WELL KNOWN INC., City, State   1992 – 1993
Zone Sales Designate
Domestic sales and management leading to senior career opportunity with Popular Foods
International.

POPULAR INDUSTRIES, INC., City, State   1988 – 1992
Operations Project Manager (1992)
Developed purchasing and inventory control models for operations, and analyzed mergers and
acquisitions for finance.
Market Planning Manager (1988 – 1991)
Designed and implemented marketing strategies and promotions. Integrated and executed national
and regional marketing programs. Ensured compliance, evaluated results, and developed responsive
strategies. Supervised media buying for television, radio, and print.

U.S. INTERNATIONAL TRADE COMMISSION, Washington, D.C.   1982 – 1988
Advisor to Commissioner/Chairman
Counseled Chairman on investigations conducted under U.S. trade statutes. Analyzed financial,
economic, and legal issues of foreign and domestic producers involved in international trade
disputes. Also served as a Commission representative with the White House, Congress, Department
of Commerce, and U.S. Trade Representative.

U.S. HOUSE OF REPRESENTATIVES, Washington, D.C.   1981 – 1982
Legislative Assistant
Congressman Bob Rathers (D-ST)
Analyzed legislation and assisted the Congressman with the Committee on Armed Services.
Significant effort was devoted to public relations.
Congressman Jack Collier (R-ST)
Advised the Congressman on international concerns, domestic agricultural issues, and media affairs.

Earlier experience with POPULAR, INC., as *Marketing Analyst* in Feltham Middlesex, England and
Purchase, New York.

EDUCATION

PACE UNIVERSITY SCHOOL OF LAW, White Plains, New York
Juris Doctor degree
HAGUE ACADEMY OF INTERNATIONAL LAW, The Hague, Netherlands
Public International Law
UNIVERITE LIBRE de BRUXELLES and VIRGE UNIVERSITEIT BRUSSEL, Brussels, Belgium
Law of the European Community
STETSON UNIVERSITY, DeLand, Florida
Bachelor of Arts, Social Science

ASSOCIATIONS

American, California, and New York Bar Associations – Member
Professional Marketing Association of America – Law Committee

142

Chronological. *Lorie Lebert, Novi, Michigan*
A resume that is just a summary. Full credentials were given in a curriculum vitae—a type of
resume used by academics and executives. Hanging indents make company names seen.

Judith Levin
55 Fifth Avenue
New York, New York 55555
(212) 555-5555

LEGAL EXPERIENCE

CITY OF NEW YORK HUMAN RESOURCES ADMINISTRATION
Assistant General Counsel, Office of Legal Affairs
March xxxx - Present

Supervision of five attorneys within Medicaid Litigation Unit; management and litigation of cases involving trusts, estates and related Medicaid issues.

SUPREME COURT OF THE STATE OF NEW YORK
Law Clerk
September xxxx - February xxxx

Principal Law Clerk to the Honorable Stanley L. Sklar during leave of absence of the Judge's Law Clerk.

SMOLLENS, GURALNICK & FRAZER, LLP
Of Counsel
September xxxx - August xxxx

Real Estate Litigation - represented individual clients, cooperative corporations and condominiums both as plaintiffs and defendants; extensive writing, motion practice, discovery and consulting with cooperative boards.

NEW YORK STATE ATTORNEY GENERAL'S OFFICE
Assistant Attorney General - Litigation and Real Estate Financing Bureau
January xxxx - September xxxx

Represented state agencies in federal and state trial and appellate courts; federal litigation included class actions; 1983 cases, Bankruptcy, and constitutional issues; handled motion practice, discovery, preparation of briefs; assisted in drafting and reviewing agreements and opinions.

Enforced New York State law regulating the offer and sale of real estate securities; negotiated workouts with banks, sponsors, boards of cooperatives and condominiums; mediated disputes between sponsors and board.

SPECIAL PROSECUTOR FOR HEALTH AND SOCIAL SERVICES
Special Assistant Attorney General
January xxxx - January xxxx

Supervision of investigators and auditors in the investigation and prosecution of criminal offenses in the health care field within New York State; consultant for community groups regarding nursing and adult homes; drafted proposals, commentary and supporting memoranda regarding state and federal legislation.

LEGAL AID SOCIETY
Associate Attorney - Civil Division
September xxxx - December xxxx

Litigated federal class action law reform cases and public benefits entitlement cases; state court litigation included landlord/tenant disputes; consumer advocacy and matrimonial matters for senior citizens; provided outreach to tenant and community groups.

- continued -

143

Chronological. *Judith Friedler, New York, New York*
"A fairly straightforward legal resume" that differs in listing Academic Experience as well. Hanging indents make the side headings stand out. All-uppercase letters are used for firm names and

Judith Levin
Page Two

ACADEMIC EXPERIENCE

NEW YORK LAW SCHOOL
Adjunct Instructor, Legal Writing Program
September xxxx - Present

SETON HALL LAW SCHOOL
Adjunct Instructor, Legal Writing Program
September xxxx - June xxxx

MONTCLAIR STATE UNIVERSITY
Adjunct Instructor - Paralegal Studies Program
August xxxx - June xxxx

Executive Assistant to Academic Vice President
September xxxx - August xxxx

Responsibilities included liaison with Board of Trustees, N.J. Department of Education, Department of Higher Education and Attorney General's Office; labor relations; academic program coordination; and budget planning.

EDUCATION

BROOKLYN LAW SCHOOL - *J.D., 1978*
Honors: *Moot Court Honor Society*

HARVARD UNIVERSITY - *M.A. Spanish Language & Literature, 1972*
Honors: *graduated with distinction*

HUNTER COLLEGE, C.U.N.Y. - *B.A. Spanish Literature, 1971*
Honors: *Cum Laude, Fulbright Scholarship, Emma Wagner Ackerele Award*

BAR ADMISSIONS

New York, New Jersey
United States District Court, Southern and Eastern District of New York
United States District Court of New Jersey

AFFILIATIONS / ACTIVITIES

New York City Civil Court
Volunteer Small Claims Court Arbitrator, 1993 - Present

Community Dispute Resolution Project, *1981 - 1984*
Volunteer Mediator for evening project to resolve pending Municipal Court cases at pretrial level in Essex County, NJ.

Association of the Bar of the City of New York

New York County Lawyers' Association

Association of Arbitrators

school names, and bold italic enhances the positions. The wide left margin for the main information and consistent use of blank lines ensure that the resume has adequate white space to avoid a crowded look. Sections for Bar Admissions and Affiliations/Activities display ties to New Jersey as well as New York.

FRANCINE NUMANN, ESQ
14 Banbury Court • Robbins, New Jersey 00000
(555) 555-5555

SUMMARY of QUALIFICATIONS:

A highly dedicated professional with a successful career and the capacity to contribute to the development of a progressive organization. Excellent organizational skills are evident in handling large caseloads and managing time effectively. Demonstrated strengths include the capacity to analyze large volumes of complex information, strong interpersonal skills with the ability to interface with individuals at all levels and strong follow-up skills.

AREAS of EXPERTISE:

GENERAL NEGLIGENCE • MEDICAL MALPRACTICE • LITIGATION
AUTOMOBILE NEGLIGENCE • PRODUCTS LIABILITY

PROFESSIONAL AFFILIATIONS:

BROTHERS INSURANCE GROUP (formerly American Reliance Insurance Company)   Lawrenceville, NJ
Staff Attorney   *1990 - Present*
- Serve as in-house counsel handling liability claims with a caseload of 100 files concurrently.
- Examine complaints, analyze legality of suits and prepare/file answers/pleadings on behalf of clients.
- Prepare and participate in all phases of pretrial discovery.
- Organize materials required for defense of negligence suits.
- Evaluate pending suits, review settlement demands and negotiate settlements.
- Participate in jury and nonjury trials.

Selected Achievements:
- *Consistently achieve a high success rate in obtaining dismissals of automobile negligence suits for failure to meet verbal threshold.*
- *Specifically requested by the Claims Department to handle verbal threshold cases.*

REISEMAN, MATTIA & SHARP   Roseland and Wall Township, NJ
A law firm specializing in insurance defense litigation, automobile negligence, medical malpractice defense, and product liability defense.
Associate   *1986 - 1990*
- Assisted partners in all phases of pretrial discovery, including drafting/filing pleadings and reviewing legality of suits.
- Prepared for and participated in jury and nonjury trials.

Selected Achievement:
- *Successfully obtained a high rate in suit dismissals for failure to meet the statute of limitations.*

(continued...)

Combination. *Alesia Benedict, Rochelle Park, New Jersey*
Just as there is tempo in music, there is tempo in reading, which means the speed at which a reader can read text because of the text. In a resume, factors influencing reading speed include

FRANCINE NUMANN   (555) 555-5555   Page Two

PROFESSIONAL AFFILIATIONS continued...

THE HONORABLE B. THOMAS LEAHY, J.S.C./THE HONORABLE BERNARD RUDD, J.S.C.
SUPERIOR COURT of NEW JERSEY   Newark, NJ
Law Clerk   *1985 - 1986*
- Assisted Family Court and Special Civil Part judges in daily court activities including motions and trials.
- Researched case law and assisted in drafting legal opinions.
- Assisted in the drafting of three legal opinions selected for publication in N.J. Super.

HOSPITAL of the UNIVERSITY of PENNSYLVANIA, Legal Department   Philadelphia, PA
Legal Intern   *1984 - 1985*
- Assisted legal counsel in drafting hospital policies and contracts.
- Assessed merit and monetary value of medical malpractice suits.

EDUCATIONAL BACKGROUND:

Rutgers School of Law • Camden, NJ
Juris Doctor

S.U.N.Y. at Binghamton • Binghamton, NY
Bachelor of Arts • History

BAR ADMISSIONS:

New Jersey • New York

MEMBERSHIPS:

New Jersey State Bar Association
Mercer County Bar Association
American Bar Association

References and Writing Samples furnished upon request

line width and spacing; font size, enhancement, and case; text alignment; and blank lines making white space. This resume promotes changes of tempo mainly through changes in alignment and line width. The reader can read fast at the beginning, must slow down for achievements, and can speed up at the end.

JUDY D. STEFANS, JD, CPCU
8 Residential Court
City, State 22222
(555) 555-5555

SUMMARY: *Skilled Manager and Attorney with extensive experience in the insurance industry. Successful project management and sales/marketing track record, including planning and implementing marketing strategies. Proven capability to supervise staff, promote staff development, and achieve performance objectives. Demonstrated ability to institute cost savings initiatives.*

PROFESSIONAL EXPERIENCE:

1987 - Present   **AMERICAN INSURANCE, LTD.**
Claims Market Manager; City, State   **Jan. 1996 - Present**
Accountable for Claims Adjustment in nine county western region. Directly supervise 32 Claims Adjusters and support staff. Maintain relationships with over 40 local sales agents.
- Serve on Marketing Committee with senior managers and agents.
- Provide professional training, motivation, and support to individual agents.
- Recruit, train, and evaluate performance of Claims Representatives.
- Manage facilities and company-owned fleet of vehicles.
- Assist Sales Agents in achieving sales goals in various market segments.
- Design and implement marketing plans to achieve regional objectives.
- Coordinate activities of Claims Representatives, Claims Technical Manager, and outside counsel on cases in litigation for western New York region.

Accomplishments:
- *Reduced Bodily Injury Claims payout by 8%, in line with targeted goals.*
- *Increased Net Salvage Recovery in line with targeted goals.*
- *Reduced pending Subrogation Claims by $414,000 for 1996 calendar year.*
- *Enhanced use of automated estimating systems for auto claims, achieving over 95% utilization.*
- *Promoted the increased use of non-OEM parts on auto repairs, resulting in substantial cost savings.*

Division Claims Manager -
American General Insurance; City, State   **1994 - 1995**
Accountable for strategic claims planning in 15 states where NGI operates. Gained valuable staff experience.
- Monitored Reserve Fund requirements in various states and worked to influence regulatory trends in each state.
- Counseled senior management on legal and claims matters.
- Conducted training programs relating to state laws and insurance regulations.
- Participated in state audits of legal and claims cases.
- Maintained oversight relationship with NGI claims operations in each state.
- Negotiated claims handling contracts with customers.
- Participated in strategic planning involving marketing and operations functions.

Claims Manager - Central Region   **1987 - 1994**
- Participated in project planning and implementation.
- Supervised commercial and personal lines litigation.
- Managed claims adjusters and support staff in a multicounty territory.
- Motivated Claims Supervisors and outside vendors to achieve planned objectives.
- Developed and delivered ongoing training on litigation and general insurance issues.

145

Combination. *Arnold G. Boldt, Rochester, New York*
A resume for an attorney who became a CLU and CPCU and uses her law and insurance expertise, together with her managerial ability, to manage Claims Adjustment for an insurance

Judy D. Stefans
Résumé - Page Two

PROFESSIONAL EXPERIENCE (continued):

1986 - 1987   **FARMERS' MUTUAL INSURANCE COMPANY; City, State**
Claims Attorney
Managed litigation of personal lines and commercial lawsuits.

1983 - 1986   **JOHNSON, WILLIAMS, BROWN, ET AL.; City, State**
Attorney - Associate / Law Clerk
Engaged in general private legal practice.

ADDITIONAL EXPERIENCE:

1996 - Present   **Consultant, Riverside Bike Shoppe; City, State**
Participated in the launch of this family-owned business to enhance marketing, business, and entrepreneurial skills. Assisted in developing Business Plan, planning marketing strategies, and setting up operations for retail bike shop.

1995   **Loaned Executive, United Way of Franklin County; City, State**
Solicited corporate donations from previously nongiving companies. Recognized for raising the most new dollars during 1995 Business Development Campaign.

LICENSURE:

Admitted to the Bar in New York and Ohio.
Life and Health Insurance (New York).

EDUCATION:

October 1995   **Chartered Property Casualty Underwriter (CPCU)**

Chartered Life Underwriter (CLU)
Five courses complete:
- Personal Risk Management   - Individual Life Insurance
- Fundamentals of Financial Planning   - Life Insurance Law
- Income Taxation

May 1985   **Juris Doctor**
University Law School; City, State
Insurance Law Book Award (Highest Average In Class).

May 1982   **Bachelor of Science, Management / Political Science**
Bethel College of City; City, State

PROFESSIONAL ENRICHMENT:

- Superior Leadership School   - Basic Management School
- Corporate Management School   - Nationwide Insurance Model
- ACE Facilitation Training   - Lessons in Leadership Annual Seminar

COMMUNITY INVOLVEMENT / AFFILIATIONS:

Vice President, Bethel College Alumni Board.
Bethel College Board of Trustees Committee for the Capital Campaign.
WWWW Channel 99 Auction / City Marathon / State Lung Association.

American Insurance Civic Action Program.

River County Bar Association / New York State Bar Association.

company. Important text is in italic. To read just the italic text is to gain a quick overview of this individual as a candidate. If you look for bold text and sweep over the resume, you'll spot section headings, dates, company names, job titles, and a centered heading: Accomplishments. These are also bulleted.

GARY F. PERSONY

10003 Colony Dr.
Space Center, CA 55555
Telephone: 000-000-0000
Email: tome@writeme.net

PROFILE

Senior Finance Executive with over 15 years' experience building and leading financial operations for a worldwide organization.

Strong general management qualifications in impacting organizational change and improvement. Additional strengths include capturing cost reductions, business process redesign, creative problem solving and executive leadership.

PROFESSIONAL EXPERIENCE

Fast–track promotion through a series of increasingly responsible positions directing large–scale finance and budget resources. Acted in a capacity of Senior Financial Representative, Corporate Auditor, Treasurer, Senior Financial Accountant, Short–Term Operating Plan Coordinator and Financial Manager. Expertise includes:

FINANCIAL MANAGEMENT
- Managed operating budgets allocated for personnel, facilities and administrative expenses.
- Consulted with senior management personnel to evaluate long–term organizational goals and design appropriate financial systems / methods to control monetary, technological and other capital assets. Accomplishments: Developed first–of–its kind automated workforce analysis, which streamlined work processes and developed efficiencies in reporting.
- Established start–up organization. Prepared work statements, hired qualified support staff and created a series of aggressive cost control / cost reduction programs. Accomplishment: Structured State of Louisiana Environmental / Enterprise Zone reporting definitions which were subsequently adopted statewide.
- Administered multimillion–dollar sales contracts and provided general financial support to operating department. Accomplishment: Automated sales contract reporting procedure.

AUDIT MANAGEMENT
- Instituted business models for corporate auditing, group finance planning and investment services which led to the successful development of Profit / Loss analysis and development of corporate goals.
- Negotiated first joint audit of a Saudi Arabian facility. Planned and participated in more than 18 domestic and international audits company–wide and made necessary productivity recommendations. Result: Dramatic improvement in working relationship between Shell Oil and Saudi Arabia Basic Industries Corporation (SABIC).
- Conducted highly successful natural gas contract audit which resulted in company savings of $3M per year.
- Revamped and automated budgeting process which dramatically saved time and improved accuracy of forecasts.
- Restructured head office reporting procedures resulting in strong improvements in accounting accuracy.

CONTINUED...

146

Functional. *Rosa St. Julian, Houston, Texas*
A resume for an attorney who became a Senior Financial Executive for a worldwide organization. The writer uses a "drop cap" for the first letter of the individual's name to call atten-

GARY A. PERSONY
PAGE 2

CAREER PATH
ZENON CAMERAS LIMITED, Space Center, CA (a subsidiary of Cameras Corporation), 1980 – Present
– Senior Financial Representative, Zenon Cameras, Small Ville, WA
– Corporate Auditor, Zenon Cameras, Small Ville, WA
– Treasurer, Zenon Shot Cameras, Small Ville, WA
– Financial Manager, Zenon Shot Cameras, Small Ville, WA
– Short -Term Operating Plan Coordinator, Zenon Cameras, Dino Land, UT
– Senior Financial Accountant, Zenon Cameras, Dino Land, UT
– Financial Accountant, Zenon Cameras, Dino Land, UT
– Location Auditor, Zenon Cameras, Dino Land, UT
– Accountant, Zenon Cameras, Dino Land, UT

EDUCATION / LICENSES

Loyola University, Toon Town, FL
Juris Doctor, Civil Law, 1987

Northeastern University, Astroworld, TX
Bachelor of Science, Accounting, Finance, Insurance, 1980

Licensed Attorney for the State of Connecticut

AFFILIATIONS

Member, American Bar Association
Member, Louisiana Bar Association

tion to it in the contact information. Headings for the main resume sections are centered. Subheadings are left-aligned. Professional Experience is subdivided into Financial Management and Audit Management. These subsections indicate accomplishments as well as responsibilities. The Career Path on page 2 has no dates.

DAVID KING
Attorney-at-Law
22 Donizi Place
Bronx, New York 10475

H: (xxx) xxx-xxxx   O: (xxx) xxx-xxxx

SUMMARY of QUALIFICATIONS:

A highly determined professional with a desire to succeed in a progressive organization. Strong communication skills result in positive relationships with individuals at all levels. Excellent analytical skills with the ability to assess the needs of a situation and implement viable solutions/strategies. Highly respected by both peers and clientele.

AREAS of EXPERTISE:

CRIMINAL LAW • BANK REGULATION

PROFESSIONAL EXPERIENCE:

OFFICE of THRIFT SUPERVISION   Jersey City, New Jersey
Trial Attorney   1991 - xxxx
- Oversaw and coordinated the activities of the investigators and bank examiners for a regulatory agency of federally insured savings and loan associations.
- Accountable for all phases of investigations including issuing subpoenas for documents and testimony and conducting interviews, depositions and administrative hearings.
- Conducted legal research and factual analysis.
- Reviewed federal, state, local business and personal income tax returns and financial statements to determine net worth for potential assessment of civil money penalties.
- Followed through with investigators until conclusions were drawn.

Achievements:

- *Directed the investigation and successfully negotiated settlements which resulted in the resignation of 5 directors and CMPs, exceeding $200,000 from a New Jersey thrift.*
- *Negotiated restitution of embezzled funds from a former President of a New Jersey thrift.*
- *Investigated and brought charges against the President of a New York thrift.*

UNITED STATES ATTORNEY'S OFFICE   New York, New York
Paralegal Specialist   1984 - 1991
- Instrumental in all stages of the investigation and trials of major criminal cases, including high-profile narcotics and organized crime cases.
- Supervised and developed paralegal staff.
- Extensively interfaced with witnesses, conducting debriefing sessions and preparing testimony for trial and before the grand jury.
- Positioned at counsel table for seven major criminal trials.
- Assisted in juror selection and developing legal strategies during trial.
- Prepared Orders for court-authorized surveillance, arrest warrants and search warrants.

Achievements:

- *Established an indexing and retrieval system to track over 500 exhibits for search warrants executed at 14 different locations.*
- *Indexed transcripts and exhibits which were utilized in 5 major narcotics conspiracy trials.*
- *Conducted vital legal research which led to the detention of defendants who would have become fugitives: criminals are currently serving life sentences.*

(continued...)

147

Combination. *Alesia Benedict, Rochelle Park, New Jersey*
This kind of design, evident in other resumes by this writer, enables the reader to find important information quickly. Want to size up the overall design of the resume through its main

DAVID KING   Page Two

PROFESSIONAL EXPERIENCE continued...

<u>INTERNAL REVENUE SERVICE</u>   New York, New York
Employee Plans / Taxpayer Service Specialist   *1981 - 1984*
- Reviewed deferred compensation plans to determine tax deferred status under the IRS Code.
- Audited plans and ensured compliance with plans' provisions.
- Provided answers to taxpayers' inquiries on a variety of Federal taxation issues.
- Coordinated installment arrangements for taxpayers owing the IRS.
- Served as a public speaker to community organizations about IRS services.

EDUCATIONAL BACKGROUND:

Duke University • Durham, North Carolina
Juris Doctor

University of Pennsylvania • Philadelphia, Pennsylvania
Bachelor of Arts in Economics

BAR ADMISSIONS:

Pennsylvania (1987) • New Jersey (1988)

sections? Look down the center at the bold, mostly all-uppercase headings. Want an overview of the individual, his positions, and achievements? Sweep through the resume, looking for italic. Want to know his current and past employers? Look down the left side at the underlined, mostly all-uppercase side headings.

JAMES BARRISTER

55555 Dickson Court, #555 ■ Sherman Oaks, California 55555 ■ (555) 555-5555

TRIAL ATTORNEY

*Personal Injury / Products Liability / Toxic Tort / Medical Malpractice
Premises Security / Sexual Harassment / Criminal Defense*

Practicing Attorney with more than 85 complex trials to verdict with excellent qualifications in the independent planning, management, and representation of clients in state and federal courts. A skilled negotiator, mediator and advisor, experienced in a wide range of personal injury and product liability cases. Handled numerous high-profile cases to successful conclusion.

ILLUSTRATIVE EXPERIENCE

- Initiated case and assisted with preparation of Supreme Court brief in *Falwell v. Flynt*. Wrote major memoranda and motions in *Thorenson v. Penthouse* and *initiated RICO class action in Re Jerry Falwell and the PTL v. James and Tammy Faye Bakker*. Represented TV star *(confidential)* in *Doe 1 v. Doe 2* from case initiation through settlement.

- Obtained $7.5 million verdict against NNN Trucking Inc. in wrongful death action.

- Won $2.9 million settlement against Suffolk County, New York on behalf of 29-year-old paraplegic in diving accident.

- Secured $2 million recovery of disfiguring injury to a legally blind man.

- Handled cases brought under 42 USC section 1983 including highly publicized police shooting of innocent cab driver which settled for $1.5 million.

- Won $1.4 million judgment against County Island Hospital in orthopedic malpractice case.

- Received $1 million judgment in favor of motorcyclist against Best Car Rental.

- Secured $800,000 judgment in New York Police Dept. accidental shooting of an officer by another officer.

- Obtained $750,000 for wrongful death sustained in toxic explosion.

- Won $635,000 medical malpractice judgment against New York Medical Hospital in neonatology case.

- Obtained $500,000 verdict from a New York City school district in case involving consensual sex between retarded youths.

- Won verdict of $450,000 in product liability case against Major Electric.

- Secured judgment of $300,000 on behalf of railroad employee under the Federal Employer Liability Act.

148

Combination. *Vivian Van Lier, Los Angeles, California*
After a successful legal career in New York, this individual relocated to Los Angeles. Although the firms he had been associated with were highly regarded on the East Coast, they were not

ILLUSTRATIVE EXPERIENCE, continued

- Tried numerous serious felonies as a public defender, including homicides and Class A-1 narcotics cases. Secured acquittals in 27 of 43 cases tried to verdict, including 22 murder cases. Handled several high-publicity cases including the "Palm Sunday Massacre" which resulted in a reduction of 9 counts of murder to 9 counts of manslaughter.

PROFESSIONAL EXPERIENCE

Trial Counsel • xxxx to xxxx
BOURNAZOS & MATARANGAS, New York, NY
AV Rated Personal Injury Firm
    Retained in numerous high-profile cases involving products liability (including Clark Forklift, General Motors and Honda of America), personal injury and general liability. Conducted numerous trials to verdict or settlement. Successfully represented insurance carriers in personal injury defense cases.

Trial Attorney • xxxx to xxxx
JAROSLAWICSZ & JAROS, New York, NY
AV Rated Litigation Boutique Firm
    Tried numerous cases to verdict in state and federal courts, including products liability, medical malpractice, construction and labor law. Litigated employment discrimination actions, securities class actions and cases brought under 42 U.S.C. Section 1983 and the Americans with Disabilities Act.

Trial Attorney • xxxx to xxxx
PASTERNACK, POPISH, & REIFF, New York, NY
AV Rated Tort Firm
    Conducted numerous trials in state and federal courts.

Trial Attorney • xxxx to xxxx
KELNER & KELNER, New York, NY
One of New York City's top firms in tort field. Senior partner served as President of the American Association of Trial Lawyers.
    Obtained numerous multimillion-dollar verdicts in state and federal courts. Co-plaintiff in largest personal injury verdict in New York history. Conducted complex plaintiffs' trials including products liability, toxic tort, medical malpractice, 42 U.S.C. Section 1983 and sexual harassment cases.

Litigation Associate • xxxx to xxxx
GRUTMAN MILLER GREENSPOON & HENDLER, New York, NY
AV Rated Park Avenue Boutique Practice
    Performed extensive research and preparation of trial memoranda and briefs to support pleadings in commercial, First Amendment, and class action cases. Conducted numerous trials to verdict.

Senior Trial Attorney • xxxx to xxxx
LEGAL AID SOCIETY, CRIMINAL DEFENSE DIVISION, New York, NY
(Office of the Public Defender)
    Designated major crimes defense attorney for Borough of Brooklyn from xxxx to xxxx. Tried numerous serious felonies including homicides and Class A-1 narcotics cases. Secured acquittals in 27 of 43 cases tried to verdict, including 22 murder cases. Successfully utilized psychiatric, entrapment and other innovative defenses.

as well known on the West Coast. One of the writer's goals was to direct attention to this person's experience and achievements and "not leave them buried under unknown firm names." After the headline, the areas of expertise in italic, and the opening profile—all within a pair of lines—the writer then presents a powerful

EDUCATION

J.D., *Graduated in top 10%*   University of Kansas School of Law, Lawrence, KS, xxxx
M.S.W., Psychiatric Social Work   University of Missouri, Columbia, MO, xxxx
B.A., Psychology   University of Missouri, Columbia, MO, xxxx

BAR ADMISSIONS

California, New York, District of Columbia, Maryland, Kansas
Admitted to practice before the United States Supreme Court

PROFESSIONAL AFFILIATIONS

Association of Trial Lawyers of America
New York State Trial Lawyers Association
National Association of Criminal Defense Lawyers

TEACHING EXPERIENCE

New York County Lawyer's Association
"Jury Selection"

New York Legal Aid Society (Public Defender's Office)
"Criminal Defense Division Cross Examination"

list of achievements in the Illustrative Experience section. It is impressive to discover that there's more illustrative experience as the reader turns to page 2. For the benefit of West Coast readers, the writer makes a comment in italic about each East Coast law firm. Impressive credentials are on page 3.

PATRICK K. DOBSON

55 Cattleman Court
Melbourne, FL 55555
(555) 555-5555

LEGAL ADVOCATE / LEGAL ASSOCIATE

Public Interest Law / Poverty Law / Children's Law / Civil Law / Elder Law

Superior legal knowledge combined with creative talent for using it to the best advantage. Committed to high ethical standards in the legal profession. Excellent writing, research and speaking skills. Strong business background and extensive volunteer work in the legal field.

EDUCATION

Juris Doctorate, Florida State University (FSU), Tallahassee, FL - XXXX
Bachelor's degree in Legal Studies, University of Central Florida, Orlando, FL - XXXX

RELEVANT EXPERIENCE

- **Legal Aid Fellowship**, Legal Aid of America, Cocoa, FL, XXXX
- **Claim Representative Intern**, Allstate Insurance, Tallahassee, FL, XXXX
- **Vice President**, Association of Public Interest Law, Florida State University, XXXX-Present
- **Child Advocate**, Guardian Ad Litem Volunteer, XXXX-Present
- **Student Rep.**, Florida Bar Association (Student Government), XXXX
- **Legal Volunteer**, State of Florida Department of Juvenile Justice, District 3, XXXX-XXXX
- **Community Service Committee Member**, Meals on Wheels, Fall XXXX
- **Peer Counselor**, The College of Business, Florida State University, XXXX

Public Interest Law
- Elected V.P. for FSU Chapter of the Association of Public Interest Law
  - coordinated student participation in annual Spring job fair conference in New York City, and soliciting Law College Council for annual funding of trip
  - advised Pro Bono Committee, matching job orders to student volunteers
  - coordinated volunteers and organized all aspects of student fellowship drive
- Worked child advocacy case as Guardian Ad Litem Volunteer, interviewing family and teachers to determine best situation for child; prepared reports, went to hearings and gave statements
- Performed intake, interviewing clients to verify they met program guidelines for Legal Aid of America

Community Service
- Participated in Community Service Committee as Student Rep. for Florida Bar Association
- Participated in preparation and distribution of Thanksgiving dinner baskets to low-income families in the community as Community Service Committee Member for Meals on Wheels
- Initiated annual haunted house for low-income children through FSU Community Service Group

Research & Legal Writing
- Performed research, assisted in drafting proposals for new programs and new delinquency prevention plan as Legal Volunteer for State of Florida Dept. of Juvenile Justice
- Handled research on legal issues using LEXIS/NEXIS and Westlaw
- Prepared legal memoranda on family law issues; drafted manual on pleadings and procedures for child custody issues for Legal Aid of America
- Investigated insurance claims, examined clients, maintained meticulous files and determined fair compensation within the limits of various fire and casualty policies as Claims Rep. for Allstate

149

Functional. *Laura DeCarlo, Melbourne, Florida*
"The challenge in this resume was to harmonize the extensive volunteer, intern and employment experience of this new graduate." The target roles are focused clearly at the top.

Thomas L. Hume, Esq.

2798 Conklin Street • Suite 452 • Patchogue, NY 11772

(516) 555-5555 • fax (516) 000-0000 • tlhEsq@sprintmail.com

Litigation • Legal Research • Legal Writing • Special Projects

---

Summary of Qualifications

- Practicing attorney, recently relocated to Long Island, with comprehensive experience in legal writing, research and publishing through background as legal "ghostwriter" and publisher's liaison for prominent Chicago law firm.

- Adept at the coordination and implementation of all aspects of litigation or research for special legal projects. Competently and efficiently process overflow or temporary assignments. Areas of interest include family, elder, and real estate law, and related women's issues.

- Concurrent background as in-flight, senior-level international customer service coordinator for American Airlines. Manage all in-flight service activities of crews attending up to 300+ domestic and international passengers.

- Recognized for leadership, team work and exceptional anticipatory thought process. Organizational and communication abilities demonstrated by management of simultaneous full-time American job, part-time legal work and full-time law school course load.

Education and Licensure

Admitted to Bar • New York, 1999 • Illinois, 1997 • Florida, 1997

Doctor of Jurisprudence, 1997
Loyola University of Chicago, IL
Graduated fifth in class • Inducted into Jesuit Honor Society, Alpha Sigma Nu

Associate Bachelor of Journalism in Broadcast News (four year degree), 1985
University of Georgia, Athens, GA • Concentration in Accounting

---

Representative Achievements in Law

- Authored "Rule 11" chapter and all quarterly supplements for updates of national legal industry bible *Attorney Malpractice Prevention and Defense* (Spitzer and Furman, Garland Publishing).

- Wrote Securities chapter for Chicago firm's book in development on accounting malpractice.

- *Law Journal* member by invitation. Published "Illinois Law Survey": *Family Law*, Volume 18, Winter, 1986. Served as *Law Journal* Student Articles Editor. Received AmJur Contracts for highest term grade in class.

- Passed Florida and Illinois bar examinations on first attempt, while accomplishing intensive legal research and writing at part-time position, and while working full-time flight schedule for American Airlines.

150

Combination. *Deborah Wile Dib, Medford, New York*
"An attorney who put himself through law school by working as a flight administrator for a major airline and ghostwriting for attorneys." Both of these activities are evident in the

Thomas L. Hume, Esq. page two

Representative Achievements In-flight Administration

- Elected to two-year post on American Airlines scheduling committee. Using seniority and FAA layover criteria, performed complex analytical and mathematical procedures to set up all Chicago and New York hub monthly flight schedules and in-flight staffing.

- Appointed International Customer Service Coordinator, an American Airlines in-flight administrative position requiring continual level of highest competency.

- Function autonomously, with responsibility for up to 300+ in-flight crew/passengers. Cool under pressure and adaptable to any circumstance: weather conditions, flight plan changes, emergency instruction and landings.

Employment

1996 to 1999

LEGAL WRITER/RESEARCHER

Smith, Cleeves, Spitzter, Furman & Giles
Chicago, IL

- Functioned as legal researcher and writer to compose and produce new chapters and quarterly supplements for firm's book *Attorney Malpractice Prevention and Defense* (Spitzter and Furman, Garland Publishing).

- Performed continual reviews of new case law. Handled research, accessed pertinent information and chose new cases to include in book updates.

- Edited manuscripts for content and final proofing, reviewed galleys, interfaced with publisher and editor. Produced five + editions.

INTERNATIONAL CUSTOMER SERVICE COORDINATOR   **1985 to 1999**
(IN-FLIGHT CSC)

American Airlines, Chicago, IL

- Specialist in charge of in-flight passenger service and safety for domestic and international flights. Supervise up to twelve flight attendants and administer to up to 300+ passengers.

- Trained to independently and competently manage unexpected in-flight problems including unruly passengers, passenger health issues, weather conditions, flight plan changes, and emergency landings. Interface with all passenger levels from CEOs and celebrities to children and the infirm.

- Determine appropriate service for situations, delegate personnel, handle all in-flight and customs documentation, account for all liquor and video payments. Prepare flight to physical standards for customs clearance.

Computer Skills   WordPerfect • MS Word • Lexus • Westlaw • Internet

Summary of Qualifications; the two Representative Achievements sections, respectively; and the Employment section. Lines separating sections make them visible at a glance. White space from a wide left column and blank lines between sections and paragraphs prevent a crowded look. See Cover Letter 6.

Mary T. Morstan, Esq.
4221 South Rosemont Lane
Denver, Colorado 81000

✆ [303] 555-5555 (Office)
[303] 555-6666 (Home)

Admitted to the Bar, Denver, Colorado, October 1985

Legal experience:

Deputy Attorney General
(Jun 92 – Present)
  ⬧ *Promoted to* Division
    Chief for Capital
    Litigation
    (Jan 95 – Present)
  ⬧ Section Chief for
    Capital Litigation
    (Oct 93 – Jan 95)

Assistant Attorney General
(Jun 87 – Jun 92)

Colorado Attorney General's Office, Denver,
Colorado

  ⬧ Directed research of all legal issues arising in
    State of Colorado v. Walter Leroy Smith, Jr. since
    1992
      ⬧ Selected as cocounsel for this trial: the largest
        ever tried in the state
      ⬧ Guided marshaling and organizing nearly
        3,000 exhibits
      ⬧ Helped prepare more than 120 witnesses for
        pretrial hearings and trial
      ⬧ Worked closely with FBI, ATF, USPS, CBI
  ⬧ Participated in oral argument in the capital
    murder case *Harris v. Colorado* before United
    States Supreme Court
  ⬧ Actively working with legislature to cut
    unnecessary delays in the direct capital appeals
    process
  ⬧ Make time to summarize and index every Court
    of Criminal Appeals and Colorado Supreme
    Court case: some 50 each month
  ⬧ Responsible for all direct appeal and post-
    conviction proceedings work in capital cases.
    Currently directing caseload of 140 inmates –
    among the 10 largest death-row populations in
    the country
  ⬧ Serve as single point of contact for all capital
    punishment efforts in the state. Personally
    responsible for the last two executions
  ⬧ Sought often by district attorneys and judges
    statewide for advice on death penalty trial
    proceedings
  ⬧ Regularly cross-examine as part of state
    collateral and Federal habeas corpus hearings
  ⬧ Wrote the Criminal Psychopath Release
    Restriction Act of 1988. AG approved my work
    virtually without change

151

Chronological. *Donald Orlando, Montgomery, Alabama*
The goal of this individual is to become an Assistant Attorney General in Colorado. The resume
concentrates on results more than responsibilities. Notable results are listed in the bulleted items

Mary T. Morstan, Esq.   ✆ [303] 555-5555 (Office); [303] 555-6666 (Home)

Legal experience (continued):

| Assistant Attorney General (Oct 86 – Jun 87) | Colorado Department of Mental Health & Mental Retardation, Denver, Colorado |

* Helped Department prepare for and defend against suits
* Wrote and filed pleadings, motions, briefs

| Law Clerk and Bailiff (Aug 85 – Jun 86) | Honorable Josiah H. Amberly, Circuit Judge, Gunnison, Colorado |

Education:

* J.D., University of Colorado School of Law, Denver, Colorado, 85
* B.S., Public Administration, Dean's List, Colorado State University, Boulder, Colorado, 82

Courts admitted to:

* United States Supreme Court
* Eighth Circuit Court of Appeals
* United States District Courts for the Northern, Middle and Southern Districts of Colorado
* Colorado Supreme Court

Professional affiliations:

* Attended annual summer conference of the District Attorneys' Association (87, 92, 93, 95, 98)
    * Asked to speak at this three-day gathering by Executive Director.
* Member, Association of Government Attorneys in Capital Litigation
    * One of only two attorneys selected by AG from 50 eligibles to attend this group's annual conference.

Computer literacy:

* Very proficient in Westlaw
* Proficient in Law on Disk
* Working knowledge of Lexis-Nexis, WordPerfect 6.1, Word for Windows 2.0

- 2 -

in the right column on pages 1 and 2. (Note the distinctive bullets.) Especially notable is the person's research effort for Colorado's largest trial and his appearance before the United States Supreme Court for another case. The Professional Affiliations section on page 2 shows honors. See Cover Letter 4.

HIRAM B. SMYTHE

4000 Agway Court
Virginia Beach, Virginia 55555
(000) 000-0000

SUMMARY OF QUALIFICATIONS

An assertive individual with caring interest in people. Have the ability to inspire trust and confidence with top-notch debating and writing skills. Able to research and analyze cases, think conceptually and logically. Successful experience in **Litigation**, **Training**, **Management** and **Supervision** of **Law-Related Activities.**

Litigation:	**Judge/Hearing Officer**: Presided over factually complex cases . . . Assessed testimony and real evidence . . . Managed emotionally charged, "high-visibility@ cases . . . Researched and rendered written and oral legal opinions and rulings. **Litigator**: Prosecuted/Defended complex criminal cases . . . Analyzed and assessed facts . . . Persuasive oral advocate.
Management:	Set goals and evaluated their attainment . . . Implemented activities to produce the best possible morale and productivity . . . Estimated time, manpower, and requirements for various jobs . . . Assured that workload assignments were successfully brought to completion . . . Acted as liaison between coworkers and upper management . . . Supervised operational control of law activities and facilities . . . Served more than twenty years as a naval officer/lawyer.
Training/ Administration:	Supervised training, counseling, development, and motivation of personnel in their assigned duties . . . Developed, expanded and encouraged employee loyalty . . . Trained key personnel for leadership positions . . . Made certain that staff personnel cooperated with persons of varied ethnic, cultural and socio-economic backgrounds . . . Handled complaints in a manner ensuring continuing good will . . . Established continuity of effort and communication between personnel and organizational leaders to reach an ideal goal of 100% accomplishment of goals and objectives assigned.
Strengths:	Works well without supervision. Inspired and motivated individual and team efforts . . . Detail-oriented and meticulous . . . Reliable and capable under pressure . . . Hardworking and self-motivated . . . A *People Person*.

WORK HIGHLIGHTS

DEPARTMENT OF DEFENSE (United States Navy) 1970-1994

Military Judge (Felony Court Jurisdiction) 1991-94
- o Presided over more than 350 bench and jury trials involving all manner of felony, misdemeanor and military offenses; Certified NITA Instructor.

152

Combination. *Anne G. Kramer, Virginia Beach, Virginia*
This person got his legal experience in the military. After his discharge, he was limited to practicing in one state but hoped to move to another area. The writer showed him "in the

HIRAM B. SMYTHE

Chief Defense Counsel (Navy Legal Service Office) 1991
- o Supervised ten junior attorneys providing court-martial representation; successfully defended commanding officer at court-martial for ship collision with a merchant vessel.

Staff Judge Advocate (U.S. Naval Forces, Asia) 1988-90
- o Staff Counsel to Commander of U.S. naval forces in Asia; legal advisor in military justice and matters of international negotiations, including admiralty, and base debarment proceedings. Dealt directly with Asian counterparts.

Chief Prosecutor (Navy Legal Service Office) 1987
- o Directed twelve prosecutors in cases including murder, rape and armed robbery; managed all aspects of over 900 cases in a one-year period.

Head, Claims and Legal Assistance (Navy Legal Service Office) 1986-87
- o Supervised four attorneys providing legal assistance to eligible personnel; instituted client walk-in system; supervised various activities involving Navy interests in claims acts.

Assistant Staff Judge Advocate (U.S. Ocean Fleet Commander) 1985
- o Staff counsel to Commander, Submarine Forces Atlantic Fleet; advised and investigated military justice of incidents involving nuclear submarines, collisions, groundings and other accidents at sea.

Staff Judge Advocate (USS Aircraft Carrier) 1982-84
- o Sole lawyer on aircraft carrier of 5,000 men; managed all military justice matters and legal assistance; negotiated with law-enforcement and judicial personnel of numerous foreign countries for the settlement of criminal and civil matters arising out of U.S. Navy personnel activities.

EDUCATION

SUNNY UNIVERSITY, Binghamton, Virginia, B.A. (1969), J.D. (1976).
NAVAL JUSTICE SCHOOL, Newport, Rhode Island.

ACTIVITIES/AWARDS/SCHOLARSHIPS

Full academic scholarship . . . President, Alpha Beta Chi . . . President of Student Government Association . . . *Who's Who in American Colleges.*

ASSOCIATIONS

American Bar Association . . . American Judges Association . . . Virginia Bar Association.

best possible light so he could obtain suitable employment while studying for the bar in other states." In the Summary of Qualifications, phrases separated by ellipses are carefully placed to avoid "rivers of white"—the illusion of paths of white space (created by nearby ellipses above and below) snaking through the section.

Diana L. Justice

1776 Commonwealth Avenue
Boston, Massachusetts 02141
(617) 555-5555

PROFESSIONAL PROFILE

Effective trial lawyer with experience in criminal, juvenile, and appellate courts; a career history of success and advancement; and a strong ability to perform well in pressure situations.

Demonstrated ability to exercise sound judgment and work cooperatively to balance the needs of all concerned: victim, offender, law enforcement and judicial systems, and citizens.

Achieve satisfaction from resolving matters quickly and effectively, yet persistent in pursuing most effective and appropriate course of action.

Strengths include jury selection, presentation of facts, and persuasive argument abilities. Proven ability to acquire skill in essential areas such as public speaking and presenting.

EDUCATION/ CERTIFICATION

J.D., Boston College Law School, 1992
Named to Massachusetts State Bar, 1992
B.A., Boston College, 1987

EXPERIENCE

1992-Present   **Assistant Prosecutor** • SUFFOLK COUNTY PROSECUTOR'S OFFICE, Boston, Massachusetts

1995-Present   **Criminal Felony Division** • Manage all aspects of case preparation and trial of high-stakes criminal felony cases — robberies, assaults, drug crimes, rapes and other sex crimes. Establish credibility and trust with juries through a combination of logical presentation of the facts and persuasive argument skills. Negotiate plea bargains.
    In 9 months, tried and won convictions in 12 jury trials.

1994-95   **Criminal Municipal Division** • Prosecuted bench and jury trials for criminal misdemeanors such as DUI and domestic violence. Argued motions to suppress evidence. Set bond figures. Negotiated plea bargains. Trained new prosecutors.
    Selected as one of two prosecutors to pioneer the Rapid Indictment Program, instituted to speed case resolution. Working cooperatively with defense counsel, law enforcement, judges and the Grand Jury, negotiated fair resolutions to offenses. This program, which is still in use, has succeeded in significantly reducing the cost of criminal prosecutions.

1993-94   **Juvenile Division** • Tried felony and criminal misdemeanor cases involving youthful offenders.
    Selected to train new prosecutors.

1992-93   **Appellate Division** • Conducted extensive legal research, wrote briefs, and presented arguments before First District Court of Appeals. Regularly requested to perform research for other divisions of the Prosecutor's Office.
    Instrumental in conducting research that led to the institution of a highly successful Victim Advocate program.

1991   **Law Clerk** • SMITH & WESSON, Boston, Massachusetts
1990   **Legal Extern** • CITY OF QUINCY PROSECUTOR'S OFFICE, Quincy, Massachusetts

Conducted legal research for civil and criminal actions using Lexis and WestLaw. Prepared financial analyses for divorce settlements, trial briefs, complaints and motions. Prosecuted Traffic Court cases.

COMMUNITY ACTIVITIES

Participate in political campaigns for prosecutors, judges and city council representatives: fund-raising, staffing telephone banks, attending campaign functions, other campaign details.

153

Combination. *Louise M. Kursmark, Cincinnati, Ohio*
This dynamic and successful individual had "a real passion for her profession" and wanted to become a defense attorney with a private law firm. Distinctive type matches the person.

Other Professional
Resumes

Maynard J. Finance

250 SEVENTH STREET
LAKOTA, ND 58333
(701) 000-0000

FINANCE

Ambitious results-oriented individual with more than four years of experience in *finance*. Excellent problem-solving and analytical skills. Cooperative team player, yet equally effective, motivated, and hard working independently.

- ✦ Experience in working with multicultural groups
- ✦ Meet deadlines; remain calm under pressure
- ✦ Versatile; adapt quickly and easily to new environments and jobs
- ✦ Accurate
- ✦ Computer literate
- ✦ Trustworthy and dependable
- ✦ Excellent work ethic

EDUCATION

BACHELOR OF SCIENCE	University of Minnesota: Minneapolis, MN Major: **Banking and Finance**	May 1985
ASSOCIATE OF SCIENCE	University of Minnesota: Crooks, MN Major: **Business**	May 1982

SUMMARY OF EXPERIENCE

- ✦ Trained new employees
- ✦ Compiled daily reports for managers and supervisors of various departments
- ✦ Researched lost, torn, missorted, and exception checks
- ✦ Sorted personal and corporate checks on IBM check sorting computers
- ✦ Contributed money-saving ideas
- ✦ Distributed corporate statements from central bank location
- ✦ Possess outstanding sorting record; sorted CEO, Board of Directors, and other special accounts monthly
- ✦ Participated in team groups of 5-12 employees
- ✦ Distributed daily work to employees
- ✦ Worked in various positions within bank departments
- ✦ Decreased bank's expenses by repairing machines within the bank system rather than using repairmen

RELATED EMPLOYMENT HISTORY

WACHOVIA BANK OF GEORGIA: Chubbtown, GA   April 1988-May 1991
UTILITY CLERK

- ✦ Oversaw daily departmental functions, identified problems and/or potential delays, made necessary changes to keep operation progressing to provide quality service

CITIZENS AND SOUTHERN NATIONAL BANK: Holland, GA   December 1986-April 1988
STATEMENT PROCESSOR

- ✦ Processed over 1,200 customer accounts per hour operating a Bell+Howell inserting computer, the highest production rate within bank; lowest in errors

OTHER EMPLOYMENT

FINANCE FARM: Meadow, ND   Spring, Summer, and Fall 1991-1995
Self-employed Farmer

MINOT ASSEMBLY COMPANY: Minot, ND   Winters 1991-1994
Wire Cutter

WILLIAM JOHNSON FARMS: Stark, ND   Summers 1975-1986, 1991

154

Functional. *Mary Laske, Fargo, North Dakota*
The format is functional in that Employment dates are not put in descending chronological order throughout. Employment related to finance is put first; then other work is presented.

MOLLY P. SENG

550 55th Street ► Glendale, New York ► 55555 ► (555) 555-5555

GOAL

BANK MANAGEMENT/OPERATIONS SUPPORT

PROFILE

- ► Results-oriented professional with 12 years of experience in retail banking/financial operations.
- ► Proven ability to implement strategies that improve client services and increase sales volume.
- ► Dynamic leader, strongly committed to working with colleagues to achieve corporate goals.
- ► Able to analyze operations to identify potential cost-reduction and program improvement areas.
- ► Detail-oriented and organized; Effectively handle multiple tasks and meet project deadlines.

BANKING/FINANCE EXPERIENCE

NATIONAL INFORMATION SERVICES - New York, NY
Crew Leader, XXXX to XXXX

Hired, trained, and supervised a team of 15 employees. Planned and delivered training seminars for thousands of enumerators. Reviewed and certified payroll. Coordinated information review for downtown Manhattan (180,000+ households).

- ► Achieved lowest error ratio in New York (out of all NYS district offices).
- ► Implemented organizational procedures that enabled office to be the *first* to complete review in the state.
- ► Dedication and work performance earned promotion from **Administrative Assistant.**

ADVANCED GLASS SYSTEMS, INC. - Brooklyn, NY
Controller, XXXX to XXXX

Oversaw financial operations for company with $100,000 to $200,000 in monthly sales revenue. Supervised 3 bookkeepers and completed performance appraisals. Prepared company payroll and monthly sales reports. Managed short-term investment portfolio.

- ► Eliminated abuse of overtime by developing and enforcing strict personnel policies.
- ► Significantly slashed office expenses by carefully monitoring expenditures.

CITYWIDE BANK COMPANY - New York, NY
Assistant Manager, XXXX to XXXX

Supervised staff and evaluated work performance. Opened and maintained customer accounts.

- ► Implemented internal control procedures that turned stagnant operations into profitable branch.
- ► Selected by senior management to train managers and employees in other branch locations.
- ► Interim Branch Manager for World Trade Center office: Within 3 months, increased profits and resolved all deferred and abeyance account issues.
- ► Promoted from **Teller;** Completed 18-month Operations Training Program within 13 months.

ADMINISTRATIVE EXPERIENCE

Ward/Unit Clerk, XXXX to present   ST. MARY'S HOSPITAL - New Hyde Park, NY
Ward/Unit Clerk, XXXX to XXXX   SACRED HOSPITAL - Staten Island, NY

EDUCATION

BROOKLYN COLLEGE - Brooklyn, NY
Bachelor of Arts in Economics, Expected December XXXX

155

Combination. *Kim Isaacs, Jackson Heights, New York*
A partial line is used with a full line for the contact information. Information about a degree in progress is put last. Arrow tip bullets point to achievements. See Cover Letter 13.

SANDRA HOPKINS
4034 Smith Lane • Chandler, Texas 75700 • (903) 888-5555

HIGHLIGHTS OF QUALIFICATIONS

- **Challenge-driven, results-oriented professional** with comprehensive knowledge of and experience in **financial / investment industry**. Familiar with NYSE, NASDAQ, and Federal Reserve laws.
- Astute **financial / investment manager**. Cognizant of research procedures, portfolio development, and trading processes of various investment instruments. Strong accounting aptitude. Good judgment.
- Proven strengths in **consultative sales, investment marketing,** and **client relationship management**.
- Highly **organized** with ability to prioritize time / tasks to optimize productivity. **Effective problem solver** adept in analyzing critical situations and creating solutions to complex issues.
- Exemplary **integrity, trustworthiness,** and **work ethic. Advocate for superior customer service.**

EDUCATION
UNIVERSITY OF TEXAS AT TYLER – Tyler, Texas
B.S., Finance (December 1998); GPA: 3.7/4.0

RELEVANT INVESTMENT ASSIGNMENTS

- **Created, managed, and tracked model investment portfolios** for classes during two semesters; received an **"A"** in both classes for **proficiently developing and managing diversified, profitable portfolio**.
- Performed extensive research to determine appropriate stocks and yields to achieve objectives; using specified monetary funds, selected and "purchased" individual stocks; logged investments; maintained vigil on portfolio.
- Established authentic, personal investment portfolio, performing research and selecting mutual funds to meet investment objectives; track and manage funds on ongoing basis.

PROFESSIONAL EXPERIENCE

Customer Service Associate / Teller, BANK OF TYLER – Tyler, Texas   1995 – Present
- **Consistently meet sales quota for investment referrals**; analyze customers' financial status; refer customers to bank's investment analyst for advice regarding appropriate investment instruments.
- Provide personalized, superb service to individual and commercial customers; process stop payments; reconcile customers' checkbooks; research lost deposits; resolve discrepancies.
- Resolve customer complaints/disputes in professional, efficient, diplomatic manner.
- Assist in organization/coordination of and participate in United Way Walk-a-Thon events (1996–1998).
- Plan, organize, coordinate, and participate as "Adoptee" in "Spirit of Christmas" event (1995–Present).
- As Teller, provided assistance to commercial customers; logged/audited monetary instruments; processed cash and check transactions/deposits; performed daily reconciliations; issued Money Orders and Travelers Cheques. Trained tellers on procedures/processes in accordance with banking regulations. **Promoted within one year.**

Commercial Vault Teller, CITY BANK – Tyler, Texas   1993 – 1995
- Assumed responsibility for administering commercial vault; ensured security of large monetary sums.
- Processed large deposits of currency, checks, Travelers Cheques; prepared/filed currency transaction reports.

AFFILIATIONS / HONORS

Who's Who Among American High School Students (1989–1992) ➤ National Honor Society (1990–1992)
Graduated 7th in Class of 1992 ➤ Head Cheerleader (1987–1992) ➤ Miss LHS

156

Combination. *Ann Klint, Tyler, Texas*
A resume for a recent graduate who wanted to move from a Teller to an entry-level position in financial/investment management. Small caps in headings and boldfacing stress key info.

Stephanie Smithson

20 Rose Boulevard • Boca Raton, FL 33486
561-555-5555 • smithson@aol.com

Bank Brokerage Senior Executive • Financial Services Professional

Career Profile	Seventeen-year background in high-growth domestic and international brokerage services management and financial sales management with AmericasBank, AmericasBanc Investments, and Clayton Investments, Inc.
	Utilize strong implementation skills to transform corporate vision and strategy into profitable reality. Fully experienced in the upswings and declines of the full-market cycle, consistently developing proactive management and sales initiatives that ensure investor confidence, increased sales, and maximum revenue gains.
	NASD Licensed: Series 4, 7, 24, 53, 63, 65. Expert in mutual funds, fixed income securities, offshore mutual funds, stocks, options, and gold coin / bullion for investment. Risk / Compliance-oriented, with an impeccable U4. Speak fluent Spanish.

Areas of Expertise

- Series 24 Sales Force Management
- Series 7 Program Management
- Start-ups / Mergers / Turnarounds
- Budgeting / Planning / Forecasting
- Margin Improvement / Revenue Gain
- International Finance / Investment Sales
- Financial Planning / Asset Management
- Sales Automation Development / Training

- Mutual Fund Sales Management
- Contract Review and Negotiation
- Brokerage Sales
- Broker Recruiting
- High Net-Worth Customer Selling
- High-Level Relationship Management
- Customer Retention Strategies
- Relationship and Team building

Executive Performance Overview

Quantifiable track record of sales growth, revenue enhancement, and expense reduction.
Representative achievements include management of 85 direct reports and generation of full-service brokerage annual revenues of over $14 million, with $3.4 million in net income, and an average broker productivity exceeding $400 thousand.

Structure innovative programs that produce strong and sustainable results.
Increased Clayton Investments' international assets under management from $100 million in 1987 to over $1.4 billion in 1996 through the proposal and implementation of an international brokerage office and statewide international brokerage initiative.

Drive financial organizations to greater productivity, efficiency, and profitability.
Reduced costs by $2 million while increasing average sales representative productivity by $50 thousand through work as chairman of a Clayton market penetration study.

Blend a can-do management style with vision, tenacity, and team leadership.
Anticipate trends and create business-building opportunities including conception and implementation of programs in sales, sales automation, and offshore mutual fund certification. Consistently surpass objectives and develop top-ten sales performers.

Maintain revenue and employee retention during merger transition periods.
Retained 95% of Investment Consultants and their revenues during AmericasBank's acquisition of Clayton Bank. Provided constant communication and personal availability to keep employees informed and focused on the customer.

Routinely work with, and create programs for high net-worth customers.
Understand the subtleties of selling to "old money," the newly wealthy, and international customers. As producing assistant regional manager, developed $36 million book of business in under two years, with 80% of clients having over $750 thousand in assets.

157

Combination. *Deborah Wile Dib, Medford, New York*
This individual was looking for a new position in banking or investments after the company that employed her was acquired and she was retained by the new company. Horizontal lines

Stephanie Smithson

Achievements in Market and Revenue Growth

Created elite International Brokerage initiative that grew Clayton Investments' total international assets under management from $0 in 1987 to $280 million in 1997, with annual fee income of $2.1 million.
Conceived, proposed and delivered the International Brokerage initiative. Recruited and intensively trained six global brokers who traveled to Latin American with private bankers to develop new business and retain Clayton Banks' most profitable customers. In 1983, developed an international investment business that generated one third of personal production at Southeast Bank that same year.

Conceived and implemented a program that increased statewide nonresident assets from $77 million in 1992 to $360 million in 1996.
Developed an international investing achievement certification program and a fixed-income investing program, approved for continuing education credits by NASD. Provided video and/or on-site training of over 120 Clayton brokers in the sale of investment products to the bank's NRA customers. Program increased revenues from this targeted market from $737 thousand in 1992 to $2 million in 1996.

Built dealer bond department from monthly production of $100 thousand to $300 thousand in under one year.
Within first six months, expanded department from three to thirteen investment representatives. Personally ranked in the top 10% of 100 investment representatives, and managed over $36 million in assets with 80% of clients having over $750 thousand in assets. After six months was taken from production and continued to grow division to ultimately produce a third of the total revenues of four total divisions.

Increased assets in Offshore Mutual Fund line from $0 in 1992 to $50 million in 1996.
As Clayton Banks' international mutual fund product line manager, recommended and approved the selection of the bank's offshore product line. Revenues averaged $100,000 per month from this activity.

Developed Southeast Bank's international gold sale business.
Sold an average of $100 thousand monthly in gold bullion and coins from 1983 to 1986. Was considered the expert in gold sales by colleagues and international bankers. Met company expectations to provide this service on a passive basis.

Achievements in Operations' Leadership

Selected to serve as the brokerage services expert on the implementation team of Clayton Banks' newly created Asset Management Vision.
Teamed with division heads and provided information on brokerage industry practices. After implementation, was given a regional manager role to continue hiring and building company. Ultimately managed 55 brokers, five area managers and 20 sales assistants, until AmericasBank's acquisition of Clayton Bank.

As Regional Manager, handled the South Florida implementation of Clayton's Dealer Bond / Discount Brokerage merger to a full service brokerage company.
Led division during the next ten years. Brokers represented over half of the top 10% performers, while representing only a third of the sales force. Grew sales force from 13 in 1988 to 53 in 1992, with an average broker productivity of $400 million. Delivered Clayton's first million-dollar producer in 1991, and three in total.

Retained as new AmericasBanc Investments senior manager for one of the most affluent markets in the United States, after completion of AmericasBank merger,
Served as Senior Vice President and Senior Branch Manager of Palm Beach County, Florida, office. Increased revenues by 20% over previous year. Managed 21 Investment consultants and nine sales assistants, one assistant branch manager and one branch operations manager. Annual revenue responsibility was $6 million, producing at 90% of plan, 30% above prior year.

help to make the main section visible over three pages. Boldfacing, in highlighting key information, helps the reader see quickly the chief topics over the three pages. Almost all of the supportive information is quantified, which makes the document impressive. Her career path shows steady growth in responsibility.

Stephanie Smithson

Employment

AMERICASBANC INVESTMENTS, INC., WEST PALM BEACH, FL   **1998**
Senior Vice President, District Sales Manager: Palm Beach County

AmericasBanc Investments is the investment arm of AmericasBank, the largest bank in the US, with over $572 million in assets and operating revenues of $16 billion.

CLAYTON INVESTMENTS, INC., FORT LAUDERDALE, FL   **1987 to 1998**
South Florida Regional Sales Manager

Clayton, acquired by AmericasBank in 1998, was the leading bank in Florida, a $42 billion organization with 22,000 statewide employees and a 30% market share.

AMERICASBANK, MIAMI, FL   **1986 to 1987**
Assistant Vice President / Sales

In 1987 AmericasBank was an eight-state "super regional" with $24 billion in deposits.

SOUTHEAST BANKS, N. A., (Now merged with First Union)   **1981 to 1986**
Assistant Vice President (1983 to 1986)
Investment Analyst (1981 to 1983)
Accounting Analyst (1981)

Southeast was a $13 billion bank holding company, ranked #1 (at the time) in deposits in the state of Florida, with a international presence in Latin America.

Technology

Advanced user of multiple software applications.
- Microsoft Word, Excel, and PowerPoint
- Act Contact Manager, Lotus Word Pro, Lotus 1-2-3, Freelance Graphics
- Fidelity FBSI System, Fidelity Maxxes, ADP News and Quote System
- Bloomberg, Video Conferencing, Internet-based news and research services

Specialist in the effective use of technology to promote productivity.
First in company to use videoconferencing to train and communicate with investment consultants company-wide. Key member of Clayton's sales automation program development team with direct decision-making input in research, development, and implementation. Relieved of normal responsibilities for six months to devote entire effort to Asset Management Vision deployment. Earned promotion upon completion.

Professional Activities

- **Board of Governors, Florida Securities Dealers Association, 1993 to 1998**
- **Spoke as brokerage expert for National Financial Industry Conference.**
- **Served as Clayton's PAC captain; achieved 90%+ employee participation.**
- **As PAC captain, met with members of Congress and industry leaders.**
- **Coordinated all Asset Management kickoff components; spoke at breakout session.**

Education

B. A. in Business Administration. University of Miami, Miami, FL, 1982
Earned 4.0 GPA in business subjects. Attended while working full-time.

Business courses at Florida Atlantic University and Florida International University
Marketing Management, Organizational Management Behavior, Introduction to Management, Business Statistics, Business Communications, Money and Banking, Personnel Administration, International Business

Executive workshops and team-building events through Clayton Banks, Inc.
Empowering Executive Workshop, Better Management Under the Law, Effective Interviewing Skills, Supervisory and Time Management Skills, Diversity Management

Usually weak information is put last in a resume, but content about impressive professional activities, a 4.0 GPA in business subjects, additional business courses, and company-sponsored executive workshops make a strong ending. The kind of information presented justifies the use of three full pages for this resume.

Michael K. Wan
8541 Smith Street
Garden Grove, California 55555
(555) 555-5555

PROFESSIONAL OBJECTIVE & PROFILE

Highly motivated professional looking to utilize solid educational preparation and related experience within a progressive financial organization. Strong interests include Credit Analysis, Loan Underwriting, Budget Analysis and Loan Processing.

- Academic background includes course work in International Business Finance; Theory of Corporate Finance; Commercial Bank & Financial Institution Management; Financial and Managerial Accounting
- Proven expertise in credit and financial analysis, with keen mathematical abilities
- Analytical and organized; able to identify needs and implement effective solutions
- Successfully manages new challenges and responsibilities
- Proficient utilization of Excel, PowerPoint and Word

EDUCATIONAL ACHIEVEMENTS

BA degree in Business Administration - *Concentration in Finance* –
California State University, Fullerton - XXXX
GPA 3.25/4.0

Associate's degree - *Accounting*
Orange Coast College, Costa Mesa - XXXX
GPA 3.40/4.0

HONORS & ACTIVITIES

- Awarded *Talent Roster Certificate of Achievement* for achieving 3.5 GPA (Orange Coast College)
- Awarded *Certificate of Appreciation* in Airline Travel for an active 2-semester participation in Career & Community Service (Orange Coast College)
- Active participation in fund-raising and alumni events
- Successfully maintained professional positions while consistently maintaining high GPA

PROFESSIONAL EXPERIENCE

UNITED COMMERCIAL BANK - Irvine, California   June XXXX to Present
Customer Service Representative II
- Efficiently process and complete customer transactions
- Assist in selling customers various bank products and programs; demonstrate service benefits
- Maintain accurate operation of cash drawer; answer phones; manage and check reports
- Process and effectively diffuse customer complaints

WONG NGA VAN CLINIC - Huntington Beach, California   January XXXX to May XXXX
Receptionist
- Assist in performing basic office functions, answer and appropriately direct phone calls
- Direct accurate billing of insurance and Medicare forms

Excellent Work References and Letters of Recommendation Available

158

Combination. *Kim Little, Victor, New York*
The distinctive feature of this resume for a recent graduate is the white-on-black format for the section headings and closing remark about references and letters.

Marilyn Commodities
197 Success Drive
Scenic, NJ 11111

555-555-1212
555-555-1212

CAREER PROFILE

Extremely well-organized professional. Welcomes challenge and is motivated to begin new and different projects. Excellent interpersonal skills enhanced by an ability to communicate well with all levels of management. Takes ownership of projects and responsibilities and is tenacious in reaching resolution. Makes well-informed decisions quickly and confidently.

PROFESSIONAL EMPLOYMENT

Bank of Banks, Allendale, NJ   1987 - present
Ten-year career demonstrates continuous professional development with increasing responsibilities and advancement to key financial positions.

Assistant Vice President - Investment Manager   1996 - present
Individually manage customer accounts and maintain investment portfolio. Service accounts and accompany sales reps on new business calls to represent the Specialty Fixed Income product.
- Manage and direct the activities of three clerical staff members.
- Introduced consistency to the banking compliance process.
- Initiated a reorganization to streamline processes and eliminate duplication.
- Successfully create and maintain productive business relationships.
- Consistently exceed targets on project completion dates for investment analyses and presentations for sales.

Assistant Vice President - Securities Trader   1989 - 1996
Managed three mutual funds with a total value of $1B. Researched the market for best values and executed trades for portfolios. Communicated daily with Wall Street traders to make carefully researched, quick decisions. Executed securities trades for portfolio managers in Trust Department.
- Created and maintained an approved list of securities that reflected investment quality.
- Sustained performance of eight years without a monetary loss on a trade.
- Consistently outperformed industry benchmarks.
- Established and maintained productive business relationships.
- Monitored portfolios consistently to diversify risk through verbal communication and research on financial investments.
- Designed and implemented solutions to business problems.
- Trained two employees to cover this position.

159

Combination. *Fran Kelley, Waldwick, New Jersey*
If you look just for boldfacing, you can size up this resume quickly. You will see the person's name in the contact information (repeated on page 2), the Career Profile, the headings, the

Marilyn Commodities

555-555-1212
555-555-1212

page two

Trust Specialist   1987 - 1989

Responsible for all mutual fund accounting: posting to accounts, noting dividends or interest. Worked with auditors to create prospectus/annual report. Interacted with shareholders via phone on buys or sells.

- Created spreadsheets to automate what had been a paper process.
- Managed relationships in the department to improve productivity and took responsibility for resolving disputes.

Staff Accountant

Accounting Associates, Bristol, CT   1986 - 1987

Responsible for varied accounting projects, as assigned. Conducted income and expense analyses for commercial rental properties.

- Automated financial reporting from a former paper process.
- Created financial reports readily understandable to all levels.
- Managed and directed the activities of four bookkeepers. This included assessment of training and development needs as well as performance reviews.

Fund Accountant

Kelley and Co., Inc., Bristol, CT   1985 - 1986

Responsible for all mutual fund accounting.

- Started with responsibility of accounting for one fund and given responsibility for four funds within one year.

EDUCATION

BS   Business Administration/Accounting
Wharton School

COMPUTER SKILLS

Proficient in Lotus 1-2-3, Microsoft Word, WordPerfect

COMMUNITY SERVICE

School Board President

italic statement under the name of the current workplace, the job positions, and the degree near the end. The bold italic text in the Profile and under the reference to the current employer is center-justified to look different and stand out. The last three sections are short and centered to increase reading tempo at the end.

Robert A. Kelly

104 Madison Avenue
New York, NY 00000
(555) 555-5555

Banking Operations Officer ▪ Letters of Credit ▪ Trade Finance

---

Professional Profile

- Highly regarded operations manager and accounting professional with more than ten years' experience in high-volume, fast-paced banking and brokerage environments.

- Progressive record of promotions to increasingly responsible decision-making roles.

- Productive team player with strong vision of company goals. Consistent performance in improving quality, accountability and efficiency.

- Well-developed analytical skills support ability to meet deadlines with accuracy and discretion.

- Known for open, fair and cooperative communication style toward all levels of management, peers, staff and clients. Actively mentor colleagues and rely on network to achieve common objectives.

Management Accomplishments

LETTERS OF CREDIT

- Successfully manage current Letter of Credit portfolio of $2.3B. Bottom-line responsibility for all invoicing of clients and tracking of unpaid fees.

- Led team in reconciliation project on open monies totaling over $48M in bank's account. Reduced 900 unreconciled items to less than 80 items. Recovered $1.2M of open debits of which the bank was unaware it was due, and restored order to a chaotic situation.

- Devised new, automated reporting system for the Information Systems Department to process liability reports. Reduced the manual proof time by 100% and allowed portfolios to be seen more rapidly. Automated system was adopted bankwide, e.g., loan and audit departments.

- Ensured departmental targets were met by training team members on all upgrades to internal loan liability and fee accrual systems. Implemented and reinforced training by using immediate, common-sense applications.

- Designed several Excel spreadsheets to reduce time spent on monitoring participation deals. Enabled a 20% staff reduction, with an increase in productivity and portfolio size.

- Collaborated with senior management on review committee to determine potential effectiveness of outside loan systems. Identified specific loan needs and demonstrated intuitive grasp of system applications and accounting details.

TRADE FINANCE

- Aggressively monitored $700M Trade Finance portfolio. Ensured compliance with accuracy, up-to-date and complete data and necessary adjustments made to eliminate risk exposure. Kept informed of market conditions on a daily basis.

- Reduced losses on agricultural deals under the Commodity Credit Corporation by recovering defaulted money on approximately 24 loans. Meticulously prepared a huge volume of paperwork that was 100% error-free.

- Handled client account problems on syndicated deals with diplomacy and confidence. Cultivated client loyalty and trust by using bilingual skills and ensuring that needs were totally met.

160

Functional. *Phyllis B. Shabad, Ossining, New York*
The individual had limited education but excellent career growth. The writer's strategy was to make clear the individual's strengths and accomplishments in the workplace. Boldfacing for the

Robert A. Kelly

Areas of Expertise and Experience

- Portfolio Management
- Loan Administration
- Export Documents

- Trade Finance Instruments
- Asset Valuation/ Reconciliation
- Fronting Bank Letters of Credit

- Cash Management
- Default Claims
- Syndicated Credits

Employment

Multinational Bank, New York, NY	Bank Officer–Associate	xxxx to present
Eastern Conglomerate Brokerage, New York, NY	Operations Manager	xxxx to xxxx
BlueChip Investments, Inc., New York, NY	Research Specialist	xxxx to xxxx

Related Prior Employment: xxxx to xxxx
Bank and brokerage securities processing

Education

Pace University, New York, NY–two years
Accounting Major

Related Skills and Achievements

AWARDS
In recognition of exceptional performance, received Multinational Bank Award for implementing a securities tracking system.

PROFESSIONAL DEVELOPMENT
Successfully completed numerous accounting courses at the American Institute of Banking.

Attended training workshops on specialized systems software and applications.

Seminar: Letters of Credit.

LANGUAGES
Native English speaker fluent in written and spoken French.

COMPUTER LITERACY
Hardware: IBM platform; Windows 95.

Software: Microsoft Excel; Microsoft Word; specialized financial software.

contact information, headline, headings and subheadings, Areas of Expertise and Experience, and labels (Hardware, Software) helps to ensure that key information will be seen. Equally bold horizontal lines separate the sections, making their size evident. A half-page of Accomplishments makes page 1 strong.

Carlo Howard

56 Spruce Drive, Syosset, NY 11791 ▪ 516-55-5555

Consultative Sales Professional ▪ Banking Industry Specialist

- Comprehensive senior-level consultative sales experience with Dun & Bradstreet, the world's premier provider of business information.

- Extensive background in Fortune 100, Fortune 500, National, and Global account oversight with strategic expertise in finance and banking.

- Consistently overcome major competition and sell ROI value through meticulous preparation, including quality initiative studies, business test samples and head-to-head quality studies.

- Recognized for strong contributions in customized program development and solution-based selling. Achieved six D & B "Presidential Citation" top sales performer awards and numerous national / regional sales awards.

Areas of Knowledge in Banking and Finance

Banking Segments

Community
Global
Retail
Wholesale
Private
Small business

Portfolio Risk Management

Mergers / Consolidations
Due diligence
Risk management
Portfolio managemnet
Credit and risk scoring
Loan recovery

Underwriting Decisions

Credit policy
Commercial credit
Consumer credit
Benchmarking
Preapproval
Automated systems
Cutoffs / Score card
Response rate

Administration

Householding
Outsourcing
Community reinvestment
Fair Credit Reporting Act

Career Highlights

- Developed $1 million Citibank program highlighted in *BusinessWeek* magazine. As member of two-person team, built an automated equipment leasing system connected to an outsourcing group. Increased profits and reduced staff by improving application review / approval turnaround.

- Aided merger of Chase and Chemical banks through the solution-based sale of a $200 thousand system and $150 thousand software application (first sale in the nation of D&B SMART STREAM) that identified matching vendors, totaled expenditures and increased buying power.

- Achieved $100 thousand contract increase through creation of a voice-activated credit information system (DUNS VOICE) for Olsten Corporation's branch operations, enabling automatic retrieval of ingrained credit matrix scores and approvals via DUNS number input.

- Instrumental in a four-year, $100 thousand-per-annum sale for the building of marketing and prospecting databases for Citibank's small business direct marketing campaigns. Actively involved in a $100 thousand sale for building of Chase's NY Metro area middle-market / small business prospect database.

- Developed a five-year, $150 thousand-per-annum Citibank corporate-level sale for the building of a platform to identify corporate family linkage for Global accounts using D&B Worldbase software.

- Constructed a vendor platform for identification of over $6 billion in Time Warner subsidiary total expenditures. Platform saved millions of dollars by linking vendor patterns for leveraging of corporate buying agreements.

- Created $200 thousand revenue opportunity with Chubb through the sale of a D&B underwriting guide that increased turnaround time and approval rates by improving underwriters' efficiency.

- Produced a $100 thousand Risk Assessment Manager (D&B RAM) software sale to Chemical Bank to project allocation of future loans and provide framework to build portfolio of financial data and tie in risk scores to determine forward-moving industries.

161

Combination. *Deborah Wile Dib, Medford, New York*
An exceptional resume design for a high-performance Banking and Finance Strategic Industry Specialist. The right-aligned left column on pages 1 and 2 displays Areas of Knowledge,

Carlo Howard

Representative Accounts

Chase
Chemical
Citibank
Sterling National Bank
Republic National Bank
North Fork Bank
First Data Merchant Services
Time Warner
Sumatomo
Olsten
Canon
Chubb Group

Sales and Marketing Skills

Fortune 100 / 500
Consultative selling
Solution selling
Relationship management
Strategic sales
Market planning
Business development
Senior-level negotiation
Customized solutions
Channel selling
Cross-selling
Cross-functional teaming
Market penetration
Outsourcing solutions
ROI selling
Technology sales

Presentation Skills

Text development
Graphic development
Multimedia
CEO / CFO level interface
Small to large groups
Sales and systems training

Awards and Recognition

Achieved six D&B "Presidential Citations." Earned coveted national "Chairmans Discretionary Award" and "Customer Focus Award." Placed on top of list for innovative "Personal Sales Solutions." Won national sales contests, first and second place; regional sales contest; and numerous local and regional "salesman of the month" awards.

Employment

The Dun & Bradstreet Corporation **New York, NY**	**1980 to present**
■ **Senior Strategic Account Manager**	1997 to present
■ **Senior National Account Manager**	1994 to 1997
■ **National Account Manager**	1989 to 1994
■ **Senior Account Executive**	1985 to 1989
■ **Account Executive**	1983 to 1985
■ **Account Representative**	1980 to 1983

Currently function as Strategic Account Manager with responsibility for oversight of National, Global, and Fortune 100 / 500 accounts. Carry revenue responsibility of up to $4.5 million. Have met or exceeded 100% of quota every year and led national sales force in multiple categories.

As Banking and Finance Strategic Industry Specialist, design and sell national and global applications to international banking and finance customer base. Identify and address revenue opportunities. Interface at CEO / CFO / CIO levels to plan and present innovative "value added" and "return on investment" information solutions.

Manage a $1.6 million account portfolio for Chase, a $1.3 million budget for Citibank's credit/risk management portfolio of accounts, and a $1.6 million portfolio for second-tier financial institutions.

Blend marketing, risk management and portfolio management to cross-sell solution-based contracts for cutting-edge business information software and programs. Coordinate D&B team specialists to implement customized business information, credit, and marketing applications.

Sell RAM (Risk Assessment Manager), SPECTRUM, SAM (Supplier Assessment Manager), and other D&B proprietary software including scoring applications. Interface D&B products with third parties (ex. Fair, Isaac), to utilize company services / data for marketing and credit programs. Proficient in Windows 95, MS Word, PowerPoint, and Excel.

Education

Bachelor of Science in Economics, Queens College, Flushing, NY

Professional Development Courses and Seminars
- Spin Selling, Banking, and Financial Services training (IBM)
- Credit and Finance course (13 weeks, D & B)
- Industry-specific software training (D & B)
- The Power of Negotiation Skills (Karrass Group)
- Dale Carnegie

Representative Accounts, Sales and Marketing Skills, and Presentation Skills by lists of categories. The right column presents in detail quantified Career Highlights, impressive Awards and Recognition, and a career path of steady growth. This person's record displays imagination, innovation, and computer expertise.

JOAN C. BRAVES

1234 TREE LANE
Columbia, MD 34261
(000) 000-0000

FINANCIAL PLANNING INSTRUCTOR

◇ **Enthusiastic Communicator** ◇ **Corporate Financial Trainer** ◇ **Superior Platform Skills** ◇
◇ **Executive Liaison** ◇ **Bank Management** ◇ **Quality Control** ◇

- Reduced the organization's financial exposure by providing comprehensive training impacting branch audits, budget, and compliance.
- Skillful interaction with people; train multicultural workforces.
- Proven experience in presentation and adult learning techniques.
- Develop and monitor project resources, work plans, schedules, and budgets, all within contract specifications.

PROFESSIONAL EXPERIENCE—ABC BANK (XXXX - PRESENT)

- Eight years' direct experience as a trainer for a major banking facility with a loan portfolio of $100M servicing a customer base of 100,000. Trained over 900 bank employees.

- Refined in-depth knowledge and demonstrated proficiency of training in credit management, services and financial planning. Developed curricula, created materials, updated course materials, and facilitated eight two-week classes annually at a centrally located corporate training facility. Counseled students attending 15 different courses presented in 50 sessions a year.

- Conducted seminars and workshops. Prepared all experimental exercises, interactive activities, games, role-plays, case studies, test questions, and evaluation forms. Highly skilled in group processes, team building, questioning, negotiations, conflict management, and offering productive feedback. Delivered on-site training ensuring continuity among customer service personnel. Acted as a consultant to branches with unique or unusual situations.

SENIOR TRAINING INSTRUCTOR

- Trained and instructed entry- and advanced-level employees in credit services. Analyzed and wrote measurable objectives, training design plans, instructional and testing strategies, and evaluation plans. Designed instructor and participant guides, workbooks, formal classroom instructions (lesson plans), and self-study materials. Researched trade publications, home pages/Web sites, financial periodicals and training newsletters to incorporate new techniques, tools and relevant information into the credit training curriculum.

- Reviewed changes to branch operational manuals to ensure easy readability and clarity of policy and procedures. Served as a member of the bank's Consumer Lending Committee which developed marketing strategies and loan promotions; reviewed policies and procedures and recommended changes for credit services.

INTERIM MANAGER

- Served as Interim Manager of the training center. Participated in the preparation of the department budget totaling $800M; wrote justifications for expenditures; scheduled and enrolled employees; coordinated requirements and accommodations for conferences, classes, and seminar participants.

162

Combination. *Diane Burns, Columbia, Maryland*
A number of features make this a strong, competitive resume: the lines enclosing the heading, profile information, and areas of expertise; the hollow diamond bullets here and in the Training

Bank Branch Manager (xxxx – xxxx)

- Directly managed a branch. Scheduled and counseled personnel to maximize services. Ensured that quality customer service was always provided. Recruited and selected qualified, motivated employees. Delivered all in-branch training providing continuity among customer service personnel. Conducted performance spot checks. Participated in the formulation of action steps to reach branch goals and enabled subordinates to successfully meet and achieve the goals.

- Supervised subordinates. Familiar with all aspects of bank management including office operations, credit and loan services, customer service, teller functions, and ATM operations.

- Prepared, presented and marketed financial services at community programs, information fairs, town hall meetings, in-processing briefings for new soldiers, family forums, and community retailers, improving the bank's image, account penetration, and average balance. Created a new column in the company's newspaper, improving the information network and increasing conformity in interpretation of policy and procedures.

Other
- Completed H&R Block Income Tax Course
- International Board of Certified Trainers
- Financial Counselor, Regional Hospital, xxxx – xxxx
- Teller and Teller Trainer, xxxx – xxxx

Education
- B.A. Accounting

Computers
- Sharp working knowledge of a variety of computer programs including spreadsheets, graphics, WordPerfect, Lotus 1-2-3, dBASE, Harvard Graphics, Microsoft Windows, PowerPoint, Word, and Office 95.

Training

◇Training Facilitator Training Program	◇Law/Labor Mgmt. Training	◇Chief Teller
◇Teams and Tool TQM	◇Advanced Customer Service	◇VA Home Loan
◇Credit Services	◇Business Writing	◇Computers
◇Selling Skills for Bankers	◇BSA/LTC Training	◇Word Processing
◇Principles of Banking	◇Financial Counseling	◇Train the Trainer

Professional Associations
- American Society for Training and Development
- American Society for American Comptrollers

section near the end; the three-dimensional shaded box featuring training strengths; bulleted paragraphs in the Professional Experience that display training experience and skills; and three other sections (Other, Training, and Professional Associations) that present more information about training qualifications.

JEFF T. GARRETT

505 Valley Street · Smalltown NY 55555 · 555/555-5555

PROFILE

Quality Manager with ISO and TQM expertise and ISO certification. Background includes training and extensive experience as an instructor of Quality Management and diverse related subjects. Proven track record of establishing quality departments and developing, documenting and implementing quality control procedures and processes.

PROFESSIONAL EXPERIENCE

BIGBOX CONTAINER MANUFACTURING – Bigcity NY

Quality Manager   *June XXXX-present*

Effectively develop, implement and monitor Total Quality Management as ISO 9000 Coordinator, Lead Auditor and Management Representative, which includes:

- Train all employees in performance-related quality, Statistics, TQM, Theory of Quality, and a variety of other subjects
- Coordinate most seminars and on-the-job training relating to manufacturing (i.e., bar-coding, ink, print plates)
- Accompany sales representatives on client visits
- Compile and implement the ISO 9001 Quality Procedure Manuals, Machine Specifications Manual, and Printing Specification Manual
- Design, organize and implement incoming inspection process of all raw materials with monthly reporting and internal inspection process, which includes inspection of the first piece prior to manufacture, during manufacture and the last piece following manufacture
- Implement complaint reporting system (internally and externally), charted by dollars
- Member of Interviewing Committee using the Nowlin System
- Coordinate monthly physical inventory and waste program
- Supervise one staff member and eight auditors

ANOTHER CONTAINER COMPANY – Smallcity NY   *August XXXX-June XXXX*

Regional Quality Manager

- Promoted to this position; established Quality Assurance Departments in six plants and educated all employees in the use of Statistical Process Control

Quality Manager

- Managed the Quality Department in the Smallcity plant and supervised two technicians
- Trained managers and supervisors in six plants using the Philip Crosby TQM Education System

ADDITIONAL EXPERIENCE

FLOWER SHOPPE – Smalltown NY   *July XXXX-March XXXX*

Partner/Owner

- Assisted in the operations of this family-owned business in the areas of purchasing; routine bookkeeping; and managing relationships with suppliers, banks and accountants

EDUCATION & CREDENTIALS

AAS, Quality & Reliability Technology: County Community College – Smallcity NY; XXXX

Certified ISO 9000 Lead Assessor: Perry Johnson Inc.; February XXXX

Certified Quality System Instructor: Philip Crosby Quality College; June XXXX

AFFILIATIONS

- Member – American Society of Quality Control
- Past Member – Board of Advisors of the Quality Program at County Community College
- Guest Lecturer – Total Quality Management, SUNY College
- School Board Trustee – Smalltown Central School, Smalltown NY
- Faith Formation Catechist – St. John's, Smalltown NY
- Red Cross Blood Donor

163

Combination. *Salome Randall Tripi, Mt. Morris, New York*
The person was driving 150 miles each day and wanted to work closer to home. The writer created this resume, updating an old one. The individual now drives 50 miles each day.

JANE M. SMITH
94 Main Street
Franklin Round, NY XXXXX
516-XXX-XXXX

OBJECTIVE: PRODUCTION MANAGER/EDITOR IN A NEWSPAPER OR MAGAZINE SETTING.

SUMMARY OF QUALIFICATIONS

- 15 years' experience in production coordination, supervision of production personnel, proofreading and copyediting.
- Experienced contract negotiator with typesetters, printers and designers.
- Excellent management experience. Proven ability to obtain high workforce productivity.
- Strong background in accounting and complete handling of books.

RELEVANT EXPERIENCE AND ACCOMPLISHMENTS

PRODUCTION MANAGER
- Developed promotional materials.
- Liaised with outside vendors in the areas of database management, photocomposition, typesetting, designing, copyediting and printing.
- Trained and managed a staff of 15 people.
- Managed books and accounts.
- Implemented an in-house binding system that saved $20,000 per year.

SENIOR PRODUCTION EDITOR
- Oversaw production process from start to finish.
- Supervised copyediting and proofreading.
- Designed mock-ups and layouts.
- Generated graphics and editorial formats.
- Coordinated production schedules with graphic designers and copywriters.

EMPLOYMENT HISTORY

- xxxx-Present VP, General Manager **RISE AND FALL DELIVERY SERVICE**, Short Beach, NY
  Coordinated the work and assigned duties to over 15 workers.
- xxxx-xxxx Sr. Production Editor **INTERNATIONAL STUDIES INSTITUTE,** Old York, NY
  Supervised copyediting and performed proofreading. Designed mock-ups and layouts.
- xxxx-xxxx Product Supervision **SCIENTIFIC INFORMATION, INC.,** Old York, NY
  Saved $20,000 per year by reducing the production schedule by 5 days.
- xxxx-xxxx Production Editor **AMERICAN DEPARTMENT STORES, LTD.,** Old York, NY
  Edited and proofread merchandise copy from original copy through final color proofs.

EDUCATION

Sarah Lee College, Muffinville, NY
Bachelor of Arts Degree, XXXX
Cum Laude Graduate - Distinguished Academic Scholarship
Earned 50% of College Tuition by Managing a Leather Goods Store

164

Functional. *John Tisano, Stewart Manor, New York*
This person wanted to return to publishing after a timeout to help her spouse launch a delivery service. Functional form downplays this hiatus. In two weeks she had three interviews.

JEFFREY M. ANDREWS

██████████████████████

P. O. Box 000 • Dovetail Road
Gaines, PA 11111
(555) 555-5555

CAREER SUMMARY

Provisions Executive with more than 20 years of continuous advancement and increased responsiblities offers demonstrated strengths in financial management, cost reductions, international sourcing, and contract administration. Consistently recognized for excellence in job performance. Experience includes:

■ Accounting	■ Financial Planning	■ Budgeting	■ Auditing
■ Forecasting	■ Purchasing	■ Government Procurement	■ Vendor Negotiations
■ Materials Control	■ Facility Operations	■ Order Fulfillment	■ Quality Control

EXPERIENCE

FLIGHT HELICOPTER DIVISION • Edison, PA   1991 to 1998
Facilities Provisioner

- Established over 110 multiyear contracts for procurement of materials and services required to maintain this 6 to 7 thousand employee operation. Expedited purchase order turnaround of equipment in less than 48 hours.

- Key financial responsibilities involved establishing, maintaining, controlling, and forecasting procurement activity relative to maximizing facility operations. Planned and administered in excess of $15 million of an overall department budget of $45 to 55 million. Established multiyear contracts with vendors to ensure operational objectives were attained. Also maintained automotive fleet of 50 to 100 vehicles.

AEROSPACE, INC. • Lansing, PA   1990 to 1991
Production Control Manager

- Managed and directed 8 to 10 employees in the areas of planning, project coordination, and production. Maintained schedules for multiplant operations. Collaborated with procurement manager for materials. Fulfilled customer orders.

ELECTRONICS CORPORATION • Frenchtown, NJ   1983 to 1990
Manager of Material Control

- Reported directly to the director of procurement / program management and the division vice president. Held overall responsibility for material procurement of government contracts for the purpose of building secure military communications equipment. Activities included purchasing, inventory management, planning, meeting with production schedulers, customer program reviews, and expediting customer deliveries. Assisted with corporate audits. Supervised 15 employees in stock control, planning, expediting, clerical, and systems functions, and oversaw daily activities of the program office, purchasing, engineering, production management, and quality control departments.

- Achievement Highlights:
  - Reduced inventory procurement on expendable items from an excess of 10% to 2%.
  - Planned, conducted, and analyzed an audit. Final inventory came to within less than .5% variance of $250 million material volume.

165

Combination. *Deborah S. Edwards, Wellsboro, Pennsylvania*
The individual was interested in a position with a rural electric cooperative. He did not have a background with an electric producer, so the writer played up his experience with government

JEFFREY M. ANDREWS

EXPERIENCE (CONTINUED)

WAREHOUSE ELECTRIC • Lighting, PA   1966 to 1982

International Service Sales Planner
- Fully responsible for meeting customer needs in an international market shipping $150 million of power generation equipment per year. Planned and controlled major outages and fulfilled major maintenance requirements for all customers. Coordinated ordering, consolidating, invoicing, and delivery of multimillion-dollar service parts orders. Served as company courier on various business trips to hand-deliver parts to customers' job sites overseas.

- Achievement Highlights
  - Awarded excess of $5,000 for manufacturing improvements.
  - Shipped and billed the largest service sales order account of approximately $6 million in the shortest amount of time (72 hrs.) to a foreign country.

Advance Planning
- Planned manufacturing operations for three plant locations (North and South Carolina, and Pennsylvania) to facilitate the manufacture of power generation equipment. Forecasted 5 to 10 year production schedules. Performed site surveys to identify manufacturing capabilities and assigned work to appropriate plants.

Production Control Coordinator
- Coordinated the manufacturing assembly of various power generation equipment for utility companies, and met production schedules.

MILITARY EXPERIENCE

U. S. ARMY • Viet Nam Veteran   1968 to 1970
  - Stock Control
  - Accounting Specialist
  - Communications / Electronics Parts Specialist

EDUCATION & PROFESSIONAL DEVELOPMENT

Courses completed toward an MBA — Financial management, auditing, and business
WIDENER UNIVERSITY • Widener, PA

B. S. Accounting • GLASSBORO STATE COLLEGE • Glassboro, NJ   1977

Various employer sponsored management development courses in management, procurement, and traffic control.

contracts because the cooperative had dealings with government procurement. The writer also made conspicuous his veteran status because the company had a reputation for hiring veterans. The thick, short black line draws attention to the name. Note the use of filled triangles for bullets. See Cover Letter 3.

Eleanor Fong, CPHM   35-21 45th Avenue, Bayside, NY 11360
phone / fax 516-555-5555 ▪ efong@aol.com

Resource and Materials Management ▪ Purchasing Administration

Career Profile

- Bottom-line-oriented manager with comprehensive experience in resource management, materials management, contract negotiations, purchasing logistics and nonsalary expense reduction. Utilize anticipatory management style that drives results in a rapidly changing industry.

- Control operating budget of nearly $.5 million, with purchasing volume of more than $70 million. Personally handle large transactions of over $100 thousand. Representative resources include supplies, equipment, contracts, computers, office supplies, professional services and outsourced functions.

- Respond to competitive change by strategically transforming the purchasing and materials management function to the comprehensive management of resources. Exercise critical thinking and action-focused leadership to develop beneficial business partnerships, innovative resource utilization and effective expense control.

Areas of Experience

▪ Materials Management	▪ Expense Reduction	▪ Contract Development/Review
▪ Resource Management	▪ Value Analysis Methodology	▪ Informational Writing
▪ Purchasing Logistics	▪ Win-Win Negotiations	▪ Formal/Informal Presentations
▪ Program Administration	▪ Construction Planning	▪ Team Building
▪ Project Planning/Budgets	▪ Capital Equipment Procurement	▪ Facilitation/Group Dynamics

Representative Accomplishments

- Generated inventory expense reductions exceeding $400 thousand over two years and simultaneously increased customer satisfaction by negotiation and implementation of a stockless inventory system for forms management and office supplies.

- Implemented a customized Purchasing Department Information System featuring computerized purchase orders, fax and EDI to suppliers; bar-coded receipt management; and integration with accounting/general ledger functions. System actualized $3.5 million in savings through improved production and staff reductions.

- Attacked a persistent problem of multimillion-dollar inventory of excess useable equipment by creating an innovative surplus equipment recycling program. Educated all department heads in program's benefits and importance. Realized annual savings of $150 thousand.

- Negotiated annual savings of over $1 million in medical record transcription / correspondence services, patient laboratory testing, pager / beeper rental, elevator maintenance, exterminating, archive record storage, MRI services, pacemakers, linen / laundry service, furniture purchases and copier maintenance.

166

Combination. *Deborah Wile Dib, Medford, New York*
This "highly accomplished executive" wanted to move from a shrinking health care field to an expanding industry. Page 1 mentions management experience, other areas of experience, and

Eleanor Fong, CPHM page two

Career Development

LONG ISLAND JEWISH MEDICAL CENTER, INC., NEW HYDE PARK, NY   1993 to present
Director of Corporate Purchasing

- Coordinated and negotiated nonsalary supply savings of $5.9 million for fiscal 1998. Utilized internal staff and group purchasing contracts to reduce expense structure while maintaining quality and service.

- Reduced equipment maintenance expense by over $1.5 million in three years through implementation of an innovative technology assessment program.

- Saved $500 thousand on an outsourced food services contract and significantly improved customer satisfaction by competitive bidding and negotiation of an agreement with Aramark Corporation.

- Negotiated a recycling, municipal waste, regulated medical waste, and sharps removal agreement that saved over $250 thousand in three years.

- Produced annual revenue enhancements of over $700 thousand in areas such as pay telephone services, parking, patient television rental and infant formula grants.

- Chaired a multidisciplinary team of business and clinical professionals empowered to review and implement a nonsalary expense reduction program.

- Developed and implemented a unique cosourcing contract utilizing external expertise to collaboratively manage the processing of medical-surgical supply purchases.

- Implemented a total integrated materials management and purchasing information system as key member of team involved in system planning and development.

NORTH SHORE UNIVERSITY MEDICAL CENTER, MANHASSET, NY   1980 to 1993
Director of Purchasing (restructured division title)   1986 to 1993
Director of Purchasing, Material Management   1981 to 1986
Assistant Director, Material Services (acting director)   1980 to 1981

- Developed and initiated innovative value analysis and savings programs that produced savings of $3.5 million in 3 years. Programs were featured in *Materials Management* magazine. This program enabled buyers to utilize preestablished guidelines to track cost avoidance on purchasing transactions.

- Improved requisition and purchase order time lag from 4 days to 2 days on 90% of all requisitions processed by designing a computerized program to track buyer processing lead time. This initiative dramatically increased productivity and enabled the redeployment of 2 employees.

- Constructed an integrated systems contract (buying) approach to improve quality, timeliness, and costs to the medical and scientific community. System included on-site vendor representatives; purchasing, vendor, accounts payable and user department computer interface; and an enhanced distribution delivery system.

- Negotiated and instituted a vendor prompt payment cash discount policy with over 300 key suppliers. Developed numerous innovative corporate partnership agreements that actualized revenue enhancement, value-added services and highly competitive prices. Companies included Corporate Express, Fisher Scientific, Bard Medical, Baxter Scientific and Abbott Laboratories.

- Created 3 senior buyer/contract specialist positions for advanced interface with user departments, M.I.S., and the legal and insurance departments. This expedited the contract review process and resulted in more beneficial terms to the entire organization.

accomplishments, but hardly refers to heath care topics. The person "obtained a job as procurement director for a major university." All of the bulleted items on page 2 point to accomplishments. Therefore, half of a three-page resume consists of accomplishments! Three headings—Internal Publications and Projects,

Eleanor Fong, CPHM   page three

Internal Publications and Projects

- Materials Management Manual
- Procedures Manual for the Acquisition of Computer Software
- Information System Project Justification Report
- Purchasing Department Procedure Information and Policy Booklet
- Work Effort Statistics Report
- Purchasing Department Management Evaluation Criteria
- Requisition and Purchase Order Flow Chart for Purchasing Department Information System
- Direct Distribution Network Organizational Chart
- Buyer Category/Cross Reference Chart

Professional Memberships

- American Society for Purchasing and Materials Management (Senior member)
- American Purchasing Society
- Hospital Purchasing and Materials Management Association
- National Association of Educational Buyers
- National Association of Purchasing Management
- Purchasing Management Association of New York
- Metropolitan Health Administrators' Association

Technology Skills

- Employ Enterprise Nova and customized, industry specific, materials management and purchasing programs
- Proficient in Microsoft Word, Excel and Windows 95

Education and Professional Development

CPHM, Certified Professional in Healthcare Material Management
International Material Management Society, Health Care Section

Bachelor of Science in Business Management and Economics
State University of New York at Stony Brook

Coursework: Hospital Purchasing and Materials Management Association of Greater New York

- Materials Management: Surviving in the 90s
- Legal Issues Confronting the Health Care Materials Manager
- Process and Techniques of Negotiating

Community Activities

Founder and director of renowned *Model Train and Toy Show* that raises annual net/net income of $40,000 per year for St. John Bosco's Parish in Bayside, NY. Show is run 5 times per year and is now in its 12th year of operation with 200 dealers and 2,000 attendees per event. Directly responsible for planning and implementation of all activities including advertising, vendor solicitation and logistics.

Chairman, School Board Tuition Committee   ■   Volunteer, Community Outreach Program

Professional Memberships, and Technology Skills—appear in one section on page 3. (The lines on page 3 indicate that the writer thought of these three topics as making up one section.) The Community Activities section at the end of the resume is yet another part that shows achievements.

PAMELA M. JOHNSON

(770) 555-5555 • 3333 Glynview Circle • Lawrenceville, Georgia 33333

Business Management Consultant

PROFILE

Over ten years of experience in design and implementation of successful administrative procedures for start-up companies with dynamic growth. Strengths:

- Able to readily assess opportunities in departmental procedures for maximizing productivity and profits: Highly creative and intuitive problem solving.
- Effective in establishing and maintaining business relations resulting in compliance and adherence to new procedures by company employees at all levels of organization.
- Proficient development and writing of employee policy and procedural manuals.

RELEVANT ACCOMPLISHMENTS

Administrative
- Extensive experience in all aspects of start-up company business including:

    Bookkeeping • Purchasing • Human Resources • Advertising / Marketing • Project Management • Sales / Customer Service • Transportation • Warehousing

- Maintained optimum cash flow and credit with vendors and banking institutions by designing and implementing timely and effective Purchasing, A/R, and A/P procedures.
- Effectively managed all aspects of company expansion in *dynamic 375% growth* over eight-year period.
- Successfully ensured adherence to project budget guidelines and restrictions.

Business Relations Development
- Instrumental in establishing and maintaining vendor / supplier relations, negotiating terms and higher lines of credit.
- Cultivated positive employee relations and motivation resulting in maximum productivity.
- Able to counsel and develop employees in problem-solving skills.
- Mediated company buyout resulting in smooth acquisition.
- Experienced in writing and implementing personnel policy / procedures and manuals, including drug policy.

Company Needs Assessment
- Experienced in analyzing individual department and company personnel needs for maximum productivity and minimal waste, including interviewing, hiring, and employee development.
- Assessment of effectiveness of existing departmental procedures and advisement on design and implementation.
- Expansive resource of referrals as needed.

WORK HISTORY

Vice President	XXXX - Present	Famous Design Communications - Atlanta, GA
General Manager	XXXX - XXXX	Famous Design Communications - Atlanta, GA
Vice President of Purchasing	XXXX - XXXX	Computer Warehouse, Corp.- Atlanta, GA
Advertising Manager	XXXX - XXXX	Cody Management - Atlanta, GA

167

Functional. *Karen D. Wrigley, Round Rock, Texas*
A strong, thick-thin page border is accompanied by a thick-thin line under the contact information. Bold italic calls attention to the person's name, the headings, and key text.

ROBERT J. THOMAS
964 Leaf Circle * San Diego, CA 55555
Tel: 555-555-5555

BUSINESS CONSULTANT

Managed one of the most remarkable financial turnarounds in the history of overseas military services.

CONTRACT/FINANCE MANAGER

FINANCIAL PLANNING

WORK CONTROL MANAGER

OPERATIONS MANAGEMENT

PERSONNEL ADMINISTRATION

SUPPLY/LOGISTICS

SUPPORT SERVICES

MULTINATIONAL WORK FORCES

BILLETING MANAGER

FOOD SERVICE OPERATIONS

WRITE, FORMULATE, SURVEY, AND DEVELOP MAINTENANCE CONTRACTS

MANAGE/MONITOR THE BIDDING PROCESS

CONTROL NEGOTIATIONS, ARBITRATION AND RESOLUTION

COMPENSATION AND BENEFITS

MICROSOFT OFFICE

CAREER PROFILE

*E*xecutive experience directing community activities and facilities to include housing/billeting, contracts, business operations, budgets, financial programs and administration. Articulate writer and speaker. Formulate policy, plans, and procedures applying a thorough knowledge of international, military, legal and regulatory requirements; sharp analysis of complex issues.

*A*ctively engaged as a Business Operations Consultant/Adviser and Clubs Operations Director. Expert knowledge of military policies governing such operations, with an adept ability to plan, direct, control, and supervise multinational workforces through subordinate managers. Flawless aggressive ability in planning, justifying, and executing budgets and activity finances.

PROFESSIONAL EXPERIENCE

Business Operations Manager, xxxx to xxxx

- Direct the business operations for community activities inclusive of Bowling Lanes, a Skating Rink, Clubs, a Rod and Gun Club, and Hotels (all activities reap high revenues). Develop, prepare, and distribute fiscal year program calendars. Determine funding, supplies, and facilities. Meet and exceed budget goals and objectives. Write or formulate executive-level staff papers, justifications, and base maintenance contracts. Articulate performance standards.

- Execute budget authorization. Adept experience planning and formulating budgets and objectives with written justifications including setting objectives for revenue-making facilities, salaries, acquisition, maintenance and repair, transportation, and other requirements. Monitor Capital Purchases and Minor Construction (CPMC) Projects. Maintain strict control over business operations, practices, and methods appropriate for the effective management of revenue-producing operations.

- Exercise stringent controls over accounting documentation, overtime requirements, supply requisitions, and inventories. Conduct regular analysis and evaluation of programs, activities, facilities, revenue, objectives and budgets. Analyze financial program data strengths and weaknesses and apply that information directly to budget preparation, enhancing financial programming and solvency for future years/months.

168

Functional. *Diane Burns, Columbia, Maryland*
This individual "responded to a specific announcement for military posts." The writer had to review a background that was diverse and covered a lot of ground. She then had "to zero in

Marketing and Sales Executive, xxxx-xxxx
- Recruited and established sales agents to represent the Middle East and U.S. Companies throughout the Middle East. Trained sales personnel; called on major clients, maintaining excellent liaison; and coordinated all transactions related to quotations, confirmations, banking payments, shipping, and the customers' receipt of products.

Community Services Assistant Director (xxxx-xxxx)
- Full executive control and direction for ten divisions: Funds Management, Business Operations, Recreation Services, Contracting/Purchasing, Drug and Alcohol/Substance Abuse Center, Army Community Services, School's Officer, Personnel, Family Support Division, Remote Site Coordinator and the numerous programs which fell under each division. Formulated and executed annual budgets exceeding $20 million.

- Developed a five-year plan with staff requirements, supply and equipment needs, program improvements, facility renovations, funding sources, and program modifications. Executed CPMC and major construction per scheduling. Reviewed internal controls. Managed $10 million in gross income and $15 million in assets. (In xxxx the community was experiencing losses of over $600,000 per annum. One year later there was a $1 million turnaround and in xxxx a net of over $800,000.)

- Directed a large and diverse workforce. Effectively trained, directed, and motivated employees. Prepared individual development plans for each subordinate. Provided performance standards.

- *The community won the USA Community of Excellence Award in xxxx and xxxx. Directly hired, trained, and managed a team of winners.*

Regional Clubs Manager, xxxx-xxxx
- Controlled and directed resources management requirements including staffing, contract negotiations, briefings, and other program requirements. Served as custodian of individual funds instrumentalities within the club system. Negotiated and monitored contracts. Renegotiated all vendor contracts providing a more stabilized income for the club system.

- *Appointed transition officer and business manager for the implementation of a special fund account. The transition was successfully completed on time despite manpower shortages. Developed a stable and self-sustaining, quality-of-life enhancement program.*

AWARDS/HONORS/SKILLS
- Business Director of the Year Award, xxxx (Military Services).
- Technical Representative of Contracting Officer (Housing Referral, Food Service, Billeting, Recreation Services) for a base maintenance contract in Spain.
- Active Community Volunteer and Charity supporter.
- Worked throughout the world: Thailand, France, Germany, Dubai, America, Spain.

on a few specific aspects of his business expertise." The three-dimensional shaded box enclosing the headline and a "remarkable" achievement is eye-catching. Areas of experience listed down the left column also capture the reader's attention. Italic is used on page 2 to direct the reader to notable achievements.

10000 Woodlands Drive
Tampa, Florida 33600

GEOFF L. ABRAMSON

(813) 000-0000

CAREER PROFILE

Senior-Level Corporate Accounting and Management Professional with progressive career reflecting successive advancement achieved via executing proactive leadership, generating revenues, and producing bottom-line results for a global organization. Seven-year tenure combines diverse scope of controllership-related experience and sales management responsibilities with strong technical knowledge, business savvy, and keen analytical ability. Self-directed and entrepreneurial-minded achiever; earned recognition for proficiency in streamlining automated accounting systems, maximizing operations, training personnel, and upholding fiscal efficiency. Effective communicator possessing strong public speaking, public relations, and interpersonal skills; demonstrated strengths in projecting high-level motivation, problem solving and decision making. *Willing to relocate.*

TECHNICAL SKILLS

DOS/Windows-based programs; Microsoft Word, Excel, PowerPoint; QuickBooks; Real-T Pro; Windows 95; Internet

EXPERIENCE SUMMARY

Sales Management

- **Business/Management Consultant** responsible for successfully directing and supporting managerial operations inclusive of P&L for 100 offices in 14-county area located throughout the south and central Florida region.

- **Dynamic record of accomplishments** stemming from ability to motivate people, conduct effective training seminars, achieve bottom-line results and consistently outperforming other regions.

- **Expertise in consultative sales management**, strategic business planning, sales forecasting and implementing developmental programs within high-growth, competitive markets.

- **Corporate leader,** facilitating acceleration of sales volume/profits and outperforming other regions; chosen to serve as ownership's chief liaison at geographical council meetings communicating goals and assisting in developing cooperative advertising campaigns.

- **Conversant with performing due diligence**, market analyses, needs assessment and formulating short- and long-term financial projections for start-up and conversion operations.

- **Thorough knowledge** of coordinating, structuring and negotiating company mergers focused on increasing revenues and expanding marketshare.

Accounting/Financial Management

- **Integral role as Financial Services Representative** charged with providing consulting assistance to strategically plan, develop and execute fiscal directives for 100 independent companies.

- **Skilled in corporate accounting procedures**, budgeting, conducting financial/operational audits, presiding over accounts receivable process, preparing/analyzing financial statements and overseeing collections.

- **Orchestrated improvements** of automated accounting systems, documentation and internal controls to eliminate operational deficiencies and provide a monitoring system to ensure compliance with policies/procedures.

- **Spearheaded training** of accounting staff in automated accounting systems and financial statement preparation.

169

Combination. *Diane McGoldrick, Tampa, Florida*
The candidate wanted to pursue two areas: corporate financial (accounting) management and business (sales) management. These themes are evident in the Experience Summary, the

GEOFF L. ABRAMSON

EMPLOYMENT HISTORY

XYZ, INC.   **1990 - 1997**
(World's largest franchisor of hotels and residential real estate brokerage offices; acquired ABC Real Estate Corporation in 1996.)

Exceptional record of consistently exceeding corporate expectations resulted in successive promotions to visible, senior management positions and highly demanding, pivotal role of diverse responsibilities amplified by the acquisition/restructuring of corporate parameters.

Business Consultant (1996 - 1997)
Reported to Vice President/Director of Broker Services, Southern Division. Spearheaded development and growth of existing real estate franchises, start-up and conversion businesses in four dominant market areas consisting of 100 independent offices throughout south and central Florida. Provided leadership and consulting services delineating managerial policies/procedures, strategic business planning, market penetration/profitability and financial management.

- **Expedited planning, negotiating and approval process for three separate affiliate franchise mergers generating gain in marketshare and profitability for franchisor.**
- **Facilitated implementation of business operating systems**.
- **Key role in providing detailed analyzes for expansion, marketing, and return on investment for franchisees.**
- **Increased revenue 15% within first year following the acquisition.**
- **1996: Received bonus for increasing sales growth and volume.**

Management Consultant (1993 - 1996)
Served under direction of President. Charged with providing sales management training, detailed business development plans, market analyses, monitoring compliance with franchise agreement, ensuring operations adhere to legal and corporate parameters, and coordinating support for franchise businesses marketing the ABC Real Estate name. Assisted in sale of franchises, presided over orientations programs for prospective buyers and conducted career-oriented presentations to recruit potential sales agents.

- **Designed profitability models to identify sales results and expense variances by category producing a more effective decision-making process for cost reductions.**
- **Pioneered benchmarking study of top franchises to initiate standardized corporate procedures focused on improving organizational structure, financial performance, sales training, recruiting methods and motivational/team building techniques.**
- **Consistently outperformed other regions; grew territory sales 38% over three-year period.**
- **1993/1994/1995: Earned bonus for outstanding performance.**

Auditor/Financial Services Representative (1990 - 1993)
Worked in correlation with Controller. Extensively interacted with franchise members to provide financial consulting services involving all aspects of corporate accounting functions. Participated in preparation of documentation for year-end audit.

- **Wrote operational audit program incorporating follow-up procedures to increase franchise efficiency.**
- **Devised automated collection process that reduced active A/R by 50%.**
- **Created standardized chart of accounts implemented by corporate throughout the region.**
- **Instrumental in training accounting staff in automated accounting systems and financial statement preparation.**

EDUCATION / PROFESSIONAL DEVELOPMENT

B.A. - Accounting UNIVERSITY OF WEST FLORIDA , 1990 (Dean's List)

Certified Management Operations Facilitator ABC Real Estate

SEMINAR TRAINING
Sales Management. . .Accounting. . .Automated Accounting Systems for Real Estate
Sales Training. . .Consultative Management. . .Recruiting Techniques. . .Computer Training

Employment History, and the cover letter. A distinctive feature is the three-line bar under the contact information and as part of a header on page 2. Another feature is the use of two horizontal lines to enclose each section heading. Bold, bold italic, italic, and underlining are all used for emphasis. See Cover Letter 9.

CONFIDENTIAL RÉSUMÉ

ATTENTION EMPLOYERS and RECRUITERS:
For more information concerning this résumé,
please contact by fax, telephone or e-mail and send for the candidate's identity on company letterhead to:
RÉSUMÉ CONNECTION
33 Waln Street, PO Box 361, Wellsboro, PA 16901
Ph. (570) 724-3610 - Fax (570) 724-5492 - E-mail: resume@epix.net
This is done for confidentiality reasons only. No fee will be charged. Thank you for your interest.

PROFESSIONAL SUMMARY

An administrator and leader with 13 years experience in credit administration, planning, directing, budgeting and cost control of branch operations. A dependable, thorough, energetic, and well-organized problem solver, who is proactive and communicates effectively. Skilled in the use of computers for communications and financial reports.

PROFESSIONAL EXPERIENCE

CREDIT ADMINISTRATION, PENNSYLVANIA   March 1995 to Present & December 1989 to June 1991
A Credit Association with assets of $200 million that provides funds for commercial credit for agriculture and forest industry, and the retail market.

Commercial Loan Officer (April 1997 to Present)
Administer portfolio of more than $10 million with credit approval authority of $250,000. Branch assets total $17 million. Serve as financial consultant primarily to the dairy industry working with herds of over 150 animals, as well as to the swine and veal industries. Assess needs, review costs, develop budgets, and provide direction for business development and expansion. Provide training and support to new credit officers. Responsible to develop new agricultural business.

Division Manager (June 1996 to April 1997)
Managed division technical, operations, and human resources activities serving a seven county area with assets of $50 million. Performed credit audit reviews, established and maintained credit quality, ensured agriculture industry compliance, and classified loans. Developed new business in Dairy sector, Veal industry, and Swine industry.

Branch Manager (March 1995 to June 1996)
Provided leadership for a branch operation serving a two-county area. Administered a $22 million loan portfolio. Supervised, evaluated, and oversaw branch personnel activities of a five-member staff serving as loan officers, consumer service representatives, and loan specialist.

Senior Loan Officer (December 1989 to June 1991)
Held the responsibility for new business development and servicing large complex loans. Conceived and conducted several branch marketing programs. Negotiated and developed new loans that increased branch volume by 10% and improved credit quality by 15%.

Achievements:
- Member of the Board of Directors / Treasurer of a timber industry association.
- Serve as Financial Consultant participating in a three-year live case study project involving veterinary studies at Penn State University, 1996.
- Conceived/Conducted a direct target marketing campaign to promote the Swine Industry in 1996, and also for the Veal Industry Convention in 1996. Swine industry promotion resulted in $1.5 million of new business.

170

Combination. *Deborah S. Edwards, Wellsboro, Pennsylvania*
A Confidential Resume for an acquaintance who was working for a competitor of the company that was offering a position, and who lived in a small town in which word about his applying

VOCA, WASHINGTON, DC.   October 1994 to November 1994

Volunteers of Overseas Cooperative Assistance is an international people to people volunteer organization.

Credit Consultant working with the Romanian Development Bank (third largest Bank in Romania) and the Tiriac Bank (newest bank in Romania) providing support to better understand and work with agricultural credit in a free market economy.

CREDIT ADMINISTRATION, CENTRAL ATLANTIC STATES   January 1992 to September 1994

A Credit Association, with assets over $112 million, that provides funds for commercial credit for the agriculture and forest industry.

Vice President of Credit/Operations
Provided leadership for the Association and branch operations, with many diverse responsibilities including directing, planning, developing and organizing the management of credit practices, policies and procedures; generating reports for analysis and control.

Achievements:
- Organized and implemented credit standards that raised portfolio credit quality 34%, reduced delinquencies by 50% and acquired property volume by 90%.
- Implemented internal credit review program, scheduled and conducted the internal examination of association credit underwriting. This resulted in satisfactory external audits and examinations assessing the association management as effective.
- Administered the merger of eight branch offices into four to improve efficiencies and reduce operating expenses.
- Supervised and evaluated branch personnel activities, coordinated goal setting for an 18-member credit staff team, resulting in a cohesive staff. Directed budget planning for branch operations.
- Marketed, developed, and underwrote a new $2.3 million dollar timber industry loan. This represented 2 percent of total loan portfolio volume.

CREDIT ADMINISTRATION, CENTRAL ATLANTIC STATES   June 1991 to December 1991
A Credit Association with assets of $60 million.

Vice President Credit / Operations & Acting President
Provided leadership for the association. Coordinated the merger of two associations. Administered the $60 million loan portfolio. Implemented training programs and internal controls.

Previous employment includes a series of positions related to finance, sales, and income tax preparation.

EDUCATION / AFFILIATIONS

B.S. Business Administration, Southeast Missouri University, 1981
    Major - Management, Minor - Mathematics

Numerous continuing education classes with credits in accounting, sales, and finance.

Business Professional Membership

for another job would travel fast. This resume was thus a probe from an anonymous person to explore the possibility of a job change without revealing personal identity. See Cover Letter 5, which was sent by the resume writer. Note the special contact information at the top of the resume.

Julie M. Daniels

555 Cambridge Manor Drive · Scofield, New York · 55555 · (555) 555-5555

PROFILE

Accomplished, results-oriented professional with 12+ years experience in the financial services industry with extensive knowledge of credit and lending, investment management, financial planning/analysis, banking products and operations. Possess strong planning and organizational skills with the ability to coordinate all aspects of business operations/project management. Expertise in introducing systems and strategies that build revenues, boost productivity, enhance customer service and strengthen employee performance.

Exceptional interpersonal and communication skills allow development of strong rapport with individuals on all levels. Equally effective in self-managed projects or as a cooperative team member. Proficient in the use of computerized equipment with basic knowledge of computer programming, LAN Systems and various computer equipment/software applications. Bottom-line-oriented with a consistent record of exceeding standards and expectations – delivered strong operating and financial results in highly competitive markets.

Prepared to adapt a variety of talents toward a new challenge!

PROFESSIONAL EXPERIENCE

COMMERCIAL CREDIT SERVICES, Scofield, NY · 1996 - present
<u>Senior Customer Service Representative</u>
· Work closely with members of the financial community to develop new business sources; encourage existing customers to invest additional funds.
· Initiate applications over the telephone; determine creditworthiness of applicants; approve credit within authority and recommend approval/disapproval for accounts exceeding credit lending authority.
· Handle customer inquiries and concerns in a timely/efficient manner; develop appropriate solutions.
· Analyze/review payment trends to identify potential credit problems; initiate efforts to reduce delinquencies.

FIRST NATIONAL BANK OF THE MOHAWK VALLEY, Pendleton Square, NY · 1987 - 1996

Steady career progression through a series of increasingly responsible positions to assignment as Merchant/Credit Card Representative with daily operations management and financial accountability for the department.

Merchant / Credit Card Representative · 1995 - 1996
· Managed/coordinated plans for daily operation of the department; directed, trained/motivated and evaluated staff.
· Served as liaison for 20 branch offices in addressing/resolving customer credit card/merchant-related service issues.
· Implemented merchant application system from point of application to actual setup.
· Developed and implemented branch procedures to monitor $4.5 million annual cash advance volume.
· Provided assistance to merchants in need of research regarding deposits and other merchant-related matters.
· Provided training both on-site and over the telephone to new and existing merchants.
· Conducted periodic reviews of the merchant portfolio to determine profitability and monitor pricing mechanisms.
· Created, implemented/maintained spreadsheets to monitor daily/quarterly/annual cash advance activities for risk management, credit card adjustments, fee reversals, income and payments, and deposit corrections for merchants.

Senior Adjustor / Collector · 1991 - 1995
· Compiled data and produced weekly/monthly reports on delinquent accounts.
· Contacted customers regarding delinquent accounts; established reason for delinquency; arranged payment plan and coordinated collection of past due amount.
· Implemented effective follow-up procedures and resolutions of customer disputes.
· Worked with bank attorneys on accounts requiring legal action other than foreclosure; coordinated foreclosure procedure with attorneys when required.
· Streamlined and organized existing reporting methods and developed new methods of reporting.

Continued...

171

Combination. *Barbara M. Beaulieu, Scotia, New York*
A resume for an individual with paralegal training but whose exposure to computer science and programming got her onto a career path in the financial services industry leading to

Julie M. Daniels

Secondary Market Representative · 1988 - 1990
· Provided daily servicing as required by investors such as Freddie Mac.
· Performed monthly account reconciliations of various investor loans.
· Monitored an investor portfolio of approximately $20 million.
· Reviewed newly booked loans sold into the secondary market.
· Packaged and delivered loans to individual investors.
· Developed a network of potential investors; documented internal secondary marketing service procedures and administered collection activities for the entire mortgage portfolio.
· Conducted field inspections of properties under construction and those secured by secondary market mortgages.
· Increased investor portfolio from $5 million to about $20 million within an 18 month period.

Merchant / Credit Card Services · 1993 - 1994
Mortgage Processor / Underwriter · 1987 - 1988

ADDITIONAL EXPERIENCE
AMERICAN CREDIT SERVICES, Pendleton Square, NY · 1977 - 1981
Computer Operator / Programmer Trainee

NATIONAL CREDIT SERVICES, Port Chester, VT · 1981 - 1982
Programmer Trainee

ST. MATTHEW'S COLLEGE, Westhaven, VT · 1982 - 1983
Coordinator of Computer Services

EDUCATION
New York State Banker's Association Consumer Credit School, West Point, NY
Curriculum: Direct Lending, Indirect Lending, Credit Cards, Residential Mortgage Lending, Home Equity Loans, Asset Liability Management, Costing, Pricing and Funding, Collections and Bankruptcy, Compliance, Small Business Lending, Customer Service

Paralegal Studies, Completed June 1992, Dutchess Community College, Poughkeepsie, NY
Areas of Study: Computer Science, Business, Photography

Real Estate Appraisal, Marist College, Poughkeepsie, NY

Dental Assisting, Hudson Valley Community College, Troy, NY

PROFESSIONAL DEVELOPMENT

How to Handle Difficult People	Stress Management for Women	Secondary Marketing School
Project Management	Improving Management Skills	Fannie Mae Orientation Workshop
Getting It All Done		

COMPUTER SKILLS
PC, Windows 95, MS Word, MS Excel, MS Publisher, WordPerfect, SuperCalc$_5$ E-mail, Internet

References Available on Request

commercial credit services. The Profile section indicates the person's skills. Bold italic and italic are used to characterize the individual and her career path for one of her employers. Boldface and underlining distinguish her current job title. Bulleted items under job titles contain a mix of responsibilities and achievements.

Claudia T. James

12 Orange Tree Lane
Port Washington, NY 11050
(516) 000-0000

Credit and Financial Analyst • *Business Information Specialist*

Career
and Personal
Profile

- Twelve years of advancement to senior level credit and financial analyst with Dun & Bradstreet, the world's premier provider of business information.

- Consult with officers and management of Fortune 100, 500 and 1000 companies on a daily basis to procure vital corporate financial information.

- Focused and self-directed. Achieve corporate and departmental objectives using financial acuity, prioritization, persistence, and team leadership skills.

- MBA in progress. Possess broad knowledge of accounting, commercial law, communication, taxes, business trends, and the general cycle of business.

Areas of
Knowledge

- Credit/Financial analysis
- Executive-level consultation
- Business information collection
- Database creation

- Sales and marketing support
- Team building and management
- High-performance assignments
- Training and mentoring

Employment

Dun & Bradstreet Corporation   **1987 to present**
Information Resources Division, New York, NY

Senior Information Consultant	1995 to present
District Business Analyst	1994 to 1995
Senior Business Analyst	1989 to 1994
Business Analyst	1987 to 1989

Recent Accomplishments

- Achieved the highest office percentage (130%) of objective for financial statement replacement.

- Consistently attain 100% to 110% of direct sales volume and indirect sales lead generation revenue goals.

- Built comprehensive marketing database, producing highest office objective (152%) for project.

- Currently running highest percentage in D&B nationwide for financial statement information timeliness.

- Generated highest number of leads and sales in office for the past three years.

172

Combination. *Deborah Wile Dib, Medford, New York*
This individual wanted to move to "another industry leader in the credit information field."
Two full lines enclose the headline, two partial lines enclose the Areas of Knowledge, and

Claudia T. James   *page two*

Employment
(continued)

Dun & Bradstreet Corporation (continued)

Analysis, Sales, and Supervisory Activities

- Compile data from a broad spectrum of businesses including manufacturers, wholesalers, services and retailers with volumes up to $100 million.

- Interface with CFOs, presidents, vice-presidents, controllers and credit managers to acquire industry information that many are reluctant to reveal.

- Maintain a very high, 85% success rate for procuring personal or telephone management and officer interviews to access financial information.

- Obtain interviews and data using targeted questioning, interpersonal skills and absolute persistence to overcome objections.

- Generate substantial revenue through the sale of D&B financial, marketing, database and reference services as peripherals to information compilation process.

- Assist potential/current D&B customers with advice and facts on customer-oriented financial analysis and business information reports and services.

- Mentor and train groups in all aspects of self-directed teaming process. Group leader responsible for training and mentoring new employees.

Corporate
Awards

- Customer Focus Award (for information quality and customer service)
- Analyst of the Year
- Analyst of the Month (multiple times)

Computer Skills

- Daily user of Microsoft Office Suite: Word 6.0, Access, Excel and PowerPoint.
- Expert in use and sales of D&B software: RAM, SAM, and Market Spectrum.

Education

MBA program in progress — fifteen credits accrued to date
New York University, New York, NY

Bachelor of Science in Education with a minor in Economics
State University of New York at Stony Brook

Professional
Development

Spin Selling and Consultative Interviewing (Dun & Bradstreet)
Facilitating Meetings for Self-Directed Work Teams (Zengler-Miller)

---

another pair of partial lines encloses the Corporate Awards on page 2. The writer used bold italic for the contact information, the headline, the side section headings, and the name in the header on page 2. With a wide left column and many blank lines, the resume has plenty of white space for easy reading.

Karen A. Librarian

000 Any Street • Anywhere, Michigan 00000 • (000) 000-0000

Summary of Qualifications

Over 10 years of Librarian experience with 8 years at the supervisory level, maintaining a positive working environment. Possess excellent verbal and written communications skills and significant knowledge in reference materials. Conscientious and detail-oriented with ability to plan, organize, and direct library services and programs. Substantial computer experience, including Internet support.

Professional Experience

Any Public Library – Anywhere, Michigan   *XXXX – Present*
Assistant to the Director
- ✓ Supervise, instruct, and schedule 11 staff members, including entire faculty in director's absence
- ✓ Automation Project Manager in regards to interlibrary loans, book status, and budgeting
- ✓ Administer reference and reader advisory services to patrons, provide outreach services to senior center, and schedule various meetings
- ✓ Lead adult book discussions including book selections and conduct library tours
- ✓ Assisted in library expansion, design, and construction (XXXX-XXXX)

Another Public Library – Anywhere, Michigan   *XXXX – XXXX*
Assistant to the Director, (XXXX – XXXX)
- ✓ Supervised, instructed, and scheduled 9 staff members
- ✓ Maintained microfiche and microfilm storage
- ✓ Handled bookkeeping responsibilities and routine operations of the library

Children's and Young Adult Librarian, (XXXX – XXXX)
- ✓ Selected books, periodicals, and nonprint material for collection development
- ✓ Planned and implemented "Story Time" programs for preschool students, summer reading programs for grade school students, and "Computer Pix" for young adults
- ✓ Updated reference and library materials to exhibit most current information

Another Branch Library – Anywhere, California   *XXXX – XXXX*
Reference Librarian (Temporary)
- ✓ Examined ordered resources for collection development
- ✓ Assisted coworkers and patrons in microfiche operation and computer usage
- ✓ Handled book reservations and answered reference inquiries

Computer Experience

- ✓ Microsoft Word, Excel, and PowerPoint
- ✓ Michigan Occupational Information Systems (MOIS)
- ✓ Data Research Associates (DRA), Intelligent Catalog-Bibliofile, TDD, Magnifiers, RLIN, CLSI, OCLC, GEAC, ERIC Data Base, and Info Track – Magazine Index

Education

Texas Woman's University – Denton, Texas
- Master of Library Science, XXXX • Bachelor of Library Science, XXXX

173

Combination. *Maria E. Hebda, Trenton, Michigan*
The writer fixed a weak resume, providing a Summary of Qualifications, check marks for the Experience section, and many other changes. The person got a Head Librarian job in Florida.

Olivia Sanchez

555 Vera Street
Grove, IL 55555
(555) 555-5555

Professional Experience

Grove Area Public Library   Grove, IL
July 1993 to Present
Adult Services Librarian. Assisted with the transfer of all library materials to a new facility; involved in the initial shelving and file setups. Answer questions at the Reference Desk, including those related to various CD-ROM products and online catalogs. Taught classes in how to use various library resources. Expand and maintain the annual report collection. Maintain genre card files for readers advisory service. Update and preserve local history files. Assist in collection development and the acquisitions process. From 1989 to 1993, focused on family responsibilities.

B.T. Jarvis, Inc.   Chicago, IL
July 1988 to April 1989
Research Associate. Responsibilities included reference and research using various print sources and online databases including DIALOG, NEXIS/LEXIS, DOW JONES NEWS RETRIEVAL, DUN & BRADSTREET REPORTS. Controlled records of payment for standing order accounts and computer search services. Provided tours of the department to new employees. Assumed responsibilities of overseeing the Information Center in the absence of the manager.

Brant Hedler   Chicago, IL
August 1986 to July 1988
Head Librarian for National and Chicago offices. Responsibilities included administrating and overseeing entire library operation, supervising a full-time assistant, research for Chicago and nationwide offices, library maintenance, materials acquisition, billing, cataloging, online database searching using NEXIS/LEXIS, word processing and microfiche printing.

Green Financial   Chicago, IL
September 1985 to August 1986
Project Manager of Corporate Library and Research. Responsibilities included library setup, research, records control for off-site storage, word processing, material acquisition and supervising a full-time assistant.

Professional Affiliations: American Library Association; Special Library Association
Certification: State of Illinois, Type 03 Teacher Certification, K-9

Education

University of Arizona   Tucson, AZ
Master of Library Science, August 1985
   Honors: Graduate Academic Scholarship
   Also worked as a Student Assistant at the College of Architecture Library.
Bachelor of Arts in Elementary Education/Early Childhood, with Distinction, May 1983
   Participated in the "Block Program" for intensive study and classroom experience.
   Honors: Golden Key National Honor Society, Dean's List, Kappa Delta Pi Honor Society

References provided upon request.

174

Chronological. *Christine L. Dennison, Lincolnshire, Illinois*
This individual wanted to return to full-time employment in information science after a few years at home raising her children. Bold type calls attention to former employers and jobs.

Candice B. Robinson
663 Belle Grande Way
City, State 14166
(555) 555-5555
E-mail: cbrobb@aol.com

SUMMARY: *Librarian with over nine years' experience in leadership roles as Manager of a busy suburban branch and Acting Director of a multibranch suburban library. Experience developing and administering budgets, supervising professional and clerical staff, and dealing with community relations issues. Excellent project management capabilities, including overseeing building renovation projects and information systems implementations.*

RELEVANT EXPERIENCE:

1984 - Present   **INDIAN BAY PUBLIC LIBRARY; City, State.**
Acting Director (Library Director IV)   **June 1998 - Present**
Assume duties of Library Director during position vacancy. Accountable for management and operation of suburban library with two branches, $1.4 million annual budget, and yearly circulation of 700,000 items (projected XXXX).
- Prepare proposed budget for presentation to Town Board of Indian Bay.
- Manage expenditures and approve disbursements based on operating guidelines.
- Purchase capital equipment, supplies, and new library materials.
- Address human resource issues related to professional staff performance and staff development.
- Represent library at relevant Middle County Library System (MCLS) meetings and at community events.

Accomplishments:
Collaborated with local schools to implement Summer Reading Program serving 2,400 students.

Negotiated new contract for maintenance and service of HVAC systems at two branch buildings.

Updated job descriptions for various positions to reflect changes in duties and job responsibilities.

Branch Head - Evan St. Paul Branch (Librarian III)   **1992 - 1998**
Accountable for daily operations of branch library with 80,000 item collection and annual circulation of 340,000 items.
- Supervised up to 20 full-time and part-time employees; hired, trained, and evaluated staff.
- Established work schedules and assigned duties.
- Monitored maintenance and upkeep of building and capital equipment.
- Managed acquisitions and processing for both branches.
- Supported Library Director in preparing budgets, facilitating community outreach programs, and implementing long-range capital plans.
- Answered patron questions and otherwise fulfilled public service duties.

Accomplishments:
Managed reorganization of St. Paul and McGuiness branches. Designed new floor plan and coordinated the installation of new carpet and shelving with movement of collection to minimize disruption of public service.

Directed the reconstruction of entrances at Evans Branch to comply with Americans with Disabilities Act (ADA) requirements.

Supervised the installation of new Local Area Network in St. Paul Branch.

Coordinated Summer Reading Program that served over 1,600 children annually at St. Paul Branch.

Acting Director   1991 - 1992
Branch Head - Evan St. Paul Branch (Librarian III)   1989 - 1991
Librarian I - West Branch (Part-Time)   1984 - 1988

175

Combination. *Arnold G. Boldt, Rochester, New York*
This individual has worked in libraries ever since she got her bachelor's degree. After she received her M.L.S., she found part-time library work for several years. In 1986 she began working full-

Candice B. Robinson   *Résumé - Page Two*

ADDITIONAL PROFESSIONAL EXPERIENCE:

1983 - 1988   **CITY PUBLIC LIBRARY; City, State.**
Interlibrary Loan (Librarian I)   **1987 - 1988**
Compiled materials in response to subject reference questions from patrons. Served the needs of patrons in a five-county area, utilizing RPL, MCLS, and OCLC resources.

Science & Technology Division (Librarian I)   **1986 - 1987**
Responded to reference questions and instructed patrons in use of library resources. Maintained vertical files, selected automotive materials/assigned subject headings, and planned/prepared displays.

Library Assistant, Science & Technology Division (Part-Time)   **1983 - 1984**
Clipped newspaper articles for vertical files, answered reference questions, and worked on special projects.

1981 - 1982   **INDIAN BAY PUBLIC LIBRARY; City, State.**
Librarian I - West Branch (Part-Time)
Fulfilled public service functions and participated in Rolling Library (bookmobile) program.

1981   **HEALTH SCIENCE LIBRARY - SCOTTSMAN HOSPITAL; City, NY.**
Librarian (Part-Time)
Substituted for regular Librarian during vacations. Responded to reference questions and interlibrary loan requests. Reorganized medical journal storage room.

1979 - 1980   **INDIAN BAY PUBLIC LIBRARY; City, State.**
Library Clerk (Part-Time)

1971 - 1977   **SALT CITY UNIVERSITY; Salt City, State.**
Library Clerk - Geology Library   **1976 - 1977**
Supervisor, Processing & Circulation - Engineering Library   **1973 - 1976**
Technical Associate - Engineering Library   **1972 - 1973**
Pre-Order Searcher - Science & Technology Libraries   **1971 - 1972**

EDUCATION:

1981   **Master of Library Science**
State University of State, College at Cuylerville; Cuylerville, State.

1971   **Bachelor of Arts, Sociology**
Ivy University, College of Arts & Sciences; City, State.

PROFESSIONAL ENRICHMENT:

Grant Writing   NYS Employment & Labor Law
Customer Focused Organizations   Public Relations / Media Relations
Conflict Resolution   Creative Problem Solving

How To Design & Conduct Library Surveys
Planning A Library Building, Renovation, or Expansion

AFFILIATIONS:

American Library Association
  - Public Library Section

State Library Association:
  - Adult Services Section

time for a public library and has been on an upward career path since that time. Italic for some of the contact information stands out. Italic is used again in this resume to draw attention to important information, including Accomplishments. For a reading strategy, first look at all the bold text; then, the italic.

Mark M. Allen

401 Lane Allen Road #432 ● Lexington, KY 40505 ● (606) 555-1234 ● mallen@sprynet.com

CAREER OBJECTIVE
Library Automation Coordinator/
Network Services Implementor

Experience History

Technology Coordinator 11/97–present
Fayette County Regional Library System, Lexington, KY
Responsibilities
- Manage computer network
- Plan, develop and implement new technologies
- Supervise assistant technology coordinator
- Design, update and support Web pages
- Service and maintain Library Automated System
- Analyze and secure vendor contracts and bids
- Evaluate and purchase new equipment

Accomplishments
- Implemented new mail and Web server
- Created and employed FoxPro database system
- Recovered from major UNIX crash in three days
- Redefined networking methodology to help provide full browseability across WAN
- Introduced new WAN-supported scheduling and timeclock software
- Begun founding regional support group for Sirsi Automated System users

Computer Services Assistant 8/96–8/97
University of Louisville, Louisville, KY
- Designed, installed, and upgraded Web pages
- Conducted seminars on home page design
- Instructed staff in Web page management
- Created course syllabi Web pages

Instructor of English 8/94–8/96
Transylvania University, Lexington, KY
- Taught English Composition, Speech, and Business English courses
- Tutored in English and computer applications; assisted in library

Education

M.S.L.S. 8/97
University of Louisville, Louisville, KY
M.A., Comparative Literature 7/95
Indiana University, Bloomington, IN
B.A., English 5/90
Indiana University, Bloomington, IN

Summary of Qualifications

→ **Enthusiastic**, dependable, self-motivated; assumes responsibility necessary to accomplish jobs quickly and efficiently
→ **Skillful**; organizes work flow, materials, ideas, and people for maximum productivity
→ **Efficient**; prioritizes and delegates responsibilities and work assignments
→ **Resourceful**, innovative, quick learner; responds and adapts quickly to challenges
→ **Persistent**; approaches and solves problems thoroughly and precisely
→ **Effective;** works productively, either alone or as a member of a team
→ **Diplomatic**; relates to superiors, coworkers, and the public with professionalism and tact
→ **Cooperative**; works seamlessly and constructively with all personality types

Networking / Telecommunications Protocols
- TCP/IP
- NetBEUI
- SIRSI
- H.323
- LANS
- WANS
- FTP
- IPX/SPX

Networking / Operating Systems
- Windows NT 4.0
- UNIX, AIX 4.1
- Win 98
- Redhat Linux 5.0
- Mac System 7.5
- DOS

Server Software
- Netscape Enterprise
- Streaming Video
- WarFTP
- Netscape Collabra
- Webstar for Macintosh

General Applications
- MS Office Pro 97
- WordPerfect 8
- NetFusion Web Editor
- Adobe Photoshop
- Adobe Web Editor
- Adobe PageMaker
- Adobe Acrobat
- Adobe Premier Video
- RealNetworks Audio and Video Encoding packages

Web Page Competencies
- In-depth knowledge of HTML
- Working knowledge of Javascript
- Adept with all popular Web page editing packages

Other General Computer Skills
- Proven ability to troubleshoot, repair, swap, maintain and configure hardware componentry
- Comprehensive understanding of scanning and other TWAIN-compliant devices
- Extensive knowledge of Internet searching

176

Combination. *David W. Adler, Lexington, Kentucky*
A striking resume because of the distinctive type in the contact information, shadowed box for the Objective, and two-column format. Note the different bullets. See Cover Letter 22.

Jeanne Shannon

44 Cambridge Street
Watertown, MA 02072
(555) 555-5555

SUMMARY

Diligent, accurate, and detail-oriented **Lease Administrator** who combines exceptional analytical and decision-making abilities with outstanding interpersonal skills. Effective in high-pressure situations requiring multitasking. Proven track record of generating financial savings. High rate of productivity. Recognized for consistently exceeding expectations. Computer skills include proficiency in Excel, Access, Lotus 1-2-3, Filemaker Pro, Microsoft Windows, and Internet research.

EXPERIENCE

Lease Administrator   **Hallmark,** Watertown, MA   xxxx–present

➤ Interpret and administer leases for up to 225 stores, producing expense savings of $90,000 in less than a year.
➤ Generate correspondence and coordinate information for landlords, store managers, and multiple corporate departments, resulting in reconciled disputes and reduced costs.
➤ Conduct research and prepare reports, accurately and ahead of schedule in fast-paced environment.
➤ Calculate and analyze rent, percentage rent, monthly and yearly sales figures, utility bills; reconcile real estate taxes, common area maintenance expenses, and insurance; and perform other mathematically based functions with high degree of accuracy and precision.
➤ Recommend new operational procedures to streamline departmental processes.
➤ Establish and maintain positive professional relationship with colleagues and clients.
➤ Identify excessive expenditures and institute cost-saving procedures.

Manager	**Pier Four,** Boston, MA	xxxx–xxxx
Assistant Manager	**Jimmy's Harborside,** Boston, MA	xxxx–xxxx
Operations Manager	**Pier Four,** Boston, MA	xxxx–xxxx
Supervisor	**Pillar House,** Newton Lower Falls, MA	xxxx–xxxx
Supervisor	**Pier Four,** Boston, MA	xxxx–xxxx

➤ Managed day-to-day operations including inventory for restaurant generating $4 million in revenue.
➤ Reduced labor costs and improved efficiency of the operations.
➤ Implemented changes in menu content and design to increase customer base.
➤ Supervised staff of up to 50 people and motivated high levels of performance while generating high employee morale.
➤ Fostered repeat business and increased clientele by setting and maintaining high standards of customer satisfaction.

EDUCATION

Bachelor of Arts   **Regis College,** Weston, MA   xxxx

177

Combination. *Wendy Gelberg, Needham, Massachusetts*
A resume for a person with a B.A. degree whose career path has led to lease administration and the analysis of rents, sales, utility bills, taxes, maintenance expenses, and insurance.

SALLY A. JEFFERSON

1111 China Boulevard North ◆ Apartment 1414 Southern Tower
Saigon, Vietnam 000000
1234 / 1111-0000 *(Office)* ◆ 1234 / 1111-0001 *(Home)* ◆ 1234 / 1111-0002 *(Fax)*
sajefferson@internet.sa.vn

BUSINESS DEVELOPMENT EXECUTIVE
Combining extensive experience in Asia and a global market understanding with an ability to position and execute international business for a United States-based organization

Top-producing manager with 15 years' experience — including 10 years in Asia — creating, marketing, positioning, and producing corporate imaging and brand development projects for multinational companies. Highly motivated and creative professional with an entrepreneurial focus and a demonstrated ability to plan and execute strategic business objectives. Recognized as a business catalyst with keen ability to marshal resources and produce results. Respected as a manager and producer for integrity and skills in communication, organization, and team building.

Notable Proficiencies Include:

- Sponsorship Development & Management
- Arts, Sports & Entertainment Property
- Negotiations & Contract Administration
- Alliances & Joint Ventures
- Operations & Financial Management
- International Business Techniques
- Market Requirements Analysis
- Consultant & Vendor Relationships
- Communications & Presentations

- Worldwide Marketing & Sales
- Producer & Promoter
- Advertising & Media Buys
- Strategic & Business Planning
- Human Resource Management
- Business Licensing & Government Relations
- Real Estate & Leasing
- Innovative Problem Solving
- Conflict Management & Resolution

Contributed to significant revenue and profit growth through decisive, proactive management and an ability to promote and generate business

EXPERIENCE

LIBERATION ENTERTAINMENT & CONFERENCE, Saigon, Vietnam   XXXX to Present
A property management company with a $250 million mixed-use complex, including 25,000 square meters of office space, a 700-room 5-Star hotel, 472 apartments, restaurants, retail plaza, theatre, and exhibition hall.

Director of Theatre & Exhibitions *(XXXX to Present)*
Deputy Director of Exhibitions & Conferences *(XXXX to XXXX)*

- Manage 1,000-seat performing arts center, 4,000-square-meter exhibition hall, and 900-square-meter Atrium for Vietnam's premiere international commercial and residential complex.
- Produce special events ranging from Vietnamese touring companies to international orchestras, ballets, and music concerts with celebrities such as Mariah Carey, Manhattan Transfer, Roger Whittaker, REM, and Tony Bennett.
- Executed 146 events involving multinational sponsors, agents, promoters, cultural bodies, and local and international media firms.
- Produced over 750 hours of original programming for Vietnamese television. Managed pre- and postproduction and all media buys and advertising.
- Created and organized a 28-show entertainment property featuring 12 international music concerts and 16 Vietnamese arts performances presented in subscription format.
- Increased gross operating profits of exhibition and theatre divisions by over 50% each year.
- Supervise a 43-person Vietnamese staff and manage all related human resources.

Continued

178

Combination. *Carole S. Barns, Woodinville, Washington*
After a lengthy career in Asia, this person wanted to return to the United States to be closer to her children. From a new base in the United States, she still wanted to work throughout the Far

SALLY A. JEFFERSON / Page 2

◆ Clients include:

➤ Boeing	➤ Chevrolet	➤ British Petroleum
➤ Pepsi-Cola	➤ Ford Motor Company	➤ MasterCard
➤ NBC	➤ Miller Brewing Co.	➤ American Express
➤ Microsoft	➤ Johnnie Walker	➤ GTE

◆ Established exhibition and conference themes, arranged Vietnamese host organizations, and secured international co-organizers and sponsors.

➤ Managed venue rentals, event consulting, advertising, press conferences, and event logistics.

◆ Planned, created, and executed annual trade shows, including:

➤ International Software Developers	➤ Culinary Exposition
➤ International Jewelry Show	➤ Pharmaceutical Exposition
➤ Telecommunications Exposition	➤ Bookbinders International

◆ Achieved most successful annual trade show program of any exhibition hall in Asia.

◆ Retained as an outside consultant to sports and entertainment groups.

MERRILL LYNCH, Seattle, Washington   XXXX to XXXX

Financial Consultant

◆ Developed and marketed successful financial strategies for investments in stocks, bonds, retirement plans, and insurance to individuals and businesses.

◆ Built and managed an account base of 280 investors and $10.3 million in assets.

◆ Achieved 125% of sales plan.

SELECT MARKETERS, INC., New York, New York   XXXX to XXXX

International Marketing Manager

◆ Planned, organized, and managed 4 exhibitions and conferences in Japan and China.

◆ Directed and managed the North American exhibition space sales campaign, including advertising, floor plan and database management, budgets, and on-site assistance.

◆ Coordinated global sales efforts and interfaced with the U.S. Department of Commerce, trade associations, and various supporting organizations.

◆ Exceeded annual sales plan by 73%.

COMP*USA*, Baltimore, Maryland   XXXX to XXXX

Senior Marketing Representative

◆ Marketed business automation systems, including microcomputers, peripherals, software, networks, and PC-to-mainframe communications, meeting and exceeding sales plan by up to 112% each year.

EDUCATION & TRAINING

Bachelor of Arts, Wisconsin State University, *XXXX*
Majored in Economics, with a minor in Business Administration
(Achieved NCAA Division I All-American Swimming Honors)
Merrill Lynch Management Trainee Program
Comp*USA* Sales Training Program

East, making use of her many contacts and her talent for business imaging and finding multinational sponsors for events. Full and partial horizontal lines are used effectively. Important comments and positions are center-justified and enhanced with bold italic. Various columns and indentation patterns create interest.

JOHN HONG
555 55th Street, Apt. 55
Kew Gardens, NY 55555
(555) 555-5555

PROFILE	Extensive experience in the financial industry with proven experience in investment analysis of U.S. and emerging market equities. Consistently received excellent evaluations by leading investment bank.
EXPERIENCE 1/96-xxxx	**EQUITY INVESTMENT CORP.,** New York, NY *Investment Associate/Portfolio Management Associate*

- Promoted to lead position in charge of 6 investment associates for upcoming departmental reorganization.
- Member of team overseeing $500 million in discretionary assets for institutional clients: pension funds, annuity funds, charities, corporate entities, and high net worth individuals.
- Research and select a wide range of undervalued, high growth, value-oriented stocks for U.S. and emerging markets in Hong Kong, China, and Southeast Asia.
- Review and evaluate numerous Equity Investment Corp. and outside research reports spotlighting U.S. and emerging market companies.
- Perform extensive fundamental and technical research analysis on equities, utilizing various spreadsheet and investment tools such as Advent Professional Portfolio/Axys software.

Achievements:
- Investment Management Group achieved the following performance record for equity investments:

	Balanced Composite Equity Performance	S&P 500
xxxx YTD xxxx-xxxx	21.39%	20.54%
1 Year xxxx-xxxx	36.82%	34.72%
Inception to Date xxxx-xxxx (annualized)	24.38%	22.08%

- Personally brought the following finance projects to company during period xxxx-xxxx:

China Telecommunication Development & Investment Fund with total capital of USD $1 billion
Eastern Communications Co. Ltd. International placing of B shares
Luyuan Dawson Cashmere Co. Ltd. To raise capital of $10 million through private placement or IPO offering

- Increased productivity by 300% by replacing 3 employees.
- Initially selected for position out of a pool of 250 applicants.
- Developed performance record analysis for new business development.

10/94-1/96	**MONEY GROWTH INSTITUTE, INC.,** New York, NY *Investment Assistant/Portfolio Administrator* • Actively participated in investment decisions regarding equities, fixed income, governmental securities, futures and options instruments.
EDUCATION 4/94	**GOLDEN GATE UNIVERSITY,** San Francisco, CA *Master in Business Administration-Corporate Finance major*
7/84	**SHANGHAI UNIVERSITY,** Shanghai, China *Bachelor of Arts in Liberal Arts*
SKILLS	Computer: DOS, Windows, Excel, Lotus 1-2-3, Advent Professional Languages: Bilingual English/Chinese
LICENSES	• Series 7, General Securities Representative Examination • Series 63, Uniform Securities Agent state Law Examination

179

Combination. *Etta R. Barmann, New York, New York*
The design of this resume is effective because it fits on one page. Factors which made that possible are narrow top and bottom margins, small print, and reduced leading (line spacing).

MELANIE E. PALMER
2000 Woodstock Drive
Tyler, Texas 75700
(903) 555-3333

HIGHLIGHTS OF QUALIFICATIONS

♦ **Astute, goal-oriented professional** with experience and proficiency in **finance / investment management, strategic analysis / planning / development**, and **technical research / analysis**.

♦ Familiar with NYSE and NASDAQ requirements / regulations; knowledgeable of and experience in common / preferred / foreign stocks, options, mutual funds, and IRA investments.

♦ Outstanding **organizational**, **time management**, **analytical**, and **problem-solving** abilities.

♦ Computer literate: Windows 95; MS Word, Excel, Access, Lotus 1-2-3; Internet; database design.

♦ Savvy, compliant **team player**. **Ambitious**. **Trustworthy**. Bonded.

EDUCATION / PROFESSIONAL DEVELOPMENT

UNIVERSITY OF TEXAS AT TYLER – Tyler, Texas
Bachelor of Business Administration – Finance (December 1997)

Money Banking and the Federal Reserve ♦ **Investments / Financial Administration**
Strategic Planning / Development ♦ **Retirement Planning**

PROFESSIONAL EXPERIENCE

SANGER STORES INC.   Tyler, Texas
Vendor Analyst / Manager–Trouble Expeditor   1998 – Present
♦ Initiated database system for corporate reporting requirements within distribution center; created customized databases for various departments, including Distribution Management, Merchandising/Structure, HR.
♦ Created and implemented employee skills tracking system for Human Resources Department.
♦ Supervise team of 12 in analyzing and resolving shipping problems.
♦ Prepare and submit various weekly/monthly reports to corporate office.

Independent Private Trader   1995 – 1998
♦ Researched technical indicators and investments; analyzed data to determine appropriate investment strategies.
♦ Created model portfolio to achieve desired financial goals; traded stocks and options on NYSE and NASDAQ.
♦ Collaborated with Momentum Securities to acquire in-depth knowledge about NASDAQ stocks and system.

FINANCIAL SECURITIES, INC.   Dallas / Tyler, Texas
Assistant to Vice Presidents and Brokers / Stocks Wire Operator   1993 – 1995
♦ Provided administrative support to vice presidents and stockbrokers (1993–1994); promoted to Stocks Wire Operator in corporate office (1994–1995). Functioned efficiently in fast-paced, critical-timing environment.
♦ Performed comprehensive research and analysis of investments; placed orders approved by brokers.
♦ Interfaced extensively with clients; resolved account discrepancies; received/submitted checks; mailed financial documents, prospectuses, and research/investment materials to clients and prospective clients.
♦ Assisted in planning and coordinating investment seminars. Created form letters and client profiles.
♦ Worked closely with area attorneys to coordinate special projects related to trusts and wills and CPAs regarding preparation of tax returns.
♦ Completely renovated/reorganized filing system; **significantly improved efficiency and accessibility**.
♦ Served as backup Receptionist and Wire Operator.
♦ As Stocks Wire Operator, received all OTC orders from Principal Financial branches throughout U.S.; redistributed orders to proper traders. Returned executed orders to branch offices.
♦ Researched and provided quotes on foreign stocks to branch offices.

180

Combination. *Ann Klint, Tyler, Texas*
This resume has a shadowed page border in which the shadow is shaded and not black. Boldface plays an important role in this resume. In some sections key information is bold.

JOHN POWERS

555 West 55th Street, #5E
New York, NY 55555
(555) 555-5555

EXPERIENCE

Scott Fitzerald, Inc.   New York, NY
OTC Trader   xxxx-xxxx

Aggressively trade a wide variety of domestic over-the-counter equities and ADRs for both proprietary trading and institutional clients. Work closely with senior trader in a team-oriented environment.

- Gained experience in risk taking by providing liquidity in very thin, high beta post IPO stocks.
- Selected for special two-week assignment in the firm's Paris office to assume responsibilities of senior trader. Traded on the Easdaq, Nouveau Marchaux, and Neuer Market for H & Q's European institutional clients.
- Developed a strong understanding of European customers' trading styles and execution expectations.
- Traded IPOs and secondary offerings, for both lead and comanaged deals, including Amazon.com, Inktomi Corp., Broadcast.com, and Platinum Technology.
- Developed knowledge of rules governing stock buy-backs and insider transactions.
- Worked on the Agency Desk. Formulated and enhanced Scott Fitzerald's relationship with other broker-dealers.
- Cultivated and maintained direct relationships with the firm's major institutional customers.
- Responsible for maintaining direct communications with institutional salesmen and institutional coverage traders, research analysts, venture and syndicate services personnel.

John Smith, Inc., Member of NYSE   New York, NY
Head Clerk   1994-1995

- Executed orders for principal's customers on the floor of NYSE, working directly with three floor brokers.
- Worked directly with listed trading desks and gained valuable experience in listed markets.
- Served as an intermediary with other "$2 brokers" and clerks in the booth.

Manning Company Ltd.   New York, NY
Account Executive   1993-1994

- Directly collaborated with Senior Vice President in the successful expansion and cultivation of institutional client base.
- Prospected and managed institutional and high net work individuals' equity accounts.
- Developed strong understanding of securities and other financial instruments. Garnered a strong ability to interpret and analyze financial statements.

Intern   1992-1993
- Performed research, prepared reports and conducted cold-calling of institutional accounts to establish viable prospects.

EDUCATION

New York University, New York, NY   May 1993
B.S. degree in Business Administration; Major In Finance

SKILLS

Series 7 and 63.

181

Chronological. *Etta R. Barmann, New York, New York*
Most of the Experience section is devoted to the individual's position as an OTC Trader. The bulleted items for this position contain a mix of responsibilities and notable achievements.

GARY ANDRICH

111 Gomer Court   Toms River, New Jersey 08533   (732) 992-9999

**WALL STREET WHIZ BOASTS A PROVEN TRACK RECORD IN LEADERSHIP,
PROBLEM SOLVING AND COMMUNICATIONS**

"I feel that Mr. Andrich is a Stand Out Professional in a profession where there are few standouts."
- -Stephen Leeb, Editor, Personal Finance

EXPERIENCE SUMMARY

Financial Administration	Business Development
Strategic Planning	Staff Recruitment & Training
Marketing & Public Relations	Public Speaking

ACCOMPLISHMENTS

- Achieved significant positions and notoriety via hard work, honesty and a commitment to the workplace.
- Provided high-quality customer service and nurtured a loyal client following throughout career.
- A national television and radio personality, provided more than 500 interviews, was quoted frequently, and was the subject of numerous articles in leading financial publications and daily newspapers.
- Published a financial newsletter that received international attention.
- Spoke before worldwide audiences at major investment conferences.
- Assisted publicly held companies with financing and corporate development.
- Provided investment guidance to a staff of 300 salesmen.

CAREER HISTORY

President/Consultant/Investment Advisor: 4/93-Present
> **PETER GRANDICH COMPANY, INC.,** Wall Township, Englishtown, NJ

Stockbroker/Market Strategist/Investment Strategist: 4/84-4/93
> **WASIK AND DAVIDSON,** Freehold, NJ
> **AFM INVESTMENTS,** Howell, NJ
> **MUNICIPAL AND GOVERNMENT SECURITIES,** Freehold, NJ
> **PHILLIPS, APPEL & WALDEN,** Eatontown, NJ
> **UNDERHILL ASSOCIATES/BROWN KNAPP & COMPANY,** Red Bank/Freehold, NJ

Warehouse Manager: 7/81-3/84
> **TOSHIBA AMERICA,** Fairfield, NJ

HONORS

"Distinguished Businessman" New Jersey State Assembly Resolution, 1996

References Furnished upon Request.

182

Functional. *Nina K. Ebert, Toms River, New Jersey*
Few resumes exhibit vitality, but this one does. The light tone of the headline, followed by a strong quote, establishes the resume's tone, which is kept to the end.

CRAIG L. SIMMS

Phone/Fax: (555) 555-5555	55-55 55th Street, #55
E-mail: CraigLS@msn.com	New Springville, New York 55555

Profile
- **Equities/Securities Trader** with 6 years of progressively responsible experience.
- Assertive and self-motivated professional with a proven record of sales achievements.
- Talent for understanding market trends; knowledge of international and emerging markets.
- Articulate communicator; relate well to people from varied backgrounds and cultures.
- Analytical with strong problem-solving abilities; knowledge of company/economic research.
- Familiar with computerized trading; proficient in Microsoft Word and Excel.

Related Employment

A & H SECURITIES, LTD. - Essex, England
Equities Trader, XXXX to XXXX

Executed stocks trading and ensured regulatory compliance. Coordinated trades with back office. Interfaced with brokers and traders from different stock exchanges. Advised company sales personnel. Informed fund dealers about market trends and developments. Worked with research department to devise effective market strategies. Reported to Country Head.

- Implemented strategies that helped company grow from ground zero to a market leader.
- Instrumental in activating seats on the London Stock Exchange and National Stock Exchange of England.
- Successfully set up dealing desk for the company and established a panel of brokers.
- Achieved nearly 100% compensation increase within 2 years.

ROYAL SECURITIES, LTD. - London, England
Chief Equities Trader, XXXX to XXXX

Supervised the execution of trades for institutional and corporate clients. Monitored stock price movements and client portfolios. Liaised with exchange authorities to settle transactions. Established strong client relationships. Reported to Chief Executive Officer.

- Received Merit Award for Star Performer of the Year.
- Promoted from Trader to Chief Equities Trader.
- Earned an industry reputation as a leader in equities trading.
- Actively assisted with setting up branches across the country.

ACTION STOCK BROKERS, LTD. - London, England
Executive - Primary Markets, XXXX to XXXX

Handled brokerage of bonds for companies and government institutions. Marketed these instruments to corporate and individual clients, government institutions, and banks. Reported to General Manager of Company.

- Recognized for achievements in sales, new account development, and strong closing ratios.
- Sales achievements earned promotion from **Accounts Executive** (XXXX to XXXX).

Employment (other)

CAPITAL ACCOUNTING CO. - London, England
Manager, Audit and Tax, XXXX to XXXX

Completed statutory, internal, and taxation audits.

SUPERIOR ACCOUNTING CO. - London, England
Article Clerk, XXXX to XXXX

Performed accounting and auditing. Completed individual and corporate tax reports.

Education

THE INSTITUTE OF CHARTERED ACCOUNTANTS - London, England
Associate Chartered Accountant, Accounts and Auditing, Corporate Law, and Tax, XXXX

THE CITY UNIVERSITY - London, England
Bachelor's degree in Commerce, Accounts & Finance Major / Export Management Minor, XXXX

183

Combination. *Kim Isaacs, Jackson Heights, New York*
This person was seeking a job in the United States, so his English "job titles and credentials had to be 'Americanized.'" Now the "English" focus is not evident. See Cover Letter 19.

DONALD S. ALLEN

740 Blair Mill Drive
Edison, New Jersey 07000
(973) 000-0000

SENIOR FINANCIAL CONSULTANT

Combine excellent qualifications in financial planning, investment management, and securities analysis with dynamic record of directing effective sales and marketing initiatives that successfully drive revenue gains.

PROFESSIONAL EXPERIENCE

Senior Internal Wholesaler - Financial Institution Division
NATIONAL FUNDS INC.

November 1995 - Present
New York, New York

- Serve as Financial Wholesaler to banks in FID territory; provide mentoring/training to Branch Investment Representatives in areas such as facilitating efficient prospecting/networking campaigns and augmenting effective servicing.
- Create asset allocation models; furnish economic and market analyses to bank representatives territorywide.
- Design and implement innovative sales/marketing strategies for referral training programs in multistate bank branches.
- Promoted to Division's Team Leader and Retirement Investment Specialist charged with serving as liaison to upper management.

Achievements:
- **Grew territory business $48MM in 1995; $76MM in 1996 and $138MM in 1997. (1st Quarter 1998: $51MM).**
- **Exceeded production goals 25 consecutive months.**
- **Achieved quarterly bonus level 9 successive quarters (earned top level bonus 5 times).**

Assistant Vice President/Financial Consultant
LYLE ROSEN & ASSOCIATES

March 1992 - November 1995
Tampa, Florida

- Spearheaded operational functions involving the development and implementation of client/prospect management and marketing campaigns; supervised support staff.
- Key role in performing due diligence and marketing of Private Placement Equity and Debt Offerings.
- Presided over client base of up to 500 accounts; extensively interacted with New York Traders; and coordinated stock, mutual fund, and municipal bond transactions.
- Resolved service-related problems involving cash and margin accounts and ensured proper documentation, delivery and transfer of funds and securities.

Achievements:
- **Increased gross production by 120% over two-year period.**
- **Expanded client base by approximately 150% within three years.**

Floor Trader
ABC COMMODITIES

January 1988 - January 1992
New York, New York

- Personal account trading in all commodity futures listed on the COMEX and N.Y. Cotton Exchange including precious metals, options and the U.S. Dollar.
- Supervised three staff members and ensured proper trade execution and clearing activities.

Vice President Floor Operations / Floor Trader
JONAS MILLER COMMODITIES

March 1981 - January 1988
New York, New York

- Managed customer relations and support operations. Executed customer outright, spread and arbitrage orders for domestic/overseas clients.
- Monitored activities of gold/silver/copper futures and options markets; supervised floor staff — 10 brokers and 20 clerical employees.
- Participated as a member of COMEX Arbitration Committee and the COMEX Childrens Fund Committee.

Floor Clerk

- Worked as phone clerk taking retail outright, spread and arbitrage orders; assisted clearing staff in reconciliation of unmatched trades.

EDUCATION / LICENSURE

B.S. degree - Finance, PENNSYLVANIA STATE UNIVERSITY

Licensure: Series 7, 63, Life/Annuity

184

Combination. *Diane McGoldrick, Tampa, Florida*
A resume prepared for an internal promotion. The resume has features of an executive resume: narrow margins, wide lines, small print, reduced line spacing, and white space.

Jonathan T. Doe, CFA

Home Address, Home Telephone, E-mail Address

CAREER SUMMARY

Extensive experience in financial services and banking to broad range of individuals, companies and institutional investors. Provide finest-quality client service through diligent responsiveness and thorough follow-up. Maintain excellent long-term relationships with clients by furnishing conceptual solutions to serve their long-term interests. Impeccable personal integrity.

PROFESSIONAL EXPERIENCE

1982-present FIRST RATE INVESTMENT BANK, Los Angeles, CA
Vice President, Private Client Services, 1987-present
Associate, 1982-1987
High Net Worth Individuals ($5 million-$1 billion)
Clients include 18 current/former CEOs of public companies and venture capital firms.
- Direct all aspects of wealth management including goal identification, asset allocation, and portfolio construction and implementation.
- Constructed special-purpose fixed-income portfolios to achieve specific current income goals. Investments include municipal bonds, master limited partnerships and real estate investment trusts.
- Performed special projects for clients such as location and analysis of third-party niche managers who specialize in foreign equities, hedged investments and commodities.
- Single stock risk management: possess thorough knowledge of all aspects of managing concentrated stock positions including hedging strategies and restricted stock transactions involving Rules 144 and 145 and their tax implications.
Corporate Cash Management (from small startups to publically held corporations)
- Working closely with company treasury staff, design investment policy guidelines for emerging growth companies and implement portfolio strategies.
- Invest corporate funds in wide range of instruments including repurchase agreements, taxable and tax-exempt commercial paper, taxable and tax-exempt variable rate preferred stock, short-term U.S. agency and municipal notes, and high yield corporate notes.
Small Institution Equity Management
Clients include small institutional equity managers with niche strategies including Asian equity funds, technology funds, small capitalization managers and short sellers.
- Provide research and trading coverage to chief portfolio managers and traders.
Membership on Firm Committees
- Private Client Services Client Web Project - client focus group discussion leader
- Private Client Services Presentation Committee
- Private Client Services Compensation Committee

1978-1982 AMERICAN BANK - CORPORATE BANKING GROUP, Chicago, IL
Assistant Vice President, Chicago Office
Held line responsibility for Midwest Fortune 500 accounts. Managed all aspects of corporate relationships: lending agreements, export finance facilities, foreign exchange lines

(continued on next page)

185

Combination. *Pamela Condie, Oakland, California*
A resume for a Chartered Financial Analyst whose private clients are multimillionaires. The individual's career path is one of stability and growth. He got an M.B.A. two years after

Jonathan T. Doe, CFA

Home Address, Home Telephone, E-mail Address

of credit and cash management services.

EDUCATION

MBA with Finance Concentration, Anderson School of Management, University of California at Los Angeles, 1978; member, Dean's Honor List.

BA magna cum laude, Business Administration, University of Washington, 1976; member Phi Beta Kappa.

CONTINUING EDUCATION

Chartered Financial Analyst Program - completed all three levels of preparation in 2½ years. Passed each of 3 examinations on first attempt. Current membership as CFA Charterholder with Los Angeles Society of Security Analysts.

COMMUNITY ACTIVITIES

- Member and past Chairman, Fund Raising Committee, Alpha Boys' Club of Los Angeles, a nonprofit educational institution providing after school tutoring and college scholarship funds to disadvantaged high school students.

- Member of the Board, Surfrider Foundation, an independent nonprofit environmental organization dedicated to the protection and enjoyment of the world's oceans and beaches.

graduating *magna cum laude* from college and then worked four years at a bank. He then moved to his second company and has been there ever since. Underlined text indicates the range and diversity of his activities. The Continuing Education and Community Activities sections show expertise beyond work.

James Porelli

555 Forest Avenue
Northwoods, IL 55555
(555) 555-5555

Summary

Portfolio Manager with consistent record of success in structuring accounts and advising businesses and individuals. Worked with taxable and tax-exempt portfolios in the $500,000 to $20 million range. Direct experience with equities, fixed income securities and derivatives. Record of almost 100% client retention.

Professional Experience

Trustee / Manager / Broker
XXXX to Present
Since June XXXX, **Assistant Vice President** with XYZ Illinois, managing over 50 of XYZ's most investment-sensitive accounts requiring a high level of attention and client contact. Daily interaction with stock analysts; frequent trading of ideas with outside managers. Persuaded XYZ to add a particular stock to the approved list. Developed a statement of account review procedure for the investment department. Instrumental in closing 6 new trust accounts, including one for $6 million.

From XXXX to XXXX, a Registered Representative for The Equitable, emphasizing estate-planning products and services. Top 2nd Year Producer for Chicago in XXXX.

Since XXXX, trustee and client of an investment counseling firm, gaining valuable insight into the client's perspective.

Manager of the Premiere Equity Hedge Fund
1982 to 1989
A limited partnership operating as a broker dealer. Generated average annual returns of 66%; 121% in 1983; no down years. Discovered an inefficiency in the market for high priced stocks and created a computer program to capture it.

ABCD -- Market Maker
Great Plains Stock Exchange -- Specialist
1981
Direct experience arbitraging a primary market against its derivatives and seeing the effects of various institutional execution strategies. During the previous two years, bought, rehabbed and sold a Chicago apartment building.

Illinois National Bank   Chicago, IL
1980
Commercial Loan Officer

First National Bank of the Bay   Boston, MA
1972 to 1979
Assistant Vice President. Progressive assignments consulting to savings banks on portfolio construction and on asset/liability management. Handled stock and bond portfolios up to $20 million and all-stock portfolios up to $9 million.

Education

Chartered Financial Analyst

Yale University, Bachelor of Arts, 1971

Additional Skills: Windows, Lotus 1-2-3, Harvard Graphics

186

Combination. *Christine L. Dennison, Lincolnshire, Illinois*
This individual had "many years of investment management experience, much of it overlapping." The writer wove together a number of achievements "into a clear, concise whole."

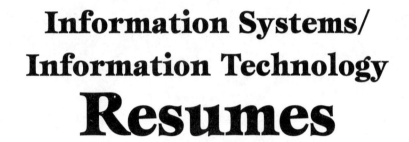

Information Systems/
Information Technology
Resumes

Roxanne Johanson

35 North Station Avenue
Oakdale, NY 11769

phone ■ 516-555-5555
e-mail ■ roxjohan@aol.com

Information Systems Group Management ■ Technology Administration

Career Profile

■ Bottom-line-oriented executive with over fifteen years of comprehensive experience in innovative oversight of teams *and* technology. Utilize an anticipatory management style to drive results in a rapidly changing industry. Produce consistent achievements in cutting-edge information systems management, team management, contract negotiations, purchasing logistics and expense reduction.

■ Managed information systems group supporting production and business operations for *Newsday*, the nation's seventh largest newspaper. Supervised 48 direct reports and controlled $5 million + operating budget. Researched, assessed and approved technology purchases. Implemented system improvements to maintain profitable, competitive, and quality-driven production processes.

Key Management and Technology Abilities

- Advanced Technologies
- Resource Management
- Project Planning/Budgets
- Project Management
- Expense Reduction
- Team Building/Motivation
- Presentations
- Capital Expenditure Planning

- Technology Needs Assessment
- Technology Rightsizing/Upgrades
- Win-Win Negotiations
- RFP Development/Review
- Vendor Partnerships
- Network Administration
- Project Lifecycle
- UNIX, SUN, LAN, WAN

- Systems Configuration
- Systems Implementation
- Parallel Systems Operation
- Intranet Development
- Technology Integration
- Disaster Recovery
- Systems Security
- Year 2000 Solutions

Summary of Major Accomplishments

■ Reorganized entire Newsday Business Systems operation and hardware for 20% productivity improvement and a $230 thousand savings against operating expenses. Reduced footprint, allowing department's relocation to main building, freeing old location for lucrative commercial rental.

■ Recruited and led team of volunteers to independently develop Information Systems Department's Intranet Server. Program was so successful that it was adopted company-wide and became part of Information Systems Department's long-range strategic plan.

■ Led project team that planned and implemented Newsday $4.8 million pagination project representing cutting-edge production technology. Project ROI was only 2.5 years.

■ Increased productivity and reduced expenses by purchase of new Tivoli system, replacing "manual" monitoring/installation method, which provided fast-response central network monitoring, asset management and LAN central software distribution to 1,200 desktops and 35 servers.

■ Developed and implemented $680 thousand network project that replaced old copper Ethernets with a fiber optic backbone and Cat5 10baseT wiring to the desktop utilizing dynamic switching hubs.

187

Functional. *Deborah Wile Dib, Medford, New York*
A resume for an Information Systems Director for a newspaper that recently reorganized. She had both management and technology skills. The resume does justice to both. In fact, the writer

Roxanne Johanson

Career Development

NEWSDAY, INC., LONG ISLAND, NY   1980 to XXXX

Director, Information Systems Group (Publishing, Business, Networking)	1997 to XXXX
Publishing Systems Manager	1990 to 1997
Editorial Project Manager	1986 to 1990
Systems Maintenance and Operations Supervisor	1982 to 1986
Senior Computer Technician	1980 to 1982

Managed all Newsday Information System groups to provide support to the Editorial, Advertising, and Production Departments in all areas of system design, maintenance, training and disaster recovery. Information Systems group reports included:

Publishing Group—handles all support for print functions of publication: software, hardware, operating systems, desktop installations, upgrades, repairs 24X7 365 days.

Business Systems Group—the actual operations team. Includes systems programmers and data center staff for *Newsday* and the *Baltimore Sun*. Team also handles testing and implementation of the business systems disaster recovery plan for 24-hour data center catastrophe recovery.

Networking Group—the technical team. Designs, implements, installs, monitors and repairs LAN and WAN systems in New York City; Long Island; and Washington, DC.

Information Systems Group Management Overview

- Managed 48 employees and oversaw a $5.6 million budget to research, plan, install, integrate and maintain hardware, software and networks to support 2,000 internal and external customers at Newsday's New York, Long Island, and Washington, DC facilities.

- Conducted strategic planning including system upgrades, and capital, operating and line-item budgets. Developed RFPs, executed ROI analysis, and negotiated/reviewed contracts. Performed system reliability analysis and cost justifications on system replacements.

- Controlled departmental purchasing and resource management. Tracked expenses and crossed with finance department's fixed asset reports and accounts payable to maintain budget integrity. Produced management and staff reviews, determined salary increases and payroll budget.

- Led project teams, and managed projects using Microsoft Project and Support Magic to direct teams handling internal and client hardware and software installations. Reviewed incident report summary and analyzed to determine repetitive problems and diagnostics.

- Headed Newsday Standards Committee to determine minimum standards for desktops, servers, software packages, printers and laptops. Member of Year 2,000 problem-solving team.

- Partnered with Newsday's Electronic Publishing Department to develop an RFP and select an Internet provider. Obtained Newsday's Class B Internet license.

Early Technical Employment

Q1 CORPORATION, LONG ISLAND, NY	POTTER INSTRUMENT COMPANY, LONG ISLAND, NY
System Test Technician	System Test Supervisor

used a third page with a technical summary "to expand on technology and keep technical terms from confusing the management pages." This individual is savvy not only about management and technology but also about finance, budgets, capital expenditures, ROI, expense tracking, cost reduction, payroll, and so on.

Roxanne Johanson

Technical Achievements Summary

- Researched, purchased and implemented multimillion-dollar systems. Set up parallel systems to prove reliability before production. Authored Information Services training curriculum.

- Increased processing power and reduced system footprint by conversion to IBM C-MOSS OS390 (R52 Model) from IBM 3090/400J. Scrapped older disk drives, installed new Symetrics disk drives from EMC Corp., and utilized Storage Tech tape silo.

- Developed original version of Newsday's NT Intranet Server. Planned and implemented Newsday's $4.8 million pagination project.

- Installed Tivoli system providing fast-response central network monitoring, asset management and LAN central software distribution to 1,200 desktops and 35 servers.

- Developed and implemented $680 thousand network project that replaced old copper Ethernets with a fiber optic backbone and Cat5 10baseT wiring to the desktop utilizing dynamic switching hubs.

- Moved Editorial Department from proprietary dumb terminals at desktops, to PC-based desktop terminals. Expanded Editorial front-end system from single to multiple networks.

- Constructed and implemented network and file server. Managed system queues. Maintained spooler queues and worklists for automatic file routing. Developed CAWT files and ran typesetting goal posts.

- Created system failure troubleshooting and preventative maintenance procedures. Instituted spare parts online inventory system. Maintained, repaired and operated front-end systems.

Network, Client Server and Software Technology

- Fiber Optic Backbone
- LAN and WAN
- Wide Area Networks Through T-1 lines
- Class B Internet license
- TCP/IP
- Firewall One
- HubWatch
- Wellfleet and Cisco Routers
- Dial and Dedicated Remote Communications
- Frame Relay
- DEC 900 Dynamic Switching Hubs
- Switched and Shared Ethernet Circuits
- Tivoli LAN Management system

- UNIX Operating Systems
- SUN Solaris and Raid Disk Technology
- Sybase Relational Database
- WinFrame Syntrex for Thin Client/Fat Server
- NT Alpha Server with Microsoft Mail
- Windows 3.1
- Windows 95
- Windows NT (Client and Server)
- Microsoft Mail
- Microsoft Office
- Microsoft Project and Support Magic
- Norton AntiVirus
- Total Intranet Development and HTML Code

Education and Professional Development

Bachelor of Science, Business (Magna cum Laude), 1980
Dowling College, Oakdale, NY

Associates in Applied Sciences in Electricity and Electronics, 1977
Suffolk County Community College, Selden, NY

It's difficult to understand why a company undergoing reorganization would agree to the release of someone with such diverse experience and multiple areas of expertise. That a reader of a resume should feel this way attests to the success of the resume as well as to the multiple merits of the individual.

HOWARD EDWIN

55555 Rainbow Trail
Portland, OR 44444

Home: (555) 555-5555
Voice Mail: (555) 333-3333

MANAGEMENT EXECUTIVE · HIGH TECH INDUSTRIES
· FINANCE - INFORMATION TECHNOLOGY - STRATEGIC PLANNING ·

EXECUTIVE PROFILE

Significant expertise in managing and directing financial, information technology and strategic planning for world-class, high-tech companies.

☒ *Strategic Planning:*
- Manage & plan for system upgrades
- Plan new systems architecture
- Develop & implement IT changes
- Significant analytical expertise
- Proven time & cost saving skills

☒ *Financial / Budget Management:*
- Budget analysis & strategies
- Established financial objectives
- Planning for global business
- Chair capital expenditure committees

☒ *Contract Negotiations:*
- Negotiate worldwide vendor contracts
- Focus on Information Systems
- Prequalify all vendors

☒ *International Management:*
- Manage offshore operations
- Maximize Operational Assets
- Improve quality standards/processes
- Established, new, overseas divisions

☒ *Operational Management:*
- Strong Team Leader expertise
- Lead on a worldwide scale
- Prescribe system standards

PROFESSIONAL EXPERIENCE

·· *Ferman Technology...Beaverton, Oregon*

Director Information Technology
xxxx to present

- Manage worldwide Information Technology needs for this $600M division, assisted by a team of 7 in the U.S., plus 5 in Ireland and Hong Kong.

- Spearheaded conversion of all business systems for 570 users, to Ferman standards, within 6 months of acquisition.

- Initiated conversion to Oracle applications using client/server technology to achieve "Best of Class" operating results.

- Upgraded IT infrastructure from bridged to routed network. Introduced Lotus Notes, MS Office XX, and decision support tools running on Novell networks.

- Recognized with the "Presidents Award for Excellence" Summer, xxxx.

Strategic Planning Director
xxxx - xxxx

- Promoted with a corporate mandate to focus on a $40 million upgrade of IT applications to client/server computing.

- Chaired three committees for evaluation and selection of enterprise resource management applications, consulting partners, and server platforms.

- Planned and established a new overseas software Development Center in France with 60 Developers, increased resources 400%.

188

Combination. *Carl L. Bascom, Fremont, California*
A dual-line page border, checkerboard-style bullets for headings, and decorative graphics before the Education and Honors & Awards sections add interest to this two-column resume.

HOWARD EDWIN
page - two

• Negotiated a worldwide database licensing agreement from node based to concurrent user model, that saved over $600,000.

Financial Systems Manager   *xxxx - xxxx*

• Primary architect and project coordinator for Financial Systems Integration of a $1.6 billion acquisition.

• Dynamically reduced financial close cycle from 15 days to 5 days, by developing an innovative program of consolidation.

• With a team of 5 Developers designed and implemented a global accounts receivable system, reducing days sales outstanding from 60 to 45.

• Created an Automatic Matching System for accounts payable, slashing overhead by nearly $500,000 annually.

• • *Prudoh Semiconductor...Portland, Oregon*

Corporate Planning Manager   *xxxx - xxxx*

• Consolidated & reported worldwide results for this $1.7 billion company, covering manufacturing cost, sales variance, margin analysis, inventory, capacity utilization, production levels, headcount, capital, yield variance, and support group spending.

• Directed the corporate budgeting process and recommended targets for inventory turns, profit, capital and headcount.

• • *Santiago Computers, Inc...Hillsboro, Oregon*

MIS Controller   *xxxx - xxxx*

• Managed a $32 million MIS Budget and orchestrated a highly successful strategic application development.

• Saved $1 million, annually, by conceiving of strategy for change winning approval to consolidate computer operations.

• • *Marcus Micro, Inc...Portland, Oregon*

Manager Operations Logistics   *xxxx - xxxx*

• Initiated development of a new Production Planning Model using Linear Programming and established a JIT program for Strategic Customers.

PROM Product Line Controller *xxxx - xxxx*

• Directly responsible for close, forecast, annual plan, capital spending inventory valuation and inventory production.

Corporate Operations Analyst   *xxxx - xxxx*

• Developed a new Corporate Financial Forecast System that saved $250,000 in time-sharing costs.

EDUCATION

M.B.A. DEGREE   *xxxx*
Major: Finance & Information Systems
Harvard University, School of Business
Boston, Massachusetts

Bachelor of Technology   *xxxx*
Major: Mechanical Engineering
Missouri State University, Saint Louis

HONORS & AWARDS

International Scholarship
Awarded the Kiwanis International Scholarship from among 1,400 candidates for study at Harvard University.

National Merit Scholarship
Awarded the National Merit Scholarship for placing in "Top 100" students in the Senior Scholarship Examinations.

The outline font for the section headings looks gray compared to the bold uppercase characters in the person's name in the contact information and in the headline and areas of expertise listed on one line below it. Profile information is clustered, and achievements in the Experience section are heavily quantified.

John Stevens   *1321 Tiffany, Littleton, Florida 32068 • (904) 555-5555*

Objective: **Manager of Technical Services / Systems Administrator**

Professional Experience:

ACR SYSTEMS, INC., Jacksonville, Florida   1996-Present
    Corporate Network & Telecommunication Administrator
    Provide system support for 100 local workstations as well as 70 remote workstations connected to an Ethernet LAN via Frame Relay. Maintain servers that include NetWare 3.12, NetWare 4.10, Windows NT 4.0 and UNIX Open Server 5. Authored Policies & Procedures for LAN & WAN security for the corporation.

Highlights   • Installed, implemented, and support Microsoft Exchange Server 5.5, Microsoft IIS 4.0, and Microsoft SQL Server 6.5.
       • Researched, coordinated, and directed the installation of two Firewalls for offices in Jacksonville and Los Angeles.
       • Installed and implemented the Frame Relay between 2 Jacksonville, Florida, locations and 1 Los Angeles Location.

KEYBOARD CONNECTION, Orange Park, Florida   1993-Present
    Consultant
    Design business advertisements. Create Web pages and provide technical maintenance. Write computer applications in Microsoft Access, dBASE III and dBASE IV.

Highlights   • Created and published a 40-page publication for a local church utilizing DTP software: Microsoft Publisher, QuarkXpress and Adobe PageMaker.

GE CAPITAL CORPORATION, Jacksonville, Florida   1995-1996
    LAN Administrator
    Managed and personally supported 182 users on a NetWare 3.12/ NetWare 4.1 Token Ring LAN. Monitored and configured LAN/WAN equipment as needed to ensure uninterrupted operations. Designed and presented training presentation for field representatives for Windows 95 and Microsoft Office products.

Highlights   • Participated as an integral part of project planning for the migration process from NetWare 3.12 and Windows 3.1 to NetWare 4.1 and Windows 95.
       • Received the "Manager's Award" in December of 1995.
       • Received several Special Recognition Awards from fellow employees and managers for ideas that were implemented into the business to help increase productivity and cost reduction.

SHERATON CHICAGO HOTEL & TOWERS, Chicago, Illinois   1993-1995
    Systems Manager
    Provided software and hardware support for 140 users on Ethernet LAN. Performed troubleshooting and found resolutions for network and workstation problems.

Highlights   • Planned and trained hotel staff in software packages which included WordPerfect 5.1, Microsoft Work, Microsoft Excel, and Lotus 1-2-3 for DOS and Windows.

Business Center Assistant Manager
    Provided technical support for all computer equipment rented from our Business Center to the Hotel Guests. Designed customized forms. Trained and managed four Business Center employees and achieved significant improvements in their productivity.

Highlights   • Restructured and improved pricing structure for Business Center, increasing profits by over 40%.

189

Chronological. *Valerie Roberts, Middleburg, Florida*
A resume for an individual who has been successful in LAN Administration. Boldface makes the job titles easy to spot. The Highlights side headings in italic direct attention to the person's

John Stevens   *1321 Tiffany, Littleton, Florida 32068 • (904) 555-5555*

Education/Training

PRODUCTIVITY POINT, Jacksonville, Florida – May 1998
Microsoft IIS 4.0
Microsoft Course #936 – Create and Configure a Web Server Using Microsoft Tools
Course toward MCP and MCSE

DUN & BRADSTREET, Jacksonville, Florida – October 1997
Supervisor's Workshop
How to be an Effective Supervisor and/or Manager

EXECUTONE BUSINESS SYSTEMS, Milford, Connecticut – May 1997
Basic System Administration
Certification for telephone system administration for Executone phone systems.

ADVANCED COMPUTER TRAINING, Jacksonville, Florida
NetWare 4.1 Systems Administration – May 1996
NetWare 3.12 Systems Administration – January 1995

HYLES-ANDERSON COLLEGE, Crown Point, Indiana – Graduated 1992
Bachelor of Science

accomplishments for each position held. In the Education section on page 2, boldface enables you to see quickly the different kinds of training experiences the individual has had since graduation from college. If you read page 1 from the bottom up, you trace the person's career path as one of steady growth.

BARBARA ANNE BLACK
1234 Western Avenue, #D-17 ◆ Anytown, WA 98000 ◆ (555) 123-1212

TECHNICAL PROJECT MANAGEMENT
Utilizing experience and excellence in project, people, and systems management to interface between the technical and nontechnical

---

Innovative, results-oriented, information technology professional with strong interpersonal relationship skills and the ability to successfully interface between the technical and the non-technical. Highly regarded by customers/users for focused, clear communication skills and the ability to effectively collaborate; assess needs; and deliver creative, appropriate solutions. Strong problem analysis talents, driven by global view/attention to detail approach. Hands-on, mentoring leader with a solid track record of creating, cultivating, and supervising high-performance teams. Comfortable handling numerous tasks simultaneously in high-pressure, demanding environments. Eagerly accept risk, ownership, and decision making. Skilled in PCs and UNIX.

Management proficiencies include:

- Project Management
- Planning & Organization
- Quality Assurance & Control
- Customer Service

- Software & Hardware Configuration Management
- Problem Analysis & Resolution
- Communications, Negotiations & Persuasion
- Training, Team Leadership, Matrix & Dotted Line Supervision

Technological proficiencies include:

- Test Methodologies
- File Transfer Protocol
- Desktop Image Building
- Web Technologies

- LAN/WAN Implementation, Troubleshooting & Repair
- Data Recovery, Dial Backups Maintenance & Upgrades
- Documentation Development & Writing
- End-User Requirements & Cost Appropriations

Languages: UNIX, C++, JCL ***Software:*** Windows 95, Office Pro, Harvard Graphics, Photoshop

LAN/WAN/Telecommunications/Voicelink expertise includes:

◆ UNIX/HP 9000	◆ UNIX/DEC	◆ TOKEN RING	◆ NT 4.0
◆ TCP/IP	◆ IBM AS/400	◆ Northern Telcom	◆ Router
◆ Controlled Access Unit	◆ Maclayer Bridge	◆ Cellular Modem	◆ Gateway
◆ Lobe Attachment Modules	◆ MOSIAX I, II, III	◆ Summa 4 Digital Switch	

EXPERIENCE

THE AIRPLANE COMPANY, Anytown, XXXX to Present   *LAN Administrator*

- Serve as the technical focal for implementation of Spacetop, an Airplane Company-based and written inventory tool, readying PCs for deployment and training 100 professionals on its use.
  - ➤ Built images for PC desktop configuration.
  - ➤ Adjusted The Airplane Company version of Windows 95 to accept Spacetop program.
  - ➤ Tested program to ensure PCs and system worked together.
- Developed a solution when 1,200 PCs crashed during Spacetop testing period.
  - ➤ Designed method to fix problem via a double-click through e-mail. Sent it to 1,200 users.
  - ➤ Spacetop implemented without repair tickets.
- Worked with NT staff to create an informational Web site on Spacetop.
- Collected the documentation and scheduled implementation of The Airplane Company Software Standard Server (S³) to reduce corporate costs under a business tailoring program.
  - ➤ Gained buy-in among 1,200 PC users, despite strong resistance from individuals accustomed to selecting and using own choices in software and hardware.
  - ➤ Provided hands-on training to more than 1,200 users and support staff.
- Drove the formation of a planning board to manage the overtime required for S³ implementation.
- Created a Web page with hot links for dissemination of training tips and information.

Continued

190

Combination. *Carole S. Barns, Woodinville, Washington*
A highly technical individual who is skilled in talking to those who don't know the technical jargon. The first half of page 1 details the "various proficiencies she has." Whenever this person

BARBARA ANNE BLACK / Page 2

- Began S³ project in a 6-month assignment as a contractor for The Airplane Company, working with a mix of 500 professional and nonprofessional internal customers.
  - ➤ Awarded a Certificate of Achievement, a rare occurrence for contractors.
- Selected to serve on 2 specialized teams:
  - ➤ Internal department team to manage and schedule customer buy-in, downtimes, and training and to coordinate communications, using a cascading approach.
  - ➤ External department team composed of upper management, the architectural designer, a NT representative, project managers from other sites, and an S³ board member.
- Initiated use of laptop computers to gather information, follow-up data, lessons learned, and documentation. Laptops have now become SOP for this process.

SPORTS & ROCK MEMORABILIA, Anytown, XXXX to XXXX   *Technical Consultant*

- Created 2 Web sites in a UNIX-based system for this international seller of rock music and sports memorabilia, enabling the company to scan photos of items for sale on the Internet.
- Used Andorra System to develop a bulk mailing procedure for Internet customers.

CITY OF ANYTOWN, XXXX to XXXX   *Computer Software Specialist*

- Transformed a collage of systems for 120 users into a unified NT system, finding ways to use or refurbish equipment while staying within the city's budget and bidding/purchasing procedures.
- Implemented a metering payment software program to allow bill backs for time spent on an Oracle database and assisted Police with operation and backup of its Alpha UNIX/DEC server.
- Provided technical support for Banyan Vines and UNIX/DEC servers and network support that included troubleshooting attachment of remote servers to CISCO router via T1s.

INTERNATIONAL COMPUTERS, Anytown, XXXX to XXXX   *UNIX/Technical Representative*

- Provided hardware/software support for UNIX/HP9000 servers and Summa 4 IC switches.
- Handled on-site and after-hour technical support for premier accounts, including AT&T Puerto Rico, PacBell, US West, and pager duty for 2,000 Hong Kong-based users.

BIG SOFTWARE CO., Anytown, XXXX   *Technical Support Representative*

- Furnished help desk support and instruction for PowerPoint and for troubleshooting DOS, Windows, and related applications and software.

FEDERAL EXPRESS, Los Angeles, XXXX to XXXX   *Technical Support Representative*

- Provided technical support for Novell NetWare 3.12 and IBM AS/400 and performed backup, data recovery, dial backups, maintenance, and upgrades.
- Installed and handled troubleshooting of modems, Northern Telecom, Maclayer bridge, routers, and gateways; and provided documentation, training, and after-hours user support.

EDUCATION & TRAINING

B.S., Computer Information Systems, XXXX, *Any State University*
Microsoft Certified Professional, *Scheduled for Completion, July XXXX*
"Windows 98 Support," XXXX, *The Airplane Company*
"ATEMS Training," XXXX, *The Airplane Company*
"Internetworking MS TCP/IP on MS Windows NT 4.0," XXXX, *The Airplane Company*
"Windows NT 4.0 Support Fundamentals," 1997, *Anycity Community College*
"Supporting Windows NT 4.0 Server," 1997, *Anycity Community College*
"Computing Security, Doing Business on the Web," XXXX, *The Airplane Company*
"Fundamental Support Training," XXXX, *PSS Worldwide Training, Microsoft*
"Windows Support Training," XXXX, *PSS Worldwide Training, Microsoft*

sends her resume, she tweaks it by adding an objective in which she specifies the target job title and company name. The contrast between bold type and regular type is strong, so anything in boldface noticeably stands out. Job titles are flush right, which makes them easy to see in a sweep down the right margin.

THEODORE BUCHMANN

555 Pinewood Avenue, Apt. B00, New Rochelle, NY 00000

Home: (000) 000-0000   E-mail: theodoreb@product.net   Work: (000) 000-0000

INFORMATION TECHNOLOGY / NETWORK MANAGEMENT

- **LAN/WAN Technologies**
- **Client/Server Architecture**

- **Applications Development**
- **Internet/Intranet Design**

Highly qualified manager offers extensive background in developing computer networks for multisite organization.... Instrumental in improving communications and expanding corporate capabilities through automation.... Guided management team in long-range planning and system implementation.

CAREER EXPERIENCE

FREIGHT MOVERS, INC., New York, NY   xxxx-Present
MIS Manager

Manage computer system operations for this international freight forwarder/consolidator and customs broker with ten offices in North America. Supervise technical staff of four in addition to outside consultants. Maintain a networked system of seven LANs and a WAN, troubleshooting problems and providing user support on daily basis. Promoted from Systems Administrator based on performance.

Accomplishments

- Led company in setting up fully networked computer system, including user support procedures and training programs.
- Designed and implemented current Frame Relay WAN, including a PPP dial-up solution.
- Set up e-mail function for all employees in US and South America. Reduced communications overhead by approximately 40%.
- Headed up design team that developed company's client server Logistics Tracking System. Significantly improved freight tracking, allowing company to bid on larger jobs.
- Standardized and upgraded software in all offices. Achieved more efficient maintenance as well as improved data exchange.
- Secured savings of $250,000 annually from long distance carrier by negotiating contract based on combined usage of all offices as one account.

NATIONAL POWER, Hamburg, Germany   xxxx-xxxx
Application Developer

Developed UNIX-based application for the remote control of power plants and substations for second largest power supply company in Germany.

- Responsible for testing and implementing program on-site and at main control.

PREVIOUS EXPERIENCE includes position of Technical Coordinator for major project sponsored by UNICEF, which rebuilt Kurdish Hospitals destroyed by Iraqi Army after Gulf War.

EDUCATION/LANGUAGES

EE Degree, Hamburg Technical College, Hamburg, Germany
Fluent in German / Basic French

TECHNICAL

Operating Systems	*Networking*
Windows NT 4.0	Windows NT Server 4.0
Workstation Windows 95 & 3.1	Novell NetWare 2.2,3.12, 4.11

Software	*Hardware*
MS-SQL Server 6.5 / MS-IIS 3.0	Workstations / Servers / Notebooks / Tape
ARCserve (NT & NetWare)	Libraries / RAID storage system
PowerPoint / Word / Excel / Access / Act	Hubs / Bridges / Routers (Cisco)

191

Combination. *Vivian Belen, Fair Lawn, New Jersey*
This resume "emphasizes on-the-job results for a highly technical candidate with a short work history. The strong profile section . . . captures the reader's attention immediately."

Stephen F. Douglas

55555 Systems Drive
San Romano, CA 99999

Home (510) 555-5555
Pager (510) 999-9999

Self-motivated **IS Operations Manager** with 20+ years of diverse experience and proven ability to build department from startup to fully functional, multifacility operation. Developed and provided consistently strong leadership for operations team that services 500+ internal customers and maintains a 98% system uptime rate. Background includes systems administration, programming, applications training, and standards development and documentation.

OPTIMAL BUSINESS SYSTEMS, Belleflower, CA
IS Operations Manager   XXXX-Present
Systems Administrator   XXXX-XXXX

Built and manage Computer Operations function essential to automated manufacturing for international Fortune 500 company. Supported this high-tech startup's growth from $10M to $600M in yearly revenues.

- Developed Computer Operations from a one-person S36 system into an international organization with 14 operators and 2 Operations Analysts supporting 10 AS/400s and 2 RS/6000s at 3 major sites.

- Maintain 7-by-24 schedule with 4 weekly shifts, generate 75 daily reports critical to management's decision making, and install cumulative packages and system upgrades with only 2 down days per year.

- Played major role in expansion into international operations through performance analysis, system selection and on-site implementation, and ongoing remote support for two Malaysian sites.

- Developed and implemented escalation procedures for troubleshooting IS problems that have kept downtime to less than 2% at all facilities.

- Manage and track $1M Computer Operations' budget, including payroll, capital, and noncapital expenses.

MANIFOLD INC., Lexington, CA
Division MIS Specialist   19XX-19XX

Ensured efficient MIS operations for the Telecommunications and Corporate Human Resources Divisions.

- Developed and implemented worldwide division's first automated financial reporting package, which provided timely performance data while reducing analyst verification time by 2 days.

- Created COBOL programs for employee time analysis and product standard costing systems.

EDUCATION & TRAINING

B.A., Mathematics, Minor: Economics, California State College
Frontline Leadership Training (52 hours) plus numerous professional courses

EQUIPMENT: IBM AS/400, S38, S36, RS/6000, Novell, IBM and Macintosh PCs

SYSTEMS/   OS/400, UNIX (AIX), CL Programming, Office 97, Lawson, MESA,
SOFTWARE: Pansophic, COBOL

192

Combination. *Sydney J. Reuben, Menlo Park, California*
The writer stressed two of the most important qualifications for an IS Manager: the ability to keep a system up and running (uptime) and to expand both the system and the staff.

PETER PIPER

33 Garden Court
Harvest Township, PA 55555

Phone: 555-555-5555
Fax: 000-000-0000
E-mail: ppiper@bol.com

SENIOR TECHNOLOGY CONSULTANT
VOICE & DATA COMMUNICATIONS / INFORMATION TECHNOLOGIES
DATA CENTER OPERATIONS / PROJECT MANAGEMENT / CLIENT / SERVER

Top-level technology management skills based on 19 years of broad-based experience in the domestic and Canadian telecom industries. Proven track record of enhancing revenue and profits. Pioneer in complex networking, client/server and telecommunications technologies. Solid technical training, team building, management development and customer service skills. Experienced in telecom start-ups, improvements and maintenance. Core competencies include:

- Strategic Analysis and Planning
- Operations Management / Logistics
- Creative Problem Solving

- New Business Services Development
- Frame Relay and ATM Networks
- Executive Negotiations

SELECTED ACHIEVEMENTS

WORLD TECHNOLOGY GLOBAL ISDN
Life Cycle Manager for Disaster Recovery
Tier Three Technical Support – GISDN Video Conferencing

XXXX-PRESENT

- Oversee and manage ongoing technical support for pre-sales and post-sales of Global ISDN services and Video Conferencing, the 2nd largest growing service for World Technology.

- Provide direct project management for special GISDN projects and manage disaster recovery of large customer networks as Life Cycle Manager of Virtual Gateway Services.

WORLD/DATA COMMUNICATION SERVICES
Level 2 Capacity Manager – Domestic Frame Relay

19XX-XXXX

- Implemented Manchester Frame Relay to ATM network on deadline and within specifications, avoiding potential daily $10K fines to be imposed for missing critical due dates.

- Selected as Team Leader for Divisions Task Force to eliminate obstacles preventing future growth of the Frame Relay Service; responsible for forecasting, planning, managing and improving Domestic and Canadian Frame Relay network.

- Process owner for Large Customer Reservation Process which successfully implemented and scheduled 38 of World's largest Frame Relay customers.

- Project Manager for frame relay emerging services including ISDN, PSN (SNA over Frame), and Disaster Recovery; negotiated with systems engineers for development of systems to design and monitor emerging services as well as life cycle management of the network.

- CONTINUED -

193

Combination. *Susan Guarneri, Lawrenceville, New Jersey*
This person's job was secure, but he wanted a new position that offered "greater responsibility and challenge." Note that "Selected Achievements" is the heading for the work experience

PETER PIPER

33 Garden Court
Harvest Township, PA 55555

Phone: 555-555-5555
Fax: 000-000-0000
E-mail: ppiper@bol.com

SELECTED ACHIEVEMENTS
continued

WORLD/DATA COMMUNICATION SERVICES

L2 Capacity Manager BMS-E Product   19XX-19XX

♦ Managed and coordinated the installation, maintenance, process, and spare part inventory of 12 separate customer networks, including all customer upgrades.

♦ Reduced product overcharges by $4.75MM over a three-year period through detailed reexaminations of engineering estimates and charges.

♦ Reduced the cost of FAA spare parts inventories by consolidating three warehouses to one warehouse and by reducing the maintenance time in finding spare parts.

NMC Technician   19XX-19XX

♦ Project-managed the conversion of T1 and ABM circuits to T45 facilities as well as DSO to T45 circuits; directly provided installation and maintenance of ABM, 745 ACCULINK, SDN, ISDN, Mega 800 and 800 circuits, and GE Video Conference network.

♦ Key technical investigator in troubleshooting chronic telecommunications problems, from initial investigation to total resolution.

Team Coordinator for Access Verification   19XX-19XX

♦ Recipient of the VP Hall of Fame Award for design and implementation of a special process to verify LEC access billing for Pennsylvania which saved $6MM in one year.

♦ Coordinated the re-homing and migration of 9500 serving links and 250 T1.5 facilities in a 24-month period for the Newtown central office to the new digital office.

TECHNICAL SKILLS

HARDWARE	SOFTWARE
IBM PC's and Sun Work Stations	MS Office 97 (Excel, Word, PowerPoint)
Cisco/Stratacom Frame Relay Switch	MS Exchange / Outlook
Picture Tell Video Equipment	UNIX for Work Stations
Paradyne ACCULINK Bandwidth Switches	Windows 95
Ascend MAX's	Lotus Notes

EDUCATION

BS, Mathematics (in progress), Central State University, Millertown, PA
Focus: Mathematics and Economics
Courses in Electronic Technology, New York Technology Center, New York, NY

- 2 -

section! That is a bold departure from using Achievements as a subheading within the Experience section. The achievements are technical, and the technical terms in the descriptions of the achievements must be handled carefully to avoid errors that will be evident to technical readers. See Cover Letter 12.

MARIANNE FIGARO
1 Tudor City Place, Apt. 0000
New York, NY 10000
212-111-0000

AUDITING - INFORMATION SYSTEMS

- EDP Auditor with wide range of financial and nonfinancial system applications
- MBA with strong combination of technical, communication, and quantitative analysis skills
- Effective during implementation of projects requiring analysis, complex testing, and strong internal controls
- International experience: fluent in French, proficient in Spanish and Portuguese
- Available for travel • CISA candidate

Hardware:	IBM AS/400, Model 9406-D60 with IPL 6900 Raid-5, IBM RS/6000, DEC VAX 3800.
Software:	COBOL, RPGIII, CL, RUMBA, TURNOVER, DOS, Lotus for Windows, Word for Windows, WordPerfect 6.1, Turbo Pascal.
Applications:	Payroll, Accounts Payable, General Ledger and Billing Systems, LAN, NOVELL, Distributive Processing, Statistical Sampling, Regression Analysis, and Forecasting.

PROFESSIONAL EXPERIENCE

ROCKEFELLER GROUP, INC., New York, NY   xxxx-xxxx
Performs real estate management of Rockefeller Center's nineteen buildings, with several subsidiaries, including
Cushman & Wakefield, Radio City Music Hall, Rockefeller Telecommunications, Inc., New Jersey Foreign Trade Zone.
Three Data Centers (Minicomputers); over 4000 employees.
EDP Audit Manager
Responsible for all EDP audits and review of financial and nonfinancial Information Systems. Hands-on Manager,
supervising up to two auditors. Conduct Data Center Reviews and Contingency Planning / Disaster Recovery and Testing.
Significant accomplishments include:
- Analyzed, evaluated and established internal controls features during design or preimplementation of systems
- Tested financial and nonfinancial systems applications before release to production, including computer security
- Identified excessive overtime in operating subsidiary, resulting in significant savings
- Established 3 contingency sites in Tristate area and performed annual contingency testing of financial systems
- Performed Quality Assurance functions

HOME LIFE INSURANCE, New York, NY   xxxx-xxxx
Senior EDP Auditor
- Reviewed internal controls on Brokers' Compensation module of Life-Comm system during implementation.

AMERICAN EXPRESS, New York, NY   xxxx-xxxx
Senior EDP Auditor
- Resolved difficult operation problem involving $23 million of unsettled transactions
- Performed audits and operational reviews of five Data Centers (Mainframes and Minicomputers)
- Participated as team member in fraud audit of Bank (BCDE) in City, Switzerland, xxxx-xxxx
- Selected by American Express, on behalf of The Institute of Internal Auditors, to be consultant on loan to
  New York City Municipal Government, for one year (xxxx)

EDUCATION

NEW YORK UNIVERSITY, Stern School of Business, New York, NY **M.B.A.** Accounting, xxxx
HUNTER COLLEGE, CUNY, New York, NY **B.A.** Economics, xxxx

PROFESSIONAL AFFILIATIONS

The Institute of Internal Auditors, Information Systems Audit and Control Association
IEEE Computer Society, Computer Security Institute, ACM.

194

Combination. *Linsey Levine, Chappaqua, New York*
A resume for an individual whose employers are well known. The layout switches between
center- and left-justification. Boldface makes a strong first impression in the opening profile.

CARL S. TEMPLE   444 Halcione Drive
(555) 333-3333   e-mail: cstemple@aol.com   Dublin, CA 55555

PROFESSIONAL HIGHLIGHTS

- Significant, hands-on, electronic engineering experience focused on the computer industry.
- Proven ability for analyzing and troubleshooting software problems and providing solutions.
- Strong experience as a team member with engineers and managers for planning & troubleshooting.
- Recognized by senior management—several times—for promotions, awards and bonuses.

PROFESSIONAL EXPERIENCE

De Havolyn Research Corporation...San Jose, California

SYSTEMS DESIGN ENGINEERING MANAGER   xxxx to present

- Manage a team of 6 Systems Design Engineers in the Storage Product Engineering Department.
- Interact with engineers from other department to coordinate activities, and for special projects.
- Team member of the Product Planning Committee for new product development.
- Produce a weekly "Hot List" and make monthly presentations to a senior management group.

STAFF SYSTEMS DESIGN ENGINEER   xxxx - xxxx

- Promoted to "Staff" from the "Senior" level in less than 2 years, normally a 4-6 year progression.
- Tested, analyzed and corrected firmware design problems, then created microcode "patches."
- Created a unique, new series of Procedures Manuals for microcode projects that replaced three configuration managers and was a significant, production cost savings for the company.
- Received the *"Directors Award"*—twice in 3 years—plus a generous cash bonus for outstanding development of "extra" projects.
- Selected by the Executive Management for a special and confidential program that is still ongoing.
- Chairperson for the Problem Reporting Committee, which met with engineers and managers to ensure timely support for Field Engineering.
- Success in this position earned a promotion to Systems Design Engineering Manager, noted above.

SENIOR SYSTEMS DESIGN ENGINEER   xxxx - xxxx

- Provided the Technical Support Group with training on future microcode releases.
- Researched, corrected problems and validated corrections to ensure IBM compatibility.

FIELD ENGINEER SPECIALIST - *Production Department*   xxxx - xxxx

- Supported the Field Support team—worldwide—as a corporate Field Engineer Specialist.
- Interfaced—daily—with Systems Design Engineering to resolve problems for the Field Engineers.
- Traveled, worldwide, to assist Field Engineers at customer sites for troubleshooting and resolution.

EDUCATION & CERTIFICATIONS

B.S. DEGREE - *Major: Business Information Systems (BIS)* - University of California, Davis xxxx
A.S. DEGREE - *Major: Electrical Engineering Technology (EET)* - De Anza College, Cupertino, CA
CERTIFICATIONS • SCSI Nuts & Bolts • Legal Aspects of Management • C & Advanced C

COMPUTER SKILLS

- Experienced with PCs using DOS, Windows 3.1 & 95, MS Word, Excel, PowerPoint, Access, MS Project, Visual Analyst, plus C & Advanced C, Pascal and Assembler language, IBM's MVS/ESA 390, VM and UNIX operating systems, and considerable Internet business research.

195

Combination. *Carl L. Bascom, Fremont, California*
The design of this resume is easy to grasp because of lines separating main sections; all-upper-case letters for the person's name, headings, job titles, and degrees; and underlining.

Gemma Martinez
150 Prairie Road
Abilene, TX 10232

voice ▪ 972-555-5555
work ▪ 817-000-0000
e-mail ▪ GMartf@aol.com

Project Manager ▪ Applications Developer ▪ Project Troubleshooter

Career Profile

- Bottom-line-oriented, hands-on senior-level executive with over twenty years of comprehensive experience in profitable direction of teams *and* technology. Utilize an anticipatory management style to drive results in a rapidly changing industry. Produce consistent achievements in cutting-edge project management, applications development, team management, project troubleshooting, and systems implementation.

- Currently manage multimillion-dollar projects supporting human resources operations for Sabre Group, the corporate arm of American Airlines. Throughout career, have led technology teams of up to 40 persons, managed project budgets of up to $2,000,000, and developed numerous software applications for human resources, payroll, pension, benefits, and financial operations.

- Recipient of multiple awards for excellence, featured speaker at numerous professional organizations and author of public relations documents, marketing pieces, business plans, proposals, design documents, etc. Adjunct professor of computer concepts, applications instruction for two colleges.

Key Management and Technology Abilities

▪ Full Project Lifecycle	▪ RFP/RFI Development / Procurement	▪ Team Building / Motivation
▪ Year 2000 Solutions	▪ Contract Evaluation	▪ Strategic Planning / Turnarounds
▪ Advanced Technologies	▪ Cost Containment	▪ Vendor Partnerships
▪ Project Planning / Budgets	▪ Applications Development	▪ Presentations
▪ Project Management	▪ Systems Implementation	▪ Marketing Strategies / Plans
▪ Multiproject Management	▪ Quality Management	▪ Business Plans
▪ Project Methodologies	▪ Sales Support	▪ College-Level Teaching

Accomplishments as Project Manager and Developer

- Developed strong Year 2,000 team project methodology and structure of human resources segment currently representing June, 1999 deadline and work of 36 developers, tens-of-thousands of man-hours, and multimillion-dollar budget. Defined scope of actual deliverables from thousands of objects and implemented into manageable components—organizing, defining and controlling process to realistic expectations.

- Selected by Sabre Group to troubleshoot, take over, and turn around failing IEF project for development of American Airlines' award-redemption banking system (created to manage redemption of $7,000,000 in awards for 85,000 employees). Project was $1,500,000 over budget, 18 months behind schedule and had escalated to CEO level. Restructured team of developers, ran new confirmation process to reaffirm deliverable phases for customer / developer segment sign-offs, and created delivery time and confirmation process road maps. Delivered project on time and on budget.

- Designed and implemented new IEF American Airlines proprietary employee suggestion system with budget of $750,000 dollars. This new system is now the leading commercial employee suggestion system in the world, processes 300 suggestions per day (previous was 300 month), has tracked $50,000,000 in first-year savings for American, and has maintained over 300,000 suggestions to date. Wrote business plan, job descriptions and RFP.

196

Combination. *Deborah Wile Dib, Medford, New York*
A three-page resume full of information but with white space supplied by enough blank lines so that no page seems cluttered. The eye is guided through the document by bold black: bold

Gemma Martinez

Accomplishments (continued)

- Revitalized the production of an accounts receivable system for Chanel, Inc. Project was two years behind schedule with cost overruns of over a half million dollars. Met with customer to learn business and develop required system functionality. Reevaluated processes and reconfirmed to determine controllable manageable deliverables. Project delivered on time per revised plan.

- Managed nationwide Employee Information System product line with total P&L, marketing, product development, and implementation responsibilities. Enhanced design of product to make it more robust to become market leader. Product line was integral in corporation's annual revenue increase from $50,000 to $5,500,000.

- Installed accounting system and developed chart of accounts for Cartier Jewelry. Developed processing requirements through proactive business information meetings with Cartier's CFO designed to elicit important nuances of Cartier's needs. Additional projects required creating RFI estimates for three different types of custom systems.

- Designed software systems for Chase Manhattan Bank to perform affirmative action planning; job requisitioning for 300 daily openings, 300 daily temp requirements, and 6,000 annual jobs; demographic employee analysis; pension and benefit support; and management report production. Managed a staff of 30 professionals in human resources and personnel application software.

Technology Summary

Human Resources Applications	■ Personnel / HR ■ Applicant Tracking	■ Pension (ERISA) ■ Suggestion Programs	■ Pension / Benefits ■ Award Programs
Financial Applications	■ Payroll ■ General Ledger	■ Accounts Receivable ■ P/O and Order Entry	■ Accounts Payable ■ Inventory
Personal Computer Applications	■ Spreadsheets ■ Utilities	■ Word Processors ■ Operating Systems	■ Databases
Project Management	■ MS Project, IEF	■ Project Workbench	■ Visible Analyst
Languages and Databases	■ ICASE (IEF-Composer) ■ SQL	■ Oracle ■ QMF	■ DB2 ■ COBOL
Hardware	■ IBM 30xx and 43xx	■ IBM AS400	■ Personal Computers
Operating Systems	■ DOS	■ Windows 3.11 and 95	■ OS/2

Education and Professional Development

- **Bachelor of Science in Electrical Technology, concentration in Computer Science and Pure Math**
  Cornell University, Ithaca, NY

- **24 credits toward Master's in Business Administration (Accounting, Marketing, Information Systems)**
  Fordham University, New York, NY, and Columbia University, New York, NY

- **Continuing Education, Workshops and Seminars** SQL, ISPF, Project Management, Project Planning, Risk Assessment, Business Writing, Employee Management, IEF, Structured Analysis, Data Flow Diagramming, Motivation and Team-building

contact information, thick lines, a bold headline, bold headings, filled square bullets, a bold header on pages 2 and 3, bold side headings in the Technology Summary, bold first lines in the Education and Professional Development section, bold job titles in the Career Development Summary, and bold column heads in

Gemma Martinez

Career Development Summary

Project Manager and Developer 1989 to present
Sabre Group (corporate-side), a subsidiary of American Airlines, Abilene, TX

Manage Year 2000 human resource initiatives as well as key projects for human resources software development and internal / external business opportunities. Manage multimillion-dollar employee suggestion and award-redemption systems that have produced over $50,000,000 in first-year savings. Personally develop and implement numerous software modifications and custom programs.

Adjunct Professor 1992 to present
Parsons Technical Institute (four-year accredited college)
Abilene Community College

Create and teach beginner-to-advanced computer courses including: DOS, Windows, Systems Analysis and Design, Qbasic, Operating Systems, Excel, and Personal Oracle.

Project Manager, Systems Analyst 1987 to 1989
Chryson Associates, Inc., Dallas, TX

Managed and designed up to 30 simultaneous projects for financial and human resources payroll application software packages. Projects represented over $1,000,000 in software accounts. Interfaced with top client management to understand needs and develop project parameters.

President, Chief Operating Officer, and Owner 1984 to 1987
Tech-Link, Inc., Dallas, TX

Specialized in hardware sales and training support for the computer industry. Brought in first year sales revenue of $1,000,000. Devised and implemented corporate business plan, marketing plan and sales strategies. Marketed products throughout the U.S.

Vice President of Marketing 1982 to 1984
Stanley Computing Publishers, Dallas, TX

Created sales department and distribution channels for start-up microcomputer publisher of systems development utility software. Increased monthly revenue to over $100,000 through development of cohesive marketing strategy and strong publicity programs including cover of BYTE magazine.

Vice President, Chief Operating Officer, and Owner 1981 to 1982
Computer Solutions Incorporated, Dallas, TX

Firm functioned as a privately held, venture-capital-based microcomputer holding company. Intensely involved with acquisitions, procurement, negotiations, contract evaluations, business and marketing plans, and retail and distribution marketing philosophy development.

Manager, Human Resource Systems 1980 to 1981
Quatro Systems Incorporated, Dallas, TX

Designed, developed and managed implementation of human resource systems on all levels. Independently identified market opportunity; created product and marketing initiatives for visibility and credibility that shortened sales cycle and increased closing percentages.

Early Technical Employment

| **Product / Project Manager** | **Applications Manager** | **System Analyst / Consultant** |
| Information Science Incorporated | Chase Manhattan Bank | Digital Applications |

the Early Technical Employment section. The headings are spread out through the use of a character space between letters. Quantified accomplishments distributed over two pages make a strong impression. Reading page 3 from the bottom up gives an impression of the individual's career path to the present.

Maggie Morris

(304) 555-0444 - Work

1234 Ballerina Blvd. • Belle, WV 25015 • (304) 555-8888 - Home

Skills Overview

- Twelve years' experience in information systems management
- Over 20 years' experience with computer operations, including:
  - » IBM AS/400 Model D70   » LAN Network
  - » IBM 4341-2 operating under CICS, NCP, VTAM, OS/VS
- Highly skilled at streamlining information processing operations, reducing administrative costs, and increasing reporting efficiency
- Results-oriented with a reputation for reliably meeting deadlines
- Excellent at coordinating projects from inception through implementation
- Self-disciplined team player with outstanding organizational skills
- Highly ethical, consistently productive, and even-tempered

Employment History

Data Center Supervisor   1976-Present
WEST SERVICES, INC., Belle, West Virginia
- Manage systems to ensure quality and timely distribution of reports
- Troubleshoot and monitor computer operations to reduce downtime
- Manage time-sensitive check runs of over $1 million weekly
- Hire, train, and supervise computer operators and data entry personnel

Selected Highlights :
- Currently involved in developing and implementing new computer facilities as well as a Disaster Recovery Plan for the Data Center
- Developed and maintain procedure manuals and training models, detailing steps necessary for accurate completion of 10-15 separate processes
- Initiated centralization of data processing from three regional offices
- Separated data entry and operations, markedly increasing efficiency

Account Manager   1973-1975
DATA SYSTEMS CORPORATION, St. Albans, West Virginia
- Trained new users of Medic 80 software and WordStar word processing
- Provided ongoing customer support to numerous medical office employees
- Position required excellent problem-solving and interpersonal skills

System Operator   1968-1973
WALKER & COMPANY, Columbus, Ohio
- Began in data entry position and promoted to supervisor of 7 operators
- Processed payroll for 300, requiring a high degree of confidentiality
- Prepared and distributed daily, weekly, and monthly operations reports

Education

West Virginia State College, Institute, West Virginia
Computer Science and Management major, with course work in systems analysis, programming, and COBOL.

IBM Shortcourse, Atlanta, Georgia
Data Processing Operations Management—In-depth course featuring hands-on applications through case studies.

197

Combination. *Barbie Dallmann, Charleston, West Virginia*
Without a degree, this person had moved into "a responsible management position." To help her find a similar position in another state, the writer stressed skills and achievements.

JOHN THURSTON
114 Park Street
New York, New York 00000
555-777-0000

PROFESSIONAL SUMMARY

MIS · Project Management · System Conversions · Technical Training & Support · Documentation

Experienced computer professional with extensive qualifications in all aspects of microcomputers and systems administration, management and maintenance, including multisite networks, hardware/software acquisition, data integrity, security and backup. Proficient in selection and implementation of computer systems that provide business solutions and increase organizational efficiency/productivity. Contributed to bottom line through design, development and implementation of systems to reduce/save costs. Strong customer service focus and solid communication skills with departmental staffs. Demonstrated talent for learning new systems and software quickly; ability to explain complex technical information in terms easily understood by nontechnical users. Well-versed and experienced in all areas of manufacturing operations and processes including MRP, inventory management and production planning/scheduling.

SELECTED ACCOMPLISHMENTS & PROJECTS

♦ Overhauled antiquated system at Allen Machine Company and completed conversion to new, more efficient system (DG Aviion) in just 2 weeks without any downtime or loss of data.

♦ Created and generated over 350 different reports, including MRP, inventory, sales, shipping and forecasting, to support all departments.

♦ Recommended and installed new manufacturing and accounting software, including data conversion, which was integrated with existing system. Concurrently maintained both systems, minimizing disruption while preserving data integrity during testing and cutover.

♦ Saved Anderson Company $100K annually through design, development and implementation of aircraft maintenance system, learning new programming language in only 1 month.

♦ Streamlined use of diverse software throughout corporation and standardized software applications achieving unity, consistency and transferability of data.

♦ Created integrated microcomputers planning system package at Branden Systems, now utilized by national service company.

♦ Designed program at Smith Manufacturing that dramatically cut product backorders from $220K down to $10K, resulting in on-time shipments and improved customer satisfaction.

♦ Trained and supported end users on utilizing microcomputers, Windows and DOS-based operating systems, word processing, spreadsheet and database applications.

PROFESSIONAL EXPERIENCE

<u>ALLEN MACHINE COMPANY</u>   New York, New York
Data Processing Manager   *1989-1997*

Managed company-wide IT operations for a manufacturer of motion control devices. Accountable for DG/UX/System V UNIX network including hardware and software sourcing, evaluation and acquisition, data integrity, systems security and backup procedures. Provided technical training and support to all company personnel. Accountable for physical inventory and maintaining MCS manufacturing and RealWorld accounting software programs.

198

Combination. *Louise Garver, Enfield, Connecticut*

With his original chronological resume, this person was getting no interviews during almost a year of unemployment. The writer reorganized the resume to showcase the person's strongest

ANDERSON COMPANY   New York, New York
Manager of Data Processing   *1987-1989*

Managed entire operations for multiuser, multisite microcomputer network system for corporation providing aircraft charter and maintenance services for Aetna, Travelers and other corporate customers across the country. Designed aircraft maintenance system and developed several reports for sales, maintenance, customer service, accounting, accounts payable, and other activities. Coordinated purchasing for all computer software/hardware company-wide.

BRANDEN SYSTEMS   New York, New York
Programmer/Analyst   *1983-1986*

Created commercial microcomputer software packages and in-house programs for software developer serving clients in the telecommunications industry, including AT&T. Wrote and maintained software programs to meet customer requirements and provided end-user training/technical support. Performed programming in CBASIC and prepared thorough, accurate documentation.

SMITH MANUFACTURING   New York, New York
Senior Inventory Planner   *1979-1983*

Coordinated inventory control, production planning and scheduling, and expediting functions for manufacturer of tools and fasteners. Liaison between production and other departments, overseeing staff/activities in the expediting area to ensure production schedules were achieved. Automated inventory control and production planning function, creating computer programs in BASIC for scheduling primary manufacturing machines and work-in-process.

EDUCATION

M.S. (Computer Information Systems) New York University • Troy, New York

B.A. (Accounting) City College • New York, New York

Additional Training:
Advanced Windows 95 • Windows NT 4.0 Administration • Windows NT 4.0 Core Technologies

COMPUTER PROFICIENCY

Operating & Network Systems: Windows 95 and 3.1 • Windows NT 4.0 • MS-DOS • Novell • DG/UX UNIX • AT&T System V UNIX • Ethernet • Thoroughbred • Corvus
Hardware: All x86 Intel processor microcomputers • DG Aviion 4605 • AT&T 3B2/400 minicomputers
Languages: BASIC • CBASIC • DERPG • DBL
Applications: dBASE • Lotus 1-2-3 • Intelligent Query Report Writer • WordPerfect • Quattro Pro

ASSOCIATIONS

Association of Computing Machinery

accomplishments first and to place his technical skills on page 2. The new resume, which you see here in fictional form, emphasized the best of what the person had to offer. With this new resume, the person got interviews every week. Within 30 days he was offered four positions—"a complete turnaround."

JOHN P. FORRESTER
43 Colorado Drive • New Haven, New York 12345 • (123) 456-7890

Operation Management / Business Development ... Results-oriented, general management executive with record of top-level accomplishments in financial and operations management. Demonstrated ability to improve productivity and profit. Able to build and motivate positive, productive teams. Consistent record of achieving high-quality standards.

GENERAL MANAGEMENT:
NATIONAL PROPERTY MAINTENANCE, INC. Albany, New York   (2/xx – present)
Branch Operations: Oversee 250 employees at 372 sites throughout eastern NY, VT and NH with annual sales $11 million.
Fiscal Controls: Establish financial systems and monitor profitability for contracted and ad hoc services, negotiate prices.
Quality Assurance: Develop operational systems and procedures to ensure contract compliance, develop training program.
Trade Relations: Primary contact for principal customers and professional associations, enhance trade and public relations.

WAL-MART DISCOUNT DEPARTMENT STORES New York and Texas   (3/xx-2/xx, 7/xx-6/xx)
Store Operations: Accountable for $28 million sales, $7.2 million inventory, 226 associates and 125,000 square ft. of space.
District Management - Specialty Division: Oversaw 14 stores, 364 associates, $56 million annual sales in four divisions.
Fiscal Responsibility: Direct Profit and Loss accountability resulting in a 12% increased net profit, 4.3% reduction in expenses and sales/sq. ft. rising from $21 to $38 within 9 months. Conducted business seminars for department managers.
Human Resources: Installed computerized personnel scheduling program for planning, tracking and management. Recruited from nontraditional sources, executed corporate legal process for harassment, discrimination, and diversity issues.
Instruction: Taught regional "Personal Development" Course for 58 Management Trainees, numerous in-store workshops.
Market Analysis: Completed market assessments for geographical merchandising and assisted in store site selection.
Additional Training: Graduated from Walton Institute.

CAPITAL INVESTMENTS (General Contractors) Dallas, Texas   (6/xx-3/xx)
Project Development: Coordinated construction of McDonald's restaurants: blueprint to occupancy, costing $500- $700,000.
Contract Administration: Accepted vendor bids, negotiated contracts, met stringent deadlines, secured payment and controlled costs through material pricing, subcontractor scheduling, and implementing quality assurance checkpoints.
Partnership Selling: Assisted McDonald's in securing leasing contracts with Wal-Mart through strong partner relationships.
Accounting: Restructured accounting periods and reporting for 4 independent businesses while developing a computerized financial tracking system. Implemented customized system and trained accounting personnel over 6-month period.
General Management: Directed turnaround of 2 businesses through cost control, customer services, marketing, training.
Compensation Administration: Developed benefits portfolios for employees to include health insurance, retirement planning, incentive bonuses and competitive wages. Negotiated with contract vendors for services and prices.

UNITED STATES ARMY   (10/xx-3/xx)
Finance and Accounting Management: Supervised 13 military personnel in financial tracking controls for 9 automated sites on 3 military bases through mainframe systems. Trained personnel in computer operation and finance systems.
Reconciliation: Prioritized spending, controlled budgets, transferred funds, and tracked inventory for entire military installation averaging $700,000 in daily transactions. Verified purchase order release amounts within budgetary restraints.
Active Duty: Served in Korea and Desert Storm.

TECHNICAL SKILLS:
Hardware/Operating Systems: Mainframes, personal computers, DOS, IBM, Macintosh.
Software: Microsoft Windows, OS/2, Word, WordPerfect, Excel, Lotus 1-2-3, PowerPoint, Quicken, Peachtree, OneWrite Plus, AutoCAD III, Internet, and customized software for networking and small businesses.
Computer Assembly: Constructed personalized computers for business proprietors.

EDUCATION:
WESTERN KENTUCKY UNIVERSITY Bowling Green, Kentucky
Associate of Applied Science: Finance and Accounting   (May xxxx)

UNIVERSITY OF MARYLAND Fort Ord, California
Bachelor of Science: Business Law and Management   (December xxxx)

PROFESSIONAL AWARDS:
Wal-Mart District Manager of the Year xxxx   **US Army Soldier of the Year** xxxx - Korea
National Expeditionary Medals: Saudi Arabia & Panama   **Army Primary Leadership Development Award**

199

Combination. *Elizabeth M. Daugherty, East Greenbush, New York*
While in the Army, this individual supervised personnel in using mainframes for financial tracking. This full, one-page resume displays his operations management in civilian life.

Michael J. Sampson
56 35th St. NW
Progressiveville MN 55555

(555) 555-5555

Great minds think "out of the box." Creativity expands to fit the surroundings ... and beyond.

Technology Skills

Computer consulting ... Teaching and training ... Programming ... Systems design ... Systems analysis ... Installation, builds, setup and configuration ... Network engineering ... Troubleshooting of hardware and software problems ... Beta testing ... Web site standards ... Interpretation of blueprints and schematics ... Year 2000 problem ... Design of adaptive software for Windows NT ... Experience with satellite communications and microwave systems ... Installation of answering services and ESS switches ... PBX systems ... Past FCC licensing

Systems, Hardware, Software and Programming

UNIX ... Linux ... IBM systems 34, 36, 37 ... Sun ... Apple ... HP ... PCs ... Novell, Windows 3.1 / 95 / NT ... DOS ... CPM ... machine code ... assembly ... object-oriented ... client server ... C, C++ ... COBOL/85 ... RPGII ... FORTRAN ... Pascal ... BASIC ... Ada ... WordPerfect ... Word ... Excel

Work History

1995-XX	Technical Consultant / Trainer, Disabled Student Services, Sunny State Polytechnic University, Lakeland NC
1993-95	Instructor, Computer Lab, College of the Lakes, Lakeland NC
1986-93	Self-employed Computer Consultant / Cabinet Maker, Atlantis GA
1980-86	Engineering Consultant, Electronics Consulting and Engineering, Atlantis GA
1978-80	Broadcast Engineering Instructor, The Techie Broadcast School, Roe NC
1976-78	House & Stage Manager, Community Theater, Roe NC
1975-76	Asst. Chief Engineer, KMKI Radio Station, Roe NC

Accomplishments / Experience

➡ Assisted in developing Y2K university course in COBOL ➡ Wrote and developed Kurzweil-to-PC software used by state and county agencies ➡ Taught computer science classes at Sunny State Polytech University ➡ Instructed learning disabled students in computer lab at Computer Lab ➡ Responsible for accessibility to Internet by handicapped students and ADA Web page compliance ➡ Private consulting for City Broadcasting, KFFF TV, KTUU Channel 2 and KGLN radio ➡ Developed computer lab policies and procedures ➡ Responsible for day-to-day operations of Adaptive Computer Labs, as well as training equipment setup

Education / Continuing Ed

➡ 100+ credit hours toward BS degree
➡ Microsoft Systems Certification pending
➡ Seminars on Adaptive Technology

Profile

Talented ... Enthusiastic ... Flexible ... Zest for learning ... Able to think abstractly, as well as concretely ... Productive

Michael Sampson is highly self-motivated, creative and technologically astute – and has been working with electronics since age 15. His "can do" attitude allows him to work effectively in an independent environment, or as a vital part of a team. His zest for life is demonstrated by the many interests and hobbies he pursues:

➡ Collecting old mainframes ... Working on an Internet-based Morse Code training program ... Math programs for children ... Custom furniture and woodworking ... Kinetic sculpture contests ... Auto mechanics and restoration of motor homes ... Re-stringing of pianos ... Gourmet cooking.

Michael strives to remain up-to-date on leadership techniques, trends and theories: JIT ... TQM ... ISO 9001 ... Continuous flow manufacturing.

Miscellaneous skills:

➡ Setup and training on adaptive computer equipment ➡ Refitting and maintenance of technical centers on campuses ➡ Building and setup of sound studios and theatre sets, including lighting, weights and counterbalances ➡ Installation of radio station transmitters and towers ➡ Training of broadcast engineers in theory and practice ➡ Field testing / measuring of radio broadcast signals for FCC certification ➡ Maintenance of AM/FM stations ➡ Installation of large-scale VTRs and hydraulic heads

200

Functional. *Beverley Drake, Rochester, Minnesota*
Read this gifted individual's entire resume and then be surprised to learn that he has a severe sight disability! The resume's exceptional design matches the exceptional person.

GEORGE HOFFMAN
2 Overlook, Poughkeepsie, NY 12603

voice ■ 914-555-5555
e-mail ■ hoffg@aol.com

INFORMATION TECHNOLOGY ARCHITECT ■ **SYSTEMS MANAGER AND CONSULTANT**

CAREER PROFILE

■ Information technology, disaster recovery, and systems professional with comprehensive experience in development and oversight of leading-edge Virtual Machine/ESA-based business support and disaster recovery technologies for IBM internal and external customers. Recognized for history of VM/ESA and related systems expertise, meticulous follow-up abilities, and dedicated work ethic.

■ Believe strongly in impeccable and dedicated customer support, with a foundation of personal initiative, persistence, and the desire to meet those technical and business challenges presented by a rapidly changing industry. Accounts supported include major banks and other customers with critical workloads, IBM Testing Services, and other IBM Business Units.

■ Produce consistent achievements in progressive project management, applications development, team leadership, project troubleshooting, and systems implementation.

PROJECT / SYSTEM DEVELOPMENT	HARDWARE, PROTOCOLS, IMPLEMENTATION	SYSTEMS, LANGUAGES
■ Project Lifecycle	■ S/390 CMOS Processors, RX family	■ VM/ESA (all components)
■ Project Planning / Management	■ S/390 Water Cooled Processors	■ MVS/ESA and OS/390
■ Systems Architecture	■ I/O Devices and Connectivity Planning	■ Windows 95, 98, 3.1
■ Multiproject Development	■ Directors, Switching Devices	■ OS/2
■ Applications Development	■ IOCP Support	■ MVS Parallel Sysplex Support
■ Systems Design / Development	■ Basic and LPAR-mode Systems	■ S/390 Assembler
■ Systems Implementation	■ Network Skills: VTAM (SNA), TCP/IP	■ PL/I
■ Disaster Recovery	■ VM RSCS and PVM IP Link Implementation	■ FORTRAN
■ Cross-System Data Sharing	■ VM/ESA-based WWW Servers	■ COBOL
■ H/W and S/W Product Installation		■ REXX
■ H/W and S/W Product Customization		■ CMS Pipelines
■ Y2K Solutions and Testbed Support		■ CGI Scripts
■ Customer Technical Support		

SUMMARY OF TECHNOLOGY EXPERTISE

■ VM/ESA (through version 2 release 3.0) structure and logic, including all components (CP, CMS, GCS, AVS, RACF); problem determination and debugging; performance monitoring and capacity planning.

■ MVS/ESA specialist since early '80s.

■ VM guest system implementation and support, including V=R and V=F guests and the S/390 Multiple High-Performance Guest facility.

■ Particular emphasis on MVS and OS/390 parallel sysplex guests and support.

■ Highly proficient with lpar-mode systems.

■ Communications software and protocols, including VM/VTAM, TCP/IP, PVM and RSCS (BSC, SNA and IP link implementation).

■ RACF system administration.

■ S/390 large systems, including 9021-class hardware and CMOS processors (RX3, RX4, RX5, RX6); management, operations, and installation planning.

■ Workstation proficiency with DOS, Windows 95, Windows 98, Windows 3.1, OS/2, and Lotus Notes client software.

201

Functional. *Deborah Wile Dib, Medford, New York*
A resume for an individual who was "highly specialized in a specific area" of his firm's products. He wanted to use this resume either for internal promotion or for "testing the waters" of

GEORGE HOFFMAN

RECENT PROJECT HIGHLIGHTS

Converted High Availability System from an RX3 to an R74 processor.

- Project duration: 1998 to 1999.
- Completed as I/T Specialist / Systems Management Consultant: IBM Global Services, BRS.

Migration required expertise in CMOS architecture, IOCP and I/O planning, and VM/ESA and MVS design and implementation. Severe time pressures with very little possibility of fallback required focused team-leadership abilities. Project provided for future usage growth and took advantage of the new microcode features available with newer processor family. Completed hardware and system software conversion on time, after numerous 60-70+ hour weeks, with no disruption of customer work (primarily MVS parallel sysplex) and no resulting problems with customer projects.

Initiated, planned, and implemented installation, production beta testing, and ESP (IBM Early Support Program) validation of VM/ESA version 2 release 3 parallel sysplex support.

- Project duration: 1997 to 1998.
- Completed as I/T Specialist / Systems Management Consultant: IBM Global Services, BRS.

VM sysplex support makes it possible for IBM to meet growing customer demand for testing (and in some cases production use of) sysplex systems in an efficient and cost-effective manner, reducing high hardware expenses and the level of operational complexity.

Implemented first VM host High Availability System for IBM's Poughkeepsie and external customers, with both guest-system and lpar support.

- Project duration: 1996 to 1997.
- Completed as I/T Specialist / Systems Management Consultant: IBM Global Services, BRS.

System is based on a "peer" production VM/ESA host on which all new software service is first installed and tested to ensure stability and proper functioning. Led implementation team to completion of a system with an outstanding overall measured availability exceeding 99%.

Designed and led team implementation of common VM/ESA host system layout and distribution mechanism for production use at multiple geographic sites — Poughkeepsie, Raleigh, and Dallas.

- Project duration: 1993 to 1998.
- Began as Consulting Marketing Support Representative: IBM ISSC.
- Completed as I/T Specialist / Systems Management Consultant: IBM Global Services, BRS.

All target processors support multiple customers, both internal and external; hundreds of interactive users; and all major IBM operating systems as guests. VM system design and layout promotes efficiency, reduces software installation / personnel costs, and ensures that all participating systems are as up-to-date as possible. Basic scheme has been extended to incorporate a new IBM BRS installation in Boulder, Colorado, as well as use by BRS Canada.

Developed VM/PVM release 2.0 Multiple Session Facility (MPVM) Auto-Signon feature.

- Project duration: 1993-1996.
- Began as Consulting Marketing Support Representative: IBM ISSC.
- Completed as IBM I/T Specialist / Systems Management Consultant: Global Services / BRS.

Code based on IBM internal-use-only predecessor product. Supplied official documentation and assisted IBM development in its release as a product feature.

employment elsewhere. Areas of expertise (not so labeled) are listed in three columns between the Career Profile and the Summary of Technology Expertise. The column heads are categories according to which the areas of expertise are grouped. In the Recent Project Highlights section, the duration of each project is

GEORGE HOFFMAN

CAREER DEVELOPMENT SUMMARY

IBM CORPORATION, Poughkeepsie, NY   1985 to present

- I/T Specialist / Systems Management Consultant: Global Services / BRS   1997 to present
- Consulting Marketing Support Representative: ISSC   1995 to 1997
- Senior Marketing Support Specialist: Washington Systems Center   1992 to 1995
- Advisory Marketing Support Specialist: Washington Systems Center   1988 to 1992
- Researcher, Research Division: Yorktown Heights   1985 to 1988

Representative Contributions and Responsibilities include:

Multiple host processor shared VM/ESA systems environment, supporting IBM product development, competitive customer benchmarks, guest (OS/390, MVS, VSE, VM) systems, and networking subsystems. Design, implement, and manage this environment for customers including Business Recovery Services itself, IBM Testing Services, and other IBM internal and external users.

VM host systems for IBM Business Recovery Services (BRS). Support IBM High Availability System and disaster-recovery tests, with target processors ranging from 9021-9X2 systems to RX6 CMOS systems.

I/O configuration and connectivity planning. Including ESCON director switching, along with the administration of IOCPs for multiple hosts, including processors in lpar mode.

Parallel sysplex support. Consult and provide all VM support of parallel sysplex MVS systems in Poughkeepsie.

Guest design and implementation. Consult and ensure that customer requirements and guest testing or production goals can be met.

Y2K testing. Support Year 2000 testing using standard VM timer controls or new VM/ESAv2.3 (SET VTOD) facilities.

Three-site RSCS and PVM network design and management. Implement wide range of protocols including IP, SNA, and BSC. Support remote and local customer access to various VM and MVS hosts using multiple production VTAM systems, Netview Access Services, PVMG (PVM SNA server), etc.

VM/ESA, PVM, and RSCS development organizations. Provide chief interface to IBM development for Poughkeepsie, and BRS Boulder and Canada.

SFS and APPC-based data sharing applications. Develop as needed for BRS customers.

EARLY EMPLOYMENT

IBM Corporation: Systems Engineer for Army Programs Branch Office. Advisory Systems Engineer for Federal Programs Branch.

U.S. Air Force: Programmer/Operational logistics applications (Honorable discharge as Staff Sergeant).

EDUCATION

- **B.S. in Mathematics,** Boston University, Boston, MA
- **Graduate studies in Theoretical Mathematics,** Columbia University, New York, NY

specified. Separate Began and Completed statements are provided for projects whose duration was three or more years. The Career Development Summary begins with a work history (not so labeled) and provides a list of Representative Contributions and Responsibilities. Opening phrases are in boldface.

3
P·A·R·T

Best Cover Letter Tips

Best Cover Letter Tips at a Glance

Best Cover Letter Tips

$\mathbf{I}$n an active job search, your cover letter and resume should complement one another. Both are tailored to a particular reader you have contacted or to a specific job target. To help you create the "best" cover letters for your resumes, this part of the book mentions some common myths about cover letters and presents tips for polishing the letters you write.

Myths about Cover Letters

1. **Resumes and cover letters are two separate documents that have little relation to each other.** The resume and cover letter work together in presenting you effectively to a prospective employer. The cover letter should mention the resume and call attention to some important aspect of it.

2. **The main purpose of the cover letter is to establish friendly rapport with the reader.** Resumes show that you *can* do the work required. Cover letters express that you *want* to do the work required. But it doesn't hurt to display enthusiasm in your resumes and refer to your abilities in your cover letters.

3. **You can use the same cover letter for each reader of your resume.** Modify your cover letter for each reader so that it sounds fresh rather than canned. Chances are that in an active job search, you have already talked with the person who will interview you. Your cover letter should reflect that conversation and build on it.

4. **In a cover letter, you should mention any negative things about your life experience, work experience, health, or education in order to prepare the reader in advance of an interview.** This is not the purpose of the cover letter. You might bring up these topics in the first or second interview, but only after the interviewer has shown interest in you or offered you a job. Even then, if you feel that you must mention something negative about your past, present it in a positive way, perhaps by saying how that experience has strengthened your resolve to work hard at any new job.

5. **It is more important to remove errors from a resume than from a cover letter, because the resume is more important than the cover letter.** Both your resume and your cover letter should be free of errors. The cover letter is usually the first document a prospective employer sees. The first impression is often the most important one. If your cover letter has an embarrassing error in it, the chances are good that the reader may not bother to read your resume or may read it with less interest.

6. **To make certain that your cover letter has no errors, all you need to do is proofread it or ask a friend to "proof" it.** Trying to proofread your own cover letter is risky, even if you are good at grammar and writing. Once a document is typewritten or printed, it has an aura about it that may make it seem better written than it is. For this reason, you are likely to miss typos or other kinds of errors.

    Relying on someone else is risky too. If your friend is not good at grammar and writing, that person may not see any mistakes either. Try to find a proofreader, a professional editor, an English teacher, a professional writer, or an experienced secretary who can point out any errors you may have missed.

7. **After someone has proofread your letter, you can make a few changes to it and not have it looked at again.** More errors creep into a document this way than you would think possible. The reason is that such changes are often done hastily, and haste can waste an error-free document. If you make *any* change to a document, ask someone to proofread it a final time just to make sure that you haven't introduced an error during the last stage of composition.

Tips for Polishing Cover Letters

You might spend several days working on your resume, getting it "just right" and free of errors. But if you send it with a cover letter that is written quickly and contains even one conspicuous error, all of your good effort may be wasted. That error could be just the kind of mistake the reader is looking for to screen you out.

You can prevent this kind of tragedy by polishing your cover letter so that it is free of all errors. The following tips can help you avoid or eliminate common errors in cover letters. If you become aware of these kinds of errors and know how to fix them, you can be more confident about the cover letters you send with your resumes.

Using Good Strategies for Letters

1. **Use the postal abbreviation for the state in your mailing address.** See best resume-writing strategy 1 in Part 1.

2. **Make certain that the letter is addressed to a specific person and that you use this person's name in the salutation.** Avoid using such general salutations as Dear Sir or Madam, To Whom It May Concern, Dear Administrator, Dear Prospective Employer, and Dear Committee. (To ensure anonymity, some of the resume writers who have provided sample cover letters for this book have used general saluations.) In an active job search, you should do everything possible to send your cover letter and resume to a particular individual, preferably someone you've already talked with in person or by phone, and with whom you have arranged an interview. If you have not been able to make a personal contact, at least do everything possible to find out the name of the person who will read your letter and resume. Then address the letter to that person.

3. **Adjust the margins for a short letter.** If your cover letter is 300 words or longer, use left, right, top, and bottom margins of one inch. If the letter is

shorter, the width of the margins should increase. How much they increase is a matter of personal taste. One way to take care of the width of the top and bottom margins is to center a shorter letter vertically on the page. A maximum width for a short cover letter of 100 words or fewer might be two-inch left and right margins. As the number of words increases by 50 words, you might decrease the width of the left and right margins by two-tenths of an inch.

4. **If you write your letter with word processing or desktop publishing software, use left-justification to ensure that the lines of text are readable with fixed spacing between words.** The letter will have a "ragged right" look along the right margin, but the words will be evenly spaced horizontally. Be wary of using full justification in an attempt to give a letter a printed look. Unless you do other typesetting procedures, like kerning and hyphenating words at the end of some lines, full justification can make your letter look worse with some extra wide spaces between words.

Using Pronouns Correctly

5. **Use *I* and *My* sparingly.** When most of the sentences in a cover letter begin with *I* or *My*, the writer may appear self-absorbed, self-centered, or egotistical. If the reader of the letter is turned off by this kind of impression (even if it is a false one for you), you could be screened out without ever having an interview. Of course, you will need to use these first-person pronouns because most of the information you put in your cover letter will be personal. But try to avoid using *I* and *My* at the beginnings of sentences and paragraphs.

6. **Refer to a business, company, corporation, or organization as "it" rather than "they."** Members of the Board may be referred to as "they," but a company is a singular subject requiring a singular verb. Note this example:

   > New Products, Inc., was established in 1980. It grossed over a million dollars in sales during its first year.

7. **If you start a sentence with *This*, be sure that what *This* refers to is clear.** If the reference is not clear, insert some word or phrase to clarify what *This* means. Compare the following lines:

   > My revised application for the new position will be faxed to you by noon on Friday. You indicated by phone that *this* is acceptable to you.

   > My revised application for the new position will be faxed to you by noon on Friday. You indicated by phone that this *method of sending the application* is acceptable to you.

   A reader of the first sentence wouldn't know what *This* refers to. Friday? By noon on Friday? The revised application for the new position? The insertion after *This* in the second sentence, however, tells the reader that *This* refers to the use of faxing.

8. **Use *as follows* after a singular subject.** Literally, *as follows* means *as it follows*, so the phrase is illogical after a plural subject. Compare the following lines:

Incorrect:	My plans for the day of the interview are as follows:
Fixed:	My plans for the day of the interview are these:
Correct:	My plan for the day of the interview is as follows:
Better:	Here is my plan for the day of the interview:

In the second set, the improved version avoids a hidden reference problem—the possible association of the silent "it" with *interview*. Whenever you want to use *as follows*, check to see whether the subject that precedes *as follows* is plural. If it is, don't use this phrase.

Using Verb Forms Correctly

9. **Make certain that subjects and verbs agree in number.** Plural subjects require plural forms of verbs. Singular subjects require singular verb forms. Most writers know these things, but problems arise when subject and verb agreement gets tricky. Compare the following lines:

Incorrect:	My education and experience has prepared me. . . .
Correct:	My education and experience have prepared me. . . .

Incorrect:	Making plans plus scheduling conferences were. . . .
Correct:	Making plans plus scheduling conferences was. . . .

In the first set, *education* and *experience* are two things (you can have one without the other) and require a plural verb. A hasty writer might lump them together and use a singular verb. When you reread what you have written, look out for this kind of improper agreement between a plural subject and a singular verb.

In the second set, *making plans* is the subject. It is singular, so the verb must be singular. The misleading part of this sentence is the phrase *plus scheduling conferences*. It may seem to make the subject plural, but it doesn't. In English, phrases that begin with such words as *plus, together with, in addition to, along with*, and *as well as* usually don't make a singular subject plural.

10. **Whenever possible, use active forms of verbs rather than passive forms.** Compare these lines:

Passive:	My report will be sent by my assistant tomorrow.
Active:	My assistant will send my report tomorrow.

Passive:	Your interest is appreciated.
Active:	I appreciate your interest.

Passive:	Your letter was received yesterday.
Active:	I received your letter yesterday.

Sentences with passive verbs are usually longer and clumsier than sentences with active verbs. Spot passive verbs by looking for some form of the verb *to be* (such as *be, will be, have been, is, was*, and *were*) used with another verb.

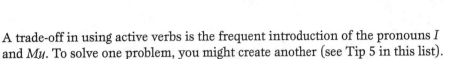

A trade-off in using active verbs is the frequent introduction of the pronouns *I* and *My*. To solve one problem, you might create another (see Tip 5 in this list). The task then becomes one of finding some other way to start a sentence.

11. **Be sure that present and past participles are grammatically parallel in a list.** See Tip 62 in Part 1. What is true about parallel forms in resumes is true also in cover letters. Present participles are action words ending in *-ing*, such as *creating, testing,* and *implementing.* Past participles are action words usually ending in *-ed,* such as *created, tested,* and *implemented.* These are called *verbals* because they are derived from verbs but are not strong enough to function as verbs in a sentence. When you use a string of verbals, control them by keeping them parallel.

12. **Use split infinitives only when *not* splitting them is misleading or awkward.** An *infinitive* is a verb preceded by the preposition *to,* as in *to create, to test,* and *to implement.* You split an infinitive when you insert an adverb between the preposition and the verb, as in *to quickly create, to repeatedly test,* and *to slowly implement.* About 50 years ago, split infinitives were considered grammatical errors, but opinion about them has changed. Many grammar handbooks now recommend that you split your infinitives to avoid awkward or misleading sentences. Compare the following lines:

Split infinitive:	I plan to periodically send updated reports on my progress in school.
Misleading:	I plan periodically to send updated reports on my progress in school.
Misleading:	I plan to send periodically updated reports on my progress in school.

The first example is clear enough, but the second and third examples may be misleading. If you are uncomfortable with split infinitives, one solution is to move *periodically* further into the sentence: "I plan to send updated reports periodically on my progress in school."

Most handbooks that allow split infinitives also recommend that they not be split by more than one word, as in *to quickly and easily write.* A gold medal for splitting an infinitive should go to Lowell Schmalz, an Archie Bunker prototype in "The Man Who Knew Coolidge" by Sinclair Lewis. Schmalz, who thought that Coolidge was one of America's greatest presidents, split an infinitive this way: "*to instantly and without the least loss of time or effort find. . . .*"[1]

Using Punctuation Correctly

13. **Punctuate a compound sentence with a comma.** A compound sentence is one that contains two main clauses joined by one of seven conjunctions (*and, but, or, nor, for, yet,* and *so*). In English, a comma is customarily put before the conjunction if the sentence isn't unusually short. Here is an example of a compound sentence punctuated correctly:

---

[1]Sinclair Lewis, "The Man Who Knew Ccoolidge," *The Man Who Knew Coolidge* (New York: Books for Libraries Press, 1956, p. 297.

I plan to arrive at O'Hare at 9:35 a.m. on Thursday, and my trip by cab to your office should take no longer than 40 minutes.

The comma is important because it signals that a new grammatical subject (*trip*, the subject of the second main clause) is about to be expressed. If you use this kind of comma consistently, the reader will rely on your punctuation and be on the lookout for the next subject in a compound sentence.

14. **Be certain not to put a comma between compound verbs.** When a sentence has two verbs joined by the conjunction *and*, these verbs are called *compound verbs*. Usually, they should not be separated by a comma before the conjunction. Note the following examples:

> I *started* the letter last night *and finished* it this morning.
>
> I *am sending* my resume separately *and would like* you to keep the information confidential.

Both examples are simple sentences containing compound verbs. Therefore, no comma appears before *and*. In either case, a comma would send a wrong signal that a new subject in another main clause is coming, but no such subject exists.

Note: In a sentence with a series of three or more verbs, use commas between the verbs. The comma before the last verb is called the *serial comma*. The serial comma is optional; many writers of business documents omit this comma. For more information on using the serial comma, see resume-writing style Tip 77 in Part 1.

15. **Avoid using *as well as* for *and* in a series.** Compare the following lines:

Incorrect:	Your company is impressive because it has offices in Canada, Mexico, as well as the United States.
Correct:	Your company is impressive because it has offices in Canada and Mexico, as well as in the United States.

Usually, what is considered exceptional precedes *as well as*, and what is considered customary follows it. Note this example:

> Your company is impressive because its managerial openings are filled by women as well as men.

16. **Put a comma after the year when it appears after the month.** Similarly, put a comma after the state when it appears after the city. Compare the following pairs of lines:

Incorrect:	In January, 1998 I was promoted to senior analyst.
Correct:	In January, 1998, I was promoted to senior analyst.

Incorrect:	I worked in Chicago, Illinois before moving to Dallas.
Correct:	I worked in Chicago, Illinois, before moving to Dallas.

17. **Put a comma after an opening dependent clause.** Compare the following lines:

Incorrect:	If you have any questions you may contact me by phone or fax.
Correct:	If you have any questions, you may contact me by phone or fax.

Actually, many writers of fiction and nonfiction don't use this kind of comma. The comma is useful, though, because it signals where the main clause begins. If you glance at the example with the comma, you can tell where the main clause is without even reading the opening clause. For a step up in clarity and readability, use this comma. It can give you a "feel" for a sentence even before you begin to read the words.

18. **Use semicolons when they are needed.** See resume-writing style Tip 78 in Part 1 for the use of semicolons between items in a series. Semicolons are used also to separate main clauses when the second clause starts with a *conjunctive adverb* like *however*, *moreover*, and *therefore*. Compare the following lines:

Incorrect:	Your position in sales looks interesting, however, I would like more information about it.
Correct:	Your position in sales looks interesting; however, I would like more information about it.

The first example is incorrect because the comma before *however* is a *comma splice*, which is a comma that joins two sentences. It's like putting a comma instead of a period at the end of the first sentence and then starting the second sentence. A comma may be a small punctuation mark, but a comma splice is a huge grammatical mistake. What are your chances for getting hired if your cover letter tells your reader that you don't recognize where a sentence ends, especially if a requirement for the job is good communication skills? Yes, you could be screened out because of one little comma!

19. **Avoid putting a colon after a verb or a preposition to introduce information.** The reason is that the colon interrupts a continuing clause. Compare the following lines:

Incorrect:	My interests in your company *are:* its reputation, the review of salary after six months, and your personal desire to hire handicapped persons.
Correct:	My interests in your company *are these:* its reputation, the review of salary after six months, and your personal desire to hire handicapped persons.
Incorrect:	In my interview with you, I would like *to:* learn how your company was started, get your reaction to my updated portfolio, and discuss your department's plans to move to a new building.
Correct:	In my interview with you, I would like to discuss *these issues:* how your company was started, what you think of my updated portfolio, and when your department may move to a new building.

Although some people may say that it is OK to put a colon after a verb like *include* if the list of information is long, it is better to be consistent and avoid colons after verbs altogether.

20. **Understand colons clearly.** People often associate colons with semicolons because they sound alike, but colons and semicolons have nothing to do with each other. Colons are the opposite of dashes. Dashes look backward (see resume-writing style Tip 80 in Part 1), and colons usually look forward to information about to be delivered. One common use of the colon does look backward, however. Here are two examples:

> My experience with computers is limited: I have had only one course on programming, and I don't own a computer.

> I must make a decision by Monday: that is the deadline for renewing the lease for my apartment.

In each example, what follows the colon explains what was said before the colon. Using a colon this way in a cover letter can impress a knowledgeable reader who is looking for evidence of writing skills.

21. **Use slashes correctly.** Information about slashes is sometimes hard to find because *slash* often is listed under a different name, such as *virgule* or *solidus*. If you are not familiar with these terms, your hunt for advice on slashes may lead to nothing.

At least know that one important meaning of a slash is *or*. For this reason, you often see a slash in an expression like ON/OFF. This means that a condition or state, like that of electricity activated by a switch, is either ON or OFF but never ON and OFF at the same time. As you saw in resume-writing style Tip 75 in Part 1, this condition may be one in which a change means going from the current state to the opposite (or alternate) state. If the current state is ON and there is a change, the next state will be OFF, and vice versa. With this understanding, you can recognize the logic behind the following examples:

Incorrect:	ON-OFF switch (on and off at the same time!)
Correct:	ON/OFF switch (on or off at any time)
Correct:	his-her clothes (unisex clothes, worn by both sexes)
Correct:	his/her clothes (each sex had different clothes)

Note: Although the slash is correct in *his/her* and is one way to avoid sexism, many people consider this expression clumsy. Consider some other wording, such as "clothes that both men and women wear" or "unisex clothes."

22. **Think twice about using *and/or*.** This stilted expression is commonly misunderstood to mean *two* alternatives, but it literally means *three*. Look at the following example:

> If you don't hear from me by Friday, please phone and/or fax me the information on Monday.

What is the person at the other end to do? The sentence really states three alternatives: just phone, just fax, or phone *and* fax the information by Monday. For better clarity, use the connectives *and* or *or* whenever possible.

23. **Use punctuation correctly with quotation marks.** A common misconception is that commas and periods should be placed outside closing quotation marks, but the opposite is true. Compare the following lines:

    Incorrect: Your company certainly has the "leading edge", which means that its razor blades are the best on the market.

    Correct: Your company certainly has the "leading edge," which means that its razor blades are the best on the market.

    Incorrect: In the engineering department, my classmates referred to me as "the guru in pigtails". I was the youngest expert in programming languages on campus.

    Correct: In the engineering department, my classmates referred to me as "the guru in pigtails." I was the youngest expert in programming languages on campus.

Unlike commas and periods, colons and semicolons go *outside* double quotation marks.

Using Words Correctly

24. **Avoid using lofty language in your cover letter.** A real turn-off in a cover letter is the use of elevated diction (high-sounding words and phrases) as a bid to seem important. Note the following examples, along with their straight-talk translations:

    Elevated: My background has afforded me experience in. . . .
    Better: In my previous jobs, I. . . .

    Elevated: Prior to that term of employment. . . .
    Better: Before I worked at. . . .

    Elevated: I am someone with a results-driven profit orientation.
    Better: I want to make your company more profitable.

    Elevated: I hope to utilize my qualifications. . . .
    Better: I want to use my skills. . . .

In letter writing, the shortest distance between the writer and the reader is the most direct idea.

25. **Check your sentences for an excessive use of compounds joined by *and*.** A cheap way to make your letters longer is to join words with *and* and do this repeatedly. Note the following wordy sentence:

Because of my background and preparation for work and advancement with your company and new enterprise, I have a concern and commitment to implement and put into effect my skills and abilities for new solutions and achievements above and beyond your dreams and expectations. [44 words]

Just one inflated sentence like that would drive a reader to say, "No way!" The writer of the inflated sentence has said only this:

Because of my background and skills, I want to contribute to your new venture. [14 words]

If, during rereading, you eliminate the wordiness caused by this common writing weakness, your letter will have a better chance of being read completely.

26. **Avoid using abstract nouns excessively.** Look again at the inflated sentence of the preceding tip, but this time with the abstract nouns in italic:

Because of my *background* and *preparation* for *work* and *advancement* with your *company* and new *enterprise*, I have a *concern* and *commitment* to implement and put into *effect* my skills and *abilities* for new *solutions* and *achievements* above and beyond your *dreams* and *expectations*.

Try picturing in your mind any of the words in italic. You can't because they are *abstract nouns*, which means that they are ideas and not images of things you can see, taste, hear, smell, or touch. One certain way to turn off the reader of your cover letter is to load it with abstract nouns. The following sentence, containing some images, has a better chance of capturing the reader's attention:

Having created seven multimedia tutorials with my videocamera and Gateway Pentium computer, I now want to create some breakthrough adult-learning packages so that your company, New Century Instructional Technologies, will exceed $50,000,000 in contracts by 1995.

Compare this sentence with the one loaded with abstract nouns. The one with images is obviously the better attention grabber.

27. **Avoid wordy expressions in your cover letters.** Note the following examples:

at the location of (at)
for the reason that (because)
in a short time (soon)
in a timely manner (on time)
in spite of everything to the contrary (nevertheless)
in the event of (if)
in the proximity of (near)
now and then (occasionally)
on a daily basis (daily)
on a regular basis (regularly)
on account of (because)

one day from now (tomorrow)

would you be so kind as to (please)

After each of these phrases is a suitable substitute in parentheses. Trim the fat wherever you can, and your reader will appreciate the leanness of your cover letter.

28. **At the end of your cover letter, don't make a statement that the reader can use to reject you.** For example, suppose that you close your letter with this statement:

> If you wish to discuss this matter further, please call me at (555) 555-5555.

This statement gives the reader a chance to think, "I don't wish it, so I don't have to call." Here is another example:

> If you know of the right opportunity for me, please call me at (555) 555-5555.

The reader may think, "I don't know of any such opportunity. How would I know what is right for you?" Avoid questions that prompt yes or no answers, such as, "Do you want to discuss this matter further?" If you ask this kind of a question, you give the reader a chance to say no. Instead, make a closing statement that indicates your optimism about a positive response from the reader. Such a statement might begin with one of the following:

> I am confident that. . . .
>
> I look forward to. . . .

In this way, you invite the reader to say yes to further consideration.

Exhibit of Cover Letters

The following Exhibit contains sample cover letters that were prepared by professional resume writers to accompany resumes submitted for this book. In most cases, the names, addresses, and facts have been changed to ensure the confidentiality of the original sender and receiver of the letter. For each letter, however, the essential substance of the original remains intact.

Use the Exhibit of cover letters as a reference whenever you need to write a cover letter for your resume. If you have trouble starting and ending letters, look at the beginnings and ends of the letters. If you need help on writing about your work experience, describing your abilities and skills, or mentioning some of your best achievements, look at the middle paragraph(s). Search for features that will give you ideas for making your own cover letters more effective. As you examine the Exhibit, consider the following questions:

1. **Does the person show a genuine interest in the reader?** One way to tell is to count the number of times the pronouns *you* or *your* appear in the letter. Then count the number of times the pronouns *I*, *me*, and *my* occur in the letter. Although this method is simplistic, it nevertheless helps you see where the writer's interests lie. When you write a cover letter, make your first paragraph *you*-centered rather than *I*-centered. See also Tip 5 earlier in Part 3.

2.   **Where does the cover letter mention the resume specifically?** The purpose of a cover letter is to call attention to the resume. If the letter fails to mention the resume, the letter has not fulfilled its purpose. Besides mentioning the resume, the cover letter might direct the reader's attention to one or more parts of the resume, increasing the chances that the most important part(s) will be seen by the reader. It is not a good idea, however, to put a lot of resume facts in the cover letter. Let each document do its own job. The job of the cover letter is to point to the resume.

3.   **Where and how does the letter express interest in an interview?** The immediate purpose of a cover letter is to call attention to the resume, but the *ultimate* purpose of both the cover letter and the resume is to help you get an interview with the person who can hire you. If the letter doesn't display your interest in getting an interview, the letter has not fulfilled its ultimate purpose.

4.   **How decisive is the person's language?** This question is closely related to the preceding question. Is interest in an interview expressed directly or indirectly? Does the person specifically request an interview on a date when the writer will be in the reader's vicinity, or does the person only hint at a desire to "meet" the reader some day? When you write your own cover letters, be sure to be direct and convincing in expressing your interest for an interview. Avoid being timid or wishy-washy.

5.   **How does the person display self-confidence?** As you look through the Exhibit, notice the cover letters in which the phrase "I am confident that. . ." (or a similar expression) appears. Self-confidence is a sign of management ability but also of essential job-worthiness. Many of the letters display self-confidence or self-assertiveness in various ways.

6.   **Does a letter indicate whether the person is a team player?** From an employer's point of view, an employee who is self-assertive but not a team player can spell T-R-O-U-B-L-E. As you look at the cover letters in the Exhibit, notice whether any letter mentions the word *team*.

7.   **How does the letter make the person stand out?** As you read the letters in the Exhibit, do some letters present the person more vividly than other letters? If so, what does the trick? The middle paragraphs or the opening and closing paragraphs? The paragraphs or the bulleted lists? Use what you learn here to help you write distinctive cover letters.

8.   **How familiar is the person with the reader?** In a passive job search, the reader will most likely be a total stranger. In an active job search, the chances are good that the writer will have had at least one conversation with the reader by phone or in person. In that case, the letter can refer to any previous communication.

After you have examined the cover letters in the Exhibit, you will be better able to write an attention-getting letter—one that leads the reader to your resume and to scheduling an interview with you.

JANE E. SIMMONS, C.P.A.

18015 Prestwick Drive
Tampa, Florida 33600
(813) 000-0000

May 13, 1998

XYZ Corporation
Director - Employee Services
Attn: Job Code 0000
P.O. Box 30000
Tampa, Florida   33600-0000

Dear Director:

I am a well-qualified, senior-level Accounting Professional writing to express my interest in the **Director-Financial Accounting** position advertised in the May 10, 1998, edition of the *Tampa Tribune*. As requested, I have enclosed my resume and salary history for your review. Although secure in my current position, I am **confidentially** exploring new professional roles where my experience in a broad range of accounting, auditing, state and federal tax, and business management functions would bring measurable value to a progressive company.

In perusing my resume, you will note that throughout my career I have achieved an excellent record of advancement and excelled in positions of increased responsibilities. I offer excellent qualifications in financial analysis; summarizing and interpreting data; automated accounting software programs; and presiding over managerial, supervisory and administrative tasks. My expertise lies in my ability to effectively interact with clients, identify problems/concerns, and develop applicable strategies for achieving financial goals. Just as significant is the quality control experience I have gained as an active member of an internal inspection team.

As a person who takes pride in bringing integrity and professionalism to the workplace, I am confident my skill sets would serve as an asset to the financial infrastructure of XYZ Company. Thank you for taking the time to review my credentials; I look forward to your reply.

Sincerely,

Jane E. Simmons

Enclosure

For Resume 53. *Diane McGoldrick, Tampa, Florida*
The first of three paragraphs introduces the writer and reveals her goal and strategy; the second indicates her transferable skills; the third expresses her confidence and thanks.

DONALD P. ROWING
15 Church Street
East-West, PA 11111
(123) 456-7890

June 3, XXXX

Ms. Kim S. Goodyear
Personnel Administrator
Field Craft, Inc.
7733 Route 15
Mansfield, PA 55555

Dear Ms. Goodyear:

If you are seeking someone with a solid track record of improving cash management systems, developing information systems and establishing key analytical tools for a management team, then I would like to be considered.

As a top performer with 12 years' experience in general accounting, I have the knowledge and expertise it takes to bring about positive change. My enclosed résumé highlights my contributions and accomplishments in the areas of general and cost accounting, conversion and consolidation, procedures and policies development, strategic planning, leveraged buyout accounting, and forecasts and financial analysis. I take pride in my work and abilities. I have made great strides in being recognized as a key player on the management team and consider myself "more than just a bean counter." My accomplishments speak for themselves.

My objective is to find a management-level position where my talents can contribute to Field Crafts' growth and profitability. My present compensation package is in the mid-fifty-thousand bracket, but the right opportunity is the motivating factor. In researching your organization, I found that you recognize your employees as a valuable resource and take a holistic approach toward their spiritual, physical, and mental well being in the workplace. I was pleased to learn that Field Craft shares my beliefs, and I would be proud to become a member of your team. I am sure we could come to terms for compensation considering the benefits that are provided.

I would be excited to have an opportunity to speak with you personally about my qualifications. I can be available for an interview at your convenience.

Sincerely,

Donald P. Rowing

Enclosure

2

For Resume 97. *Deborah S. Edwards, Wellsboro, Pennsylvania*
An employer wants to know whether a candidate *can do* the job and whether the person *wants* to. The first two paragraphs show the person's ability; the second two, his eagerness.

JEFFREY M. ANDREWS

P. O. Box 000 • 3 Dovetail Road
Gaines, PA 11111
(555) 555-5555

September 10, XXXX

Mr. Keith C. Bender
County Electric Company
South Main Street
Kelsey Creek, PA 12345

Dear Mr. Bender:

Please accept the enclosed résumé for consideration for the position of Manager of Financial
Services which you have posted with the County Job Center. As an executive with more than 20
years of experience in accounting, finance, budgeting, forecasting, purchasing and auditing, I am
confident my qualifications match your requirements.

I would like to bring your attention to specific aspects of my experience which I believe
demonstrate what I have to offer your organization. Throughout my career, I have been involved
with power generation equipment—manufacturing and service. I am knowledgeable about
keeping a facility running and maintaining it to maximize operations.

My background reflects accomplishments in purchasing and establishing many multiyear
contracts to cut expenses and improve the bottom line. Vendor contracts were negotiated which
locked in prices for 3-5 years. This also afforded our company the ability to minimize our
inventory because most of our vendors stocked the materials with turnaround time within 24
hours. I was instrumental in streamlining processes to the extent that production didn't have any
excuses not to have things operational.

I would appreciate an opportunity to meet with you personally to discuss my qualifications and
how I may contribute to the position in greater detail. Please call me at the above telephone
number to schedule an appointment.

Sincerely,

Jeffrey M. Andrews

Enclosure

3

For Resume 165. *Deborah S. Edwards, Wellsboro, Pennsylvania*
The four-paragraph design is *goal, particularly relevant experience, accomplishments,* and
interest in an interview. The heavy black bar under the person's name matches the resume.

Mary T. Morstan, Esq.
4221 South Rosemont Lane
Denver, Colorado 81000
℘ [303] 555-5555 (Office); [303] 555-6666 (Home)

January 15, XXXX

Hon. Paul McChesney
District Attorney
Office of the Routt County District Attorney
416 Stapleton Road
P. O. Box 168
Hot Sulphur Springs, Colorado 80451

Dear Mr. McChesney:

Let me put the bottom line on the top: I would like to join your team as an Assistant District Attorney.

Even before graduating from law school, I wanted to work for state or local government. Now, with more than a decade of successful experience, I still find great rewards in public service.

My résumé should help you learn more about me. In putting it together, I tried to go beyond reciting responsibilities to concentrate on results. Behind the specifics are a wealth of skills I had to master quickly. The law in this field changes constantly; mistakes could mean convicted killers go free. Because Colorado's system of jury selection requires a more searching *voire dire*, my skills at helping select juries are in constant demand. Finally, because I must know "cold" what a prosecutor can and cannot say in these high-profile cases, my hard-won reputation is tested every day.

The Attorney General's office rewards me regularly for my work. I enjoy what I do. However, I want to put my experience and energy to work in a broader arena. May I call in a few days to explore the possibility of a confidential interview?

Sincerely,

Mary T. Morstan

One enclosure: Résumé

4

For Resume 151. *Donald Orlando, Montgomery, Alabama*
An energetic, enthusiastic letter. The sequence of topics per paragraph is *goal, motivation, skills,* and *desire for an interview.* Some letters never get off the ground. This one soars.

RÉSUMÉ CONNECTION   Career Management Resources for Job Transition

June 27, XXXX

Mr. J. Robert Dalton
Human Resources Director
Citizens Bank & Trust
10 North Union Street
Twin Tiers, PA 11111

Dear Bob:

As a follow-up of our telephone conversation today, I am forwarding the enclosed résumé for the new operations position you are currently developing. I think you will want to consider this friend of mine whom I am recommending as a strong candidate for the position because of his solid background and exceptional skills in the areas of lending and branch operations.

I am not at liberty to disclose his identity at this time. He is currently employed with one of your competitor's organizations in another area of Pennsylvania and does not want to jeopardize his position there. I can tell you, however, that he is exploring other opportunities due to the transition and merger taking place within the organization he is currently working for. He feels that it may be time for a change, although he would like to remain in credit administration.

You will note from his résumé that besides his expertise in operations, he also has outstanding experience administering portfolios of as much as $22 million; he has been involved with leading branch personnel within a two-county area; and he is effective in planning, directing, budgeting and cost control. In short, I believe Citizens Bank & Trust would gain a valuable resource in adding him to their growing organization.

I'll call you next week to see how you would like to proceed in setting up an appointment for a personal interview. If you would prefer to move this along sooner, just let me know, and I'll see what can be arranged. Thank you for your time. As always, it's a pleasure to be of service.

Sincerely,

Deborah S. Edwards, NCRW/CPRW

Enclosure

33 Waln Street • PO Box 361 • Wellsboro, PA 16901 • (570) 724-3610
319 Main Street • Towanda, PA 18848 • (570) 265-9459

5

For Resume 170. *Deborah S. Edwards, Wellsboro, Pennsylvania*
A confidential letter for a friend whose identity is kept unknown. The writer is an intermediary. The third paragraph directs the reader to the resume; the fourth gives follow-up plans.

Thomas L. Hume, Esq. 2798 Conklin Street • Suite 452 • Patchogue, NY 11772

(516) 555-5555 • fax (516) 000-0000 • tlhEsq@sprintmail.com

June 14, xxxx

Granger & Corbin, LLP
92 West Main Street
Patchogue, NY 11772

Dear Mr. Granger:

As a practicing attorney experienced in general law as well as intensive legal research and writing, I have credentials that match the requirements stated in your recent advertisement for a staff attorney. If you are looking for a seriously focused professional who can work independently or function as part of a dynamic firm, we should meet.

You will find that I offer an unusual combination of practical experience acquired from a dual career as an attorney and as an international in-flight administrator for American Airlines. Although I have done very well at American, I recently moved from Chicago to Long Island and plan to devote all my energies to building a legal career.

You may feel that flight administration experience is a strange background for an attorney. However, the nature of my demanding work for American taught me the same people skills, leadership qualities, tenacity, and cool headedness needed by a good lawyer. These traits were essential when I was in control of a cabin of 300+ passengers and crew in daily and emergency situations.

These same abilities have made me an effective attorney with an exceptional work ethic. I attended law school—graduating fifth in my class—while working as a legal writer and researcher for a prominent Chicago law firm and fulfilling my full-time obligations with American.

There are many attorneys who can *meet* your requirements. If offered the opportunity, I will *exceed* your expectations. I know I can be an asset to Granger & Corbin, making immediate and beneficial contributions as a member of your legal team. I look forward to hearing from you!

Sincerely,

Thomas L. Hume, Esq.

6

For Resume 150. *Deborah Wile Dib, Medford, New York*
Each of the five paragraphs says something beyond the usual: (1) the need to meet, (2) the dual careers, (3) the work for American, (4) the exceptional work ethic, and (5) excelling.

BEVERLY BARRINGER
222 Anthem Drive
Hancock, NH 55555
Telephone: (555) 555-5555
Fax: (000) 000-0000

September 17, XXXX

Mr. Chester Field, President
Tri-State Capital Markets
441 Chivalry Square, Suite 111
Palmer Ridge, NH 55555

Dear Mr. Field,

Does your organization anticipate the need for a **Financial Analyst**? As a Finance professional with over eight years' experience in Financial Investments and Accounting in the global marketplace, perhaps I can be of service. My resume is enclosed for your review. I can offer your organization:

Solid Expertise in Financial Investments - Venture Capital and Asset Management. With an MBA from Post University in Finance and International Finance, I am currently the Vice President for Finance and Investments with a start-up company, Acme Arms Inc. My duties include strategic planning, business plan development, financial planning, preparation of the balance sheet, budgeting, pricing, marketing, troubleshooting, and positioning the firm for the global market and an IPO. Additionally, I have spent several years as a Mutual Fund Broker.

Key Analytical and Organizational Skills. These skills have enabled me to implement more efficient and effective methods for accounting and researching investment instruments, consistently meeting crucial deadlines as well as the insight for strategic planning. Often I have been called upon to provide problem solving, and I have always enjoyed the challenge.

Excellent Interpersonal Skills. Increasing communication between finance and operations and establishing cooperative relationships with managers and directors have also been successful. I have made financial presentations, complete with financial analysis, while serving as Treasurer and board member for a credit union. In the Credit and Loan Department I collaborated with others to initiate new collections policies and procedures and provided financial counseling to the credit union membership.

An Ambition to Succeed. My positions over the last eight years have increased in scope and responsibility with excellent evaluations from all of my former employers. The opportunity to expand my professional knowledge is a serious commitment for me.

As you can see, I would be an asset to your organization. I will call your office next week to set up a mutually convenient appointment. Thank you for your time and consideration.

Sincerely,

Beverly Barringer

Enclosure

For Resume 103. *Susan Guarneri, Lawrenceville, New Jersey*
The opening question is a setup for the information in the next four paragraphs. Words in boldface indicate expertise, skills, and successfulness. The letter ends with follow-up plans.

JACK T. SMITH, CPA

550 Harris Street • **Anytown, ST 55555** • **(555) 555-5555**

September 15, XXXX

Mr. Robert J. Spane, CEO
American Manufacturing, Inc.
555 University Blvd.
Suite 332
Mailstop PKSOJQ0456
Atlanta, GA 33333

Dear Mr. Spane:

It was a pleasure to speak with you today! Having heard more about the position, I am very interested in securing employment as **Senior Accountant** with American Manufacturing, Inc.
Per your request, the enclosed résumé will provide a brief overview of my verifiable work record of accomplishments and employment history.

My qualifications _**include**_:

- **Over ten years of experience that includes extensive accounting, auditing and financial analysis of medium-size corporations, sole proprietorships, businesses and individuals.**

- **Excellent ability to communicate effectively with individuals from a wide range of backgrounds, age groups and management levels.**

- **Highly motivated with a strong desire to accept and conquer increasingly difficult challenges.**

The opportunity of a personal interview where we may further discuss how my qualifications will match the particular needs of American Manufacturing, Inc., would be appreciated. I will call this week to verify your receipt of this information and to arrange for an interview.

Your consideration is greatly appreciated!

Sincerely,

Jack T. Smith, CPA

Enclosure

For Resume 45. *Karen D. Wrigley, Round Rock, Texas*
This letter follows up a phone call. Bullets point to qualifications: experience, skills, and motivation. Another follow-up is planned. Like the resume, the letter has a page border.

GEOFF L. ABRAMSON

10000 Woodlands Drive
Tampa, Florida 33600

(813) 000-0000

September 12, 1997

Mr. Henry Benner
Director, Executive Recruitment
KLM & Associates
5555 Franklin Parkway
Tampa, FL 33600

Dear Mr. Benner:

As a corporate accounting and management professional with excellent qualifications in consultative sales, business development, and financial services, I am seeking to align myself with a company poised for growth. Based on my knowledge of KLM & Associates, it may be a company where my high-level motivation and entrepreneurial attitude would parallel your endeavors for corporate success. To that end, I have enclosed my resume for your review.

Highlights of my qualifications and select achievements include:

- Senior-level, managerial experience emphasizing corporate leadership, P&L responsibilities and ability to grow sales volume/revenues for 100 independent companies. **Increased revenue an additional 15% first year after a major acquisition.**

- Solid track record of high-level professionalism, consistently exceeding corporate expectations and achieving rapid promotions to visible, key role positions. **Grew territory sales 38% over three-year period; outperformed other regions.**

- Proficiency in strategic planning, optimizing efficiency, motivational sales management training, financial management and automated accounting systems. **Developed automated collection process that reduced active A/R by 50%.**

If you could benefit from my well-developed experience and are looking for a person who has a successful track record of continually fulfilling challenges, I am available to meet with you at your convenience.

Sincerely,

Geoff L. Abramson

Enclosure

9

For Resume 169. *Diane McGoldrick, Tampa, Florida*
The first paragraph indicates the individual's purpose. Bulleted items display qualifications and selected achievements. The closing paragraph expresses an interest in an interview.

TANYA A. VIOLA
9999 Puritan Road
City, State 44444
(555) 555-5555
E-mail: viola@website.com

August 14, XXXX

Ms. Mary Manager
Lexis Law Publishing
1000 I Street
City, State 44444

Dear Ms. Manager:

As an office professional with significant legal experience, I am writing to you to inquiry about possible contract employment with your organization. It is my understanding that there may be opportunities to perform proofreading or other services for Lexis on a contract basis. I would be interested in such opportunities and have enclosed for your review a résumé that outlines my background.

Over a career that has spanned eleven years, most of that with one company, I have acquired a number of skills that I believe are relevant to your business. These include:

- *Extensive knowledge of personal injury and personal liability law. As a Legal Assistant and as an Insurance Claims Representative, I have directly dealt with liability cases, including researching points of law and assisting an attorney in drafting pleadings.*

- *Superb written and verbal communication skills. These include an excellent grasp of grammar and spelling, and experience reading and interpreting legal writings.*

- *A strong aptitude for information systems. Throughout my career, I have utilized a variety of computer applications to prepare documentation and conduct research. I am confident that I can quickly acquire any specialized computer skills necessary to meet your particular needs.*

I would enjoy meeting with you to discuss the opportunities available and how I might best serve your needs. Please contact me by phone or e-mail to arrange a convenient date and time for us to begin a dialogue. I look forward to speaking with you soon.

Thank you.

Sincerely,

Tanya A. Viola

Enclosure

10

For Resume 121. *Arnold G. Boldt, Rochester, New York*
The person's goal is given in the first paragraph. Bulleted items indicate skills acquired over 11 years of experience. The last paragraph states the person's interest in an interview.

RAYMOND MONROE

12 Main Street
New York, New York 00000
(555) 555-5555

Dear _____:

Perhaps your company could benefit from a strong chief financial officer with a record of major contributions to business and profit growth.

The scope of my expertise is extensive and includes the full complement of corporate finance, accounting, budgeting, banking, tax, treasury, internal controls, and reporting functions. Equally important are my qualifications in business planning, operations, MIS technology, administration, and general management.

A business partner to management, I have been effective in working with all departments, linking finance with operations to improve productivity, efficiency and bottom-line results. Recruited at The Southington Company to provide finance and systems technology expertise, I created a solid infrastructure to support corporate growth as the company transitioned from a wholesale-retail distributor to a retail operator. Recent accomplishments include:

- **Significant contributor to the increase in operating profits from under $400K to more than $4M.**

- **Key member of due diligence team in the acquisition of 25 operating units that increased market penetration 27% and gross sales 32%.**

- **Spearheaded leading-edge MIS design and implementation, streamlining systems and procedures that dramatically enhanced productivity while cutting costs.**

A "hands-on" manager effective in building team work and cultivating strong internal/external relationships, I am flexible and responsive to the quickly changing demands of the business, industry and marketplace. If you are seeking a talented and proactive finance executive to complement your management team, I would welcome a personal interview. Thank you for your consideration.

Very truly yours,

Raymond Monroe

Enclosure

For Resume 100. *Louise Garver, Enfield, Connecticut*
The first paragraph expresses the person's best role, and the second indicates his expertise. Areas of effectiveness are followed by bulleted achievements. Interest in an interview is last.

PETER PIPER

33 Garden Court
Harvest Township, PA 55555
Phone: 555-555-5555
Fax: 000-000-0000
ppiper@bol.com

Dear Hiring Executive:

Developing innovative telecommunications technology and networking solutions is my expertise. As the Life Cycle Manager for Disaster Recovery and Technical Support manager for Global ISDN Video Conferencing at World Technology, I have provided strategic, technical and operational leadership critical to our market success.

My greatest strength lies in my ability to merge the strategic with the practical, to understand needs and expectations, and to deliver and support the client/server and telecommunications technologies and applications appropriate for each functional organization. Some of my more recent achievements (resume enclosed) include:

- Spearheading the development of world class network GISDN projects as well as overseeing technology support of Video Conferencing, the 2nd largest growing service for World Technology.
- Project oversight and management for disaster recovery of large customer telecommunications networks as Life Cycle Manager of Virtual Gateway Services.
- Pioneering frame relay emerging services including ISDN, PSN (SNA over Frame), and Disaster Recovery for World Data Communications Sevices.
- Evaluating technology requirements and integrating the personnel and resources critical to systems development, operability and marketability for the successful implementation of Manchester Frame Relay to ATM network on deadline and within all technical specifications.

My success thus far is the result of attention to detail as well as the ability to see the "big picture." If you are interested in quality performance, dependable action and innovative solutions, my proven track record demonstrates what I can do. Although my position is secure, I feel it is time for a change to a position that offers greater responsibility and challenge. I would welcome a personal interview at your convenience and would also appreciate your keeping this inquiry confidential. Thank you.

Best regards,

Peter Piper

Enclosure

12

For Resume 193. *Susan Guarneri, Lawrenceville, New Jersey*
The letter compresses much information: the person's expertise, current position, leadership, greatest strength, recent achievements, reason for change, and interest in an interview.

MOLLY P. SENG

550 55ᵗʰ Street ➤ Glendale, New York ➤ 55555 ➤ (555) 555-5555

September 8, XXXX

Vivian Capell
Human Resource Director
National Bank
55 Oak Street
New York, NY 55555

Dear Ms. Capell:

In response to your Internet advertisement for an Operations Support Analyst, I am forwarding a scannable résumé for your review. In learning about this challenging opportunity, I believe that my credentials are an excellent match for the position.

Detailed on my résumé is a solid background in the banking and financial services industry. My accomplishments demonstrate my managerial skills and ability to increase revenues, while improving operations and motivating employees. Highlights of my qualifications include:

> ➤ National Information Services - As Crew Leader, was instrumental in achieving the lowest error ratio in NYC.

> ➤ Advanced Glass Systems - As Controller, directed the company's financial operations, prepared business reports, supervised employees, and managed short-term investments.

> ➤ Citywide Bank Company - As Assistant Manger, increased profits and provided training sessions to managers in other branches.

> ➤ Solid foundation in banking procedures, principles of banking, and bank management.

Currently, I am pursing a Bachelor's degree in Economics, which I expect to receive in December XXX. As a former government employee, I have had federal security clearance. I am committed to achieving excellence and meeting and exceeding financial and operational goals. I would welcome an interview to discuss the Operations Support Analyst position. Please call me at (555) 555-5555.

I look forward to speaking with you.

Best regards,

Molly P. Seng

enclosure

13

13 For Resume 155. *Kim Isaacs, Jackson Heights, New York*
The opening mentions the occasion and the resume. The letter refers next to background, achievements, and skills. Bullets point to qualifications. Wanting an interview is last.

ANGELA C. ARNOLD
18 French Court
City, State 00000
(555) 555-5555
E-mail: aaaaaa@aol.com

August 31, XXXX

Ms. Jane J. Jones
Accounting Manager
XYZ Corporation
1234 Industrial Parkway
City, State 99999

Dear Ms. Jones:

As an Office Professional with extensive accounting/bookkeeping experience, I am most interested in opportunities with your firm that would utilize my skills and offer further professional growth. With this in mind, I have enclosed for your consideration a résumé that briefly outlines my qualifications.

Over the past twenty years, I have developed a number of capabilities that could benefit your company. These include:

- **Administering Accounts Payable and Accounts Receivable, with exposure to Purchasing and Collections.**

- **Processing payroll for employees and payments to subcontractors. I have also prepared filings related to payroll taxes.**

- **Maintaining General Ledgers, making Journal Entries and performing Bank Reconciliations for a variety of businesses.**

- **Tracking job costs for complex construction projects, including posting charges to 120 cost centers.**

In addition, I routinely prepare documentation relating to real estate closings, which requires a high level of attention to detail and the ability to effectively interact with buyers, attorneys, and banks.

I am confident that my knowledge and expertise would allow me to significantly contribute to the efficient operation of your accounting department and to your bottom-line success. I would enjoy meeting with you in person to discuss the potential opportunities and how I could best serve your needs. Please call me at (555) 555-5555 to arrange an interview. I look forward to speaking with you soon.

Thank you.

Sincerely,

Angela C. Arnold

Enclosure

14

For Resume 7. *Arnold G. Boldt, Rochester, New York*
Boldfacing the bulleted capabilities makes them stand out in this letter for an Office Manager. The closing paragraph expresses the person's interest in scheduling an interview.

James T. Robertson

June 14, xxxx

Mr. Jonathan Booth
President
Media Three Corp.
12 Corporate Road
Hauppague, NY 11788

Dear Mr. Booth:

As an experienced, senior-level finance professional with quantifiable, profit-making achievements, I would like to speak with you about the possibility of a financial leadership position with Media Three.

Building corporate value, orchestrating aggressive turnarounds, and steering organizations through accelerated growth are my expertise. As a CFO, Vice President for Business, and Financial Consultant for profit and not-for-profit companies, my strengths and vision have produced highly imaginative *and* highly profitable growth opportunities including:

- The financial and visionary leadership that directly contributed to the building of a small Long Island waste management firm from a $400 thousand gross to a profitable $5 million gross revenue stream in only eight years.

- The 18-month turnaround and development of a $100 thousand cash flow surplus from a $125 thousand deficit for the YMCA's seven-branch Long Island Chapter.

- The total overhaul of the New Hampshire division of the Visiting Nurses Association Hospice, including securing $200 thousand line of credit and rebuilding finance department.

- The building of a profitable cross-industry business and tax consulting practice.

After over 15 years of consistent challenge and success with companies on Long Island, I moved to New Hampshire. Although I love the area, I find that I sorely miss the energy and pace of the Metro marketplace. I plan to return to Long Island and am looking for a new endeavor in Metro New York where I can fully utilize my marketing and development capabilities while continuing to provide integrated operating and financial leadership.

If you are in need of a visionary leader with a proven portfolio of accomplishments, I would like to explore the opportunity. The enclosed resume demonstrates the absolute value that I will bring to Media Three's current and long-term business ventures. I look forward to speaking with you to discuss the possibility of a mutually beneficial relationship.

Sincerely,

James T. Robertson

enclosure

300 Hemlock Road • Nashua, NH 00000 • 603-555-5555

15

For Resume 114. *Deborah Wile Dib, Medford, New York*
The topical sequence of paragraphs is *purpose, expertise, bulleted achievements, reason for relocating,* and *interest in an interview.* The last paragraph also refers to the resume.

CLARE FARRELL
6820 Cattrell Avenue ▪ Sunnyvale CA 94000
(408) 000-0000

October 30, XXXX

Mr. Frank Carter
Vice President of Finance & Administration
Thompson-Kittridge Industries
18220 Hollis Boulevard
Palo Alto CA 94000

Dear Mr. Carter:

If your organization could use an experienced accounting professional with strong analytical, problem-solving and team-building skills, I believe you will find the enclosed résumé worth a close look. It reflects my diverse responsibilities and accomplishments as Accounting Manager for a rapidly growing company.

As the résumé indicates, I perform extensive accounting management responsibilities within my organization. In addition, I serve as the focal point for financial interaction with another company that my employer has formed an alliance with; this has placed special responsibilities and demands on me, all of which I have met successfully.

One reason I've been able to meet the diverse challenges I've encountered is that I adopt a proactive approach to change and actually enjoy it. Another key factor is that I have recruited and molded my staff into a close-knit, supportive team focused on achieving goals in a timely, professional manner. Recent accomplishments have included:

- Created the current-year corporate budget independently, from scratch.
- Set up books for the joint company, including a change from incorporated to LLC structure.
- Devised a simplified allocation method for overhead billing that ensures smooth funding flow.
- Played a key role in successful completion of the company's first external audit.

I have thoroughly enjoyed the challenges provided by my current position. At this time, however, no additional growth opportunities are available to me within the organization. After evaluating my situation, I have decided it's time to find a new environment that will enable me to continue expanding my professional capabilities while contributing to the ongoing success of my employer.

If you would like additional information, or if a personal interview is appropriate, I would welcome the opportunity to speak with you. Feel free to contact me at the number shown above. Please note that my job search is confidential at this time.

Sincerely,

Clare Farrell

Encl.

16

For Resume 28. *Georgia Adamson, Campbell, California*
The topical sequence of these paragraphs is *who I am, what I do, what I've accomplished, why I want a new position elsewhere,* and *my interest in an interview—and confidentiality.*

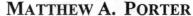

MATTHEW A. PORTER
8910 Stillwell Avenue, #1234
Lutz, Florida   33549
(813) 000-0000

March 10, 1997

Mr. Richard James
R & J Associates, P. A.
2300 Ashley Drive
Suite 555
Tampa, Florida 33600

Dear Mr. James:

I am interested in exploring your firm's need for a senior-level, corporate accountant. At this juncture of my career, I am pursuing more challenging, professional roles where my broad scope of accounting and MIS experience will bring immediate value to corporate operations.

Highlights of my qualifications include:

- B.S. degree in Accounting from the University of Florida.

- Senior-level management experience emphasizing corporate leadership, P&L accountability, progressive accomplishments and successive advancement.

- Expertise in strategic planning, business operations, automated accounting systems, software applications, and upholding fiscal efficiency.

- Peak performance in orchestrating directives, producing bottom-line results, problem solving, and making prudent decisions.

- Well-developed time management, organizational, communication and interpersonal skills.

Enclosed is my resume, which will provide a more detailed summation of my experience and key accomplishments. If you have a need, I could do an excellent job for you. May we talk?

Sincerely,

Matthew Porter

Enclosure

For Resume 21. *Diane McGoldrick, Tampa, Florida*
This letter can be read quickly without seeming too brief. The bulleted highlights include *a degree, experience, expertise, performance,* and *skills.* The letter ends with a question.

MarciaWard
385 Grove Street
Freeport, New York 11111
(516) 555-5555

November 18, 19XX

Ms. Linda Samson
Director of Human Resources
Law Offices of Judge Bean
555 Madison Avenue
New York, New York 10016

Dear Ms. Samson:

Please accept this letter and enclosed résumé as expressed interest in a position with your firm. My experience lies in **legal and financial services** settings. For the past several years I have worked as a **legal assistant / paralegal** at a corporate and securities practice.

In this position I have developed expertise and strengths in a number of areas, including:

- Drafting agreements, regulatory filings and Blue-Sky registrations.

- Acquiring knowledge of various compliance issues as they relate to the various exchanges.

- Drawing up documentation for corporate filings, legal opinions and sole proprietorships.

- Interacting with high-profile clients, exercising discretion, and ensuring confidentiality at all times.

- Proficiency in an array of computer applications including Microsoft Word, Excel and PowerPoint; WordPerfect; Lotus; Lexis-Nexis and Westlaw legal research systems; and Time Slips Deluxe client billing system.

I believe that my qualifications and experience speak for themselves and indicate that I would be a valuable asset to your team. I would like to meet with you personally, at your convenience, to discuss this further. If you need any additional information, please feel free to contact me at the above address or telephone number.

Thank you very much for your time and consideration. I will contact you next week to arrange for an appointment.

Sincerely,

Marcia Ward

Marcia Ward

Enclosure

18

For Resume 122. *Judith Friedler, New York, New York*
The person indicates first her interest and experience. Bullets point to her strengths and areas of expertise. She then expresses interest in a meeting and how she will follow up.

CRAIG L. SIMMS

Phone/Fax: (555) 555-5555	55-55 55th Street, #55
E-mail: CraigLS@msn.com	New Springville, New York 55555

April 6, XXXX

Dept. F
P.O. Box 5555
New York, NY 55555

Dear Hiring Manager:

Please accept this letter and résumé as an application for the Equities Trader position advertised in <u>The New York Times</u>. Based on your listed requirements for the position, I believe that I am highly qualified. Most notably, I offer:

- 6 years of professional experience in equities trading.

- Proven strengths in developing new accounts, managing portfolios, implementing effective marketing strategies, and evaluating market trends.

- Strong understanding of international and emerging markets.

- Computer literate with knowledge of computerized trading.

- Excellent verbal and written communication skills.

In my most recent position as Equities Trader for A & H Securities, Ltd. (England), I helped the company grow from obscurity to a market leader. In this capacity, I helped institute a dealing desk, organize a panel of brokers, and activate seats on the London Stock Exchange and National Stock Exchange of England. The strategies that I implemented brought the company to top-level operations and market performance.

My sales achievements are equally significant—throughout my career, I have been recognized for above-average sales performance. I am able to generate new accounts and maintain existing accounts. I am also self-motivated to produce high-quality work and motivate others to do the same. My energy, enthusiasm, market knowledge, and outstanding performance will be an asset to your company's equities trading team.

Currently, I am seeking new opportunities and challenges within the United States. I have achieved significant results within the British market and would like to apply my talents to impact performance within the U.S. market. If you are interested in a candidate with proven talents in equities trading, I would welcome a personal interview to discuss the Equities Trader position. Thank you in advance for your consideration.

Sincerely yours,

Craig L. Simms

enclosure

For Resume 183. *Kim Isaacs, Jackson Heights, New York*
The letter indicates the purpose. Then bullets call attention to the person's qualifications. After a paragraph each for achievements and sales results, the person asks for an interview.

WALTER J. BRADFORD, ESQ.
433 State Highway
City, State 00000
555-555-5555

November 28, XXXX

Mr. Sam S. Suspicious
Box 999
999 Washington Avenue
City, State 00000

Dear Mr. Suspicious:

Your advertisement for a Manager of Investigations has caught my attention. As a legal professional with twenty years experience in the criminal justice system, I believe that my knowledge and expertise uniquely qualifies me for this position. Accordingly, I have enclosed for your review a resume that briefly outlines my career.

During my tenure with the District Attorney's Office, I served for eight years as Bureau Chief of Investigations. This management team role encompassed several responsibilities that are relevant to the position you are seeking to fill. These include:

- **Supervising the Chief Investigator, with ultimate accountability for ten investigators working out of the DA's office.**

- **Directing investigations of organized crime, gambling, narcotics, and criminal conspiracy cases.**

- **Approving warrants for electronic surveillance and supervising undercover investigations.**

- **Conducting internal investigations of police officers for both criminal and civil violations of established police operating standards.**

- **Advising the County Drug Enforcement Task Force on legal matters.**

- **Prosecuting major narcotics and organized crime cases.**

In addition, I have spent the past four years as Legal Counsel to State Supreme Court Justice Carl Smith. I research cases and advise the Justice on legal matters relating to cases before the court. This involves points of evidentiary law and procedural issues. Justice Smith has been appointed to the federal bench, and circumstances do not make it practical for me to join his staff in Federal District Court.

I am convinced that my legal background and professional diligence would allow me to meet the challenges of this managerial role and protect your corporate interests. I would enjoy speaking with you in person about the position and how my unique talents can be utilized to your benefit. Please call me at (555) 555-5555 to arrange a convenient date and time for us to open our discussions.

Thank you.

Sincerely,

Walter J. Bradford, Esq.

Enclosure

20

For Resume 140. *Arnold G. Boldt, Rochester, New York*
The letter begins with the reason for writing. Bullets point to important responsibilities. The next paragraph gives the reason for a change. The letter ends with a request for a meeting.

Jennifer Trevalian

June 14, xxxx

Ms. Catharine Armond
Investment Recruiters
71 Broadway
New York, NY 11010

Dear Ms. Armond:

Does one of your clients have a need for an experienced investment banking officer with demonstrated industry expertise in media and telecommunications?

As Vice President in Investment Banking for IBIS Investment Banking, and as Senior Associate in Investment Banking for Merrill Lynch, I have been instrumental in the origination and closing of transactions representing a career total of $5.6 billion. Here's a short representation of my accomplishments in the media and telecommunications area; I'd like to make similar contributions to your client:

- Originated and am currently executing a $10 mm private placement mandate for an Internet retailer of entertainment collectibles.

- Originated and closed a $15 mm convertible mandate for TELEX.

- Originated and closed a research relationship with Seattle Tech Group.

- Originated a $100 mm IPO mandate for UHC Japan.

- Assisted the origination and closing of a $100 mm sell-side M&A mandate for Blueside N.A.

- Assisted the closing of a $275 mm buy-side M&A mandate for NA Communications, Inc.

- Assisted the origination of a $320 mm IPO mandate for CRT International, Inc.

My résumé and deal sheet are enclosed for your review. You will find that broad analytical experience, creativity, tenacity, and boundless energy have been key components in my generation of bottom-line results. My aggressive origination of new business has required strong client relations skills and proactive development of industry-specific expertise.

If my qualifications are of interest to you, I'd like to meet and discuss the ways in which I can contribute my experience and energy to your client's bottom line. Until we speak, please regard this inquiry as confidential and do not release my résumé without consent. I look forward to the possibility of a mutually beneficial association.

Sincerely,

Jennifer Trevalian

150 Spring St., 2A, New York, NY 10003   voice/fax 212-555-5555   e-mail Jtre@aol.com

21

For Resume 107. *Deborah Wile Dib, Medford, New York*
The person uses a question to introduce herself. Bullets call attention to accomplishments. The next paragraph indicates transferable skills. The person then asks for an interview.

Mark M. Allen

401 Lane Allen Road #432 ● Lexington, KY 40505 ● (606) 555-1234 ● mallen@sprynet.com

August 12, XXXX

Mr. George Pankow
Director of Recruitment
Louisville Free Public Library   **RE**: Position of Library
301 York Street   Automation Coordinator
Louisville, KY 40220

Dear Mr. Pankow:

I am pleased to submit my résumé for this position. As you can see, my education, training, and experience uniquely qualify me to meet and surpass your specifications.

Your requirements:	**My qualifications:**
Knowledge of information systems in a client/server environment.	Broad experience working with and troubleshooting WAN and LAN systems.
Facility in various desktop applications.	Extensive familiarity with most major, and many minor, desktop applications.
Knowledge of *SCO, UNIX, Redhat Linux*, and *Netscape Collabra.*	Working, to expert, competence with these programs and environments.
Four-year degree.	Three degrees (B.A., M.A., M.S.L.S.).
Ability to work well with and train end users and other county employees.	Exceptional skills in working with others. Teaching is my greatest joy.
Ability to communicate effectively orally and in writing.	Former English teacher. Adept at business, technical, or expository writing.

I believe I am exceptionally qualified to help your library continue fully to automate its most needed functions while keeping your costs to an absolute minimum. As I'm sure you'll agree, automation doesn't cost money, it saves money. I will contact your office early next week in order to schedule an interview where we can discuss my candidacy more fully.

Sincerely,

Mark M. Allen

22

For Resume 176. *David W. Adler, Lexington, Kentucky*
Two-column format is useful for showing how an individual's qualifications in experience, knowledge, education, and skills meet the requirements of an announced position.

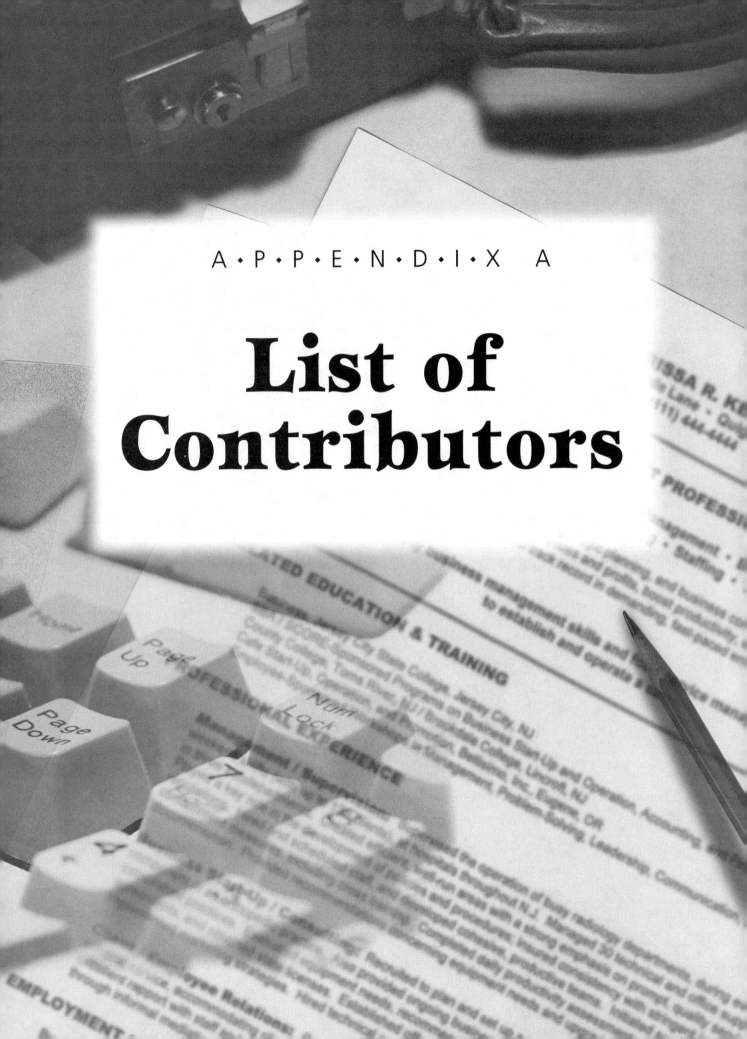

A·P·P·E·N·D·I·X A

List of Contributors

—List of Contributors

The following persons are the contributors of the resumes and cover letters in this book. All of the contributors are professional resume writers. To include in this appendix the names of these writers and information about their business is to acknowledge with appreciation their voluntary submissions and the insights expressed in the letters that accompanied the submissions. Resume and cover letter numbers after a writer's contact information are the numbers of the writer's resumes and cover letters included in the Gallery, not page numbers.

Alabama

Montgomery

Donald Orlando
The McLean Group
640 S. McDonough
Montgomery, AL 36104
Phone: (334) 264-2020
Fax: (334) 264-9227
E-mail: orlandores@aol.com
Member: PARW, CMI Training Master
Certification: MBA, CPRW
Resume: 151
Cover Letter: 4

Arizona

Phoenix

Bernard Stopfer
Resumes Plus
2855 W. Cactus Rd., Ste. 28B
Phoenix, AZ 85029
Phone: (602) 789-1200
(800) 505-9596
Fax: (602) 789-6014
E-mail: reswiz@aol.com or
respro@jobsaz.com
Web site: www.jobsaz.com
Member: PARW, Pres. of Resume
Writers Council of Arizona
Resume: 17

California

Anaheim

Denise C. Ross
More Than Just Words
9852 W. Katella Ave., PMB 187
Anaheim, CA 92804
Voice/Fax: (714) 828-8220
E-mail: mtjwords@aol.com
Member: PARW, NRWA, CMI
Resume: 1

Campbell

Georgia Adamson
Adept Business Services
180-A W. Rincon Ave.
Campbell, CA 95008
Phone: (408) 866-6859
Fax: (408) 866-8915
E-mail: georgiaa@ix.netcom.com
Web site: www.adeptbussvcs.com
Member: NRWA, PARW, PASS
Certification: CPRW
Resumes: 28, 95
Cover Letter: 16

Fremont

Carl L. Bascom
American Marketing Associates
555 Mowry Ave., Unit D
Fremont, CA 94536
Phone: (510) 713-7133
E-mail: ama_dtp@hotmail.com
Member: PARW
Resumes: 29, 79, 188, 195

Fresno

Susan Britton Whitcomb
Alpha Omega Services
1255 W. Shaw Ave., #100A
Fresno, CA 93711
Phone: (559) 222-7474
Fax: (559) 222-9538
E-mail: topresume@aol.com
Web site: www.careerwriter.com
Member: NRWA, PARW
Certification: NCRW, CPRW
Resumes: 46, 56, 69, 91

Los Angeles

Vivian Van Lier
Advantage Resume and Career Services
6701 Murietta Ave.
Valley Glen, CA 91405
Phone: (818) 994-6655
Fax: (818) 994-6620
E-mail: vvanlier@aol.com
Web site: AdvantageCareerService.com
Member: PARW, NRWA
Certification: CPRW, JCTC
Resumes: 113, 130, 148

Menlo Park

Sydney J. Reuben
854 Coleman Ave., #L
Menlo Park, CA 94025
Phone: (650) 323-2643
E-mail: SReubenMA@aol.com
Member: NRWA, PARW
Certification: CPRW, MA
Resumes: 54, 78, 192

Oakland

Pamela Condie
Compleat Small Business Services
Oakland, CA
Phone: (510) 540-8555
E-mail: magoose@sirius.com
Member: PARW
Certification: CPRW
Resume: 185

Orange

Nita Busby
Resumes, Etc.
438 E. Katella, Ste. F
Orange, CA 92867
Phone: (714) 633-2783
Fax: (714) 633-2745
E-mail: resumes100@aol.com
Web site: www.resumesetc.net
Member: NRWA, CA Assn. of
  Personnel Consultants,
  contributing writer to
  www.smallbusinessresources.com
Certification: CPRW, ValueStar
Resume: 18

Christine Edick
Action Résumés
1740 W. Katella Ave., Ste. J
Orange, CA 92867
Phone: (714) 639-0942
Fax: (714) 639-3262
E-mail: Christine@actionresumes.com
Web site: actionresumes.com
Member: NRWA, PARW, CDP, CMI
Certification: CPRW
Resume: 74

Santa Monica

Sonja A. Wittich
Résumés (with a little help from a friend)
58 Village Park Way
Santa Monica, CA 90405
Phone: (310) 392-1682
Member: PARW
Certification: CPRW
Resume: 37

Connecticut

Enfield

Louise Garver
Career Directions
115 Elm St., Ste. 104
Enfield, CT 06082
Phone: (860) 623-9476
Fax: (860) 623-9473
E-mail: CAREERDIRS@aol.com
Web site: www.resumeimpact.com
Member: PARW, NRWA, IACMP, NCDA, ACA,
  CPADN
Certification: CPRW, CMP, MA, JCTC
Resumes: 66, 100, 119, 198
Cover Letter: 11

Florida

Ft. Lauderdale

Shelley Nachum
Career Development Services
4801 S. University Dr., Ste. 201
Ft. Lauderdale, FL 33328
Phone: (954) 434-0989
Fax: (954) 434-4284
E-mail: cardevsv@bellsouth.net
Web site: www.ExpertResumes.com
Member: PARW, NRWA, SHRM, NCDA
Resumes: 47, 94

Melbourne

Laura A. DeCarlo
Competitive Edge Career Service
1665 Clover Circle
Melbourne, FL 32935
Phone: (407) 752-0880
          (800) 715-3442
Fax: (407) 752-7513
E-mail: getanedge@aol.com
Web site: www.acompetitiveedge.com
Member: NRWA, PARW
Certification: CPRW, ICCC
Resumes: 26, 117, 149

Middleburg

Valerie Roberts
Roberts' Keyboard Connection
1803 Dahlia Ct.
Middleburg, FL 32068
Phone: (904) 269-9226
Fax: (904) 908-0986
E-mail: valerie@kbdconnection.com
Web site: www.kbdconnection.com
Member: PARW
Resume: 189

St. Petersburg

Anita L. Babcock
B.O.S.S.
Babcock Office Services & Solutions
9500 Koger Blvd. North, Ste. 222
St. Petersburg, FL 33702
Phone: (727) 577-1737
Fax: (727) 577-9498
E-mail: BOSS1FL@aol.com
Member: PARW
Resume: 63

Tampa

Cathleen M. Fahrman
Heider's Resume Center
4860 W. Kennedy Blvd.
Tampa, FL 33609
Phone: (813) 282-0105
Fax: (813) 639-9288
E-mail: HSSHEIDER@aol.com
Web site:
   http://members.aol.com/HSSHEIDER/
   HSSWebPage.html
Member: PARW, NRWA
Certification: CPRW
Resume: 84

Diane McGoldrick
Business Services of Tampa Bay
2803 W. Busch Blvd., #103
Tampa, FL 33618
Phone: (813) 935-2700
Fax: (813) 935-4777
E-mail: mcgoldrk@ix.netcom.com
Member: PARW, NAJST, *Who's Who Among
   Professionals,* CMI
Certification: CPRW
Resumes: 21, 53, 120, 136, 169, 184
Cover Letters: 1, 9, 17

Valrico

Cynthia Kraft
Executive Essentials
P.O. Box 336
Valrico, FL 33595
Phone: (813) 655-0658
Fax: (813) 685-4287
E-mail: CPRWck@aol.com
Web site: www.exec-essentials.com
Member: PARW, NRWA, CMI
Certification: CPRW
Resume: 109

Illinois

Arlington Heights

Joellyn Wittenstein
A-1 Quality Résumés & Career Services
2786 Buffalo Grove Rd., Ste. 206
Arlington Heights, IL 60004
Phone: (847) 255-1686
Fax: (847) 255-7224
E-mail: joellyn@interaccess.com
Web site: a-1qualityresumes.com
Member: NRWA, PARW
Certification: CPRW
Resume: 23

Chicago

Cathleen M. Hunt
Write Works
6645 N. Oliphant Ave., Ste. H
Chicago, IL 60631
Phone: (773) 774-4420
Fax: (773) 774-4602
E-mail: cmhunt@ibm.net
Member: PARW, NRWA, Board of
  Edison Park C of C
Certification: CPRW
Resumes: 15, 71, 76

Jacksonville

Sally McIntosh
Advantage Resumes
35 Westfair Dr.
Jacksonville, IL 62650
Phone: (217) 245-0752
Fax: (217) 243-4451
E-mail: sally@reswriter.com
Web site: www.reswriter.com
Member: NRWA
Certification: NCRW, CPRW, JCTC
Resume: 16

Lincolnshire

Christine L. Dennison
Dennison Career Services
16 Cambridge Lane
Lincolnshire, IL 60069
Phone: (847) 405-9775
Fax: (847) 405-9775
E-mail: chrisdennison@hotmail.com
Member: PARW
Certification: CPC
Resumes: 174, 186

Troy

John A. Suarez
Executive Career Fitness
519 Nottingham
Troy, IL 62294
Phone: (888) 521-3483
E-mail: JASUAREZ@aol.com
Member: PARW
Certification: CPRW, MA
Resumes: 2, 59, 129

Indiana

Hebron

Susan K. Schumm
The Printed Page
805 S. County Line Rd.
Hebron, IN 46341
Phone: (219) 996-6110
E-mail: theprintedpage@email.com
Web site: http://theprintedpage.cjb.net
Resume: 126

Kansas

Lawrence

Linda Morton
Transcriptions
1012 Massachusetts, Suite 201
Lawrence, KS 66044
Phone: (785) 842-4619
Fax: (785) 842-2846
E-mail: morton_sscm@compuserve.com
Member: PARW
Certification: CPRW
Resume: 92

Kentucky

Lexington

David Adler
Reliable Résumé
243 Chinoe Rd.
Lexington, KY 40502
Phone: (606) 269-8229
Fax: (606) 266-4337
E-mail: relresume@aol.com
Member: PARW, NRWA
Resume: 176
Cover Letter: 22

Maine

Bangor

Joan M. Roberts
CareerMasters
61 Main Street, Suite 55
Bangor, ME 04401
Phone: (207) 990-2102
Fax: (207) 990-1197
E-mail: jobsrch@aol.com
Web site: www.careercounseling.com
Member: NRWA, ACA
Certification: MA, CAGS, CPRW
Resume: 81

Maryland

Columbia

Audrey A. Boatwright
The Executive Desktop Publishing & Résumé
    Services, Inc.
8955 Guilford Rd., Ste. 140
Columbia, MD 21045
Phone: (410) 290-8277
Fax: (410) 290-7077
E-mail: careers@execdtp.com
Web site: www.execdtp.com
Member: PARW
Certification: CPRW
Resumes: 6, 72

Diane Burns
Career Marketing Techniques
5219 Thunder Hill Rd.
Columbia, MD 21045
Phone: (410) 884-0213
E-mail: dianecprw@aol.com
Web site: www.polishedresumes.com
Member: PARW, CMI
Certification: CPRW
Resume: 162

Ms. Earl M. Melvin
The Executive Desktop Publishing & Résumé
    Services, Inc.
8955 Guilford Rd., Ste. 140
Columbia, MD 21046
Phone: (410) 290-8277
Fax: (410) 290-7077
E-mail: careers@execdtp.com
Web site: www.execdtp.com
Member: PARW
Resume: 75

Easton

Thomas E. Spann
Lee Edwards Associates
7605 Dover Woods Rd.
Easton, MD 21601
Phone: (410) 822-2876
E-mail: resumes@skipjack.bluecrab.org
Web site: http://www.bluecrab.org/members/
    resumes
Resume: 32

Massachusetts

Needham

Wendy Gelberg
Advantage Résumés
21 Hawthorn Ave.
Needham, MA 02492
Phone: (781) 444-0778
Fax: (781) 444-2778
E-mail: wgelberg@aol.com
Member: NRWA
Certification: CPRW, JCTC
Resumes: 25, 105, 177

Northboro

Steven P. Green
Career Path
242 Brewer St.
Northboro, MA 01532
Phone: (508) 393-5548
Fax: (508) 393-6120
E-mail: Steven@WorkingSmart.com
Certification: MA, MPA
Resume: 134

Michigan

Battle Creek

Peggy Weeks
CompuPage
3914 W. Michigan Ave.
Battle Creek, MI 49017
Phone: (616) 964-7533
Fax: (616) 964-7843
E-mail: pweeks@voyager.net
Member: PARW, NRWA, ABSSI
Resume: 89

Flint

Janet L. Beckstrom
Word Crafter
1717 Montclair Ave.
Flint, MI 48503
Voice/Fax: (800) 351-9818
Voice/Fax: (810) 232-9257
E-mail: wordcrafter@voyager.net
Member: PARW
Resumes: 58, 125

Novi

Lorie Lebert
Résumés for Results
P.O. Box 267
Novi, MI 48376
Phone: (248) 380-6101
(800) 870-9059
Fax: (248) 380-0169
E-mail: llebert@aol.com
Web site: www.resumes4results.com
Member: PARW, *Who's Who for Entrepreneurs,* BBB
Certification: CPRW
Resume: 142

Trenton

Maria E. Hebda
Premier Résumé Writing Service, LLC
Trenton, MI 48183
Phone: (734) 676-9170
(877) 777-7242
Fax: (877) 777-7307
E-mail: maria@writingresumes.com
Web site: www.writingresumes.com
Member: PARW
Certification: CPRW
Resume: 173

Vicksburg

Betty A. Callahan
Professional Results
P.O. Box 45
Vicksburg, MI 49097
Phone: (616) 649-4299
Fax: (616) 649-4910
Certification: CPRW, PC
Resumes: 24, 65

Minnesota

Duluth

Linda Wunner
A Hire Image Résumé Service
4891 Miller Trunk Hwy., #208
Duluth, MN 55811
Phone/Fax: (218) 723-1995
E-mail: ahireimagemn.com
Web site: www.ahireimagemn.com
Member: PARW, NRWA
Certification: CPRW
Resume: 88

Rochester

Beverley Drake
CareerVision Resume & Job Search Systems
3936 Highway 52N, #224
Rochester, MN 55901
Phone: (507) 252-9825
Fax: (507) 252-1525
E-mail: bdcprw@aol.com
Member: PARW, NAJST
Certification: CPRW
Resumes: 118, 200

New Jersey

Brick

Carol Rossi
Computerized Documents
4 Baywood Blvd.
Brick, NJ 08723
Phone: (732) 477-5172
Fax: (732) 477-5172
E-mail: comp-docs@juno.com
Web site: http://members.aol.com/compdocsCR
Member: PARW
Certification: CPRW
Resume: 116

Fair Lawn

Vivian Belen
The Job Search Specialist
1102 Bellair Ave.
Fair Lawn, NJ 07410
Phone: (201) 797-2883
Fax: (201) 797-5566
E-mail: vivian@jobsearchspecialist.com
Web site: www.jobsearchspecialist.com
Member: NRWA, AJST, CPADN, Five O'Clock Club
Certification: NCRW, CPRW, JCTC
Resumes: 99, 191

Lawrenceville

Susan Guarneri
Guarneri Associates
1101 Lawrence Rd.
Lawrenceville, NJ 08648
Phone: (609) 771-1669
Fax: (609) 637-0449
E-mail: resumagic@aol.com
Member: PARW, NRWA, Middle Atlantic
Career Counselors Assn.
Certification: CPRW, NCC, NCCC, JCTC
Resumes: 103, 193
Cover Letters: 7, 12

Marlboro

Beverly Baskin
Baskin Business & Career Services
6 Alberta Dr.
Marlboro, NJ 07746
Other offices: 120 Wood Ave. S,
Iselin, NJ, 08830; 116 Forrestal Blvd.,
Princeton, NJ 08540
Phone: (800) 300-4079
Fax: (732) 972-8846
E-mail: bbcs@att.net
Member: NRWA, PARW, NCDA, NECA, ACA
Certification: MA, NCC, CPRW, LPC, NAJST
Resumes: 91, 124

Rochelle Park

Alesia Benedict
Career Objectives
151 W. Passaic St.
Rochelle Park, NJ 07662
Phone: (800) 206-5353
Fax: (800) 206-5454
E-mail: careerobj@aol.com
Web site: www.getinterviews.com
Member: PARW (Board), CMI (Board), NAJST
Certification: CPRW, IJCTC
Resumes: 60, 135, 138, 144, 147

Toms River

Nina K. Ebert
A Word's Worth Résumé & Writing Service
808 Lowell Ave.
Toms River, NJ 08753
Phone: (732) 349-2225
(609) 758-7799
Fax: (732) 286-9323
E-mail: wrdswrth@gbsias.com
Member: PARW
Certification: CPRW
Resume: 182

Waldwick

Fran Kelley
The Résumé Works
71 Highwood Ave.
Waldwick, NJ 07463
Phone/Fax: (201) 670-9643
E-mail: twofreespirits@worldnet.att.net
Web site:
http://home.att.net/ ~ twofreespirits/index.html
Member: PARW, NRWA, CPADN, SHRM,
IACMP
Certification: MA, CPRW, SPHR, JCTC
Resume: 159

West Paterson

Melanie A. Noonan
Peripheral Pro
560 Lackawanna Ave.
West Paterson, NJ 07424
Phone: (973) 785-3011
Fax: (973) 785-3071
E-mail: PeriPro1@aol.com
Member: PARW, NRWA, ABSSI, IAAP
Certification: CPS
Resumes: 8, 12, 13, 34, 62, 139

New York

Chappaqua

Linsey Levine
CareerCounsel
11 Hillside Place
Chappaqua, NY 10514
Phone: (914) 238-1065
Fax: (914) 238-5822
E-mail: LinZlev@aol.com
Member: PARW, NRWA, NCDA, IACMP, NAJST
Certification: MS, JCTC
Resumes: 90, 104

East Greenbush

Elizabeth M. Daugherty
1st Impressions Business & Resume Services
2 Columbia Dr.
East Greenbush, NY 12061
Phone: (518) 477-8753
Fax: (518) 477-8753
E-mail: wedothat@aol.com
Web site: www.CapitalConcierge.com
Member: PARW
Resume: 199

Elmira

Betty Geller
Apple Résumé & Typing Service
456 W. Water St., Ste. 1
Elmira, NY 14905
Phone: (607) 734-2090
Fax: (607) 734-2090
E-mail: BGellerRes@aol.com
Member: NRWA, PARW
Certification: CPRW, NCRW
Resumes: 82, 128

Jackson Heights

Kim Isaacs
Advanced Career Systems
34-41 85th St., Ste. 6-G
Jackson Heights, NY 11372
Phone: (888) 565-9290
Fax: (718) 565-1611
E-mail: support@resumesystems.com
Web site: http://www.resumesystems.com
Member: NRWA, PARW
Certification: CPRW, NCRW
Resumes: 3, 11, 73, 127, 155, 183
Cover Letters: 13, 19

Medford

Deborah Wile Dib
Advantage Résumés of New York
77 Buffalo Ave.
Medford, NY 11763
Phone: (516) 475-8513
Fax: (516) 475-8513
E-mail: gethired@advantageresumes.com
Web site: http://www.advantageresumes.com
Member: NRWA, PARW, AJST, CMI, CPADN
Certification: NCRW, CPRW, JCTC
Resumes: 107, 114, 150, 157, 161, 166, 172, 187,
    196, 201
Cover Letters: 6, 15, 21

Mt. Morris

Salome Randall Tripi
The Office Outsource
3123 Moyer Rd.
Mt. Morris, NY 14510
Phone: (716) 658-2480
Fax: (716) 658-2480
E-mail: srttoo@frontiernet.net
Web site: http://www.frontiernet.net/ ~ srttoo/
Member: PARW, CMI
Resume: 163

New York

Etta R. Barmann
Compu-Craft Business Services, Inc.
124 E. 40th St., Ste. 403
New York, NY 10016
Phone: (212) 697-4005
Fax: (212) 697-6475
E-mail: erbarmann@aol.com
Member: PARW
Certification: CSW, CPRW
Resumes: 31, 57, 101, 102, 133, 179, 181

Judith Friedler
CareerPro Résumé Services
150 Nassau St., Ste. 1624
New York, NY 10038
Phone: (212) 227-1434
Fax: (212) 766-2772
E-mail: JudyCPro@aol.com
Member: Founding Member of NRWA
Certification: NCRW, CPRW, IJCTC,
    The Five O'Clock Club Guild
Resumes: 44, 110, 122, 143

Ossining

Phyllis B. Shabad
CareerMasters
95 Woods Brooke Circle
Ossining, NY 10562
Phone/Fax: (914) 944-9577
E-mail: careermasters@cyburban.com
Member: NRWA, PARW
Certification: NCRW, JCTC
Resumes: 40, 87, 160

Poughkeepsie

Kristin Mroz Coleman
Custom Career Services
44 Hillcrest Dr.
Poughkeepsie, NY 12603
Phone: (914) 452-8274
Fax: (914) 452-7789
E-mail: kcoleman@idsi.net
Member: PARW, NRWA
Resume: 106

Marian K. Kozlowski
MKK Resume Consulting Service
47 S. Gate Dr.
Poughkeepsie, NY 12601
Phone/Fax: (914) 462-0654
E-mail: MKozlo4371@aol.com
Member: SHRM
Resume: 22

Rochester

Arnold G. Boldt
Arnold-Smith Associates
625 Panorama Trail, Bldg. 2, Ste. 200
Rochester, NY 14625
Phone: (716) 383-0350
Fax: (716) 387-0516
E-mail: Arnoldsmth@aol.com
Web site: www.resumesos.com
Member: PARW
Certification: CPRW
Resumes: 7, 14, 70, 121, 140, 145, 175
Cover Letters: 10, 14, 20

Scotia

Barbara M. Beaulieu
Academic Concepts
214 Second St.
Scotia, NY 12302
Phone: (518) 377-1080
Fax: (518) 382-8462
E-mail: barbra2@banet.net
Member: PARW, NRWA
Certification: CPRW
Resumes: 104, 171

Stewart Manor

John Tisano
Accurate Résumé Services
217 Dover Parkway
Stewart Manor, NY 11530
Phone: (516) 327-4811
Fax: (516) 327-4811
E-mail: accuresume@aol.com
Web site: www.accurateresume.com
Member: PARW, NRWA
Certification: CPRW
Resume: 164

Victor

Kim Little
Fast Track Resumes
1281 Courtney Dr.
Victor, NY 14564
Phone: (716) 742-1907
Fax: (716) 742-1907
E-mail: ServPCR@aol.com
Web site: www.fast-trackresumes.com
Member: NRWA
Certification: JCTC
Resume: 158

Yorktown Heights

Mark D. Berkowitz
Career Development Resources
1312 Walter Rd.
Yorktown Heights, NY 10598
Phone: (888) 277-9778
        (914) 962-1548
Fax: (914) 962-0325
E-mail: cardevres@aol.com
Web site: CareerDevResources.com
Member: CMI, PARW, NCDA, ACA
Certification: NCC, NCCC, CPRW, JCTC
Resumes: 9, 33, 83

North Carolina

Asheville

Dayna J. Feist
Gatehouse Business Services
265 Charlotte St.
Asheville, NC 28801
Phone: (828) 254-7893
Fax: (828) 254-7894
E-mail: Gatehous@aol.com
Member: PARW
Certification: CPRW
Resumes: 68, 85

North Dakota

Fargo

Mary Laske
ExecPro Résumé Service
1304 23rd St., SW
Fargo, ND 58103
Phone: (701) 235-8007
Fax: (701) 235-7983
E-mail: mlaske@aol.com
Member: PARW, NRWA
Certification: CPRW
Resumes: 4, 38, 39

Ohio

Athens

Melissa L. Kasler
Resume Impressions
One N. Lancaster St.
Athens, OH 45701
Phone: (740) 592-3993
             (800) 516-0334
Fax: (740) 592-1352
E-mail: mkasler2@eurekanet.com
Member: PARW, NRWA
Certification: CPRW
Resume: 131

Cincinnati

Louise M. Kursmark
Best Impression
9847 Catalpa Woods Ct.
Cincinnati, OH 45242
Phone: (888) 792-0030
Fax: (513) 792-0961
E-mail: LK@yourbestimpression.com
Web site: www.yourbestimpression.com
Member: NRWA, PARW, NAJST
Certification: CPRW, JCTC
Resumes: 20, 153

Oregon

Aloha

Pat Kendall
Advanced Résumé Concepts
18580 S.W. Rosa Rd.
Aloha, OR 97007
Phone: (503) 591-9143
Fax: (503) 642-2535
E-mail: reslady@aol.com
Web site: www.reslady.com
Member: NRWA
Certification: JCTC, NCRW
Resumes: 48, 52, 64, 67

Pennsylvania

Wellsboro

Deborah S. Edwards
Résumé Connection
33 Waln St., P.O. Box 361
Wellsboro, PA 16901
Phone: (570) 724-3610
Fax: (570) 724-5492
E-mail: resume@epix.net
Web site: http://members.tripod.com/
    dedwardsgroup/resume.htm
Member: NRWA, PARW, The Five O'Clock Club
Certification: NCRW, CPRW
Resumes: 93, 97, 165, 170
Cover Letters: 2, 3, 5

Rhode Island

Smithfield

Mary Sward Hurley
Best Impression
P.O. Box 17271
Smithfield, RI 02917
Phone: (401) 231-7551
Fax: (401) 231-7510
E-mail: Resume99@aol.com
Member: NRWA
Certification: NCRW
Resume: 80

Tennessee

Hendersonville

Carolyn Braden
Braden Resume & Secretarial
108 La Plaza Dr.
Hendersonville, TN 37075
Phone: (615) 822-3317
Fax: (615) 826-9611
Member: PARW
Certification: CPRW
Resumes: 5, 50, 96

Knoxville

Lynda Lowry
Absolutely Write
8240 Hunter Hill Dr.
Knoxville, TN 37923
Phone: (423) 690-1489
Fax: (423) 531-7083
E-mail: ResWritr@aol.com
Member: NRWA
Resume: 115

Texas

Austin

Tracy A. Bumpus
First Impressions Career and Résumé Services
1807 Slaughter Ln., #200
PMB-366
Austin, TX 78760
Phone: (512) 291-1404
(888) 277-4270
Fax: (512) 291-1160
E-mail: tbumpus@rezamaze.com
Web site: www.rezamaze.com
Member: PARW, CMI
Certification: CPRW
Resume: 61

Denton

Dorothy E. Smith
Resumes, Etc.
3309 N. Bonnie Brae St.
Denton, TX 76207
Phone: (940) 566-3343
Fax: (940) 565-0776
Member: PARW
Resume: 55

El Paso

Shari Favela
342 Vista Del Rey
El Paso, TX 79912
E-mail: afavela1@worldnet.att.net
Certification: NCC
Resume: 51

Houston

Rosa St. Julian
Aicron Career & Resume Services
9597 Jones Rd., #189
Houston, TX 77065
Phone: (888) 209-6577
Fax: (281) 894-6214
E-mail: info@aicron.com
Web site: www.aicron.com
Member: PARW, NRWA
Certification: CPRW
Resume: 146

Round Rock

Karen D. Wrigley
AMW Résumé Service
3102 Scarlet Oak Cove
Round Rock, TX 78664
Phone: (512) 246-7423
(800) 880-7088
Fax: (512) 246-7433
E-mail: amwrig@ibm.net
Web site: amwresumes.com
Member: PARW, NRWA (Board), CMI
Certification: CPRW
Resumes: 10, 36, 45, 167
Cover Letter: 8

Sugar Land

Kelley Smith
Advantage Résumé Services
P.O. Box 391
Sugar Land, TX 77487
Phone: (281) 494-3330
(877) 478-4999
Fax: (281) 494-0173
E-mail: info@advantage-resume.com
Web site: www.advantage-resume.com
Member: PARW, NRWA
Certification: CPRW
Resume: 30

Tyler

Ann Klint
Ann's Professional Résumé Service
1608 Cimmarron Trail
Tyler, TX 75703
Phone: (903) 509-8333
Fax: (903) 509-8333
E-mail: Resumes-Ann@tyler.net
Member: PARW, NRWA
Certification: NCRW, CPRW
Resumes: 156, 180

The Woodlands

Cheryl Ann Harland
Résumés By Design
25227 Grogan's Mill Rd., Ste. 125
The Woodlands, TX 77380
Phone: (281) 296-1659
Fax: (281) 296-1601
E-mail: cah@resumesbydesign.com
Web site: www.resumesbydesign.com
Member: PARW
Certification: CPRW
Resume: 132

Virginia

Lynchburg

Rebecca Stokes
The Advantage, Inc.
1330 Walnut Hollow Rd.
Lynchburg, VA 24503
Phone: (800) 922-5353
Fax: (804) 384-4700
E-mail: Advresume@aol.com or
    Advanresume@earthlink.net
Web site: www.advantageresume.com
Member: PARW
Certification: CPRW
Resumes: 98, 108, 111, 112

Richmond

Betty H. Williams
BW Custom Résumés
Richmond, VA
Phone: (804) 359-1065
Fax: (804) 359-4150
E-mail: VaBHW@aol.com
Member: PARW, NRWA
Certification: CPRW, NCRW
Resume: 43

Virginia Beach

Anne G. Kramer
Alpha Bits
4411 Trinity Ct.
Virginia Beach, VA 23455
Phone: (757) 464-1914
E-mail: akramer@livenet.net
Web site: members.about.com/AnneKramer
Member: PARW, Phi Theta Kappa, contributing writer
    to womenCONNECT.com, VIRTUAL INK
Certification: CPRW
Resume: 152

Washington

Issaquah

Kathryn Vargo
Words at Work
P.O. Box 83
Issaquah, WA 98027
Phone: (425) 392-2577
Fax: (425) 391-2604
E-mail: AllWrite01@aol.com
Member: PARW, NRWA
Certification: CPRW, NCRW, Certified
    Technical Writer
Resume: 137

Woodinville

Carole S. Barns
Barns & Associates, Complete Career Services
22432-76th Ave. SE, Ste. 201
Woodinville, WA 98072
Phone: (425) 487-4008
        (800) 501-4008
Fax: (425) 489-1995
E-mail: BarnsAssoc@aol.com
Member: PARW, NRWA, ICF, PSCDA, CMI
Resumes: 27, 35, 41, 49, 77, 86, 141, 178, 190

West Virginia

Charleston

Barbie Dallmann
Happy Fingers Word Processing & Résumé Service
1205 Wilkie Dr.
Charleston, WV 25314
Phone: (304) 345-4495
Fax: (304) 343-2017
E-mail: BarbieDall@mindspring.com
Web site: www.ibssn.com/happyfingers
Member: NRWA, ABSSI
Certification: CPRW
Resume: 197

Wisconsin

Appleton

Kathy Keshemberg
A Career Advantage
1615 E. Roeland, #3
Appleton, WI 54915
Phone: (920) 731-5167
Fax: (920) 739-6471
E-mail: kathyKC@aol.com
Web site: www.acareeradvantage.com
Member: NRWA
Certification: NCRW
Resume: 123

Milwaukee

Tina Merwin
Consultancy In Action, Ltd.
152 W. Wisconsin Ave., Ste. 531
Milwaukee, WI 53203
Phone: (414) 272-3151
Fax: (414) 272-2747
E-mail: cialtd@naspa.net
Web site: www.naspa.net/members/cialtd
Member: PARW, APCC
Resume: 42

For those who would like to contact the Professional Association of Résumé Writers, its address is as follows:

Professional Association of Résumé Writers
3637 Fourth Street North, Suite 330
St. Petersburg, FL 33704
Phone: (813) 821-2274
Fax: (813) 894-1277
Web site: www.parw.com

For those who would like to contact the National Résumé Writers' Association, write to Ms. Phyllis Shabad, NRWA Secretary, Career Masters, 95 Woods Broke Circle, Ossining, NY 10562. NRWA's e-mail address is reslady@aol.com (Pat Kendall, NRWA President). NRWA's Web site is www.nrwa.com.

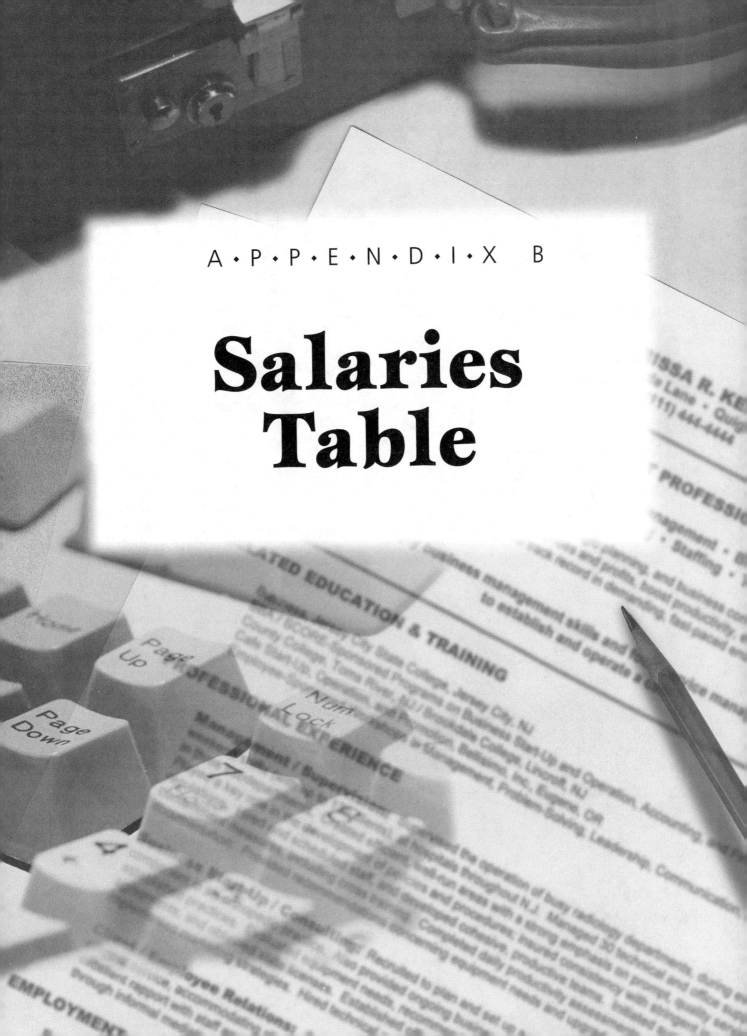

APPENDIX B

Salaries Table

Salaries Table

Annual Salaries of Selected Occupations

The values shown in the following table are relative. Dollar amounts may be higher or lower, depending on factors such as the following: academic degree(s), academic major, and relation of job to major; worker's age, years of experience, skills, knowledge, other qualifications, and previous job performance; size, health, and growth of the company; region, industry strength, and health of the national economy; and any other economic conditions that affect salaries. Amounts shown are from 1997 and 1998 tables.

Occupation	Salary	Occupation	Salary
Accountant, Cost, Senior	$43,700	Financial Manager	$54,392
Accountant, Cost, Staff	$34,900	General Manager	$58,344
Accountant, Senior	$42,650	Information Systems Consultant	$66,000
Accountant, Staff	$35,150	Information Systems Director	$87,000
Accountant, Tax	$37,600	Information Systems Operations	
Accounting Clerk	$19,500	Manager	$72,400
Accounting Manager	$63,600	Information Technology, Director	$78,000
Attorney	$70,117	Information Technology, Manager	$73,250
Attorney, Corporate	$92,000	Judge	$58,864
Auditor, Accounting	$35,250	LAN Administrator	$45,000
Auditor, Tax	$35,900	Law Clerk	$42,952
Bookkeeper	$19,500	Legal Assistant	$25,792
Budget Analyst	$33,020	Librarian	$35,750
Cash Manager	$55,700	Loan Officer	$33,020
Chief Financial Officer	$89,250	Management Consultant	$42,000
Collections Specialist	$26,000	Operations Research Analyst	$45,760
Controller, Assistant	$51,000	Paralegal	$25,792
Controller, Corporate	$64,750	Payroll and Timekeeping Clerk	$21,320
Credit Analyst	$32,000	Purchasing Manager	$39,780
Credit and Collections, Manager	$43,500	Real Estate, Lease Administrator	$61,670
Customer Service Representative	$27,061	Software Development Consultant	$48,100
Data Center Supervisor	$65,300	Tax Preparer	$19,500
Database Administrator	$67,900	Tax Manager	$67,500
Financial Analyst	$37,300	Teller	$15,392
Financial Analyst, Senior	$45,300	Treasurer	$89,250

Sources

Farr, J. Michael, and LaVerne L. Ludden, Ed.D. With database work by Paul Mangin. *Best Jobs for the 21st Century.* Indianapolis: JIST Works, Inc., 1999.

Fogg, Neeta P., Paul E. Harrington, and Thomas F. Harrington. *The College Majors Handbook: The Actual Jobs, Earnings, and Trends for Graduates of 60 College Majors.* Indianapolis: JIST Works, Inc., 1999.

The O*NET Dictionary of Occupational Titles™. 1998 Edition. Developed by J. Michael Farr and LaVerne Ludden, with database work by Paul Mangin. Indianapolis: JIST Works, Inc., 1998.

The *Wall Street Journal* Web site: http://www.wsj.com/.

Occupation Index

Current or Last Position

Note: Numbers are resume numbers in the Gallery, not page numbers.

Features Index

Note: Numbers are resume numbers in the Gallery, not page numbers.

The following commonly appearing sections are not included in this Features Index: Work Experience, Work History, Professional Experience, Related Experience, Other Experience, Education (by itself), and References. Variations of these sections, however, *are* included if they are distinctive in some way or have combined headings. As you look for features that interest you, be sure to browse through *all* the resumes. Some important information, such as Accomplishments, may not be listed here because it is presented in *sub*sections of Professional Experience.

Best Jobs for the 21st Century

Expert Reference on the Jobs of Tomorrow

By J. Michael Farr and LaVerne L. Ludden, Ed.D.

Whether you're preparing to enter the job market for the first time or simply wish to remain competitive in your current field, this information-packed reference contains data on the latest employment trends.

✦ Contains over 50 lists of jobs with best pay, high growth, and most openings by numerous categories

✦ Describes 686 jobs with fast growth or high pay

✦ Based on expert analysis of labor and economic trends

ISBN: 1-56370-486-2 • $16.95 • Order Code: LP-J4862

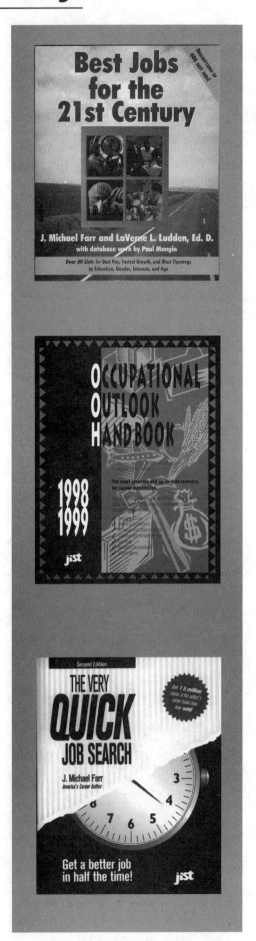

Occupational Outlook Handbook

By the U.S. Department of Labor

The *OOH* is the most widely used career exploration resource. This is a quality reprint of the government's *OOH*, only at a less-expensive price. It describes 250 jobs—jobs held by 85% of the American workforce—making the book ideal for students, counselors, teachers, librarians, and job seekers.

✦ Well-written narrative with many charts and photos

✦ Gives DOT numbers for the occupation and related occupations

✦ Sections on nature of the work, working conditions, training, job outlook, earnings

ISBN: 1-56370-464-1   **ISBN: 1-56370-475-7**
$17.95 Softcover   **$22.95 Hardcover**
Order Code: LP-J4641   **Order Code: LP-J4757**

The Very Quick Job Search

Get a Better Job in Half the Time!

By J. Michael Farr

Mike Farr, one of the most important architects of the self-directed job search, has done it again! Nowhere else will you find such excellent, timeless job search information. This award-winning title has been an important resource for more than 150,000 people just like you!

✦ Thorough coverage of all career planning and job search topics—in one book!

✦ Proven, effective advice for *all* job seekers

✦ Latest information on market trends and results-oriented search techniques

ISBN: 1-56370-181-2 • $16.95 • Order Code: LP-J1812

Résumé Magic

Trade Secrets of a Professional Résumé Writer

By Susan Britton Whitcomb

Make your ordinary resume extraordinary by following the proven techniques presented in this excellent resource. Many resume books only offer a finished product of how a resume should look. *Résumé Magic* presents examples that will teach you *why* certain techniques work and shows you how to produce a powerful, effective resume. Techniques include

✦ Using advertising strategies to gain an audience
  with your boss-to-be
✦ Choosing the most flattering format
✦ Writing great copy
✦ Resume-style editing

ISBN: 1-56370-522-2 • $18.95 • Order Code: LP-J5222

The Resume Solution, 2ⁿᵈ Edition

How to Write (and Use) a Resume That Gets Results

By David Swanson

An interactive workbook designed to help you create a more effective resume. Get powerful advice in short, to-the-point sentences—exactly the style for resumes. You'll find 90 pages of sample resumes and worksheets that take you step-by-step through the resume-writing process. The author provides solid advice on how to use a resume to secure more interviews and offers and also gives information on electronic job seeking.

ISBN: 1-56370-180-4 • $12.95 • Order Code: LP-J1804

Professional Resumes for Executives, Managers, and Other Administrators

A New Gallery of Best Resumes by Professional Resume Writers

By David F. Noble, Ph.D.

A great collection of 342 new professionally designed resumes assembled to meet the needs of anyone seeking an upper-management position. Résumés were submitted by members of the Professional Association of Résumé Writers and the National Résumé Writers Association. For each resume, comments explain strengths and useful features.

ISBN: 1-56370-483-8 • $19.95 • Order Code: LP-J4838

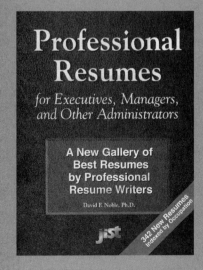

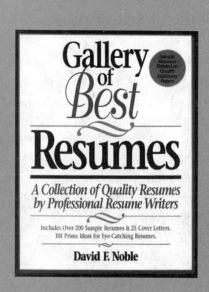

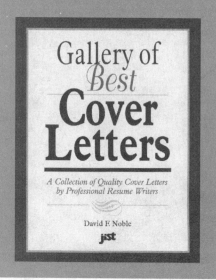